# The Harmonization of Civil and Commercial Law in Europe

# A Guide to European Private Law

# The Harmonization of Civil and Commercial Law in Europe

*by*

Barbara Pasa and Gian Antonio Benacchio

*Translated by*

Lesley Orme

CEU PRESS

Central European University Press
Budapest New York

Published in 2005 by

*Central European University Press*
An imprint of the
Central European University Share Company
Nádor utca 11, H-1051 Budapest, Hungary
*Tel:* +36-1-327-3138 or 327-3000
*Fax*: +36-1-327-3183
*E-mail*: ceupress@ceu.hu
*Website*: www.ceupress.com

400 West 59th Street, New York NY 10019, USA
*Tel:* +1-212-547-6932
*Fax*: +1-646-557-2416
*E-mail*: mgreenwald@sorosny.org

Translated by Lesley Orme



ISBN 963 7326 36 7 paperback
ISSN 1786-1438

Library of Congress Cataloging-in-Publication Data
Pasa, Barbara.
The harmonization of civil and commercial law / by Barbara Pasa and Gian Antonio Benacchio.—1st ed.
p. cm.
Includes bibliographical references and index.
ISBN 9637326359
1. Commercial law--European Union countries. 2. Contracts--European Union countries. 3. Consumer protection--European Union countries. 4. Products liability--European Union countries. 5. Restraint of trade—European Union countries. I. Benacchio, Gian Antonio. II. Title.
KJE2045.P37 2005
346.24—dc22
2005023705

Printed in Hungary by
Akaprint Nyomda

# TABLE OF CONTENTS

## Chapter V: Industrial and Commercial Property Rights 409



## Chapter VI: Competition Law . . . 477

*EU law "is an incoming tide. It flows into the estuaries and up the rivers. It cannot be held back"* – per Lord Denning, *HP Bulmer Ltd v Bollinger SA* (1974)

# Introduction

*The Harmonization of Civil and Commercial Law in Europe* is the second volume in the series *A Guide to European Private Law,* which is intended to give an account of the building of a new 'European common law,' enhanced by the perspective provided by the enlargement process of 2004.

The book is dedicated to reconstructing the important parts in the formation of the new, common, private law, which is no longer domestic, but European (or Community) in nature: consumer protection and contract law, product liability, the insurance, credit and finance industries, company law, industrial and commercial property rights and competition law.

We look at those Community measures which affect the so-called '*one-sided business transactions,*' and impinge on the bulk of private law of national legal systems, i.e. the law of contracts and the law of torts. The aim of the enquiry is substantive law only, as we are not considering rules relating to private international law. Moreover, we comment on those Community measures which affect '*business transactions*' in which only professionals participate, the so-called 'commercial contracts.'

The areas of substantive private law which are subject to harmonization, with which we shall be concerned in this book, are as follows: 1. *Competition law.* It is *par excellence* the classic theme of private Community law, which has engaged the Community institutions most profoundly from the beginning—the Council, the Commission, the Court of Justice. It is the field which has always characterized European Community activity and has demonstrated the great capacity to create new law which is effective and above all, uniform. The exclusive activity of the Commission, charged with ensuring compliance with the competition rules and with investigating cases of suspected infringements or behavior which do not conform, together with the rulings of the Court of Justice, which has jurisdiction in disputes relating to decisions of the Commission, have developed Community competition law over the course of time, composed of written rules, rulings and doctrines which, taken together, have given rise to a considerable body of substantive Community law in relation to this subject. 2. *Company law.* After competition, this is certainly the biggest area, since it includes a large number of issues which, in a more or less important way, have been respectively unified or harmonized by regulations or directives. One thinks in particular of the following: the company directives, which have dictated new rules on disclosure, nullity of companies with limited liability, on formation of public liability companies and maintenance and alteration of their capital, on mergers and divisions, on annual accounts, on consolidated accounts, on single-member private limited liability companies, etc.; the regulations on 'European Economic Interest Grouping' (EEIG), on 'European company' (EC) and 'European Cooperative Society' (ECS); the draft regulations on the European Mutual Society and European Association. 3. *Intellectual Property rights.* If the main target of the Community is the formation of a common market where professional suppliers are put in the position of being able to compete under uniform rules, the classic themes of protection of intellectual property such as patent rights, trademarks, and copyrights cannot be omitted, any more than can subjects of more recent origin, such as software protection. In this field too, Community action has shown itself in directives and regulations, which have highlighted the near uselessness and inadequacy of the Community and European Conventions as a means of uniformization, which were the only recourse in previous years. 4. *Civil Liability.* For the moment, there are only two aspects within the ambit of tortious liability which the Community legislature has concerned itself: manufacturers' liability for damage caused by defective products, which originated in the 1985 Directive, and service providers' liability, where the directive is still in the formative phase. 5. *Contract law.* This is the part of private law which lends itself to the most stimulating observation and which offers a vast number of points for reflection, concerning the development and evolution of European private law. As in company law, harmonization of national laws with Community acts are numerous in the area of contract law. Think of the directives on unfair terms, on package travel, on contracts negotiated away from business premises, on contracts relating the purchase of the right to use immovable property on a time–share basis, on consumer credit, on banking & insurance contracts, and on factoring, franchising, and leasing contracts.

This concerns a body of law which, having been conceived, elaborated on, and finally approved by case-law over the last twenty years, is causing really fundamental changes in the national legal systems because of its innovative content and frequent contrast with operative, age-old rules and principles. The characteristic features marking the development of research in comparative law are mastery of the method and awareness of the problem which must be confronted.

In particular, the book provides examples illustrating how European Community private law has been transposed into the domestic law of both the Member States and of those countries which are going to join the Union.

It will be noted that such examples are frequently drawn from the transposition of private Community law into the Italian legal system. This is for two reasons: on the one hand, because the authors' research activity is in this particular field; on the other, because we wanted to remedy the shortcomings in the availability of data on the Italian legal system, since there is, as yet, only a limited amount of material published in English on the relationship between private Community law and the Italian legal system.

The ebb and flow of judicial tides is noted, the hybridization between differing legal species, including the fact that rules and principles usually only make sense in the context of the institutions and processes in which they are meant to operate and in the context of the mindset of those institutions and processes. We are not particularly concerned with examining the provisions of all the directives and regulations one by one, nor with all the detail of the rules contained in the national implementing legislation, a task to be left for a second level of analysis, in all likelihood to be carried out in textbooks on commercial and civil law available at national levels. This is true for all the chapters in this book. And this is why each chapter contains ample bibliographical reference to manuals, treaties and academic commentaries, where the subjects may be studied in more depth.

The bibliography for reference accompanying each chapter is, naturally, not intended to be exhaustive, but is aimed at suggesting further reading on the topics of greater interest which are covered in the book; bibliographical references are given in the three languages most widely known or spoken in Europe (English, French and German) and in Italian, to provide the reader with a logical framework of reference (by topic and chronological order).

Last but not least, we have favored the editorial approach of using small fonts in the main text in order to achieve the following aims. In the first place it makes the text more attractive for students and legal professionals, avoiding cluttered pages with explanatory notes or detailed bibliographies. In the second place, this method presents the reader with material drawn directly from the legal sources, without interpolation or interference by the authors. Finally, further explanation and detailed commentary can be provided which the student or legal professional may also decide to pass over, without losing the thread of the argument in the main text.

Trento–Turin, May 2005

*Gian Antonio Benacchio*
*Barbara Pasa*

Particular thanks are due to Prof. Gianmaria Ajani (Univ. of Turin) and Prof. Luisa Antoniolli (Univ. of Trento), whose help was crucial in conceiving the book.

Heartfelt thanks are likewise due to the professors and researchers at the University of Warsaw, where a fruitful month of research was spent in June 2003: Professors Jerzy Rajski, Grzegorz Domański, Tadeusz Ereciński, Ewa Łetowska, and Doctors Tomasz Kozłowski, Hanna Machińska, Katarzyna Michalowska, Marcin Olechowski.

Particular thanks are due to Prof. Carl Gustaf Spangenberg at the University of Uppsala, where some fruitful months of both teaching and research were spent in Spring 2000 and 2001.

Finally, I would like to offer my warmest thanks to all the scholars, both Italian and those from abroad, who have collaborated in suggesting or checking the bibliography at the end of each chapter: Dr. Michel Cannarsa (Univ. of Lyon), Michele Carpagnano (Univ. of Trento), Claudio Comparato (Univ. of Trento), Dr. Stefan Greving (Univ. of Münster), Dr. Elise Poillot (Univ. of Reims, Champagne Ardenne), Dr. Eva Suwara (Univ. of Toruń), Andrea Toigo (Univ. of Trento) and Michał Zaremba (Univ. of Warsaw).

Last but not least, a special word of thanks to Lesley Orme, who translated the book from Italian into English, following a lengthy comparison of legal terminology to determine which translation to favor.

Chapters I, II and IV were written by Barbara Pasa (Univ. of Turin). The book states the law as it stood on December 31st 2004.

*Barbara Pasa*

This publication has been written within the Research Network "Uniform Terminology for European Private Law." *The member universities are Turin (Co-ordinator), Barcelona, Lyon, Muenster, Nijmegen, Oxford, and Warsaw. The research network is part of the Improving Human Potential (IHP) Programme financed by the European Commission (Contract n° HPRN-CT-2002-00229).*

# CHAPTER I

# Consumer Protection and the Law of Contracts

**KEY WORDS**: Consumer Protection – Historical Development – Community Intervention – Implementation – Member States – CEECs – Consumer Contracts – Taxonomy – Limits – Contracts negotiated away from business premises – Package travel, package holidays, and package tours contracts – Unfair terms – Timesharing – Distance sellings – Injunctions – Cross-border disputes – Sale of consumer goods and associated guarantees – Electronic signatures – E-commerce

## 1. Social and Economic Policy in Consumer Protection

"Consumerism" is the term denoting the social phenomenon which plays a central part in the protection of individuals who are consumers in the context of the organization of the global market.

A standardized definition of *consumer* is difficult to identify: in legal terms, a consumer is a natural person who acquires goods or services to meet personal or family needs, but not professional ones. As defined in terms of economics and social sciences, the consumer is a passive element in the system of mass production and distribution, given the superior bargaining power of business, and is exposed to the external stimuli of a market aimed at influencing her/his choice.

The movement started in the United States during the first decades of the 20th century, with the founding of the first Consumer Union. Mid-way through the last century, "consumerism" achieved its first concrete results, when what had been merely isolated socio-political instances became leading precedents or important legislative or administrative provisions. The issues arising in the areas of commercial advertising, standard contracts and product liability were the first to engage the attention of the U.S. courts. The legal solutions which they reached have formed the basis of reference to which European legal systems have looked when developing their own systems of protection.

After the Second World War, the movement expanded in Europe, in Denmark to be precise, where, in 1947, the Consumer Council was established—the first private consumers' organization. In the 1970's, in Great Britain, France, Germany, Spain, and Sweden, where the first Consumer *Ombudsman* was established in 1971, many administrative, constitutional, procedural, or private-law provisions identified the consumer as someone in particular need of protection.

Among the most important provisions: in Germany, the *Allgemeinen Geschäftsbedingungen Gesetz* of 1976, which introduced controls on general conditions of contracts (this is the reference model on which the Community Directive concerning unfair terms was based, see above § 11); in France, act no. 23 of January 23rd 1978 (known as the *loi Scrivener*) on the right to information and consumer protection regarding products and services, right after the act no. 22 of January 10th 1978 on consumer credit; in Great Britain, the Consumer Credit Act 1974 and the Unfair Contract Terms Act of 1977, which introduced a close check on clauses that remove a duty which would otherwise exist or which exclude or modify the remedies available on breach of that duty; in Spain, the 1978 Constitution, which contains an express provision regarding consumer protection (art. 51).

However, the individual national initiatives were not coordinated with one another and were in response to different socio-cultural conditions, to differing plans and political considerations. As such, some countries gave preference to *administrative* and others to *statutory* types of intervention, or adopted a mixed model in between these two types of intervention; some preferred to leave ample margin to self-regulation by the markets, others again favored legislation by sector, such as for example, the food industry.

By an *administrative* type of intervention, we mean the type which operates by means of checks and balances carried out by institutions under governmental direction (the French system in the 70's and 80's, the British system under the Office of Fair Trading), or else autonomous and independent, with their own functions (the Swedish system). By a *statutory* type of intervention, we mean that operating by means of special legal provisions directly enforced by the ordinary courts (the German and French systems). As far as the Italian legal system is concerned, until the recent provisions adopted in order to comply with Community directives, the expression "consumer protection" was practically unknown. Only academics devoted time to the study of this issue.

The mixed nature of national responses in this area hindered the growth of the common market; hence the need for a supranational harmonization initiative.

At first, Community law was influenced by those States which already had a consolidated basis of experience in the field; later, an independent policy for consumer protection was promoted by the EC institutions themselves. The Commission, as well as the Court of Justice, have played an important part in this evolutionary process. The latter has in fact accelerated the development of a consumer protection policy by means of an increasingly decisive affirmation of the direct and immediate effect of Community directives.[1]

At the moment, the strategy of Community policy relating to the consumer has a double objective, one social and the other economic.

On the one hand, it provides rules to afford more adequate protection to natural persons in the face of business activity, fulfilling, first and foremost, the function of protecting the health and safety of the consumer within the systems of mass production and distribution.

On the other, it promotes efficient application of the rules on consumer protection in all the Member States, through the provision of uniform legal measures. This is in order to eliminate differences among national markets, avoiding the distortion of competition, and allocating the risks of economic activity to businessmen in their dealings with consumers.

A uniform consumer protection system would, indeed, function to safeguard the health, security and economic interests of the consumer, as well as the fair competition in the internal market.

At the time of the first legislative steps in this area by the Community, the EEC (as it was then known) developed consumer protection provisions aimed at achieving the principle goal set out in the Treaty of Rome, i.e. the protection of the common market and fair competition. The pursuit of this latter aim may seem of small account compared to the intrinsic purpose of the welfare of the individual/consumer, but it certainly was not 'irrational,' since it was a valid justification of a program open to possible objections of 'lack of competence' on the part of dissenting States. In other words, the reasons for the apparent ambiguity in Community policy (formal protection of competition and freedom of economic initiative *versus* concrete protection of the consumer) must be sought in the context of the apportionment of competence between the Community and the Member States.

For many years the Community institutions legislated in the consumer sector without having express legislative competence.

> Originally the only provisions of the EEC which contained the term 'consumer' were those in art. 39 (1) e), (now art. 33 (1) e),

[1] See *Océano Grupo Editorial and Salvat Editores SA v. Roció Murciano Quintero et al.*, Cases C-240/98 to C- 244/98 (2000) ECR I-4941; EC *Commission v. Kingdom of the Netherlands*, Case C-144/99, (2001), ECR I-3541. Cf. the first volume in this series, *A Common Law for Europe*, chapter V.

> on common agricultural policy, in arts. 85 (3) and 86 (now arts. 81 (3) and 82), on competition.
>
> When the Treaty of Rome was signed, the motivating forces operating on the EEC were mainly economic ones. The very fact that that free movement of goods was mentioned before free movement of persons is a telling one, in understanding that the primary aim of the Community's founders was the achievement of a European free market rather than a Europe where citizens' interests were paramount. Nonetheless, there were various arguments to justify the central role of consumer protection: for example, weight was given to the declarations of principle contained in the preamble to the Treaty of Rome, where the common objectives of the European States included that of "improving living standards of citizens." A second argument was based on the premise that the whole of Community law was impliedly a function of protecting the consumer, the ultimate beneficiary of the economic aims of the Treaty.

Legislative competence was introduced by the Single European Act of 1986[2] and was decisively conferred on the Community by the Treaty of Maastricht of 1992;[3] finally, with new art. 153 TEC as modified by the Treaty of Amsterdam, the relationship between Community policy and consumer protection has been sanctioned by a constitutional type of formulation. In this way the interventionist policy of the Community institutions in the area of consumer protection has assumed an important autonomous role, as a social goal of the European Union, and is no longer seen as merely instrumental in the protection of competition.

## 2. The Historical Development of Consumer Protection by Community Institutions

The original 1957 version of the Treaty of Rome contained no provisions which conferred specific competence on Community institutions in the area of protection of consumers' rights. Up until the early 70's, the word *consumer* was used in the language of the Community with no technical

---

[2] See art. 18 of the Single European Act. The Single European Act came into force on July 1st 1987. See chapter IV of the first volume in this "Guide to European Private Law," *A Common Law for Europe*.

[3] See Title XI (now Title XIV) concerning Community activity in this area. See chapter IV of the first volume in this "Guide to European Private Law," *A Common Law for Europe*. See also this chapter and following §§.

or qualified meaning to it, and there was nothing to indicate that within a few years this area would become a key sector of Community policy.

In 1972, at the Paris summit, the heads of State and of Government of the EEC charged the Commission with the task of planning a program for consumer protection.

In 1973 the Commission established the Consumers' Consultative Committee, with the task of gathering the opinions of consumers and their associations in relation to initiatives which had been or were to be adopted by the Community institutions. In 1989 the Committee was reformed and was established as an institution in the form of the Consumers' Council, at which the representatives of the major consumers' associations participate at European level.

In 1975 the Commission adopted the first multi-year *action program* for consumer protection.[4] The aims identified by the plan were:

- The protection of consumer health and safety.
- The protection of the economic interests of the consumer (in the sense of adjusting the contractual balance between consumer and seller or supplier, in particular against one-sided standard contracts).
- The right to damages for defective goods.
- The provision of consumer information and education.
- Consultation with and representation of consumers at institutional sessions, in the framing of decisions affecting them.

In 1981 the Commission launched the second *action program*, more detailed but substantially the same as the first, where the same conclusions were reaffirmed, both in terms of objectives as well as rights which were to be accorded to consumers. 1986 was the year in which the policy of consumer protection was formalized in fundamental Community documents.

The Single European Act, in fact, recognized for the first time the competence of the Community to intervene in new areas, such as environment and consumer protection, with the insertion of art. 100A (now art. 95 TEC) on completing the internal market.

The third paragraph of this provision lays down that "the Commission, in its proposals envisaged in paragraph 1 concerning health, safety, environmental protection and consumer protection, will take as a base a high level of protection, taking account in particular of any new development based on scientific facts. Within their respective powers, the European Parliament and the Council will also seek to achieve this objective."

---

[4] O.J., C 92/1, 04/25/1975.

The provision refers only incidentally to the role of Community law in the protection of the consumer. Nonetheless, this represented the first notable legal recognition, which was then followed by increasingly important initiatives.

The introduction, by art. 189B (now art. 251 TEC), of the procedure of qualified majority voting is equally important: it repealed the Treaty provisions which provided for unanimity among the Council members in the adoption of directives in a range of sectors, including, as the case in point, that of consumer protection.

In 1989, the Community adopted the first three-year *action plan,* launched by the Commission for the years 1990–1992, which proposed to have recourse to directives in order to intervene in those areas which have now become *par excellence* the main ones, such as:

- Representation of consumers' associations in Community institutions and bodies.
- The right to information (on products, legal instruments concerning protection and whatever else may be of use for the protection of the health and economic interests of the consumer).
- Product safety.
- Regulation of contracts concluded between undertakings and consumers.

> It was as a result of this plan that some of the most important directives in this area were adopted, such as that on general product safety (1992), on labeling of food products (1990–1991–1992), on package travel, package holidays, and package tours (1990) and in the area of consumer credit (1990).
>
> One should also remember the presentation of some draft directives at that time, which were later adopted, such as for example those on distance selling (1992), on the liability of the provider of services (1991), on misleading and comparative advertising (1991), and on timesharing (1992).

Community policy in the area of consumer protection took on a whole new importance with the Maastricht Treaty. In fact a fundamental article was introduced, i.e. art. 129A (now art. 153 TEC), which constituted the new Title XI (now Title XIV) dedicated exclusively to consumer protection.

> **Art. 153 TEC:** "**(1)** In order to promote the interests of consumers and to ensure a high level of consumer protection, the Community shall contribute to protecting the health, safety and economic interests of consumers, as well as to promoting their right to information, education and to organise themselves in order

> to safeguard their interests. **(2)** Consumer protection requirements shall be taken into account in defining and implementing other Community policies and activities."

Paragraph 3 (b) affirms that the Community may intervene by "measures which support, supplement and monitor the policy pursued by the Member States."

This provision concerns the same objectives established by the Commission in the *first action program* of 1975, transposed into the Treaty substantially unchanged, some twenty years later.

In 1993, the second three-year *action plan* was launched, which, beside reaffirming intervention in the areas described above (consumer information, safety and protection of economic interests),[5] stressed the role and functions of the consumers' associations,[6] in particular through the Consumers' Council created in 1989, to which new tasks were given, alongside the merely consultative ones, as well as new ways of operating. Besides this, the Commission set up a new Consumers' Committee, which must now be consulted regarding all initiatives which may involve consumers' interests and, above all, with the task of formulating its own opinion, which must follow each phase of Community policy.

> A Consumer Committee was set up by Decision 95/260/EC (*O.J., L 162, 07/13/1995, p. 37)*. The Commission Decision 2000/ 323/ EC of May 4th 2000 improves the Consumer Committee so that the new Committee would be representative of consumers in all Member States of the European Community, whether they be organized at national or European level. The Committee is made up of delegates from the principle national associations in addition to the five main European organizations, that is: EUROCOOP (*Communauté Européenne des Coopératives*), COFACE (*Comité des Organisations familiales de la Communauté Européenne*), BEUC (*Bureau Européen des Unions des Consommateurs*), ANEC (*European Association for the Co-ordination of Consumer Representation in Standardisation*), AEC (*Association of European Consumers)*.

The second three-year action plan moved attention away from mere abstract recognition of consumer rights to their concrete implementation by the Member States, providing, among Community objectives, for the harmonization of the right of access to justice by consumers and their respective associations. This initiative then led to the publication of a

---

[5] The central theme was consumer information, see § 25 of the action plan.

[6] See § 32 of the action plan.

Green Paper on the access of consumers to justice and the settlement of consumer disputes in the context of the single market, prepared by the Commission in 1993.[7]

The document is of particular significance since it offers a precise and detailed view on the state of national legislation in the area of access to the courts, whether regarding legal or extra-legal procedures.

The comparative analysis carried out by the Commission has shown that the procedural rules governing access to justice can influence the effectiveness of consumers' rights, and that national differences involve little protection for the consumer. As we shall see in the following paragraphs, such considerations have induced the Community institutions to develop directives and draft directives which bear directly upon the domestic rules of procedure.

In 1995, when the new Directorate-General XXIV was established within the Commission, dedicated solely to consumer protection matters, the Commission presented the third three-year *action plan* for the period 1996–1998.[8]

The main feature was that, for the first time, the consumer policy was not inserted into the more general context of the policy for the development of the internal market. Moreover, among the objectives of the new policy, there were three priorities:

- To adopt protection measures in the areas of financial services, essential public utility services and food products.
- To adopt suitable measures in relation to consumer education, aimed mainly at encouraging sustainable consumption behavior and facilitating access to the "information society."
- To provide assistance to the ex-communist countries of Eastern Europe and developing countries in order to help them develop their own consumer-oriented policy.

> More concretely, the third plan proposed, among other things, to approve certain directives and regulations concerning the following matters: Statute for a European Company, Statute for a European Mutual Society, Statute for a European Cooperative Society, mergers of public limited liability companies, late payments, electronic signature, sale of consumer goods and associated guarantees, financial services, and supplementary pensions.

---

[7] COM (93) 576 final; compare the later Green paper on EU consumer protection, COM (2001) 531 final, 10/02/2001.

[8] COM (95) 519 final, 11/03/1995; Opinion of the Economic and Social Committee O.J., C 295, 10/07/1996, p. 64.

The 1997 Treaty of Amsterdam had strengthened the instruments available to the Community institutions, as was expected, and it had amended art. 129A (now 153 TEC) by inserting two new paragraphs, more in keeping with the importance which the Community intervention in this sector had assumed.

The 1999–2000 *action plan* for consumer policy has shown, from certain aspects, a partial departure from the policy direction of the Community on this subject, evaluating as a priority aims which are more economic than social. Thus consumer protection has reverted to being an instrument of EU economic policy, to confront new challenges posed by the rapid development of communication techniques and electronic commerce, or by genetic engineering; with this important difference: whereas up to a short time ago, attention was directed exclusively towards harmonization of the domestic laws of the Member States, now, however, the need to harmonize Community law—and that of its Member States—with the law of the Community's main economic competitors, is becoming increasingly clear.

In 1999, the European Parliament and the Council adopted a general framework for Community activities in favor of consumers.[9] The decision establishes, at Community level, a general framework for activities promoting the interests of consumers and providing them with a high level of protection. Community actions aim to protect the health, safety, and economic interests of consumers and promote their right to receive information and education and to join forces in order to protect their interests. It is open to the countries of Central and Eastern Europe, as well as Cyprus and the countries of the European Economic Area.

In 2001, the Commission presented a new *Green Paper on European Union Consumer Protection*,[10] which drew attention to the existence of gaps in the legislation in the field of protection of the economic interests of consumers in the internal market and demonstrating the need for more far-reaching Community action, aimed at increasing cooperation between the public consumer protection authorities in the various Member States.

The following year, in 2002, the *Follow-up Communication to the Green Paper on EU Consumer Protection*[11] was published, in which the Commission presented a draft law (through the use of a framework directive) to encourage cooperation between Member States in the consumer protection field, but only after further consultation processes with national

---

[9] Decision No. 283/1999/EC of January 25th 1999 (O.J., L 34, 02/09/1999). This general framework covers a five-year period (January 1th 1999 to December 31th 2003).

[10] COM (2001) 531 final, 10/02/2001.

[11] COM (2002) 289 final, 06/04/2002.

governments had taken place.[12] This was a response to the Green Paper on consumer protection which had caused much reaction from business, consumers' organizations, governments and national bodies, from which the unanimous consensus emerged on the need to reform European legislation in the area of consumer protection.

The Commission has gathered together the suggestions of the other Community institutions in the *Strategic plan for consumer policy 2002–2006*.[13] The fundamental strategic objective is to ensure "a better quality of life for everyone,"[14] in addition to the modernization of the European economy. The success of the new policy towards consumers will be measured on the basis of the impact it has on the citizens of the Community. For the time being the Commission believes it essential firstly to present the reasoning which underpins the basis of its strategy, and, regarding the future, to subject progress in the implementation of its strategy to regular monitoring, in order to evaluate its effectiveness.

There are five key elements conditioning the new strategy:

- The adoption of the Euro, which has potentially eliminated barriers to trans-national trade.
- The use of the internet and its spread throughout European families, which has had an impact on new ways of buying (e-commerce).
- The notable price differences within the EU Member States, which reduce consumer confidence in buying beyond their own frontiers.
- The reform of European Governance and the simplification of Community legislation.
- The enlargement of the internal market to include the candidate countries, which has increased the heterogeneity of legal rules.

The main medium term objectives are three:

- A high and harmonized level of consumer protection for the EU as a whole. This goal would have to be achieved via a more general legislative framework so as to respond more rapidly to market changes.
- Enforcement of consumer protection measures, thanks to better cooperation at EU level but also to raising consumers' awareness and providing them with more information.
- Involvement of consumers in decision making at Community level.

---

[12] The tendency in this direction was also repeated in the later *Strategy for the Internal Market (2003–2006* (COM (2003) 238 final), in which Parliament and the Council agree upon the need to pursue the aim of greater efficiency in the area of consumer protection, to ensure consumer confidence in the internal market, resulting in its further development.

[13] COM (2002) 208 final, 06/08/2002.

[14] An objective already highlighted in another Communication: COM (2000) 154 final, 02/09/2000.

More importance should be given to consumer education and to supporting consumer organizations in applicant countries.

The objectives will be achieved by means of action undertaken in a short-term program[15] to be regularly reviewed by the Commission as circumstances evolve.

Regulation (EC) no. 2006/2004 of October 27th 2004 on cooperation between national authorities responsible for the enforcement of consumer protection laws (the Regulation on consumer protection cooperation)[16] was approved in December 2004, implementing the proposals set out in the preceding documents. In this, the European Parliament and the Council accept the draft formulation of the Commission in its Communication 2002 to establish a real network of public authorities to protect consumer interests, including a framework of rights and duties of reciprocal assistance, which might ensure the quicker and better application of Community provisions, in particular where consumers have dealings with dishonest professionals.

> **Reg. 2006/2004**, recitals: "Existing national enforcement arrangements for the laws that protect consumers' interests are not adapted to the challenges of enforcement in the internal market and effective and efficient enforcement cooperation in these cases is not currently possible. These difficulties give rise to barriers to cooperation between public enforcement authorities to detect, investigate and bring about the cessation or prohibition of intra-Community infringements of the laws that protect consumers' interests. The resulting lack of effective enforcement in cross-border cases enables sellers and suppliers to evade enforcement attempts by relocating within the Community. This gives rise to a distortion of competition for law-abiding sellers and suppliers operating either domestically or cross-border. The difficulties of enforcement in cross-border cases also undermine the confidence of consumers in taking up cross-border offers and hence their confidence in the internal market. It is therefore appropriate to facilitate cooperation between public authorities responsible for enforcement of the laws that protect consumers' interests in dealing with intra-Community infringements, and to contribute to the smooth functioning of the internal market, the quality and consistency of enforcement of the laws that protect consumers' interests and the monitoring of the protection of consumers' economic interests."

---

[15] See COM (2002) 208 final, *cit.*, Appendix at page 15.

[16] O.J., L 364, 12/09/2004 p.1. It shall apply from December 29th 2005, while the provisions on mutual assistance set out in Chapters II and III Reg. shall apply from December 29th 2006.

The objective of the Regulation is the cooperation between national authorities responsible for the enforcement of consumer protection law; since it cannot be sufficiently achieved by the Member States because they cannot ensure cooperation and coordination by acting alone, and can therefore be better achieved at Community level, the Community may adopt measures, in accordance with the principle of subsidiarity and the principle of proportionality as set out in art. 5 TEC.
The challenges of enforcement in the internal market derives from what art. 3 Reg. defines *intra-Community infringements*. Intra-Community infringement means "any act or omission contrary to the laws that protect consumers' interests (...), that harms, or is likely to harm, the collective interests of consumers residing in a Member State or Member States other than the Member State where the act or omission originated or took place; or where the responsible seller or supplier is established; or where evidence or assets pertaining to the act or omission are to be found."

According to the Regulation, each Member State shall communicate to the Commission and the other Member States the identities of the competent authorities, of other public authorities and bodies having a legitimate interest in the cessation or prohibition of intra-Community infringements, and of the single liaison office. The Commission shall publish and update the list of single liaison offices and competent authorities in the Official Journal of the European Union.

Following up what was expressed in the preceding Communication and the Green Paper, the Commission has also made provisions for close administrative cooperation between Member States, and between the latter and the Commission, in projects of common interest aimed at informing and educating consumers. The Commission Decision 2003/709/EC of October 9th 2003, setting up a *European Consumer Consultative Group,*[17] can take its place in the context of this strengthening of the instruments for consumer protection; this is a new body equipped with consultative functions regarding all issues concerning the protection of consumers' interests at Community level.[18]

Consumer protection and in particular the high degree of such protection had already earned an independent place in the *Charter of fundamental rights of the European Union* (art. 38); it has also been reconfirmed in the new *European Constitution* (art. III-120 & art. III-235, Constitution Treaty, which should replace art. 153 TEC).

---

[17] O.J., L 258, 10/10/2003, p. 35.

[18] However, it should be noted that the consultation by the Commission is merely optional, thus greatly reducing its actual utility.

**Constitution for Europe. Art. III-120**: "Consumer protection requirements shall be taken into account in defining and implementing other Union policies and activities."

**Constitution for Europe. Section 6: Consumer Protection. Art. III-235:** "**(1)** In order to promote the interests of consumers and to ensure a high level of consumer protection, the Union shall contribute to protecting the health, safety and economic interests of consumers, as well as to promoting their right to information, education and to organise themselves in order to safeguard their interests. **(2)** The Union shall contribute to the attainment of the objectives referred to in paragraph 1 through: (a) measures adopted pursuant to Article III-172 in the context of the establishment and functioning of the internal market; (b) measures which support, supplement and monitor the policy pursued by the Member States. **(3)** European laws or framework laws shall establish the measures referred to in paragraph 2(b). Such laws shall be adopted after consultation of the Economic and Social Committee. **(4)** Acts adopted pursuant to paragraph 3 shall not prevent any Member State from maintaining or introducing more stringent protective provisions. Such provisions must be compatible with the Constitution. They shall be notified to the Commission."

In general, for these purposes the Commission encourages the other European institutions to sustain *maximum harmonization* measures and to reform existing directives by means of framework directives. Maximum harmonization seeks to remove the freedom of Member States to maintain or introduce protective measures, so that the Community law becomes the ceiling of protection. The shift from minimum to maximum harmonization is now at the very core of academic debate.

## 3. Beyond a Definition of 'Consumer'

We have referred to the difficulty of attributing a single meaning to the term *consumer*. Let us look at the definitions proposed at Community level.

The Community legislature has not involved itself in any specific way with this; in fact the Treaty, the primary source of Community law, makes use of the term, but does not define it; instead it falls to the directives to define what a consumer is, although it is sometimes rather blurred.

The Court of Justice, in the case of *Bertrand v. Paul Ott K.G.*[19] has

[19] Case C-150/77, June 22nd 1978, (1977) ECR I-1431, especially point 21 and the conclusions of Advocate-General Capotorti.

ventured the definition of the consumer as "weaker party" ("*parte debole*" in Italian, "*partie faible*" in French, "*schwächer partei*" in German) and as "natural person" ("*personne physique*" in French, "*natürliche person*" in German, "*persona fisica*" in Italian) in the cases *Cape Snc* v. *Idealservice Srl* and *Idealservice MN RE Sas* v. *OMAI Srl*.[20]

The legal scholars who study Community law have advanced their interpretation of the concept.[21] The fact is that when regarding the consumer, various legal situations are envisaged: sometimes s/he is the buyer of a product, sometimes the person who has suffered damage, other times the user of a public service, or the insured, sometimes the investor, the saver, or even the client. Some systems extend the protection due to natural persons to include those who represent associations or non-profit making bodies.

Following an informal meeting of experts called by the Directorate–General XXIV, held in Brussels on April 10th 1995, some important considerations on the point were made.

First of all, it was recognized that the term consumer is variously applied in the Community directives and its meaning may change according to which economic operation requires regulation. A "consumer" may sometimes be understood to mean a natural person who acquires goods, or a natural person who uses services and therefore is a "user," or as a person who borrows money or who invests their own savings, thus a "saver."

Secondly, it emerged from the meeting that the term consumer is used in a residual way, in that s/he is considered to be a "non-professional," i.e. someone who acquires goods or services for purposes which are unconnected to the exercise of a professional activity.

Thirdly, an analysis of the EC provisions demonstrates that in practice, the intervention of the Community law-makers concentrates on "professionals," who are the principle actors in the integration of the internal market, and it is at the cost of the non-professionals (also called *pure civilians*), who undertake non-commercial transactions. The main goal pursued by harmonization is, in fact, the correction of market failures.

We may therefore catalogue the Community provisions in the field of consumer protection according to their varying degrees of intensity.

The first type of intervention is aimed at safeguarding the health of Community citizens and is represented by the collection of rules, directed primarily at States and businesses, and concerns the adaptations which

---

[20] Case C-541/99, C-542/99, November 22nd 2001, (2001) ECR I-9049.

[21] The reader is referred to the bibliography at the end of the chapter.

must be made by those whose activity may result in damage or be dangerous for the health and safety of the citizen. Rules of this kind are to be found in the directives on product labeling, food advertising, contents of cosmetic products, toy safety, pharmaceutical advertising, and, in part, on misleading advertising.[22]

The second type of intervention is aimed at protecting the economic interests of the consumer and consists in the harmonization of domestic laws applicable to legal relations between private parties, and, in particular, to the relationship between a natural person on one side, and an undertaking on the other (i.e. *one-sided business transactions or business-to-consumer contracts*). The Community intervention here concentrates on adopting directives which rebalance the information asymmetry which represents the qualifying aspect of consumer contracts.

The third type of intervention, which achieves the objective of protecting the consumer only indirectly, is directed towards regulating commercial transactions which can restrict competition, in which only professionals participate (i.e. *commercial contracts or business-to-business transactions*). These are represented by the rules concerning company law, for protecting intellectual property and for ensuring fair competition.

In chapters I, II & III of this book we will be looking at the second type of intervention, namely those Community measures which affect the so-called *one-sided business transactions*, and impinge on the bulk of private law of national legal systems, *i.e.* the law of contracts and the law of torts. The aim of the enquiry will be substantive law only, as we shall not be concerning ourselves with rules relating to private international law.[23]

In chapters IV, V & VI we will be commenting on the third type of intervention, namely those Community measures which affect business transactions in which professionals participate, the so-called *commercial contracts*.

---

[22] According to the Strategic plan for consumer policy 2002–2006, cited at note 10, all these directives will be subject to revision and reform. They will not be dealt with in this book.

[23] This sector is dominated, so far as contractual obligations are concerned, by the 1980 Rome Convention, promoted by the European Community (O.J., L 266, p. 1, 10/09/1980). The Commission, in the Green Paper published on January 14th 2003—COM (2002) 654 final—proposed to convert the Convention into a Regulation (Rome I): *cf.* above chapter I § 11 and chapter VI § 2; *cf.* also below § 8 this chapter.

## 4. The Relevant Issues in the Domestic Private Laws of Member States

In the last fifteen years, so-called *Community consumer law* has erupted into the domestic private laws of Member States, altering rules and time-honored practices, introducing new rights, overturning apparently untouchable principles, and, on more than one occasion, upsetting the order of the European Civil Codes.

The analysis of both Community legal provisions and national implementing measures will be divided, for ease of explanation, into the following three parts:

- *Consumer contracts,*[24] where both rules of a general nature are relevant (e.g. directives on unfair terms in consumer contracts, sales of consumer goods and associated guarantees), as well as rules applicable to certain types of contract (e.g. directives on contracts negotiated away from business premises, on package holidays, tours and package travel, on timeshare, etc). The weight of the sources of Community law in the context of the law of contracts is extremely significant, such that in academic circles the expression 'Europeanization of the law of contracts' is widely used.
- *Product Liability,*[25] where the Community provisions on manufacturers' strict liability for defective products, as well as the draft Directive on the liability of provider of services are relevant.
- *Insurance, banking, and financial services law;*[26] this part concerns sectors which are detailed enough to require separate treatment, in that they arose from a series of interventions which have had an impact beyond the law of contracts or torts. The separate analysis of these areas is also justified by the variety of Community interventions concerning consumer credit, banking contracts and investment funds.

## 5. The Consequences of Community Intervention in the Law of Contracts

The considerations which have made the Community legislature develop special rules in contract law, in the context of consumer protection policy, may be summarized in the following way:

---

[24] See below in this chapter.

[25] See below in chapter II.

[26] See below in chapter III.

– *Legal considerations.* "Standard form contracts" prepared by the business enterprise are becoming more and more common; these may be concluded by a signature at the foot of a pre-printed form, or may take place over the telephone, even in the course of a television program, or via the internet. The exponential development of such contracts, together with new technology, has often taken judges and legal practitioners by surprise, who have then had to find solutions which are not always appreciated.
– *Economic considerations.* The lack of coordination among national legal systems has caused a diversification of applicable rules which is unsatisfactory for a market aspiring to unity. The disparity in legal regimes in trans-national contracts, according to whether they are subject to more rigid or more lenient legislation, leads to economic disparity.

Proposals on the subject of protecting buyers of goods or services from the abuse of power on the part of sellers or providers, have been discussed for some time in Brussels.[27] It would be fifteen years before these initiatives were achieved, after a lengthy planning phase between Member States and as a result of a process of continual mediation between different models in search of a balanced compromise, rather than an efficient model. To have a precise idea of the development time for Community provisions in this area, just consider that the draft proposal which was to introduce the Directive on unfair terms was in place in 1975, while the Directive only saw the light of day in 1993.[28]

Apart from a minority of jurists always eagerly watching what was going on in Brussels, generally such draft proposals (which are subject to the uncertainty of whether and when they may be approved) did not arouse much interest, and remained confined to the political arena, a sphere in which they seemed to be of no interest to legal professionals.

The situation changed radically over the course of a few years. The fact is that the activity of the Community legislators in the area of civil and commercial law, and particularly the law of contracts, expanded both quantitatively and qualitatively. The Brussels legislature has not only progressively extended its work of harmonization to cover an increasing number of contracts, but at the same time has proceeded to issue detailed regulation in contract matters. The means adopted is the directive, which

---

[27] As we have seen, already (§ 2, this chapter) in the first action plan of 1975, the Community policy was inclined towards protection of the economic interests of consumers, through a series of interventions which would have involved the law of contracts.

[28] See also chapter II, in first volume of this series, *A Common Law for Europe*.

frequently does not stop at laying down essential principles, but governs in detail the obligations and duties of the parties, to the point that it has lost its original connotation and is used as a standardizing instrument rather than a means of harmonization.

This large-scale intervention by the Community, the detail of the legal solutions introduced, together with the common substrate, which has been laid down in this area, has led to the formation of a new law of contracts. Today, at the national level, every lawyer or judge must deal with an ever-increasing number of provisions which, with the aim of implementing Community directives, have transformed the domestic law of contracts.

At least two new fundamental features, among other things, characterize this new set of rules, which we will pause to look at in the following pages: for one, the introduction of new legal instruments which protect only one of the contracting parties; for another, the introduction of a classification which distinguishes between commercial and consumer contracts.

These are not the only consequences of the phenomenon which we are examining.

In the chapter on the circulation of legal rules and models,[29] we saw that the Community law-makers are, in the design of the texts of the directives and regulations, in debt to the experience of the Member States, and, in particular, those States which have most political influence within the Community. Examples of the circulation of models in the field of consumer contracts are too numerous. For instance, the Directive on door-to-door contracts refers to principles from the French legal system; the Directive on consumer credit has adopted some of the rules from British common law; the Directive on unfair terms was inspired by the German and, in some cases, French rules.

This intense reference to heterogeneous, mainly European, models may have the effect of bringing national lawyers *et al*, who are called upon to use the new instruments based on a different experience, closer to the interpretative ways of the jurisprudence and case law of the country from which the model derives, much more so than at present. Familiarity with trans-national legal rules and solutions thus becomes not only (and not so much) the chance for an excursion into comparative law, as a necessary undertaking with a view to a correct interpretation of non-native rules.

These are the main directives concerning *consumer contracts*, which will be occupying us in the following paragraphs:

---

[29] See chapter II, in first volume of this series, *A Common Law for Europe*.

- Contracts negotiated away from business premises: Directive of October 20th 1985, no. 85/577 (§ 9, this chapter).
- Package travel, package holidays, and package tours: Directive of June 13th 1990, no. 90/314 (§ 10, this chapter).
- Contracts containing unfair terms: Directive of April 5th 1993, no. 93/13 (§ 11, this chapter).
- Contracts for the purchase of the right to use immovable property on a timeshare basis: Directive of October 26th 1994, no. 94/47 (§ 12, this chapter).
- Distance selling: Directive of May 20th 1997, no. 97/7 (§ 13, this chapter).
- Injunctions for the protection of consumers' interests: Directive of May 19th 1998, no. 98/27 (§ 14, this chapter).
- Access to justice in cross-border disputes: Directive of January 27th 2003, no. 2003/8 (§ 15, this chapter).
- Sale of consumer goods and associated guarantees: Directive of May 25th 1999, no. 99/44 (§ 16, this chapter).
- Electronic signatures: Directive of December 13th 1999, no. 99/93 (§ 17, this chapter).
- E-commerce: Directive of June 8th 2000, no. 2000/31 (§ 18, this chapter).

Other directives concerning consumer contracts—such as the Directive of February 2nd 1990, no. 90/88 on consumer credit contracts, the Directive of May 10th 1993, no. 93/22 on investment services in the securities fields, the Directive of September 23rd 2002, no. 2002/65 on distance marketing of consumer financial services—which have had an impact beyond the law of contracts will be analyzed in chapter III.

## 6. A New Taxonomy: Consumer Contracts

As is well known, the authoritative intervention by the *State* or other supranational institutions different from the *Market*, with the aim of correcting an alleged imbalance, has been viewed as a disturbing factor. The principles which govern the law of contracts arose in the first half of the 19th century: they are those of freedom of contract, *caveat emptor*, privacy of contract, etc., which presuppose both that the individual is aware of her/ his own interests and that it is for her/him alone to put her/ himself in a position of understanding the significance of the contract and to be in possession of all the information necessary to conclude the contract.

The mere imbalance in the contracting power of the parties was insufficient to justify and permit a possible corrective intervention by the

State; there had to have been a particular weakness, in the specific case, of the party, by which is meant 'individual,' not merely by reason of belonging to an intrinsically weaker category.

In this sense, in the 20th century, the legislature only intervened where a situation of *abuse* (or exploitation by one of the contracting parties) had been identified. One only needs to consider the provisions contained in the national Civil Codes on contracts entered into under duress, or contracts where consent was a consequence of error or undue influence.

It would therefore be inaccurate to suppose that it is only in recent times that lawmakers have realized formal respect for the freedom to contract may conceal abuses which damage the other party.

What differentiates the model of protection introduced by the Community with respect to the legal systems of the Member States, is the fact that the Community model applies to all cases where there is a contractual relationship between a business/professional on the one side, and a consumer/natural person on the other, quite apart from establishing the existence or otherwise of abuse on the part of the former.

A contract between a professional and a consumer is always subject to the new special rules, and testing whether there is effectively a difference in contractual power between the parties counts for nothing. In fact the consumer is generally (but not always) the weaker contracting party, having generally less expertise than the other party regarding the goods or services s/he wishes to buy or which are offered to her/him; s/he usually does not have all the necessary information at hand to conclude the deal and generally finds her/himself confronting a "take it or leave it" situation, due to the widespread practice of using standard contracts prepared by one party.

Thus the set of directives has given rise to a new category of contracts, *consumer contracts,* unknown, for example, to the Italian legal system, but well-known to the French, German, and Scandinavian systems which, in the 70's, gave voice to the first examples of consumer protection.

The creation of new kinds of *consumer contracts* has caused a definitive break-up of contract law, which, up until then, had been a coherent and homogeneous system in itself, as a set of rules codified (in civil law systems) or developed through judicial case-law, and in any case coherent within itself due to the principle of *stare decisis* (e.g. the rule of precedent).

> An early fragmentation of contract law happened as a result of the European codifications of the 19th century, which kept the Civil Codes separate from the Commercial ones (the French, German, and Spanish ones are examples). However, unification was pursued in the 20th century codifications, which denied a bi-par-

tite approach and codified the commercial aspect within the Civil Code (see the Swiss, Italian, Dutch, and Russian Civil Codes).

The countries which had been under the communist sphere of influence, when reforming their own legal systems preferred the bi-partite approach in many cases, by adopting separate Civil and Commercial Codes, although their renewed Civil Codes also contain general commercial provisions (*cf.* for example, the Polish, Czech, and Slovak Civil Codes).

To sum up, with the adoption of a new policy for the protection of consumers, the legal systems of the European States have undergone two fundamental changes:

- The introduction of differentiated legal rules and solutions for consumer contracts (*one-sided business transactions)* in respect of commercial transactions in which only professionals participate (*commercial contracts*).
- The recognition of *a double system of rules and remedies* applicable in cases where at least one of the parties is a consumer: the ordinary provisions, already contained in the Civil Codes or special acts, on the one hand, and the new rules which implement the directives, on the other.

## 7. The Limits of Consumer Protection

Some legal scholars are highly critical of the dichotomy between consumer contracts and non-consumer (both commercial and ordinary) contracts and have viewed with disfavor the tendency of national legal interpreters to liken the consumer to the so-called "weaker party" in a contract.

As we have seen, the intrinsic weakness of the consumer can derive from the following:

– Limited access to information and the knowledge s/he has of the goods or service which form the subject-matter of the contract.

– The limited interest a consumer has in understanding the technicalities of the contract.

Regarding the first aspect, the consumer, even if diligent, cannot make an informed choice because s/he is at a cognitive disadvantage and therefore, at the time of signing the contract, is not correctly informed as to what is truly in his/her best interest. But what matters more, from the second aspect, is that the consumer has no motivation to inform her/himself more fully about the purchase regarding the technicalities of the contract, since his/her intrinsic weakness derives from a standardized system of acquisition and distribution, where the consumer has little chance to intervene (one thinks of contracts for the supply of electricity, gas, mobile telephone, internet services, etc).

Thus the consumer may certainly be considered, in general, as a "weaker party," so long as it is kept in mind that:

– A business entrepreneur *may*, sometimes, be a weaker party.

– A consumer *may not* always be a weaker party.

Legal scholars also note the fact that Community directives on this subject place emphasis on the *function* underlying a consumer contract (which must be outside professional activity), and not on the effective weakness of the contractor involved in an individual contractual negotiation.

It cannot be categorically asserted that whoever may be considered weak *in the abstract* within the economic system, namely the person who makes a contract with a professional for their own or their family's benefit, is *in actual fact* weak in relation to the specific negotiation. One thinks for example, of a consumer who buys goods from an entrepreneur who is about to go into liquidation, when the former is aware of this fact: it is difficult in this case for the entrepreneur to impose his/her own conditions. Another instance, where the consumer-buyer is not without resources but has equal or superior competence to the professional, is the solicitor who makes a contract for a bank mortgage on his/her own account. Such a person is fully able to recognize the significance of the other party's standard conditions of contract.

The small businessman who wants to expand her/his business and seeks a bank loan for this purpose is not in a very different position with respect to someone who exercises the same profession, but is asking for the loan to buy his/her own dwelling house. Both of these are potentially inexpert and subject to possible abuse.

As can be seen from this empirical type of observation, the set of rules provided by the Community directives is not aimed at the protection of the weaker contracting party. The aim is protection of the consumer, simply that.

The weaker party, be they entrepreneur, businessman, professional person, or natural person who makes a contract with another natural person who is not an entrepreneur, can have recourse (if necessary) to national legal instruments/remedies such as rescission or termination of the contract for mistake, duress, undue influence or misrepresentation, provided that all the pre-requisites exist to sustain the action. But they cannot avail themselves of the consumer protection laws unless the national courts decide to give a wide interpretation to the rules in question, so as to apply them also to someone who is not, in the strict sense, a consumer.

Conversely, a natural person who has made a contract as a consumer will always be able to make use of the available Community remedies, without having to prove that s/he is a weaker party.

## 8. The Legal Instruments for Consumer Protection: Procedural Fairness and International Private Law

Intervention by the Community legislature in the area of consumer contracts may be of two kinds, *sectoral* and *general.*

Intervention is *sectoral* (or "vertical") when the directive concerns a particular contract or economic operation. This is the case, for example, of the directives on package tours, timesharing, contracts negotiated away from business premises, consumer credit contracts, and others besides.

Intervention is *general* (or "horizontal") when the directive governs some general characteristics of the contracting process, independently of the kind of economic operation or particular contract it concerns. The archetypal example is the Directive on unfair contract terms, whose content refers to a vast array of contracts, or the Directive on sale of consumer goods and associated guarantees, which places the obligation on the seller to supply goods in conformity with the contract concluded with the consumer.

All the directives, involving both sectoral and general interventions, are characterized by some common rules whose implementation has given rise to remarkable innovation within the European legal systems.

1. First and foremost there is the introduction of the so-called *cooling-off period* in favor of the consumer-contractor. This *Jus Poenitendi*, in legal terms, according to the case in question, translates into a right of withdrawal, a right to cancel the contract or to terminate it (when the contract has been performed immediately); or into a temporary suspension of the effects of the contract (when the contract is to be performed at a different time with respect to the expiry date of the cooling-off period).

Initially, the right to a cooling-off period was applied to contracts made in situations where the other party sought out the consumer, often taking her/him unawares (so-called "surprise effect"), for example, contracts with door-to-door salesmen or outside business premises. However, over time, the recognition of the cooling-off period has been extended to situations which have nothing to do with an "ambush," such as in the case of insurance contracts, where the contracting buyer has a right of withdrawal in every case, even if it was she herself or he himself who paid a visit to the insurer's office.

The unilateral termination of the contract sounds like the recognition of an undecided state of mind which may therefore be changed, submitting the contract to a kind of anomalous precariousness which makes it subject to revocation and cancellation.

2. Secondly, all the directives on the subject have in common a particular attention to the *right to information*. This right consists of two aspects, namely (i) information on a whole range of elements to do with the contract, clearly listed in each directive, (the object and reciprocal duties, the form); and (ii) information about the contractor's rights which are recognized by the specific provision, including the time-limits within which they must be exercised.

Immediately apparent is the impact of Community directives on contract forms. There is quite an emphasis on formal rigor, which the supranational legislator intends to correspond to a more engaged consent on the part of the consumer. The form functions as a guarantee of the interests of the person who concludes the negotiations quickly, following standardized procedures which are not subject to modification by the purchaser. Diffusion of information is therefore left to the form of the contract, which protects the interests of certainty and transparency, and works both ways, in respect of the consumer, as well as the business, with the aim of producing beneficial effects on competition.

3. Lastly, almost all the directives in question establish a range of new rules which impinge on the *performance of the contract*, increasing its potential for being invalid or of no effect.

To summarize, it seems that the Community legislature places most emphasis on guaranteeing *procedural fairness* rather than *substantial fairness*; it is concerned with creating the pre-conditions so that the contractual process takes place according to criteria of reasonableness, leaving to the courts (the national ones, through the interpretative contribution of the Court of Justice) the task of judicial intervention to restore the balance which is unfavorable, or missing from the start, using the remedial apparatus available in the case of failure to observe Community law.

The principle of State liability for damage caused to individuals through violation of Community law is important in this connection, as established by the well-known case of *Francovich* (see chapter V of the first volume of this series, *A Common Law for Europe).*

*Cf.* also the ECJ case, September 20th 2001, C-453/99, *Courage ltd. v. Crehan*, ECR I-6297: a person can, in certain cases, rely on a breach of art. 81 TEC to claim damages before a national court, even where s/he is a party to a restrictive trade agreement. In particular, it is for the national court to ascertain whether the party who claims to have suffered loss through concluding a contract

> that is liable to restrict or distort competition found himself in a markedly weaker position than the other party, such as to seriously compromise or even eliminate his freedom to negotiate the terms of the contract and his capacity to avoid the loss or reduce its extent, in particular by availing himself in good time of all the legal remedies available to him. (See §§ 26–27, 29, 31, 33, 36 and operative part 2–3 of the Judgment).

The aim is to ensure that the consumer is not taken by surprise, but may choose to contract after careful consideration: once "informed choice" is guaranteed, it is no longer of any account if the subject-matter of the contract should prove disadvantageous to the consumer. In this sense the Community law of consumer contracts seems to respect the traditional principle of freedom of contract.

However, the new law of contracts which has emerged following Community intervention has not resolved the problems of the functioning of the internal market which derive from the coexistence of different national laws. For this reason, as we saw in the first volume of this series, *A Common Law for Europe,* the Commission has published three Communications[30] to stimulate debate in national and supranational institutions (courts and legislative bodies), among professional suppliers and consumers (both associations and private individuals), professors and lawyers, as to what may represent a desirable level of harmonization in the law of contracts of the Member States of the EU.

The need for homogenous and incisive action by the Community in the area of contract law has led the Commission to ask interested parties for an opinion as to possible and desirable solutions. To assist the various parties to define possible solutions, the *Communication 2001* presented a list of options for future EU initiatives in the area of contract law. These are four in number, but interested parties could add their own proposals to this list:

- Leave the solution of the problem to the market (option I).
- Promote the development of common, non-binding principles, possibly to be collected together in a Restatement (option II).
- Improve the quality of existing EC law (option III).
- Adopt exhaustive new legislative measures at Community level (option IV).

[30] COM (2001) 398 final, 07/11/2001; COM (2003) 68 final, 02/12/2003 and COM (2004) 651 final, 10/11/2004.

As a result of the consultation process, *Communication 2003* proposed an Action Plan, which suggested a mix of regulatory and non-regulatory measures. The Commission put the drafting of a European Civil Code[31] off the agenda and announced the creation of a *Common Frame of Reference* (CFR) establishing common principles and terminology in the area of contract law, in the form of a non-binding document, for achieving a higher degree of convergence between the contract laws of Member States.

The *Communication 2004* presented the "way forward" for reviewing the existing *acquis* through the CFR and for improving European contract law. With respect to the non-binding measure, an Optional Code on general contract law and certain specific contracts,[32] the Commission took into consideration the respondents' position in the debate launched with the Action Plan 2001 and supported the 'opt in' model—a purely optional model which would have to be chosen by the parties through a choice of law clause. It should cover business-to-business transactions as well as business-to-consumer contracts, with two consequences.[33]

Firstly, the introduction in the optional instrument of mandatory provisions concerning consumer protection, within the meaning of arts. 5 and 7 of the Rome Convention, would represent a great advantage. In fact the parties, by choosing the optional instrument as applicable law to their contract on the basis of art. 3(1) of the Rome Convention, would know—from the moment of the conclusion of the contract—which mandatory rules are applicable to their contractual relationship. This possibility nevertheless seems to be precluded for the time being, at least according to the leading interpretation of the Rome Convention: the expression "law chosen by the parties" is generally regarded as precluding the election of *non-national law* (such as it would be an Optional Code on general contract law and certain specific contracts).

> **Rome Convention: Art. 3. 1.** "A contract shall be governed by the law chosen by the parties. The choice must be expressed or demonstrated with reasonable certainty by the terms of the contract or the circumstances of the case. By their choice the parties can select the law applicable to the whole or a part only of the contract. (…)".
>
> **Rome Convention: Art. 5. 1.** "This Article applies to a contract the object of which is the supply of goods or services to a person ("the consumer") for a purpose which can be regarded as

[31] *Cf.* COM (2003) 68 final, Executive summary and point 1.6., cit. above.

[32] The Commission set out clearly that it is not its intention to propose a 'European Civil or Contract Code.' *Cf.* the volume *A Common Law for Europe*, chapters I and VI.

[33] *Cf.* COM (2004) 651 final, point 2.3 and Annex II, cit. above.

being outside his trade or profession, or a contract for the provision of credit for that object. **2.** Notwithstanding the provisions of Article 3, a choice of law made by the parties shall not have the result of depriving the consumer of the protection afforded to him by the mandatory rules of the law of the country in which he has his habitual residence—if in that country the conclusion of the contract was preceded by a specific invitation addressed to him or by advertising, and he had taken in that country all the steps necessary on his part for the conclusion of the contract, or if the other party or his agent received the consumer's order in that country, or if the contract is for the sale of goods and the consumer travelled from that country to another country and there gave his order, provided that the consumer's journey was arranged by the seller for the purpose of inducing the consumer to buy. **3.** Notwithstanding the provisions of Article 4, a contract to which this Article applies shall, in the absence of choice in accordance with Article 3, be governed by the law of the country in which the consumer has his habitual residence if it is entered into in the circumstances described in paragraph 2 of this Article."

**Rome Convention: Art. 7., 1.** "When applying under this Convention the law of a country, effect may be given to the mandatory rules of the law of another country with which the situation has a close connection, if and in so far as, under the law of the latter country, those rules must be applied whatever the law applicable to the contract. In considering whether to give effect to these mandatory rules, regard shall be had to their nature and purpose and to the consequences of their application or non-application. **2.** Nothing in this Convention shall restrict the application of the rules of the law of the forum in a situation where they are mandatory irrespective of the law otherwise applicable to the contract."

Secondly, the introduction of the business-to-business transaction within the scope of the optional instrument would raise the issue of coherence and compatibility with the Vienna Convention (CISG). If the optional instruments will be an 'opt in' measure, by choosing the optional instrument as applicable law to their contract, the parties would have tacitly excluded the application of the CISG on the base of art. 6 CISG.

**CISG, Art. 6**: "The parties may exclude the application of this Convention or, subject to art. 12, derogate from or vary the effect of any of it provisions."

In the opinion of the Commission, this Optional Code would give parties the greatest degree of contractual freedom. It could take the legal form of a Regulation. In the field of consumer contracts, the Commission concluded that there is a need for *maximum harmonization* (very close to unification),[34] considered to be particularly suited to the *new law of contracts*, in view of the importance of this sector of private law in relation to commerce between the States of the Community.

## 9. Contracts Negotiated away from Business Premises

Council Directive no. 85/577 of December 20th 1985 for the protection of consumers in the case of contracts negotiated away from business premises[35] was the first to harmonize some aspects of the national contract laws.

The Directive caused much comment at the time: on the one hand for its content, in that it regulated widespread commercial practice and introduced some innovative rules; on the other because it demonstrated that the EEC was able to concern itself not just with commercial policy, but also with issues of civil law, with which, apart from the area of competition, it had not hitherto involved itself. The Community had taken its first step towards the uniformization of European private law.

The Directive originated in the first program for consumer protection of April 1975.[36] There was a lengthy process involved in the approval of the Directive (the draft was dated May 29th 1977, and it became a Directive on December 20th 1985), reflecting the time required to overcome the opposition of the German federal government. The Federal Republic of Germany blocked the adoption of the Directive using its veto, until the German *Haustürwiderrufsgestz* was approved, on November 14th 1985. There was therefore a contemporaneous initiative at both Community level and that of German domestic law.

> Another law which stimulated the Community debate on the subject was a French statute dating from 1972, on the subject of doorstep selling (*loi* no. 72-1137 of December 22nd 1972). In 1989, with *loi* no. 89-421 of June 23rd 1989, the French legal system harmonized its own legislation to the Community Directive, which were later amalgamated in the Consumer Code (*Code de la consommation)*.

Dir. 85/577 is aimed at all contracts ready-made by an enterprise and normally contained in a standard form, which is then given to an "unpre-

---

[34] *Cf.* above, this chapter, § 2.

[35] O.J. L 372, 12/31/1985, p. 31. Transposed by all the member States.

[36] See above, this chapter, § 2.

pared" consumer to sign. The consumer-contractor is often accosted at her/his own front door and, embarrassed by receiving such a visit at home and anxious to extricate her/himself from an importunate salesman, won over by his persuasive capacity, s/he ends up agreeing to the deal without being fully convinced of all the consequences which her/his signature on the contract implies. In other words, the basic idea behind the Directive is the protection of the privacy of the individual. The context for the application of the Directive are contracts under which a trader supplies goods or services to a consumer, who has negotiated a deal for purposes which exclude business or professional activity (art. 1):

- During a sales-trip arranged by the trader away from business premises.
- In the course of a visit to the consumer's home.
- In the course of a visit to the consumer's place of work.

The Directive therefore makes no reference, as the French would have wished, to contracts made in the street or public areas, and differs from the provisions of the original 1977 draft proposal, which was closer to the German model.

Contracts concerning the supply of food and drink or other products for current domestic consumption are expressly excluded, as it is thought that such goods are indispensable in daily life and no particular protection of the buyer is necessary. Contracts made through catalogues and those involving the sale of real property are also excluded. Another limitation provided by the Directive is the minimum sum (€ 60) below which the new provisions may not be applied, should the States think it inopportune. Insurance contracts and those involving transferable securities are also excluded, in that they are already governed by specific Community and national legal rules.[37]

> See ECJ Judgment March 17th 1998, case C-45/96 *Bayerische Hypotheken-und Wechsellbank AG v. Edgar Dietzinger* (1998) ECR I-1199, regarding the interpretation of arts. 1 & 2 of the Directive. The main actor in the case was the German Federal Supreme Court (the ninth division of the BGH) which referred to the Court of Justice the question as to whether the Directive under consideration was applicable to the performance of a contract of guarantee concluded by Mr. *Dietzinger* with the bank.
>
> ***Edgar Dietzinger* ruling:** "(**§22**) However, it is apparent from the wording of Article 1 of Directive 85/577 and from the ancil-

[37] See below, chapter III.

> lary nature of guarantees that the directive covers only a guarantee ancillary to a contract whereby, in the context of 'doorstep selling', a consumer assumes obligations towards the trader with a view to obtaining goods or services from him. Furthermore, since the directive is designed to protect only consumers, a guarantee comes within the scope of the directive only where, in accordance with the first indent of Article 2, the guarantor has entered into a commitment for a purpose which can be regarded as unconnected with his trade or profession. (§ **23**) The answer to the question referred to the Court must therefore be that, on a proper construction of the first indent of Article 2 of Directive 85/577, a contract of guarantee concluded by a natural person who is not acting in the course of his trade or profession does not come within the scope of the directive where it guarantees repayment of a debt contracted by another person who, for his part, is acting within the course of his trade or profession."

The Directive prescribes only a minimum standard of protection; Member States may maintain a higher standard of protection domestically (art. 4).

The two main features of the Directive are the right of cancellation and a set of rules concerning the so-called right to information.

On the first point, overturning traditional and common principles in the law of contract, the Directive introduced the rule which allows the consumer, even having signed the contract, to withdraw from the contract within seven days, even without a justifiable cause. Time runs from when the consumer receives adequate information regarding her/his right to a cooling-off period (art. 5). The first crack that appeared in the dogma concerned the binding effect of the contract and its reciprocal enforceability. The right of withdrawal cannot be waived or renounced. The Directive provides, in respect of this, that the legal effects of withdrawal, in particular the reimbursement of payments and restitution of the goods, shall be governed in conformity with national law (art. 7).

On the second point, the information which the seller must provide to the buyer concerning the right of withdrawal and its application, becomes an element which may determine the length of time over which the right may be exercised, in the sense that a lack of requisite information prolongs the time-limit for withdrawal to 60 days. But what is more important is the detail established by the Community legislature regarding the content of the information, including the fact that this should be supplied in writing (art. 4).

## *9.1. Examples of National Transposition*

At the time of the notification of the time-limit for adoption of the Directive by Member States, Germany had already substantially provided for this by the federal act of November 14th 1985.[38] A comparison of this German act and the implementation of the Directive in Italy, by legislative decree of January 15th 1992 no. 50,[39] readily reminds us of the danger in badly-managed harmonization of national laws, as a result of different domestic implementing measures (cf. *A Common Law for Europe,* the first volume of this series, already cit.).

For example, regarding the right to withdrawal, whose exercise in both German and Italian legal systems is provided for in writing, it is clear that the theoretical basis is different, as are the methods, terms, and conditions for its exercise.

In Italy, the pre-conditions of the right to withdrawal are *material fact:* that the contract has been signed or the contractual offer made in places and circumstances set out in letters *a)–d)*, art. 1 (1) of the legislative decree. The consumer has the right to withdraw (in Italian: "*diritto di recedere*") quite apart from having a justifiable reason, and such right cannot be waived or renounced (art. 4 & 6 of legislative decree). The circumstances in which the right can be exercised are wider, but the Italian law lists more cases where exclusions of the right of withdrawal operate. Moreover, in derogation of the discipline set out in the Civil Code, the consumer may return the goods, even if they have been used (art. 7 of legislative decree).

In Germany, the pre-condition of the right of withdrawal is a *mental state*: the consumer's intention to buy must have been influenced or determined by the professional seller exercising his trade in the places set out in clauses *1–3,* § 1 (1), of the German federal act. The right of withdrawal (in German: *Widerruf*), in this case too, quite apart from having a justifiable reason, cannot be waived or renounced. The cases where this right is not available are limited only to contracts of minimal value and to contracts which are immediately executed.

Thus the right of cancellation set out in the Directive has been implemented differently in the two countries.

> To turn to legal terminology, which often reveals different substantive rules, we should note that the German term corresponds to

---

[38] Published on January 16th 1986 and entered into force on May 1st 1986.

[39] Published in the *Gazz.Uff., Suppl.ord.,* February 3rd 1992, no. 27. It came into force on March 3rd 1992, whereas the Directive should have come into force by December 23rd 1987.

> the Italian *recesso* (a unilateral act of terminating a contract which has been signed, under art. 1373 of the Italian Civil Code), and not to the Italian *revoca* (the right to cancel a contract upon the occurrence of certain kinds of default by the other contracting party).

Finally, concerning the field of application of the Italian legislative decree, it should be noted that it is broader than that provided by the Directive. Indeed the Italian rules go beyond the hypotheses contemplated in art. 3 Dir. 85/577, but extends to contracts concluded in any public place as well, for example in the street, or via television (art. 9 of legislative decree). In this case the Italian legislature, taking advantage of the French example,[40] anticipated events, given that in May 1997 the Council of the Community approved the Directive on the subject of distance selling.

This shows that often the breach opened by Community harmonization measures permits more far-reaching solutions to enter the national legal system, than those contemplated by the Community's specific provisions themselves.

The harmonization of CEEC's legal systems in respect to this Directive came about with the issuing, in each country, of a single implementation act transposing several directives together, generally those on unfair terms, on liability for defective products, on distance selling, and on doorstep selling.[41]

## 10. Package Travel, Package Holidays and Package Tours Contracts

Council Directive 90/314/CEE of June 13th 1990 concerning package travel, package holidays and package tours[42] was not intended to control the activity of travel agents or organizers or promoters of holidays; its objective was consumer protection.

The reason for this lies in the fact that the uniform regulation of legal relations which are established between the various actors involved (tourist, travel agency, tour operator) was already contained in the international *Convention concerning travel contracts*, signed in Brussels on April 23rd 1970,[43] and developed essentially for this purpose.

---

[40] We are referring to act no. 88-3 of January 6th 1988, which however governs only TV sales.

[41] For this reason the issue is treated below, § 11 in this chapter.

[42] O.J., L 158, 06/23/1990, p. 59. Transposed by all the Member States.

[43] See on the internet, at http://www.unidroit.org/British/conventions/c-trav.htm.

The Brussels Convention 1970 defines the concept of *travel contract*, which means either an organized travel contract or an intermediary travel contract. The Convention identifies two contractual situations: *organized travel contract*, that is any contract whereby a person undertakes in her/his own name to provide for another, for an inclusive price, a combination of services comprising transportation, accommodation separate from the transportation, or any other service relating thereto; *intermediary travel contract*, which means any contract whereby a person undertakes to provide for another, for a price, either an organized travel contract or one or more separate services rendering possible a journey or sojourn. 'Interline' or other similar operations between carriers shall not be considered as intermediary travel contracts.

Three actors are mainly involved: the traveler, the travel intermediary, and the travel organizer. Various others with the duty of supplying the material services (transport personnel, hotelier, etc.,) remain in the background.

The Convention is essentially designed to regulate this particular three-way legal relationship, producing a legal scheme based on maintaining the balance of interests of the beneficiary of the service and those who perform the entrepreneurial activity (the intermediary or operator).

The Convention is not concerned with protection of the beneficiary of the service, the tourist.

The Directive does not apply to all travel contracts, but only to the sale of so-called *packages tours/package holidays*, namely those contracts which contain a series of services including at least transport and accommodation, or transport and accommodation together with other services. The offer must be for more than 24 hours or include an overnight stay.

The ECJ has ruled that the Directive must be interpreted so as to include holidays organized in accordance with the consumer's specifications, as well as combinations of tourist services put together at the time when the contract is concluded between the travel agency and the consumer.

*Cf.* the ruling of the April 30th 2002, C-400/00, *Club-Tour and Viagens–Turismo SA v. Alberto Carlos Lobo Gonçalves Garrii*, (2002) ECR I-4051:

**Clubtour and Viagens Turismo Ruling:** "(**§ 19**) As it has been held in paragraph 16 of this judgment that the term 'package' in Article 2(1) of the Directive must be interpreted so as to include holidays organised in accordance with the consumer's specifications, the term 'pre-arranged combination' which constitutes one of the elements of the definition of 'package', necessar-

> ily covers cases where the combination of tourist services is the result of the wishes expressed by the consumer up to the moment when the parties reach an agreement and conclude the contract. (§ **20**) The answer to the second question must therefore be that the term 'pre-arranged combination' used in Article 2(1) of the Directive must be interpreted so as to include combinations of tourist services put together at the time when the contract is concluded between the travel agency and the consumer."

As with the Directive on doorstep selling, the information that must be provided to the client is fundamental. Among others, there is the obligation to provide all *information* necessary to identify precisely the nature of the *tourist package* which has been acquired; to indicate the exchange rate used to set the prices; to make available all the conditions regarding methods of and time for payment, cancellations, changes of arrangements, etc. But in the case of package tours, the inadequacy (or absence) of the information is not so clearly subject to sanction by the Community legislature (art. 4).

Besides, although the contract may have been made within business premises, a right of withdrawal is provided for the consumer where there has been an upward revision of the global cost of the holiday stipulated in the contract. Price increases are only allowed where this is expressly provided by the contract, and only as a result of certain events (changes in transport costs, petrol price rises, etc). In the same way, the consumer may withdraw from the contract when there has been a significant alteration of one or more of the contract's essential terms, such as price, by the professional (art. 4[6]). Cancellation takes place with no penalty payment and brings with it the right to reimbursement of the money already paid.

On the subject of failure to perform or improper performance of the contract, the Directive provides that the organizer and the retailer/intermediary of the package holiday shall be jointly liable to the consumer for obligations assumed by either one of the professionals involved (art. 5 [1]).

This provision introduces a kind of *strict liability*: for example, the travel agency must pay compensation for loss of which the provider of material services is actually responsible, and may then seek restitution of the loss from the latter. As we will be seeing below in this paragraph, in Germany, the strict liability of travel agencies was provided for by the 1977 Act; in France and the UK, it was introduced with the provisions adopting this Directive. In Italy, on the other hand, the implementation provisions provide that liability is apportioned between the tour operator and the retailer according to their respective degrees of responsibility:

for this reason, the rule of strict liability contained in the Directive has not become part of the Italian implementation act.

> As far as this provision is concerned, the Court of Justice gave its interpretation in the case of March 12th 2002, C-168/00, *Simone Leitner v. TUI Deutschland GmbH & Co. KG.*, (2002) ECR I-2631. *Cf.* the first volume of this *Guide, A Common Law for Europe,* Chapter V.
>
> ***Simone Leitner* ruling:** "(**§ 23**) It is in light of those considerations that Article 5 of the Directive is to be interpreted. Although the first subparagraph of Article 5(2) merely refers in a general manner to the concept of damage, the fact that the fourth subparagraph of Article 5(2) provides that Member States may, in the matter of damage other than personal injury, allow compensation to be limited under the contract provided that such limitation is not unreasonable, means that the Directive implicitly recognises the existence of a right to compensation for damage other than personal injury, including non-material damage."

Article 7 Dir. 90/314 is of fundamental importance, because it protects consumers from the risk of financial loss involved in buying an "all-in" package holiday: "The organizer and/or the retailer party to the contract shall provide sufficient evidence of security for the refund of money paid over and the repatriation of the consumer in the event of insolvency."

This Community provision has put the responsibility upon Member States for adopting measures aimed at ensuring that operators as well as simple retailers, provide suitable guarantees for the repayment of the price paid and any consequent expenses of repatriation incurred by the consumer as a result of their insolvency or liquidation.

It is only possible fully to understand the purpose and scope of this provision if one recalls that the Community legislature, inspired by the Brussels Convention on travel contracts, has definitively established, for the protection of the consumer, a regime of responsibility for failure to adopt measures on the part of the organizer and/or the retailer of package holidays, based on strict liability and no longer on the basis of professional negligence.

Article 7 is the *core rule* of the Directive: its function is to guarantee the consumer reimbursement of the price paid for services not delivered and repatriation expenses incurred by the insolvency or liquidation of the operator and/or the retailer. In this way the rights of the consumer are not just merely formally recognized, but can be concretely and effectively satisfied.

The Court of Justice has pronounced both incidentally and directly on the interpretation of art. 7.

The first interpretation given by the Court of Justice was in 1996, in the case of ***Dillenkofer***, ECJ Judgment October 8th 1996, joined cases C-178/94, C-179/94, C-188/94, C-189/94 e C-190/94, *Erich Dillenkofer, Christian Erdmann, Hans-Jürgen Schulte, Anke Heuer, Werner, Ursula and Trosten Knor v Bundesrepublik Deutschland*, ECR I-4845.

The case concerned the actions for compensation which some individuals brought against the Federal Republic of Germany for damage they suffered because the Directive on package holidays and tours was not transposed within the prescribed period. Their holidays were ruined as a result of the financial failure of the operator, and they were unable to benefit from the system of guarantees deriving from the implementation of art. 7, because the State was late in adopting the Directive. The Court affirmed *obiter* that art. 7 of the Directive is a provision which confers directly on the consumer the right to obtain reimbursement of the price paid and the repatriation expenses incurred as a result of the insolvency or liquidation of the package holiday organizer. The Court expressly stated that the aim of the Directive was to protect the consumer from financial risk resulting from the insolvency of package holiday operators.

In 1998, in the case of ***Österreichische Kreditversicherungs*** (ECJ Judgment of May 14th 1998, C-364/96, *Verein für Konsumenteninformation v Österreichische Kreditversicherungs AG.*, (1998) ECR I-2949), following a preliminary reference of the district commercial court of Vienna (*Bezirksegericht für Handelssachen Wien*), the Court of Justice pronounced *directly* for the first time on the interpretation of art. 7. The Austrian court was petitioned by the consumers' association, which had been approached by some Austrian tourists who had acquired a package holiday in which the holiday destination was the island of Crete, and had, as was the practice, paid the whole price of the trip. The travel agent had not arranged to forward the payment to the hotelier, who, as a result, had made the two tourists pay a second time for the services used, threatening to prevent them from returning home.

The Austrian Regulation 881/94, which implemented Dir. 90/314, provides, by art. 3, that holiday operators take out insurance to guarantee the reimbursement of money paid by the consumer equal to the value of the services which are the subject-matter of the package holiday, not performed due to the insolvency of the operator, including expenses incurred for repatriation. The Austrian court asked the Court of Justice whether art. 7 of the Directive is to be interpreted as covering a situation in which the purchaser of a package holiday who has paid the travel organizer for the costs of his accommodation before travelling on his holiday is compelled, following the travel organizer's insolvency, to pay the hotelier for his accommodation again in order to be able to leave the hotel and return home.

In the ***Rechberger*** case, (ECJ Judgment June 15th 1999, C-140/97, *Walter Rechberger, Renate Greindl, Hermann Hofmeister et al. v. Republic of Austria*, (1999) ECR I-3499) the Court returned to the interpretation of art. 7 and reiterated that the aim is to protect the consumer from financial risk resulting from the insolvency of the travel organizers and/or retailers. The case concerned some subscribers to the Austrian daily newspaper *Kronenzeitung*, who had decided to participate in a prize offer, promoted by the newspaper's management. As a result of the enormous number of participants, the travel organizer who had provided the package tours, unable to satisfy all the bookings, was forced to start bankruptcy proceedings. The unsatisfied participants therefore applied to the judicial authorities to obtain the repayment of their money, seeking a ruling, in concrete terms, against the Republic of Austria, together with the travel organizer, for failure to transpose the Directive properly into national law, which prevented the plaintiffs from obtaining the reimbursement of money paid to a travel organizer who became insolvent.

(§§ 1–4–5 of the operative part of the ruling): "(1) Article 7 of Council Directive 90/314/EEC of June 13th 1990 on package travel, package holidays and package tours applies to trips which are offered by a daily newspaper as a gift exclusively to its subscribers as part of an advertising campaign that contravenes national competition law and for which the principal contractor, if he travels alone, pays airport taxes and a single-room supplement or, if he is accompanied by one or more persons paying the full rate, airport taxes only. (4) Article 7 of Directive 90/314 has not been properly transposed where national legislation does no more than require, for the coverage of the risk, a contract of insurance or a bank guarantee under which the amount of cover provided must be no less than 5% of the organizer's turnover during the corresponding quarter of the previous calendar year, and which requires an organizer just starting up in business to base the amount of cover on his estimated turnover from his intended business as a travel organizer and does not take account of any increase in the organizer's turnover in the current year. (5) Once a direct causal link has been established, a Member State's liability for breach of Article 7 of Directive 90/314 cannot be precluded by imprudent conduct on the part of the travel organizer or by the occurrence of exceptional or unforeseeable events."

The ECJ ruled that art. 7 places the responsibility on Member States to adopt procedures which ensure the complete and effective repayment of the price paid and the expenses of repatriation incurred due to the financial failure of the operator; and consequently affirmed that the adoption of provisions which guarantee only partial repayment must be considered as an incomplete adoption of the Directive, resulting in the liability of the State to the unsatisfied consumers. Therefore, a Member State which fails to put in place provisions capable of guaranteeing full repayment, risks a ruling ordering it to pay compensation for loss sustained by consumers.

### *10.1. Examples of National Transposition*

The Directive has been by all the Member States, but the resulting national disciplines differ notably from one another, because the Directive leaves ample room for interpretation by national lawmakers. Thus the Commission has expressed doubts as to whether it has been correctly adopted.[44]

For example, Germany is one of the States which decided not to sign the Brussels Convention on package travel, because the text appeared rather unclear regarding the limits of the organizer's liability in relation to third parties involved in the provision of the individual services. The fact of not signing the Convention led to the passing of a specific act, *Reisevertragsgesetz* of May 4th 1979, which inserted the travel contract into §§ 651a–651k of the German Civil Code (BGB). The delay by Germany in adopting the Directive, which came about with the act of June 24th 1994, was conditioned by the existence of this 1979 act.

At present, German legal practice focuses on the relationship between the organizer and the traveler, concentrating attention on the package holiday (*Pauschalreise*). It is in fact in this sector that problems arise, due to the fact that the organizer was accustomed to decline all liability by making use of general clauses in the contract, which defined the services as being provided by an intermediary, thus obliging the traveler to have recourse to each individual provider for any loss sustained; a procedure which put the tourist in serious difficulty.

The new § 651a BGB defines a travel contract as one which operates between the organizer and the traveler, where the former is bound to provide the totality of the services and the latter to pay the price for those services. The organizer must supply at least two services: therefore the

[44] See the Report of the Commission, SEC (1999) 1800 final.

other circumstances, where a single service is offered, are not included, but they are, however, subject to the ordinary provisions of the BGB.

The individuality of the Spanish system is due to the fact that the national act *Ley* 21/1995, which transposed Dir. 90/314, established that there are 17 *Comunidades Autonomas* which can issue detailed regulations in the area of tourism.[45] For issues not governed by the autonomous legislation, there remains in force the Royal decree of 1988 on travel agencies.[46]

In the United Kingdom, the implementation of Dir. 90/314 was provided for by a range of provisions passed on December 23rd 1992, The Package Travel, Package Holiday and Package Tours Regulations 1992[47] developed by the *Department of Trade and Industry* (DTI). The DTI itself published a guide for the application of the new legislative provisions, the Guidance Notes, without binding legal effect, but full of effects of noteworthy importance, given that tour operators who follow the guidelines contained in it are indirectly obeying the law laid down in the Regulations. The main aspects which are important to emphasize are those contained in the guarantees which must be taken out by tour operators and travel agents. Following the implementation of Dir. 90/314, Regulations 16–21 establish the method by which these guarantee the financial protection of the tourist, ensuring the repayment of deposits or repatriation in the event that the tour operator becomes insolvent and ceases commercial activity.

In France, Dir. 90/314 was adopted by act no. 645 of July 13th 1992,[48] whereby art. 31 of the act conferred upon the *Conseil d'Etat* the power to issue an administrative decree governing all the details. Decree no. 490 of June 15th 1994 lists the conditions necessary to carry on the activity of travel agent including the detailed legal requirements concerning finan-

---

[45] See *Ley* no. 21/1995, July 6th 1995, *reguladora de los Viajes Combinados (*BOE n. 161, 07/07/1995, p. 20652). See for example the regulations adopted by Catalonia (*Decreto* 168/1994, *de 30 de mayo, de Regolamentaciòn de las Agencias de Viajes*), by the Balearic Islands (*Decreto* 43/1995, *de 6 de abril, de Regolamento de Agencias de Viajes)* and by the Canaries (*Decreto* 176/1997, *de 24 de julio, por el que se regulan las agencias de viajes*).

[46] *Real Decreto* 271/1988 of March 25th *por el que se regula el ejercicio de las actividades proprias de las Agencias de Viajes*; *Orden* of April 14th 1988 *por la que se aprueban las normas reguladores de las Agencias de Viajes.*

[47] Statutory Instrument no. 3288 of 1992.

[48] *Loi* no. 92-645 du 07/13/1992 *relative à l'élimination des déchets ainsi qu'aux installations classées pour la protection de l'environnement, JO du* 07/14/1992 p. 9457; *Décret* no. 94-490 du 06/15/1994 *pris en application de l'article 31 de la loi Numéro 92-645 du 07/13/1992 fixant les conditions d'exercice des activités relatives à l'organisation et à la vente de voyages ou de séjours, JO* 06/17/1994 p. 8746.

cial guarantees (in French: *garantie financière*), an indispensable element for obtaining the administrative authorization necessary to operate as a travel agent.

In Italy the Directive was implemented by legislative decree no. 111 of March 17th 1995. The contract must be produced "in written form, in clear and precise terms" (art. 6 of the legislative decree). All the elements which the contract must contain are identified in minute detail (among these are: destination, length and dates of starting and finishing, name, address and telephone no. of the operator or retailer, price and landing fees, insurance details, means of transport and their type and characteristics, itineraries, visits, excursions, presence of tour guides, and many others besides, art. 7, letters a–p, legislative decree), following a legislative technique inspired by commercial models. As a consequence, there is a difference between provisions deriving from the transposition of Community legislation, which are contained in a special act, and those from the Italian Civil Code, where the contents of various typical contracts are not described in detail, but are confined to essential elements only.

Later, provision was made for the establishment of a Fund managed by the Department of Tourism of the Industry Ministry, with the aim of reimbursing users in the case of the financial failure of travel agents and tour operators, and to organize the return trip in the event of the insolvency of the tour operator vis-à-vis the foreign tourist establishments.[49]

In the transitional phase characterized by the liberalization of all sectors of the economy and profound institutional reforms, the countries of Central and Eastern Europe were not equipped with a specific set of rules governing the tourism sector.

Let us take the case of Poland as an example. To avoid fraudulent conduct by travel agencies which exist only "on paper," Poland harmonized its own previous measures with Community law in 1997, with the act regarding tourist services, which came into force on July 1st 1998.[50]

> Before the harmonization, pursuant to the Act of December 23rd 1988, on business activity (*Dz. U.* no. 41, at 324, and later amendments), any person could set up a travel agency. In order to establish one, it was sufficient to register the business in the local community office. Pursuant to the Act of June 14th 1991, on

---

[49] Ministerial Decree July 23rd 1999, no. 349, Regulation listing rules for the management and functioning of the national guarantee Fund for package holiday consumers.

[50] Act of August 29th 1997, in Polish Journal of Laws (*Dz. U.*) no. 133 at 884, and subsequent amendment of April 10th 1999 (*Dz. U.* no. 40, at 401). Unified text in 2001 *Dz. U.* no. 55, at 578.

joint-venture companies (*Dz. U.* no. 60, at 253 and later amendments) any foreign business person could open a travel agency (usually in the form of a limited liability company or by purchasing shares in such companies).

The act introduces a new system of licenses which both the operator and the retailer of package holidays must obtain from the administrative authorities, but there are some exceptions (art. 4 [2]): *a)* retailers who permanently act as brokers contracting for the licensed organizers of packages or for hotels or sanatoria; *b)* schools, churches, and religious associations for their pupils, members, or believers. The licenses are granted only to undertakings able to satisfy a list of further requirements: the activities have to be managed by persons who possess 'experience and training' (*cf.* decree of the Prime Minister of Dec. 12th 1998 for what constitutes 'experience' in organizing tourist packages or in tourist services); the applicant has to provide evidence of financial security for the refund of the cost of repatriation when the organizer, contrary to her/his obligation, has not provided transport back to the country and the repayment of all moneys paid by the consumers under the contract, in case of nonfulfillment of the contract. The security should be provided in the form of a bank guarantee, insurer's guarantee or liability insurance. The minimum sum of the guarantee, has been set at 4 percent of the annual income of the business. Finally the licenses are registered in the Central Registry. In the case of failure to obtain a license, the subject concerned may appeal to the President of the Office for Sport and Tourism in Warsaw, and has the right to request the intervention, on the grounds of law, of the Supreme Administrative Court (art. 7 [2]).

The other provisions introduced by the act reflect the contents of Dir. 90/314 and concern the large amount of information to be supplied to the tourist (set out at length in art. 14), the occasions for rescission, and the liability of the operator for failure to perform or improper performance of the contract.

The rule of vicarious liability, provided by art. 474 of the Civil Code, applies. The debtor shall be liable, as for her/his own act or omission, for any act or omission by persons who assist him or perform the contract on her/his behalf as if s/he acted by her/himself.[51]

Some limitation on liability is permitted solely on grounds of international Conventions and special regulations expressly set out in the con-

---

[51] The Polish Supreme Court has applied this rule to travel agencies since the case of March 28th 1968, published in 1 CR 64/68, PUG 4/1969.

tract (art. 18). The act concludes with a clause relating to interpretation: the terms in the contract which are less beneficial to the consumer are void and are replaced by the statutory regulation (art. 19).

On the basis of this internal act, which substantially adopts the Community legislation, the Commission for the Codification of Civil Law has developed a draft "Contract of Travel" to be inserted into the Civil Code as a new type of contract.

## 11. Unfair Terms in Consumer Contracts

Directive 93/13 regarding unfair terms in consumer contracts was approved by the Council on April 5th 1993.[52]

This represents one of the most interesting of the Community interventions in the area of contracts, both because it is *substantive* and not merely procedural, and because its implementation has remarkable consequences for commercial practice in the European legal systems.

Unfair terms are to be found in any contracts containing corresponding contractual duties, when the information asymmetry which characterizes the relationship between the parties shows up an imbalance between the rights and reciprocal obligations.

Generally, unfair terms are to be found in standard contracts, pre-printed forms supplied by one of the two parties, usually the entrepreneur, and offered to the consumer. The consumer does not have the option of negotiating the terms of the contract individually; s/he must accept or refuse the offer of the entrepreneur-professional (the so-called "take it or leave it" technique).

To the well-known *standard-form contracts*, such as insurance and banking contracts, contracts for supply and the majority of contracts made with public administration and public bodies, transport contracts etc., we can add, in huge numbers in the last few years, those concerning the sale of consumer goods and financial services from leasing to share-dealing.

The problem of the terms in consumer contracts involves important interests from the social and economic point of view. For some economic sectors, the acceptance of one proposal rather than another, the insertion of one word or phrase, could cause a real revolution in commercial practice. All the business associations paid unusually close attention to the passage of the Directive and the successive implementation provisions. Proof of this lies as much in the lengthy journey from the draft

[52] O.J., L95, 04/21/1993, p. 29. Transposed in all the Member States.

Directive, lasting over 20 years, as in the debate which accompanied the implementation of the Directive in the individual national governments. Implementation brought with it serious problems of consistency, given that the new legal framework in most cases had to co-exist with the pre-existing national provisions.

The Community legislature has explained the reasoning behind the intervention in this area, placing emphasis on the objective of achieving an internal market. The diversity of national legislation, the differentiation between the single markets and possible distortion of competition which follows, are expressly mentioned as the principle reasons which have led to harmonization of the law relating to unfair terms in Europe, reasons which, even in the Preamble of Dir. 93/13, precede those concerning consumer protection.

> **6th Whereas Dir. 93/13**: "In order to facilitate the establishment of the internal market and to safeguard the citizen in his role as consumer when acquiring goods and services under contracts which are governed by the laws of Member States other than his own, it is essential to remove unfair terms from those contracts; (…)"

As mentioned at the beginning of the chapter, the debate regarding standard form contracts arose at the beginning of the last century and assumed definite form in the 1970's. Before the Community intervened, some Member States had regulated this sector.

In Sweden, the Act Prohibiting Unfair Contract Terms was passed in 1970, which codified a mixed control system, employing both a special court for the protection of the consumer and an administrative body, the Ombudsman. Powers to involve the court in the most serious cases were conferred on this body, the negotiation of standard-form contracts with business and prohibitory provisions to prevent the use of clauses which were "improper" or "excessive" having regard to the balance of corresponding duties contained in the contract.

In Denmark, the act of 1975, which modified the law of contracts dating back to 1917, established the general rule that every contract is void if it is unfair or contrary to commercial practice, and established the Ombudsman, with the task of overseeing contractual terms.

In the German Federal Republic, the Act of December 9th 1976 on General Terms and Conditions in Business (*AGB Gesetz*) rendered ineffective (in the sense that a contract entails no legal effect) clauses which create undue disadvantage to the party at whom they are directed (the customer), in contravention of good faith (§ 9 *AGB Gesetz*); the German act, moreover, provided the famous "black list" of prohibited clauses, and the "grey list" of clauses whose validity depends on the courts' appraisal (§§ 10-11 *AGB Gesetz*) and it applied to contracts between persons acting in the course of business (e.g. between professionals) as well.

In the United Kingdom, the Unfair Contract Terms Act 1977 (UCTA) rendered ineffective "exclusion clauses" (not necessarily the standard ones) which are "unreasonable," seeking to limit liability for negligence in the case of death or injury of the customer in contracts for the sale of goods and the supply of goods and services, while the Sale of Goods Act 1979 imposed a requirement that goods are fit for the purpose for which they are sold.

In France, the act no. 78 of January 10th 1978 prohibited clauses imposed on the non-professional with abuse of economic power (*abus de la puissance économique*) by the professional and which conferred undue advantage (*avantage excessif*) on the latter.

In the Netherlands, the act of June 18th 1987 on standard contracts (later incorporated into the Civil Code of 1992 at § 6.5.2A.2 provided for the voidability of the unfair and burdensome contract terms.

In Italy, legal rules for the purpose did not exist, but the courts developed a doctrine using a combination of articles 1341, 1342 & 1370 of the Civil Code.

In this European legal context, the Commission drafted the Directive, which guarantees new regulatory measures in the area of standard contracts, ensuring that they conform to the aims of Community policy.

The principle features of Dir. 93/13, which consists of only 11 articles, as well as an important Appendix, can be summarized as follows:[53]

– The Directive applies only to contracts made between a *consumer* and a *professional*, a person acting in the course of business, (seller or supplier, arts. 1 & 2). A consumer is any natural person who is acting for purposes which are outside her/his trade, business or profession; a seller or supplier is any natural or legal person who, in contracts covered by this Directive, is acting for purposes relating to her/his trade, business or profession, whether publicly owned or privately owned (art. 2 [b]–[c]).

> See ECJ Judgment of November 22th 2001, Joined cases C-541/99 and C-542/99, **Cape Snc v Idealservice Srl** and **Idealservice MN RE Sas v OMAI Srl**:
>
> "(§ **16**) It is thus clear from the wording of Article 2 of the Directive that a person other than a natural person who concludes

[53] *Cf.* the European conference of July 1999 at Brussels, at www.europa.eu.int/comm/ dgs/healt_consumer/index.en.htm.

a contract with a seller or supplier cannot be regarded as a consumer within the meaning of that provision." See also supra § 3.

– The Directive introduces the concept of an *unfair term*: a contractual term which has not been individually negotiated shall be regarded as unfair if, contrary to the requirement of good faith, it causes a significant imbalance in the parties' rights and obligations arising under the contract, to the detriment of the consumer (art. 3 [1]).

Some Member States (the Scandinavian countries, France, and in some measure Austria and The Netherlands) have not given effect to the requirement of "not individually negotiated terms," without this having caused the slightest practical problem (see COM (2000) 248 final). However, the new practice of some firms, who prepare contracts on the computer, on a case-by-case basis, which contain a declaration by the consumer that s/he has negotiated and expressly accepted the general contractual terms, create serious prejudice for the consumer, by going around the area of application of the Directive.

The text of the previous version of the Directive (draft presented by the Commission, COM (90) 322 final, O.J., C 243, 09/28/1990, p. 2.) did not make terms "not individually negotiated" a requirement, at least for certain contractual terms. The need to achieve the consent of all the Member States, has meant, after lengthy disagreement, that the text was published in its present form.

– This general criterion is completed by a list indicative of clauses *normally considered unfair* (Annex, art. 3 [3]).

In the previous draft of the Directive of 1990, the list of clauses held to be unfair was considered binding on the States (see the Preamble, recital no. 11, and art. 2, no. 2). The final version of the Directive confines itself to affirming that such clauses "may" be declared unfair, so leaving the advisability of choosing directly to the Member States, at the implementation stage.

Recital no. 17 of the Preamble expressly provides that the annexed list is to be regarded as of indicative value only and, because of the cause of the minimal character of the Directive, the scope of these terms may be the subject of amplification or more restrictive editing by the Member States in their national laws.

This means not only that the States may not, at the implementation phase, eliminate the list of terms provided in the Annex, but also that, if such were the case, the terms not so transferred could in any case be invoked by the consumer by recourse to the principle of the direct effect of directives which are "sufficiently clear and unconditional." Therefore, the contents of the list must appear in their entirety in the national implementation law with the object of ensuring judicial certainty, so that individual citizens may fully know their rights. In this regard, see the ruling of the Court of Justice in the case of *Commission v Greece*, C-236/95, (1996) ECR I-4459, pt. 13. But some countries have refused to adopt the list (Finland, Sweden, and Denmark), and infringement proceedings are in train against them.

- The Directive sets out the *principle of transparency* of the contract, meaning that in contracts which contain terms proposed to the consumer in writing, such terms must always be drafted in plain, intelligible language. Where there is doubt about the meaning of a term, the interpretation most favorable to the consumer shall prevail (so called principle of interpretation *contra stipulatorem,* art. 5).

Violation of the principle of transparency does not imply nullity, or inefficacy of the term: however, the national courts hearing the case have, in some cases, declared the term illegal, for lack of clarity: *cf.* ruling of September 20th 1989, *Court of Appeal of Créteil* (CLAB FR 000012). CLAB is a database which collects national case law, the decisions of administrative bodies, voluntary agreements and arbitration decisions on unfair terms: access is free on the Commission's server at www.europa.eu.int/clab/index.htm.

- The sanction resulting from the inclusion of an unfair term is that it is not binding; it is up to the States to establish the most appropriate judicial formula (*invalidity*, *inefficacy*, *nullity*, *voidability*, *inapplicability*) (art. 6) in order to save the contract wherever possible. However, the Report of the Commission[54] has emphasized that, with a view to dissuading the professional in a tangible way from making use of unfair terms, it seems advisable to provide other sanctions (in the form of liability for economic loss or of a penal nature).

- The Directive allows a choice between *judicial* or *administrative* procedure to prevent the insertion of unfair terms into the contract (art. 7 [1]).

The national legislatures have opted for the judicial procedure,

[54] See COM (2000) 248 final.

with important differences: ordinary courts usually have jurisdiction over the matter, but in some cases other courts have special jurisdiction (e.g. the High Court and recently the County Courts in the UK, and the Market Court in the Nordic countries, which have jurisdiction over the entire national territory). Various systems have an "administrative component" which cannot be overlooked: in the UK, a request may be made to the Director of the Office of Fair Trading to end the insertion of unfair terms; in Ireland, to the Director of Consumer Affairs; in Nordic countries, to the Ombudsman; in Germany to the *Verbraucherschutzverein* (a body of the private law sector financed by public funds to carry out projects of general interest). In Spain and Portugal, even the public prosecutor may petition the courts. In Italy, the system of control of unfair terms is efficient above all from the point of view of preventive action carried out by various bodies (the Chamber of Commerce, the Isvap—Authority for the insurance sector—the Bank of Italy, the antitrust Authority).

- The Directive introduces rules of *prevention* and *collective protection*, thanks to which the consumers' associations (and other interested parties) have a right to go to court to certify abuses regarding contractual terms and bring about an end to their deployment (art. 7 [2]).

With the object of achieving the effective elimination of unfair terms, some national systems of control (e.g. the Ombudsman and the Office of Fair Trading) have preferred "direct negotiation" with individual professionals and associations of professionals, in an effort to persuade them to bring about the necessary changes.

- The Directive allows States either to maintain these provisions or bring in *stricter* ones for the protection of the consumer (art. 8).

### *11.1. The Implementation of Directive 93/13 in Member States*

The Directive should have come into force on December 31st 1994, but some States have not observed the time limits. The Commission has therefore begun infringement proceedings against the States which are out of time, and which have given notification of implementation measures before the Court makes the ruling. Later, the Court examined the national implementation texts for the Directive and has started new infringement procedures against all the States for failure to adopt or incorrect adoption (mainly in respect of art. 3 (5); art. 5; art. 6 (2); and art. 7 (2) Dir. 93/13).

Generally speaking, the implementation of the Directive in the Member States has been achieved in some countries by departing somewhat from the original text, through amendments made to the pre-existing legislation: Germany is one such case, through the amendment of the 1976 *AGB Gesetz* by the act of January 19th 1996, and France, which has amended the 1978 act by a new act no. 95–96 of February 1st 1995, the provisions of which have been inserted in the Consumer Code, at art. L. 132-1.

In other countries, the adoption has been faithful to the letter of the Directive, and the new Community provisions have been superimposed upon the previous domestic law (creating evident problems of coherence within the system): this is the case in the UK, where the Unfair Terms in Consumer Contracts Regulations 1994[55] have been placed alongside the provisions of the Unfair Contract Terms Act 1977, which has not been repealed.[56]

The Regulations enable a consumer (and in certain cases the Director General of Fair Trading acting on behalf of consumer) to challenge certain contractual terms as being "unfair." The unfairness of the terms, under Regulation 4(1) 1994 and Regulation 5(1) 1999, is tested by the OFT.

The OFT was set up as a result of the Fair Trading Act 1973; the provisions are concerned with restrictive practice monopolies and mergers, but the Director of the OFT (appointed by the Secretary of State for Trade and Industry) is also given powers in relation to consumer protection matters. In particular, it keeps under review the commercial supply of goods and services to consumers in the UK, makes recommendations to Department of Trade and Industry (DTI), encourages trade associations in preparing Codes of practice for their members, and takes action against traders whose conduct is unfair to the consumer.

The test of unfairness goes beyond the one of reasonableness required by the UCTA 1977. The OFT' s starting point in assessing the fairness of the term is normally to ask what would be the position for the consumer if the term did not appear in the contract. In the Unfair Contract Terms Guidance of 2001,[57] the OFT observes that the principle of freedom of contract can no longer be said to justify using standard terms to take away protection consumers would otherwise enjoy.

---

[55] S.I. 1994 no. 1590, as amended in 1999, S.I. 1999, no. 2083.

[56] The British Law Commission is working on a consolidation in one text of both UCTA and Regulations provisions: see on the Internet at www.lawcom.gov.uk/misc/common.-htm.

[57] See at www.oft.gov.uk/html/reasearch/reports/oft311.htm.

When the supplier refuses to modify the unfair clause, the OFT can claim an injunction before the Chancery Division of the High Court (and now also before the County Courts). The clause will be ineffective, but the rest of the contract will remain in force.

In any case, the consumer can recover the price s/he has already paid at least in three cases: when the contract is rescinded for misrepresentation; where specific goods perish before the risk has passed to the buyer; where a contract for the sale of goods is discharged as a result of the supplier's breaches.

It is worth pointing out as well, that the indirect effect of the Directive on Common Law has been to acclimatize the British courts to the doctrine of good faith. In the case of *Director General of Fair Trading v. First National Bank plc,*[58] the Court of Appeal commented that "good faith has a special meaning in the regulations, having its conceptual roots in civil law systems," citing the German Standard Contract Terms Act 1976, which played an important role in the drafting of the Directive. The House of Lords gave leave to appeal and the case was argued before their Lordships in 2001.[59] Lord Bingham, in his opinion, observes that "the requirement of good faith in this context is one of fair and open dealing. Openness requires that terms should be expressly fully, clearly and legibly, containing no concealed pitfalls or traps (…) Fair dealing requires that a supplier should not, whether deliberately or unconsciously, take advantage of the consumer's necessity indigence, lack of experience, unfamiliarity with the subject matter of the contract, weak bargaining position or any other factor listed in or analogous to those listed in Schedule 3 of Regulations. Good faith in this context is not an artificial or technical concept; nor, since Lord Mansfield was its champion, is it a concept wholly unfamiliar to British lawyers. It looks to good standards of commercial morality and practice."

In other countries, the Community provision has been introduced into the national legal systems *ex novo:* this is the case with Italian law,[60] which has implemented the Directive by the insertion of five new articles into Book IV (Title II, new Section XIV) of the Civil Code, from 1469-*bis* to 1469-*sexies*, on consumer contracts.

---

[58] (2000) 2 *All ER* 759.

[59] *Director General of Fair Trading v. First National Bank plc*, October 25th 2001, (2001) 3 *WLR*. 1297; (2002) 1 *Lloyd's Rep*. 489.

[60] See also the Italian *Community Act for 1999*, no. 562/99 (in *Gazz.Uff., Suppl. Ord.*, January 18th 2000, no. 13), which, following infringement proceedings, have amended some provisions previously brought into the Civil Code by the first implementation act (art. 1469 *bis*, 1469 *quarter*, 1469 *quinquies* and 1469 *sexies*). *Cf.* the first volume of this *Guide, A Common Law for Europe* above cit., chapter IV.

The Italian legislature has remained essentially faithful to the contents of the Directive, but the unhappy Italian translation of art. 3 (1) of the Directive "contrary to the requirement of good faith" as "*malgrado la buona fede*," has caused much discussion regarding interpretation.

The reference to good faith may be taken to mean that a clause is unfair which, while conforming to good faith, still produces an imbalance, or in the sense that a clause is unfair if, in violation of the principle of good faith, it causes imbalance.

The new system of unfair terms (in Italian: *clausole vessatorie*) is now made up of a double set of rules:

- Those just mentioned, intended to govern the practice of contracts made between a professional and a consumer, to which the new articles of the Civil Code are applied.
- Those intended to govern all other cases, i.e. contracts between two persons both acting respectively in the course of their business, or natural persons neither of whom is acting in the course of business, contracts to which the old general rules of the Civil Code apply.

The adaptation by the Italian legislature to the Directive on unfair terms confirms the tendency of the Community institutions to advance towards the harmonization of private law through the construction of many "legal micro-systems," each of which represents a set of solutions which are increasingly specific and specialized.

The present micro-system concerning unfair terms in Italy is denoted by a triple classification:

- Those coming under the general definition which allows the judge to determine whether the clause is unfair (art.1469-*bis*, (1), Civil Code).
- Those treated as unfair unless the contrary is proved, the so-called "grey list," (art. 1469-*bis*, (3) Civil Code) (*rebuttable presumption*). As distinct from what is provided in the Directive, there is a presumption that these clauses are unfair, which may be rebutted only if the professional can supply proof to the contrary, namely that there has been individual negotiation or that in any case no significant imbalance has been caused in the rights and obligations under the contract.
- Those always treated as unfair and for which no proof to the contrary is available, the so-called "black list" (art. 1469-*quinquies*, (2) Civil Code) (*irrebuttable presumption*).

The Italian legislature has opted for the solution of deeming the unfair clause ineffective (but not the whole of the contract, which remains valid and effective), so remedying the criticisms made of the previous program for implementation of the Directive, which had provided for the inefficacy of the clause, without however concerning itself with the results this sanction could have had at a practical level. Its inefficacy is relative, in the sense that it operates only to the advantage of the consumer, and can also be removed by the judge *ex officio*.

Finally, an inhibitory measure has been introduced into the Italian Civil Code in the implementation of art. 7 Dir. 93/13, in favor of the associations which represent consumers and professionals, as well as the Chambers of Commerce, by which they have the right to take to court businesses or associations which *use*[61] standard form contracts containing unfair terms. The judge can prevent the use of the unfair terms and can even publicize the ruling in the national press.

### *11.2. The Reception of Directive 93/13 in CEECs*

Harmonization of national legislation in the area of consumer protection in the CEECs is at an advanced stage, at least from the point of view of formal adoption of the Community provisions. As we saw in Chapter III of the first volume of this *Guide*, *A Common Law for Europe*, all interested governments in fact have to satisfy the Copenhagen criteria to be able to join the EU; among these there is the adoption of the *acquis communautaire,* which includes the whole area of consumer contracts.

However, difficulties remain at the level of enforcement, explicable in terms of *path dependency*. This expression aims to describe how the process of transformation is conditioned by the point of departure, and explains how the past may influence the present and the future.

> The intellectual who first drew the attention of economic historians to the thesis of the development process being conditioned by the point of departure was P. David, *Clio and the Economics of QWERTY*, (1985). The author endeavored to explain how and why the particular arrangement of letters on typewriter keyboards became standardized and what accidental factors may have influenced the success of this result, despite the existence of other, more efficient layouts. A reading of this writer's work suggests that a

[61] Following the ECJ Judgment of January 24th 2002, C-372/99, *European Commission v. Italian Republic*, the Italian Parliament, by the Community Act for 2002 (*Legge comunitaria per il 2002*, Act of February 3rd 2003, no. 14) has provided for the redrafting of the first clause of art. 1469 *sexies*, to permit consumers' associations and Chambers of Commerce to take action against professionals who "*recommend the use of...*" general contract terms which are unfair.

high level of continuity with the past is the result of limits imposed on change to institutions that are highly *path dependent*.

The principle reason lies in the holistic attitude of communist doctrine, in the conviction that what is right and good for the state enterprises must also automatically be so for society, and therefore for the individual.

The obstacles to consumer protection were already evident in the 1980's, despite the fact that some of the Eastern European countries, above all Poland and Hungary, had begun to reform their centrally-planned economies, opening up to structural innovations typical of western market economies.

In the early 90's, the neo-liberal enthusiasm which greeted the change-over from the planned to the market economy caused further 'errors of perspective,' such as, for example, the widespread belief that, since privileges had been eliminated for state enterprises, special privileges for consumers could not be tolerated.

In the context of consumer protection, the legal systems of these countries continued to train their attention on warranties and guarantees, as could not be otherwise in an extremely weak market, where the offer of goods and services was rather scarce and where the fundamental problem was to find someone who sold goods or provided services at all. This, in essence, is the reason why the right to cancel the contract (or the right of withdrawal from the contract) which can carry with it the corresponding duty to repay the money, was not thought to be a satisfactory remedy and was not included in the codification of the first post-communist acts relating to consumer protection in this area.[62] The current rules were not 'consumer-focused,' but worked to protect the interests of the professionals, above all in relation to the burden of proof, which fell entirely on the consumer.

By the end of the wave of privatization brought about by the second half of the 90's, with the flood of private capital into the markets and along with the arrival of many foreign investors, the new commercial or marketing techniques which took consumers by surprise and new aggressive selling methods spread throughout the CEEC's.

In the last three years, the legislators have issued new rules for consumer protection which are closer to the aims and objectives of the European Community. The fact remains that these are relatively recent

---

[62] See for example the protection afforded to the consumer in Romania, by Government Ordinance 21 of 08/28/92 on consumer protection and by Government Decision 482 of 08/28/92 on the Office for the Protection of the Consumer.

phenomena and the judges and public prosecutors of Eastern Europe, called upon to apply the new legal rules, show more indulgence, in spite of everything, towards suppliers' duties, than sensitivity towards consumers' rights.

Despite the specific difficulties outlined above, which go against the present process of adopting the *acquis communautaire,* there is a feature which may facilitate the effective capacity of the CEEC's to implement the Community rules: in fact, this transplant has found fertile ground in the prevailing legal climate of this area, whose roots go deep in the Roman–Germanic tradition.

As has been noted, the pre-communist Civil Codes of the CEEC's were strongly influenced by Germanic models, in particular the German BGB (1900) and the Swiss ZGB (1912).

Moreover, looked at properly, the Civil Codes of the communist era contained some general principles which could be used for the protection of the individual/consumer, in relation to consumer goods over which a kind of communist ownership known as "personal property" was exercised. Some Codes contained a practice reference for consumer protection (for example, the Polish Civil Code of 1964, or the Hungarian Civil Code of 1959, following amendments introduced in 1977, during the course of reform to introduce a special type of mixed 'market and planned' economy).

The transposition process of the Community directives therefore has found fertile ground in the CEECs, and it generally happens through the promulgation of statutory measures which adopts several directives, sometimes without their content being inserted into the Civil Codes. These implementing acts have to be considered as *lex specialis* in respect to the ordinary provisions contained in the Civil Codes, which in any case remain available to the consumers as *lex generalis.*

In Poland, for example, the Act on the protection of consumer rights and liability for damage caused by a dangerous product[63] has implemented the Community provisions concerning liability for a defective product (85/374/EEC), on contracts concluded outside commercial premises (85/577/EEC), on unfair terms (91/13/EEC), and on distance selling (97/7/EC). Later the Directives on injunctions (98/27/EC) and on sales of consumer goods and associated guarantees (99/44/EC) were implemented too.[64]

---

[63] Act of March 2nd 2000, in Polish Journal of Laws (*Dz. U.)* no. 22/2000, item 271, which entered into force on July 1st 2000.

[64] Respectively Act of July 5th 2002 (*Dz. U.*, no. 129/2002, item 1102) and Act of July 27th 2002 (*Dz. U.*, no. 141/2002, item 1176).

As far as consumer protection is concerned, the 2000 Act amended the Polish Civil Code of 1964, introducing a definition of consumer under art. 384 (3). It was quite broad: both natural persons and legal ones could be considered to be "consumers." The aim was to protect medium and small enterprises, since their weakness derives, still today, from a standardized system of acquisition and distribution, where they have little chance to intervene. But in 2003, in order to avoid non-conformity in respect to Community legislation, a new Act amending the Civil Code and other acts[65] has repealed art. 384 (3), and has introduced a new art. $22^1$ in the General Part (Book I) of the Polish Civil Code. According to this provision, a consumer can only be a natural person who performs acts in law, which are not in direct connection with her/his economic or professional activity.

The legal regime of consumer protection is set out in Arts. $385^1$ *ff.* Polish Civil Code, introduced by the 2000 Act. Under art. $385^1$ (1) the protection may be accorded when the clauses are against *bones mores* and, contrary to the requirement of good faith, they cause a significant imbalance in the parties' rights and obligations arising under the contract, to the detriment of the consumer.

Moreover, the rule also applies to contracts concluded between two consumers.

At paragraph 3, the article specifies that clauses included in standard forms prepared by a professional are to be regarded as "not individually negotiated terms." The professional can supply proof to the contrary, namely that there has been individual negotiation or that, in any case, no significant imbalance has been caused in the rights and obligations under the contract. Art. $385^2$ adopts the same case by case approach of Dir. 93/13, listing 23 clauses to be treated as unfair, unless the contrary is proved (it is the so-called "grey list"). There is no "black list," e.g. clauses always treated as unfair and for which no proof to the contrary is available.

The monitoring of unfairness (as provided by art. 7 (2) Dir. 93/13) comes under the jurisdiction of the Anti-monopoly Tribunal of Warsaw, a specialized civil court established by the Ministry of Justice in 1990; in all the other cases the ordinary civil law courts have jurisdiction over this matter. An appeal on the facts, or on mixed fact and law, can normally be taken as far as the Court of Appeal, whereas appeals to the Supreme Court, which are very few in number per year, are only admissible on points of law.

---

[65] Act of February 14th 2003 (*Dz. U.* no. 49/2003, item 408).

Under arts. 479[36] to 479[45] of the Polish Code of Civil Procedure, as amended by the 2000 Act, the clauses which have been "prohibited" and declared void by the courts are to be listed in a public register managed by the president of the Competition and Consumer Protection Office,[66] and in newspapers with nationwide distribution. The judgments delivered in individual cases obtain an *ultra partes* effectiveness, and become effective *vis à vis* third parties.

In Bulgaria, the Act protecting consumers of 1999 (but its enforcement has undergone delays) has implemented the Community provisions regarding product safety (92/59/EEC), unfair terms (91/13/EEC), and distance selling (97/7/EC). The national Consumers' Council, an independent institution established in 2000, is responsible for the application of the law, with jurisdiction over the whole territory, under the auspices of the Ministry of Economy (established by the merger of the Ministry of Industry and the Ministry of Trade and Tourism in December 1999).

In Slovakia too, the institution responsible for consumer policy is the Ministry of Economy: this defines policy in cooperation with other ministries and monitors the application of legal rules in relation to consumer protection.

In Romania some governmental provisions,[67] later approved by Parliament, have essentially adopted the Directive on liability for a defective product (85/374/EEC) and that on unfair terms (93/13/EEC), providing the following kinds of protection of consumers' rights, whether in the acquisition of goods or performance of services:

- Compensation for personal injuries (protection of life, health and safety) and economic loss to their legitimate rights or interests (§ 3 of the Act).
- The right to receive detailed and complete information on goods and services with the aim of making informed choices in the marketplace (§ 18 *ff.* of the Act).
- The right to be represented before the courts by consumer associations (§31 *ff.* of the Act), to prevent the future insertion of such clauses in contracts.

Furthermore, the Romanian provisions concerning consumer sale contracts establish that all types of clauses and commercial practices which

[66] *Cf.* chapter VI on competition law.

[67] Government Ordinance no. 21 of 08/28/92 on consumer protection, and Government Decision no. 482 of 08/28/92 on the Office for the Protection of Consumers, cited above.

may interfere with the free choice of the consumer are prohibited. The contractual clauses, above all those to do with quality, guarantees, price and interest rates of the goods or service, must be put in writing, in clear terms; if not, they will be considered unfair. In 2001, the National Authority for Consumer Protection was created: an independent body subordinate to government, with centers all over the country, whose functions will range from internal consumer policy, to supervision and inspection of the market, and the imposition of penal or administrative sanctions in cases of infringement of the law; in 2002 it published a guide for consumers.

Hungary has preferred to pass new legislation to bring its domestic law into conformity with the directives (such as the Act CLV of 1997 on Consumer Protection), rather than make amendments to the Civil Code (*Ptk*) or establish a consumers' Code on the French model. However, the current Project for the reform of the *Ptk* contained in governmental decree no. 1050/1998 (IV. 24) as amended by decree no. 1061/99 (V.28)[68] tends towards the direct transposition and integration of the European Directive into the text of the Code, above all with regard to contract law, which requires greater changes. The Government approved the Project of Reform of the new *Pkt* by decree 1003/2003 (I.25),[69] and has fixed the time limit for re-codification at September 30th 2005.

As things stand the legal remedies of which the Hungarian consumer can avail her/himself are variously regulated by a number of sources of law: from the Act on Domestic Trade of 1978 to various government and ministerial decrees, which protect consumers' right and interests concerning packaging, suitable quality, prohibition of misleading advertisements and liability for damages. Further, the Competition Act of 1996, s. 21, governs unfair contract terms and forbids all sales activity which is misleading to consumers.

The Hungarian Civil Code (art. 209 *ff.*), as amended in 1977 and further elaborated by Act CXLIX of 1997, also governs the area of general conditions of contract. There remains, however, a difference, primarily terminological, as regards Dir. 93/13: the Hungarian Civil Code uses the expression "unjustified term, with unilateral benefit of general conditions of contracts" as equivalent to "unfair term." In addition, as a result of some translation errors made when rendering the text of the Code compatible with the Directive, art. 209 *Ptk* provides protection for every type of consumer contract, without the imposition of the limitation provided under the original wording of art. 3 Dir. 93/13 (*which was not individu-*

---

[68] Published in *Magyar Közlöny*, n. 15, 2002, vol. II.

[69] Published in *Magyar Közlöny*, n. 8, 2003.

*ally negotiated)*. However, an intention of adopting a more aware and focused transposition technique can be identified, as demonstrated by Act XXXVI of 2002 on the Amendment of the Civil Code, which introduced some novelties to the definition of 'consumer contract' (art. 685 [e]), as suggested by the legal profession.

> On the transposition of Dir. 93/13 into the Hungarian legal system, on its interpretation and enforcement see the case *Ynos Kft. v. János Varga* still pending in the Court of Justice.
>
> Pending case C-302/04. Reference for a preliminary ruling by the Szombathelyi Városi Bíróság by order of that court on June 10th 2004 in the case ***Ynos Kft. v János Varga***:
>
> "May Art. 6(1)of Council Directive 93/13/EEC on unfair terms in consumer contracts, which provides that Member States are to lay down that unfair terms used in a contract concluded with a consumer by a seller or supplier are, as provided for under their national law, not to be binding on the consumer, be interpreted as meaning that it may constitute the basis of a national provision such as Article 209 of Law No IV of 1959 on the Civil Code, applicable when a general condition in a contract stating that unfair terms do not cease to bind the consumer *ipso jure*, but do so only where an express declaration to that effect is made, that is to say, when they are successfully contested, is found to be unfair? Does it follow from that provision of the Directive, according to which the contract is to continue to bind the parties upon those terms if it is capable of continuing in existence without the unfair terms, that where the unfair terms inserted by a seller or supplier are not binding on the consumer as provided for under national law, but where in the absence of those terms, which form part of the contract, the seller or supplier would not have concluded the contract with the consumer, the validity of the contract as a whole cannot be affected if it is capable of continuing in existence without the unfair terms? From the point of view of the application of Community law, is it relevant that the main dispute arose before the accession of the Republic of Hungary to the European Union, but after the adaptation of its domestic law to the Directive?"

Further differences can be found between the Hungarian legal system and Community law: the provisions of the Civil Code are confined to regulating general contractual conditions created by legal entities; the other national sources apply to all kinds of contracts, not just to consumer contracts (as between a professional seller and a consumer); the burden of proof is reversed: the injured party must prove that s/he had no opportunity to modify the contract.

Finally, the main omissions are noticeable at the level of effects: an unfair term is declared void if the contract is still in the course of performance or is still to be performed; once it has been performed, no claim for invalidation can be entertained. What is more, the Directive covers not only exclusion, but also limitation of claims. The Hungarian Competition Act (§§ 21–22) prohibits only the exclusion of enforcement of claims, and then only on condition that the other contracting party is in a position of economic dominance.

In the three Baltic States, a system of consumer protection in line with the Brussels Directive has been operational since 1994, the year that the statutes on the subject came into force. Since then, various regulations have been added which reinforce their efficacy. The Latvian and Estonian systems of control are similar to each other: the Council (Estonia, 1999) and the Center (Latvia, 1998) for consumer protection supervise the market and report cases of violations of the law; they check information directed at consumers and business.

Furthermore, the Baltic States participate in the TRAPEX program, based on the European RAPEX one.

> RAPEX is a system for the rapid exchange of information on dangers arising from the use of consumer products established by Council Decision no. 84/133, of March 2nd 1984 (as amended). Participation is mandatory for all Member States.
>
> TRAPEX is a system which follows the structure of the Union's RAPEX system, hence its name, Transitional Rapid Exchange of Information on Dangerous Products for the CEECs. The central market surveillance agencies of Bulgaria, Estonia, Hungary, Latvia, Lithuania, Poland, Romania, and Slovakia created the market surveillance rapid information system for the Region on March 23rd 1999. An observer at the time, the Slovenian agency, is also among the founding members. It is a transitory system and, unlike RAPEX, it is based upon voluntary membership and operates on an informal basis outside the European Union.

The Estonian legislature has transposed the Community *acquis* on consumer contracts most evidently in the area of invalidity of unfair standard terms. Indeed, in June 2002 the Law of Obligations Act[70] was passed. This act, which has introduced a new definition of *obligation* into the Estonian legal system, has modified the national law of contracts.

---

[70] It entered into force 07/01/2002, *RT* I 2002, 53, 336.

> § **2 of the Estonian Act**: "Definition of obligation: (1) An obligation is a legal relationship which gives rise to the obligation of one person (obligated person or obligor) to perform an act or omission (perform an obligation) for the benefit of another person (entitled person or obligee), and to the right of the obligee to demand that the obligor perform the obligation. (2) The nature of an obligation may oblige the parties to the obligation to take the other party's rights and interests into account in a certain manner. An obligation may also be confined thereto."

However, in applying what was literally provided in Directive 93/13 and its annex, the new Estonian national regime allows certain exceptions precisely for the financial services sector.[71]

In Slovenia in 2000, Parliament debated and adopted a "Two-year Policy Programming Paper on Consumer Protection," prepared by the government: this indicates that an important shift in perspective is under way and that the new approach is giving above all political priority to consumer affairs.

The concluding remarks concern the practical difficulty in applying the legal rules mentioned above, which was emphasized in the Regular Reports of the Commission on progress towards accession.[72] Remedies available to consumers are not equivalent to those proposed by Community law. Moreover, despite the fact that non-governmental organizations exist in all the countries of the region, they are under-financed, as are the reconciliatory committees and arbitration committees. These organizations which, according to the country, are known as 'National Consumers' Association,' 'Federation of Consumers' and so on, operate in all the CEECs. Certain administrative agencies (a kind of consumer ombudsman), established on a regional basis, are more efficient; for instance, those in Poland by the Act of 1998, which monitor consumer and commercial transactions.

The only alternative for the consumer is to apply to the national courts, but court proceedings are time-consuming and not efficient. The question, therefore, remains open; it probably will not be resolved until all the governments in the area work out domestic policies for consumer protection along Community guidelines, so that the consumer becomes the central figure in the law-making process.

---

71 See chapter III, § 13 ff.

72 See above, chapter III, in the first volume of this *Guide, A Common Law for Europe*.

## 12. Timesharing

Directive 94/47 of October 26th 1994 concerns the protection for the buyer for some aspects of contracts relating to the purchase of the right to use immovable property on a timeshare basis.[73]

The Community legislature did not wish to harmonize the various legal rules of the Member States which governed a particular type of contract, or adopt a particular position regarding the legal nature of an institution which was atypical and unregulated in many legal systems.

The Directive confines itself simply to governing some aspects of the purchasing process, with the aim of affording adequate protection to the buyer.

In this case, too, the *right of withdrawal* and *to information* are of essential importance in the harmonization legislation: in fact, the Directive covers only those aspects of the provisions concerning contractual transactions that relate to information on the constituent parts of a contract and the arrangements for the communication of that information, and the procedures and arrangements for cancellation and withdrawal (art. 1 [2]).

The solutions adopted by the Member States regarding these aspects are many and varied, and this is attributable to their belonging to different legal systems.

As a preliminary remark, theories about the legal nature of *timeshare* (in French *multipropriété*) are many and varied, too.

In the USA, where timesharing originated, this practice was introduced to facilitate and strengthen international tourism. A factual reconstruction of the techniques arising from the various legal solutions adopted in practice by the Member States includes the following phenomena: in

---

[73] O.J., L 280, 10/29/94, p.83. The Directive should have been brought into force by April 29th 1997. The Italian legislature implemented the Directive with a considerable degree of delay, on November 9th 1998, by legislative decree no. 427/1998. The same is true for Belgium, France, and Spain. *Cf.* in Belgium: *Loi modifiant la loi du 11 avril 1999 relative aux contrats portant sur l'acquisition d'un droit d'utilisation d'immeubles à temps partagé*, 02/19/2001, *MB* 02/21/2001; Spain: *Ley n° 42/98 de 12/15/1998 sobre derechos de aprovechamiento por turno de bienes inmuebles de uso turístico y normas tributarias*; France: *Loi n° 98-566 du 07/08/1998 portant transposition de la directive 94/47/CE du Parlement européen et du Conseil du 10/26/1994 concernant la protection des acquéreurs pour certains aspects des contrats portant sur l'acquisition d'un droit d'utilisation à temps partiel de biens immobiliers, JO* 07/9/1998, p. 10486. In Germany, the Directive was transposed by the *Schuldrechtsmodernisierungsgesetz*, 11/21/2001, *BGBl* I 3138, and inserted in the BGB at §§ 481–487 (*Teilzeit-Wohnrechteverträge*). It has not been transposed in all the Member States.

France, the use of the *société d'attribution d'immeubles en jouissance a temps partagé* introduced by act no. 86 of 1986; in the UK, the technique of a trust and the constitution of a "club trustee;" in Germany, the mechanism of using a joint stock liability company; in Italy, the phenomenon has been regulated by means of the law of real property, with different nuances.

All these different practical solutions have generated great interest in academic circles: a vast quantity of articles have been written on this theme to explain the diversity of models which operate in the different Community legal systems.

In France, where a specific legal discipline has been in use since the beginning of the 1970's,[74] after an early attempt to frame the *multipropriété* within the law of real property, the difficulty involved in the management of large building complexes induced the French legislature to use company law to confer personal rights of different types, which could only be attributed to specially designed legal institutions. The method adopted was that of a construction and/or development company, conceived specifically as a property company granting beneficial enjoyment only.

The company can grant any beneficial rights, even of a personal nature. It is provided that, in the place of ordinary shares, the company may assign "preferred" shares, which confer rights to "*en jouissance à temps partagé*." The form is analogous to a *commodatum* in civil law systems: a loan for use is an agreement by which a person delivers a thing to another, to use the thing and return it after s/he has finished using it.

In common law countries, "timesharing" is organized on a different basis: the developer grants a right of use for part of the property to individual multiple-owners, on the basis of a contract which creates a merely personal relationship; occasionally a trust may be set up in favor of purchasers who are part of a "club" (members' club), which has power to grant beneficial use respectively to its members on a time-share basis. A multiple owner's rights never grant her/him title to the property.

The timesharing system in the USA, on the other hand, may permit the registration of an interest in the real estate, limited to beneficial use taken in turns, on the basis of a scheme which governs the exclusive rights of individual owners of a *fee-interest,* that is a right which can be asserted against third parties.

---

[74] It is contained in many *Lois*, but notably in those of July 15th 1971 and January 6th 1986.

In Portugal, on the other hand, the multiple-owner is considered to have a title to real property *sui generis*.

In Italy, the scheme which has been adopted in practice and supported by the law assures the purchaser of a beneficial title to the property, without, however, excluding the possibility of setting up a company/*condominium* arrangement, at the stage when the rights are being granted. According to some commentators, the concept of timesharing could be considered as a development of the *condominium* (Residents' Association/management company) and the multiple owner as one of the co-owners of the single units. But there are those who maintain that timesharing is a new way of owning property. Others classify it as a personal beneficial right, considering that the multiple owner generally has beneficial use of the property but not the right to manage/direct.

It was in consideration of all these differences seen in practice in the legal systems of the Member States that Dir. 94/47 avoids describing the legal nature of the rights which may become the subject of timesharing, thus allowing free choice to the individual Member States as to how to regulate what the Directive defines as a "contract relating directly or indirectly to the purchase of the right to use one or more immovable properties on a timeshare basis." According to the provisions of the Directive, "it shall mean any contract or group of contracts concluded for at least three years under which, directly or indirectly, on payment of a certain global price, a real property right or any other right relating to the use of one or more immovable properties for a specified or specifiable period of the year, which may not be less than one week, is established or is the subject of a transfer or an undertaking to transfer" (art. 2 [1]).

It is from this perspective that the provisions of the Directive should be seen, which are concerned exclusively with some aspects of the relationship between the seller and purchaser of the right to use immovable property on a timeshare basis.

In particular, the Directive contains three categories of rules to protect the purchaser:

- Those providing for detailed *information* to be supplied to the purchaser at the negotiation stage.

> The information contained in the prospectus must include the identity of the proposer, the nature of the right which is the subject-matter of the contract, the period such right is to be enjoyed, a precise description of the property, details of planning permission, services and common parts which can be used by the purchaser, costs and other related financial charges, the service charges on the property, the state of completion of the construction work,

a warranty that all the conditions stipulated in the planning permission have been met, a guarantee that it will in effect be completed, including also a certificate that it is fit to be inhabited.

- Those which govern the *right to withdraw.*

  Art. 5 establishes that the right to withdraw, which is British in origin (see the Timeshare Act 1992, March 16th), exercisable only by the purchaser, may be exercised within ten days of the definitive or preliminary signing of the contract. In the event that the contract does not contain all the information required by the Directive, the time limit runs from the moment all the requisite information has been supplied, and, in any event, not before three months from drawing up the contract.

- Those *prohibiting payments* by the purchaser before the time limits for exercising the right to withdraw have expired.

The Directive, which is closer to common law solutions than those of the civil law systems, supplies many provisions, especially for purposes of transparency, which protect the purchaser both during pre-contractual negotiations and when the contract is drawn up.

However, it seems to concern itself more with the regular development of contractual relations between the parties than the safety and preservation of the right acquired.

### *12.1. Examples of National Transposition*

The implementation of the Directive has been insufficient to resolve the very serious problem in legal systems such as in France and Italy. It concerns the risk for the purchaser of losing both the right and the money paid on account, should the seller be in financial difficulty or be dishonest, and who, in the interval between the "preliminary contract" and the "definitive" one, may burden the right to use the immovable property with extra charges or even assign it to third parties.

In Italy, decree no. 669 of December 31st 1996[75] has remedied this, by requiring the registration (in Italian: *trascrizione*) of the preliminary contract (*contratto preliminare*) of sale of real property. The registration requirement makes the transfer of ownership of immovable property a

---

[75] Transformed, with modifications, into Act no. 30, of February 28th 1997.

complicated situation, similar to the US "Race Notice Statute" (a deed recorded before another deed is recorded by a *bona fide* purchaser prevails over the other conveyances).

In France, in the particular instance of the purchase of a property-right in a building at project stage (in French: *en l'état future d'achévement*), the deed (*l'acte authentique*) is registered as if the building were already completed (art. 7, *loi* no. 67-3) and the payment, even part-payment, of the purchase price before the building is finished and the completion documents drawn up, is forbidden; in the meanwhile, any sums requested during the course of the building work must be deposited in escrow with a bank until work is completed.

At judicial level, the only case so far decided by the Court of Justice concerns the Directive on timeshare only indirectly.[76]

> On September 14th 1996, ***Sanchis*** signed a contract, away from the seller's premises and inside a tourist complex, with the company *Travel Vac* to purchase the right to use an immovable property on timeshare basis. At that time, the Directive on timesharing had been issued, but Spain had not yet implemented it, and the time limits for implementation had not yet expired. The contract provided that the purchaser could withdraw from the contract, on prior notice and prior payment of 25% of the price as a penalty, within seven days of signing. After three days the purchaser went to the seller's commercial premises saying he wished to withdraw, but refused to pay the required penalty payment, asserting that the contract was of no effect.
>
> The Spanish court referred the question to the Court of Justice, regarding the interpretation to be given to Dir. 85/577 on contracts made away from business premises, in relation to the case in point concerning timesharing. In particular, one of the fundamental questions raised by the national court was whether Dir. 85/577 applied to the case and, if so, whether it could grant the counterclaim for cancellation of the contract made by Mr. Sanchís.
>
> The Luxembourg judges, without entering into the merits of what constitutes timesharing rights, affirmed, however, that Dir. 85/577 applied to timesharing on the basis of these considerations. Though it may be true that timesharing contracts are the subject of the provisions of Dir. 94/47, this does not exclude that a contract containing a right to use immovable property on time-

---

[76] ECJ Judgment of April 22nd 1999, C-423/97, *Travel Vac SL v Manuel José Antelm Sanchis*, (1999) ECR I-2195. See also chapter V, in the first volume of this *Guide, A Common Law for Europe*.

share basis may equally be brought within the application of Dir. 85/577, when the conditions for its application have in some way or another been satisfied. Indeed, neither of the two directives contain provisions intended to exclude the application of the other. Further, an interpretation which meant that the protection provided by it were to be excluded for the simple reason that the contract in principle fell within the ambit of application of Dir. 94/47, would be contrary to the objective of Dir. 85/577. An interpretation which would have the effect of depriving the consumer of the chance to avail himself of the protective provisions of Dir. 85/577, the more so since the contract had been negotiated away from business premises.

The central and eastern countries which joined the EU in 2004 have also begun to implement this Directive over the course of the last few years: a case in point is, for example, to be found in the Polish law of July 13th 2000,[77] or in the Hungarian Government Decree 20/1999 (II. 5.) *Korm.* on Contracts Relating to the Purchase of the Right to Use Immovable Properties on a Timeshare Basis.

## 13. Distance Contracts

The Directive of the European Parliament and Council no. 97/7 of May 20th 1997 concerns consumer protection in the field of distance contracts.[78]

This has been produced with greater precision with respect to the other directives concerning consumer protection; however, like the others, it imposes a minimum of harmonization of domestic laws, authorizing States to adopt or maintain stricter provisions, as long as they are compatible with the Treaty, which may ensure a higher level of protection for the consumer (art. 14). When adopted, all these directives taken together give a glimpse of the arrival of a Community legal scheme for consumer contracts.

---

[77] In the Polish Journal of Laws (*Dz. U.*) of 2000, no. 74, item 855.

[78] O.J., L 144, 06/04/1997, p. 19. The time limits for adoption of the Directive in the Member States was May 20th 2000. All of the Member States have transposed the Directive: finally Spain and Luxembourg as well: *cf. Ley* 47/2002, 12/19/2002, *de reforma de la Ley 7/1996, de 15 de enero, de Ordenacion del Comercio Minorista, para la transposicion al Ordenamiento juridico espanol de la Directive 97/7/CE, en materia de contratos a distancia, y para la adaptacion de la Ley a diversas Directivas comunitarias*, in BOE n° 304 de 12/20/2002, p. 44759; *Loi* du 16 avril 2003 *concernant la protection des consommateurs en matière de contrats à distance*, in *Memorial A*, n° 61 du 8 mai 2003, p. 1026.

The fixed aims of Dir. 97/7 can be deduced from the twenty-four recitals *(whereas clauses)* in the Preamble, and are 'the old favorites' which recur consistently in every discussion on the subject of consumer law:

- Necessity to consolidate the internal market (1st *recital*).
- Necessity to harmonize the various legal disciplines of the Member States (4th *recital*).
- Advisability of protecting the purchaser against aggressive sales methods (5th *recital*).
- Protection of competition between professionals (20th *recital*).

Besides, the Preamble to the Directive (18th *recital*) makes express reference to the *Convention on Human Rights and Fundamental Freedoms*, quoting art. 8 (protection of privacy) and art. 10 (freedom of information). This represents a methodical connection between the aims and contents of the Directive from one point of view, and protection of human rights on the other. The reason for the protection of the private life of the consumer emerges clearly from the desire of the Community legislature to protect the privacy of individuals from commercial contacts established via the most modern instruments of communication.

The field of application of the Directive is very large indeed (art. 2) and is extended by a provision of the Directive (art. 12 [2]) which refers to *international private law*, obliging Member States to check that the consumer is not in fact deprived of available protection by reason of the choice of law of a third country as the law applicable to the contract.

It concerns the main distance-selling techniques in relation to goods or services, such as sales via printed media catalogues, telephone, answering machine, e-mail, fax, radio, television, etc., the provision of services, the location, just as they are listed (not comrehensively) in Annex I.

The decisive moment is the *performance at 'a distance'* of a contract between the supplier of goods or services and a consumer. The new rules are therefore destined to become one of the main remedies to meet the problems arising from the use, one must now say massive use, of electronic commerce.

In any case, the Community legislation and that adopted at national level for distance-selling are not applied to a list of contracts, at least not exhaustively, in Annex II:

- To contracts for investment services;
- Insurance and reinsurance operations;
- Contracts inherent in banking services;
- Contracts regarding pension funds;
- Contracts concluded by means of automatic vending machines or automated commercial premises;

- Contracts for the construction or sale of real property and other property rights (except for rental);
- Contracts made at auction sales;
- Contracts concluded with telecommunications operators through the use of public payphones.

The instruments for achieving the objectives set by the Directive are the classic ones which recur in all the Community provisions that are dedicated to consumer protection: the right to information and to withdraw, even though the methods and conditions under which these rights are exercised change.

The right to *information* has a more precise purpose, namely to protect the contractual agreement.

At the first stage, the seller must supply the consumer with certain information "in a clear and comprehensible way" (art. 4) before the contract is concluded: in particular, information concerning the supplier's identity, the essential characteristics of the goods or service, the price, the delivery charges, payment methods, etc., including, above all, the existence of the consumer's right to withdraw. Bearing in mind the specific nature of the various distance selling systems, the Directive was unable to avoid a generalized provision that the information supplied must be "clear (…), provided in a clear and comprehensible manner in any way appropriate to the means of distance communication used, with due regard, in particular, to the principles of good faith in commercial transactions, and the principles governing the protection of those who are unable, pursuant to the legislation of the Member States, to give their consent, such as minors" (art. 4 [2]).

At the second stage, after the contract has been completed, but not after the goods are delivered, the seller must send the consumer written confirmation of the preliminary information (art. 5).

A third type of information concerns instead events inherent in the performance of the contractual obligations, such as the non-availability of the goods which have been ordered or the intention to send goods of a different description, but of equivalent quality and value. This possibility is allowed, on condition that it is brought to the consumer's attention at the time the contract is being concluded (art. 7).

Also, regarding the right of *withdrawal*, the Directive confirms what must now be seen as a constant rule in all consumer contracts, i.e. the possibility of exercising this right unilaterally, without penalty, freely and at the consumer's discretion, independently of the existence or otherwise of a situation which might take the consumer by surprise. Consumer contracts, therefore, become definitive only after the passage of some time following the consumer's acceptance, the so-called cooling-off period. Consent is definitive and binds the consumer only when this period of time has passed. Further, in order to motivate the enterprise to supply all the requisite information, the normal expiry time of at least seven working days for the exercise of the right of withdrawal is extended to three months from the day the goods are received (art. 6).

The Directive further affirms the principle of *lex specialis,* which was not particularly favorably viewed by the Member States. According to art. 13 (1) "The provisions of this Directive shall apply insofar as there are no particular provisions in rules of Community law governing certain types of distance contracts in their entirety."

This means that the Community legislature, aware that its intervention in the area of contract law has been somewhat fragmentary, has been concerned to coordinate these provisions and those contained in other directives, with a view to avoiding or reducing the problems of interpretation caused when provisions overlap one another.

A further link is provided by the rule which makes it clear that wherever a specific Community provision exists, containing legislation which concerns individual aspects to do with the supply of goods or services, the specific rules will be the ones that apply to these aspects, even where the issue is a distance contract, and not the provisions of Dir. 97/7 (art. 13 [2]).

### *13.1. Examples of National Transposition*

The transposition of Dir. 97/7 into the Member States' legal systems, as with previous directives, has proved to be more or less consonant with the content and fixed objectives of the Community legislature, according to the context in which it has been implemented.

> Note that, prior to the Directive, the area under consideration was partially regulated in some Member States: for example, in Luxembourg by the act of August 25th 1983 *sur le contrats conclus par correspondance*, in France by the act of January 6th 1988 *sur les opérations de vente à distance et le téléchat,* and in Italy by legislative decree no. 50 of January 15th 1992, which adopted the Directive on contracts negotiated away from business premises (see infra § 9 this chapter).

In Italy,[79] for example, the Directive's text has been faithfully followed

---

[79] For Italy see legislative decree no. 185 of May 22nd 1999, in *Gazz Uff.*, June 21st 1999, no. 143, under the delegated powers set out in the *Italian Community Act* no. 128/98 of April 24th 1998.

and implemented in a legislative decree, except for art. 7 concerning events inherent in the performance of the contractual obligations: as distinct from what is set out in the Directive, the Italian legislative decree provides for the possibility of consigning goods which are different from those ordered, but of equivalent quality and value, with the 'consent' of the consumer, to be expressed prior to or at the time of concluding the contract.

In France[80] the transplantation has provided only illusory protection for the consumer, both because of the uncertainty caused by the mechanism for adoption of the Directive, and for the incoherence created with respect to the existing provisions in the Consumer Code (*Code de la consommation)*. The French government has recently obtained Parliamentary authorization to transpose the contents of certain directives in emergency circumstances, arising when it becomes necessary to avoid infringement proceedings which could be brought against the State should there be delay in transposition. Hence, this Directive has been transposed by executive means, with no debate or discussion. The gaps are revealed most clearly in the context of application of the law, both regarding the kinds of contract to which it applies, and to the parties, in the protection conferred (here there is a conflict between the old provisions contained in art. L. 121-27 Consumer Code, which does not impose the obligation to confirm the offer in writing, and the new L. 121-19 Consumer Code, which introduces it), and in the sanctions provided to guarantee the efficacy of the protection (the text of the *ordonnance* provides for a decree of the *Conseil d'Etat* to be made for concrete regulations preventing the use of the new techniques of distance selling which are contrary to the Directive).

Among the central and eastern countries the picture is equally mixed; Directive 97/7 has been adopted in Poland, by the act of 2000 which transposed several directives for consumer protection into the domestic legal system,[81] or in Hungary with Government Decree 17/1999 (II. 5.) *Korm.* on Distance Contracts, while in other countries (Bulgaria and Romania) this Directive has not yet been adopted.

---

80 For France, see the *ordonnance* no. 2001-741 of August 23rd 2001, which was inserted into the *Code de la consommation*, art. L. 121-16 and following, issued by the Government under parliamentary delegated legislation contained in *Loi* no. 2001-1 of January 3rd 2001, in *JO*, January 4th 2001, p. 93.

81 We refer the reader to what was said in § 11.2. p. 93 of this chapter.

## 14. The Directive on Injunctions and New Systems of Protection

On May 19th 1998, Directive no. 98/27 was approved, whose objective is the approximation of legislative, regulatory, and administrative provisions of the Member States relating to *injunctions* for the protection of consumers' interests.[82]

Directive 98/27 has been partly modified by Dir. 99/44 of May 25th 1999[83] regarding some aspects of the sale of and guarantees on consumer goods, in order to bring up to date the list of directives concerning the collective interests of consumers which are capable of protection by injunction (*infra*, this §).

Dir. 98/27 is aimed at the harmonization of national legal rules on the use of injunctions to prevent practices and behavior contrary to Community law. In effect, the picture that emerges of the situation within the Member States shows a greatly varied selection of legal solutions, as set out in the Report that accompanies the draft directive.

Regarding the areas protected by injunction, in Belgium, for example, the remedy is available in the fields of misleading advertising, consumer credit, financial services, advertising within the legal profession and package holidays; in France, Greece, Denmark, Sweden, and the UK it is available wherever consumer interests are prejudiced; in Austria, for unfair terms and misleading advertising; in Portugal, only for unfair terms; in Italy for misleading advertising, protection of the environment and the ozone layer, and, since 1996, unfair terms too.

Regarding those to whom the remedy is available, in certain cases this may be any organization whose object is the protection of consumer interests, or associations with a minimum number of active members, or in other cases the administrative authorities such as the Ombudsman or the Director General of Fair Trading, or, as in Italy, even individual consumers.

The Directive has only 10 articles and contains in art. 1 a reference to a list of directives (in the Annex) which define the area concerned and whose violation may lead to injunction proceedings.

> **Art. 1 Dir. 98/27**: "The purpose of this Directive is to approximate the laws, regulations and administrative provisions of the

---

[82] O.J., L 166/51, 06/11/98, p. 83. The time limit for adopting the Directive expired on January 1st 2001. All of Member States transposed the Directive, except for Luxembourg, for which no references are available.

[83] O.J., L 171, 07/07/1999, p. 12, below § 15, this chapter.

> Member States relating to actions for an injunction referred to in Article 2 aimed at the protection of the collective interests of consumers included in the Directives listed in the Annex, with a view to ensuring the smooth functioning of the internal market. 2. For the purpose of this Directive, an infringement shall mean any act contrary to the Directives listed in the Annex as transposed into the internal legal order of the Member States which harms the collective interests referred to in paragraph 1."

The list consists of:

- Council Directive 84/450/EEC of September 10th 1984 relating to the approximation of the laws, regulations, and administrative provisions of the Member States concerning misleading advertising.
- Council Directive 85/577/EEC of December 20th 1985 to protect the consumer in respect of contracts negotiated away from business premises.
- Council Directive 87/102/EEC of December 22th 1986 for the approximation of the laws, regulations, and administrative provisions of the Member States concerning consumer credit, as last amended by Directive 98/7/EC.
- Council Directive 89/552/EEC of October 3rd 1989 on the coordination of certain provisions laid down by law, regulation or administrative action in Member States concerning the pursuit of television broadcasting activities: Articles 10 to 21, as amended by Directive 97/36/EC.
- Council Directive 90/314/EEC of June 13th 1990 on package travel, package holidays, and package tours.
- Council Directive 92/28/EEC of March 31th 1992 on the advertising of medicinal products for human use.
- Council Directive 93/13/EEC of April 5th 1993 on unfair terms in consumer contracts.
- Directive 94/47/EC of the European Parliament and of the Council of October 26th 1994 on the protection of purchasers in respect of certain aspects of contracts relating to the purchase of the right to use immovable properties on a timeshare basis.
- Directive 97/7/EC of the European Parliament and of the Council of May 20th 1997 on the protection of consumers in respect of distance contracts.

The right of action provided by Community law is not of a general nature, but one which must at least be recognized in the cases considered in the Annex to the Directive. This therefore is another example of so-called minimum harmonization.

Art. 3 Dir. 98/27 sets out the *entities* who are qualified to bring an action: a "qualified entity" means any body or organization which, being properly constituted according to the law of a Member State, has a legitimate interest in ensuring that the provisions referred to in Article 1 are complied with, in particular: (a) one or more independent public bodies, specifically responsible for protecting the interests referred to in Article 1, in Member States in which such bodies exist and/or (b) organizations whose purpose is to protect the interests referred to in Article 1, in accordance with the criteria laid down by their national law.[84]

### *14.1. Examples of National Transposition*

In the Member States the implementation of the Directive on injunctions is very recent.

In Italy it was implemented by legislative decree no. 224 of April 23rd 2001, entitled "Implementation of Dir. 98/27 concerning injunction proceedings to protect the interests of consumers"[85] which amended act no. 281 of July 30th 1998 on the "Regulation of consumers and users' rights,"[86] which was issued by chance a few days after the Community adoption of the Directive.

The content of the Italian act 281/1998 was not far removed from that of Dir. 98/27: the requirements for bringing the action for the protection of consumers and users was set out in the act, together with the methods of enrollment of the consumers' associations in an appropriate Register containing the list of associations qualified to bring this action.

The Italian decree 224/2001 recognizes the collective interests of big business down to the small craftsman,[87] which emerge from the Directives listed in the Annex, due to be updated by ministerial decree.

Moreover the Italian decree provides that independent public bodies and organizations, recognized in other European States and enrolled in the list of institutions qualified to bring injunction proceedings in the

---

[84] Concerning the entities qualified to bring an action under art. 2 of this Directive see the Communication of the Commission concerning Article 4 (3) of Dir. 98/27 of the European Parliament and of the Council on injunctions for the protection of consumers' interests, (2001/C 222/07).

[85] Published in *Gazz. Uff.* no. 137 of June 15th 2001.

[86] Published in *Gazz. Uff.* no. 189 of August 14th 1998. Later ministerial decree (*D.M.*) no. 20 of January 19th 1999 (in *Gazz.Uff.* no. 29 of February 5th 1999) adopted the Regulation for inclusion in the list representative consumers and users' associations at national level.

[87] Art. 1 of the *d.lgs. 224/2001*, which introduces a new 2 *bis* in art. 1 of act July 30th 1998, no. 281.

collective interests of consumers, published in the Official Gazette of the EU, may act to protect such positions when confronted by conduct in any part of Italian territory,[88] which is treated as harmful to consumers in their own country.

> The rule gives these bodies and organizations the capacity to activate the conciliation procedure and confers upon the Minister for Industry and Commerce the task of communicating to the European Commission the list of representative consumers and users' associations at the national level, with a view to their being enrolled in the list of entities qualified to bring injunction proceedings to protect the collective interests of consumers.
>
> Giving independent organizations and bodies charged with ensuring the protection of collective interests the right to take cases to court completes the approximation of the Italian legal system to the provisions of articles 3 and 4 of Directive 98/27.

Regarding the importance of implementation of Community legislation, it should be emphasized that, with respect to the reference made in the Directive to infringements "originating" in the territory of the State, the Italian legislation is wider than this, and evaluates the circumstances, as to whether "wholly or partly" in the national territory, under which the acts and behavior took place.

From another point of view, the indication of the kinds of acts and behavior must be taken as summarizing all the ways by which an infringement of the collective interests of consumers may take place, following the principle which requires the interpretation which is closest to the intention of the Community legislature.

In the UK, The Stop Now Orders (E.C. Directive) Regulations 2001 implement Directive 98/27/EC, referred to in the Regulations as the "Injunctions Directive."[89] The Regulations apply to any act contrary to a provision in certain EC consumer protection directives as transposed into the legal order of a Member State and which harms the collective interests of consumers.

For the purpose of these Regulations, these acts are defined as "Community infringements." The ten relevant Directives, which cover a wide range of consumer protection measures, are listed in Schedule 1.

---

[88] Art. 2 of the *d.l. 224/2001*, which introduces a new 1 *bis* in art. 3 of act July 30th 1998, no. 281.

[89] Statutory Instrument no. 1422 of 2001. The text and commentary (which follows the text) can be found at the following address: http://www.hmso.gov.uk/si/si2001/20011422.htm.

The Regulations also contain a non-exhaustive list of the United Kingdom legislation which, for the purposes of the definition of Community infringement, are to be regarded as transposing the ten EC directives into the United Kingdom legal order.

The Regulations provide that the provisions of Schedule 2 have effect in place of the corresponding provisions in Part III of the Fair Trading Act 1973 in relation to Community infringements.

> **The Stop Now Order Regulations 2001; Regulation 3**: "Schedule 2 provides that the Director General of Fair Trading and any qualified entity have the power to bring proceedings under section 35 of the Fair Trading Act in relation to any Community infringement. In addition, to widening the range of bodies who may bring proceedings under section 35 of the Act, it displaces the existing requirement that before bringing proceedings under this section the Director General must first use his best endeavours to obtain a satisfactory written assurance from the trader that he will refrain from continuing that course of conduct or a similar one."

The existing provisions of Part III of the Fair Trading Act 1973 provide a means of dealing with traders who persist in a course of conduct which breaches the constraints imposed by civil or criminal law, in a way which is detrimental to the interests of consumers. Under section 35 of the Fair Trading Act, the Director General of Fair Trading can apply for an order that the trader refrain from carrying on that course of conduct.

Where the relevant court is satisfied that the trader has engaged in conduct which constitutes a Community infringement or is likely to do so, the court may make an order (including an interim order) under section 37 of the Fair Trading Act. The order, to be known as a Stop Now Order, must require the trader to stop the infringement or not to engage in the conduct which would constitute an infringement. In addition, the court may, where appropriate, order the publication of the decision to make the order (in full or in part) and/or the publication of a corrective statement with a view to eliminating effects of the infringement.

The Regulations identify three categories of qualified entities: "public UK qualified entities" listed in Schedule 3 to the Regulations (statutory regulators and trading standards departments); "other UK qualified entities;" and "Community qualified entities."

> **The Stop Now Order Regulations 2001, Regulation 4** "Community qualified entities" are defined as entities from other Member States which are listed in the Official Journal of the European

> Communities under Article 4.3 of the Injunctions Directive. "Other UK qualified entities" are private consumer organisations meeting objective criteria set out in Regulation 4 (2) who have been designated for this purpose by the Secretary of State. Private consumer organisations may be designated for all purposes under these Regulations or in relation only to particular types of Community infringement. The names of other UK qualified entities are to be published in a manner that appears to the Secretary of State best calculated for bringing it to the attention of persons who may be concerned. At the request of an other UK qualified entity, the Secretary of State is required to notify the European Commission that it should be added to the list of bodies qualified to bring proceedings which is published in the Official Journal."

Regulation 5 empowers the Director General and public UK qualified entities to bring proceedings in other Member States and to bring proceedings in the UK on behalf of Community qualified entities. The Director General, public UK qualified entities and other UK qualified entities on the Official Journal list may co-operate with each other and with Community qualified entities for the purpose of bringing proceedings under these Regulations or in other Member States.

The CEECs have not yet transposed this Directive into national law, with the exception of some countries, such as Poland.[90]

## 15. Improving Consumer Access to Justice in Cross-Border Disputes

Council Directive 2002/8/EC of January 27th 2003 should be noted in relation to consumer protection, which improves access to justice in cross-border disputes by establishing minimum common rules relating to legal aid for such disputes.[91]

The Directive aims to ease consumer *access to courts and tribunals* in a foreign country.

According to art. 2 (1) & (3), for the purposes of the Directive, a cross-border dispute is one where the party applying for legal aid in the context of this Directive is domiciled or habitually resident in a Member State other than the Member State where the court is sitting or where the decision is to be enforced. The relevant moment to determine if there is a cross-border dispute is the *time when the application is submitted.*

---

[90] See Act of July 5th 2002 (*Dz. U.*), no. 129/2002, item 1102.

[91] O.J., L 26, 01/31/2003. The time limit expired on November 30th 2004.

Only natural persons involved in a dispute covered by this Directive shall be entitled to receive appropriate legal aid in order to ensure their effective access to justice (art. 3).

This differs from the draft from which Directive 2002/8 derives,[92] which extended legal aid to legal persons which were non-profit organizations.

The Directive's field of action is vast, and includes the following *costs*:

– Interpretation.

– Translation of the documents necessary for the resolution of the case and required by the court or by the competent authority and presented by the recipient.

– Travel costs to be borne by the applicant where the physical presence of the persons concerned with the presentation of the applicant's case is required in court by the law or by the court of that Member State, and the court decides that the persons concerned cannot be heard to the satisfaction of the court by any other means.

– The assistance of a lawyer both at the pre-litigation phase, as well as representation in court).

– The trial costs (wholly or in part).

– The trial costs of the other party, where such costs are to be borne by the losing party in the State where the court is sitting.

– Extra-judicial procedures, under the conditions defined in this Directive, if the law requires the parties to use them, or if the parties to the dispute are ordered by the court to have recourse to them.

– Expenses incurred in having a judgment enforced in the Member State where the court is sitting.

The award of these costs by the *State* where the party is domiciled or where the court is sitting is determined either at first instance, or on appeal, regardless of whether the request is made by the plaintiff or defendant. However, the award of the costs may be partial, the State having the power to require the beneficiary to make a reasonable contribution, based on demonstrable criteria, including total or partial reimbursement if the latter's financial standing should noticeably improve or where the awards were granted on the basis of inexact information supplied by the beneficiary.

The economic situation of a person shall be assessed by the *competent authority* of the Member State in which the court is sitting, in the light of various objective factors such as income, capital, or family situ-

[92] COM (2002) 13 final.

ation, including an assessment of the resources of persons who are financially dependant on the applicant (art. 5).

Member States may define *thresholds* above which legal aid applicants are deemed partly or totally able to bear the costs of proceedings set out in art. 3(2). These thresholds shall be defined on the basis of the criteria defined in paragraph 2 of this article. Thresholds defined according to paragraph 3 of this article may not prevent legal aid applicants who are above the thresholds from being granted legal aid if they prove that they are unable to pay the costs of the proceedings referred to in art. 3(2) as a result of differences in the cost of living between the Member States of domicile or habitual residence and of the forum.

Art. 13 Dir. 2002/8 provides for the establishment of competent authorities to determine, at no cost, applications for possible allocation of legal aid, sub-divided as follows:

- *Transmitting authorities*, the competent authorities of the Member State in which the applicant is domiciled or habitually resident.
- *Receiving authorities*, the competent authorities of the Member State in which the court is sitting or where the decision is to be enforced.

The former must forward the application within 15 days of its receipt. Reasons must be given for the rejection of the application, which is subject to appeal. The competent transmitting authorities may decide to refuse transmitting an application if it is manifestly: (a) unfounded; or (b) outside the scope of this Directive. The standard form for the transmission of legal aid applications should have been established by May 30th 2003 at the latest. The standard form for legal aid applications should have been established by November 30th 2004 at the latest.

It is worth emphasizing that adoption of the provisions regarding costs of pre-litigation advice under art. 3 (2) (a) of Dir. 2002/8, with a view to reaching a settlement prior to bringing legal proceedings, has been postponed to May 30th 2006.

## 16. Sale of Consumer Goods and Associated Guarantees

Directive 99/44 of the European Parliament and Council, approved May 25th 1999, concerning the guarantees which the seller must provide in consumer sales,[93] represents another intervention of particular importance in consumer contract law. Among the priorities of the Directive is that of

[93] O.J., L 171, 07/17/1999, p. 12. The time limit was fixed for expiry on January 1st 2002.

conferring on European consumers the same opportunity to obtain effective legal protection for defects in goods sold, independently of where the sale took place (i.e. within or beyond State boundaries).

The Directive's contents are also interesting for the fact that, once adopted by the Member States, a series of new rules concerning legal *remedies* for consumer protection will have to be put in place in the national legal systems.

First and foremost, the Directive distinguishes two types of *guarantees*: 'legal and commercial.'

The *legal guarantee* is the one directly provided for by the law, in relation to defects in goods sold, and cannot be derogated by either party in any circumstances (art. 7). The guarantee takes effect when the goods acquired do not conform to the contract of sale (art. 2).

The *commercial warranty*, on the other hand, originates intentionally on the seller's part whereby s/he voluntarily assumes an express liability towards the buyer, with a precise description of the extent of the guarantee and the essential elements to validate it (art. 6).

All *movable consumer goods* are subject to the guarantee, with the following exclusions:

- Goods sold as a consequence of a liquidation/bankruptcy sale, following a court order.
- Sales of gas or water, where these are not supplied in limited quantities.
- Electricity.

Member States may also exclude the application of these rules to sales by public auction.

A *lack of conformity* occurs when the goods supplied:

- Do not conform to the seller's description and are not of merchantable/suitable quality.
- Are not fit for the purpose to be usually expected of goods of the same type.
- Are not fit for the customer's specific purpose, provided that such purpose was made known to the seller at the time of purchase and accepted by her/him.
- Are not of such quality and standard as is normally to be expected of goods of that description, as advertised in the seller or producer's publicity materials (art. 2).

The seller is liable to the consumer for any lack of conformity which exists at the time the goods were delivered (art. 3).

Another important feature with respect to the national models of sellers' legal guarantees is represented by the *hierarchy of remedies*, ordered according to the time that the lack of conformity is discovered (art. 3).

The length of the guarantee is one of the striking features of the Directive: the provision of two years is a longer period than the average in the Member States, which is six months. A fundamental aspect has to do with the limitation period for bringing an action and the differing burden of proof.

If the lack of conformity appears within two years of delivery, the consumer may request the repair or substitution of the item, obviously at no cost. Only where these solutions cannot be achieved (impossible due to loss/destruction of the goods), or because the result would be disproportionate (according to a balancing of costs for the seller and the nature of the defect), or are not achievable in a short time and with no inconvenience to the consumer, the buyer has the right to ask for a price reduction or alternatively the termination of the contract, under certain conditions (for example, the consumer is not entitled to have the contract terminated if the lack of conformity is minor, so-called *de minimis rule*).

If the lack of conformity appears within six months of delivery, there is a rebuttable presumption that it was present at the time of delivery; therefore, in this instance, the burden of proving otherwise rests with the seller. If, on the other hand, the defect should appear after the first six months, the buyer has the burden of proving that it was already present at the time of delivery.

Finally, the Member States may establish a *time-limit* of not less than two months, from the discovery of the lack of conformity, within which the buyer must communicate the existence of the defect to the seller in order to benefit from his rights (art. 5 [2]). This last provision seems to contradict the spirit of the whole Directive since it reduces protection for the consumer. In fact, in this case the time limit for communicating the lack of conformity starts to run from the day the consumer effectively ascertained the defect in the goods acquired. The disadvantage for the consumer is obvious: s/he will only have two months to assert her/his version of events. From the other point of view, the rule seems to favor the producer, who would be put in the position of having an immediate verification of the impact of the item on the market, or to monitor consumer reaction and to intervene with a notable saving of time and costs to improve the quality of the merchandise and his production, with evident benefits for the internal market of the EU.

As for the regime of liability provided by the Directive, commentators have found it inadequate, mainly for one fundamental reason: there is no provision for joint liability of the manufacturer and the other intermediaries who form part of the chain of production; therefore the protection for the consumer is ineffective.

## *16.1. Examples of National Transposition*

All the Member States have transposed the Directive into their national law, except Belgium and Luxembourg.

Austria, the first to transpose the Directive by a federal act of August 5th 2001,[94] has modified its own Civil Code in the part concerning guarantees, as well as the law on consumer protection and on insurance contracts.

Italy implemented the Directive in 2002, by legislative decree no. 24 of February 2nd 2002, inserting it into the text of the Civil Code by means of new articles, from 1519 *bis* to 1519 *nonies*,[95] a special statute for the sale of movable goods to consumers.

But the most interesting case is in Germany.[96]

Here the implementation of Dir. 99/44 has rekindled the debate on the reform of the *Kaufrecht* and, more generally, on the law of obligations. The enthusiasm with which it has been greeted and its explosive effect demonstrate how far it has provided the opportunity to launch far-reaching reform of Book I (the *Allgemeiner Teil*, General Part) and Book II (the Law of Obligations and Contracts) of the BGB, which has been in train since the beginning of the 80's. Three volumes of studies (the well-known *Gutachten und Vorschläge*), were published between 1981 and 1983; this is a collection of papers and proposals by distinguished German legal scholars, which represented the point of departure for the parliamentary debate.

The rules regarding limitation periods for contractual claims (*Verjährungsrecht*) have been simplified, as has the law of non-performance.

The various forms of non-performance were: supervening impossibility (*Unmöglichkeit*), default (*Verzug*), breach of pre-contractual duties (*culpa in contrahendo*), and positive violation of contractual duties (*Positive Vertragsverletzung*). Most of these forms of action now revolve around a new single concept, namely *breach of contractual duties* (*Pflichtverletzung*), although a special statute for it has been redrafted for contracts containing reciprocal duties, with provision for withdrawal (*Rücktritt*) and claims for compensation, which repeatedly defeats the aim of simplification.

New clauses are devoted to consumer sales, whose provisions are not

---

[94] *Gewährleistungsrechts-Änderungsgesetz* (*GewRÄG*), in *BGBl*. I, no. 48/2001.

[95] Art. 1 (paragraphs 1 & 3) of Act no. 422 of September 29th 2000 (the *Italian Community Act* 2000) gave the Government the power to implement the Directive.

[96] *Gesetz zur Modernisierung des Schuldrechts*, in *Bundesgesetzblatt* n° 61, Jahrgang 2001, Teil I, 11/29/2001, Seite 3138.

default rules, but mandatory; they render void conventional derogations and provisions which negatively affect the consumer. The reform introduces the reunification of the legal consequences deriving from defective goods, no longer making a distinction between material defects (*Sachmängel*) and legal defects (*Rechtsmängel*).

The hierarchy of remedies provided by Dir. 99/44 is introduced; this, however, is no novelty to German law, which already gave prime position to the cherished remedy of restitution or *restitutio in integrum* (*Nacherfüllung*). The federal act approving the modification of the BGB was passed by the *Bundestag* on October 11th 2001 and the *Bundesrat* on November 9th 2001.

Thus consumer contracts were inserted into the BGB following the reform, and the *Schuldrechtsreform* became law, coming into force on January 1st 2002.

The BGB has incorporated new features following the transposition of various Directives: in particular it now contains the specific provisions of some domestic acts which have adopted the contents of Directives no. 1994/47, 1997/7, 1999/44, 2000/31, and 2000/35.

The CEECs have not as yet transposed this Directive into their own national legal systems, with some exceptions. Poland, for example, implemented the Directive with the Act of July 27th 2002 on consumer sales and guarantees.[97] Hungary introduced those rules in the *Ptk* (art. 306 and 306/a) and adopted a terminology coherent with the texts of the preceding Directives on consumer protection contracts by amendments contained in Act XXXVI of 2002 and Act XXXDI of 2002.

## 17. Electronic Signatures

Directive 99/93/EC of the European Parliament and Council was approved on December 13th 1999, on a Community framework for electronic signatures.[98] The Directive resolves to favor the use of electronic signatures in e-commerce transactions, and furthermore without regulating specific issues, such as those concerning the validity of the contract.

> **4th Whereas, Dir. 99/93**: "Electronic communication and commerce necessitate 'electronic signatures' and related services allowing data authentication; divergent rules with respect to legal

---

97 Published in Journals of Laws (*Dz. U.*), September 5th 2002, item 141.

98 O.J., L 13, 01/19/2000, p. 12. The time limit was fixed for expiry on July 19th 2001. The Directive has been transposed in all member States, except for Ireland and the Netherlands.

> recognition of electronic signatures and the accreditation of certification-service providers in the Member States may create a significant barrier to the use of electronic communications and electronic commerce; on the other hand, a clear Community framework regarding the conditions applying to electronic signatures will strengthen confidence in, and general acceptance of, the new technologies; legislation in the Member States should not hinder the free movement of goods and services in the internal market; management of certificates, but should also encompass any other service and product using, or ancillary to, electronic signatures, such as registration services, time-stamping services, directory services, computing services or consultancy services related to electronic signatures."

The requirements as to the form of the contract remain within the competence of Member States by express reference in the Directive. The following provisions are of particular importance:

- *Electronic signature* means data in electronic form which are attached to or logically associated with other electronic data and which serve as a method of authentication; "advanced electronic signature" means an electronic signature which meets the following requirements: (a) it is uniquely linked to the signatory; (b) it is capable of identifying the signatory; (c) it is created using means that the signatory can maintain under his sole control; and (d) it is linked to the data to which it relates in such a manner that any subsequent change of the data is detectable; "certification-service-provider" means an entity or a legal or natural person who issues certificates or provides other services related to electronic signatures (art. 2).
- Member States shall ensure that *advanced electronic signatures*, which are based on a qualified certificate and which are created by a secure-signature-creation device: (a) satisfy the legal requirements of a signature in relation to data in electronic form in the same manner as a hand-written signature satisfies those requirements in relation to paper-based data; and (b) are admissible as evidence in legal proceedings (art. 5).
- The *certification-service-provider* is liable for damage caused to any entity or legal or natural person who reasonably relies on that certificate: (a) regarding the accuracy at the time of issuance of all information contained in the qualified certificate and regarding the fact that the certificate contains all the details prescribed for a qualified certificate; (b) for assurance that at the time of the issuance of the certificate, the signatory identified in the qualified certificate held the signature-creation data corresponding to the signature-verification data given or identified in the certificate; (c) for assurance

that the signature-creation data and the signature-verification data can be used in a complementary manner in cases where the certification-service-provider generates them both; unless the certification-service-provider proves that he has not acted negligently (art. 6).

– Member States shall ensure that certification-service-providers and national bodies, responsible for accreditation or supervision, comply with the requirements laid down in Dir. 95/46/EC of October 24th 1995 on protection of individuals with regard to the processing of personal data and on the free movement of such data (art. 8).

### *17.1. Examples of National Transposition*

The transposition of the Directive has necessitated a reform program of the Civil Codes of the Member States regarding the provisions of both substantive and procedural law on the admissibility of evidence.

Directive 99/93 was implemented into Italian law on January 23rd 2002 by legislative decree 10/02.[99] There already existed a domestic provision in the Italian legal system on electronic documents and digital signatures, before the Directive: it was art. 15 (2) of the act (*L. Bassanini),* no. 59/97, followed by presidential decrees *(DPR)* no. 513/98 and no. 445/00.[100]

The first result of the implementation of Dir. 99/93 is the introduction into the Italian legal system of two types of electronic signatures, having differing levels of security, related to the mechanism of their formation/certification, and with differing effectiveness to the computer-generated documents to which they are affixed:

– The *simple* electronic signature, namely the type of signature where the signatory writes his/her name at the end of an electronic text; while it does not include the requisites for a "digital signature," and is thus less secure, is nevertheless legally valid.

– The *advanced* electronic signature, so-called "digital signature," used for identifying the signatory and for connecting him/her to the content of the document by technical means that render perceptible any modification made to the document after the signature is apposed. It is certified by a verification service provider company.

---

[99] Published in the *Gazz. Uff.* no. 39, of February 15th 2002.

[100] The presidential decree of November 10th 1998, no. 513, provides criteria and models for the formation, storage, and transmission of documents by means of computer and telecommunications technology (in *Gazz.Uff.* no. 60 of March 13th 1998); the second decree of December 28th 2000, no. 445 (in *Gazz Uff.* no. 42, of February 20th 2001), is the so-called Single Text on administrative documentation.

Apart from the technology used, the important aspect is the level of effectiveness, in terms of security, integrity, authentication, and impossibility of repudiation of the signed electronic document. The choice of the type of signature shall be determined by the parties according to the case, the requirements, and the level of security which they wish to achieve for the smooth running of their contractual relations.

The transposition of the Directive under consideration operates so that the electronic document has the same probative value as mechanical reproductions do under art. 2712 Italian Civil Code. This means, in practical terms, that any electronic document electronically signed is admissible as evidence in court. Further, according to the Italian legislation adopting this Directive, the electronic document satisfies legal requirements as to the written form. Moreover, the requirement provided by articles 2214 *ff.* of the Civil Code and every other analogous legislative or regulatory provision is likewise satisfied.

The electronic document, signed with a digital signature or other advanced electronic signature, based on a qualified certificate and generated by means of an arrangement for creating a secure signature, provides full proof even against a challenge to authenticity, of the provenance of the declaration of the signatory.

The document so signed cannot be repudiated by the signatory (according to art. 214 of the Italian Civil Procedure Code). Therefore, to counteract its probative value it will always be necessary to challenge the validity of the document within the meaning of art. 221 *ff.* of the Civil Procedure Code.

This innovation is of great importance because a *third type* of documentary proof has been introduced, alongside the '*notarial act*' (Italian: *atto pubblico*) and the '*written document*' (Italian: *scrittura privata*), and certainly deserves further consideration in special commentary.

Furthermore, Italian legislative decree no. 10/02 has introduced far-reaching innovation into the practices of certification-service-provider, to whom free right of establishment and services is granted, without further need of previous authorization. The certification-service-provider's liability has been specifically regulated for the first time. In particular, where the certification-service-provider releases a qualified certificate to the public or guarantees the reliability of the certification to the public, s/he is liable for damage sustained by whomsoever has reasonably relied on her/him, in the three instances provided by art. 8 Dir. 99/93, unless the certification-service-provider can prove to have acted without negligence, with a reversal of the burden of proof with respect to the general rule for extra-contractual liability, under art. 2043 Italian Civil Code.

The introduction of legislative decree 10/02 has had important political repercussions too. In fact, the activity carried out by AIPA (the Independent Authority for Information Technology in the Public Administration) has passed into the hands of the new Department for Innovation and Technology, a governmental body.

In France, the probative value of electronic documents and electronic signatures has been regulated by the act of March 13th 2000, in view of what has been provided by the Directive.[101] The act represents a significant improvement over the previous practice and was much awaited by French lawyers and an ever-increasing number of users of electronic means for commercial transactions. It redefines the concept of written proof (*preuve littéral*) in the new art. 1316 of the French Civil Code, with the aim of freeing it from its electronic support. According to the act, *La preuve littérale, ou preuve par écrit, résulte d'une suite de lettre, de caractère, de chiffres ou de tous autres signes ou symboles dotés d'une signification intelligible, quels que soient leur support et leurs modalités de transmission.*[102]

The definition, as may be understood, does not limit this evidence to the requirement of writing. It confirms the fact that that the terms '*littéral*' and '*écrit*' should be taken as synonymous and spells out what constitutes the elements of written proof (signs or symbols of letters, characters, figures which possess intelligible meaning, whatever their electronic support and method of transmission may be).

Furthermore, the French law defines the limits of application. According to art. 1316.1 of the Civil Code, *l'écrit sous forme électronique est admis en preuve au même titre que l'écrit sur support papier, sous réserve que puisse être dûment identifiée la personne dont il émane et qu'il soit établi et conservé dans des conditions de nature à en garantir l'intégrité.*[103] Electronic writing is admissible in evidence with the same validity as written evidence on paper, with the condition that the person who pro-

---

[101] *Loi* no. 2000-230 of March 13th 2000, published in *Journel Officiel*, March 13th and 14th 2000, p. 3968.

*Cf.* also *Décret* 2001-272 du 30 mars 2001, *Décret pris pour l'application de l'article 1316-4 du Code civil et relatif à la signature électronique, entrée en vigueur le 03/31/2001*, in *JO* 03/31/2001, p. 5070; *Arrêté* du *05/31/2002 relatif à la reconnaissance de la qualification des prestataires de certification électronique et à l'accréditation des organismes chargés de l'évaluation*, in *JO* 06/08/2002, p. 10223.

[102] Approx: the written proof, or proof of letter, comes from a set of letters, characters, figures or any other signs or symbols which have an intelligible significance, regardless of their vehicle or way of transmission.

[103] Approx: digital texts can be accepted under the same condition as texts on paper, provided that the person who has emitted it can be duly identified and that the texts are created and preserved under conditions that guarantee integrity.

duced it is duly identifiable and that the electronic writing is created and preserved as it should be, in such a way that its integrity is guaranteed.

The new legislation basically adopts the decisions of the French courts, which had already separated the written part from its electronic means or support. Among the other features which deserve attention, it should be remembered that the new French law likewise provides that an electronic document cannot be admitted in evidence if the source from which it derives cannot be identified, and if it has not been preserved in a way that ensures its integrity. The purpose of this is to ensure certainty in the law and to guarantee the security of the electronic document.

Among the CEECs, various countries have adopted national measures which faithfully follow the Directive's contents and have therefore transposed it. The Czech Republic passed the Electronic Signature Act in June 2000 and Hungary as well in the same year.[104]

In Lithuania experts drew up an act on electronic signatures that is in compliance with EU Dir. 99/93, as well as with the requirements of the Council on a Community Framework for Electronic Signatures. The act was drafted by the Faculty of Mathematics and Informatics of Vilnius University, in collaboration with the Information Systems Section of the Department of Information and Informatics of the Ministry of Public Administration Reforms and Local Authorities. By adopting the Act on Digital Signatures, effective on July 26th 2000, Lithuania has taken the first steps in the creation of a legal basis for electronic commerce. The provisions regulate the creation, checking and validity of the digital signature, rights and responsibility of users of digital signatures, certification services, and requirements to the providers of such services. A safe digital signature now has the same legal effect as a signature in written documents and must be considered as evidence in court proceedings.

The Polish Parliament adopted the Electronic Signature Act on September 2001.[105] The act is quite compatible with EC legislation regarding the rules introduced. It amended the Polish Civil Code at arts. 60 (declaration of intents) and 78 (written form of an act), and other provisions (banking, etc.) as well.

In Estonia the Digital Signatures Act was passed on March 8th 2000, and it entered into force on the of December 15th 2000.

In Bulgaria, the Act on Electronic Documents and Electronic Signatures was adopted by the National Assembly in March 2001 and became law on April 6th 2001. It came into force on September 6th 2001.

---

[104] Respectively Act no. 227/2000 *Coll.*, and Government Resolution no. 1075/2000 (IX.13.) on the legislative principles of the bill on electronic signatures and other necessary related measures, and Act no. XXXV. of 2001 on electronic signatures.

[105] Journal of Laws (*Dz. U.*) of 2001, no. 130, item 1450.

We must await the first reactions to how these provisions have been applied in practice and what problems have arisen in interpretation by the courts, before being in a position to evaluate their beneficial effects on trans-national trade.

## 18. E-commerce

Directive 2000/31/EC on certain legal aspects of the services of the information society, in particular electronic commerce in the internal market, presented by the Commission on December 23rd 1998, was approved by the Council on June 8th 2000.[106]

In the long Preamble, which contains a full 65 points, the Community legislature dwells upon its motivations and the reasons for the choices, and this seems to indicate the difficulty of achieving general agreement among the Member States about the regulation of this sector.

*Electronic commerce* is an economic phenomenon which is evolving rapidly and, perhaps for this very reason, the Directive only aims at minimum harmonization.

The Directive, consisting of 24 articles and two Annexes, requires Member States to provide, by means of suitable legislation, that contracts made through electronic means are recognized as valid and effective. The Community legislature intends to avoid the situation where the internal market is seen as unattractive by undertakings, so that they decide to set up in businesses elsewhere. Consumer protection is not the aim of Community policy, but the means of establishing the trust of consumers in business.

---

[106] In O.J., L 178, 07/17/2000, p. 1. The time-limit for implementation was July 17th 2003. France, Portugal, and the Netherlands have not yet transposed the Directive. On the other hand, see for example Germany: *Gesetz über rechtliche Rahmenbedingungen für den Elektronischen Geschäftsverkehr (Elektronischer Geschäftsverkehr-Gesetz [EGG]),* in *Bundesgesetzblatt*, 2001, Teil I no.. 70, vom 12/20/2001, Seite 3721; *Landesgesetz zu dem Sechsten Rundfunkänderungsstaatsvertrag und zur änderung des Landesrundfunkgesetz*es vom 07/04/2002 in *GVBl. Rheinland-Pfalz* n° 10 du 06/12/2002 p. 255; Belgium: *Loi du 11 mars 2003 sur certains aspects juridiques des services de la sociétè de l'information visés à l'article 77 de la Constitution*, in *MB Ed.* 2 du 03/17/2003, p. 12960 (C-2003/11126); Spain: *Ley 34/2002 de 11de julio, de servicios de la sociedad de la informacion y de comercio electronico,* in *BOE* n° 166 du 07/12/2002 p. 25388; Italy: *Decreto legislativo 04/09/2003 n. 70 – Attuazione delle direttiva 2000/31/CE relativa a taluni aspetti giuridici dei servizi della societa dell'informazione nel mercato interno, con particolare riferimento al commercio elettronico,* in *Gazz.Uff., Serie gen.*, n° 87, 04/14/2003; the UK: *The Electronic Commerce (EC Directive) Regulations 2002*, in *SI* n° 2013, 07/31/2002 coming into force 08/21/2002 (Regulation 16: 10/23/2002).

Here too, in the context of electronic commerce, one of the most noticeable features of private Community law in recent years is again in evidence, namely the tendency towards '*external harmonization,*' that is, harmonization not only aimed at creating uniform market conditions within the Community, but above all directed at accomplishing a Community market which can compete internationally.

To this end, the Community legal system must not impose features which penalize business with respect to those in other non-EU States. This principle prevails not only in relation to the main commercial competitors of the EC (Japan and the USA), but also to other places, geographically closer to EU territory, which could represent more advantageous alternatives to entrepreneurs.

As the 60th recital of the Preamble sets out, "in order to allow the unhampered development of electronic commerce, the legal framework must be clear and simple, predictable and consistent with the rules applicable at international level so that it does not adversely affect the competitiveness of European industry or impede innovation in that sector."

Thus, while art. 15, eloquently entitled "No general obligation to monitor" provides that "Member States shall not impose a general obligation on providers (...) to monitor the information which they transmit or store, nor a general obligation actively to seek facts or circumstances indicating illegal activity," the 65th recital hastily adds that "the Council, in its resolution of January 19th 1999 on the consumer dimension of the information society,[107] stressed that the protection of consumers deserved special attention in this field; the Commission will examine the degree to which existing consumer protection rules provide insufficient protection in the context of the information society and will identify, where necessary, the deficiencies of this legislation and those issues which could require additional measures; if need be, the Commission should make specific additional proposals to resolve such deficiencies that will thereby have been identified."[108]

It is noteworthy too, that the Directive, in contradistinction to the preceding draft, refers to *business-to-business contracts* and not just to the so-called business-to-consumer ones. This very significant alteration is collocated in the objectives in respect of which the States achieved consent. Indeed, there was no sense in limiting the effect of Dir. 2000/31 to contracts where one party is a consumer, given that consumer protection is not the essential aim of the Directive.

---

[107] OJ., C 23, 01/28/1999, p. 1.

[108] See also, previously, the Commission action plan for consumer policy 1999–2001, above *cit.*

The complex rules, present in the draft, for establishing the moment when the electronic contract is concluded, have been taken out of the definitive text of the Directive, too. Significantly, it was considered prudent to relinquish one of the most delicate issues, since it involved a confrontation between the various national traditions, in order to achieve speedy approval of the harmonizing legislation.

Article 4 contains one of the fundamental principles of the Directive, which allows any operator to sell, via electronic means, in all Member States without needing to approximate to the laws of each State, due to the application of the *home country control principle*, already applied in the banking and insurance sectors.[109]

As a result, the Dir. 2000/13 does not impose particular duties or obligations to fulfil on interested undertakings, unless those linked to the *information* which economic operators must supply when the goods are put on the market and which concern their details, the head office, register entries if any, and so on.

It should finally be noted that art. 9 Dir. 2000/31 allows Member States to exclude the possibility of making valid and effective contracts where the intervention of a court is required, or whose validity is subject to registration with public authorities, in contracts of suretyship granted and on collateral securities furnished by persons acting for purposes outside their trade, business, or profession and in contracts governed by family law and those concerning the law of succession.

This Directive fits into a wider context of long-term development over the next ten years, presented at the EC Lisbon summit, in March 2000.

The Commission's Report, *On e-Europe: An Information Society for all*,[110] presented at that meeting, the later Communication from the Commission on *Realizing the EU's Potential*: *consolidating and extending the Lisbon strategy*,[111] and the Santa Maria de Feira EU Summit with the adoption of the *Action Plan on e-Europe 2002*,[112] define the outlines of the ambitious Community strategy to make the EU "the most competitive and dynamic knowledge-based economy in the world, capable of sustainable economic growth and better jobs and greater social cohesion."

The Swedish Presidency at the Gothenburg summit in June 2001[113] concluded with a message directed at the candidate countries for enlarge-

---

[109] See below, chapter III.

[110] *Cf.* the document in internet at: http://europa.eu.int/information_society/eeurope/action_plan/index_en.htm.

[111] COM (2001) 79 final. European Council, Stockholm March 23–24th 2001.

[112] Brussels, 06/14/2002, at http://europa.eu.int/information_society/eeurope/action_plan/pdf/actionplan_en.pdf.

[113] In internet at http://europa.eu.int/comm/gothenburg_council/index_en.htm.

ment of the EU: from spring of 2003, in drawing up the annual synthesis report on e-Europe, the Commission will take into account the candidate countries as well and their national policies.

Further, at the Gothenburg summit the *Common Action Plan on e-Europe 2003* was adopted, which establishes the deadlines and tasks which must be respected by the candidate countries before accession. The Action Plan was based on four objectives: to accelerate the construction of the Information Society; to invest in professional training for the new economy; to facilitate access to the Internet to an ever-increasing number of citizens; to render such access safe. According to this plan, the candidate countries must undertake more than 100 concrete actions before the end of 2003. This indubitably represented a *new acquis*, an additional effort required of the candidates and imposed unilaterally by the Community, given that the concept of e-Europe was not even mentioned in the Europe Agreements.

Hungary was one of the first of the candidate countries to take action after the Lisbon and Santa Maria de Feira summits. The Hungarian government established a special Government Commissioner for Informatics within the Prime Minister's Office and a Parliamentary Committee on the Information Society; it also adopted a National Information Society Strategy, and adopted a legislative program for the construction of an Information Society. It introduced new provisions on e-commerce in a separate text, the Act CVIII of 2002 and its further amendments by Act XCVII of 2003, in compliance with Directive 2000/31.

Poland, by the Act 2003,[114] introduced new contractual provisions on electronic declarations of intention and offer directly into the Civil Code.

However, the difficulties which the all the Member States and forthcoming members from the CEEC's must face in the next few years are still numerous:

- The new legal terminology which the e-Europe *acquis* requires to be developed and adopted.
- The new "codification techniques" required by the new e-commerce (where and how to regulate these topics, whether in civil, commercial, or special consumer protection Codes).
- The interpretation of the new laws which concern judges, law-enforcement agents, prosecutors, attorneys, and notaries, who must all be educated by means of suitable apprenticeships to ensure effective consumer protection.
- The Codes of Civil Procedure which have to be amended.

---

[114] See Act of February 14th 2003 (*Dz. U.* no. 49/2003, item 408) *cit.*, at art. 66.

# Bibliography Chapter I

## *Selected Books/Commentary:*

*§ In English:*

HOWELLS G., JANSSEN A., SCHULZE R., *Information Rights and Obligations, Ashgate, 2004; NIGLIA L., The Transformation of Contract Europe,* The Hague/London, Kluwer Law International, 2003; GRUNDMANN S., STUYCK J. (eds), *An Academic Green Paper on European Contract Law,* Kluwer Law International, 2002; SCHULZE R., SCHULTE–NÖLKE H. & JONES J. (eds.), *A Casebook on European Consumer Law,* Oxford, Hart publishing, 2002; SCHULTE–NÖLKE H., SCHULZE R., BERNARDEAU L. (eds.), *European Contract law in Community Law,* Köln, 2002; VUKOWICH W. T., *Consumer Protection in the 21st Century: A Global Perspective,* Transnational Publ., 2002; WILHELMSSON T., TUOMINEN S., TUOMOLA H., *Consumer Law in the Information Society,* The Hague, 2001; LOWE R., WOODROFFE G. (eds.), *Consumer Law and Practice, 5th ed.,* London, 1999; MARSH G. A., *Consumer Protection Law in a Nutshell (Nutshell Series),* West Wadsworth, 3rd edition, 1999; HOLLAND D., *European Consumer Law,* Informa UK Ltd., 1999; WEATHERILL S., *EC Consumer law and policy,* London, 1997; KÖTZ H., FLESSNER A., *European Contract Law. Vol. I: Formation, Validity, and Content of Contracts; Contract and Third Parties,* trans. by T. Weir, Oxford, 1997; WILHELMSSON TH., *Social Contract Law and European Integration,* Dartmouth, 1995; REICH N.– WOODROFFE G. (eds.), *European Consumer Policy after Maastricht,* Kluwer 1994; WILHELMSSON TH. (ed.), *Perspectives of Critical Contract Law,* Dartmouth, 1993; BOURGOIGNIE T., TRUBEK D., *Consumer Law, Common Markets and Federalism in Europe and the United States,* CAPPELLETTI–SECCOMBE–WEILER, *Integration Through Law. Europe and the American Federal Experience,* vol. III, De Gruyter, 1987; BORRIE–DIAMOND, *Consumer, Society and Law,* London, 1977.

*§ In Italian:*

ALPA–PATTI (a cura di), *Clausole vessatorie nei contratti del consumatore, in Commentario al Codice Civile fondato da Piero Schlesinger,* diretto da Francesco D. Busnelli, Milano, 2003, 1231; AMATO C., *Per un diritto Europeo dei contratti con i consumatori,* Milano, 2003;COMANDÈ G., SICA S., *Il commercio elettronico,* Torino, 2001; SMORTO G., *Clausole abusive e diritti dei consumatori,* Padova, 2001; CHINÉ G., *Il diritto comunitario dei contratti,* in TIZZANO (ed), *Il diritto privato dell'Unione europea,* in BESSONE, *Trattato di diritto privato,* vol. I, Torino, 2000, 608; TRIMARCHI, *La multiproprietà,* in TIZZANO (ed)., *Il diritto privato dell'Unione europea,* in BESSONE, *Trattato di diritto privato,* vol. I, Torino, 2000, 245; PATTARO E., *Codice di diritto dell'informatica,* Padova, 2000; ZAGAMI R., *Firma digitale e sicurezza informatica,* Padova, 2000; DE CRISTOFARO G., *Difetto di conformità al contratto e diritti del consumatore,* Padova, 2000; TORIELLO F., *I contratti di vendita stipulati dai consumatori. Recenti sviluppi,* in TIZZANO (ed.), *Il diritto privato dell'Unione europea,* in BESSONE, *Il diritto privato dell'Unione europea,* vol. I, Torino, 2000, 669; ALPA G., *Il diritto dei consumatori,* Roma–Bari, 1999; BARTOLINI A., *Guida ai diritti dei consumatori,* Hoepli, 1999; MOLFESE F., *Il contratto di viaggio e le agenzie turistiche,* Padova, 1999; AA. VV., *Tendenze evolutive nella tutela dei consumatori,* Napoli, 1998; GAROSCI R., *Consumatori d'Europa: come l'Unione europea difende i cittadini prima, durante e dopo i consumi,* Venezia, 1998; CHINÉ G., *Il consumatore,* in LIPARI (ed.), *Diritto privato europeo,* Padova, 1997, vol. I, 164; JANNARELLI A., *La disciplina dell'atto e dell'attività: i contratti tra imprese e tra imprese e consumatori,* in LIPARI (ed.), *Diritto privato europeo,* Padova, 1997, vol. II, 489.

*§ In French:*

POILLOT E., *Droit européen de la consommation et uniformisation du droit des contrats*, thèse dactylographiée, sous la direction de P. de Vareilles-Sommières, Reims 2004; LEWANDOWSKI H., MAKOWSKI D. (eds.), *Influence du droit communautaire sur le droit interne, Cas De la France e de la Pologne*, Warszawa, 2003; CALAIS-AULOY J., F. STEINMETZ, *Droit de la consommation*, 6ème éd. Paris, 2003; FASQUELLE D., P. MEUNIER (sous la direction de), *Le droit communautaire de la consommation, bilans et perspectives*, La documentation française, 2002; GAVALDA CH., G. PARLEANI, *Droit des affaires de l'Union européenne*, Litec, 4ème édition, 2002; GAUDEMET-TALLON H., *Compétences et exécution des jugements en Europe, règlement n. 44/2001: Conventions de Bruxelles et de Lugano*, LGDJ, 3ème éd., 2002; DE MATOS A.- M. (préface de R. Bout), *Les contrats transfrontières conclus par les consommateurs au sein de l'Union européenne*, PUAM 2001; VERBIEST T., WERY E., *Le droit de l'internet et de la société de l'information, Droits européen, belge et français*, Coll. Création–Information–Communication, 2001; DE NAYER B., LAFFINEUR J., *Le consentement électronique*, Actes du colloque de Bruxelles des 23 et 24 septembre 1999, Louvain-la-Neuve, Coll. *'Droit et Consommation'* 2000; BOUCQUEY N., (ed.) *Le droit européen des consommateurs et la gestion des déchets / European Consumer Law and Waste Management*, Louvain-la-Neuve, Coll. *'Droit et Consommation'*, Volume XXXIX, 1999; CHILLON S. (préface de J. Calais-Auloy), *Le droit communautaire de la consommation après les Traités de Maastricht et d'Amsterdam*, Story Scientia LGDJ, 1999; HEUSEL W. (sous la direction de), *Le nouveau droit des contrats et la protection des consommateurs. Concepts de la réglementation communautaire et leurs conséquences pour le droit civil national*, ERA Trèves 1999; BOULANGER F., *Tourisme et loisirs dans les droits privés européens*, Economica, 1996; BOURGOIGNIE TH., *Éléments pour une théorie du droit de la consommation: au regard des développements du droit belge et du droit de la Communauté économique européenne*, LGDJ/ Story scientia, Bruxelles-Louvain la Neuve, 1988; BIHL L., WILLETTE L., *Une histoire du mouvement consommateur, mille ans de lutte*, Paris, 1984; *Les contrats d'adhésion et la protection du consommateur*, Colloque Droit et Commerce 1978, ENAJ 1978.

***§ In German:***

KAMMERER C., *Harmonisierung des Verbraucherrechts in Europa: das verbraucherschützende Widerrufsrecht der Paragr. 355 ff. BGB im Lichte der europarechtlichen Vorgaben und im Vergleich zum Code de la consommation*, Hamburg, 2004; HEIDERHOFF B., *Grundstrukturen des nationalen und europäischen Verbrauchervertragsrechts: insbesondere zur Reichweite europäischer Auslegung*, München, 2004; DAUNER-LIEB; *Das Neue Schuldrecht in der Praxis*, Köln, 2003; PALANDT; *Kommentar zum BGB*, 62nd ed., München, 2003; REICH N., MICKLITZ H.-W., *Europäisches Verbraucherrecht*, Baden–Baden, 2003; DAUNER-LIEB, HEIDEL, LEPA, RING (eds.), *Das Neue Schuldrecht*, Heidelberg 2002; DILGER P., *Verbraucherschutz bei Vertragsabschlüssen im Internet*, München, 2002; GRUNDMANN S., BIANCA C.M., *EU-Kaufrechts-Richtlinie*, Köln, 2002; KOLLER, ROTH, ZIMMERMANN, *Schuldrechtsmodernisierungsgesetz 2002*, München, 2002; MICKLITZ, *Schuldrechtsreform und Verbraucherschutz*, Baden–Baden, 2001; SCHWARTZE A., *Europäische Sachmängelgewährleistung beim Warenkauf, Mohr Siebeck*, 2000; SCHULZE R., SCHULTE-NÖLKE H. (eds.), *Europaeische Rechtsangleichung und nationale Privatrechte*, Baden– Baden, 1999; TONNER K., *Der Reisevertrag*, 4. Auflage, Berlin, 2000; GRUNDMANN S., *Europäisches Schuldvertragsrecht*, Brussels, 1999; GRABITZ/HILF II/ WOLF, *Das Recht der Europäischen Union*, Kommentar, 1999; ID., *Das Recht des Time-Sharing an Ferienimmobilien*, 1997; HILDENBRAND T., KAPPUS A., MÄSCH G., *Time-Sharing und Teilzeit-Wohnrechtegesetz, Handbuch, Kommentar und Leitentscheidungen*, Stuttgart, 1997.

***§ In Spanish:***

LETE ACHIRICA J. (ed.), *Garantías en la venta de bienes de consumo/Les garanties dans la vente de biens de consommation,* Santiago de Compostela, Servicio de Publicaciones de la Universidad, 2004; VERGEZ SÁNCHEZ M., *La protección del consumidor en la Ley de garautias en la veuta de bieues de consumo,* cizur meuor, 2004; AÑOVEROS TERRADAS B., *Los contratos de consumo intracomunitarios,* Barcelona–Madrid, Marcial Pons, 2003; CLEMENTE MEORO M., CAVANILLAS MÚGICA S., *Responsabilidad civil y contratos en internet. Su regulación en la Ley de Servicios de la Sociedad de la Información y del Comercio Electrónico,* Granada, Comares-Asociación de Profesores de Derecho Civil, 2003; ESTEBAN DE LA ROSA F., *La protección de los consumidores en el mercado interior europeo,* Granada, Comares, 2003; GUILLÉN CARAMÉS J., *El estatuto jurídico del consumidor. Política comunitaria, bases constitucionales y actividad de la Administración,* Madrid, Cívitas, 2002.

***Selected Articles:***

HESSELINK M., *The European Commission's Action Plan: towards a more coherent Contract Law?* 11 ERPL 113, 2004; ERVINE W. COWAN H., *The Unfair Terms in Consumer Contracts regulations in the courts,* 21 The Scots Law Times, 2004; BAKAR M. A., *Unsolicited commercial e-mail: implementing the EU Directive,* 10 Computer and telecommunications law review, 2004; Study Group on Social Justice in European Private Law, *Social Justice in European Contract Law: A Manifesto,* 10 ELJ 653, 2004; CALLIESS, *Coherence and consistency in European Consumer Contract Law: a progress report,* 4 German Law Journal 333, 2003; HOWELLS G., WILHELMSSON T., *EC Consumer Law: has it come of age?* 4 ELJ 370, 2003; HONDIOUS E., JELOSCHER C., *Towards a European Sales law / Legal Challenges posed by the Directive on the Sale of Consumer Goods and Associated Guarantees,* 4 ERPL, 158, 2001; GRUNDMANN S., *The Structure of European Contract Law* 9 ERPL 505, 2001; SCHWARTZ D. J., *Loose Teeth in European Union Consumer Protection Policy: The Injunction Directive and the Mass Default Scenario,* 28 Ga. J. Int'l & Comp. L., 527, 2000; LETWOSKA E., *Consumer Protection as Public Interest Law,* Droit Polonais Contemporain/Polish Contemporay Law 39, 1999; REEVES T., *Opposites Attract: Plain British with a European Interpretation,* 147 New Journal 576, 1997; REICH S. N., *European Consumer Law and its Relationship to Private Law,* 3 ERPL 285, 1995; HONDIUS E., *The Reception of the Directive on Unfair Terms in Consumer Contracts by Member States,* 3 ERPL 242, 1995; REICH S.N., *Protection of Diffusive Interest in the EEC and the Perspective of "progressively establishing" an Internal Market,* Journal of Consumer Policy 11, 1988.

GRANZIERA, E., *Tutela dei consumatori: la Corte di giustizia condanna l'Italia,* Il diritto dell'economia, 171, 2004; MASUCCI A., *Documento informatico e sottoscrizione elettronica: la nuova normativa del T.U. sulla documentazione amministrativa tra direttiva europea e specificità italiana,* Rivista italiana di diritto pubblico comunitario 541, 2004; TRIPODI E. M., *Alcuni interrogativi sul d.lgs. n. 70/2003 di recepimento della direttiva sul commercio elettronico,* 6 Il corriere giuridico, 829, 2004; ALPA G., *Ancora sulla definizione di consumatore,* Contratti, 205, 2001; ALESSI R., *Diritto europeo dei contratti e regole dello scambio,* Europa e dir. priv. 961, 2000; BUONOCORE V., *Gli effetti sulle operazioni della nuova disciplina dei contratti con i consumatori,* Giur. comm., III, 237, 2000; MARCATAJO G., *Asimmetrie informative e tutela della trasparenza nella politica comunitaria di consumer protection,* Europa e dir. priv. 751, 2000; PIZZOLANTE G., *Contrattazione a distanza e tutela del consumatore in diritto comunitario,* Dir. comm. internaz. 389, 2000; GABRIELLI G., *L'attuazione in Germania e in Italia della direttiva europea sui contratti negoziati fuori dei locali commerciali,* Europa e dir. priv. 715, 2000; BONINO E., *Strategia comunitaria per la politica dei consumatori,* Contratti 621, 1999; CIMINO A., *Diritto europeo dei consumatori: il summer programme in European Community consumer law* (Louvain-la-Neuve, 7/17 luglio 1998), Contratto e impr./Europa 1058, 1998; CASTRONOVO C., *Profili della disciplina nuova delle clausole c.d. vessatorie cioè abusive,* Europa e dir. priv. 5, 1998; MAZZAMUTO S., *L'inefficacia delle clausole abusive,* Europa e dir. priv. 45, 1998; SERIO M., *Profili comparatistici delle clausole vessatorie,* Europa e dir. priv. 77, 1998; ZENO ZENCOVICH V., *voce Consumatore (tutela del): I, Diritto civile,* Enciclopedia giuridica italiana, VIII; BIN M., *Clausole vessatorie: una svolta storica (ma si attuano così le direttive comunitarie?),* Contratto e impr./Europa, 431, 1996; PARDOLESI R., *Clausole abusive, pardon vessatorie: verso l'attuazione di una direttiva abusata,* Riv. critica dir. privato 523, 1995.

BASEDOW J., *Internationales Verbrauchervertragsrecht: Erfahrungen, Prinzipien und europäische Reform, Festschrift für Erik Jayme,* Bd. 1, 3, 2004; HAHN P., BROCKMANN P., *Das Haustürwiderrufsrecht bei finanzierten Immobilienanlagen auf dem Weg zu einem wirksamen Verbraucherschutzrecht?* 19 VuR Heft 6, 207, 2004; MAKRIS S., *Die Umsetzung der E-Commerce-Richtlinie in griechisches Recht und der Schutz des Verbrauchers im elektronischen Handel: Vergleich zum deutschen Recht,* 4 The European legal forum Heft 3, 160, 2004; ROTT P., *Effektiver Rechtsschutz vor missbräuchlichen AGB—Zum Cofidis-Urteil des EuGH,* EuZW Heft 1, 2003; BÜLOW P., *Verbraucherkreditrecht im BGB,* NJW 1145, 2002; TONNER K., *Probleme des novellierten Widerrufsrecht: Nachbelehrung, verbundene Geschäfte, Übergangsvorschriften,* BKR 856, 2002; HOFFMANN J., *Verbrauchsgüterkaufrechtsrichtlinie und Schuldrechtsmodernisierungsgesetz,* ZRP 347, 2001; REICH N., *Anmerkungen zu EuGH, Rs. C-381/98, Ingmar,* EuZW 51, 2001; RICHTER W., *Die Praxis des Insolvenzschutzes bei Pauschalreisen,* RRa, 131, 2000; FRITZE U., HOLZBACH C., *Die Electronic-Commerce-Richtlinie,* WRP 872, 2000; MICKLITZ H.-W., *Die Fernabsatzrichtlinie 97/7/EG,* ZEuP 875, 1999; JOERGES C., *Die Europäisierung des Privatrechts als Rationalisierungsprozeß und als Streit der Disziplinen. Eine Analyse der Richtlinie über mißbräuchliche Klauseln Verbraucherverträgen,* Zeitschrift für Europäisches Privatrecht 1995, 181 (English version: *The Europeanisation of Private Law as a Rationalisation Process and as a Contest of Legal Disciplines—an Analysis of the Directive on Unfair Terms in Consumer Contracts,* 3 European Review of Private Law 1995, 175); REICH N., *Zur Umsetzung der EG-Richtlinie 93/13/EWG in deutsches Recht,* VuR 1, 1995.

BOURGOIGNIE TH., *Droit et politique communautaire de la consommation,* in *Etudes de droit de la consommation, Liber amicorum Jean Calais-Auloy,* Dalloz 2004, 95; LUBY M., *Trop ne vaut rien! (Ou quand la CJCE ébranle le régime juridique des clauses abusives),* Contrats, conc., consomm. 6, 2004; DE MATOS A.-M., *Transposition en droit français de la directive du 25 mai 1999: un large débat et une amorce de réponse,* Rev. eur. dr. consomm. 18, 2003; JOURDAIN P., *Transposition de la directive sur la vente du 25 mai 1999: ne pas manquer une occasion de progrès, D.* 4, 2003; MAZEAUD D., *Transposition de la directive sur la vente du 25 mai 1999: la parole est à la défense, D.* 6, 2003; SAUPHANOR-BROUILLAUD N., A. CERMOLACCE, Image électronique et consommateur, 6 Communication, commerce électronique 23, 2003; LARGARDE X., *Mouvement sur la forclusion (à propos de l'article L 311-37 du Code de la consommation),* Les Petites Affiches, n. 6, 08/01/2003, 4; VARII AUCTORES, *La transposition en droit français de la directive européenne du 25 mai 1999 relative à la vente,* Colloque du 8 novembre 2002, Université Paris I Panthéon–Sorbonne, J.C.P. éd. Entr. n. 1, supplément à la Semaine

Juridique n° 9 du 27 février 2003; LEVENEUR L., *Les contrats de consommation et le droit européen*, 3 Contrats, conc. consomm., 3, 2002; MAZEAUD D., *Les vices de la protection du consentement du consommateur*, Recueil Dalloz Sirey, n. 1, 01/03/2002, 71; MOREAU F., *La protection du consommateur dans les contrats à distance*, Les petites affiches, n. 57, 03/20/2002, 4; PAISANT,G., L. LEVENEUR, *Quelle transposition pour la directive du 25 mai 1999 sur les garanties dans la vente de biens de consommation*?, J.C.P., I, 135, 2002; PIZZIO J.-P., *L'apport du droit communautaire à la protection contractuelle des consommateurs, in Protection du consommateur dans l'espace européen*, 108 Droit et Patrimoine, 59, 2002; SAUPHANOR-BROUILLAUD N., *Application de la réglementation sur les clauses abusives à un service public industriel et commercial—Note sous arrêt du Conseil d'Etat, 11 juillet 2001, no 221458, Sté des eaux du Nord*, J.C.P. E Semaine Juridique (édition entreprise), n. 3, 01/17/2002, 134; TOURNAFOND O., *De la transposition de la directive du 25 mai 1999 á la réforme du Code civil, D.* 159, 2002; VINEY G., *Quel domaine assigner à la loi de transposition de la directive européenne sur la vente?*, J.C.P., I, 158, 2002; BAZIN E., *De l'exercice du droit par les associations de consommateurs,* Dalloz Sirey, n. 29, 08/30/2001, 2395; BERNARDEAU L., *La notion de consommateur en droit communautaire (à la suite de l'arrêt Idealservice, aff. Jointe C-541/99 et C-542/ 99)*, Rev. eur. dr. consomm. 341, 2001; HUET J., *Éléments de réflexion sur le droit de la consommation*, Les Petites Affiches, n. 223, 11/08/2001, 4; LEBAUT-FERRARESE B., *Le droit communautaire au soutien du consommateur (à propos du délai de forclusion de l'article L. 311-37 du Code de la consommation*, P. A., 21 mai 2001, 16; LEVENEUR L., *Directive du 25 mai 1999: quelle transposition?*, Contrats conc. consomm., repères, 2, août-septembre 2001; MAINGUY D., *Propos dissidents sur la transposition de la directive du 25 mai 1999 sur certains aspects de la vente et des garanties des biens de consommation*, J.C.P., I, 183, 2001; RAYMOND G., *Ordonnance du 23 août 2001 portant transposition de directives communautaires en matière de droit de la consommation*, J.C.P. G Semaine Juridique (édition générale), n. 50, 12/12/2001, 2281; TOURNAFOND O., *La transposition de la directive du 25 mai 1999 sur la vente et les garanties des biens de consommation, D.* 3051, 2001; ID., *De la transposition de la directive du 25 mai 1999 à la réforme du code civil, D.* 2883, chron., 2002; BERNARDEAU L., *Le droit de rétraction du consommateur un pas vers une doctrine d'ensemble*, J.C.P. G Semaine Juridique (édition générale), n. 14, 04/05/2000, 623; ID., *Le droit de rétractation du consommateur, un pas de vers une doctrine d'ensemble. A propos de l'arrêt CJCE, 22 avril 1999, Travel Vac, aff. C-423/97*, J.C.P., I, 218, 2000; ID., *Clauses abusives, l'illicéité des clauses attributives de compétence et l'autonomie de leur contrôle judiciaire*, Rev. dr. eur. consomm. 261, 2000; GRYNBAUM L., *La fusion de l'action en garantie des vices cachés et de l'obligation de délivrance opérée par la directive du 25 mai 1999*, Contrats conc. consomm., 4, 2000; LAFFINEUR J., *Les contrats de consommation en droit communautaire*, in *Les contrats de consommation*, Actes des journées d'études de Poitiers des 18 et 19 octobre 2000, PUF, 157; LUBY M., *La notion de consommateur en droit communautaire: une commode inconstance*, Contrats, conc., consom. 2000, chron. 1; PELET S., *L'impact de la directive 99/44/CE relative à certains aspects de la vente et des garanties des biens de consommation*, Rev. eur. dr. consom. 2000, 56; RAYNARD J., *Droit communautaire et vente: les enjeux d'une transposition à venir (directive du 25 mai 1999 sur certains aspects de la vente et des biens de consommation)*, Rev. trim. dr. civ. 440, 2000; TOURNAFOND O., *Remarques critiques sur la directive européenne du 25 mai 1999, relative à certains aspects de la vente et des garanties des biens de consommation*, D. cah. dr. aff., 2000, 159; TROCHU M., *Vente et garantie des biens de consommation: directive CE n. 1999-44 du 25 mai 1999*, D. cah. dr. aff., 2000,

119; TONNER K., *Politique du tourisme de l'Union européenne et protection des consommateurs*, Rev. eur. dr. consomm. 1998, 26; BASEDOW J., *Un droit commun des contrats pour le Marché commun*, R.I.D.C. 7, 1998; RADE C., *L autonomie de l-action en garantie des vices cachés*, J.C.P. I, 4009, 1997; HUET J., *Propos amers sur la directive du 5 avril 1993 relative aux clauses abusives*, J.C.P., I, 309 1994; ESPERIQUETTE M., *La législation communautaire des contrats conclus avec les consommateurs*, Rec. concu. consomm. 7, 1993; TESTU F.-X., *La transposition en droit interne de la directive communautaire sur les clauses abusives (loi n. 95-96du 1er février 1995)*, 16 Dalloz Affaires 372, 1993; SAVY, R., *La protection des consommateurs en France*, R.I.D.C. 501, 1974; STERBERG H., *L'Ombudsman suédois pour les consommateurs*, R.I.D.C. 577, 1974.

# CHAPTER II

# Product Liability

**Key words**: National product liability rules – Directive on product liability – Implementation – Member States – Transposition – CEECs – Directive on general product safety – Draft directive on the liability of service providers – Directive on the liability for environmental damage

## 1. Product Liability in the Member States before the 1985 Directive

No country in the European Union had had specific legislation on product liability before the 1985 Directive.[1]

Despite this, the courts of each Member State, applying some provisions of the national Civil Codes, have developed precedents to the point of constructing differing national legal models, which apply in the case of design, production, and distribution of goods capable of causing damage to the individual consumer. Furthermore, European States transplanted the USA legal rules at least to a certain degree.

In the USA, the law on product liability has changed from that of *caveat emptor* ("let the buyer beware") to strict liability for manufacturing defects that make a product unreasonably dangerous. The history of the law of product liability is largely a history of the erosion of the doctrine of privity that dominated the 19th Century. The doctrine stated that an injured person could sue the defendant only if s/he were a party to the transaction with the injured person. The seminal case, which abolished the privity requirement in negligence cases, was *MacPherson v. Buick Motor Co.*;[2] with respect to implied warranties, the leading case which abolished the privity limitation was *Henningsen v. Bloomfield Motors, Inc.*;[3]

---

[1] In Europe, unlike the United States, the area of product liability comes under the much bigger subject of consumer protection. We are devoting to it a separate chapter from that of consumer contracts because the rules which sustain product liability answer to different needs and criteria.

[2] 217 NY 382, 111 NE 1050 (NY 1916).

[3] 32 N.J. 358, 161 A.2d 69 (1960).

finally, in 1963 the California Supreme Court adopted strict tort liability for defective products in *Greenman v. Yuba Power Products Inc.*[4]

In most jurisdictions, a plaintiff's cause of action may be based on one or more of four different theories:

– Negligence (duty of care).

– Breach of warranty (warranties are certain kinds of express or implied representations of fact that the law will enforce against the warrantor; they are codified in the Uniform Commercial Code, which every State has adopted).

– Misrepresentation (this refers to the process of giving consumers false security about the safety of a particular product).

– Strict tort liability (in the absence of fault).

There are federal laws and regulations (and sometimes State ones, for example, in Colorado, District of Columbia, and Illinois) that protect the consumer from defective and harmful products: on the federal level see the *Consumer Product Safety Act*, the *Food, Drug and Cosmetic Act*, and the *National Traffic and Motor Vehicle Safety Act.*

Finally, the fundamental part played in this sector by the *Restatement* should be emphasized. As is well known, the idea of "restating the law" in a form resembling a code has been developed by the American Law Institute, beginning in 1923. It is not a statute or a true codification, but it attempts to bring uniformity to the law. The Restatement on product liability has been widely accepted and followed by the courts in most States.

Strict liability in tort for product defects was usually based upon section 402A of the *Restatement of Torts (Second)*, published in 1965. The product must be "unreasonably dangerous" for its intended use in order to be "defective" The interpretation of these words has caused difficulty for the US courts: many courts have adopted a cost–benefit approach to defectiveness; others have been in favor of the more intuitive consumer expectation test.

In 1998, the *Restatement of Torts (Third)* has been published. The strict liability rule has been maintained, but with important amendments and limitations on the subject of design defects and development risks, with respect to some previous solutions accepted by the American courts. In particular, Section 2 gives separate treatment to three classes of product defects: manufacturing defects, design defects, and warning defects.

[4] 59 Cal. 2d 57, 377 P.2d 897 (1963).

**Restatement of Torts (Third), Section 2** "A product is defective when, at the time of sale or distribution, it contains a manufacturing defect, is defective in design, or is defective because of inadequate instructions or warnings. A product:
- Contains a manufacturing defect when the product departs from its intended design even though all possible case was exercised in the preparation and marketing of the product.
- Is defective by design when the foreseeable risks of harm posed by the product could have been reduced or avoided by the adoption of a reasonable alternative design by the seller or other distributor, or a predecessor in the commercial chain of distribution, and the omission of the alternative design renders the product not reasonably safe.
- Is defective because of inadequate instructions or warnings when the foreseeable risks of harm posed by the product or could have been reduced or avoided by the provisions of reasonable instructions by the seller or other distributor, or a predecessor in the commercial chain of distribution, and the omission of the instructions or warnings renders the product not reasonably safe."

The academic debate has been very lively in all the countries of the Union and has been followed by a remarkable variety of case-law results. What we are interested in achieving in this book is not an analysis or presentation of the particular solutions which have been adopted by each legal system, but rather highlighting the general tendency towards the adoption of a European model of product liability. In this subject, too, we shall be confining ourselves to a short analysis of the scope and declared aims of the Directive, the reflections this has had in the domestic systems following its adoption, to make an evaluation as to whether or not the fixed objectives of the Community legislature have been achieved, among which is the harmonization of the national models for product liability.

In Italy, a fairly well functioning system of product liability has been constructed on precedents, starting out from the rules contained in the Civil Code. The views of legal scholars, which have played an essential part in this area, have also been fundamental.

The Italian model of product liability was at first constrained within the "narrow limits" of the classic *doctrine of unjustified injury*, which the national courts developed from the 1950s onwards, interpreting art. 2043 of the Civil Code. The general clause on civil liability requires intention or negligent behavior of the wrongdoer as a general condition of liability (both misfeasance and nonfeasance are taken into account).

On these "narrow limits," see the judgment of the *Tribunale di Monza*, July 20th 1993, in *Foro it.*, 1994, I, 253, which is famous for being the first ruling to be based on the Italian implementation act of the product liability Directive.

The application of art. 2043 CC which, according to ordinary principles of interpretation, requires the proof of intention (Italian: *dolo*) or fault (*colpa*) by the tortfeasor, came up against great limitation which had the effect of worsening the plaintiff's legal position. Indeed, the plaintiff had to prove damage, wrongdoing, the causal nexus, and negligence on the part of the manufacturer, which were certainly not easy to prove.

Judgments which have made use of a scheme of liability based on contract have been quite rare; this was used whenever the producer and the seller of the defective product were the same.

Impelled by the need to offer the plaintiff a more effective remedy, some academic commentators, and judges making case law, attempted to reverse the burden of proof which was borne by the plaintiff under art. 2043 CC, finding a sort of presumption of liability against the manufacturer: if a product causes damage, it means the product is dangerous/ defective; if the product is dangerous *per se*, it is not necessary to prove negligence against the manufacturer of the product. Liability is presumed in so far as it is implied by the fact of having produced and distributed a product which may cause damage.

See the famous case of *Saiwa*, decided by the Supreme Court (*Cassazione civile)*, on May 25th 1964, no. 1270. The Italian Supreme Court for the first time confirmed the liability of the manufacturer, basing its reasoning on a process of logical assumptions.

In this way, wide use has been made of art. 2043 CC, to establish precedents, which have in any case removed from the plaintiff the burden of proof of the manufacturer's liability, which is assumed by way of *res ipsa loquitur*, implied by the fact itself of the proven harmfulness of the product.

This forced reading of the Italian Civil Code later impelled lawyers and judges towards the use of a different group of provisions, represented both by those which permitted a sort of strict liability, without the defendant being able to provide any exonerating proof (art. 2049 Civil Code) and others which provided for vicarious liability, with the defendant being able to provide certain exonerating proof (i.e. of "having taken all necessary steps to avoid the harm" within the meaning of art. 2050 Civil Code or of "an Act of God" within the meaning of arts. 2051 & 2052 Civil Code).

Art. 2049 bases the liability rule on a special relationship between the parties: employers are liable for the acts committed by the employees, agents, and servants within the course and scope of employment: *cf.*, among the rare examples of the use of this provision, *Corte d'Appello di Roma*, February 24th 1976, in *Giur. it.*, 1978, 1, 2, 430.

Art. 2050 establishes the rule on liability arising out the exercise of dangerous activities and bases the right to damages on the proof of the harmfulness of that activity carried on by the defendant: see, for example, *Cass. civ.*, January 13th 1982, no. 182, in *Resp. civ. prev.*, 1982, 746; *Cass. civ.*, July 20th 1979, no. 4352, in *Resp. civ. prev.*, 1980, 84; *Cass. civ.*, October 28th 1980, no. 5749, in *Giust. civ., Mass.*, 1980.

Art. 2051 & 2052: respectively liability for injury caused either by things or by animals which the defendant uses or controls; art. 2051 has been used to prove the liability of the distributor: *cf. Tribunale di Monza*, November 10th 1982, in *Resp. civ. prev.*, 1983, 793; *Tribunale di Roma*, July 23rd 1984, in *Foro it.*, 1985, I, 588.

In France, legal scholars and judges have followed a different path. France was the country which had perhaps the most efficient model of product liability in Europe, so far as protecting consumers' interests was concerned, until the approval of the 1985 Directive. Here, product liability was developed through the application of contractual rules on the seller's liability for the defects of the goods sold, under arts. 1641 and 1645 *Code Civil*.

French case law, therefore, used a form of contractual rather than extra-contractual liability in the decade from the 60's to the 70's.

*Cour de Cassation, 1re civ.*, January 19th 1965 (*D.* 1965, *Jur.p.* 389; *RTD civ.* 1965, commentary by Cornu).

Given that there was almost always a contract for the sale of goods in existence, judges had recourse to the rules provided on the subject of contractual non-performance and seller's liability, in cases of damage caused by defective products. The starting point of their assumptions was the prohibition on accumulating contractual and tortious liability, a principle which is in force in the French legal system. The prohibition consists in the fact that extra-contractual liability (French: *responsabilité délictuelle*), may not be invoked by someone who, having a duty based on contract, has a cause of action in contract (*responsabilité contractuelle*).

The legal basis was provided by art. 1641 of the Civil Code, which makes the seller liable for the defects of a product which are unknown to the buyer and which render it unfit for the purpose for which it is sold. In the beginning, French law had adopted a rather complex system, by which the plaintiff made a claim for damages against the defendant-seller, who could then take action against the party causing her/his own damage, such as the supplier, who—in her/his turn—could take action against the manufacturer. The interpretative solution was based on the assumption that the warranty for latent defects is considered as an "accessory," which is transferred with ownership of the goods. So that the consumer may take action directly against the producer of the goods, it has to be shown that none of the intermediaries were aware of the defect in the product. Such solutions involved high costs and lengthy trials which extended over a long period, with many parties being involved in the case. For this reason, the French courts developed rules which favored the plaintiff, who could sue the product manufacturer directly as well, under art. 1641 *Code civil.* In this way, the plaintiff could, in a single action, leapfrog all the links in the chain of supply and sue the manufacturer.

> *Cour de Cassation, 1re.civ.*, January 5th 1972 (*JCP* 1973, II no. 17340, commentary by Malinvaud); *Cour de Cassation, 1re. civ.*, October 9th 1979 (*D.* 1980, *IR* p. 222, commentary by Larroumet).

The inadequacies of the system of the 'chain of actions' on the guarantee were overcome with the introduction of an *action directe*, taken by the last person acquiring the goods against the manufacturer directly, considered as the original seller. This *escamotage* was criticized in academic commentary, which emphasized the fact that the solution arrived at by the Courts involved the fiction that there was a contractual relationship between plaintiff and manufacturer, which in reality was not (always) the case.

French case law has further strengthened the plaintiff's protection, still under arts. 1645 and 1646 Civil Code, by extending the absolute presumption of bad faith on the part of the professional seller to the manufacturer of the defective goods, as well. As a result, the manufacturer cannot show that s/he was unaware of the defect in the product, nor of having had any opportunity to discover the existence of the defect, nor of having exercised due care and attention in the design and manufacture of the product.

> *Cour de Cassation, comm.*, November 15th 1971 (*DP*, 1972, 211).

Another road taken by the French Supreme Court in the 90's was to hold that professional sellers assume a special 'duty of care' (French: *obligation de sécurité*) which is distinct from and goes beyond that regarding latent defects of a product.

> *Cour de Cassation 1re.civ.*, March 20th 1989 (*D.* 1989, p. 381, commentary by Malaurie; *RTD civ.*, 1989, p. 756, commentary by Jourdain); *Cour de Cassation 1re.civ.*, June 11th 1991 (*JCP* 1992, I no. 3572, commentary by Viney; *RTD civ.* 1992, p. 114, commentary by Jourdain; *D.* 1993, *Somm.* p. 241, commentary by Tournafond); *Cour de Cassation 1re.civ.*, January 27th 1993 (*D.* 1994, *Somm.* p. 238, commentary by Tournafond); *Cour de Cassation 1re.civ.*, January 17th 1995 (*D.* 1995, *Jurisp.* p. 350, commentary by Jourdain, 1996 *Somm.* p. 15, commentary by Paisant); *Cour de Cassation 1re.civ.*, March 3rd 1998 (*D.* 1999, *Jurisp.* p. 36, commentary by Pignarre & Brun; *JCP* 1998, p. 1102, commentary by Revel; *RTD civ.* 1998, p. 683, commentary by Jourdain); *Cour de Cassation 1re.civ.*, April 28th 1998 (*JCP* 1998, II no. 10088, Rapport Sargos; *RTD civ.* 1998, p. 684, commentary by Jourdain; *D.* 1998, *IR* p. 142).

This was based on art. L-221-1 *Code de consommation*, which derived from a 1983 act providing that goods and services, under normal use and other circumstances which were reasonably foreseeable by the professional, should demonstrate a level of safety which it is reasonable to expect and which must not depend on the state of health of the individual. The courts apply the rule both to contracting parties and to third parties who are outside the contractual relationship.

The advantages accruing to the consumer from the French legal model for product liability, developed before the Directive's adoption (which occurred late in 1998) are obvious, since both the action on the warranty for defects in goods sold and the special duty of care with which a professional seller is charged, do not involve proving negligence against the latter. In short, it concerns strict liability, achieved through the application of rules provided for the breach of contract, where the plaintiff need not prove fault in the defendant.

By suing under the defects warranty, the plaintiff must prove the following, besides the damage sustained:

– The existence of defects in the product acquired which pre-existed the sale to her/him.

– That such defects were latent, or that s/he was unaware of them when s/he bought the product.

– The causal link (*nexus*) between the defect and the damage sustained.

In an action based on art. L. 221-1 *Code de consommation,* the plaintiff enjoys better protection than strict liability provides, without the manufacturer being able to plead even the exemption regarding development risk (the only exemption from liability allowed by law being *force majeur*).

These features of the French legal system, upon which the whole regime of consumer protection was built, are to be contrasted with one which part of the case law had drawn from arts. 1382 *Code civil* (the general principle of *neminem laedere:* whenever a person causes damage to another there may be liability), 1384(1) *Code civil* (liability for things which the defendant possesses/controls) and 1384(5), *Code civil* (employer's liability). Relying on a general action of extra-contractual (tortious) liability (art. 1382), which requires proof of the defendant's fault/negligence, some judges have tried to construct a strict liability model within the specific area of product liability.

Indeed, in aiming to establish a plaintiff's right to damages for loss sustained, the courts have developed some evaluation criteria regarding the conduct of the manufacturer which may be used as proof of illegality, and have arrived at the point of holding the defendant's negligence as irrelevant, simple proof of the defectiveness of the product being sufficient.

> *Cour de Cassation, 2e civ.*, October 3rd 1979 (*RTD civ.* 1980, p. 358, commentary by Durry); July 20th 1981 *(RTD civ.* 1982, p. 423, commentary by Durry). For example, some French judgments have based product liability on the following hypotheses concerning *a)* the way the product was made; *b)* the information, taken as a whole, supplied regarding the product's use; *c)* the adequacy of warnings about dangers involved in using the product.

In Spain, the 1978 Constitution confers the status of a general principle of law upon consumer protection, through provisions under arts. 51 and 53. These provisions are neither merely a declaration, nor self-executing. Rather, they affirmatively direct public authorities, positive law, and the courts to their implementation. Until the mid-1980's, matters of product liability were addressed within the statutory framework provided by the Spanish Civil Code, and supplemented by judicial interventions. The *Codigo Civil* supplied a number of general rules of contract and tort liability. The contract-based product liability was advanced both under the general law of obligation (through art. 1101 Civil Code) and under the law of sales (through art. 1484 Civil Code). The tort-based product liability was modeled on art. 1902 Civil Code (which is a transplant of the French Civil Code provisions). Spanish courts had developed a practice of inverting the burden of proof, with the result that it was up to the defendant to prove his/her lack of fault. Hence, the presumption was subject to rebuttal.

The regime was altered in 1984, before the adoption of the Directive, with the consumer protection act, the General Law for the Defence of Consumers and Users.[5] Chapter VIII, arts. 25–31 of the act contains a complex set of provisions dealing with liability for harm arising from the consumption or use of goods, products and services.

The act establishes two separate regimes of product liability: the general regime (arts. 26 and 27); the special regime (art. 28). The first one largely codifies existing case law under art. 1902 *Codigo civil*. The second is qualitatively different from any preceding it. This regime is one of strict liability, since it does not provide that a defendant's fault is at all relevant to the plaintiff's case for recovery, either by way of proof or presumption.

In Germany, following the evolution of product liability in America, academics and case precedent brought about the reformation of the institution from the 60's onwards. The legal basis was provided by some sections of the BGB, § 459 and § 635 in particular, concerning contractual liability, and § 823 concerning extra-contractual (tortious) liability.

> The landmark decision to enhance the consumer's protection from defective products under the principles of tort law is the "fowl pest case" (1968) of the Federal Supreme Court: *BGH, Urt. V.* 26 th November 1968, *BGHZ* 51, 91 (102).

Both in the context of contractual remedies and tortious ones, judges have always used criteria favorable to the plaintiff in proving the elements necessary to succeed in a product liability action.

Under § 823 (1) BGB, there may be liability only in certain situations. Indeed, a plaintiff bringing a case under the tort provisions, is required to prove all the facts upon which her/his claim is based (violation of one of the interests or rights enumerated in the provision—life, person, health, freedom, property, and other rights—unlawful and negligent infringements).

Within this realm, the German Federal Supreme Court has introduced the duty of care into German tort law. A duty of care arises from the basic idea that whoever creates a potential danger is required to take the necessary measures to protect the interests and the rights of others who might be injured. The courts have then ruled on the duties of care on a case-by-case basis.

---

[5] *Ley* 26/1984, *de 19 de julio, General para la Defensa de los Consumidores y Usuarios*, in *BOE* no. 175–176, 07/24/1984.

Apart from defining duty of care, the German courts and legal scholars have developed a system which distinguishes between *Hertstellungsfehler* (manufacturing defects), *Konstruktionsfehler* (design defects), and *Instruktionsfehler* (failure to warn and instruct).

In this way, German case-law (as the Italian and French systems have also done in part) has reversed the burden of proof, placing it upon the defendant, with the aim of extending protection to those areas of non-liability, which a literal reading of the provisions of the BGB could leave open, so far as negligent manufacturers are concerned. The case law concerning burden of proof is problematic to study because courts classify their decisions according to defects and duties; moreover, the law on the burden of proof has not always developed uniformly and some issues have not yet found a clear solution.

Basically, the burden is on the plaintiff to show that the product, at time it was put into circulation, did not meet the manufacturer's own standard (the intended design) and that the defect arising therefrom caused injury and damage. The defendant must show the defect is not due to the breach of duty by the manufacturer or any of its employees.

If, on the other hand, there is a contractual relationship between plaintiff and defendant, we are back in the area of contract law, where compensation for damages resulting from a defective product is granted under narrowly defined conditions. The buyer may only claim damages if the seller fraudulently concealed a defect, or if the goods did not conform to a statement regarding its quality (i.e. a breach of an express or implied warranty). German courts have filled some gaps in contract law, developing the previously mentioned concept called *Positive Vertragsverletzung* (now incorporated in the BGB at § 280) and extending contractual protection to relatives and employees of the buyer who foreseeably come in contact with the product.

In the UK, product liability was confined to the area of contract law, where there was a contractual relationship binding the defendant (producer, supplier, seller, etc.) and the plaintiff (the consumer). However, where the contractual link was absent, the doctrine of privity of contract meant that product liability was excluded from the ambit of contract law, and entered into the area of tortious liability, through the notion of duty of care. This duty required proof of the manufacturer's fault in the context of the facts of the particular case and the forseeability of damage, in addition to the application of the criterion of remoteness of damage. These were the means by which dangerous activity was identified by the courts.

We wish to emphasize here that the British courts have also shown a greater consideration for the subjective element of the manufacturer's conduct, in the sense that there must always be negligence on the manufacturer's part in order for her/him to be held liable for the damage.

## 2. The Aims of the Directive on Product Liability

All European countries, therefore, had constructed their own legal model of product liability. From this point of view, Council Directive of July 25th 1985 no. 374,[6] on the approximation of the laws, regulations, and administrative provisions of the Member States concerning liability for defective products did not introduce a totally unknown concept.

The real importance of the Directive lay rather in its objective, that is, the unification of criteria for liability for damage caused by defective products, and to encourage the establishment of a European system of protection in this area which was valid throughout all the Member States.

The difficulty in finding a broad consensus on strict liability imposed on manufacturers, even if it was limited to cases of personal injuries, became clear from the following fact: no Member State ratified the 1977 *Convention of the Council of Europe on Product Liability in regard to Personal Injury and Death.*[7]

The uniformization of rules on product liability answers the same need that we have seen as a feature of all the directives, that is, the assurance of freedom of competition among all the undertakings in the single market. As Dir. 85/374 lays down in its Preamble, diversity of legislation may distort the free play of competition and prejudice the free movement of goods:

> **1st Whereas Dir. 85/374**: "(…) approximation of the laws of the Member States concerning the liability of the producer for damage caused by the defectiveness of his products is necessary because the existing divergences may distort competition and affect the movement of goods within the common market and entail a differing degree of protection of the consumer against damage caused by a defective product to his health or property (…)"
>
> In effect, in so far as the differences in legal solutions adopted by the various Member States has the effect that there are some countries where manufacturers are more exposed to the risk of actions for damages on the part of injured parties, it is inevitable that in such States, manufacturers will have more frequent recourse to product liability insurance, which will have an impact on the cost of the finished product.

---

[6] O.J., L 210, 08/07/1985, p. 29.

[7] Strasbourg, January 27th 1977, available at http://conventions.coe.int/treaty/en/Treaties/html/091.htm.

Indeed, a possible consequence might be that the entrepreneur would choose to export her/his goods only to those countries where there is less risk of having to pay compensation.

On the other hand, the many assertions made in Dir. 85/374 concerning the aims of consumer protection, emphasized rather heavily in the Preamble, seem less convincing:

> "(…) Whereas the protection of the consumer requires that the liability of the producer remains unaffected by acts or omissions of other persons having contributed to cause the damage; (…) Whereas the protection of the consumer requires compensation for death and personal injury as well as compensation for damage to property; (…) Whereas, to achieve effective protection of consumers, no contractual derogation should be permitted as regards the liability of the producer in relation to the injured person (…)"

We need only compare the text of the 1985 Directive with the draft presented to the Council in 1976, to see how far the Directive is from the results which had been anticipated earlier.

The 1976 draft provided that the manufacturer/producer of goods was liable for damage caused by a defect in the goods, regardless of whether s/he was aware of the defect or not. The manufacturer/producer was to be held liable even if, given the prevailing state of scientific knowledge and technique at the time the goods were put into circulation by her/him, they could not be considered as defective (art. 1 of the draft).

Clearly, this product liability model was much closer to a type of strict liability, since the producer was liable, even though s/he was blameless in her/his ignorance of the defect in the product.

In addition, art. 5 of the 1976 draft provided only two exceptions from liability:

- The fact that the producer had not put the product into circulation.
- The fact that the defect was not present at the time the product was put into circulation.

But subsequently the Community legislature thought again, possibly assisted by the business associations of various industrial sectors, or by some academic theorists who were critical of the recourse to a regime of purely strict liability.

## 3. Some Features of the Community Regime

*The ambit of applicability.*
Article 1 of Dir. 85/374 lays down that the producer shall be liable for damage caused by a *defect* in her/his product.

Article 2 defines *product* as all movables, including electricity, even if it forms part of other movable or immovable property, with the exception of game and primary agricultural products (products of the soil, of stock farming and of fisheries) which have not undergone initial processing.

> It should be noted that the first version of the 1976 draft included agricultural products. Subsequently, these were excluded in the definitive version, but the option was left to the Member States to include them in the national implementing legislation. This option was exercised by Greece, Luxembourg, Sweden, and Finland.

*À propos* of primary agricultural products, following the numerous cases of "mad cow disease" during the BSE epidemic,[8] the Community legislature intervened with Directive 99/34/EC of May 10th 1999, which extends the scope of the product liability Directive to include primary agricultural products.[9]

The precise circumstances for the applicability of the Directive, so as to include goods which form an integral part of immovable property as well, has raised many issues, particularly in French academic circles. Here, in fact, frequent precedents were by now familiar, which had extended the application of the rules of tortious liability to cases of damage

---

[8] Some data may give the idea of the magnitude of the problem: by March 2002, BSE cases in the UK cattle population numbered 191,000 and 5.5 million cattle had been slaughtered in an attempt to contain the plague. The infection has spread abroad, across Europe. See BSE statistics at http://www.defra.gov.uk/animalh/bse/index.html.

[9] In O.J., L 141, 1999 p. 20. The Directive has been implemented in almost all the Member States: for example, in France by *Loi* no. 98-388 *du 14 mai 1998 relative à la responsabilité du fait des produits défectueux, JO* no. 48 11/07/2000 p. 1478; in Germany by *Gesetz zur Änderung produkthaftungsrechtlicher Vorschriften, BGBl* Teil I 2000; in Italy by *d.lgs.* no. 25 of February 2nd 2001, in *Gazz. Uff., Serie gen*, no. 49 of February 28th 2001; in the UK, by *The Consumer protection Act 1987 (Product liability)* (Modification) order 2000 (implements the directive in England and Wales) in *SI* no. 2771, coming into force on 12/20/2000 (SG(2001)A/5971 of 05/23/2001); *The Consumer protection Act 1987 (Product liability)* (Modification) (Scotland) Order 2001, in *SI* 2001/265, coming into force on 07/19/2001 (SG(2001)A/7345 of 06/29/2001 and SG(2001)A/10176 of 09/17/2001); *Consumer protection (Product Liability) (Amendment) Act* (Northern Ireland) 2001 (SG(2001)A/10176 of 09/17/2001).

caused by immovable property as a result of building defects, by which compensation could be claimed for any damage arising, including loss of value of the immovable property.

Now, however, since immovable property was no more than the result of an assembly of several movable goods, the Directive in question would very likely be applicable in many cases, which proves to be less advantageous for the plaintiff, in that loss of value of the defective goods is not admissible as a head of damage for the plaintiff, given the limitation imposed by art. 9(b) of Dir. 85/374.

The concepts of *producer* and *defective product* require more detailed examination.

As regards the definition of the economic actors involved, it should be noted that the concept of a "producer" to be derived from art. 3 of Dir. 85/374 is much broader than the literal definition, and includes the following:

- The manufacturer of a finished product.
- The producer of any raw material.
- The manufacturer of a component part.
- As regards farming products produced by cultivation of the soil or animal husbandry, fishing or hunting, respectively the farmer, breeder, fisherman, and hunter.[10]
- Any person who, by putting her/his name, trade mark, or other distinguishing feature on the product presents her/himself as its producer.
- Any person who imports into the Community a product for sale, hire, leasing, or any form of distribution in the course of his business.
- Any supplier of the product, who is, for the purposes of the Directive, treated as the producer unless s/he informs the injured person, within a reasonable time, of the identity of the producer or of the person who supplied her/him with the product.

The coercive and punitive nature of this provision is evident; it seeks to avoid defective products being put into circulation and to penalize those who manufacture or distribute them, or who in some way make a profit out of them.

As far as what constitutes a *defective product* is concerned, art. 6 of Dir. 85/374 is cryptic and quite vague. A product is defined as defective

[10] These categories have been included as a result of the amendments introduced by Directive 99/34/EC.

when it does not provide the safety which a person is entitled to expect, taking all circumstances into account, including:
- The presentation of the product.
- The use to which it could reasonably be expected that the product would be put.
- The time when the product was put into circulation.

Further, the second sub-clause continues, a product shall not be considered defective for the sole reason that a better product is subsequently put into circulation.

We shall be returning to art. 6 later, when considering the reasons for the exclusion of product liability, with which it is strictly linked. For the moment we shall confine ourselves to the observation that this concept of defect places heavy emphasis on the conduct of the producer taken as a whole, which is to be considered as a key element in judging her/his liability. In other words, in order for the producer/defendant to be found liable, it will not be enough for the plaintiff to show inadequacy of the goods for the purpose for which they were intended, but it will be essential for the judge to evaluate the defendant's conduct.

The point is that the Directive tries 'to square the circle': it uses the rhetoric of strict liability and yet in art. 6 (and 7 [e]), it seems to provide solid protection for reasonable businesses, a compromise demanded by the UK government.

*Heads of damage.*

Within the meaning of art. 9 of Dir. 85/374, recoverable damage means:
- Damage caused by death or by personal injuries.
- Damage to, or destruction of, any item of property other than the defective product itself, with a lower threshold of 500 ECU, provided that the item is property.

Furthermore, if the damage is to property, the product must be of a type ordinarily intended for private use or consumption, and was used by the injured person mainly for her/his own private use or consumption.

> A comparison between the Community solution and that of the German legal system, shows that, while § 823 BGB is interpreted to ensure the payment of compensation resulting from the violation of an absolute right of the victim, such as ownership, liberty, life, etc., it excludes the plaintiff being able to claim compensation from the producer for the loss of or damage to the product itself. If anything, such a right is exercisable against the retailer from whom the plaintiff acquired the goods.

This means that this specific legislation does not apply to damage caused by a defective product to another businessman, or to whomever has acquired the product for resale or use in the context of his/her own professional activity. It can therefore only concern a product destined for consumers.

If the damage is by way of personal injury, this limitation does not apply.

The Directive does not address the issue of compensation for pain and suffering and other non-material damages; in this case, Dir. 85/374 is confined to permitting Member States to continue to apply their own rules. In other words, the Directive made no attempt towards harmonizing the rules of damages. The fact is that the rules of damages still vary enormously in different Member States: German producers pay nothing in respect of grief when the product proves fatal, and not much for loss of support, British producers at one time did not have to pay for medical treatment needed by the injured victim, French producers pay even for mere economic loss due to a defect. The problems are still to be solved, although the Court of Justice has delivered its opinion on the point:

> *Cf.* the judgment of *Leitner* of March 12th 2002, C-168/00, *Simone Leitner v. TUI Deutschland GmbH & Co. KG*, 2002, ECR I-2631, at paragraphs 21–24 (on the facts of the case see chapter I, § 10, and in the first volume of this *Guide*, chapter V).

> ***Leitner* ruling:** (§ **21**) "It is not in dispute that, in the field of package holidays, the existence in some Member States but not in others of an obligation to provide compensation for non-material damage would cause significant distortions of competition, given that, as the Commission has pointed out, non-material damage is a frequent occurrence in that field. (§ **22**) Furthermore, the Directive, and in particular Article 5 thereof, is designed to offer protection to consumers and, in connection with tourist holidays, compensation for non-material damage arising from the loss of enjoyment of the holiday is of particular importance to consumers. (§ **23**) It is in light of those considerations that Article 5 of the Directive is to be interpreted. Although the first subparagraph of Article 5(2) merely refers in a general manner to the concept of damage, the fact that the fourth subparagraph of Article 5(2) provides that Member States may, in the matter of damage other than personal injury, allow compensation to be limited under the contract provided that such limitation is not unreasonable, means that the Directive implicitly recognises the existence of a right to compensation for damage other than personal injury, including non-material damage. (§ **24**) The answer to be given to the question

> referred must therefore be that Article 5 of the Directive is to be interpreted as conferring, in principle, on consumers a right to compensation for non-material damage resulting from the non-performance or improper performance of the services constituting a package holiday."

Legal scholars have been critical on the point, emphasizing that there could have been an effort, at least, to try to take steps towards approximation of the national laws, in an area which is in no way secondary in importance to product liability.

*The burden of proof.*
The Directive provides, by art. 1, that the producer shall be liable for damage caused by a defect in her/his product and then, by art. 4, states that the injured person shall be required to prove the damage, the defect and the causal relationship between defect and damage.

The Community model therefore seems to favor a type of strict liability, free of any reference to fault.

The reality is rather different.

If the expression "strict liability" means that a certain person (natural or legal) is to be held liable with no possibility of providing exculpatory evidence, then the liability provided by the Community legislature is not a strict liability model. In fact, art. 7 lists a series of facts which the producer can adduce, in order to escape the obligation to pay damages.

As far as the Community model is concerned, we may rather refer to the reversal of the burden of proof, in the sense that in a case of damage caused by a defective product, the plaintiff must prove the causal link and the defect as well as the damage, and the defendant-producer will be obliged to make restitution, unless s/he is able to adduce some fact which would exonerate her/him.

*Reasons for exclusion of liability.*
As background to the issue, it will be necessary to consider the exclusions which the Directive recognizes in favor of the producer and which are set out in art. 7 (and which the interpreter must evaluate in the light of the Preamble):

> **Art. 7 Dir. 85/374**: "The producer shall not be liable as a result of this Directive if he proves: *(a)* that he did not put the product into circulation; or *(b)* that, having regard to the circumstances, it is probable that the defect which caused the damage did not exist at the time when the product was put into circulation by him or

that this defect came into being afterwards; or *(c)* that the product was neither manufactured by him for sale or any form of distribution for economic purpose nor manufactured or distributed by him in the course of his business; or *(d)* that the defect is due to compliance of the product with mandatory regulations issued by the public authorities; or *(e)* that the state of scientific and technical knowledge at the time when he put the product into circulation was not such as to enable the existence of the defect to be discovered; or *(f)* in the case of a manufacturer of a component, that the defect is attributable to the design of the product in which the component has been fitted or to the instructions given by the manufacturer of the product."

**Preamble Dir. 85/374**: "(…) Whereas the protection of the consumer requires compensation for death and personal injury as well as compensation for damage to property; whereas the latter should nevertheless be limited to goods for private use or consumption and be subject to a deduction of a lower threshold of a fixed amount in order to avoid litigation in an excessive number of cases; whereas this Directive should not prejudice compensation for pain and suffering and other non-material damages payable, where appropriate, under the law applicable to the case; (…) Whereas products age in the course of time, higher safety standards are developed and the state of science and technology progresses; whereas, therefore, it would not be reasonable to make the producer liable for an unlimited period for the defectiveness of his product; whereas, therefore, liability should expire after a reasonable length of time, without prejudice to claims pending at law (…)"

An examination of the exculpatory evidence leads to consideration of the Community model and the consequences in relation to its transplant into the national legal systems, from the viewpoint of the reinforcement or weakening of consumer protection.

Particular attention should be paid to sub-clauses *(b)*, *(d)*, and *(e)*.

As regards art. 7, sub-clause (*c*), the Court of Justice held, in the ruling of May 10th 2001, case C-203/99, *Henning Veedfald v. Århus Amtskommune*, (2001) ECR I-3569, that:

**(§22 and operative part 2)** "… Article 7(c) of the Directive is to be interpreted as meaning that the exemption from liability where an activity has no economic or business purpose does not extend to the case of a defective product which has been manufactured and used in the course of a specific medical service

> which is financed entirely from public funds and for which the patient is not required to pay any consideration."

Sub-clause *(b)* is the basis of exclusion of liability for lack of a causal link between the manufacturer and the defect, since it provides the producer with the opportunity to show that the defect was not present when s/he had put the product into circulation. Sub-clause *(b)* is so drafted that the judge must exclude the producer from liability, even without her/his having provided effective proof of the lack of defect. It will be sufficient to show that in all the circumstances it can be legitimately held that the defect was not in existence at the time the goods were put into circulation. In this way, however, the judge's analysis must shift to the producer's conduct rather than objective criteria, thereby reconfiguring the regime based on liability through negligence.

For this reason, the producer can simply provide proof that none of the other identical products sold had that defect, or that all the required standards of care were being observed at the time of the production of the goods, and so on.

The consequences of this state of affairs are extremely important, for at least two reasons.

In the first place, it is obvious that proceeding in this way reverses the burden of proof, placing it on the plaintiff to prove the contrary, namely that the defect did in fact exist, despite the presumption to the contrary. In such a case, not only is the manufacturer's liability not strict, but the reversal of the burden of proof operates only partially, in that the manufacturer need not supply contrary proof, but only a set of circumstances from which, *juris tantum*, the lack of defect can be presumed. The plaintiff will only succeed if s/he can show that the defect in fact existed: only then will s/he have the right to compensation for the damage sustained.

In the second place, sub-clause *(b)* tends to shift the analysis of the presumption of liability of the producer to the level of her/his conduct, where, in order to escape liability, s/he must demonstrate that s/he exercised all due diligence and took all the required precautions. As we have already remarked, product liability in this way tends to become liability for negligence.

Sub-clause (*d*) of art. 7 Dir. 85/374, seems to lead to the same conclusion. In this case too, the important feature is the evaluation of the defendant's conduct, rather than elements which can be objectively assessed. In fact, so long as the producer manages to show that the product, though defective, is in conformity with the mandatory regulations issued by public authorities, s/he will not be held liable.

However, the exclusion from liability for defective products which has provoked the biggest argument is the one set out at sub-clause (*e*).

This has proved to be one of the most controversial points in the whole Directive, and about which there has been a confrontation between two models, Continental on the one hand and Anglo-American on the other, since the beginning of the development of this Community legislation.

> Moreover under **art. 15 (3) Dir. 85/374,** it is provided that ten years after the date of notification of this Directive, the Commission shall submit to the Council a report on the effect that rulings by the courts as to the application of Article 7 *(e)* and of paragraph 1 *(b)* of this Article have on consumer protection and the functioning of the common market.
>
> In the light of this report the Council, acting on a proposal from the Commission and pursuant to the terms of Article 100 of the Treaty, shall decide whether to repeal Article 7 *(e)*.
>
> A similar revision is in view in relation to another particularly controversial provision, **art. 16 (1) Dir. 85/374**: "any Member State may provide that a producer's total liability for damage resulting from a death or personal injury and caused by identical items with the same defect shall be limited to an amount which may not be less than 70 million ECU."

In effect, sub-clause (*e*), which excludes the liability of the producer when "the state of scientific and technical knowledge at the time when s/he put the product into circulation was not such as to enable the existence of the defect to be discovered," is none other than the application of the *principle*, characteristic of the common law legal tradition, of the *development risk defense*.

French jurists and lawyers, who feared a retrograde step with respect to the strict liability model which had been developed by their system, were strongly opposed to this principle. According to the development risk defense, the producer is not liable for damage caused by a defect in a product if s/he was unable to discover the risks associated with the product, or s/he could not be certain of the safety of the product given the state of knowledge at the time.

*The conclusive definition of defect.*

What emerges from these considerations is the fact that the full definition of *defect* in the common market can be construed from a combination of the provisions of articles 6 and 7 of Dir. 85/374.

A defect consists of the lack of a standard of safety which a consumer could legitimately expect from a producer (*art. 6)*, on the basis of the presentation of the product [*art. 7 (a)*], in relation to its normal use [*art. 7 (b)*] with reference to the time when the product was put into circulation [*art. 7 (c)*], having regard to the state of scientific and technical knowledge at the time when the product was put into circulation [art. 7 (*e*)].

Among other things, contrary to the impression given by a first reading of articles 1 and 4, the Community model seems to tend towards attributing liability for negligence rather than imputing strict liability. It is not by chance that it is precisely the commentators from within the common law tradition who were among the first to assert that the Community model expresses the principle of liability founded on negligence.

In this way, the significance of art. 15 (1) (b) Dir. 85/374 can be better understood, which allows Member States the important option of opting-out (strongly desired by France):

> **Art. 15(1)(b) Dir. 85/374**: "Each Member State may by way of derogation from Article 7 (e), maintain or, subject to the procedure set out in paragraph 2 of this Article, provide in this legislation that the producer shall be liable even if he proves that the state of scientific and technical knowledge at the time when he put the product into circulation was not such as to enable the existence of a defect to be discovered."

It is worthwhile reproducing some parts of the Preamble, where the reasons for the waiver in art. 15 are explained:

> "(...) Whereas, for similar reasons, the possibility offered to a producer to free himself from liability if he proves that the state of scientific and technical knowledge at the time when he put the product into circulation was not such as to enable the existence of a defect to be discovered may be felt in certain Member States to restrict unduly the protection of the consumer; whereas it should therefore be possible for a Member State to maintain in its legislation or to provide by new legislation that this exonerating circumstance is not admitted; whereas, in the case of new legislation, making use of this derogation should, however, be subject to a Community stand-still procedure, in order to raise, if possible, the level of protection in a uniform manner throughout the Community (...)"

The Member States, in implementing the legislation, could therefore provide (or maintain) in their own legal systems, despite the provisions of art. 7 *(e)* of Dir. 85/374, the rule fixing the producer with liability even if s/he is able to prove that the state of scientific or technical knowledge at the time did not enable her/him to discover the existence of the defect.

But the solution provided by the waiver cannot help but raise doubts, when it involves, as has in fact happened, diversification in the national implementing legislation, precisely in regard to one of the most important aspects of the subject, by contributing to a reduction of the harmonizing effect of the Directive.

## 4. Implementation of the Directive in Member States

The product liability Directive is probably the clearest example of the difficulties and limitations of the Community harmonization program. Only rarely has the implementation of a directive brought together, as in this case, so many instances of conflict between the various legal models.

The Community legislature considered that, in order to resolve these conflicts, it was sufficient to introduce the option of waiver for the Member States:

> **Art. 8 (2) Dir. 85/374**: "The liability of the producer may be reduced or disallowed when, having regard to all the circumstances, the damage is caused both by a defect in the product and by the fault of the injured person or any person for whom the injured person is responsible."
>
> **Art. 9 (2) Dir. 85/374**: "This Article shall be without prejudice to national provisions relating to non-material damage."
>
> **Art. 13 Dir. 85/374**: "This Directive shall not affect any rights which an injured person may have according to the rules of the law of contractual or non-contractual liability or a special liability system existing at the moment when this Directive is notified."
>
> **Art. 15 (1) Dir. 85/374**: "Each Member State may: (a) by way of derogation from Article 2, provide in its legislation that within the meaning of Article 1 of this Directive 'product' also means primary agricultural products and game; (b) by way of derogation from Article 7 (e), maintain or, subject to the procedure set out in paragraph 2 of this Article, provide in this legislation that the producer shall be liable even if he proves that the state of scientific and technical knowledge at the time when he put the product into circulation was not such as to enable the existence of a defect to be discovered."
>
> **Art. 16 (1) Dir. 85/374**: "Any Member State may provide that a producer's total liability for damage resulting from a death or

personal injury and caused by identical items with the same defect shall be limited to an amount which may not be less than 70 million ECU."

In other instances, it was thought that a sufficiently broad formulation of some of the harmonization provisions could serve to overcome the difficulties (such as the Preamble to articles 6 and 7).

The reality is that such strategies may work to obtain the consent of the Member States, but they do not function as far as harmonizing the national laws is concerned.

In effect, when we consider the reaction of Member States when obliged to implement the Directive, we can see that each has interpreted it and therefore implemented it according to its own legal tradition. Pre-existing differences have, for the most part, remained unaltered.

It is not by chance that all this has happened precisely in relation to a directive which is so important from the point of view of legal technicality. The harmonization process has encountered remarkable limitation since, despite the fact that the Community legislature wanted to approximate the national legal rules in a highly technical area, the national interpreters of the law were not ready for this.

Hence a whole debate was opened up, which may be summarized as a lack of jurisprudential way of thinking, or a common European school of thought.[11]

The arguments adduced in the ECJ's 2002 rulings[12] seem to be sending a clear message in this direction to national interpreters of the law.

All the Member States have transposed Dir. 85/374, using different implementation techniques: France[13] was the last country to introduce implementing legislation under act no. 98/389 of 1998, which amended the *Code civil* from arts. 1386-1 to 1386-18; Italy transposed the Directive by means of a special act, presidential decree no. 224/1988,[14] avoiding the insertion of the new set of rules into the Civil Code, as had been done on other occasions (e.g. company mergers, single-member compa-

---

[11] See the first volume of this *Guide, A common law for Europe*, chapters II & VI.

[12] See below, § 5, this chapter.

[13] *Loi n.98-389 du 05/19/1998 relative à la responsabilité du fait des produits défectueux*, in *JO* 05/21/1998, no. 117, p. 7744. This delay also involved a ruling by the Court of Justice against France under art. 169 (now art. 226) TEC for failure to fulfil its Treaty obligations under the terms of the directive (ECJ, January 13th 1993, C-293/91, ECR I-1993, p. 1. and the consequent opening, in 1995, of infringement proceedings by the Commission with a view to imposing a fine of four million francs for every day's delay.

[14] *D.p.r.* May 24th 1988, no. 224, in *Gazz. Uff.* 06/23/1988, no. 146.

nies, unfair contract terms); Spain intervened with Act no. 22/1994[15] amending the previous 1984 Act (in fact, it repealed arts. 25–28 for damages caused by defective products); in Germany the *Produkthaftungsgesetz* (Product Liability Act of December 15th 1989) entered into force on January 1st 1990;[16] in the UK, transposition came about in the form of Part I of the Consumer Protection Act 1987.[17]

The implementation of Dir. 85/374 was an improvement in that the area of product liability was better defined, but with some differences: the most important (at least for individual consumers) being that in some States, the plaintiff's position was made worse.

On the basis of the definition of 'defect' under article 6 of Dir. 85/374, some implementing acts formulated a strict liability model, others created a model based on liability founded on negligence.

Hence, the French implementing act affirms that a product is defective when it does not offer the safety which is legitimately to be expected, having regard to the presentation of the product, the use to which it may reasonably be put, and the time it was put into circulation (art. 1386-4 *Code civil*): reference to the manufacturer's conduct and its evaluation is hardly mentioned.

> In the French draft, there was the affirmation that a product is defective when "it does not conform to the terms of the contract or does not possess the characteristic features of a product of that type having regard to the use for which it is intended." This, substantially, would have led the French State to an imprecise implementation of the directive, as if it concerned a latent defect in a category typical of sales warranties and coming within the legal area of contractual liability.
>
> The draft legislation, which respected the French case law model, made no reference to the conduct of the manufacturer. However, the draft was completely disregarded when the act came to be approved in 1998.

The UK implementing legislation, the Consumer Protection Act, passed on May 15th 1987, was intended to establish a regime of strict, rather than fault-based, liability in respect of loss caused by detective products. It focused primarily on the condition of a product rather than the conduct

[15] *Ley* no. 22/94 of 07/06/1994, *de responsabilidad civil por los daños causados por productos defectuosos*, in *BOE* no. 161, 07/07/1994, p. 21737, Marginal 14797.

[16] *Gesetz über die Haftung für fehlerhafte Produkte (Produkthaftungsgesetz – ProdHaftG)* of 12/15/1989, in *BGBl* Teil I, 12/22/1989, Seite 2198.

[17] *The Consumer Protection Act 1987*, in *Statutory Instrument* 1987 no. 1680 (C.51).

of its producer. However, the spirit of the reasonable man has not been fully exorcised and some of the language and concepts of negligence reappear in the new rules. Section 3, containing the central provisions on product liability, supplies the definition of 'defect.' Having offered the first part of the Community concept (a lack of the safety standard which could legitimately be expected), it adds a list of circumstances to determine whether the consumer's expectation is legitimate or not, which end up shifting attention to the manufacturer's conduct.

The act, in fact, refers expressly to the manner in which and purposes for which the product has been marketed, to what might reasonably be expected to be done with or in relation to the product, to the use of warnings or instructions, and the time when the product was supplied by its producer to another.

This criterion for defectiveness, the so called "consumer expectation test," therefore takes account of the subjective aspect of the producer's conduct. In this sense, the legislature has transposed the Directive without deviating from the path made by judicial precedent, thereby ratifying by statute what the national judges have always done.

Since the adoption of the Directive, the plaintiff no longer has to show the existence of the duty of care owed by the manufacturer and its breach, but just the damage suffered, the defect alleged, and the causal link (or nexus) between the defect and the damage for the presumption of fault on the manufacturer's part to arise. However, this concerns a rebuttable presumption (*juris tantum*), in that proof to the contrary is admissible. In other words, under the common law system, a manufacturer who has put goods into circulation which have caused damage may not be held liable, if s/he can show that s/he took all reasonable care in the design and manufacture of the goods.

The German implementing legislation, in determining the concept of 'defect,' has laid emphasis on the "presentation" of the product, on the set of instructions and information given to the consumer and the use to which the consumer may reasonably put the product, also having regard to the time when the product was launched on the market. The German act makes no reference at all to the manufacturer's conduct. The objective standard taken is the relationship between what was promised and asserted by the "presentation" (every activity by which the manufacturer or an authorized third party presents the product to the general public and to the consumer, as far as the qualities presented are directly related to safety expectation, including warnings and instructions) on the one hand, and what has in effect been acquired by the consumer, on the other.

In Italy, the solution reached represents a middle course between the provisions of two previous models, the German model and the common law one. Article 5 (2) of the presidential decree faithfully reproduces art. 6, Dir. 85/374, but it amplifies it with the addition of circumstances such as the "instructions and warnings supplied," which refer to an evaluation of the manufacturer's conduct. However, sub-clause (3) offers an objective type of formula: "a product is defective if it does not offer the standard of safety normally to be expected of other goods of the same type."

In Spain, the definition of defect contained in art. 3 of the 1994 act follows art. 6 Dir. 85/374 at least in part, defining a defective product as one not offering the safety that might legitimately be expected under the circumstances; however, the concept proposed by the Italian legislation is partly followed, to the effect that "in any event, a product is defective if it does not offer the safety normally offered by other examples in the same series." With this more objective test, the Spanish law eases the burden of proof borne by the plaintiff.

A fundamental problem consists in establishing what the relationship is between the law implementing the Directive and the pre-existing national law (contained in codes, special acts, or precedent) in the area of product liability, which may apply when the defendant is also the producer.

The solution to this problem is not as easy as it may seem. Indeed, the Directive itself contains an express provision in art. 13, which would appear to provide an option of waiver in the specific product liability regime, wherever a different regime, which is more favorable to the plaintiff, exists in the national legal system.

> **Art. 13 Dir. 85/374**: "This Directive shall not affect any rights which an injured person may have according to the rules of the law of contractual or non-contractual liability or a special liability system existing at the moment when this Directive is notified."

The fate (and the success) of the Directive hangs on the significance which may be given to this provision; the question is open.

On the one hand, there are those who tend towards broadening, or at least not restricting, the protection of plaintiff's rights, partially compromised by the Community Directive, and support the need to maintain the central position of national laws, which are the result of decades of careful development through case-law and by academics.

On the other, there are those who believe that the Community solution is sufficient to safeguard the consumer and serves to avoid the distortions and forced positions which case-law has too often provoked in the national legal systems.

The positions adopted by interpreters of the law cover an ample range and include various grades of differences.

Those who are most critical of the Community model hold the view that the legislation implementing the Directive should give way, when there are possibilities offered by domestic law which are more favorable to the consumer.

For example, according to this interpretation, there is nothing to prevent French judges from applying, even today, the rules of *obligation de sécurité*, where these are more advantageous to the plaintiff;[18] or else, in Italy, it would be possible to bring a case under art. 2049 Civil Code, which is well-known for being more severe to manufacturers, in that no contrary proof is admissible, and to invoke the five-year limitation period provided for non-contractual actions, rather than the three-year period provided by the Community model.[19] And the same could be said for the Spanish legal system, too.

The point is that by accepting this interpretation, the approximation process of the national laws is thrown into doubt and deep uncertainty results: indeed, the disparity of treatment between entrepreneurs who operate in different States re-emerges, the very thing that the Community legislature wanted to eliminate by issuing Dir. 85/374.

For these reasons there are those who propose considering the relationship between the Community Directive, national implementing legislation and pre-existing domestic law as a relationship between *lex generalis* and *lex specialis*: the Community regime, transposed into domestic law, becomes the *lex generalis* for defective products, and may be disregarded only where there are special provisions which stand apart from it in relation to particular groups of producers, products, or consumers.

Another approach is represented by the view that the various legal regimes, either domestic or those deriving from the Community, may exist side by side, keeping their own special characteristics distinct, without interfering with one another and indeed ensuring that the plaintiff has several possible causes of action (general non-contractual, special non-contractual, and contractual). The plaintiff will be able to choose which action to take, evaluating, on a case by case basis, the appropriate remedy offered by the legal system.

Each theory of interpretation set out here has suitable and acceptable arguments.

Whoever prefers an interpretation of art. 13 which is in tune with Community thinking[20] must bear in mind the aims and objectives of this

---

[18] *Cf.* above § 1.

[19] *Cf.* above § 1.

[20] As after all, the ECJ has done, see below, § 5, this chapter.

as they would in the case of any other Community directive. If Dir. 85/374 has the objective of harmonizing the legal rules, legal results and practice of the Member States in the area of product liability, it seems essential not to permit waiver on the part of Member States.

On the other hand, whoever chooses an interpretation which favors the consumer, excluding the source of the rules at stake, will find in art. 13 Dir. 85/374 a provision which must not penalize the plaintiff: for this reason someone of this view will believe that it is up to the plaintiff, on a case-by-case basis, to select the action which suits her/him best and which is most closely adapted to her/his concrete requirements.

The fact remains that whatever interpretation is chosen in order to resolve the problem, a logical, rational solution, which is in perfect harmony with the aims of the Directive, cannot be achieved so long as art. 13 exists in this form.

Article 13 is not the result of a hasty or uninformed formulation, nor is it because of faulty translation. It was formulated in those terms with full knowledge, because of the circumstances in which the Directive was conceived.

It is another of those numerous cases cited in the first volume of this *Guide, A Common Law for Europe*, where lack of coherence, uncertainty of the result, and the contradictory nature of one individual law with respect to the premises of the whole set of Community laws, is the price that has to be paid for harmonizing the legislation. As long as some Member States do not have the least intention of changing their own practices or legal rules, there is no other option than to abandon the whole uniformization program, or to proceed with intermediate, compromise solutions, or to allow the possibility of waiver and exceptions. The latter solution was the one chosen so far as the harmonization of laws relating to product liability is concerned. However, for many commentators, the insertion of art. 13 contradicts the whole point of the Directive. So long as art. 13 exists, there will always be a danger that the Community measure will either not achieve its fixed objective, or will do so only partially.

## 5. The Cost of Harmonizing National Legal Systems

Product liability legislation, in establishing standard rules concerning the conditions, limitations, and methods of compensation, has undoubtedly brought advantages for consumers. Not, however, for all European consumers.

The concern in the Directive was to fix standard criteria regarding the risks inherent in manufacturing within the single market. The fact is that such criteria, precisely because it was thought desirable to overcome the existing diversity between the various Member States, have given rise to a new product liability model, which we can call a *Community model.* This new model is by its very nature a compromise, in the sense that there had to be a negotiation process between the various solutions, smoothing away excessive differences and permitting the various States to retain the features they were unwilling to give up.

This middle-course solution has shown itself to be less than perfect: indeed, the imaginary line of protection drawn by the new Community model follows a course which is above the protection threshold provided by some European legal systems, but below that provided by others. Hence, in those countries which did not possess a highly-developed system of protection for the injured party, the advantages for the consumer of the new Community model are obvious; however, in those countries which had developed a liability system which paid particular attention to the plaintiff's needs, the model offered by the Directive proved less of a safeguard.

In this connection, it is worthwhile drawing attention to some Court of Justice rulings from 2002, which undoubtedly represent an inconvenient precedent for the individual consumers in the countries concerned (France, Spain, and Greece) and which have been welcomed with something less than enthusiasm by European academics.

The rulings concerned the following:

– The failure by the French Republic to fulfil its obligations under arts. 9, 3 (3), and 7 of Dir. 85/374.[21] Indeed, the act implementing the Directive issued in 1998 had been omitted to provide immunity, had extended the ambit of liability to all professional individuals concerned in the distribution chain even where the manufacturer was known, had limited the sphere of operation of the development risk exemption, and extended product liability to agricultural produce as well, which was not

[21] Case C-52/00, *Commission of the European Communities v French Republic,* (2002), ECR I-3827.

subject to industrial processing, and expressly provided for compensation for pain and suffering and other non-material damages.

– The failure by the Hellenic Republic to fulfil its obligations concerning the threshold of EUR 500 laid down in art. 9(b) of the Directive, because act no. 225/94 had not been correctly transposed (only partially).[22]

– A preliminary ruling under art. 234 TEC by the *Juzgado de Primera Instancia e Instrucción no. 5 de Oviedo* (Spain) on the interpretation of art. 13 of Dir. 85/374.[23] The question was raised in proceedings between *María Victoria González Sánchez* and *Medicina Asturiana SA* for compensation for damage allegedly caused in premises belonging to *Medicina Asturiana* in the course of a blood transfusion. The Spanish judge wished to understand if the 1994 implementing act had reduced the protection previously afforded by the national legislation to the plaintiff injured by a defective product, so reducing constitutional safeguards (arts. 51 & 53 const.) in favor of the consumer as well. Indeed, under the 1984 Spanish act (by arts. 25 *ff.*) the plaintiff had only to prove damage and causation (not the defect as well). A further difference was represented by the plaintiff's option to claim damages against the manufacturer, the importer or the seller, events which the 1994 act changed for the worse, permitting it only in the case of a failure to identify the manufacturer.

The issue underlying the individual cases is the same: can the national law (Codes provisions, statutes and case-law in force before the implementation of the Directive, or the law which transposes the directive in question into national law) go further than European law in protecting the victims of defective products?

The answer from the ECJ is in the negative: the price to be paid for harmonizing European legal systems in this case falls directly upon consumers.

The arguments used by the Court to justify doing away with national laws is as follows: regarding the French and Greek cases, the Court starts with the fact that the Directive dates from 1985 and, according to art. 19 (1), the Member States were to bring into force the laws, regulations, and administrative provisions necessary to comply with the Directive by July 30th 1988 at the latest. Moreover, at that time the Treaty did not

[22] Case C-154/00, *Commission of the European Communities v Hellenic Republic*, (2002), ECR I-3879.

[23] Case C-183/00, *María Victoria González Sánchez v Medicina Asturiana SA*, (2002), ECR I-3901.

contain art. 153 (5) TEC, and therefore both the French act implementing the Directive (no. 98-389 of 1998) and the Greek one (no. 2251 of 1994) could not rely on this provision of the Treaty.

Regarding the Spanish case, the Court starts with the assumption that effective harmonization requires that, so far as product liability is concerned, law predating the Directive which contain provisions in conflict with it—such as in the case of the Spanish 1984 act no. 26—are repealed and replaced by new provisions which faithfully implement its contents; and the Spanish act which does this, transposing the Directive faithfully into the Spanish legal system, is no. 22 of 1994.

In other words, far from affirming that the Directive sets up a model which is "absolutely" inferior with respect to the ones in force in the Member States, the Court confirms the impression that the Directive's draughtsmen have been conditioned more by the needs of the business world than by consumer-plaintiffs' expectations.

The development of the *Community model for product liability* has pursued the goal of eliminating barriers to the free movement of goods and encouraging freedom of competition between the undertakings in the Community. It is this which has brought the Community legislature to insert various limitations on product liability into the Directive, which has in certain cases caused a lowering of the protection threshold with respect to the legal solutions developed in some countries, over the years, through case-law and by academics.

## 6. No Harmonization at all?

Precisely to avoid the Directive becoming the standard model only in those systems with a less comprehensive scheme for consumer protection than the Community one, that is, to avoid the Directive becoming the lowest common denominator for harmonization which must be adopted by all the States, while maintaining more severe and protective regimes, the Court of Justice has expressed itself on the point.

This still concerns the 2002 judgments cited above,[24] in particular points 21–24 in the ruling against France, 17–20 in the one against Greece and 30–34 in the preliminary ruling referred by a Spanish judge. In the words of the ECJ directed at national interpreters of the law:

> **Excerpt from the 2002 rulings**: "Art. 13 of the directive cannot be interpreted as giving the Member States the possibility of

---

[24] Cases cited in previous footnotes.

> maintaining a general system of product liability different form that provided for in the directive;" (...)
>
> "(...) the legislation of a Member State on the victims of damage caused by a defective product under a general system of liability, having the same basis as that put in place by the directive, may be limited or restricted as result of the directive's transposition into domestic law of the State."

An injured person can rely on a special liability system, but only on certain express conditions:

– If this special regime was existing at the time when the Directive was notified.

– If this specific regime is limited to a given sector of production.

In all the other hypotheses, the Directive seeks to achieve, in the matters regulated by it, complete harmonization of the laws, regulations, and administrative provisions of the Member States.

Countries such as France, which possess a national model of product liability founded on the same legal basis as the Directive (an obligation of safety in regard to the product which falls on the producer), cannot maintain, according to the ECJ 2002 rulings cited above, a system of liability which is in competition with the one which transposed the Directive. Hence, the French case law in the 1990's on the *obligation de sécurité* must be abandoned in favor of applying the regime laid down by the Directive and transposed into art. 1386-18 *Code civil*, which rests on the same foundation.

In any case, the rules developed by earlier case law (before the adoption and notification of the Directive) remain available to the consumer, namely those imputing liability to the manufacturer under arts. 1641 and 1645 *Code civil* (warranties for defects in goods sold) or else under arts. 1382 *ff. Code civil* (the *neminem laedere* principle). The point is that the national interpreters of law have felt no need to modify tried and tested rules and solutions, which have been in use over the years and found to work reasonably satisfactorily, being stricter against the producer compared to the Directive's provisions,[25] and this emerges forcefully in academic commentary.

Where the unwillingness of national systems really becomes evident, namely to adopt large-scale harmonization and the introduction of rules

---

[25] This explains why France was the last country of the Fifteen to implement the Community Directive.

which are foreign to their own legal system or practice, is in connection with art. 7 of Dir. 85/374, in the case of exclusion of liability.

Setting great store by article 7 (*e*), which allows Member States to exclude liability where the state of scientific and technical knowledge were not such as to enable the product defect to be known (the so-called *development risk defense*), the British implementing legislation did not confine itself to affirming that the producer is not liable when the defect depends on insufficient technical/scientific knowledge, but also required that the judge take into account the normal practice of other producers of similar goods. This means placing emphasis on the producer's conduct in manufacturing those particular goods, and not on the defect *per se* of the goods in question.

This formulation brought the United Kingdom before the Commission under the art. 169 procedure (now art. 226) TEC, for failure to fulfil Treaty obligations by incorrect implementation of art. 7 (*e*) of the Directive.[26] The Court of Justice held that the Commission's action was unfounded. Contrary to what may appear to be the case, the ruling does not absolve the conduct of the British legislature: rather than a ruling dismissing the action, it seems to be a warning addressed to British judges to interpret the implementing act in a way which corresponds to the spirit and aims of the Directive. Leaving aside an analysis of the contents of the judgment, we shall confine ourselves to highlighting the final part of the ruling, where it states:

> ***Commission v. United Kingdom and Northern Ireland* 1997 ruling:** (**§ 37**) "(…) the Court has consistently held that the scope of national laws, regulations or administrative provisions must be assessed in the light of the interpretation given to them by national courts (see, in particular, Case C-382/92 Commission v United Kingdom [1994] ECR I-2435, paragraph 36). Yet in this case the Commission has not referred in support of its application to any national judicial decision which, in its view, interprets the domestic provision at issue inconsistently with the Directive. (**§ 38**) Lastly, there is nothing in the material produced to the Court to suggest that the courts in the United Kingdom, if called upon to interpret section 4 (1)(e), would not do so in the light of the wording and the purpose of the Directive so as to achieve the result which it has in view and thereby comply with the third paragraph of Article 189 of the Treaty (see, in particular, Case C-91/92 *Fac-*

---

[26] ECJ judgment of May 29th 1997, Case C-300/95, *Commission of the European Communities v. United Kingdom of Great Britain and Northern Ireland*, (1997), ECR I-2649.

> *cini Dori v Recreb* [1994] ECR I-3325, paragraph 26). Moreover, section 1(1) of the Act expressly imposes such an obligation on the national courts. (§ **39**) It follows that the Commission has failed to make out its allegation that, having regard to its general legal context, especially section 1(1) of the Act, section 4(1)(e) clearly conflicts with Article 7(e) of the Directive. As a result, the application must be dismissed."

This was the first ruling of the Court of Justice on the product liability Directive.

The French model, developed through case law and academic commentary, imputed development risk to the manufacturer, until the implementing act was approved on May 19th 1998. The 1993 draft version of this same act, by way of derogation from art. 7 (*e*), excluded the option of the entrepreneur being able to escape liability by showing that the state of scientific and technical knowledge at the time the goods were put into circulation did not enable her/him to discover the defect.

However, the French implementing legislation of 1998, to the great surprise of commentators, gave up this waiver option and reduced the operational extent of the exclusion of development risk by introducing subjective elements (the producer's duty to check the product). Furthermore, contrary to the 1993 draft provisions, precedent and practice, the new act permitted another exception, where the producer provided proof of having manufactured the goods in conformity with mandatory, legal and regulatory provisions.

This formulation (as in the British case) involved France (and Greece) in infringement proceedings brought by the Commission under art. 226 (*ex* art. 169) TEC, for failure to fulfil Treaty obligations by incorrectly implementing art. 15 (1) (*a*)–(*b*) Dir. 85/374.

The Court of Justice held that the French implementing act was in conflict with the Directive in that it limited the exemption from product liability in the case of development risk by introducing a requirement (the duty to check), which had not been laid down by the Directive.[27]

> ***Commission v. France* 2002 ruling:** "(§ **20**) Although Articles 15(1)(a) and (b) and 16 of the Directive permit the Member States to depart from the rules laid down therein, the possibility of derogation applies only in regard to the matters exhaustively specified and it is narrowly defined. Moreover, it is subject *inter alia* to conditions as to assessment with a view to further harmon-

[27] Case cited above.

> isation, to which the penultimate recital in the preamble expressly refers. An illustration of progressive harmonisation of that kind is afforded by Directive 1999/34/EC of the European Parliament and of the Council of 10 May 1999 amending Council Directive 85/374/EEC (…) (§ **47**) In regard to the arguments based on Article 15 of the Directive, it should be noted that whilst that provision enables the Member States to remove the exemption from liability provided for in Article 7(e) thereof, it does not authorise them to alter the conditions under which that exemption is applied. Nor does Article 15 authorise them to cancel or amend the rules governing derogations provided for in Article 7(d). That interpretation is not negated by Directive 92/59, which does not concern the producer's liability for products which he puts into circulation."

The German and Italian systems have remained faithful to the Directive, not because of a more refined sense of being Europeans, but because the Community legislation was already closer to the solutions developed by the national courts on the basis of the provisions in their Civil Codes.

The respective implementing legislation, in relation to art. 7 Dir. 85/374, is in an intermediate position between the French and English models: exemption from liability for development risk is provided for, which is placed on the plaintiff, but there is no reference to a subjective type of assessment of the producer's conduct. Judges are not required to make a comparison between what the manufacturer of defective goods has done and what other manufacturers of similar goods do, or did. The lack of any parameters leads one to believe that liability could be imputed, for the single reason that, from a scientific or technical point of view, it was theoretically possible to avoid the defect.

In conclusion, Dir. 85/374, with its imprecise formulation and the possibilities of creating exemptions to the model on offer, has ended up by leaving the pre-existing situation intact.

Indeed, where interpretation of provisions which had not been clearly formulated was concerned, each country implemented the Directive by interpreting the provision according to their own legal model. In these cases, the Commission invoked the intervention of the Court of Justice, to ascertain if there had been an infringement; however, the Court's rulings have not resolved the uncertainty which has arisen because of the Directive's imprecise formulation.

Furthermore, where the Directive leaves open the possibility of national opt-outs, each country has made room for its own legal model. From this perspective, the Community Directive has not substantially modified the situation. Certainly, it will serve to standardize the practice in those Member States which had not already developed a precise model, be it statutory or through precedent, but it has not been able to ensure an equal level of protection in all the Member States which had models which were tried and tested, but different.

It is interesting to note that the small success enjoyed by Dir. 85/384 with regard to harmonization has partly been compensated for by the fact that many third countries, outside the Community, have spontaneously adopted the Community product liability model, enacting legislation which incorporates its characteristic features. Included among these countries, besides Switzerland and Liechtenstein, who have reason enough to conform to Community rules, given their geographical position, and the CEECs, with whom we will be dealing in the next section, there is also Australia, Brazil, and Japan to confirm the feature which we have highlighted a number of times, namely the Community model's capacity to be successfully transplanted.

In the light of these somewhat disappointing results, the Commission presented, on July 28th 1999, the *Green Paper on liability for defective products,*[28] conceived both to ascertain the state of implementation of the Directive in Member States, and to evaluate the possibility of revising the legal instruments introduced by the Directive itself, bearing in mind the new risks which Community individuals and undertakings may run in coming years. The debate has mainly been in regard to questions of development risk, of the existence of ceilings for the amount of compensation, of the methods for discharging the plaintiff's burden of proof, of the possibility of insuring against risks deriving from defective products, of supplier's liability, and of the limitation periods.

On January 31st 2001, the Commission published its *Report on the application of Dir. 85/374 on liability for defective products.*[29] Given the lack of adequate data on the application of the implemented provision of the Directive, the Commission decided not to propose any amendments to the Directive, although it is planning to gather additional information in the future.

One fact needs to be emphasized in any case: in Italy, for example, since the presidential decree implementing the Directive came into force, there have been few rulings based on the new Community model, compared with many others based on arts. 2043 and 2050 of the Civil Code.

> Clearly, we are referring here only to those judgments concerning events which happened after the Dir. 85/374 came into force. The rulings are as follows:
>
> – *Trib. Monza*, 07/20/1993, *Tentori v. Soc. Rossin (*a case of a

[28] COM (1999) 396 final.

[29] COM (2000) 893 final.

mountain-bike which broke*), in Foro it.*, 1994, I, 251, in *Nuova giur. civ.*, 1994, I, 124; in *Resp. civ. prev.*, 1994, 517, in *Dir. comun. e scambi internaz.*, 1993, 635; in *Contratti*, 1993, 539, in *Corriere giur.*, 1993, 1456;

– *Cass. civ., sez. III*, 09/29/1995, n. 10274, *Braghini v. Comune di S. Bartolomeo al Mare* (a case concerning a swing used by a twelve-year-old*)*, in *Foro it.*, 1996, I, 954, in *Danno e resp.*, 1996, 87;

– *Trib. Milano*, 04/13/1995, *Bassi v. Soc. Poliedro* (a case concerning a bunk-bed*)*, in *Danno e resp.*, 1996, 381, in *Contratti*, 1996, 374;

– *Trib. Monza*, 09/11/1995 (a weaving machine), in *Resp. civ. prev.*, 1996, 371;

– *Giudice di Pace Monza*, 03/20/1997 (a case concerning rice), in *Arch. civ.*, 1997, 876;

– *Trib. Roma*, 03/17/1998, (a case involving a bottle of mineral water) *in Foro it.*, 1998, I, 3660, in *Danno e resp.*, 1998, 1147;

– *Trib. Firenze*, 05/05/2000, n. 903, *Bassi v. Cicli Bimm S.r.l.* (another case of a mountain-bike which broke*)*, in *Arch. Civ.*, 2001, 208.

Perhaps this gives us confirmation of what has been set out above, that the Community model is not always and in every case the most advantageous for the plaintiff. The models and solutions available under some national laws probably offer, after all, a greater range of opportunities to the plaintiff.

## 7. The Transposition of the Directive in the CEECs

All the East European countries transposed Dir. 85/374, which is part of the *acquis communautaire,* and whose standard had to be reached before they joined the Union.[30]

The most widely used technique for harmonization has been transposition by means of *ad hoc* legislation, which has often implemented the product safety Directive too: in the Czech Republic, the Act on liability for damages caused by a defective product;[31] in the Slovak Republic, the Act on Product Liability;[32] in Latvia, the Act on Liability for Defective Goods and Deficient Services;[33] in Lithuania, the Act on the Amend-

[30] See the first volume of the *Guide, A Common Law for Europe,* chapter III.

[31] Act no. 59/1998 *Sb.*, as amended by the Act no. 209/2000 *Sb.*

[32] Act no. 294/1999 *Coll.*.

[33] The Act has been adopted by the *Saeima* on June 20th 2000.

ment of the Law on Consumer Protection;[34] in Hungary, the Act X of 1993 on Product Liability;[35] in Bulgaria, the Consumer Protection and Trade Rules Act;[36] in Romania, the Government Ordinance no. 87 concerning the liability of manufacturers, distributors and sellers for losses created by deficient products;[37] in Slovenia, the Consumer Protection Act;[38] also the Slovenian Law on Obligation, in force since 1978, contains provisions on producer liability for defective products (art. 179).

In Estonia, on the other hand, the subject has been inserted into the new Law of Obligations Act,[39] which has re-codified Estonian civil law and has replaced the 1965 Code previously in force. It contains a Division on liability for defective products (§§1061–1067). In Poland, too, the subject has been inserted in the Civil Code through the Act on certain Consumer Rights and on Product Liability.[40] The Code now contains a new Title VI on liability for dangerous (not defective) products (art. 449).

> Key legislation applying in the area of product safety is as follows: in the Slovak Republic, Act. no. 634/1992 *Coll.*, on Consumer protection (as amended by Act no. 310/1999 *Coll.*). Specifically Section 6a of the Act concerns dangerous imitations and general product safety. The definition of safe product stresses product characteristic of not presenting any health, life, or property risk for consumers. An amendment, no. 310/1999, implemented the Directive on general product safety (92/59/EEC) and the Directive on dangerous imitations (87/357/EEC).

---

[34] The *Seimas* of the Republic of Lithuania adopted this Act on September 19th 2000, No. VIII-1946, to amend the Act on Consumer Protection of November 10th 1994, no. I-657. Thus the new Act on Consumer Protection entered into force on January 1st 2001.

[35] Act 1993/24, 1274 of the Official Gazette.

[36] July 2nd 1999.

[37] It was adopted on August 29th 2000; published in Journal of Laws (*Monitorul Oficial)*, no. 421 of September 1st 2000. This legislative act is meant to round off the existing laws related to product liability, especially government ordinance No. 21/1992 (as published in *Monitorul Oficial* No. 75/1994, as amended in 1998 and 2000).

[38] See arts. 4–11 in Chapter II, titled Producer Liability for Products, Official Gazette of the Republic of Slovenia, no. 20-815/1998 (as amended by act no. 23-1031/1999).

[39] The Act came into force on July 1st 2001; it was amended on June 15th 2002 and came into force on July 1st 2002 (*RT* I 2002, 53, 336). The liability for violation of consumer rights (including damage to life, health and property of good or services) was the subject of a previous statute, the Consumer Protection Act passed on December 15th 1993 (*RT* I 1994, 2, 13), as amended by the Act passed on December 15th 1999 (*RT* I 1999, 102, 907).

[40] This Act was adopted on March 2nd 2000, in the Polish Journal of Laws (*Dz. U.)* 22/2000, item 271, which came into force on July 1st 2000. See also Chapter I, § 11.2.

In Latvia, the *Saeima* on June 20th 2000 adopted the Product and Services Safety Act which transposed Dir. 92/59 and has repealed domestic law in the area of product safety.

In Lithuania, Act No. VIII-1206 of the Republic of Lithuania on Product Safety was adopted on June 1st 1999.

The Estonian Consumer Protection Act passed on December 15th 1993 (*RT* I 1994, 2, 13), as amended by the Act passed on December 15th 1999 (*RT* I 1999, 102, 907) was intended to adopt the Community directives on consumer contracts and the rules contained in 92/59 on safety products.

In Poland, the Act on general product safety was adopted on January 22nd 2000, and came into force on September 8th 2000 (*Dz. U.*, 15/2000, item 179). It transposes Dir. 92/59 and also gives the Council of Ministers the power to issue implementing regulations transposing several further Community acts, such as: safety of toys, dangerous imitations, textile names and safety, for checking for conformity with safety requirements of products imported from third countries, establishing national systems for information about dangerous products, and for monitoring consumer accidents.

Product liability therefore comes under the CEECs' consumer protection policy, whose general principles and aims are the following:

- Protection of life, safety, health, and the economic interests of consumers.
- Protection of consumers against unfair competition.
- Promotion of non-governmental consumer organizations.
- Promotion of better consumer information systems (consumer rights when buying goods and services).

The mandatory nature of the provisions contained in the national laws makes any agreement which restricts or precludes the liability of a producer void.

The acts mentioned above have a common structure and definitions, taken faithfully from Dir. 85/374 and from Dir. 92/59:

- Definition of 'producer' (the same in every country).
- Definition of 'product' (in Estonia, computer software is also deemed to be movable; in the Slovak Republic, gas for consumption is also defined as a product; in Latvia, next to the definition of goods, there is also the definition of services as a product).
- Definition of 'defective product'.
- Circumstances exempting a producer from liability (among which is included development risk).
- Limitation period for and termination of claims.

– In every case, the acts in question do not apply in the case of nuclear accident.

A feature common to all these acts is that they contain a provision for referral to types of protection which pre-dated the transposition of Dir. 85/347 and which consumers can invoke in cases of product liability. In general, these provisions specify that the injured party, according to his/her own choice, may claim damages within the general framework of the Civil Code, applying the ordinary provisions of tort liability for damages.

The Courts were already used in extensive interpretation of the rules of the Civil Codes during the communist era: for example, in Hungary, product liability has been moved into the realm of torts through the use of Civil Code, art. 339, by the Supreme Court:[41] under this article, liability was to be imposed on the basis of fault; however, according to the Court, liability was better based on the "social expectation test." In practice this meant strict liability: it was irrelevant whether the manufacturer had acted properly or had been negligent, or even if the manufacturer had met the standards imposed by a state agency. Also in Poland, product liability has been moved into the realm of torts through the use of Civil Code, art. 415 (liability based on fault principle), by the Supreme Court.[42]

At present, on the basis of the definition of 'defect' in art. 6 of Dir. 85/374 (a product is defective when it does not provide the safety which a person is entitled to expect, taking all circumstances into account), and on the basis of the French, German, and English models, the implementing legislation of the CEECs varies from strict liability models to ones based on the presumption of negligence.

Let us look at the contents of some articles which define 'defect':

> **Estonia, Civil Code (as amended by Law of Obligations Act), §1064**: "(2) A product is defective unless it is safe to an extent which corresponds to a person's legitimate expectations, bearing in mind all the circumstances, and above all: 1. the manner and conditions of presentation of the product to the public; 2. the method of use of the product which the victim can reasonably presume; 3. the time of placing the product on the market. "

---

[41] Case involving a defective television: Hungarian Supreme Court, Economic Affairs Chamber, 31.208/1984.

[42] Cases of 21 November 1980 (OSNCP 1981, text 205); of April 28th 1964 (OSNCP 1965, text 32).

**Poland, Civil Code (as amended by Act on some Consumer Rights and on Product Liability), art. 449 [1] (3):** "A product shall be considered dangerous if it does not offer the standard of safety to be expected of the normal use that the product is to serve. The circumstances of the moment when the product was introduced to the market and, in particular, the presentation of the product including the attached information to consumer, are essential to determine if a product is safe. A product shall not be considered not to offer the standard safety for the sole reason that a more perfect product have been later put into circulation. The law does not make the manufacturer liable for the development risk".

**Latvia, Act on Liability for Defective Goods and Deficient Services: Section 7. "(1)** It shall be considered that goods are defective, if the safety that a person is entitled to expect of the goods has not been guaranteed, taking into account all the circumstances, including:

1. the description of the goods—their structure and packaging;
2. the instructions (directions) for installation or utilisation;
3. the use of the goods under normal or expected circumstances; and
4. the time when the goods were put into circulation.

**(2)** It shall be considered that services are deficient if the safety of such services that a person is entitled to expect has not been guaranteed, taking into account all circumstances, including:

1. the means of providing the services, the structure and composition of the article;

2. the information that has been provided regarding the services; and

3. the time when the services were provided.

**(3)** It shall not be considered that goods are defective or services are deficient for the sole reason that better goods have been put into circulation, or better services have been provided."

**Czech Republic, Act on liability for damages caused by a defective product: art 4.** "**(1)** A product shall be considered defective according to this Act unless its use guarantees qualities that may be legitimately expected for it from the point of view of safety, in particular with regard to: *a)* the presentation of the product including the attached information, or *b)* the presumed purpose to that the product is to serve; or *c)* the moment when the product was introduced to the market. **(2)** A product shall not be considered defective only because a more perfect product was later introduced to the market."

**Slovak Republic, Act on Product Liability, art. 3: "(1)** For the purpose of this Law a product shall be deemed defective provided it does not guarantee safety of use, which can be reasonably expected from it mainly with regard to: (a) presentation of the product and information on the product, which the manufacturer provided or should have provided, (b) the use to which it could reasonably be expected and the purpose that the product would be put; (c) time when the product was put into circulation. **(2)** A product shall not be deemed defective for the sole reason that a better product is subsequently put on the market."

**Slovenia, Consumer Protection Act: art. 6:** "A product shall be considered defective if its safety is not such as may rightly be expected by the consumer. In determining what safety the consumer is entitled to expect, the following shall in particular be taken into consideration:

1. the presentation of the product with regard to its intended use,
2. the predictable use of the product in a reasonable manner,
3. the time when the product was placed on the market.

A product shall not be considered defective solely because a better-quality product subsequently appears on the market."

**Slovenian Law on Obligation 1978, art. 179**: "**(1)** The producer who has manufactured and placed on the market a product which, owing to some defect unknown to him, represents a risk of damage to persons or objects shall be held responsible for the damage caused by the mentioned defect. **(2)** The producer shall be held responsible also for not having taken all the necessary steps such as the use of warnings, safe packaging or some other measure in order to prevent possible damage caused by some hazardous characteristic of a product".

The Lithuanian legislation distinguishes itself from the others just described; in fact, the product liability regime, which comes under the Act on Consumer Protection of 2000, uses different definitions with respect to those set out above, probably because of the fact that, when the Community *acquis* was being implemented, it was decided to put almost all the Community rules (Directives on product safety, on defective products, on sales of consumer goods and associated guarantees) together, and to take into consideration draft proposals of new directives (such as the one on product safety) as well. It follows that a definition of defective product can be construed by means of provisions on 'quality and safety' of goods and services.

**Lithuanian Act of 2000, Art. 6**: "Safety Requirements for Goods" (the act provides similar rules for reference to "Services"): "Goods and services must be safe. The Law on Product Safety[43] and other laws shall establish the requirements of goods and services safety as well as compensation for damage arising from the use of unsafe goods or provided services."

**Lithuanian Act of 2000, Art. 7**: "Quality of Goods" (moreover, the act provides similar rules for reference to "Services"). "**(1)** Goods must be of appropriate quality, i.e., the properties of goods shall not be below the standards specified for this type of goods in the technical regulations (if any) and in the purchase–sales contract. **(2)** The goods shall be presumed to be in conformity with the provisions of the purchase–sales contract, if: 1. the goods meet the requirements of standard acts declared by the producer; 2. the goods are fit for the purposes for which goods of the same type are normally used; 3. the goods meet the quality indicators, which can be expected considering the goods origin and the public statements on quality of goods made by the producer, his representative or the seller. **(3)** In case the non-food products sold to a consumer appear to be of poor quality, the consumer shall be entitled, at his own choice to demand from the seller the following: 1. to replace poor quality goods by their analogue of proper quality; 2. to eliminate free of charge, the defects inherent in the goods or cover all of the expenses incurred by the consumer to remedy such defects; 3. to reduce the price of goods; 4. to terminate the purchase–sale contract and reimbursement of the price paid for such goods, except in instances when the defect inherent the goods is insignificant. An institution authorised by the Government shall set the criteria on the insignificance of inherent defect in goods **(4)** Should a guarantee of quality term be not established for the goods, the consumer may voice his demands regarding the defects inherent in the goods, within two years of acquiring the goods. **(5)** In cases whereby a guarantee of quality term has been established for the goods, demands concerning defects inherent in the defects be determined during the guarantee period. **(6)** Given that the term of quality guarantee of a product is shorter than two years and the defects inherent in the goods are determined following the expiry of the term of guarantee, however, prior to the passage of two years from the day of the acquisition of the goods, the seller shall be responsible for the defects inherent in the goods, if the consumer proves that the defects arose prior to the acquisition of the goods or due to causes which arose prior to the acqui-

---

[43] Act No. VIII-1206 of the Republic of Lithuania on Product Safety was adopted June 1st 1999. On July 5th 2001 a new draft on Product Safety was proposed.

> sition of the goods, for which the seller shall be responsible. **(7)** The consumer must inform the seller about a defect inherent in the goods within two months from the day when he noticed the defect. **(8)** Should the consumer have purchased a food product of poor quality, he shall of his own choice have the right: 1. to demand that the product be replaced by an analogue of good quality; 2. to return the goods to the seller and demand a money refund for the goods. **(9)** The consumer may exercise the rights stipulated in paragraph 8 of this Article prior to expiration of the term of the safe storage life with the exception of the case specified in Article 9. **(10)** If the seller fails to meet the requirements specified in paragraphs 3 and 8 of this Article, the consumer shall be entitled to apply to the Service or Inspection regarding consumers' rights violations or to court on the defence of the rights established in this Article. In any case the consumer shall have the right to apply to court, claiming damages incurred as a result of sales of goods failing to meet the requirements established in paragraph one of this Article. **(11)** The Government or an institution authorised by it, shall approve the regulations governing public dining, retail trade and the return and exchange of goods."

If products sold to consumers do not correspond to standards contained in their documentation, or are not in compliance with the conditions set out in a contract (unless it is proved that the defects appeared through the fault of the consumer), the consumer has the right to the following relief from the seller within the warranty period (in the event that the period is not established, within 6 months[44] and 2 years from January 1st 2004) after purchase:

- Replacement of the product that is of unsatisfactory quality.
- Elimination of the defect in the product, at no extra cost.
- Reduction in the price of the product.
- Termination of the contract and refunding of money, except when defects in the goods are insignificant.

Following the expiry of the guarantee period for storage or sale of a product, the sale of such products in the Republic of Lithuania is prohibited.

---

[44] The Civil Code of the Republic of Lithuania establishes a general warranty term of 6 months during which the buyer can make a claim to the seller concerning the defects in a particular product, provided that the defect was not discussed between the parties before delivery of the product.

To conclude, all the East European countries have adopted the Community legislation; in addition, to monitor the effective application of these rules, these countries have joined a network known as TRAPEX (Transitional Rapid Exchange of information on dangers arising from the use of dangerous products).[45] It is a network of market surveillance authorities of Central and Eastern European and other candidate countries. The aim of the TRAPEX system is to share information with the member countries on food and non-food products, which may endanger health and safety of consumers, and to encourage international cooperation among the members. The Co-ordination Secretariat of the TRAPEX system is located in Hungary, at the General Inspectorate for Consumer Protection.

## 8. The Directives on General Product Safety

Still in the area of product liability, two important directives should be mentioned: the first one, Council Directive 92/59/EEC of June 29th 1992 on general product safety,[46] which regulated the sector over the past ten years; the second one, Council Directive 2001/95/EC of December 3rd 2001, on general product safety, which replaced Dir. 92/59 with effect from January 15th 2004.

From the point of view of substantive content, Dir. 2001/95 hardly changes anything: thus, we can start by illustrating the contents of Dir. 92/59 and its origins, to then describe the aims and novelties of the new directive.

Directive 92/59, which requires undertakings to launch only safe products onto the market, does not contain innovative legal instruments; however, its importance derives from its close association with product liability legislation. Indeed, the rather complex definition of a *safe product*, offered in the 1992 Directive, is inevitably linked with that of a defective product in the 1985 Directive, and most probably will not fail to influence the legal interpreter in the evaluation, taken as a whole, of a

---

[45] See at http://www.trapex.net/. *Cf.* also chapter I, § 11.2.

[46] O.J., L 228, 08/11/1992, p. 24. The Directive has been implemented in all the Member States: in France: *Code de la consommation*, in *JO*, 07/27/1993; *Loi* no. 92-60 du 01/18/1992 *renforçant la protection des consommateurs*, in *JO*, 01/21/1992, p. 968; in Germany: *Gesetz zur Regelung der Sicherheitsanforderungen an Produkte und zum Schutz der CE-Kennzeichnung (Produktsicherheitsgesetz – ProdSG)* vom 04/22/1997, in *Bundesgesetzblatt* Teil I, Nr.27, vom 04/30/1997, Seite 934; in Italy: *d.lgs.* of March 17th 1995, no.114, in *Gazz. Uff., Serie gen*, n. 92, 04/20/1995, p. 5; in the UK:, *The product safety Act 1994*, no. 364, of May 18th, 1994.

product whose "defectiveness" s/he must ascertain. There is a remarkable affinity between the two directives.

It will be sufficient to compare art. 6 of Dir. 85/374 on product liability (*see above*) with art. 2 (2) of Dir. 92/59 on product safety, which states:

> **Art. 2 (2), Dir. 92/59**: "Safe product shall mean any product which, under normal or reasonably foreseeable conditions of use, including duration, does not present any risk or only the minimum risks compatible with the product's use, considered as acceptable and consistent with a high level of protection for the safety and health of persons, taking into account the following points in particular: the characteristics of the product, including its composition, packaging, instructions for assembly and maintenance, the effect on other products, where it is reasonably foreseeable that it will be used with other products, the presentation of the product, the labeling, any instructions for its use and disposal and any other indication or information provided by the producer, the categories of consumers at serious risk when using the product, in particular children. The feasibility of obtaining higher levels of safety or the availability of other products presenting a lesser degree of risk shall not constitute grounds for considering a product to be 'unsafe' or 'dangerous'."

The Directive on product safety, compared to all previous interventions on the subject, operates horizontally.

> It should be pointed out that it does not apply to single products, as does, for example, the Directive on toy safety (88/378 CEE), or the one on the safety of building products (89/106 CEE), but to all products in general.

It has provided the means for Member States to impose *penal* or *administrative sanctions*, according to the case, on a producer who violates the safety obligations and duties established by it. This therefore concerns an operative program, which is completely different with respect to the one in the product liability Directive.

Dir. 92/59 is also important for a new and different method of approach to the problem of protection for the citizen from a product which has been put into circulation, a new method which demonstrates awareness of the inadequacy of the measures in the civil liability system to provide a safety regime.

Indeed, the Community rules provide for the establishment of appropriate *national, public bodies*, with the task of monitoring that the products put onto the market are safe products.

> See Directive 93/68/EEC which amends Council Directive 87/404/EEC (simple pressure vessels), 88/378/EEC (toy safety), 89/106/EEC (building products), 89/336/EEC (electromagnetic compatibility), 89/392/EEC (machinery directive), 89/686/EEC (personal protective equipment), 90/384/EEC (non-automatic weighing instruments), 90/385/EEC (active implantable medical devices), 90/396/EEC (appliances burning gaseous fuels), 91/263/EEC (telecommunication terminal equipment), 92/42/EEC (requirements for new hot-water boilers fired with liquid or gaseous fuels) and 73/23/EEC (electrical equipment designed for use within certain voltage limits).

Moreover the Community rules provide for *product certification*, aimed at attesting the conformity of the product to predetermined safety regulations and standards.

> There are three European standards organizations: the European Committee for Standardization (CEN), the European Committee for Electro technical Standardization (CENELEC), and the European Telecommunications Standards Institute (ETSI). The EC has entered into an agreement by which these bodies are responsible for the creation of the European standards needed by the EC. See http://www.cenorm.be; http://www.cenelec.be;
> http://www.etsi.org

The powers of control provided by art. 6 Dir. 92/59 may be exercised both prior to or subsequent to the goods being put into circulation; moreover, they may operate both to prevent the release of the goods on to the market as well as their withdrawal from sale.

These monitoring powers represent a different conception of a protection system for the private individual: the protective intervention is brought forward to the time the goods are produced (as opposed to the occurrence of the harmful event, which is contemplated by Dir. 85/374).

But there is yet another method for increasing the *level of prevention* of harm to the users of manufactured products, which consists in extending the category of those held liable for the lack of safety of a product. In the same way that the product liability Directive had broadened the concept itself of a producer, to include the importer, the manufacturer of a component or whoever puts her/his own trademark on the goods, so art. 2 Dir. 92/59 specifies that, for its purposes, producers also include importers, manufacturer's agents whose registered offices are outside the

Community, distributors, as well as other professional operators in the distribution chain, in so far as their activity may have an impact on the safety features of the product.

The *general safety requirements* are stated in art. 3 Dir. 92/59: producers shall be obliged to place only safe products on the market; distributors shall be required to act with due care in order to help ensure compliance with the general safety requirement, in particular by not supplying products which they know or should have presumed, on the basis of the information in their possession and as professionals, do not comply with this requirement.

Notice also, finally, that the legislation applies not only to new products, but also to used or second-hand goods too (art. 2 (1) Dir. 92/59).

Following the solutions put forward by the draft Directive of Parliament and the Council on general product safety adopted by the Commission on March 29th 2000, Directive 92/59 has been replaced, with effect from January 15th 2004, by the new Directive 2001/95/EC of the European Parliament and the Council of December 3rd 2001, on general product safety.[47]

Directive 2001/95 was introduced in order to complete, reinforce or clarify some of the provisions of Dir. 92/59 in the light of experience, as well as new and relevant developments on consumer product safety, together with the changes made to the Treaty, especially in articles 152 concerning public health and 153 concerning consumer protection, and in the light of the *precautionary principle* (first recital of the Preamble Dir. 2001/95).

Moreover, it should be noted immediately that, from the point of view of substantive content, the new Directive changes hardly anything. Dir. 2001/95, like its predecessor, imposes the *general obligation* upon economic actors to supply only safe goods, establishing duties to check that Community product safety requirements have been complied with at national and Community level and establishing guidelines for the rapid exchange of information between the Member States and the Community.

Dir. 2001/95 applies to products irrespective of the selling techniques, including distance and electronic selling. It does not cover services, but in order to ensure that the protection objectives in question are achieved, its provisions should also apply to products that are supplied or made available to consumers in the context of the provision of services for their use. The safety of the equipment used by service providers themselves to supply a service to consumers does not come within the scope

---

[47] O.J., L 11, 01/15/2002, p. 4.

of this Directive, since it has to be dealt with in conjunction with the safety of the service provided.

The definition of *product* includes any product (including in the context of providing a service) which is intended for consumers or likely, under reasonably foreseeable conditions, to be used by consumers even if not intended for them, and is supplied or made available, whether for consideration or not, in the course of a commercial activity, and whether new, used, or reconditioned. This definition shall not apply to second-hand products supplied as antiques or as products to be repaired or reconditioned prior to being used, provided that the supplier clearly informs the person to whom s/he supplies the product that such is the case.

*Safe product* shall mean any product which, under normal or reasonably foreseeable conditions of use including duration and, where applicable, putting into service, installation and maintenance requirements, does not present any risk or only the minimum risks compatible with the product's use, considered to be acceptable and consistent with a high level of protection for the safety and health of persons, taking into account the following points in particular:

- The characteristics of the product, including its composition, packaging, instructions for assembly and, where applicable, for installation and maintenance.
- The effect on other products, where it is reasonably foreseeable that it will be used with other products.
- The presentation of the product, the labeling, any warnings and instructions for its use and disposal and any other indication or information regarding the product; (iv) the categories of consumers at risk when using the product, in particular children and the elderly.

*Producer* shall mean:

- The manufacturer of the product, when s/he is established in the Community, and any other person presenting her/ himself as the manufacturer by affixing to the product her/his name, trade mark or other distinctive mark, or the person who reconditions the product.
- The manufacturer's representative, when the manufacturer is not established in the Community or, if there is no representative established in the Community, the importer of the product.
- Other professionals in the supply chain, insofar as their activities may affect the safety properties of a product.

With particular reference to the distributor, the obligation rests with her/him to supply products which satisfy the general requirements of product safety, to constantly monitor the safety of products put on the market, and, where necessary, to supply documentation aimed at identifying the origin of the product; distributor shall mean any professional in the supply chain whose activity does not affect the safety properties of a product. Distributors should help in ensuring compliance with the applicable safety requirements. The obligations placed on distributors apply in proportion to their respective responsibilities. In particular, it may prove impossible, in the context of charitable activities, to provide the competent authorities with information and documentation on possible risks and origin of the product in the case of isolated used objects provided by private individuals.

To ensure the effective control of product safety at national and Community level, Dir. 2001/95 included procedures for activating the Community system of *rapid surveillance of product safety* (RAPEX). This is a European network of the enforcement authorities of the Member States to facilitate, in a coordinated manner with other Community procedures, and improve collaboration at operational level on market surveillance and other enforcement activities, in particular risk assessment, testing of products, exchange of expertise and scientific knowledge, execution of joint surveillance projects and tracing, and withdrawing or recalling dangerous products.[48]

Regarding the *remedies* for the protection of purchasers of the product, Dir. 2001/95 has conferred the option of adopting all necessary measures to avoid unsafe products being put into circulation, expressly providing that the States may also oblige businesses to withdraw unsafe goods which have already been sold, "to order or organise their actual and immediate withdrawal, and alert consumers to the risks it presents (…) to order or coordinate or, if appropriate, to organise together with producers and distributors its recall from consumers and its destruction in suitable conditions."

> **Art. 6, Dir. 2001/95. "(1)** Member States shall ensure that producers and distributors comply with their obligations under this Directive in such a way that products placed on the market are safe. **(2)** Member States shall establish or nominate authorities competent to monitor the compliance of products with the general safety requirements and arrange for such authorities to have and use the necessary powers to take the appropriate measures incumbent upon them under this Directive. **(3)** Member States shall define the tasks, powers, organisation and cooperation arrangements of the competent authorities. They shall keep the Commis-

[48] See above chapter I, § 11.2.; Cf. footnote 45, on the TRAPEX network.

sion informed, and the Commission shall pass on such information to the other Member States."

**Art. 7, Dir. 2001/95:** "Member States shall lay down the rules on penalties applicable to infringements of the national provisions adopted pursuant to this Directive and shall take all measures necessary to ensure that they are implemented. The penalties provided for shall be effective, proportionate and dissuasive. Member States shall notify those provisions to the Commission by 15 January 2004 and shall also notify it, without delay, of any amendment affecting them."

**Art. 8, Dir. 2001/95:** "**(1)** For the purposes of this Directive, and in particular of Article 6 thereof, the competent authorities of the Member States shall be entitled to take, inter alia, the measures in (a) and in (b) to (f) below, where appropriate:

(a) for any product: (i) to organise, even after its being placed on the market as being safe, appropriate checks on its safety properties, on an adequate scale, up to the final stage of use or consumption; (ii) to require all necessary information from the parties concerned; (iii) to take samples of products and subject them to safety checks;

(b) for any product that could pose risks in certain conditions: (i) to require that it be marked with suitable, clearly worded and easily comprehensible warnings, in the official languages of the Member State in which the product is marketed, on the risks it may present; (ii) to make its marketing subject to prior conditions so as to make it safe;

(c) for any product that could pose risks for certain persons: to order that they be given warning of the risk in good time and in an appropriate form, including the publication of special warnings;

(d) for any product that could be dangerous: for the period needed for the various safety evaluations, checks and controls, temporarily to ban its supply, the offer to supply it or its display;

(e) for any dangerous product: to ban its marketing and introduce the accompanying measures required to ensure the ban is complied with;

(f) for any dangerous product already on the market: (i) to order or organise its actual and immediate withdrawal, and alert consumers to the risks it presents; (ii) to order or coordinate or, if appropriate, to organise together with producers and distributors its recall from consumers and its destruction in suitable conditions."

Furthermore, in cases of *serious risk*, States can prohibit the export of an unsafe product; such extreme measures, adopted by the European Commission together with each Member State, must be fully reasoned and will be subject to appeal by the interested parties before competent courts. In exceptional circumstances, States can allow a partial ban or even no ban to be decided upon, particularly when a system of prior consent is established. In addition, the banning of exports should be examined with a view to preventing risks to the health and safety of consumers. Since such a decision is not directly applicable to economic operators, Member States should take all necessary measures for its implementation. Measures adopted under such a procedure are interim measures, save for when they apply to individually identified products or batches of products.

## 9. Draft Directive on the Liability of Service Providers and Directive on Liability for Environmental Damage

Following approval of the product liability Directive, the Commission set itself the task of proceeding with more extensive harmonization of national legislation in the broader area of *civil liability*.

On November 9th 1990, the Commission presented a Proposal for a Council Directive on the liability of providers of services.[49]

The draft was based on a system of liability for those providing professional services, founded on negligence, with reversal of the burden of proof. The service provider is liable for damage sustained through her/his negligence, in the context of the provision of the service, to the health or physical well-being of persons or damage to movable or immovable property, including those which are the subject-matter of the service. The burden of proving lack of negligence falls on the provider of the service.

The idea of intervention by means of *uniform legislation in the service area* as well, originated from the same considerations as those which had determined the adoption of the Directive on product liability. The various solutions adopted in Member States were such as to create obstacles to trade and unequal conditions in the internal services market; further, the same level of protection for injured parties and consumers would not be ensured, against damage and loss to themselves or to their movable and immovable property.

The draft, favorably welcomed by consumers' associations and the Parliamentary Commission for public health and consumer protection,

[49] O.J., C 12/8 01/18/1991.

has however encountered strong opposition, both from the economic and social Committee[50] and, above all, by various professional sectors.

In the context of this debate, on June 24th 1994, the Commission submitted a Communication to the Council, in which it described some new directions in the area of the liability of suppliers of services.[51]

The most interesting point concerned the possibility of choosing one out of the following models:

- Liability founded on negligence, with reversal of the burden of proof, to be borne by the entrepreneur or professional.
- Strict liability in certain cases.
- Liability in negligence, with reversal of the burden of proof, but with the plaintiff/consumer having to prove the defect in the service supplied.

But beyond this new proposal, the Commission decided to withdraw the 1990 draft, in view of the deep divisions which separated the various persuasions, with the announcement that it would be more suitable to reposition the liability of service providers in a broader context than that originally conceived.

In effect, over recent years and especially after Maastricht, consumer protection policy has been developed to such an extent, in defense of consumers and individuals, that to take action only in the narrow field of liability for defective services would risk having a limiting and reducing effect.

It would be better, as the Commission asserts, to review the whole problem in a broader context, which must regard not only the safety of the service offered, but also the role of the consumer in the relationship with the supplier of services or the professional, including the problem of the information which must be given to the consumer (who must specify more precisely the obligations to be assumed by the service provider), and so to identify with greater precision the rights of the contracting party or user.

At the present time, due to all the difficulties encountered, the Commission has not established a working group with a view to a new draft on civil liability of providers of services based on a broader consensus. On December 1st 2003, to give a new impulse to the Proposal for a directive on the liability of service providers, the Council approved Resolu-

---

50 The Report drawn up by the economic and social Committee, which is extremely critical of the draft directive, is dated July 3rd 1991 and is published in O.J., C 269/40, 10/14/1991.

51 The Communication was adopted on June 23rd 1994: COM (1994) 260 final.

tion no. 299/01[52] on "safety of services for consumers," in which, however, emphasis has been placed almost exclusively on the *safety* of the services and the exchange of information between Member States and the Union, leaving the issue of *liability* of the service provider for loss sustained as a result of his/her activity in the shade.

In the context of the supranational rules which may have an impact on national law constituting the civil liability regimes, we should mention the Proposal for a Directive of the European Parliament and of the Council of January 23rd 2002 on environmental liability with regard to the prevention and remedying of environmental damage, which became Directive no. 2004/35 of April 21st 2004.[53]

Besides preventive measures linked to intervention by competent institutions and authorities, needed to address effectively and efficiently site contamination and the loss of bio-diversity in the Community, there are important issues which generally concern the area of civil liability.

The key issue in the present context is not whether liability rules are desirable (many Member States have already enacted them, albeit with different approaches), but whether it is desirable *to enact rules at Community level* rather than leaving the issue entirely to the national level. The fact is that without Community action, there is little guarantee that the *polluter pays principle* will be effectively applied across all the Community.

Without a harmonized framework at Community level, economic actors could exploit differences in Member States' approaches to engage in artificial legal constructions (e.g. spin-off risky operations to legally distinct and undercapitalized companies, move the "front office" within the Community to exploit liability loopholes without changing much in terms of preventive behavior) in the hope of avoiding liability. Such behavior would defeat the ultimate purpose of Member States' liability rules and lead to wasteful allocation of resources.

The impact of the new regime is delineated in the following way:

- To those carrying on activity defined as "occupational activity," including activity (private or public) not carried on for profit (art. 2 Dir. 2004/35).
- To activities classified as involving an actual or potential risk to health or the environment (intended to mean "natural resources": protected species, natural habitats, water, and land), which are iden-

---

[52] O.J., C 299, 12/10/2003, p. 1.

[53] See respectively, for the draft: COM (2002)17 final. O.J., C 151 E , 06/25/2002, p. 132; for Directive: O.J., L 143, 04/30/2004, p. 56.

tified in principle as the dangerous activities listed in Annex III, Dir. 2004/35.
- To activities which involve an immediate threat or damage to one of the "resources" listed in the same annex.

According to the outline of the type of liability provided, in the case of dangerous activity a regime of strict liability is provided (art. 3[a]); where other activity is concerned, which involves an immediate threat or damage to protected species and natural habitats, the operator is liable only for malicious or negligent conduct (art. 3[b]).

The economic impact of the Directive consists primarily in altering the distribution of costs. The main benefit expected from these provisions is improved enforcement of environmental protection standards in line with the polluter pays principle. This should bring an indirect (but not less important) benefit: a move towards more efficient levels of prevention.

The environmental benefits should be achieved cost-effectively and consistently with principles of social and economic efficiency.

Liability requires the parties responsible for damage to remedy it. Damage is defined with reference to existing protection standards built into environmental legislation. Thus liability enforces existing standards and is a powerful deterrent against non-compliance.

# Bibliography Chapter II

## *Selected Books/Commentary/Articles:*


**§ *In English:***

MILLER, C.J., *Product liability*, Oxford, 2004; BUSSANI M., V. PALMER, *Pure Economic Loss in Europe*, Cambridge Univ. Press, 2003; *SHAPO M., The Law of Products Liability*, 2001; VAN GERVEN W., *Tort Law*, Oxford, 2000; VON BAR C., *The Common European Law of Torts*, Oxford, Vol. I (1998), Vol. II (2000); PHILLIPS J.J., *Products Liability—In a Nutshell (Nutshell Series)*, West Wadsworth, 5th edition, 1998; VOS E., *Institutional Frameworks of Community health and safety Regulations*, Oxford, 1998; STAPLETON J., *Product liability*, London, 1994; ATTREE K., *European product liability*, Butterworths, 1992; HOWELLS J., *Comparative product liability*, London, 1990.

**§ *In Italian:***

ALPA–BESSONE, *La responsabilità del produttore*, IV ed., Milano, 1999; MONATERI P.G., *La responsabilità civile*, in SACCO (ed.), *Trattato di Diritto Civile, Torino, 1998, 699; CAFAGGI F., La responsabilità dell'impresa per prodotti difettosi, in LIPARI (ed.), Diritto privato europeo, vol. II, Padova, 1997, 996; ALPA–CARBONE, Atipicità dell'illecito – vol. IV: Lesione del credito – Tutela del consumatore – Responsabilità del professionista – Illecito della P.a.*, 3 ed., Milano, 1995; DRAETTA–VACCÀ (eds.), *Responsabilità del produttore e nuove forme di tutela del consumatore*, Milano, 1993; CARNEVALI U., *La responsabilità del produttore*, Milano, 1979; CASTRONOVO C., *Problema e sistema nel danno da prodotti*, Milano, 1975; ALPA G., *Responsabilità dell'impresa e tutela del consumatore*, Milano, 1975; TRIMARCHI, *Rischio e responsabilità oggettiva*, Milano, 1961.

**§ *In French:***

LEWANDOWSKI H., MAKOWSKI D. (eds.), *Influence du droit communautaire sur le droit interne, Cas De la France e de la Pologne*, Warszawa, 2003; CALAIS–AULOY J., STEINMETZ F., *Droit de la consommation*, 6e éd. Paris, 2003; *Responsabilitè du fait des produits defectueux*, mise à jour: 2 février 2003, http://www.jurisques.com/jfc23.htm; LARROUMET CH., *La transposition française et espagnole de la directive sur la responsabilité du fait des produits défectueux devant la CJCE, D.* 2462 chron., 2002; EWALD F., GOLLIER C., DE SADELEER N., *Le principe de précaution*, coll. Que sais/je PUF, 2001; LAMBERT FAIVRE Y., *Droit du dommage corporel, systèmes d indémnisation*, 4 ed., Dalloz, 2000; TAYLOR S. (préface de G. Viney), *L'harmonisation communautaire de la responsabilité du fait des produits défectueux, étude comparative du droit anglais et du droit français*, LGDJ 1999; MARKOVITS Y. (préface de J. Ghestin), *La directive CEE du 25 juillet 1985 sur la responsabilité du fait des produits défectueux*, LGDJ 1990.

**§ *In German:***

WELSER R., RABL C., *Produkthaftungsgesetz: Kommentar*, 2. Aufl., Wien, 2004; PALANDT, *BGB, (§ 823 Rdz. ProdHaftG, 201 ff.)*, 62. AUFL München, 2003; JANN P., *Die Harmonisierung des nationalen Zivilrechts am Beispiel der Produkthaftung*, Wien, 2002; ALBER S., *Produktverantwortung und Produkthaftung in einer modernen Abfallwirtschaft aus der Sicht der Europäischen Gemeinschaft*, Berlin, 2002; SCHÄFER H.-B., OTT C., *Lehrbuch der ökonomischen Analyse des Zivilrechts*, 3. Aufl., 2000; GRAF V. WESTPHALEN F., *Produkthaftungshandbuch*, Bd. 2, 1999; GRAF V. WESTPHALEN F., LANGHEID T., STREIZ S., *Der Jahr 2000 Fehler*, 1999; ERL M. *Einführung in das Umwelthaftungsrecht*, 1998; *Münchener Kommentar zum BGB,( § 823, ProdHaftG)*, 3.

AUFL vol. 5, 1997; KULLMANN H.-J., *Produkthaftungsgesetz*, 2. Aufl., 1997; DAMM R., in HOFFMANN-RIEM/SCHMIDT-AßMANN (Hrsg.), *Öffentliches Recht und Privatrecht als wechselseitige Auffangordnungen*, 1996; BRÜGGEMEIER G., in MULLER-GRAFF (Hrsg.), *Gemeinsames Privatrecht in der EG*, 1993; ID., *Die Gefährdungshaftung der Produzenten nach der EG-Richtlinie—Ein Fortschritt der Rechtsentwicklung?*, in OTT/SCHÄFER (Hrsg.), *Allokationseffizienz in der Rechtsordnung*, 1989; JOERGES C., *Produktsicherheit und Produkthaftung im Kontext der Europäischen Rechtspolitik. Überlegungen zu G.M.F. Snijders' Monographie, Tijdschrift voor Consumentenrecht* 158, 1988; ID., *The New Approach to Technical Harmonization and the Interests of Consumers: Reflections on the Necessities and Difficulties of a Europeanization of Product Safety Policy*, in R. BIEBER, R. DEHOUSSE, J. PINDER, J. H.H. WEILER (eds.), *1992 One European Market? A Critical Analysis of the Commission's Internal Market Strategy*, Baden–Baden 1988, 157.

**§ *In Spanish:***

RUIZ MUÑOZ, M., *Derecho europeo de responsabilidad civil del fabricante (a propósito de la jurisprudencia del TJCE)*, Tirant lo Blanch, 2004; GUTIÉRREZ SANTIAGO, P., *Responsabilidad civil por productos defectuosos cuestiones prácticas*, Comares, 2004;

***Selected Articles:***

REIMANN M., *Product liability in a Global Context: the Hollow Victory of the European Model*, 11 ERPL 128, 2003; ZEKOLL J., *Liability for Defective Products and Services*, 50 Am. J. of Comp. Law (supplement) 125, 2002; TAYLOR S., *The Harmonisation of European product Liability rules, French and English law*, ICLQ, 419, 1999; TASCHNER H. C., *Harmonization of Product Liability Law in the European Community*, 34 Tex. Int'l L.J. 21, 1999; MAGNUS U., *European perspective of Tort Liability*, 7 Eur. Rev. Priv. Law 427, 1995; JOERGES C., *Product liability and product safety in the European Community*, EUI Working Paper No. 89/404, 1989; CLARK, *The Consumer Protection Act 1987*, Modern Law Review 614, 1987;

VINEY G., *L'apport du droit communautaire au droit français de la responsabilité civile, in Etudes de droit de la consommation, Liber amicorum Jean Calais-Auloy*, Dalloz 2004, 1133; VINEY G., *L interprétation par la CJCE de la directive du 25 juillet sur la responsabilité du fait des produits défectueux*, JCP, I, 177, 2002; HUET J., *La responsabilité professionnelle du fait des choses: la sécurité des produits, Les Petites Affiches*, n. 137, 11/07/2001, 84; TOURNAFOND D., *Remarques critiques sur la directive européenne du 25 mai 1999 relative á certains aspects de la vente et des garanties des biens de consommation*, D., Affaires, 159, 2000; JOURDAIN P., *Commentaire de la loi n 98-389 du 19 mai 1998 sur la responsabilité du fait des produits défectueux*, JCP N Semaine Juridique (édition notariale et immobilière), n. 27, 09/07/1999, 1089; ID., *Aperçu rapide sur la loi n 98-389 du 19 mai 1998 relative à la responsabilité du fait des produits défectueux*, JCP Entreprise et Affaires, n. 22, 1999, 821; LARROUMET M., *La responsabilité du fait des produits deffectueux après la loi du 19 mai 1998*, Dalloz 1998, Chronique, 311; RAYMOND G., *Premières vues sur la lio n 98-389 du 19 mai 1998 relative à la responsabilité du fait des produits défectueux, Contrats-Concurrence-Consommation* 1998, Chronique n. 7, 1998, 7; FOUASSIER E., *Responsabilité civile liée au médicament industriel: la nouvelle donne. Analyse critique de quelques conséquences de la directive "produits défectueux" du 25 juillet 1985 et du décret du 11 février 1998 relatif aux établissements pharmaceutiques*, Revue de Droit sanitaire et social 296, 1998; GHESTIN J., *De la responsabilité du fait des produits défectueux*, Sem. Jur., n. 27, 1998, 120; REMY P., *La responsabilité contractuelle. Histoire d un faux concept*, RTD civ., 1997, 323; MALINVAUD,

*L'application de la directive communautaire sur la responsabilité du fait des produits defecteux et le droit de la construction*, Recueil Dalloz Sirey 85, 1988; GHESTIN, *La directive communautaire du 25 juillet 1985 sur la responsabilité du fait des produits défectueux*, D. 135, 1986;

BUSNELLI F., *Prospettive europee di razionalizzazione del risarcimento del danno non economico*, Danno e resp. 5, 2001; PONZANELLI G., *Responsabilità del produttore, sintesi di informazione*, Riv. dir. civ. II, 913, 2000; PONZANELLI-OWEN, *La responsabilità del produttore negli Stati Uniti d'America*, Danno e resp. 1065, 1999; CARNEVALI U., *Responsabilità del produttore*, Encicl. dir., aggiornamento – II, Milano, 936, 1998; FRANZONI M., *Dieci anni di responsabilità del produttore*, Danno e resp. 823, 1998; PIATTELLI U., *Produttore e responsabilità nell'ambito del diritto comunitario e della sua attuazione in Italia*, Economia e dir. del terziario 259, 1998; STOPPA A., *Responsabilità del produttore*, Digesto civ., Torino, 1998, vol. XVII, 119; SERIO M., *Metodo comparatistico e responsabilità del produttore in diritto comunitario*, Riv. dir. civ. II, 469, 1996;

SOSNITZA O., *Die Folgen der BasisVO Nr. 178/2002 für Verträge, Qualitätssicherung und Produkthaftung*, 31 *ZLR* 123, 2004; HIMMELREICH A, *Produkthaftungsrecht in Litauen*, Phi: Haftpflicht international, *Recht & Versicherung*, 42, 2004; SCHAUB R., *Abschied vom nationalen Produkthaftungsrecht? Anspruch und Wirklichkeit der EG-Produkthaftung: zugleich Besprechung der Urteile des EuGH vom 25.4.2002, Rs. C-52/00, C-154/00 und C-183/00*, 11 *ZeuP* Heft 2, 562, 2003; SPITZER M., *Vollharmonisierung des Produkthaftungsrechts*, 14 Ecolex Heft 2, 141, 2003; TASCHNER H.-C., *Fortentwicklung der Produkthaftung?: "PHi" zum 20. Jahrestag ihres Bestehens*, Phi: Haftpflicht international, *Recht & Versicherung* 6, 2002; MICHALSKI; *Produktbeobachtung und Rückrufpflicht des Produzenten, Betriebsberater (BB)* 961, 1998; WESTPHALEN v., *Neue Aspekte der Produzentenhaftung, Monatsschrift für Deutsches Recht (MDR)* 805, 1998.

**§ *The transposition of Directive no. 85/374 in the CEECs.***

*Legal sources and materials are available in the English language in internet, at:*
*for Czech Republic: http://mujweb.atlas.cz/www/vaske/vyrobek.htm;*
*for Slovak Republic: http://www.economy.gov.sk/angl/legislativa.htm;*
*for Latvia: http://www.ptac.lv/en/acts.htm:*
*for Lithuania: http://www3.lrs.lt/c-bin/eng;*
*for Romania: http://www.hr.ro/rdwp/digest11_2000.pdf;*
*for Slovenia: http://europa.eu.int/comm/internal_market/en/goods/liability/085.pdf;*
*for Estonia http://www.consumer.ee/eng/index.htm.*

# CHAPTER III

## Insurance, Credit, and Financial Industries: Investment, Saving, and Consumer Protection

KEY WORDS: Insurance services – First generation Directives – Second generation Directives – Third generation Directives – Insurance contracts – Harmonization – National laws of contracts – Civil liability deriving from vehicle use – Banking services – Second Banking Directive – Financial services – Indirect protection of investors and savers – Consumer credit contracts – Harmonization – National laws on financial services – CEECs legal systems

### 1. Insurance Services

The insurance industry is among the most dynamic and is about to undergo further important changes. The crisis in the welfare sector and social security, the difficulties in the private and state pension systems, the increasing establishment of a pension culture, and new types of civil liability have brought the demand for insurance to dizzy heights over the last decade.

The movement of capital in the form of the collection of insurance and savings-policy premiums is huge, and the role of insurance companies is often a determining factor in the economy of Member States.

While the European insurance culture cannot as yet compare in scale with the U.S. insurance market, it is nonetheless clear that European citizens are increasingly discovering the benefits to be had from insurance companies, which, in their turn, offer ever more diverse products and services.

The expansion in the insurance sector, which has brought about the participation of an increasingly large number of individuals, could not have failed to arouse the interest of the Community legislature, concerned on the one hand, to make the principle of free movement of services work effectively within the Union in the insurance sector too, and on the other, to protect the rights and interests of those who find themselves signing contracts with insurance companies.

Indeed, in this field too, as is the case in the banking and financial sectors, the intervention by the Community legislature has developed on two different levels, according to the ultimate objective:

- On the one hand, an intervention aimed at harmonizing both the criteria for gaining *access to the insurance business*, and the *con-*

*trol systems over the business itself* and over guarantees for the insurer's solvency (so-called *indirect protection* of the consumer or insured party): for example, Dir. no. 87/343[1] governing suretyship insurance, Dir. no. 91/674[2] governing annual accounts and consolidated accounts of insurance undertakings, Dir. no. 92/49[3] governing non-life insurance, and Dir. no. 92/96[4] on life assurance. These Directives, having introduced major deregulation over the whole sector through the abolition of the State monopoly over the pension system, establish a range of measures concerning the conditions for carrying on an insurance business, in order to protect insured persons in the Community from events which can strike insurance companies.

– On the other, an intervention aimed at harmonizing the national laws governing the various *contracts of insurance*, with the aim of protecting the weaker contracting party (so-called *direct protection* of the consumer).

The most comprehensive intervention by the Community in the insurance sector aimed almost exclusively at the first objective, that is the creation of a Community area without frontiers, a single market where insurance companies could transact their usual business, under conditions both of freedom of establishment and of providing services.

The *principle of freedom to provide services* (arts. 49–55 TEC, *ex* arts. 59–66), when applied to the insurance sector, means that a company established in one Member State may cover a risk in another Member State, which usually coincides with the contracting party's country of residence.

---

[1] Council Directive 87/343/EEC of June 22nd 1987 amending, as regards credit insurance and suretyship insurance, First Directive 73/239/EEC on the co-ordination of laws, regulations, and administrative provisions relating to the taking-up and pursuit of the business of direct insurance other than life assurance, O. J., L 185, 07/04/1987, p. 72. See below § 5.

[2] Council Directive 91/674/EEC of December 19th 1991 on the annual accounts and consolidated accounts of insurance undertakings, O. J., L 374, 12/31/1991, p. 7.

[3] Council Directive 92/49/EEC of June 18th 1992 on the co-ordination of laws, regulations and administrative provisions relating to direct insurance other than life assurance and amending Directives 73/239/EEC and 88/357/EEC (third non-life insurance Directive), O. J., L 228, 08/11/1992, p. 1. See below, § 3.

[4] This directive has been repealed by Directive 2002/83/EC of the European Parliament and of the Council of November 5th 2002 concerning life assurance, O. J., L 345, 12/19/2002, p. 1. See below, § 3.

According to **art. 49 (*ex* art. 59) TEC**: "Within the framework of the provisions set out below, restrictions on freedom to provide services within the Community shall be prohibited in respect of nationals of Member States who are established in a State of the Community other than that of the person for whom the services are intended."

**Art. 51 (2) (*ex* art. 61) TEC**: "The liberalisation of banking and insurance services connected with movements of capital shall be effected in step with the liberalisation of movement of capital".

It should be remembered that in the previous version of amendments made by the Treaty of Amsterdam, former articles 59 and 61 did not yet provide for a prohibition on restrictions, just their gradual elimination.

The freedom of establishment (arts. 43–48 TEC, ex arts. 52–58),[5] as applied to the insurance industry means that an insurance company may exercise its business activity in other Member States as well, through branch offices, subsidiaries, agencies and so on, that is, through permanent, not temporary establishments.

The Community intervention has almost always been made by means of the administrative law of each national system. To ensure that insurance companies were able to operate in any State, it was first of all necessary to standardize the rules permitting access to this activity. The chief obstacle was represented by the protectionist measures in place in each State to protect the domestic market.

The uniformization or harmonization of the national legal rules concerning insurance contracts made with clients, on the other hand, were considered indirectly. The Community legislature only occasionally lays down specific rules to standardize contracts; indeed, true harmonizing, much less uniformizing, Community legislation in this field does not exist.

Therefore, the directives which have followed one another in recent years in the field of insurance have established standard rules concerning conditions of access to the exercise of insurance activity, but have had limited effect on the protection of the insured party, despite having introduced certain rules which have altered contract law in the Member States.

The harmonization technique adopted by Brussels has been to lay down some basic rules to allow insurance companies freedom of movement within the Union and to offer their own insurance products in any

---

[5] On which see below chapter IV.

Member State. Thereafter, the task of harmonizing the *operative rules*[6] in existence in the Member States is left to competition and the market.

In other words, although some principles remain from which there may be no derogation, such as the one establishing the insured's right of cancellation/withdrawal or the one inherent in the information given to the contracting party, the task has been left to competition between the various contractual practices among insurance companies of selecting the most efficient model, reducing regulatory intervention by the Community and/or national systems to a minimum.

### *1.1. The First and Second Generation Directives*

The legal basis of the Community intervention consists of the provisions laid down in Title III of the EC Treaty, which contain the commitment on the part of the signatory States gradually to eliminate restrictions on both the provision of services and the free movement of undertakings.

By as early as 1962, the Commission, taking these Articles of the Treaty of Rome as a starting point, had begun developing a general program to eliminate restrictions on the freedom of establishment in the insurance sector.

Among other things, the program established that the abolition of restrictions on the setting-up of subsidiaries, branch offices, and agencies was subject to an essential pre-condition, namely the *harmonization of conditions of access and the exercise of insurance activity.*

The implementation of the program was begun in the 70's: the first harmonization directives should be considered, which dealt with freedom of establishment and the exercise of reinsurance activity (Dir. 64/225)[7] and the establishment and freedom to provide services for the exercise of the activities of insurance agents and brokers (Dir. 77/92),[8] as well as in the field of Community co-insurance (Dir. 78/473).[9] In the field of

---

[6] On this concept see chapter II, of the first volume of this *Guide, A Commom Law for Europe*, cit.

[7] Council Directive 64/225/EEC of February 25th 1964 on the abolition of restrictions on freedom of establishment and freedom to provide services in respect of reinsurance and retrocession (O.J., L 56, 04/04/1964, p. 878), implemented in all the Member States.

[8] Council Directive 77/92/EEC of December 13th 1976 on measures to facilitate the effective exercise of freedom of establishment and freedom to provide services in respect of the activities of insurance agents and brokers (ex ISIC Group 630) and, in particular, transitional measures in respect of those activities (O.J., L 26, 01/31/1977, p. 14), implemented in all the Member States.

[9] Council Directive 78/473/EEC of May 30th 1978 on the co-ordination of laws, regulations, and administrative provisions relating to Community co-insurance (O.J., L 151, 06/07/1978, p. 25), implemented in all the Member States.

civil liability insurance in respect of motor-vehicle use, two Directives have been adopted: no. 72/166 of April 24$^{th}$ 1972 and no. 84/5 of December 30$^{th}$ 1983.[10]

The Community intervention developed on the basis of the distinction between the two fundamental sectors in insurance: life assurance and non-life (or "damage") insurance.

The First Council Directive 73/239/EEC of July 24$^{th}$ 1973 on the coordination of laws, regulations, and administrative provisions relating to the taking-up and pursuit of the business of direct insurance other than life assurance, and the First Council Directive 79/267/EEC of March 5$^{th}$ 1979 on the coordination of laws, regulations, and administrative provisions relating to the taking-up and pursuit of the business of direct life assurance are the two pieces of Community legislation which implement the first phase of the insurance market, and are known as the *First generation Directives*.[11] The latter has been repealed by Directive 2002/83/EC of the European Parliament and of the Council of November 5$^{th}$ 2002 concerning life assurance.[12]

Both Directives, although they have not failed to have partial effect on contract law, tended to impose standard rules on access to and the exercise of insurance business, both in the formation of branch-offices or agencies in a State which is different from the one where the head office is established. Hence the intention was that the two Directives govern exclusively the freedom of establishment of insurance undertakings within the Community.

On the other hand, the standard rules on freedom to provide services were introduced by the later Community directives.

The fundamental principle of both first-generation Directives (life and non-life) was set out in the respective articles 6 (1), where it is stated that "Each Member State shall make the taking-up of the business of direct insurance in its territory subject to an official authorization."

This meant that any insurance company already involved in the pursuit of insurance business in one Member State and which wanted to exercise its activity in another Member State through agencies or branch offices, had to be in possession of a double authorization: one granted by the country of origin (issued at the start of its activity) and the other by the host country (in order to open agencies or branches).

---

[10] Respectively in O.J., L 103, 05/02/1972, p. 2 and in O.J., L 8 , 01/11/1984, p. 17. As to which, see below, § 6.

[11] Respectively in O.J., L 228, 08/16/1973, p. 3 and in O.J., L 63 del 03/13/1979, p. 1, implemented in all the Member States.

[12] See below, § 3.

The insurance company would have to present requests for authorization to the authorities in the host country, even if it was already in possession of such authority for the exercise of its own business in its own country of origin (where the head office was), specifying the nature of the risks which the undertaking proposed to cover, the general and special policy conditions which it proposed to use, the tariffs which it proposed to apply for each category of business, and whatever else was required under national law.

The control over the conditions and pre-requisites for obtaining the authorization were within the competence of the country of origin (that is, where the head office was), which verified the state of solvency of the business as a whole, including the activity conducted by branch offices and the technical reserves assets:

> Conditions for exercise of business:
> **Art. 14, Dir. 73/239**: "The supervisory authority of the Member State in whose territory the head office of the undertaking is situated must verify the state of solvency of the undertaking with respect to its entire business. The supervisory authorities of the other Member States shall provide the former with all the information necessary to enable such verification to be effected."
>
> **Art. 15 (4), Dir. 73/239**: "The supervisory authority of the Member State in whose territory the head office of an undertaking is situated shall verify that its balance sheet shows in respect of the technical reserves assets equivalent to the underwriting liabilities assumed in all the countries where it undertakes business." (...)
>
> **Art. 16 (1), Dir. 73/239**: "Each Member State shall require every undertaking whose head office is situated in its territory to establish an adequate solvency margin in respect of its entire business. The solvency margin shall correspond to the assets of the undertaking, free of all foreseeable liabilities, less any intangible items." (...)

However, the host State kept control over technical reserves and guarantee funds, collaborating with the State of the head office: "Member States shall collaborate closely with one another in supervising the financial position of authorized undertakings" (Art. 13, Dir. 73/239).

In short, the two Directives were able to accomplish the harmonizing of prerequisites, conditions, and national procedures necessary to obtain authorization for the exercise of business.

As regards the rules of the business of insurance, on the other hand, including in general those relating to insurance contracts, the different national laws provided by each Member State continued to apply.

In addition, the subject of the freedom to provide services had not yet been tackled. The Member States maintained special conditions of access for undertakings coming from other Community countries, thereby restricting the circulation of insurance services within the single market; indeed, it was not possible for an insurance undertaking to extend its own activity to other countries as well without setting up an agency (or branch office).

The Court of Justice has intervened in this area with some rulings which, from one viewpoint, have highlighted the reasons for the difficulties of harmonization in the insurance sector, and, from another, have proposed possible solutions:

> See ECJ Judgment of January 18th 1979, *Ministère public and "Chambre syndicale des agents artistiques et impresarii de Belgique" ASBL v. Willy van Wesemael and others*, Joined cases 110 and 111/78, (1979) ECR 1979, p. 35;
>
> ECJ Judgment of December 17th 1981, *Criminal proceedings against Alfred John Webb*, Case C-279/80, (1981) ECR 1981, p. 3305;
>
> ECJ Judgment of December 4th 1986, *Commission of the European Communities v. French Republic*, Case C-220/83, (1986) ECR 1986, p. 3663;
>
> ECJ Judgment of December 4th 1986, *Commission of the European Communities v. Kingdom of Denmark*, Case C-252/83, (1986) ECR 1986, p. 3713;
>
> ECJ Judgment of December 4th 1986, *Commission of the European Communities v. Ireland,* Case 206/84, (1986) ECR 1986, p. 3817;

The case of *Commission of the European Communities v. Federal Republic of Germany* of December 4th 1986,[13] occurred as a result of the conduct of the Federal Republic of Germany which, on the basis of its own insurance supervision act, subjected all Community insurance companies intending to carry on business in German territory, to the rules of the State of establishment. The Court held that the Federal Republic of Germany had failed to fulfil its obligations under articles 59 and 60 of the EEC Treaty, on the prohibition on the restriction of the free move-

---

[13] ECJ Judgment of December 4th 1986, Case C-205/84, *Commission of the European Communities v. Federal Republic of Germany* (1986), ECR 1986, p. 3755.

ment of services, in that its legislation, which imposed the requirement of establishment in its own territory, represented of itself the negation of the freedom to provide services.

In particular, with this ruling the Court, recognizing that in such a sector the protection of the insured is particularly necessary, observes that it is understandable that certain States have adopted measures submitting foreign companies to rigorous restrictions.

In effect, the insurance sector is particularly sensitive to the issue of consumer protection, if one bears in mind that:

- It is difficult, if not impossible, for the individual contracting party to ascertain the financial position of the insurance company with a view to making a judgment on its solvency.
- Some branches of insurance have become mass phenomena, so that the safeguarding of individuals' rights has become safeguarding the rights of an entire population, both regarding the contracting insured party and the injured third party.
- The individual contracting party is not usually in a position to evaluate the contract terms.

However, the ECJ continues, such restrictions are permissible only on the condition that the laws of the country where the business has its head office (the country where it is registered) are insufficient to reach the minimum standards of protection, and that the conditions imposed by the host State do not go beyond what is strictly necessary. In any case, the fact remains that such restrictions are admissible only and until there is a uniformized Community regime guaranteeing a minimum standard of protection for the insured.

The following passages from the judgment should be noted:

> ***Commission v. Germany* 1986 ruling:** "(**§ 29**) It follows that those requirements may be regarded as compatible with articles 59 and 60 of the EEC Treaty only if it is established that in the field of activity concerned there are imperative reasons relating to the public interest which justify restrictions on the freedom to provide services, that the public interest is not already protected by the rules of the state of establishment and that the same result cannot be obtained by less restrictive rules.
>
> (**§ 30**) Being contradicted by the Commission or the United Kingdom and Netherlands governments, the insurance sector is a particularly sensitive area from the point of view of the protection of the consumer both as a policy-holder and as an insured person. This is so in particular because of the specific nature of the service provided by the insurer, which is linked to future events,

the occurrence of which, or at least the timing of which, is uncertain at the time when the contract is concluded. An insured person who does not obtain payment under a policy following an event giving rise to a claim may find himself in a very precarious position. Similarly, it is as a rule very difficult for a person seeking insurance to judge whether the likely future development of the insurer' s financial position and the terms of the contract, usually imposed by the insurer, offer him sufficient guarantees that he will receive payment under the policy if a claimable event occurs.

(§ **31**) It must also be borne in mind, as the German government has pointed out, that in certain fields insurance has become a mass phenomenon. Contracts are concluded by such enormous numbers of policy-holders that the protection of the interests of insured persons and injured third parties affects virtually the whole population.

(§ **32**) Those special characteristics, which are peculiar to the insurance sector, have led all the Member States to introduce legislation making insurance undertakings subject to mandatory rules both as regards their financial position and the conditions of insurance which they apply, and to permanent supervision to ensure that those rules are complied with.

(§ **33**) It therefore appears that in the field in question there are imperative reasons relating to the public interest which may justify restrictions on the freedom to provide services, provided, however, that the rules of the State of establishment are not adequate in order to achieve the necessary level of protection and that the requirements of the State in which the service is provided do not exceed what is necessary in that respect."

The Commission and the Council, accepting the reasoning of the Court of Justice, drafted and passed two other directives, known indeed as the *Second generation*. Thanks to these, respectively Dir. 88/357[14] concerning non-life assurance and Dir. 90/619[15] concerning life assurance, busi-

---

[14] Second Council Directive 88/357/EEC of June 22nd 1988 on the co-ordination of laws, regulations, and administrative provisions relating to direct insurance other than life assurance and laying down provisions to facilitate the effective exercise of freedom to provide services and amending Directive 73/239/EEC, O.J., L 172, 07/04/1988, p.1. The Directive has been implemented in all the Member States .

[15] Second Council Directive 90/619/EEC of November 8th 1990 on the co-ordination of laws, regulations, and administrative provisions relating to direct life assurance, laying down provisions to facilitate the effective exercise of freedom to provide services and amending Directive 79/267/EEC, O.J., L 330, 11/29/1990, p. 50. The Directive has been implemented in all the Member States.

ness activity related to the provision of services has been partially deregulated.

The latter was first amended by Directive 2002/65/EC of the European Parliament and of the Council of September 23rd 2002 concerning the distance marketing of consumer financial services (and amending Dir. 90/619/EEC, Dir. 97/7/EC and Dir. 98/27/EC);[16] subsequently it was repealed by Directive 2002/83/EC of the European Parliament and of the Council of November 5th 2002 concerning life assurance.[17]

Keeping both opposed necessities in mind, namely control by the State on the security of the insured on the one hand, and the achievement of the single market on the other, Dir. no. 88/357 concerning non-life insurance has inserted at art. 5 a distinction founded upon the nature of the risk, introducing the category of so-called *large risks*, as opposed to so-called *mass risks*.

Usually, these latter are the ones which the insurance company assumes through contracts made with natural persons, or at any rate, of not particularly high value.

The large risks, on the other hand, refer to contracts for air, sea and rail transport (of persons or goods); to credit and suretyship contracts where the contracting party operates industrial, commercial, or professional activity which is of a certain size; to contacts involving civil liability generally, where the contracting party exceeds certain minimum requirements relating to the value of its assets/liabilities, the net value of its turnover, and the number of employees.

On the basis that contracting parties concerning large risks are less in need of protection, the Directive requires host States to relax public control concerning this category of insured risks, on the assumption that, since there is no substantial disparity between insurer and insured, there is not even any need for a strict system of supervision to be added to the control already exercised by the State where the head office is situated.

On the other hand, where greater attention needs to be paid to the protection of the weaker contracting party, such as contracts covering mass risks, the host States retain the option of setting conditions for access and stricter control over business transacted in its own territory by companies with their head office in another Member State.

Regarding life assurance, too, the second generation Dir. no. 90/619 introduced at art. 13 a distinction dictated by the necessity of establish-

---

[16] O.J., L 271, 10/09/2002, p. 16, on which see below, § 10.

[17] O.J., L 345 , 12/19/2002, p. 1, on which see below, § 3.

ing stricter rules in the area of control over the activity of insurance companies.

This distinction is based on the division between:

- Contracts made on the *insured's initiative*, when the contract is signed by both parties in the State where the insurance company has its head office; when the contracting party was not originally contacted by the insurer; the contract was concluded through an insurance mediator.
- Contracts made on the *insurer's initiative*: all other cases.

In the first case, concerning contracts made on the insured's initiative, there is less need for particular safeguarding of the insured, who had freedom of choice in the selection of her/his own insurer. For this reason, further restrictions imposed by Member States on the free exercise of the activity in respect of those already in place in the country of the head office, are not justified.

In the second case, concerning situations which require greater protection for the insured, the Member State where the service is provided may impose their own (and stricter) rules and regimes for the exercise of this activity.

Directive 90/619 has therefore established de-regulation of the market only as regards contracts of the first type, those on the *insured's initiative*, whereas regarding the second type, it provides that the freedom to provide the service may be subjected to specific authorization of the host country, which also maintains control over the activity.

The circumstances just described involve certain consequences of relevance at the level of the gradual harmonization of insurance law.

Both the non-life and the life assurance directives had imparted a so-called "two-speed effect" to the de-regulation of the market: faster in certain sectors (large risks in the non-life sector, contracts at the assured's initiative in the life sector), slower in others (mass risks in the non-life sector, contracts at the initiative of the insurer in the life sector).

In any case, the deregulation of the insurance market was not brought to a conclusion in the 1980's. What was lacking was substantive uniform legislation in the area of protection for the insured/individual contracting-party. As soon as the Community legislature encouraged such standard legislation as would satisfactorily guarantee protection for the insured, the Member States would no longer have any reason to impede the pursuit of insurance business activity in the field of services provided by companies with their head office in another Member State.

## *1.2. Third Generation Directives*

To avoid the inadvisability of "two-speed" harmonization, Community legislation aimed at complete harmonization of the national laws was therefore necessary, not just on the subject of protection of the insurance companies' capital or of solvency guarantees, but also the way business was transacted, and the contents of insurance contracts.

In this way the Community institutions approved a new group of directives, known as the *Third generation Directives*, by means of which the work on the construction of a single insurance market in the Community has taken another step forward.

This concerns Dir. 92/49 for the non-life sector[18] and Dir. 92/96 for the life sector.[19] This latter Directive (as well as the first and second-generation directives of this sector) was repealed by Directive 2002/83/EC of the European Parliament and of the Council of November 5th 2002 concerning life assurance.[20]

By implementing them,[21] the Member States also recognized and applied the principles of the *single passport* and *mutual recognition.*

The principle of the *single passport* (also known as the principle of *home country authorization*) means that any insurance company may pursue its own business, both by way of establishment and provision of services, in any State of the Community, without the need to seek spe-

---

[18] Council Directive 92/49/EEC of June 18th 1992 on the co-ordination of laws, regulations, and administrative provisions relating to direct insurance other than life assurance and amending Directives 73/239/EEC and 88/357/EEC, the third non-life insurance Directive (O.J. L 228, 08/11/1992, p. 1).

[19] Council Directive 92/96/EEC of November 10th 1992 on the co-ordination of laws, regulations, and administrative provisions relating to direct life assurance and amending Directives 79/267/EEC and 90/619/EEC, the third life assurance Directive (O.J., L 360, 12/09/1992, p. 1).

[20] See below in this §.

[21] Council Directive 92/49/EEC and Council Directive 92/96/EEC were implemented in most of the Member States through one single legal act: for example, in France by *Loi* no. 94-5 du 01/04/1994 *modifiant le code des assurances (partie législative), en vue notamment de la transposition des directives n° 92-49 et n° 92-96 du 18/06/1992 et 10/11/1992 du Conseil des Communautées européennes, J.O.*, 01/05/1994, p. 236; in Germany by *Drittes Gesetz zur Durchfürhrung versicherungsrechtlicher Richtlinien (Drittes Durchführungsgesetz – EWG zum VAG)* vom 07/21/1994, *Bundesgesetzblatt* Teil I, Nr. 46, 07/28/1994, Seite 1630; in Italy by *d.lgs.* of 03/17/1995, no. 175, *Gazz. Uff.*, 05/18/1995, no. 114, *Suppl. Ord.*,. n. 56; in Spain by *Ley* no. 30/95 de 11/08/1995, *de Ordenación y Supervisión de los Seguros Privados, BOE* n° 268, 11/09/1995, p. 32480, Marginal 24262; in the UK by *The Insurance Companies Regulations 1994, S.I.* no. 1516 of 1994.

cific authorization from the State where it intends to pursue its activity. Once in possession of the original authorization, granted by the country of origin where the head office is located, it is valid throughout the Community and is sufficient to permit the company to undertake business without further authorization or controls on the part of other authorities.

As a result, an insurance company pursuing its own business in more than one State will be subject only to the control of the country of origin, in accordance with the principle of home country control.

The principle of *mutual recognition* mirrors and results from that of the single passport, according to which no Member State may question the authorization granted to the insurance company by the country where the head office is located; the original authorization, granted according to the criteria and on the basis of legally required preconditions, is sufficient in itself to allow the pursuit of insurance business in any State whatever, without satisfying any further administrative requirements.

The principles of the single passport and mutual recognition therefore represent the degree of harmonization achieved by the Member States' systems in this area. Indeed, it is clear that such principles become effective and applicable only when the national legal systems are no longer characterized by significant differences, or when such differences are considered irrelevant.

Therefore, the two principles are, at the same time, both the essential precondition for there to be a single market equipped with sufficiently uniform rules, and the result of the harmonization of the rules already in existence.

The principles of single passport and mutual recognition are indicators of the state of harmonization in this area of law. The single passport principle is an indispensable factor in the free play of competition between legal models; single passport also means that insurance companies may operate in each country under the various regulatory authorities, each of which are bound by certain regulations deriving from the application of national sources of law.

As a consequence, competition between different regulatory systems may be placed alongside competition between the companies, since no-one can prevent an insurance company which wants to undertake transnational business from establishing itself in a State with more flexible regulations, and operating through subsidiaries in another country.

In this way, thanks to the application of these principles and the adoption of the directives set out above, insurance business is now transacted over a vast commercial area, practically without internal barriers, regulated by both the national control systems and the granting of authorization, which are in the process of uniformization.

However, it was realized towards the end of the 90's that harmonization and/or uniformization of the insurance laws was placed at serious risk by the continuous proliferation of innumerable Community provisions, frequently and often substantially amended. These provisions were located in a number of diverse sources, so that whoever needed to consult them had to refer back to the original act (usually a directive), as well as the amending provisions (other directives).

### *1.3. The Life Assurance Sector*

In the European context of individual citizens, the Commission has placed great importance on the simplification and clear formulation of Community law, so that it is more understandable and accessible to the ordinary person, offering such people the chance to try out the rights which the law confers; it was therefore considered indispensable to organize all the provisions which had undergone frequent modification, with the aim of making Community law clearer and more transparent.

Directive 2002/83/EC of the European Parliament and of the Council of November 5th 2002 concerning life assurance[22] was intended to achieve this objective for the life sector.

This, at least as intended by the Community legislature, represents a coherent set of rules, which is homogenous and systematic; despite this, it may have to undergo adjustment over the course of time to allow for certain technical standards to be adapted to changed market circumstances, as is set out in the Preamble at recital no. 62:

> **Whereas (62nd)**: "Technical adjustments to the detailed rules laid down in this Directive may be necessary from time to time to take account of the future development of the assurance industry. The Commission will make such adjustments as and when necessary, after consulting the Insurance Committee set up by Council Directive 91/675/EEC, in the exercise of the implementing powers conferred on it by the Treaty. These measures being measures of general scope within the meaning of Article 2 of Decision 1999/468/EC, they should be adopted by the use of the regulatory procedure provided for in Article 5 of that Decision."

---

[22] O.J., L 345, 12/19/2002, p. 1. Member States should bring into force the laws, regulations and administrative provisions necessary to comply with this Directive not later than October 9th 2004 (Art. 21, Dir. 2002/83).

Directive 2002/83 is notable for its impressive length: there are 65 recitals, which contain much detail, 74 highly technical articles and 6 annexes.

They represent an ambitious attempt at a "systematic codification" of the life assurance sector and, precisely because of the difficulty inherent in the correct transposition into national legal systems, art. 69 allows the legislators to avail themselves of flexible implementation deadlines.

In summary, the Directive provides that, in the context of the internal market, no Member State may now prevent the simultaneous pursuit of insurance business in its own territory, both in relation to the right of establishment and the freedom to provide services.

The Directive reiterates the fundamental principle of the single passport, the conditions for possible revocation or refusal of authorization, the importance of technical reserves and guarantee funds to protect the market and individual contracting parties/consumers, such as for example, the duty to inform them of rights of withdrawal in their favor.
All this is highlighted, to begin with, in the considerations of the Directive's Preamble:

> **Whereas (for the protection of the internal market, the principle of the single passport):**
>
> "**($5^{th}$)** This Directive therefore represents an important step in the merging of national markets into an integrated market and that stage must be supplemented by other Community instruments with a view to enabling all policy holders to have recourse to any assuror with a head office in the Community who carries on business there, under the right of establishment or the freedom to provide services, while guaranteeing them adequate protection.
>
> **($7^{th}$)** The approach adopted consists in bringing about such harmonisation as is essential, necessary and sufficient to achieve the mutual recognition of authorisations and prudential control systems, thereby making it possible to grant a single authorisation valid throughout the Community and apply the principle of supervision by the home Member State.
>
> **($8^{th}$)** As a result, the taking up and the pursuit of the business of assurance are subject to the grant of a single official authorisation issued by the competent authorities of the Member State in which an assurance undertaking has its head office. Such authorisation enables an undertaking to carry on business throughout the Community, under the right of establishment or the freedom to provide services. The Member State of the branch or of the provision of services may not require assurance undertakings which wish to carry on assurance business there and which have already been authorised in their home Member State to seek fresh authorisation.
>
> **($16^{th}$)** Life assurance is subject to official authorisation and

supervision in each Member State. The conditions for the granting or withdrawal of such authorisation should be defined. Provision must be made for the right to apply to the courts should an authorisation be refused or withdrawn.

**(18th)** The competent authorities of home Member States should be responsible for monitoring the financial health of assurance undertakings, including their state of solvency, the establishment of adequate technical provisions and the covering of those provisions by matching assets.

**(47th)** The Member States must be able to ensure that the assurance products and contract documents used, under the right of establishment or the freedom to provide services, to cover commitments within their territories comply with such specific legal provisions protecting the general good as are applicable. The systems of supervision to be employed must meet the requirements of an internal market but their employment may not constitute a prior condition for carrying on assurance business. From this standpoint, systems for the prior approval of policy conditions do not appear to be justified. It is therefore necessary to provide for other systems better suited to the requirements of an internal market which enable every Member State to guarantee policyholders adequate protection.

**(48th)** It is necessary to make provision for cooperation between the competent authorities of the Member States and between those authorities and the Commission.

**(49th)** Provision should be made for a system of penalties to be imposed when, in the Member State in which the commitment is entered into, an assurance undertaking does not comply with those provisions protecting the general good that are applicable to it.

**(50th)** It is necessary to provide for measures in cases where the financial position of the undertaking becomes such that it is difficult for it to meet its underwriting liabilities. In specific situations where policy holders' rights are threatened, there is a need for the competent authorities to be empowered to intervene at a sufficiently early stage, but in the exercise of those powers, competent authorities should inform the insurance undertakings of the reasons motivating such supervisory action, in accordance with the principles of sound administration and due process. As long as such a situation exists, the competent authorities should be prevented from certifying that the insurance undertaking has a sufficient solvency margin.

**(54th)** Within the framework of the internal market, no Member State may continue to prohibit the simultaneous carrying on of assurance business within its territory under the right of establishment and the freedom to provide services.

**(57th)** The coordinated rules concerning the pursuit of the business of direct insurance within the Community should, in principle, apply to all undertakings operating on the market and, consequently, also to agencies and branches where the head office of the undertaking is situated outside the Community. As regards the methods of supervision this Directive lays down special provisions for such agencies or branches, in view of the fact that the assets of the undertakings to which they belong are situated outside the Community."

**Whereas (for the protection of the contracting-party/consumer/policy holder):**

"**(45th)** For life assurance contracts the policy holder should be given the opportunity of cancelling the contract within a period of between 14 and 30 days.

**(46th)** Within the framework of an internal market it is in the policy holder's interest that they should have access to the widest possible range of assurance products available in the Community so that they can choose that which is best suited to their needs. It is for the Member State of the commitment to ensure that there is nothing to prevent the marketing within its territory of all the assurance products offered for sale in the Community as long as they do not conflict with the legal provisions protecting the general good in force in the Member State of the commitment and in so far as the general good is not safeguarded by the rules of the home Member State, provided that such provisions must be applied without discrimination to all undertakings operating in that Member State and be objectively necessary and in proportion to the objective pursued.

**(52nd)** In an internal market for assurance the consumer will have a wider and more varied choice of contracts. If s/he is to profit fully from this diversity and from increased competition, he/she must be provided with whatever information is necessary to enable him/her to choose the contract best suited to his/her needs. This information requirement is all the more important as the duration of commitments can be very long. The minimum provisions must therefore be coordinated in order for the consumer to receive clear and accurate information on the essential characteristics of the products proposed to him/her as well as the particulars of the bodies to which any complaints of policy holders, assured persons or beneficiaries of contracts may be addressed.

**(53rd)** Publicity for assurance products is an essential means of enabling assurance business to be carried on effectively within the Community. It is necessary to leave open to assurance undertakings the use of all normal means of advertising in the Member State of the branch or of provision of services. Member States may nevertheless require compliance with their national rules on

> the form and content of advertising, whether laid down pursuant to Community legislation on advertising or adopted by Member States for reasons of the general good."

The Member States are authorized to lay down stricter rules than those contained in the Directive:

> "(**28th**) Certain provisions of this Directive define minimum standards. A home Member State may lay down stricter rules for assurance undertakings."

Furthermore, bearing in mind the differing stages of development of their own economies, Member States may opt for the gradual application of this Directive:

> "(**63rd**) Pursuant to Article 15 of the Treaty, account should be taken of the extent of the effort which must be made by certain economies at different stages of development. Therefore, transitional arrangements should be adopted for the gradual application of this Directive by certain Member States."

Finally, the Directive considers it advisable to provide for the conclusion of reciprocal agreements with one or more third countries, in order to permit the relaxation of such special conditions (contained in the Directive), while observing the principle that such agencies and branches should not obtain more favorable treatment than Community undertakings.

> "(**59th**) A provision should be made for a flexible procedure to make it possible to assess reciprocity with third countries on a Community basis. The aim of this procedure is not to close the Community's financial markets but rather, as the Community intends to keep its financial markets open to the rest of the world, to improve the liberalisation of the global financial markets in other third countries. To that end, this Directive provides for procedures for negotiating with third countries. As a last resort, the possibility of taking measures involving the suspension of new applications for authorisation or the restriction of new authorisations should be provided for using the regulatory procedure under Article 5 of Council Decision 1999/468/EC (O.J., L 184, 17.7.1999, p. 23)".

Therefore, as a result of this 'codification' of life assurance law, the identification of the law in force by legal professionals, individual citizens, and insurance companies has been made easier.

Among other things, Appendix VI of Dir. 2002/83 contains a *correlation table* for comparison of various Community legal acts which have followed one another over time, demonstrating how the Directives have been recast in the interests of clarity, which former articles of previous directives have been repealed or maintained in the new body of law and which articles have been introduced *ex novo*.

In particular, Article 72 establishes which directives have been repealed, and their correlation with the present Directive, referring to the list contained in Annex V, Part A. The repealed directives are as follows: Dir. 79/267/EEC, Dir. 90/619/EEC, Dir. 92/96/EEC, Dir. 95/26/EEC (only art. 1, second indent, art. 2(2), fourth indent, and art. 3(1) as regards the references made to Dir. 79/267/EEC), Dir. 2002/12/EC, Second Dir. 90/619/EEC, Third Dir. 92/96/EEC, Dir. 95/26/EEC (only art. 1, second indent, art. 2(1), third indent, art. 4(1), (3), (5) and art. 5, third indent, as regards the references made to Dir. 92/96/EEC), Dir. 2000/64/EC (art. 2, as regards the references made to Dir. 92/96/EEC), Dir. 2002/12/EC (art. 2).

### *1.4. The Latest Developments*

The legal framework set up at Community level is anything but certain and definitive. Dir. 2002/83 has not yet been transposed into the various Member States, but has already been modified by Directive 2004/66/EC.[23] It adapted the legislation in force relating to free movement of goods, company law, agriculture, taxation, education and training, culture, and the audiovisual field and external relations in order to facilitate transposal by the new Member States, following last enlargement of May 2004.

Moreover, the European Union is recasting the special rules relating to freedom to provide cross-frontier services in the life assurance field with a view to simplifying existing legislation. Thus, there is a Proposal for a Directive on reinsurance and amending Council Directives 73/239 (First Council Directive on taking-up and pursuit of the business), 92/49 (Third Council Directive amending the First and the Second Council Directives to facilitate the exercise of freedom to provide services), 98/78 and 2002/83.[24]

---

[23] O.J., L 168 of 05/01/2004.
[24] SEC (2004) 443.

The Commission plans to create a genuine Community market in reinsurance. To that end, it proposes that re-insurers carry out their activities under the supervision of competent authorities in their home country, subject to which they will be allowed to operate throughout the European Union. Supervision will be exercised in line with provisions which all the Member States will be required to apply. The Commission's aim is thus to reinforce international financial stability, an issue of concern to all major international bodies, and to fill a gap in Community legislation, which does not regulate specialized re-insurers, even though reinsurance activities carried out by direct insurers are subject to regulation. The Commission proposes a regulatory framework based on the existing regime introduced by the Third Insurance Directives, with a view to extending to reinsurance companies the system for the authorization and financial supervision of an insurance undertaking by the Member State in which it has its head office (*home-country control*). The proposal also sets out prudential rules on the establishment of technical provisions (i.e. the amount that a reinsurance undertaking must set aside in order to enable it to meet its contractual commitments) and rules on the investment of assets covering those technical provisions. It also lays down rules on required solvency margins and minimum capital requirements as well as rules on measures to be taken by regulators if reinsurance undertakings are in financial difficulties. Lastly, the proposal also amends Directives 73/239, 92/49, 98/78, and 2002/83 in order to guarantee the consistency of the Community provisions on insurance.

In addition, Community insurance law has been made more complex and less transparent because continual interventions are laid one upon the other, straddling the insurance and financial services markets. In this connection, for example, consider the Proposal for a Directive of the European Parliament and of the Council, amending some old non-life insurance directives (Dir. 73/239 on taking-up and pursuit of the business) and more recent life assurance directives (Dir. 2002/83 recasting the entire sector of life assurance), some financial services directives (Dir. 85/611, 91/675, 93/6, and 94/19) and directives on banking sector (Dir. 2001/12, no longer in force, because it was repealed by Dir. 2002/83, and Dir. 2002/87 on supplementary supervision of credit institutions, insurance undertakings, and investment firms in a financial conglomerate), in order to establish a new financial services committee organizational structure.[25]

---

[25] COM (2003) 659 final, O.J., C 96 of 04/21/2004. On banking and financial sector directives see the following §§.

The aim of the proposal is to establish a modern, rational committee structure in the financial services sector which will improve regulatory and prudential cooperation and, thus, enable the EU to be more responsive to developments than it is at present. The package of measures should allow cooperation among supervisory authorities, thereby strengthening European financial stability. In the opinion of the Community institutions, it is vital to introduce a new approach to committee procedures at the same time as the two essential legislative acts are being drawn up, i.e. the proposals for capital adequacy directives CAD III and Solvency II establishing a new capital adequacy framework in the banking and insurance sector.

## 2. Indirect Protection of the Interests of Clients

The harmonization of national laws of contracts has however been of less consequence than one might have expected, as a result of the third and latest generation of directives.

The fact is that the Community legislature has had to adopt a different and partly original harmonization technique, given the special difficulties and deep perplexity of European professionals (a technique also used, as we shall be seeing later, in the banking sector).

Indeed it concerned the establishment of a set of minimum, essential standard rules regarding certain aspects of the contract.

It was subsequently left to the market, namely to the effect of supply and demand, and competition, to bring about the harmonization of all the other issues which were not the object of direct regulation. The technique seemed to recommend itself, taking into consideration the fact that insurance companies operate in a competitive, free market.

The reality, however, is more complex: the insurance market, without a doubt, suffers from the existence of few providers and is still today having to pay the price of a rigid policy of control and limitation on the number of foreign insurance companies: for this reason the spontaneous harmonization of contractual regimes is slow and difficult.

As things stand at present, therefore, the effect of Community secondary legislation in the field of contract law in each Member State is confined to the harmonization of three, albeit essential, legal issues:

- The right to *information*.
- The right of *withdrawal*.
- The right to *revoke the proposal*.

The right to information and the right to withdraw are the two constantly recurring instruments in all Community directives through which the desired standard model of consumer protection is achieved.

The insurance directives, transposed by national legislatures by means of acts or implementing decrees, have only served to confirm the utility of these instruments.

In the life assurance sector, the right to information has two aspects (already highlighted by Dir. 92/96 and now defined by Dir. 2002/83):

- Information which must be supplied *before* the contract is signed.
- Information which must be supplied *during* the period of validity of the contract.

**Art. 36, Dir. 2002/83:** "Information for policy holders: **(1)** Before the assurance contract is concluded, at least the information listed in Annex III (A) shall be communicated to the policy holder. **(2)** The policyholder shall be kept informed throughout the term of the contract of any change concerning the information listed in Annex III (B). **(3)** The Member State of the commitment may require assurance undertakings to furnish information in addition to that listed in Annex III only if it is necessary for a proper understanding by the policyholder of the essential elements of the commitment. **(4)** The detailed rules for implementing this Article and Annex III shall be laid down by the Member State of the commitment."

**Annex III, Dir. 2002/83:** "Information for policy holders. The following information, which is to be communicated to the policy holder before the contract is concluded (A) or during the term of the contract (B), must be provided in a clear and accurate manner, in writing, in an official language of the Member State of the commitment. However, such information may be in another language if the policy holder so requests and the law of the Member State so permits or the policy holder is free to choose the law applicable."

"(A) Information about the assurance undertaking (the name of the undertaking and its legal form, the name of the Member State in which the head office and, where appropriate, the agency or branch concluding the contract is situated, the address of the head office and, where appropriate, of the agency or branch concluding the contract); Information about the commitment (definition of each benefit and each option, term of the contract, means of terminating the contract, means of payment of premiums and duration of payments, etc.)"

"(B) Information about the assurance undertaking (any change in the name of the undertaking, its legal form or the address of its head office and, where appropriate, of the agency or branch which concluded the contract); Information about the commitment (all the information listed in the event of a change in the policy conditions or amendment of the law applicable to the policy conditions or amendment of the law applicable to the contract, every year, information on the state of bonuses)."

The policy-holder's right of withdrawal is the principle novel element introduced by the Community legislation and, in many countries, (such as Italy and Spain, for example) this represents a remarkable exception to the strict rule against unilateral cancellation of the contract, hitherto applied in these legal systems (arts. 1372 and 1373 of the Italian Civil Code, and arts. 1091, 1256, and 1258 of the Spanish Civil Code).

The policy-holder, having signed the contract, has the right to withdraw within a certain time-limit, (called in the Directive the *cancellation period*), which the Directive leaves to the Member States to determine (in any case, between 14 and 30 days from the date of communicating to her/him that the contract has been concluded (art. 35, Dir. 2002/83). The right of withdrawal, recognized only in relation to contracts of more than six months' duration, may be exercised without needing to give a reason, and corresponds to the same reasoning which marks out the analogous right to a cooling-off period, which has been approved in recent years in favor of various individuals, all of whom come within the category of *consumers*:

- The buyer outside the normal place of business.
- The individual signing a consumer credit contract.
- A person buying a package holiday.
- A person buying a right to use on timeshare basis.

The Community and national implementing legislation in non-life sector contracts, however, is less devoted to guaranteeing individual contracting-parties' rights, where there is no provision for this right to change one's mind (right of withdrawal).

In the non-life sector, the only rule governing the contents of the contract is the one setting out the content of the information which the insurance company must give to the individual contracting-party before, during, and after the signing of the contract: this information concerns the identification of the law applicable to the contract, the rules applicable to complaints regarding the contract, indication of the State where the head office is situated and the details of the agent for dealing with claims under the contract.

This method of drafting by the Community legislature, which distinguished clearly between the two branches of insurance, both from the aspect of administrative authorization and the contractual relationship with the client, has led inevitably to a segmented system of protection for contracting parties, where the policy holder of a non-life contract seems to have a much less far-reaching form of protection than the life-policy holder.

To sum up, in the *life sector*, there has been a change from the pre-1995 state of affairs, where:

- The proposal by the individual private contracting-party was held to be irrevocable.
- The right to reconsider (or cooling-off period) for the assured was not permissible.
- National implementing legislation of the Directive on unfair contract terms did not yet exist; to the present situation of protection of the assured, who may now unilaterally cancel the contract and withdraw from it, for up to a period of a month from signing.

Similar rights are not, however, available to the insured in the *non-life insurance sector*.

If these are the only harmonization rules concerning the contents of a contract, we should not overlook other features of the directives, or national implementing acts and decrees, which have been of particular importance in the further development of Community insurance law.

For example, the almost wholesale abandonment of the distinction between large risks and mass risks in the non-life field, confirms not only the fact that the guarantees provided in the national and Community context for the protection of the policy-holder are considered sufficient, but also that the risk of encountering a two-speed harmonization, brought about by the Second non-life Directive is avoided.[26] As a result, since the necessity of protecting the category of 'policy-holders' has not materialized, the distinction between contracts made at the client's behest and those on the insurer's initiative, created by the Second life-sector Directive has also disappeared.[27]

At this point, given the overlapping of various sources of law (both national and supranational), the question arises as to what happens within the domestic law of the Member States if a concrete dispute should arise between the policyholder and an insurance company. In other words, what law applies to the insurance contract?

---

[26] See preceding §.

[27] See § 2.

First and foremost, as the 44th recital of the Preamble to Dir. 2002/83 sets out, it should be made clear that the harmonization of assurance contract law is not a prior condition for the achievement of the internal market in assurance:

> **44th Dir. 2002/83**: "The provisions in force in the Member States regarding contract law applicable to the activities referred to in this Directive differ. The harmonisation of assurance contract law is not a prior condition for the achievement of the internal market in assurance. Therefore, the opportunity afforded to the Member States of imposing the application of their law to assurance contracts covering commitments within their territories is likely to provide adequate safeguards for policyholders. The freedom to choose, as the law applicable to the contract, a law other than that of the State of the commitment may be granted in certain cases, in accordance with rules which take into account specific circumstances."

The rules which the consumer contracting-party to the policy may invoke in every Member State for his/her protection in the contract with the insurance company, therefore, are as follows:

- Those introduced by the Community legislature by the Third-generation Directives and re-codified by the last life-sector Directive, which have required considerable efforts for their implementation by national legislatures, both regarding the rules on insurance-company business as well as contractual relations with the client. In the new national systems which enshrine these provisions, the rules governing insurance contracts are less often to be found in civil or commercial codes than in Community directives and special implementing acts.
- Those contained in the Rome Convention of June 19th 1980 on the law applicable to contractual obligations.[28] The reference to it is contained in Dir. 2002/83; in addition, the national implementing acts also make express reference to it.[29] The parties to the insurance contract may decide that the law of the contract shall be of another State (saving the application of mandatory provisions).

---

[28] See chapter I §.

[29] See, for example, art. 108 of the Italian legislative decree no. 174/95 which implemented Dir. 92/96 (*cf.* above cit.), and provides that, with the objective of applying the Rome Convention 1980, there is a presumption that the contract has its strongest link with the State where the obligation arises.

– Those contained in Dir. 93/13 and in the national implementing acts in the field of unfair contract terms, already inserted into national Civil Codes or special consolidation (such as Consumers' codes).[30]

## 3. New Types of Insurance Contracts Ruled by the Directives

Both in the directives we have been considering above, which formed the basis of a single insurance market, and in other related directives issued to meet the needs of specific areas of insurance, there are many provisions aimed at harmonizing the conditions for the pursuit of insurance business, including the obligatory content of some of the commonest types of contract, of which those concerning civil liability for motor vehicle use are prominent.[31]

The uniformization of the insurance market, the creation of a huge market involving the consequent offering and circulation of various insurance products, becoming more and more sophisticated and adapted to the needs of a rapidly changing society, have launched some types of contract scarcely-used in certain legal systems (such as in Italy, for example) or at least relatively novel for the European Community.

We refer, in particular, to contracts of *credit and suretyship insurance*, *legal expenses insurance* and *legal assistance*, which have now become a full part of insurance practice and whose discipline has recently been completed by Community harmonization legislation (Dir. 87/343 and Dir. 87/344).

Credit and suretyship insurance means contracts made between an insurance company and an individual (who is usually in business) through which the insurance company provides credit guarantees for the insured in their relations with third parties, as a result of a contract made with the latter.

In practice, an enterprise makes a credit arrangement, perhaps including extended credit, with its own client and insures its own credit exposure globally by means of an insurance policy.

The credit insurance contract has been known to national legal systems for some time, but has often been accorded secondary status, not much regarded and little used, possibly because of its perceived high risk. One only has to think of the so-called "domino effect" in insolvency,

---

[30] See chapter I.

[31] See below, § 6.

which may involve the policy-holder in insolvency in spite of her/himself, as a result of the insolvency of other businesses to which s/he is bound by commercial contracts or undertakings.

In effect, the obligations assumed by an insurance company, precisely because it frequently covers risks inherent in the pursuit of business activity, are strictly dependant on a multiplicity of factors which concern not only the nature of the policy-holder her/himself, but also the market, inflationary trends, the conduct of the policy-holder's debtors, and so on.

It concerns a set of factors or elements which do not allow even the approximate degree of risk of the insured event happening to be established with any certainty.

Nowadays, considering these difficulties and a level of risk which is effectively much higher than is evident in other branches of insurance, some Member States have subjected the possibility of a cumulative assumption of credit and suretyship sectors and other kinds of insurance to severe limitations (if not actually prohibiting it, as has happened in Germany), with the object of preventing events connected with such a delicate and specific sector having a negative impact on other sectors of the insurance industry.

This is the origin of the need to compartmentalize the various forms of insurance activity by recourse to the so-called *specialization* of certain insurance sectors.

However, such specialization was not adopted as a solution in all the countries of the Community and such diversity has given rise to a different degree of protection for the mass of policy-holders, according to the country in question.

This is why the Community legislature intervened, with Dir. 87/343 of June 22nd 1987,[32] by which Member States were required to abolish such specialization in principle, and replace it with other forms of pro-

---

[32] Council Directive 87/343/EEC of June 22nd 1987 amending, as regards credit insurance and suretyship insurance, First Directive 73/239/EEC on the co-ordination of laws, regulations and administrative provisions relating to the taking-up and pursuit of the business of direct insurance other than life assurance, O.J., L 185, 07/04/198, p. 72.

The Directive was implemented in France by *Décret* no. 91-398 du 04/25/1991 *adoptant le code des assurances (partie réglementaire) à la directive 87-343 du Conseil des Communautés européennes relative à l'assurance-crédit et l'assurance-caution, JO*, 04/27/1991, p. 5696; in Germany by *Zweites Durchführungsgesetz EWG zum VAG* vom 06/28/1990, *Bundesgesetzblatt* Teil I, 06/30/1990, Seite 1249; in Italy by *d.lgs.* no. 393 of November 26th 1991 (later partially amended by *d.lgs.* no. 175 of March 17th 1995, implementing Dir. 92/49); in the UK by *The Insurance Companies (Credit Insurance) Regulations 1990, Statutory Instruments* no. 1181 of 1990.

tection for the insured: the increase in guarantee funds and a new additional fund (the *equalization reserve*), aimed at covering possible above-average technical deficits arising in that class for a financial year.

> **Art. 1 (3) Dir. 87/343:** "Council Directive 73/239/EEC is hereby amended as follows: The following Article shall be inserted: Article 15a: 1. Each Member State shall require undertakings established on its territory and underwriting risks included under class 14 in point A of the Annex (hereinafter referred to as "credit insurance") to set up an equalization reserve for the purpose of offsetting any technical deficit or above-average claims ratio arising in that class for a financial year. 2. The equalization reserve must be calculated, under the rules laid down by each Member State, in accordance with one of the four methods set out in point D of the Annex which shall be regarded as being equivalent. 3. Up to the amount calculated in accordance with the methods set out in point D of the Annex, the equalization reserve shall be disregarded for purposes of calculating the solvency margin. 4. Member States may exempt establishments from the obligation to set up an equalization reserve for credit insurance business (…)."

The contract for legal expenses indemnity was (until recently) virtually unknown to insurance practice, and, thanks to the liberalization of the market, is only nowadays spreading throughout the insurance systems of all the Member States.

This concerns a contract whereby an insurance company agrees to cover legal and expert expenses which would normally fall to the insured and to offer other services in the defense of her/his rights, both at court and outside.

Some systems within the Community also required this kind of contract to be managed by an insurance company which was distinct from those offering other kinds of insurance products. However, the specialization of this branch of activity was not due to the risks attendant upon insuring a peril which was difficult to foresee, but rather the consideration that such a policy could easily bring the policyholder into a conflict of interests with her/his own insurance company. It is obvious that whenever a business operates in other sectors as well, it is not statistically impossible that a case might arise where the company finds itself on the opposing side of another case in which it is already involved.

Directive 87/344 of June 22nd 1987[33] was concerned with eliminating the requirement of specialization in insuring legal expenses, but also had to develop, at the same time, an alternative system to avoid conflicts of interest:

> **4th Whereas Dir. 87/344**: "In order to protect insured persons, steps should be taken to preclude, as far as possible, any conflict of interests between a person with legal expenses cover and his insurer arising out of the fact that the latter is covering him in respect of any other class of insurance referred to in the Annex to Directive 73/239/EEC or is covering another person and, should such a conflict arise, to enable it to be resolved."
>
> **13th Whereas Dir. 87/344:** "The interest of persons having legal expenses cover means that the insured person must be able to choose a lawyer or other person appropriately qualified according to national law in any inquiry or proceedings and whenever a conflict of interests arises."
>
> **Art. 1, Dir. 87/344:** "The purpose of this Directive is to coordinate the provisions laid down by law, regulation or administrative action concerning legal expenses insurance as referred to in paragraph 17 of point A of the Annex to Council Directive 73/239/EEC in order to facilitate the effective exercise of freedom of establishment and preclude as far as possible any conflict of interest arising in particular out of the fact that the insurer is covering another person or is covering a person in respect of both legal expenses and any other class in that Annex and, should such a conflict arise, to enable it to be resolved."

For these reasons, national implementing acts usually require insurance companies to insert into the contracts (unilaterally prepared by the company, so-called *contract forms or adhesion contracts*) a clause giving freedom of choice for a lawyer, according to which, should a conflict of interest arise between insurer and insured, the latter has the right to choose her/his own preferred lawyer. Besides this, it must be expressly set out

---

[33] Council Directive 87/344/EEC of June 22th 1987 on the co-ordination of laws, regulations and administrative provisions relating to legal expenses insurance, O.J., L 185, 07/04/1987, p. 7. The Directive was implemented by the same legal act which implemented Dir. 87/343, both in Germany and Italy: in Germany by *Zweites Durchführungsgesetz EWG zum VAG* vom 06/28/1990, *Bundesgesetzblatt* Teil I, 06/30/1990, Seite 1249; in Italy by *d.lgs.* no. 393 of November 26th 1991 (arts. 4–9) later amended by *d.lgs.* no. 175 of March 17th 1995 (arts. 44–49), implementing Dir. 92/49. In France by *Loi* no. 89-1014 du 12/31/1989 *portant adaptation du code des assurances à l'ouverture du marché européen*, *JO*, 01/03/1990 p. 63; in the UK by *The Insurance Companies (Legal Expenses Insurance) Regulations 1990*, *Statutory Instruments* no. 1159 of 1990.

in the contract that, in the case of disagreement between the insured and the insurance company as to how an accident is to be dealt with, the parties may apply to the court or require an arbitrator's ruling, who must decide fairly.

Finally, a contract of assistance means a contract by which the insurance company agrees, upon payment of a premium, to put assistance at the immediate disposition of the insured should s/he find her/himself in difficulty following an accident of some kind, while away from home or while away from her/his permanent residence. The assistance may be in the form of money or in kind. Assistance in kind may be provided using employees or equipment of third parties.

## 4. Civil Liability Deriving from Motor Vehicle Use

The First Directive dealing with the compulsory insurance of motor vehicles was issued on April 24th 1972, no. 72/166.[34] Among other things, it abolished the requirement of green card control among Member States.

The Second Directive no. 84/5/EEC on the approximation of the laws of the Member States relating to insurance against civil liability in respect of the use of motor vehicles[35] established, among other things: minimum amounts, cover and excess, both regarding damage to property and personal injuries; a body with the task of providing compensation, at least up to the limits of the insurance obligation for damage to property or personal injuries, caused by an uninsured or unidentified vehicle; the extension to the members of the family of the insured person, driver or any other person liable, of a protection comparable to that of other third parties, in any event in respect of their personal injuries; the prohibition upon invocation against third parties of contract clauses which exclude or limit insurance liability.

In regard to this latter proposition, the Court of Justice in the case of *Bernaldez*[36] expressed its approval in the following terms:

> ***Bernaldez* ruling**: "Article 3(1) of Directive 72/166 on the approximation of the laws of the Member States relating to insurance against civil liability in respect of the use of motor vehicles, and to the enforcement of the obligation to insure against such liability, is to be interpreted as meaning that, without prejudice to

---

[34] O.J., L 103, 05/02/1972, p. 2. The Italian regime on compulsory vehicle insurance was established before the Directive came into force, by act no. 990 of December 24th 1969.

[35] O.J., L 8, 01/11/1984, p. 17. It was implemented in all the Member States.

[36] Case C-129/94, *Rafael Ruiz Bernaldez* (1996) ECR I-1829. *Cf.* above, chapters I, and the first volume of the *Guide, A Commom Law for Europe*, chapters V.

> the provisions of Article 2(1) of Directive 84/5 on the approximation of the laws of the Member States relating to insurance against civil liability in respect of the use of motor vehicles, a compulsory insurance contract may not provide that in certain cases, in particular where the driver of the vehicle was intoxicated, the insurer is not obliged to pay compensation for the damage to property and personal injuries caused to third parties by the insured vehicle.
>
> In view of the aim of ensuring protection, stated repeatedly in all the relevant directives, Article 3(1) of Directive 72/166, as developed and supplemented by the later directives, must be interpreted as meaning that compulsory motor insurance must enable third-party victims of accidents caused by vehicles to be compensated for all the damage to property and personal injuries sustained by them, without the insurer being able to rely on statutory provisions or contractual clauses to refuse such compensation. Any other interpretation would deprive that provision of its effectiveness, since it would have the effect of allowing Member States to limit payment of compensation to third-party victims of a road-traffic accident to certain types of damage, thus bringing about disparities in the treatment of victims depending on where the accident occurred, which is precisely what the directives are intended to avoid. The compulsory insurance contract may, on the other hand, provide that in such cases the insurer is to have a right of recovery against the insured."

The Third motor vehicle Directive, no. 90/232,[37] has extended the right of insurance guarantees to all carriers and has established that all insurance policies provide for valid insurance cover over the whole of the territory of the Community.

The Fourth motor vehicle Directive, no. 2000/26,[38] is intended to

---

[37] Third Council Directive 90/232/EEC of May 14th 1990 on the approximation of the laws of the Member States relating to insurance against civil liability in respect of the use of motor vehicles (O.J., L 129, 05/19/1990, p. 33). It was implemented in all the Member States.

[38] Directive 2000/26/EC of the European Parliament and of the Council of May 16th 2000 on the approximation of the laws of the Member States relating to insurance against civil liability in respect of the use of motor vehicles and amending Council Directives 73/239/EEC and 88/357/EEC (Fourth motor insurance Directive), O.J., L 181, 07/20/2000, p. 65. Member States had to adopt and publish the laws, regulations, and administrative provisions necessary to comply with the Directive before July 20th 2002. Germany implemented the Directive by *Gesetz zür Änderung des Pflichtversicherungsgesetzes und anderer versicherungsrechtlicher Vorschriften, BGBl.* no. 48, 07/17/2002, p. 2586; the UK by *The Financial Services and Markets Act 2000 (Fourth Motor Insurance Directive) Regulations 2002, SI* no. 2706, 10/28/2002, coming into force 11/20/2002; Spain by *Ley 44/2002, de 22 de noviembre, de Medidas de Reforma del Sistema Financiero, BOE* no. 281, 11/23/2002, p. 41273, but still no reference is available for some Members (France, Italy, Ireland, Luxembourg, and the Netherlands).

ensure compensation for damage to persons or things for the victims of road traffic accidents occurring in a Member State which is not that of the injured party and caused by the use of vehicles which are insured and normally kept in a Member State.

This, according to art. 1(1), is the purpose of Dir. 2000/26: "The objective of this Directive is to lay down special provisions applicable to injured parties entitled to compensation in respect of any loss or injury resulting from accidents occurring in a Member State other than the Member State of residence of the injured party which are caused by the use of vehicles insured and normally based in a Member State.

Without prejudice to the legislation of third countries on civil liability and private international law, this Directive shall also apply to injured parties resident in a Member State and entitled to compensation in respect of any loss or injury resulting from accidents occurring in third countries whose national insurer's bureau as defined in art. 1(3) of Dir. 72/166 have joined the Green Card system whenever such accidents are caused by the use of vehicles insured and normally based in a Member State."

Art. 3 Dir. 2000/26 provides that each Member State shall ensure that injured parties referred to in art. 1 in accidents within the meaning of that provision enjoy a direct right of action against the insurance undertaking covering the responsible person against civil liability.

With a view to easing the recovery of damages sustained in a Member State other than the State of residence of the injured party, art. 4 Dir. 2000/26 provides that every insurance company should designate a claims representative in each Member State. This person will have the task of gathering all the necessary information to prepare the claims dossier and to represent the insurance company both in regard to the injured party and the national courts. This solution would enable damage suffered by injured parties outside their Member State of residence to be dealt with by procedures familiar to them. Anyway, this system of having claims representatives in the injured party's Member State of residence affects neither the substantive law to be applied in each individual case, nor the matter of jurisdiction.

Within three months of the date when the injured party presented her/his claim for compensation, the insurance undertaking of the person who caused the accident or her/his claims representative is required to make reasonable offer; where liability is denied or has not been clearly determined or the damages have not been fully quantified, they must submit a reasoned reply to the points made in the claim.

In addition, art. 4(6) Dir. 2000/26 refers to interest due on the sum owed by the company and provides that Member States shall adopt provisions to ensure that where the offer is not made within the three-month time-limit, interest shall be payable on the amount of compensation offered by the insurance undertaking or awarded by the court to the injured party.

Furthermore, Dir. 2000/26 specifies that each Member State must establish Information Centers (art. 5) and Compensation Bodies (art. 6) which should ensure that the injured party may invoke her/his rights to compensation within a short period of time, even if the insurer who is liable refuses to cooperate. Where the vehicle or the insurance company proves impossible to identify, the injured party may refer to the Compensation body of the Member State where he/she resides, to claim compensation.

Still on the subject of motor vehicle insurance, Directive no. 90/618[39] should be borne in mind, which brought motor vehicle liability insurance within the ambit of large risks,[40] so permitting insurance companies to pursue insurance business in the context of the freedom to provide services.

## 5. Banking Services

The process of European integration has also involved the integration of the banking and financial services industries, which compete with the insurance industry to create the financial markets. The very nature of such services, which are heavily regulated, requires the operation of harmonization between national systems of control as well as coordination between Community institutions and national supervisory authorities.

In effect, in recent years the Community institutions have been used to permit, on the one hand a general harmonization of all the national legal rules without, on the other hand, losing sight of measures aimed at protecting certain groups of individuals as users of specific banking or financial services.

This concerns individuals who, with the object of investing some of their own savings, or to make use of a multiplicity of kinds of credit or finance, make contracts with financial or credit institutions (banks, insurance companies, financial institutions) without in most cases possessing specific knowledge which might put them in a position to evaluate all

---

[39] Council Directive 90/618/EEC of November 8th 1990 amending, particularly as regards motor vehicle liability insurance, Directive 73/239/EEC and Directive 88/357/EEC which concern the co-ordination of laws, regulations, and administrative provisions relating to direct insurance other than life assurance, O.J., L 330, 11/29/1990 p. 44.

[40] See above, § 2.

the financial and legal aspects of the contract they are about to embark upon.

It is true to say that many Community countries had already started to put various instruments for protection in place before the Community legislature, but it was precisely the diversity of the solutions which were adopted and the differing efficiency of the resulting protection for the weaker contracting party, outside any coordination among the various national legislatures, which required Community intervention aimed at harmonizing and, in some cases, standardizing this area.

Let us first look at the banking sector.

The banking system is one of the most important structural conditions affecting company and capital market law. In this area, the developments have been very different in various Member States. In Belgium, France, and the Common Law countries the principle is that bank's deposit business and bank's securities business must be *separated*. By contrast, in Germany, The Netherlands, and Austria the principle is that of *universal banking*, with no (legally prescribed) separation between the commercial credit banks and investments banks. The banks offer a comprehensive range of financial services. German banks act as underwriters, control security exchanges, maintain stock participation in corporations, and by exercising their depositors' proxies, place representatives on the supervisory boards of corporations and offer their services in investment consulting.

According to the traditional interpretation, the German *universal bank* model encourages a very close fiduciary relationship between bank and client: in particular, the banks instigate long-lasting relationships with the company clients, granting long-term loans and allowing companies to maintain a greater debt compared to what happens to companies within a system based on the efficient working of the capital markets. This close relationship also tends to reduce the costs incurred when the company fails, owing to the bank's ability to reorganize the company, providing new capital before the financial difficulty manifests itself. The banks, with their voting rights on the supervisory council, influence the relations between shareholders and directors, reducing agency costs and at the same time safeguarding the company from possible hostile takeover bids and from the short-term views of its managers.

However, this conventional view of the German system has been reformulated recently, with the observation that the German system, under competitive pressure from the Community model, is moving away from the universal bank format, as traditionally meant.

The Community intervention, remarkable both for the quantity of legislation produced and for its impact on the national systems, has frequently caused a complete reversal of the rules previously applied.

The methods employed in this intervention can be summarized as follows:

- A *structural intervention*, aimed at balancing the interests of the credit agencies which participate in the market. This involves regulating the set of mechanisms which govern the competitiveness of the banking financial markets, the conditions of access to lending activity, of controls on the economic stability of the credit institutions, and so on. Since these interventions cannot affect the sphere of interest of individual clients, in that investor security is also protected, there are those who speak of *indirect saver protection* too, in this regard.
- A *substantive type of intervention*, which has an impact on the parties' rights and obligations, aimed at re-balancing the relations between financial institution and client through a range of provisions which govern contractual relations. The basic banker–customer relationship is rooted in contract; the relationship is overlaid with a range of rights and obligations deriving from the law of torts, in the notions of equity and good faith, and in statutes. This intervention concerns provisions which have to do both with the obligatory minimum contents of a contract and the requirement to provide information to protect the client. For this reason mention is also made of *direct protection of the saver*.

In this way, above all in the 1980's and 1990's, the Community set about issuing a large number of directives aimed at the regulation of financial and lending activity, involving banks, savings banks, credit institutions and insurance companies. The chosen instrument in this case, too, was not the regulation but the directive which, owing to its greater flexibility, has proved to be the most suitable means of reaching differing legal systems, encouraging the integration of national markets in a single market and, at the same time, safeguarding some particular national features.

The process of harmonizing national laws by means of adapting to the key directives must also be followed by the enforcement of both Community and domestic legal rules through judicial case law, to achieve the aims of the internal common market.

## 6. Community Legislation Relevant to the Banking Sector

Directive 2000/12/EC of March 20th 2000 relating to the taking up and pursuit of the business of credit institutions[41] gathered all the main Directives of this sector into a single legal text, a sort of consolidation.

> Legal certainty, simplicity, and transparency, however, are not easy to guarantee: in fact, Dir. 2000/12 has been amended by Directive 2000/28/EC of the European Parliament and of the Council of September 18th 2000, according to which: "credit institution shall mean [...] an electronic money institution within the meaning of Directive 2000/46/EC of the European Parliament and of the Council of 18th September 2000 on the taking up, pursuit and prudential supervision of the business of electronic money institutions."[42]
>
> Dir. 2000/12 was also amended by Directive 2002/87/EC of the European Parliament and of the Council of December 16th 2002 on the supplementary supervision of credit institutions, insurance undertakings, and investment firms in a financial conglomerate (amending also Dir. 73/239, Dir. 79/267, Dir. 92/49, Dir. 92/96, Dir. 93/6, Dir. 93/22, Dir. 98/78). Cf. below § 6.2.
>
> In its turn, Dir. 2002/87 is going to be amended by another Directive: see the proposal for a Directive of the European Parliament and of the Council in order to establish a new financial services committee organizational structure (amending also Directives 73/239, 85/611, 91/675, 93/6, 94/19, 2001/12, 2002/83) See above § 1.4., p. 178.

The following Directives have consequently been formally repealed (art. 67 Dir. 2000/12): Dir. 73/183/EEC, 77/780/EEC (First Banking Co-ordination Directive), 89/299/EEC (Own Funds), 89/646/EEC (Second Banking Co-ordination Directive), 89/647/EEC (Solvency Ratio), 92/30/EEC (Consolidated Supervision), and 92/121/EEC (Large Exposures), as amended by the Directives set out in Annex V, Part A, which have been repealed as well, without prejudice to the obligations of the Member States concerning the deadlines for transposition of the said Directives listed in Annex V, Part B.

According to art. 67 (2), references to the repealed Directives shall be construed as references to Dir. 2000/12, and should be read in accordance with the *correlation table* in Annex VI.

[41] O.J., L 126, 05/26/2000.
[42] O.J., L 275, 10/27/2000.

For this reason, Dir. 2000/12 does not contain a deadline by which it must be implemented by the Member States, but confines itself to reference the time-limits established for each of the directives to which it refers.

Despite the embodiment in a single Directive, we think it advisable to continue to discuss the contents of those harmonization Directives, with a view to:

- Highlighting the historical development which has led to the new Community model.
- Making the judgments of the Court of Justice, which have interpreted these Directives, easier to understand.
- Making the reading of the repealed Directives easier to follow, which are to be read according to the correlation table which is to be found in Annex VI (art. 67 Dir. 2000/12).
- Permitting immediate reference to academic commentary on the Directives, which has been made in the past.

## *6.1. The Second Banking Directive and its Principles*

The internal market in the banking sector originated on January 1st 1993, the final date for implementing Directive no. 89/ 646,[43] the *Second coordinating banking Directive.*

However, the first Community provision on the subject arose in 1973, when Directive no. 73/183[44] laid down, for the first time, the duty of Member States to abolish every type of restriction on the freedom of establishment and freedom to provide services also in the areas of banking and other financial institutions. However, the provisions were conceived more as laws programmed within the Community's objective of arriving at a single market, than as effective measures to remove national barriers.

Not even the *First banking Directive* no. 77/780 of December 12th 1977, on the coordination of the laws, regulations, and administrative provisions relating to the taking up and pursuit of the business of credit institutions,[45] was able to give rise to a free market system in the area of lending activity.

Indeed, even after this Directive, a credit institution wanting to open a branch in a Member State had to obtain authorization from the rele-

---

[43] O.J., L 386, 12/30/1989. See below in this §.

[44] Council Directive 73/183/EEC of June 28th 1973 on the abolition of restrictions on freedom of establishment and freedom to provide services in respect of self-employed activities of banks and other financial institutions, O.J., L 194, 07/16/1973, p. 1, implemented in all the Member States.

[45] O.J., L 322, 12/17/1977, p. 30, implemented in all Member States.

vant authorities of the host State. Besides, the branch was subject to all the provisions governing the control of the activity by the host State, as if a national bank were involved. It should not be forgotten, either, that the host country could require an endowment fund from the branch, on a par with newly established credit institutions.

A step in the direction of a single market in the credit sector was not taken until the *Second banking Directive* 89/646/EEC of December 15th 1989[46] on the coordination of laws, regulations, and administrative provisions relating to the taking up and pursuit of the business of credit institutions and amending Dir. 77/780/EEC.

This Directive has had a notable impact on the banking systems of the countries of the Community, removing a large number of the obstacles which were still impeding freedom of establishment in the credit sector.

As in the insurance sector, the basic choice made by the Community authorities in this field, too, consisted of minimum harmonization. Instead of coordinating national legislation in a detailed way, or laying down standard and precise rules for each of the activities normally carried out by banking and credit institutions, the Community legislature has preferred the option of establishing only certain basic rules, aimed at harmonizing the laws regarding access to, and exercise of the activity, thereafter leaving to the market and free competition the task of confirming the most efficient solutions available from among the various national models.

The three fundamental principles on which the Second Banking Directive is based are:

– *Single passport*

This expression means that each bank in any Member State may operate freely in any Community country, either by establishing branches, or under a regime of freedom to provide services, without the necessity of obtaining a new authorization from the authorities in the host country. In other words, each branch operating abroad is subject to the sole control of the country of the head office, regarding the conditions of access to, and exercise of the activity (the home country control rule).

– *Mutual recognition*

This principle sets out the requirement that no Member State may make any foreign bank, operating through branches in its own territory, observe different conditions for the exercise of the activity from those required for banks which have their head office in its territory.

---

[46] O.J., L 386, 12/30/1989, implemented in all Member States.

– *Universal bank*

This expression, introduced by the Second Directive, means that a bank is able to exercise not only credit activity in the strict sense, but a whole range of other financial activity as well, such as acceptance of deposits and other repayable funds from the public, lending, financial leasing, money transmission services, issuing and administering means of payment (e.g. credit cards, travelers' checks and bankers' drafts), guarantees and commitments, safe custody services, including *inter alia*: consumer credit, factoring, and financing of commercial transactions (including forfeiting), capital management consultancy, business management consultancy on industrial strategies and financial structuring, to the issue of guarantees and letters of credit, merger consultancy, and so on, as set out in the Annex list of activities subject to mutual recognition to Dir. 89/646.

This concerns a system which has brought banks throughout the Community countries to a position of *de-specialization*, that is to say, towards the emergence of a particular type of bank, familiar for a long time in Germanic countries where it is known as a *family bank*, which is able to offer a new kind of service and be in a position to address all the individual's needs, from simple savings to loans and advisory work, to any connected operations whatever, including those of businesses.

## *6.2. The Creation of a Single Banking Market*

The deregulation of the credit market, demonstrated in particular by the adoption of the principles set out above of the single passport and mutual recognition, represented the indispensable precondition for the creation of a single banking market. However, it required at the same time the adoption of measures necessary to avoid possible negative consequences resulting from the uncontrolled opening-up of barriers.

For this reason, the Community institutions adopted the following harmonization provisions, pursuing the double objective of:

- Ensuring parity of treatment between credit institutions and therefore, conditions of effective competition of the new single market.
- Avoiding the removal of head offices to States with a less rigorous control system.

*a)* Directive 86/635 of December 8th 1986 on the annual accounts and consolidated accounts of banks and other financial institutions[47] (amended by Dir. 2001/65 of September 27th 2001), which harmonized the

[47] O.J., L 372, 12/31/1986, p. 1. It has been implemented in all the Member States.

criteria for the drawing-up of accounts by credit institutions and banking groups, analogous to what was done in relation to certain companies' annual accounts and consolidated accounts.[48] This Directive was a pre-condition for the full application of the principle of mutual recognition.

*b)* Directive 89/117 of February 13th 1989, on the obligations of branches established in a Member State of credit institutions and financial institutions having their head offices outside that Member State, regarding the publication of annual accounting documents,[49] which established the rule that every branch office operating in one Member State, with the head office in another Member State, is obliged to publish accounts in relation not only to its own activity, but also that of the head office.

*c)* Directive 89/299 of April 17th 1989 on the own funds of credit institutions,[50] completed by Dir. 91/633 of December 3rd 1991 and amended by Dir. 92/16 of March 16th 1992, finally recast in Dir. 2000/12. These provisions on own funds aimed at the harmonizing of national laws providing for certain safeguards concerning the continuity of the activity of credit institutions besides that of savings. Own funds substantially serve to absorb losses which cannot be compensated for by sufficient profits, but they also function, so far as the competent authorities are concerned, as an effective control of the solvency of such credit institutions. Own funds of credit institutions shall consist, for example, of capital invested, reserves, funds for general banking-risks, commitments of the members of credit institutions set up as cooperative societies, and joint and several commitments of the borrowers of certain institutions organized as funds, fixed-term cumulative preferential shares, and subordinated loan capital.

*d)* Directive 89/647 of December 18th 1989[51] (as partially amended by Dir. 94/7 of March 15th 1994, finally recast in Dir. 2000/12), which harmonized the criteria on a solvency ratio for credit institutions.

*e)* Directive 91/308 of June 10th 1991[52] on prevention of the use of the financial system for the purpose of money laundering (as partially amended by Dir. 2001/97 of December 4th 2001).

*f)* Directive 92/30 of April 6th 1992 on the supervision of credit insti-

---

[48] See below chapter IV.
[49] O.J., L 044, 02/16/1989, p. 40. It has been implemented in all the Member States.
[50] O.J., L 124, 05/05/1989, p. 16. Implemented by all the Member States.
[51] O.J., L 386, 12/30/1989, p. 14. Implemented by all the Member States.
[52] O.J., L 166, 06/28/1991, p. 77. Implemented by all the Member States.

tutions on a consolidated basis,[53] which replaced Dir. 83/350 & 89/646 (and finally was recast in Dir. 2000/12). The Directive imposed on Member States the requirement to adopt a system of control over the activity of banking groups, in addition to that already provided for single banking institutions.

*g)* Directive 92/121 of December 21st 1992 on the monitoring and control of large exposures of credit institutions[54] (finally recast in Dir. 2000/12), which imposed certain limits on credit risks which credit institutions could assume in respect of one or more clients. The credit extended to a client by a lending institution is considered as "large credit" if its value is equal to or exceeds 10% of the own funds of the institution itself (art. 1(3) of Dir. 92/121). In such a case, the institution is obliged to notify the competent authorities of the credit arrangement; large credits may not, however, exceed 25% of the own fund value.

*h)* Directive 94/19 of May 30th 1994 on deposit-guarantee schemes,[55] which provided that compliance with one of the systems of guarantee is a necessary pre-condition for the exercise of activity by the banking institution.

*i)* Directive 97/5 of January 27th 1997 on cross-border credit transfers, later followed by the EC Regulation no. 2560/2001 of December 19th 2001 on cross-border payments in Euro.[56]

*l)* Directive 2001/24 of April 4th 2001 on the reorganization and winding up of credit institutions.[57] The Directive establishes the principle of

---

[53] O.J., L 110, 04/28/1992, p. 52. Implemented by all the Member States (no reference available for Greece and Finland).

[54] O.J., L 029, 02/05/1993, p.1. Implemented by all the Member States (no reference available for Spain, Sweden and the UK)

[55] O.J., L 135, 05/31/1994, p. 5. The Directive was implemented in all the Member States (no reference available for Germany and Ireland).

[56] Respectively in O.J., L 43, 02/14/1997, p. 25 and OJ., L 344, 12/28/2001, p. 13.

[57] O.J., L 125, 5/05/2001, to be adopted before May 5th 2004. Among national measures of implementation see: in 2003 (Austria): Bundesgesetz, mit dem die Konkursordnung, die Ausgleichsordnung, das Insolvenzrechtseinführungsgesetz, das Bankwesengesetz und das Versicherungsaufsichtsgesetz geändert werden (Bundesgesetz über das Internationale Insolvenzrecht IIRG) *BGBl.* für die Republik Österreich, Teil I, n. 36, 06/13/2003. p. 189; (Germany): Gesetz zur Umsetzung aufsichtrechtlicher Bestimmungen zur Sanierung und Liquidation von Versicherungsunternehmen und Kreditinstituten, *BGBl.*, Teil I, n 59, 12/16/2003, p. 2487; in 2004 (Luxemburg): Loi 03/19/2004 portant transposition dans la loi modifiée du 5 avril 1993 relative au secteur financier de la Directive 2001/24/CE du Parlement européen et du Conseil du 4 avril 2001 concernant l'assainissement et la liquidation des établissements de crédit, *Mémorial A* n. 45, 03/29/2004, p. 708; (the UK): The Credit Institutions (Reorganisation and Winding up) Regulations 2004, *S.I.* 2004/1045.

equal treatment between creditors, which must be respected in the cases of liquidation and financial restructuring of a credit company. The Directive imposes upon the administrative and/or judicial authorities the duty to publish details of the refinancing measures taken in the Official Gazette of the EU and in at least two national newspapers in the Member State where the credit institution has a branch office (the so-called 'host Member State'). Publication must be so timed as to allow possible third parties to be able to exercise their rights under the law. The requirement to provide information extends to assist all creditors, both those established in the Member State where the institution has its registered office (so-called 'home Member State'), and those creditors resident, domiciled or with their registered office in another Member State. The Directive further provides that, in the case of the insolvency of a credit institution with branch-offices in other Member States, the administrative or judicial authorities of the home Member State which are responsible for winding-up shall alone be empowered to decide on the opening of winding-up proceedings concerning a credit institution, including branches established in other Member States. A decision to open winding-up proceedings taken by the administrative or judicial authority of the home Member State shall be recognized, without further formality, within the territory of all other Member States and shall be effective there when the decision is effective in the Member State in which the proceedings are opened.

*m)* Directive 2002/87 of December 16th 2002 on the supplementary supervision of credit institutions, insurance undertakings, and investment firms in a financial conglomerate and amending Dir. 73/239/EEC, 79/ 267/EEC, 92/49/EEC, 92/96/EEC, 93/6/EEC, 93/22/EEC, 98/78/EC, and 2000/12/EC.[58] The purpose of the Directive is to establish prudential supervision of credit institutions, insurance undertakings, and investment firms on a stand alone basis, along with credit institutions, insurance undertakings, and investment firms which are part of respectively a banking/ investment firm group or an insurance group, i.e. groups with homogeneous financial activities which form part of financial conglomerates, with the aim of reinforcing stability in the European financial market.

The Directive provides: (a) the definition of a financial conglomerate on the basis of threshold criteria and the nature of the type of activity

[58] O.J., L 35, 02/11/2003, to be adopted before August 11th 2004, Denmark was the first state to transpose this Directive.

carried out by these institutions [art. 2(14)]; (b) the Member States shall require regulated entities in a financial conglomerate to ensure that own funds are available at the level of the financial conglomerate which are always at least equal to the capital adequacy requirements as calculated in accordance with Annex I; (c) the Member States shall also require regulated entities to have in place adequate capital adequacy policies at the level of the financial conglomerate (art. 6); (d) the Member States shall require regulated entities to have, in place at the level of the financial conglomerate, adequate risk management processes and internal control mechanisms, including sound administrative and accounting procedures (art. 9); (e) a single coordinator, responsible for coordination and exercise of supplementary supervision, shall be appointed from among the competent authorities of the Member States concerned, including those of the Member State in which the mixed financial holding company has its head office (art. 10); (f) the Member States shall ensure that there are no legal impediments within their jurisdiction preventing the natural and legal persons included within the scope of supplementary supervision, whether or not a regulated entity, from exchanging amongst themselves any information which would be relevant for the purposes of supplementary supervision (art. 14).

> Finally, it should be kept in mind that harmonization in this area of Community law has been conducted at international level as well, by standardization bodies: an example of harmonization of the financial market regulations is the *Basel Capital Accord* of 1988, which established capital adequacy rules for banking engaging in cross-border activities.
>
> In addition to banking regulation, the legal standardization efforts include insurance regulation (within the IAIS, International Association of Insurance Supervisors) and securities market regulation (within the IOSCO, International Organization of Securities Commissions). See below this chapter.

## 7. Indirect Protection of the Interests of Investors and Savers

We are dealing here, as can be seen from the illustration above, with harmonization measures whose primary aim is to oblige the Member States to adopt uniform provisions on access to the credit market and control over lending activity, and to avoid the creation (or permanency) of regions characterized by more tolerant and flexible laws, clearly with a view to the completion of the internal market.

However, all the provisions mentioned only marginally affect European savers and investors. While it is true that effective control by the authorities over the access to and exercise of credit activity represents guarantees and protection for savings, it is also true that for some time all Member States already possessed rules, and in some cases strict rules, in this field.

Despite this, the interests of investors and savers are indirectly protected by these directives: in fact, the threshold of *minimum harmonization* which the national laws must reach is fixed in such a way that minimum conditions of protection provided at Community level are not inferior to those in force within the individual national systems.

The case is different, conversely, regarding the set of Community provisions developed with a view to harmonizing the laws of the Member States governing the *contractual relationship to be established between the bank and the client.*

This concerns directives aimed at eliminating differences in the area of contract formation and contents, or to establishing standard rules for keeping savers informed.

The most important of the Directives in this area is Dir. 87/102, of December 22nd 1986,[59] concerning consumer credit, amended by Dir. 90/88 of February 22nd 1990 and recently amended by Dir. 98/7 of February 16th 1998,[60] which has specified various means by which publication of the effective annual interest rate is to be achieved. Given its importance, it will be examined in detail below.

Another important piece of Community legislation in this regard is Dir. 93/13 on unfair terms, with which we have been dealing in the chapter on the harmonization of consumer contracts.[61] The national provisions introduced by implementing legislation[62] have an impact in the area of contracts for banking and financial services as well. They establish special rules which are different from general principles according to the nature of the parties (undertaking or professional on the one hand, consumer on the other).

This legislation, both Community and national, is considered from the point of view of specific aspects which it presents in the context of banking contracts.

In fact, the development of the bank–client relationship, on the basis

59 See below § 11.

60 See below, § 11.

61 See above, chapter I, § 11, on the far-reaching and wide-ranging reform activity both in general and in particular areas, which has been happening in the context of so-called mass or standardized contracts.

62 See above, chapter I.

of national and Community legislation regarding contract forms, is reflected in important ways in the contract schemes adopted by the banks, which signify an important moment in the management of lending relationships.

The elements of imbalance in the bank–client relationship were particularly clearly demonstrated by the use of general contract terms unilaterally prepared by the credit institution and specifically approved in writing by the client. The large-scale application of unfair terms, particularly burdensome regarding the banks' right to amend contractual rates or commission unilaterally, their right of revocation even in contractual relationships of pre-determined length, with no (or hardly any) warning and without allowing adequate time for the client to repay the debt.

The regime introduced by the national implementing laws and inserted in the Civil or Commercial Codes, or in consolidated texts concerning consumer contracts, according to the legal system concerned, has limited the powers accorded to professional providers in general, and hence to banks and any financial institutions, of inserting over-onerous clauses for consumers.

However, applying what is expressly set out in Dir. 93/13 itself, the national regimes have put certain exceptions to the provisions in place, opt-outs which were provided precisely for the financial services sector.[63]

> **Paragraph 2 (b) of the Annex to Dir. 93/13**: "Subparagraph (j) — enabling the seller or supplier to alter the terms of the contract unilaterally without a valid reason which is specified in the contract — is without hindrance to terms under which a supplier of financial services reserves the right to alter the rate of interest payable by the consumer or due to the latter, or the amount of other charges for financial services without notice where there is a valid reason, provided that the supplier is required to inform the other contracting party or parties thereof at the earliest opportunity and that the latter are free to dissolve the contract immediately."

In the case of Italy, for example, the exceptions are all contained in art. 1469-*bis* Civil Code, and may be divided into three groups.

The first concerns the consumer's right to cancellation and the professional's unilateral right to alter contractual terms.

One of the most obvious exceptions in the scheme of clauses deemed to be unfair set out in the list in art. 1469-*bis*, is in fact the one which permits the professional financial services provider to terminate a contract of indeterminate duration where there is a valid reason, even "*without rea-*

---

[63] The waivers correspond almost entirely to paragraph 2 (b) of the Annex to Dir. 93/13.

*sonable notice,*"[64] communicating the fact immediately, however, to the consumer.

Still in the area of the right unilaterally to alter contractual terms, the specific regime in the field of financial services allows an exception to the general rule of the unfair terms (in particular art. 1469-*bis,* no. 11), whereby the professional financial services provider is permitted to amend the contract conditions, albeit on justifiable grounds, notifying the consumer within an adequate time-limit, who, in her/his turn, has a right to withdraw from the contract.[65]

The second group of exceptions to the special regime for consumers (and, in particular, as exceptions to nos. 12 & 13 of the same article, 1469-*bis* Italian Civil Code) are set out in the fifth paragraph art. 1469-*bis*, which allows the professional financial services provider to amend the interest rate or any other liability "*without prior notice*" but for a valid reason, upon immediate communication to the consumer, who has the right to withdraw.

Finally, the last two exceptions to the special regime are contained in art. 1469-*bis* (6) and (7), by which paragraph nos. 8, 11, 12, and 13 of this article are not applicable to contracts concerning stock exchange securities, financial instruments, or other products whose price is connected to fluctuations in a stock exchange quotation or index or a financial market rate that the seller or supplier does not control, including foreign currency dealings, traveler's checks, or international money orders denominated in foreign currency.[66]

> **Paragraph. 2 (c) of the Annex to the Dir. 93/13:** " Sub-paragraphs (g)—enabling the seller or supplier to terminate a contract of indeterminate duration without reasonable notice except where there are serious grounds for doing so—(j)—enabling the seller or supplier to alter the terms of the contract unilaterally without a valid reason which is specified in the contract—and (l)—providing for the price of goods to be determined at the time of delivery or allowing a seller of goods or supplier of services to increase their price without in both cases giving the consumer the corresponding right to cancel the contract if the final price is too high in relation to the price agreed when the contract was concluded—do not apply to: transactions in transferable securities, financial

---

[64] "Reasonable notification" is, however, required of any other professional to terminate a contract of indeterminate length without reasonable cause (art. 1469-*bis*, no. 8).

[65] The provision corresponds almost entirely to the second part of paragraph 2 (b) of the Annex to Dir. 93/13.

[66] The provision corresponds to paragraph. 2 (c) of the Annex to the Dir. 93/13.

> instruments and other products or services where the price is linked to fluctuations in a stock exchange quotation or index or a financial market rate that the seller or supplier does not control; contracts for the purchase or sale of foreign currency, traveller's cheques or international money orders denominated in foreign currency."

This means that there is a presumption that the following clauses are unfair: those which allow the professional to terminate a contract of indeterminate duration without notice and without a valid reason (no. 8), to alter the contract (no. 11), to determine the price later (no.12), to increase it (no. 13). For contracts with a provider of financial services, such clauses are not, conversely, considered unfair.

## 8. Consumer Credit Contracts

In commercial practice, consumer credit contracts allow the individual to make use of the finance system in order to allow for the immediate use of certain goods, spreading the *payments by installments,* at pre-established rates and intervals.

Such contracts serve a double purpose.

The first concerns the consumer, who can acquire goods immediately, which s/he then pays for over a period of time; the second concerns the seller/supplier, who is able to sell to an increasing number of buyers (including those who do not have immediate financial means) and still obtain payment for the goods sold.

The consumer credit relationship may be structured following a bilateral or tri-lateral scheme, according to whether the seller/supplier is, at the same time, also the financier, or whether s/he is reliant upon a third party, formally outside the shop where the goods are sold, who will pay the cost of the goods in advance, in place of the person acquiring them. The financing arrangement will cost more or less, according to the transaction taking place, the sum paid in advance, the number and period of installments, and the costs involved.

The possibility of paying for consumer goods by installments, or having a third party, who is not the person acquiring the goods (such as a credit institution), pay for them, represents a change in the habits of modern society and, in particular, marks the passing from the cash to the credit society. Consumer credit has developed freely for many years in the European States, without particular limitations, excepting those of a general character prohibited by the usury laws and on money-lending. The post-war measures introduced to regulate the phenomenon are generally typified by the requirement on the consumer to make a down-payment on signing the contract, but do not generally involve a policy favorable to the consumer.

The early forms of consumer credit, which were none other than payments by installment operated by sellers, were later replaced, owing to the unstoppable growth of the consumer society, of payment methods which introduced third parties, the financiers, in addition to the contracting parties: at first it was the industries which produced the goods, and later, banks or other financial intermediaries.

The experience of the United States, which inspired the Community legislature and various national experiences as well, is characterized by the presence of several sources of law.

In the first place, there is the *1970 Fair Credit Reporting Act*, Title VI of the 1968 Consumer Credit Protection Act, which is mainly concerned with consumer credit. The activity of the Consumer reporting agency, which prepares background information to pass on to third-parties via the Consumer Reports, is monitored by the Federal Trade Commission, which also oversees the remedy of damages for consumers.

The rules contained in the Fair Credit Reporting Act were integrated into the *1974 Equal Credit Opportunity Act*, which is concerned with ensuring full respect for the principle of equality (of sex, religion, and race) regarding access to credit.

The expression *Truth in Lending,* which qualifies Title I of the 1968 Consumer Credit Protection Act, assumes central importance, and aims to ensure that the market is exposed to the full light of day, providing information requirements to protect the consumer. In fact, the main characteristic of the US legislation is that it accords quite reduced protection to the consumer (with the exception of the *right of rescission*). The declared aim is to achieve a very high level of disclosure in the bank–client relationship.

Since 1968, credit protection has grown rapidly. The law underwent important changes in 1980, with the *Truth in Lending Simplification and Reform Act*. This law simplified disclosure available to consumers, and markedly reduced the civil liability of banks, increasing at the same time the administrative type of control.

The concepts of *fair* and *equal* credit have been written into acts that bar unfair discrimination in credit transactions, require that consumers be told the reason when credit is denied, let borrowers find out about their credit records, and set up a way to settle billing disputes.

In a similar way to the American one, the English experience is notable since the 1970s for having concentrated administrative control in an institution under governmental direction, the Office of Fair Trading, which is still very active in this sector today.[67]

In the field of consumer credit there are three tasks which the *Consumer Credit Act 1974* has delegated to the Office of Fair Trading:

- The fixing of joint liability, so that whoever offers the product or banking service (either the seller or the provider of the credit or both) assumes full liability for the fulfillment of the contract.
- The granting of licenses for the pursuit of financial activity.
- The accurate and precise establishment of the total cost of credit for all types of operation.

Ordinary disputes arising out of consumer credit contracts are dealt with in the light of the principle of reasonableness, which is set out in the *Unfair Contract Terms Act 1977 (UCTA)*.

The French experience, too, shows signs of similarity with that of the United States, with the Act on consumer protection in the sector of certain credit operations 1978 *(loi no. 78-22 du 10 janvier 1978 relative à l'information et à la protection des consommateurs dans le domaine de certaines opérations de crédit*). The provisions contained in the French 1978 Act were consolidated in the *Code de la consommation*, and later, they were repealed by the act implementing Community measures.

The controlling role is performed by the *Comité de la réglementation bancaire et financière,* established by act no. 84-46 of 1984 (as later amended) concerning the activity of and control over credit institutions.

However, with respect to the US, the French experience is marked by copious legislation, which offers a convincing response regarding the information which must be made available to consumers, to its transparency, and to the rates of commission charged by the banks.

The so-called *taux effectif global* (i.e. effective global rate, or TEG) was defined at administrative level by decree no. 66-1010 of December 28th 1966 on money-lending and excessive interest rates (later amended by decree no. 85-944 of September 4th 1985, by decree no. 92-750 of July 29th 1992 and by decree no. 2002-927 of June 10th 2002).[68]

Other countries, such as Italy, for example, have never regulated the commercial practice of consumer credit at all.

Leaving aside existing regulations, the apparent ease of access to these forms of borrowing led to unpleasant surprises for the consumer throughout the national markets of the European Community.

---

[67] *Cf.* chapter I, § 1.

[68] *Décret relatif au calcul du taux effectif global applicable au crédit à la consommation et portant modification du code de la consommation*, in *J.O.* 06/11/2002, p. 10357.

In fact, the consumer could be taken in by the minimum amounts of the rates proposed and sign the contract without an accurate idea about the rates of interest applicable or the additional costs. The need to provide instruments in favor of consumer protection arose from these possible scenarios and complications.

The phenomenon of consumer credit was regulated for the first time in the Community context by Dir. no. 87/102 of December 22nd 1986,[69] later completed by Dir. 90/88 of February 22nd 1990[70] and Dir. no. 98/7 of February 16th 1998.[71]

### *8.1. The Directive on Consumer Credit*

The gestation of the consumer credit Directive was particularly lengthy, not only because of the existing differences on the topic among the Member States, but also because of the diverse practice in the ways of allowing credit. The draft Directive was presented to the Community Council of Ministers on February 27th 1979, after more than ten years of preparatory work, and approved by the Council on December 22nd 1986, nearly eight years later.

The context for the application of the Community Directive is set out at arts. 1 & 2:

> **Art. 1, Dir. 87/102** (…) "credit agreement" means an agreement whereby a creditor grants or promises to grant to a consumer a credit in the form of a deferred payment, a loan or other similar

---

[69] O.J., L 42, 02/12/1987, p. 48. The Directive in question and its amendment of 1990 were adopted in Italy by Act no. 142, 02/19/1992, *Gazz. Uff., Serie gen,* 02/20/1992, no. 42, p. 12, in particular by arts. 18–24, later consolidated, with certain amendments, into Section II of Title VI of the Single Text on banking and credit law (*Testo Unico in materia bancaria*) issued by *d.lgs* 09/01/1993, no. 385. In Germany by *Gesetz über Verbraucherkredite und zur Änderung der Zivilprozeßordnung und anderer Gesetze* vom 12/17/1990, *Bundesgesetzblatt* Teil I, 12/22/1990, Seite 2840. In Belgium, by *Loi du 12 juin 1991 relative au crédit à la consommation, MB,* 07/09/1991, p. 15203.

In the UK, Portugal, and France there were national provisions on this matter before the Directive was passed: in the UK, *The Consumer Credit Act of 1974;* in Portugal *Decreto-Lei* n. 457/79 de 11/21/1979, *Estabelece normas relativas a vendas a prestações,* in *Diário da República I* Série n. 269 de 11/21/1979, p. 2989; in France, *Loi* no. 78-22, 01/10/1978, *relative à l'information et à la protection des consommateurs dans le domaine de certaines opérations de crédit, JO* 01/11/1978, p. 299. After the Community Directive, French legislature passed the Act no. 89-421, 06/23/1989, *relative à l'information et à la protection des consommateurs ainsi qu'à diverses pratiques commerciales, JO,* 06/29/1989, p. 8047.

[70] O.J., L 61, 03/10/1990.

[71] O.J., L 101, 04/01/1998.

financial accommodation. Agreements for the provision on a continuing basis of a service or a utility, where the consumer has the right to pay for them, for the duration of their provision, by means of instalments, are not deemed to be credit agreements for the purpose of this Directive."

**Art. 2, Dir. 87/102**: "**(1)** This Directive shall not apply to: (a) credit agreements or agreements promising to grant credit: intended primarily for the purpose of acquiring or retaining property rights in land or in an existing or projected building, intended for the purpose of renovating or improving a building as such; (b) hiring agreements except where these provide that the title will pass ultimately to the hirer; (c) credit granted or made available without payment of interest or any other charge; (d) credit agreements under which no interest is charged provided the consumer agrees to repay the credit in a single payment; (e) credit in the form of advances on a current account granted by a credit institution or financial institution other than on credit card accounts. Nevertheless, the provisions of Article 6 shall apply to such credits; (f) credit agreements involving amounts less than 200 ECU or more than 20 000 ECU; (g) credit agreements under which the consumer is required to repay the credit: either, within a period not exceeding three months, or, by a maximum number of four payments within a period not exceeding 12 months."

The 11$^{th}$ and 12$^{th}$ recitals of the Preamble of Dir. 87/102 in fact provide for the whole or partial exclusion of the application of the Directive itself, having regard to the character of certain credit agreements or types of transaction, or else of certain forms of credit of a non-commercial character granted under particular conditions. The Community legislation expressly excludes every form of credit destined for professionals or entrepreneurs from its field of application.

Dir. 87/102 (as later amended), and consequently the national laws which have likewise implemented it, is marked by the noticeable objective of the protection of consumers' interests. It represents a further testing of the tendency towards the protection of consumer rights which, notwithstanding the difficulties set out in preceding paragraphs and chapters, has characterized the activity of the Brussels legislature, despite the primary expressed objective remaining that of avoiding distortions of competition between grantors of credit in the common market.

**Whereas Dir. 87/102**: "Whereas the programmes of the European Economic Community for a consumer protection and information policy provide, *inter alia*, that the consumer should be pro-

> tected against unfair credit terms and that a harmonization of the general conditions governing consumer credit should be undertaken as a priority; Whereas the terms of credit may be disadvantageous to the consumer; whereas better protection of consumers can be achieved by adopting certain requirements which are to apply to all forms of credit (…)"

To be more precise, Dir. 87/102 declares its aim as promoting greater transparency in contractual clauses and more detailed information on the cost and conditions of consumer credit. The information is retailed in a two-fold way: establishing strict rules to ensure the signing of the contractual agreement is treated with due seriousness; drawing the consumer's attention to the operation's economic and legal contents at the time the contract is signed.

The information requirements which have been established by the Community legislature in the field of consumer protection have had an impact on the law of contracts of the Member States, standardizing the rules on form and content, on the right of withdrawal, and the remedies available for private individuals.

In this way, the requirements for protecting transparency in contracts between the consumer and the lender are emphasized. These requirements are, substantially, to reduce the contract to writing, with a minimum information content, so as to permit the precise knowledge of the total cost of the borrowing and the conditions which may determine any variation in the performance of the contract:

> **Art. 4, Dir. 87/102**: "**(1)** Credit agreements shall be made in writing. The consumer shall receive a copy of the written agreement. **(2)** The written agreement shall include: (a) a statement of the annual percentage rate of charge; (b) a statement of the conditions under which the annual percentage rate of charge may be amended. In cases where it is not possible to state the annual percentage rate of charge, the consumer shall be provided with adequate information in the written agreement. This information shall at least include the information provided for in the second indent of Article 6 (1). **(3)** The written agreement shall further include the other essential terms of the contract. By way of illustration, the Annex to this Directive contains a list of terms, which Member States may require to be included in the written agreement as being essential."
>
> **Art. 6 (1), Dir. 87/102:** "**(1)** Notwithstanding the exclusion provided for in Article 2 (1) (e), where there is an agreement between a credit institution or financial institution and a consumer for the

granting of credit in the form of an advance on a current account, other than on credit card accounts, the consumer shall be informed at the time or before the agreement is concluded: of the credit limit, if any, of the annual rate of interest and the charges applicable from the time the agreement is concluded and the conditions under which these may be amended, of the procedure for terminating the agreement. This information shall be confirmed in writing."

Remedies available to private individuals for violation of the information requirements laid down by the Directive may be as follows, according to the case in question:

- In the whole contract being *null and void*. This provision has raised some issues, in that the contract which is no longer binding on the parties involves the requirement, by the consumer, to return the goods acquired.
- In the substitution or implication by operation of law (*ope legis*) of void or missing clauses. The substitution of void contract clauses with others established by the law has been considered by the Community and national legislatures to be an effective system for the defense of the consumer, in that it permits the contract to be maintained even where nullity strikes at one of the essential contractual elements (for example, the subject-matter of the consumer's duties), thereby safeguarding the expectations of the consumer her/himself. Missing clauses which must automatically be implied, concern *a)* the amount and method of the loan; *b)* the number, amount and date of each individual installment; *c)* the *annual percentage rate of charge* (APR); *d)* a detailed analysis of the conditions under which the APR may hypothetically be changed; *e)* the amount and reason for costs which are excluded from the APR calculation; *f)* guarantees possibly required; g) possible insurance cover required for the consumer and excluded from the APR calculation.
- Another fundamental right available to the consumer is the *right of withdrawal* (as is set out in the Directive, the consumer is entitled to discharge her/his obligations before the due date fixed by the agreement, art. 8) (in French: *droit de rétractation*), even where there is a clause to the contrary, and with no additional penalty payment.

Among the other numerous innovations introduced into the commercial practice of the Member States, an important one is to be found in art. 11 (2) Dir. 87/102:

> **Art. 11, Dir. 87/102:** "**(1)** Member States shall ensure that the existence of a credit agreement shall not in any way affect the rights of the consumer against the supplier of goods or services purchased by means of such an agreement in cases where the goods or services are not supplied or are otherwise not in conformity with the contract for their supply. **(2)** Where: (a) in order to buy goods or obtain services the consumer enters into a credit agreement with a person other than the supplier of them; and (b) the grantor of the credit and the supplier of the goods or services have a pre-existing agreement where under credit is made available exclusively by that grantor of credit to customers of that supplier for the acquisition of goods or services from that supplier; and (c) the consumer referred to in subparagraph [a] obtains his credit pursuant to that pre-existing agreement; and (d) the goods or services covered by the credit agreement are not supplied, or are supplied only in part, or are not in conformity with the contract for supply of them; and (e) the consumer has pursued his remedies against the supplier but has failed to obtain the satisfaction to which he is entitled, the consumer shall have the right to pursue remedies against the grantor of credit. Member States shall determine to what extent and under what conditions these remedies shall be exercisable."

The Directive, then, gives the consumer the possibility of taking action against the grantor of credit, within the limits of the credit advanced, where the supplier cannot be proceeded against, so long as there exists an agreement between the grantor of credit and the supplier which gives the former exclusive rights to allow credit to the supplier's clients.

The reasoning behind the rule is as follows: it is common practice for the suppliers of goods or services to rely on a particular financial institution which they trust, to guarantee the sale of goods by installments. The consumer in this way finds her/himself signing contracts with two different parties, one for the supply of the goods to her/him, the other for financing the deal, even if there is a single operation carried out by her/him which translates itself into the acquisition of goods.

If the operation is financed through a credit company proposed by the seller, it would not be reasonable to leave the consumer with the repayment obligations to this company if there should be some shortcoming on the part of the seller. In such a case, the consumer can not only fall into arrears with the seller, but also more importantly, can suspend the payment of the installments and take action against the credit company up to the limit of the credit granted.

Art. 11 Dir.87/102 is very innovative since it breaks away from the traditional principle concerning credit contracts, whereby the grantor of credit only assumes the risk of insolvency of the finance provider and not non-fulfillment by the seller as well.

The Community legislature has considered it advisable to allow each national legislature the option of including or excluding some actions from the field of application of the directive, which fulfil the following conditions: they are granted at rates of charge below those prevailing in the market, and they are not offered to the public generally.

Besides, according Art. 2 (3), the provisions of Art. 4 (disclosure) and of Arts. 6 to 12 (information requirements) shall not apply to credit agreements or agreements promising to grant credit, secured by mortgage on immovable property, in so far as these are not already excluded from the Directive under paragraph 1 (a) of Art. 2.

Finally, Member States may exempt from the provisions of Arts. 6 to 12 credit agreements in the form of an authentic act signed before a notary or judge.

Member States used different methods to determine whether the interest charges are excessive.

Thus Dir. 90/88, amending Dir. 87/102 for the approximation of the laws, regulations, and administrative provisions of the Member States concerning consumer credit, established the important contractual aspect of the annual rate of interest and other costs, indicating the *method for calculating the annual percentage rate of charge* (APR).

To this end, art. 1(2)(e) Dir. 87/102 has been replaced with the following definition of APR: "annual percentage rate of charge means the total cost of the credit to the consumer, expressed as an annual percentage of the amount of the credit granted." The APR, which shall be that equivalent, on an annual basis, to the present value of all commitments (loans, repayments and charges), future or existing, agreed by the creditor and the borrower, shall be calculated in accordance with the mathematical formula set out in Annex II, Dir. 90/88.

In implementing Dir. 90/88, the method of calculating the APR have been fixed by each Member State by acts or national decrees. The APR is designed to allow the consumer, even at the pre-contractual stage, to have access to information containing reference to all the costs to be met, avoiding all forms of trickery or lack of clarity in the contractual terms which result from aggressive marketing.

The protection factor established by Dir. 90/88 is represented by the assurance that the information on the cost of credit (calculated in accordance with mathematical formulae) is clear and easily comparable with all the various offers of credit proposed in the Community market area.

Finally, Dir. 98/7 amending Dir. 87/102 for the approximation of the laws, regulations, and administrative provisions of the Member States concerning consumer credit was intended to achieve a further level of harmonization of the criteria for calculating the APR. This was necessary in order to put the European consumer in a position to make a better comparison between the actual percentage rates of charges offered by institutions in the various Member States, thereby ensuring harmonious functioning of the internal market.

Until now, there have only been a few judgments from the Luxembourg Court interpreting the Community provisions on consumer credit. Beside the ruling already considered, which excludes the horizontal effect of the consumer credit Directive not implemented by the State (*El Corte Inglés v. Blázquez Rivero)*,[72] the Court of Justice ruling in the case of *Berliner Kindl Brauerei AG v. Andreas Siepert* of March 23rd 2000[73] should be born in mind:

> ***Berliner Kindl Brauerei* ruling: (§§ 22, 26–27):** "On a proper construction of Directive 87/102 for the approximation of the laws, regulations and administrative provisions of the Member States concerning consumer credit, it does not cover a contract of guarantee for repayment of credit where neither the guarantor nor the borrower was acting in the course of his trade or profession. Thus, the fact that the Directive both refers to guarantees when listing the terms regarded as essential to a credit agreement from the point of view of the borrower and is silent as to the legal implications of guarantees or other forms of surety shows that, in contemplating guarantees for the repayment of credit solely in terms of consumer protection, the Directive intentionally excluded agreements to act as guarantor from its scope. Furthermore, the scope of the Directive cannot be widened to cover contracts of guarantee solely on the ground that such agreements are ancillary to the principal agreement whose performance they underwrite, since there is no support for such an interpretation in the wording of the Directive, or in its scheme and aims."

## *8.2. The Reform of Consumer Credit Contracts*

In recent times, the credit contract was extended to include other forms of payment by installment as well, non-refundable, connected to the evolution of society and the needs of certain types of client, in particular to current accounts and credit cards. While the extension of credit in a current account in the simple form of an overdraft or advance is not includ-

---

[72] See the first volume of this *Guide, A Commom Law for Europe,* chapter V.

[73] See ECJ Judgment, C-208/98, (2000), ECR I-1741.

ed in the regime regarding consumer credit, a credit opening connected to the use of a credit card is included in the sets of circumstances to which the consumer credit directives apply.

This difference in the regime between the extension of credit in a current account and advances using a credit card, which has given rise to conflicting interpretation in academic circles, is caused by the possibility for a consumer to exploit a cash fund which can be used and is repayable with no expiry date established, which makes it consequently impossible to calculate in advance the effective ARP to be applied.

As a result of some consultation promoted by the Commission with the interested parties concerned in the application of the directives set out above, and the publication of some Reports (1995, 1996, and 1997),[74] it was realized that the level of protection available under the existing directives is inadequate.

The Member States have made provision in their legislation to include other types of credit and new credit agreements, which were not covered by the Directives. By resorting to the minimum clause provided by art. 15 of Dir. 87/102 and in order to protect their consumers, Member States have adopted provisions that are more detailed, more precise and more stringent than those contained in the Directive itself.

Some examples can be provided: the Member States' legislations use different procedures and apply different time limits for *withdrawal*, *cooling-off*, and *cancellation* in connection with a credit agreement. These differences in terms of periods of time and procedure create obstacles for creditors who would like to offer credit in other Member States but face a cooling-off period of three days in Luxembourg, and a period of seven days in Belgium; in the case of France they are not permitted to take any action on the credit agreement for the duration of the cooling-off period, while in other cases the credit agreement must include references to any time periods or procedures involved. The various legislations do not lay down the conditions governing the drawing up, conclusion, and cancellation of credit agreements in a uniform way and distortion of competition is the result.[75]

Such distortions and restrictions in turn affect the volume and type of credit sought as well as the purchase of goods and services.

Differences in legislation and banking/financial practices also mean that the consumer is unable to enjoy the same degree of protection in all

---

74 Communication from the Commission—Financial services: enhancing consumer confidence—follow up to the Green Paper on "Financial services: meeting consumers' expectations," COM(97)309 final.

75 COM/2002/443. See the EESC Opinion of 07/17/2003, O.J., C/2003/234.

the Member States with regards to consumer credit. Consequently, in 2002, the Commission presented a draft Directive on the harmonization of the laws, regulations, and administrative provisions of the Member States concerning credit for consumers.[76]

A revision of Dir. 87/102 calls for: changes to the legal framework to reflect new methods of credit, a realignment of the rights and obligations both of consumers and credit providers to redress the balance, a high degree of consumer protection. The aim is to pave the way for a more transparent and effective market, and to offer such a degree of protection for consumers.

To achieve these objectives the Directive would need to be revised in a way that takes account of the following six guidelines:

- A redefinition of the scope of the Directive in order to ensure that it reflects the new situation on the market and is better able to draw the line between consumer credit and housing credit.
- The inclusion of new arrangements that take account not only of creditors, but also of credit intermediaries.
- The introduction of a structured information framework for the credit provider, in order to allow her/him to assess more fully the risks involved.
- A specification requiring more comprehensive information for the consumer and any guarantors.
- A fairer sharing of responsibilities between the consumer and the professional.
- The improvement of the arrangements and practices that determine how professionals deal with payment defaults, both for the consumer and for the credit provider.

This draft Directive is intended to extend the scope of Dir. 87/102 (which applied only to credit agreements), to include any guarantor, and thus any consumer, who stands surety, whether in person or in material terms and regardless of whether it covers credit granted to a consumer or to a trader. These persons must be provided with a minimum amount of information and protection similar to that enjoyed by the consumer/borrower. The proposal improves stability by putting in place a set of provisions on responsible lending, on providing information and protection both when the credit agreement is concluded and during its performance (or in the event of its possible non-performance) that will reduce the probability of a creditor or credit intermediary being able to mislead

[76] Cit. at previous note.

consumers in another Member State or jeopardize their financial situation or even of acting irresponsibly.

The Directive being proposed, and in particular its provisions relating to the prevention of over-indebtedness, together with the rules on consulting central databases, will further improve the quality of loans and lessen the risk of consumers falling victim to disproportionate commitments that they are unable to meet, resulting in their economic exclusion and costly action on the part of Member States' social services. All types and forms of credit that are available to private individuals will, in principle, be harmonized. It is for this reason that the title of the future Directive is worded "credit for consumers" rather than "consumer credit."

The definitions of creditor, consumer and credit agreement will undergo no change compared with the text of the original Directive, with the exception of an improvement to the manner in which the concept of *agreement promising to grant credit* is included. All credit transactions are covered, including promises to conclude agreements.

This proposal for a draft Directive contains a reassessment both of the calculation conventions and of the inclusion or exclusion of certain costs on the basis of their economic justification so that a minimum of credit costs will be excluded and a maximum of clarity achieved. This should, as a rule, bring about the maximum possible harmonization of the national cost bases and a greater degree of uniformity as regards calculation.

## 9. Financial Services

After the insurance and banking sectors, the deregulation program desired by the European Community also involved the financial brokerage sector.

If from one viewpoint, *company law* in Western industrial economies has developed in a homogenous way, in an effort to reconcile the differing interests of shareholders, creditors, workers, and the State, and has followed the various stages of its own evolution which are evident in separate Codes of Commerce or special sections within Civil Codes, from another point of view, regulations for the *protection of the financial markets* were only issued at a later stage, following an alternative course with respect to company law, alongside monopoly legislation and price policy.

The European legal systems traditionally presented differing structures, which may be summarized by the formula of 'public' *versus* 'self-regulatory' framework.

Belgium was the first national system to equip itself with legislation on the circulation of financial instruments and investor protection, shortly after the 1933 US Securities Act; in France, the capital market law was adopted in 1967 and, following French administrative tradition, it stressed far reaching and clearly outlined intervention powers of the *Commission des Opérations de Borse*. In Britain (and also in Ireland and the Netherlands), the capital market law has always been a mix of company law and other legal norms on the one hand, and the rules and standards of the City and the federated stock exchange on the other. Both sets of norms are complementary and are supervised and coordinated ultimately by the Department of Trade. The institutional framework and the legal norms have been changed fundamentally by the 1986 Financial Service Act, which forms the basis of regulation in the UK securities market (the so-called *Big Bang*).

In contrast with other Member States moving in the direction of a capital market legislation, such as Italy, Germany's capital market law has remained at an early stage of development, because it is based on the assumption that capital market law problems can be regulated through company law and stock exchange law. However, company law in Germany is primarily organizational law and contains few rules on conduct when issuing shares on capital market. Nor can stock exchange law fill these gaps, since it is limited to those few companies whose securities are quoted on the exchange.[77]

As may easily be understood, the European market was fragmented into as many markets as there were States making up the Community and each market was formed of systems which tended to be closed, protectionist, and scarcely influenced by the practices and evolution of other national markets. In such a context, harmonization was hardly felt to be a pressing need.

As soon as the achievement of a single market in the banking and insurance fields was under way, harmonization of the capital market rules was shown to be an inevitable necessity for avoiding the disparity of treatment between economic institutions or professionals (with whom we have been concerned several times in the preceding pages) which could lead to distortion of competition.

We are not going to examine the quantity of Community intervention on the subject, all the respective domestic implementation acts, and all the developments and characteristics of each provision. The important

---

[77] The differences between States in the field of capital market laws involved, historically, complex interaction with other legal areas such as procedural, tax, commercial, insurance, and labor law, with which we shall not be dealing in this brief excursus.

thing is to highlight the scale of influence of the Community over domestic private law, including the way in which the Community model has managed to modify national rules in this sector.

## 10. Community Legislation Relevant to the Financial Sector

The provisions currently in force are contained in Dir. 2001/34 of May 28th 2001 on the admission of securities to official stock exchange listing and on information to be published on those securities.[78]

> Even in this sector, legal certainty and transparency are not easy to guarantee: Dir. 2001/34 has been amended by Dir. 2003/6 of January 28th 2003 on insider dealing and market manipulation (market abuse). Dir. 2001/34 was also amended by Directive 2003/ 71/EC of the European Parliament and of the Council of November 4th 2003 concerning the prospectus to be published when securities are offered to the public or admitted to trading (below § 10.2. this chapter).[79]

This Directive, according to criteria of simplification and transparency, governs the establishment of minimum conditions for the admission of securities to official listing on stock exchanges situated or operating in the Member States, without, however, giving issuers any right to listing. Secondly, it sets out the information which the listed company must make available to investors. The scope of the Directive is to harmonize the laws in force in Member States in order to provide equivalent protection for investors at Community level; because of the more uniform guarantees offered to investors in the various Member States, it will facilitate both the admission to official stock exchange listing, in each such State, of securities from other Member States, and the listing of any given security on a number of stock exchanges in the Community.

The Directive has put the main Directives in the sector together into a single text: Directives 79/279/EEC, 80/390/EEC, 82/121/EEC, and 88/ 627/EEC are consequently repealed.

The coordination provisions concern all transferable securities which are officially listed, whatever the legal nature of the issuing institutions, whether other Member States, regional authorities, or international public institutions.

---

[78] O.J., L 184, 07/06/2001.

[79] Respectively in O.J., L 96, 04/12/2003, p. 16 and in O.J., L 345 12/31/2003, p. 64.

The Directive sets out the general *conditions for admission*, making a single distinction between shares and debt securities, allowing each Member State the option of introducing stricter conditions and obligations, or supplementary ones.

In order to ensure full and transparent *information*, the Directive has made admission of securities to official stock exchange listing conditional upon the publication of a prospectus, containing the information necessary for evaluating the financial and capital situation, the economic results, and prospects of the issuing institution, including details about the transferable securities for which listing is sought. Once approved, the prospectus must be recognized by other Member States with no need for further authorization nor the possibility of requests for further information, under the principle already established by Dir. 89/298. The competent national authorities determine the applications for admission. The competent authorities may reject an application for the admission of a security to official listing if, in their opinion, the issuer's situation is such that admission would be detrimental to investors' interests. The competent authorities may also refuse to admit to official listing a security already officially listed in another Member State where the issuer fails to comply with the obligations resulting from admission in that Member State. Against the refusal of admission or discontinuance, the issuers of securities have the right to apply to the courts.

Listed companies must respect specific obligations regarding information, producing an information sheet, referred to in the Directive as *listing particulars*, for the benefit of investors, in particular making their annual accounts and management report available. Dir. 2001/34 establishes a specific Committee, composed of representatives of Member States and the Commission, with a regulatory function concerning the conditions for admission of securities to official listing, the listing particulars of the listed companies, the information to be published at the time of acquisition, and sale of large numbers of securities in listed companies.

The main changes compared with the Commission's original proposal are: introduction of enhanced disclosure standards in line with international standards for the public offer of securities and admission to trading; introduction of special Community rules for securities designed to be traded by professionals; introduction of new prospectus formats for frequent issuers, and the duty on firms whose securities are listed on a regulated market to update the information on issuers at least once a year.

To summarize, the repealed Community Directives on financial services had common essential aims. The historic phases of which these Directives have been the concrete result are as follows:

- Council Recommendation 77/534/EEC of July 25th 1977 concerning a European code of conduct in transactions concerning transferable securities. It provided the first definition of such securities in Community law: all negotiable or negotiated stocks in an organized market.
- Directive no. 79/279/EEC[80] (the First Directive) was the first in this field coordinating the conditions for the admission of securities to official stock exchange listing. Besides establishing the conditions for listing on the stock exchange, this Directive invited Member States to designate one or more authorities with monitoring powers. The Directive was repealed in 2001.[81]
- Directive no. 80/390/EEC[82] (the Second Directive) coordinating the requirements for the drawing up, scrutiny, and distribution of the listing particulars to be published for the admission of securities to official stock exchange listing. It set out the essential financial information for admission to listing, on the basis of the definition of stock exchange securities expressed in the first directive and the recommendation. Dir. 80/390 was significantly amended in 1987,[83] with the introduction of the principle of mutual recognition, which means that if a security is negotiated on a certain national market, and is negotiated at the same time on another national market, then the second stock exchange must accept as fully adequate the listing particulars that were accepted by the first stock exchange. The amendments introduced in 1994[84] were intended to promote cross-border securities dealing. The Directive was repealed in 2001.[85]
- Directive no. 82/121 (Interim Reports Directive) and Directive 88/627 (Major Holdings Directive).[86] These Directives were repealed by Dir. 2001/34 as well.

---

[80] O.J., L 66, 03/16/1979, p. 21. Implemented by all the Member States (no reference available for Ireland).

[81] O.J., L 184, 07/06/2001.

[82] O.J., L 100, 04/17/1980, p. 1. Implemented by all the Member States (no reference available for Greece).

[83] O.J., L 185, 07/04/1987, p. 81.

[84] O.J., L135, 05/31/1994, p. 1.

[85] O.J., L 184, 07/06/2001.

[86] Respectively in O.J., L 48, 02/20/1982, p. 26 and O.J., L 348, 12/17/1988, p. 62.

## *10.1. Stock Exchanges and other Securities Markets*

Directives on *undertakings for collective investment in transferable securities*, known by the acronym *UCITS*, are of fundamental importance: respectively Dir. 85/611[87] (as amended by Dir. 95/26 of December 20th 1995 on the coordination of laws, regulations, and administrative provisions relating to undertakings for collective investment in transferable securities) and Dir. 88/220 of March 22nd 1988.[88]

The undertaking can take the form of a mutual fund, a management company for a security investment fund, a unit trust, or an investment company, depending on the legal framework in each Member State. The competent supervisory authorities, according to Dir. 85/611 may be "public authorities" or "bodies appointed by the public authorities": in this way, space is left for the operation of self-regulatory bodies (on the British model), under public control. In 1998 the Commission proposed amending these Directives, in order to encourage the UCITS to offer a broader range of investments (including money market investments, options and futures) and with the objective of requiring Member States to adopt minimum prudential supervision standards.

On January 21st 2002, the Parliament and the Council adopted Dir. 2001/107/EC amending Dir. 85/611 on the coordination of laws, regulations, and administrative provisions relating to UCITS with a view to regulating management companies and simplified prospectuses, and Dir. 2001/108/EC amending Dir. 85/611 on the coordination of laws, regulations, and administrative provisions relating to UCITS, with regard to investments of UCITS.[89]

---

[87] O.J., L 375, 12/31/1985, p. 3.

[88] O.J., L 100, 04/19/1988, p. 31.

The two Directives 85/611 and 88/220 were implemented together in most of the States: in Italy by *d.lgs.* nos. 83 & 84 of January 25th 1992, *Gazz.Uff., Serie gen.*, 07/09/1992, n. 160, p. 23; in France by *Loi no. 88-1201 du 12/23/1988 relative aux organismes de placement collectif en valeurs mobilières et portant création des fonds communs de créances, JO*, 12/31/1988, p. 16736; *Décret no. 89-623 du 09/06/1989 pris en application de la loi no. 88-1201 du 09/23/1988 relative aux organismes de placement collectif en valeur mobilière et portant création des fonds communs de créances, JO*, 09/07/1989, p. 11304; *Décret no. 89-624 du 09/06/1989 pris pour l'application de la loi no. 88-1201 du 09/23/1988 relative aux organismes de placement collectif en valeurs mobilières et portant création des fonds communs de créances, JO*, 09/07/1989, p. 11305; in Germany by *Gesetz zur Verbesserung der Rahmenbedigungen der Finanzmärkte (Finanzmarktförderungsgesetz)*, 02/22/1990, *Bundesgesetzblatt* Teil I, Seite 266.

[89] Respectively in O.J., L 41, 02/13/2002, p. 20, and O.J., L 41, 02/13/2002, p. 35. To be implemented before August 13th 2003. Luxemburg has transposed the two Directives

The main objective of Dir. 2001/107 are the companies which manage collective investment undertakings (so-called *management companies*). In order to take into account recent developments in national legislation of Member States and to permit such companies to achieve important economies of scale, it is desirable to revise their regime. It is necessary, for the protection of investors, to guarantee the internal overview of every management company, in particular by means of two-man management and by adequate internal control mechanisms. The Directive permits such companies to carry out the activity of management of portfolios of investments on a client-by-client basis (individual portfolio management) including the management of pension funds as well as some specific non-core activities linked to the main business. Specific rules should be introduced preventing conflicts of interest when management companies are authorized to carry on both the business of collective and individual portfolio management.

Dir. 2001/108 maintains the view that it is necessary to widen the investment objective of UCITS in order to permit them to invest in financial instruments, other than transferable securities, which are sufficiently liquid. The financial instruments which are eligible to be investment assets of the portfolio of the UCITS are listed in this Directive. It is desirable to permit a UCITS to invest its assets in units of UCITS and/or other collective investment undertakings of the open-ended type which also invest in liquid financial assets mentioned in this Directive and which operate on the principle of risk spreading.

It is necessary that UCITS, or other collective investment undertakings in which a UCITS invests, be subject to effective supervision. In particular, in order to have access to investment activity, national authorities have to grant an authorization, which certifies that the company has adopted an internal monitoring system by means of separating the supervision and management functions. The authorization further certifies that the company has an available initial capital of at least 125.000 Euro. Once the certification has been issued, the company can carry on its own activity throughout the whole of the EU on the basis of the mutual recognition principle.[90] Finally, the Directive has introduced a simplified

by *Loi du 20 décembre 2002 concernant les organismes de placement collectif et modifiant la loi modifiée du 12 février 1979 concernant la taxe sur la valeur ajoutée, Mémorial A*, no. 151, 12/31/2002, p. 3660; Italy has transposed the Directives by *d. lgs. 1 agosto 2003 che modifica il testo unico della finanza, Gazz. Uff.*, no. 233, 10/07/2003.

[90] The so-called single passport, which other operators in the financial sector already enjoy: see above § 6.1., in this chapter.

prospectus, for easier access to information and easier consultation by investors.

On April 21th 2004, Directive 2004/39 on markets in financial instruments was approved, amending Dir. 85/611 (besides also amending no. 93/6, and repealing no. 93/22).[91] The purpose of this Directive is to cover undertakings, the regular occupation or business of which is to provide investment services and/or perform investment activities on a professional basis. Therefore its scope should not extend to any person with a different professional activity.

One of the main objectives of Dir. 2004/39 is to protect investors. Measures to protect investors should be adapted to the particularities of each category of investors (retail, professional, and counterparties). To this end, the Directive derogates from the principle of *home country authorization:* it is appropriate for the competent authority of the *host Member State* to assume responsibility for supervision and enforcement of certain obligations specified in this Directive in relation to business conducted through a branch within the territory where the branch is located, since that authority is closest to the branch, and is better placed to detect and intervene in respect of infringements of rules governing the operations of the branch.

Another objective of Dir. 2004/39 is to impose an effective *best execution obligation* to ensure that investment firms execute client orders on terms that are most favorable to the client. This obligation should apply to the firm which owes contractual or agency obligations to the client. Fair competition requires that market participants and investors be able to compare the prices that trading venues (i.e. regulated markets, multilateral trading facilities—MTFs—and intermediaries) are required to publish. To this end, it is recommended that Member States remove any obstacles which may prevent the consolidation at European level of the relevant information and its publication.

According to the Directive, MTF means a multilateral system, operated by an investment firm or a market operator, which brings together multiple third-party buying and selling interests in financial instruments.

> As the recitals summarize, **(44)**: "With the two-fold aim of protecting investors and ensuring the smooth operation of securities markets, it is necessary to ensure that transparency of transactions is achieved and that the rules laid down for that purpose apply to investment firms when they operate on the markets. In order to enable investors or market participants to assess at any time the terms of a transaction in shares that they are considering

---

[91] O.J., L 145, 04/30/2004, p. 1. See also below §.

and to verify afterwards the conditions in which it was carried out, common rules should be established for the publication of details of completed transactions in shares and for the disclosure of details of current opportunities to trade in shares. These rules are needed to ensure the effective integration of Member State equity markets, to promote the efficiency of the overall price formation process for equity instruments, and to assist the effective operation of "best execution" obligations. These considerations require a comprehensive transparency regime applicable to all transactions in shares irrespective of their execution by an investment firm on a bilateral basis or through regulated markets or MTFs. The obligations for investment firms under this Directive to quote a bid and offer price and to execute an order at the quoted price do not relieve investment firms of the obligation to route an order to another execution venue when such internalisation could prevent the firm from complying with "best execution" obligations."

## *10.2. Second Generation Securities Directives*

Following the White Paper on Completing the Internal Market 1985 recommendations,[92] the Council adopted various *Second generation Securities Directives,* focused more on the *service provider*, instead of on the *product*. The approach to the category of *securities* changed.

In particular, Dir. 89/298 of April 17th 1989 on coordinating the requirements for the drawing-up, scrutiny, and distribution of the prospectus to be published when transferable securities are offered to the public[93] has specified the concept of *transferable securities*, establishing, at art. 3 (e), a definition which differs with respect to the one used during the 70's and 80's:

> **Art. 3(e), Dir. 89/298:** "transferable securities shall mean shares in companies and other transferable securities equivalent to shares in companies, debt securities having a maturity of at least one year and other transferable securities equivalent to debt securities, and any other transferable security giving the right to acquire any such transferable securities by subscription or exchange (…)"

Dir. 89/298 was repealed by Dir. 2003/71 of November 4th 2003, with effect from June 30th 2004.[94] This last Directive constitutes an instru-

---

[92] See also the first volume of this *Guide, A Commom Law for Europe*, chapter IV.

[93] O.J., L 124, 05/05/1989, p. 8. Implemented by all the Member States.

[94] O.J., L 345, 12/31/2003, p. 64. *Cf.* above in this chapter.

ment essential to the achievement of the internal market as set out in the timetable presented in the Commission Communications (*Risk capital Action Plan* and *Implementing the framework for financial market: Action Plan*), facilitating the widest possible access to investment capital on a Community-wide basis, including for small and medium-sized enterprises (SMEs) and start-ups, by granting a single passport to the issuer.

Dir. 89/592 of November 13th 1989 on insider trading[95] defined inside information and insider dealing, prohibiting those (such as for example, managers or employers) who have obtained inside information from dealing in the stocks on the exchange. The Directive contained a provision of great importance, which directly concerned investors. Art. 7 Dir. 89/592 extended the duty to companies or businesses whose transferable securities were listed on the stock exchange or other regulated markets, to keep the public informed of important new facts which occured within their sphere of activity, when they were not already in the public domain, and which could, given their impact on the capital or financial situation or general state of affairs in the company, have brought about important changes in their share situation. The company was also obliged to inform the general shareholders of any change concerning right connected with the various categories of shares, including changes occurring in the structure of the important capital shareholdings.

This was established by § 5 of scheme C, annexed to Dir. no. 79/279 of March 5th 1979, referred to in the Dir. 89/592. The competent authorities may, however, allow companies to dispense with obeying this obligation, where the diffusion of certain information could cause prejudice to the company's interests. In 2001, the Commission announced the intention of amending the Directive with a view to adding other prohibitions regarding the manipulation of the securities market and to lay down more effective enforcement duties.[96] The new Directive on insider dealing and market manipulation, no. 2003/6 was adopted on January 28th 2003.[97]

Dir. 89/646[98] took a different approach to the regime under consideration, where the broader category of *financial instruments* has a more central place (see the Annex to the Directive at 7 (e) for securities and (c) for financial instruments).

---

[95] O.J., L 334, 11/18/1989, p. 30. Implemented by all the Member States.

[96] See Common Position no. 50/2002 of July 19th 2002 on insider dealing and market manipulation (market abuse), O.J., C 228, 09/25/2002, p. 19.

[97] O.J., L 96, 04/12/2003, p. 16.

[98] The Second Banking Co-ordination Directive, repealed by the Dir. 2000/12. See above § 6 ff.

## *10.3. A Single European Market in Investment Services*

The new approach was confirmed by Dir. 93/22/EEC of May 10th 1993 on investment services in the securities field (ISD)[99] and Dir. 93/6/EEC of March 15th 1993 on the capital adequacy of investments firms and credit institutions (CAD).[100]

These two Directives have been essential for the achievement of a single European market in investment services; they represent a compromise between the more liberal perspective of north European countries and the interventionist tradition of the Mediterranean countries, between the Continental, or German model of universal banking, and the Common Law, or British model of generally separate banking and securities activities.

As was the case with the Second banking Directive, the instruments used by the two investment Directives to achieve the goal of the internal market were again the principles of *single passport* and *mutual recognition.*

> For instance, *cf.* **3rd Whereas, Dir. 93/22:** "The approach adopted is to effect only the essential harmonisation necessary and sufficient to secure the mutual recognition of authorisation and of prudential supervision systems, making possible the grant of a single authorisation valid throughout the Community and the application of the principle of home Member State supervision."

The Directives also eliminated the advantage in favor of credit companies, ensuring full implementation of the principle of freedom of establishment and to provide services within the single market:

> **40th Whereas Dir. 93/22**: "Whereas, with the two-fold aim of protecting investors and ensuring the smooth operation of the markets in transferable securities, it is necessary to ensure that transparency of transactions is achieved and that the rules laid down for that purpose in this Directive for regulated markets apply both to investment firms and to credit institutions when they operate on the market."

In this way, all Community enterprises operating in the financial sector had the right to offer their own services within the European Union and

---

[99] O.J., L 141, 06/11/1993, p. 27. As Amended by Dir. 95/26/EC of June 29th 1995, O.J., L 168, 07/18/1995, p. 7, Dir. 97/9/EC of March 3rd 1997, O.J., L 84, 03/26/1997, p. 22, Dir. 2000/64/EC of November 7th 2000, O.J., L 290, 11/17/2000, p. 27.

[100] O.J., L 141, 06/11/1993, p. 1.

to have access to the relevant regulated markets while remaining subject to the discipline of the country of origin. Thus, a bank domiciled in an EU country that permitted universal banking could conduct universal banking in another EU country that prohibited it. With France and Germany committed to universal banking, *the single passport model* effectively opened all of Europe to universal banking. It also permitted Britain to maintain a separate regulatory framework for its non-bank securities firms.

Since the securities operations of Germany's universal banks would be competing with Britain's non-bank securities firms, there was a desire to harmonize capital requirements for the two. The solution implemented with Dir. 93/6 on the capital adequacy (CAD) was to regulate *functions* instead of *institutions*. The CAD established uniform capital requirements applicable to both universal banks' securities operations and non-bank securities firms.

The ISD developed a sophisticated new legal classification aimed at reordering the financial sector, which all the Member States transposed into their own legal systems.[101] The definitions were to be found by cross-referencing the Directive's Preamble, articles, and Annexes.

For example, 'investment service' (in German: *Wertpapierdienstleistung,* in French: *service d'investissement,* in Italian: *servizio d'investimento*) had been defined in the following way:

> **Art. 1(1), Dir. 93/22**: "For the purposes of this Directive: 1. investment service shall mean any of the services listed in Section A of the Annex relating to any of the instruments listed in Section B of the Annex that are provided for a third party (...)"
>
> **Section A of the Annex (Dir. 93/22):** "Services:
> (a) Reception and transmission, on behalf of investors, of orders in relation to one or more of the instruments listed in Section B. (b) Execution of such orders other than for own account. 2. Dealing in any of the instruments listed in Section B for own account.

---

[101] For example, Dir. 93/22 was implemented in Germany by *Gesetz über den Wertpapierhandel und zur Änderung der börsenrechtlichen und wertpapierrechtlichen Vorschriften (Zweites Finanzmarktförderungsgesetz)*, 07/26/1994, *Bundesgesetzblatt Teil I*, 07/30/1994, *Seite* 1749; in Italy, by *d.lgs.* n. 415, 07/23/1996, *di recepimento della direttiva 93/22/ CEE del 03/10/1993 relativa ai servizi di investimento del settore dei valori mobiliari e della direttiva 93/6/CEE del 03/15/1993 relativa all'adeguatezza patrimoniale delle imprese di investimento e degli enti creditizi, Gazz. Uff.*, n. 186 p. 44, *Suppl. Ord.* n. 133, 08/09/1996; in the UK by *The Investment Services Regulations 1995, S.I.* no. 3275 of 1995.

3. Managing portfolios of investments in accordance with mandates given by investors on a discretionary, client-by-client basis where such portfolios include one or more of the instruments listed in Section B. 4. Underwriting in respect of issues of any of the instruments listed in Section B and/or the placing of such issues."

**Section B of the Annex (Dir. 93/22)**: "Instruments:
(a) Transferable securities; (b) Units in collective investment undertakings. 2. Money-market instruments. 3. Financial-futures contracts, including equivalent cash-settled instruments. 4. Forward interest-rate agreements (FRAs). 5. Interest-rate, currency and equity swaps. 6. Options to acquire or dispose of any instruments falling within this section of the Annex, including equivalent cash-settled instruments. This category includes in particular options on currency and on interest rates."

**Section C of the Annex (Dir. 93/22):** "Non-core services:
1. Safekeeping and administration in relation to one or more of the instruments listed in Section B. 2. Safe custody services. 3. Granting credits or loans to an investor to allow him to carry out a transaction in one or more of the instruments listed in Section B, where the firm granting the credit or loan is involved in the transaction. 4. Advice to undertakings on capital structure, industrial strategy and related matters and advice and service relating to mergers and the purchase of undertakings. 5. Services related to underwriting. 6. Investment advice concerning one or more of the instruments listed in Section B. 7. Foreign-exchange service where these are connected with the provision of investment services."

The meaning of the expression 'transferable securities' (in German: *Wertpapiere,* in French: *valeurs mobilières,* in Italian: *valori mobiliari*) was to be obtained from the following provisions:

**Whereas, Dir. 93/22**: "transferable securities means those classes of securities which are normally dealt in on the capital market, such as government securities, shares in companies, negotiable securities giving the right to acquire shares by subscription or exchange, depositary receipts, bonds issued as part of a series, index warrants and securities giving the right to acquire such bonds by subscription."

**Art 1(4), Dir. 93/22**: "transferable securities shall mean: shares in companies and other securities equivalent to shares in companies, bonds and other forms of securitised debt which are

> negotiable on the capital market and any other securities normally dealt in giving the right to acquire any such transferable securities by subscription or exchange or giving rise to a cash settlement excluding instruments of payment."

The meaning of the term 'money-market instruments' (in German: *Geldmarktinstrumente*, in French: *instruments du marché monétaire*, in Italian: *strumenti del mercato monetario*) was to be obtained from the following:

> **Whereas, Dir. 93/22**: "money-market instruments means those classes of instruments which are normally dealt in on the money market such as treasury bills, certificates of deposit and commercial paper."
>
> **Art. 1(5), Dir. 93/22**: "money-market instruments shall mean those classes of instruments which are normally dealt in on the money market (…)."

The Directive also specified the limits of application of the definitions contained in it, excluding the possibility of a more generalized reading by those interpreting it:

> **Whereas, Dir. 93/22**: "The very wide definitions of transferable securities and money-market instruments included in this Directive are valid only for this Directive and consequently in no way affect the various definitions of financial instruments used in national legislation for other purposes such as taxation; whereas, furthermore, the definition of transferable securities covers negotiable instruments only; whereas, consequently, shares and other securities equivalent to shares issued by bodies such as building societies and industrial and provident societies, ownership of which cannot in practice be transferred except by the issuing body's buying them back, are not covered by this definition; Whereas 'instrument equivalent to a financial-futures contract' means a contract which is settled by a payment in cash calculated by reference to fluctuations in interest or exchange rates, the value of any instrument listed in Section B of the Annex or an index of any such instruments; (…)"

However, as we have already seen above, Directive 2004/39 of April $21^{th}$ 2004 on markets in financial instruments amended the CAD (besides Directives 85/611 and 2000/12, as to which see above), and repealed the

ISD.[102] In fact, the Community legislature has taken note of the fact that more investors have become active in the financial markets and are offered an even more complex wide-ranging set of services and instruments.

As specified in the *Communication of 15 November 2000 on upgrading the Investment Services Directive*,[103] the Commission considered it was necessary to update the legislative framework because of the technical changes to exchanges and clearing systems, and the arrival of the Euro and new technologies. The Communication launched extensive consultations with all the parties concerned on the best way of updating Dir. 93/22. For example, the single passport for investment firms would be sufficient for inter-professional business and could be progressively extended to cover services to retail investors. Regarding the organization of exchanges and clearing systems, it would be useful to apply common principles to trading systems, including new electronic arrangements.

According to the financial and economic studies used by the Commission, market-based financing has begun to overturn the traditional predominance of bank-based lending in most EU Member States. New companies issue shares in unprecedented numbers. Institutional investors and a new generation of competitive brokers are mobilizing household savings: in some Member States, more than one in three adults owns shares. Trading infrastructures are also undergoing profound changes. New technology facilitates entry by service providers who can compete with incumbent players at all stages in the trading system—from rudimentary order-routing systems to fully-fledged exchange—like entities. At the level of exchanges, the race is on to provide issuers, investors, and intermediaries with a platform for pan-European trading. This has spurred ambitious proposals for mergers and alliances between exchanges. Clearing (and to a lesser extent settlement) are of central importance as an important cost-center in European trading where large benefits can be reaped from consolidation.

The pressure from market users is eroding the boundary between national and European/international clearing and settlement. One third of the total volume of new shares issued on European stock exchanges in 1999 emanated from newly listed companies. Encouraged by the elimination of exchange risk in the Euro-zone, these structural developments have assumed a pan-European dimension. Market inter-dependencies are being reinforced at all levels. The investment horizons of funds and private investors are becoming more pan-European. The same financial

---

102 O.J., L 145, 04/30/2004, p. 1. See above § and also below §10.4.

103 COM (2000) 729 final (Not published in the Official Journal).

instruments are potentially tradable on competing exchanges and trading platforms across the EU. The same investment firms constitute the membership of different exchanges and serve the same national client bases. Finally, exchanges and new types of trading platforms are competing across borders for order flow and are increasingly dependent on consolidated clearing houses/central counterparty facilities.

In view of these developments, the legal framework of the Community encompasses the full range of investor-oriented activities. To this end, it provides for a higher degree of harmonization and offers a high level of protection to the investors; it allows investment firms to provide services throughout the Community, being a Single Market, on the basis of home country supervision. And in view of the preceding, Dir. 2004/39 has replaced Dir. 93/22.

> **Dir. 2004/39, Art. 2:** "Money-market instruments" means those classes of instruments which are normally dealt in on the money market, such as treasury bills, certificates of deposit, and commercial papers and excluding instruments of payment;
>
> "Transferable securities" means those classes of securities which are negotiable on the capital market, with the exception of instruments of payment, such as: (a) shares in companies and other securities equivalent to shares in companies, partnerships, or other entities, and depositary receipts in respect of shares; (b) bonds or other forms of securitized debt, including depositary receipts in respect of such securities; (c) any other securities giving the right to acquire or sell any such transferable securities or giving rise to a cash settlement determined by reference to transferable securities, currencies, interest rates, or yields, commodities or other indices or measures;
>
> "Investment services and activities" means any of the services and activities listed in Section A of Annex I relating to any of the instruments listed in Section C of Annex;

> **Dir. 2004/39. Annex I.** "LIST OF SERVICES AND ACTIVITIES AND FINANCIAL INSTRUMENTS.
>
> Section A. Investment services and activities.
>
> (1) Reception and transmission of orders in relation to one or more financial instruments. (2) Execution of orders on behalf of clients. (3) Dealing on own account. (4) Portfolio management. (5) Investment advice. (6) Underwriting of financial instruments and/or placing of financial instruments on a firm commitment basis. (7) Placing of financial instruments without a firm commitment basis. (8) Operation of Multilateral Trading Facilities.
>
> Section B Ancillary services [...]

Section C Financial Instruments. (1) Transferable securities; (2) Money-market instruments; (3) Units in collective investment undertakings; (4) Options, futures, swaps, forward rate agreements and any other derivative contracts relating to securities, currencies, interest rates or yields, or other derivatives instruments, financial indices or financial measures which may be settled physically or in cash; (5) Options, futures, swaps, forward rate agreements and any other derivative contracts relating to commodities that must be settled in cash or may be settled in cash at the option of one of the parties (otherwise than by reason of a default or other termination event); (6) Options, futures, swaps, and any other derivative contract relating to commodities that can be physically settled provided that they are traded on a regulated market and/or an MTF; (7) Options, futures, swaps, forwards and any other derivative contracts relating to commodities, that can be physically settled not otherwise mentioned in C.6 and not being for commercial purposes, which have the characteristics of other derivative financial instruments, having regard to whether, inter alia, they are cleared and settled through recognised clearing houses or are subject to regular margin calls; (8) Derivative instruments for the transfer of credit risk; (9) Financial contracts for differences; (10) Options, futures, swaps, forward rate agreements and any other derivative contracts relating to climatic variables, freight rates, emission allowances or inflation rates or other official economic statistics that must be settled in cash or may be settled in cash at the option of one of the parties (otherwise than by reason of a default or other termination event), as well as any other derivative contracts relating to assets, rights, obligations, indices and measures not otherwise mentioned in this Section, which have the characteristics of other derivative financial instruments, having regard to whether, inter alia, they are traded on a regulated market or an MTF, are cleared and settled through recognised clearing houses or are subject to regular margin calls."

## *10.4. The Ongoing Transformation of the Financial Sector*

On May 11th, 1999 the *Financial Services Action Plan* was published.[104] The Action Plan contained a range of measures to improve the single market for financial services over the "following five years," developing open and secure markets for retail financial services, eliminating tax obstacles to market integration, providing a high level of protection for

[104] COM (99) 232 final.

consumers to encourage consumer confidence, and ensure continuing stability in EU financial markets. Raising the level of consumer protection in certain areas[105] was one of the principle objectives of the Financial Services Action Plan. One of the most important challenges was the harmonization of the rules of Member States governing private company and industry-wide occupational pension plans, to align them with the internal market.

In 2000, the Commission drafted the Directive of the European Parliament and of the Council on the activities of institutions for *occupational retirement provision.*[106] As the Action Plan for Financial Services and other subsequent documents stressed, there was an urgent priority to draw up a Directive on the prudential supervision of institutions for occupational retirement provision: these institutions are major financial institutions not subject to a coherent Community legislative framework allowing them to fully benefit from the advantages of the internal market. In fact, Directive no. 2003/41 on the activities and supervision of institutions for occupational retirement provision was passed on June 3rd 2003.[107]

The Action Plan also emphasized the urgency of developing a truly integrated retail market in which the interests of consumers and service providers are properly protected. A Directive was adopted to set up a legal framework which ensures a high level of professionalism and competence among insurance intermediaries whilst guaranteeing a high level of protection of customers' interests: Dir. 2002/92/EC of the European Parliament and of the Council of December 9th 2002 on *insurance mediation.*[108]

Another centerpiece of the EU Financial Services Action Plan was the draft Directive on *prospectuses.*[109] The indications that the current Community instruments on prospectuses are not suited to the operation of capital markets have not changed. There are currently many different practices and differing interpretations based on distinct traditions within the EU, regarding the content and the layout of prospectuses. The methods used and the time required for checking the information given therein are also different. The current complex and partial mutual recognition

---

[105] *Cf.* Directive 2002/65/EC at § 11, this chapter.

[106] O.J., C 96, 03/27/2001, p. 136.

[107] O.J., L 235, 09/23/2003, p. 10.

[108] O.J., L 9, 01/15/2003, p. 3.

[109] Amended proposal for a Directive on the prospectus to be published when securities are offered to the public or admitted to trading and amending Directive 2001/34/EC, Brussels, 08/09/2002, COM(2002) 460 final.

mechanism is unable to ensure the objective of providing a single passport for issuers. To achieve this objective, harmonization of the information contained in each prospectus, including those relating to markets specially intended for professional investors, is necessary in order to provide equivalent protection for investors at Community level. The prospectus Directive draft was adopted on July 15th 2003[110] to harmonize also also this area.

In addition, the Financial Services Action Plan drew attention to the underdeveloped EU legal framework for securities markets, and the significant opportunity costs resulting from the regulatory fragmentation of EU liquidity. It identified a number of initiatives to create a legislative framework to support the emergence of a single, highly liquid financial market.

As part of this package, the Commission published a *Green Paper* in November 2000, exploring a number of themes relating to the effects of the ISD.

Since the adoption of the ISD,[111] the EU financial marketplace has become more complex and the boundary between marketplaces and intermediaries has become blurred; the functions of market intermediary and marketplace have been performed by distinct types of institutions. This institutional dichotomy has allowed a clear distinction between the reach of investor-facing protection (which applies only to intermediaries) and market-facing rules designed to uphold the transparent and efficient functioning of markets (which applies primarily to exchanges).

In the words of the Commission's Green Paper, the existing Directive no longer provides an effective framework for undertaking investment business on a cross-border basis in the EU. It does not establish clear ground-rules within which competition and consolidation of trading infrastructures can take place; it does not provide sufficient harmonization to allow effective mutual recognition of investment firm licenses; it contains outdated investor protection regimes; it does not span the full range of investor-oriented services (e.g. advice, new distribution channels) or financial dealing (e.g. in commodity derivatives); it does not address the regulatory and competitive issues that arise when exchanges start competing with each other and with new order-execution platforms; it is insufficiently clear regarding allocation of enforcement responsibili-

---

[110] It is still to be published: for more references on the Directive see the website at http://www.europa.eu.int/comm/internal_market/en/finances/mobil/prospectus_en.htm.

[111] See § 10.3. in this chapter.

ties within Member States and it does not establish a sound basis for cross-border supervisory cooperation.

For all these reasons, in 2002 the Commission proposed a draft Directive on *investment services and regulated markets,* which was amended and adopted on April 21$^{th}$ 2004, with the new title, *on markets in financial instruments* (Dir. 2004/39).[112] The Directive updates and harmonizes the regulatory conditions with which investment firms must comply, at the time of initial authorization and thereafter.

It reinforces the disciplines that investment firms must respect when acting on behalf of clients in pan-European trading. It seeks to clarify and expand the list of *financial instruments* that may be traded on regulated markets and between investment firms (Annex I). It also broadens the range of *investment services* for which authorization was required under the ISD Directive, notably to include investment advice, and clarifies the ancillary services which investment firms could provide (Annex I). Finally it defines the *professional client*, as being a client who possesses the experience, knowledge and expertise to make his/her own investment decisions and properly assess the risks that s/he incurs (Annex II). The distinction made in respect of *non-professional investors* is particularly important for the purposes of applying the relevant provisions regarding conduct. In order to promote consistent enforcement throughout the EU, the new Directive sets minimum standards for the mandate and the powers *national competent authorities* must have at their disposal. It also establishes effective mechanisms for real-time cooperation in investigating and pursuing breaches of the Directive's obligations, by upgrading the obligations of competent authorities to assist each other, exchange information and facilitate joint investigations. Dir. 2004/39, among other things, recasts the regime for the *codes of conduct* put in place for the protection of savers, taking into account the standards of protection of investors adopted by the *European Securities Committee* (ESC) (Art. 64, Dir. 2004/39).[113]

Indeed, updating the protection offered by the legal system is a priority: "The objective of creating an integrated financial market, in which investors are effectively protected and the efficiency and integrity of the overall market are safeguarded, requires the establishment of common

---

112 Respectively Brussels, 11/19/2002, COM(2002) 625 final and O.J., L 145, 04/30/2004 p. 1. See above §§.

113 The ESC (*European Securities Committee*) and CESR (*Committee of European Securities Regulators)* were formally established in June 2001 (Commission Decisions 2001/528/EC and 2001/527/EC) and held their first meetings in September 2001. The ESC primarily has a regulatory function, the CESR has an advisory function.

regulatory requirements relating to investment firms wherever they are authorized in the Community and governing the functioning of regulated markets and other trading systems so as to prevent opacity or disruption on one market from undermining the efficient operation of the European financial system as a whole."[114]

A preliminary reading of the Directive demonstrates clearly the different method (with respect to that adopted in 1993) used by the Community legislature to govern codes of conduct. Indeed, in this case it has not confined itself to laying down some general standards, but identifies rules of conduct in some detail. However, one effect of transferring to the ESC the task of drawing up more analytical rules is that they are subject to rapid obsolescence. For this reason, the regime governing *conflict of interests* is no longer limited to declaring the principle that the investment company must use its endeavors to avoid conflicts of interest, and, where that is not possible, to ensuring that its clients be treated in an equitable way. Instead, it identifies in detail such reasonable and advisable steps to take to identify conflicts (art. 18 Dir. 2004/39), conferring on the ESC the task of developing the detailed executive measures. The criteria of professionalism and good faith are thus given meaning at an operational level. In this way, the *best execution rule* is laid down and specified, with the emphasis being placed on other factors besides the price element—factors which are more difficult to evaluate, such as the speed and likelihood of the negotiation being carried out, having regard to the time, the size and the nature of the client's order, and all the specific instructions given by the client. The rules in relation to information and transparency are shaped according to the stage of negotiations to which they refer. It is laid down that an investment firm shall act honestly, fairly, and professionally in accordance with the best interests of its clients and comply, in particular, with the principles set out in paragraphs 2 to 8 (art. 19 Dir. 2004/39).

As we have seen, there is a widespread need for modernization and more flexibility. Unless the reform is enforced, the European financial market will still be fragmented. Cross-border capital raising will therefore remain the exception, rather than the rule, the antithesis of the logic of the single currency.

[114] Whereas (71), Dir. 2004/39.

## 11. Indirect Protection of the Interests of Investors and Savers

Community legislation and national implementing measures do not confine themselves to regulating the means of access and the pursuit of the activity of investment services by the authorized institutions. In fact, in this sector too,[115] the impact of Community legislation is noticeable for its effect on national laws regarding consumer contracts, their form and contents, and the right to withdrawal, whose failure to be observed leads to nullity of the contract.

Therefore, to furnish some concrete examples, the contract is void if it is not reduced to writing; an agreement containing merely a reference to usage to determine the amount and the costs to be paid by the client is likewise void; also an investment contract where the client's right of withdrawal is missing is similarly void. Clauses which exclude the client from being able to give binding instructions about the operations to be carried out, or those which provide that the firm can assume contractual obligations on behalf of the client which commit him/her beyond the amount of managed capital, or again, which prohibit the client from withdrawing from the contract, are also all void.

In all these cases the nullity is relative, in the sense that the clauses may only be enforced at the instance of the consumer (saver or investor).

In particular, as we recalled above, Dir. 2004/39, as distinct from Dir. 93/22, does not confine itself to laying down some general standards,[116] but identifies detailed rules of conduct which should provide the basis for the ESC and the Member States to draw up prudent sets of rules which financial intermediaries should observe in their relationships with clients:

> **Art. 19, Dir. 2004/39**: "Conduct of business obligations when providing investment services to clients. (**1.**) Member States shall require that, when providing investment services and/or, where appropriate, ancillary services to clients, an investment firm act honestly, fairly and professionally in accordance with the best interests of its clients and comply, in particular, with the principles set out in paragraphs 2 to 8. (**2.**) All information, including marketing communications, addressed by the investment firm to clients or potential clients shall be fair, clear and not misleading. Marketing

---

[115] As with the provisions in the directives and implementing laws which we saw in connection with consumer contracts, see chapter I.

[116] The fact is that the establishment of these rules was not accompanied by the provision of an efficient system of remedies; thus the rules of conduct continued to be very different in every Member State, in terms of content, form, and means of enforcement.

communications shall be clearly identifiable as such. (**3.**) Appropriate information shall be provided in a comprehensible form to clients or potential clients about: the investment firm and its services, financial instruments and proposed investment strategies; this should include appropriate guidance on and warnings of the risks associated with investments in those instruments or in respect of particular investment strategies, execution venues, and, costs and associated charges so that they are reasonably able to understand the nature and risks of the investment service and of the specific type of financial instrument that is being offered and, consequently, to take investment decisions on an informed basis. This information may be provided in a standardised format. (**4.**) When providing investment advice or portfolio management the investment firm shall obtain the necessary information regarding the client's or potential client's knowledge and experience in the investment field relevant to the specific type of product or service, his financial situation and his investment objectives so as to enable the firm to recommend to the client or potential client the investment services and financial instruments that are suitable for him. (**5.**) Member States shall ensure that investment firms, when providing investment services other than those referred to in paragraph 4, ask the client or potential client to provide information regarding his knowledge and experience in the investment field relevant to the specific type of product or service offered or demanded so as to enable the investment firm to assess whether the investment service or product envisaged is appropriate for the client. In case the investment firm considers, on the basis of the information received under the previous subparagraph, that the product or service is not appropriate to the client or potential client, the investment firm shall warn the client or potential client. This warning may be provided in a standardised format. In cases where the client or potential client elects not to provide the information referred to under the first subparagraph, or where he provides insufficient information regarding his knowledge and experience, the investment firm shall warn the client or potential client that such a decision will not allow the firm to determine whether the service or product envisaged is appropriate for him. This warning may be provided in a standardised format. (**6.**) Member States shall allow investment firms when providing investment services that only consist of execution and/or the reception and transmission of client orders with or without ancillary services to provide those investment services to their clients without the need to obtain the information or make the determination provided for in paragraph 5 where all the following conditions are met: the above services relate to shares admitted to trading on a regulated market or in an equivalent third country market, money market instruments, bonds

> or other forms of securitised debt (excluding those bonds or securitised debt that embed a derivative), UCITS and other non-complex financial instruments. A third country market shall be considered as equivalent to a regulated market if it complies with equivalent requirements to those established under Title III. The Commission shall publish a list of those markets that are to be considered as equivalent. This list shall be updated periodically, the service is provided at the initiative of the client or potential client; the client or potential client has been clearly informed that in the provision of this service the investment firm is not required to assess the suitability of the instrument or service provided or offered and that therefore he does not benefit from the corresponding protection of the relevant conduct of business rules; this warning may be provided in a standardised format, the investment firm complies with its obligations under Article 18. **(7.)** The investment firm shall establish a record that includes the document or documents agreed between the firm and the client that set out the rights and obligations of the parties, and the other terms on which the firm will provide services to the client. The rights and duties of the parties to the contract may be incorporated by reference to other documents or legal texts. **(8.)** The client must receive from the investment firm adequate reports on the service provided to its clients. These reports shall include, where applicable, the costs associated with the transactions and services undertaken on behalf of the client. **(9.)** In cases where an investment service is offered as part of a financial product which is already subject to other provisions of Community legislation or common European standards related to credit institutions and consumer credits with respect to risk assessment of clients and/or information requirements, this service shall not be additionally subject to the obligations set out in this Article. **(10.)** In order to ensure the necessary protection of investors and the uniform application of paragraphs 1 to 8, the Commission shall adopt, in accordance with the procedure referred to in Article 64(2), implementing measures to ensure that investment firms comply with the principles set out therein when providing investment or ancillary services to their clients. Those implementing measures shall take into account: (a) the nature of the service(s) offered or provided to the client or potential client, taking into account the type, object, size and frequency of the transactions; (b) the nature of the financial instruments being offered or considered; (c) the retail or professional nature of the client or potential clients."

These guidelines faithfully reflect the guidelines of the *International Organisation of Securities Commission* (IOSCO). Thus, the intermediary (or investment firm) must behave with diligence, correctness and transparency in the interests of the client and the integrity of the market; the investment firm must act in such a way as to keep the client *fully informed*; it must reduce the risk of a *conflict of interests* to a minimum; it must ensure the service is efficient; it must manage the business in an independent, careful way, to safeguard the interests of the clients. These are duties of diligence, correctness, transparency, and correct management which respond to the general need for the proper functioning of the market as a whole, and are not confined to a single relationship or the particular interests of the individual client.

The aim of the Community legislature is clear, since it is natural that a market which is regulated on the basis of principles which ensure proper functioning represents the fundamental element which attracts the trust of savers worldwide, ensuring them the satisfaction of their expectations.

There are other Directives which aim at harmonizing the safeguards offered to investors.

One of these is Dir. 2002/47 of June 6th 2002 on *financial collateral arrangements.*[117]

The Directive establishes a minimum uniform regime at Community level for financial instruments and cash, with the aim of limiting the credit risk in financial transactions, which is considered indispensable for sustaining the integration and stability of the markets and the efficiency of the EU's monetary policy, as well as protecting European investors.

As is explained in the Preamble, the Community legislation is intended to protect the validity of *financial collateral arrangements* (Italian: *contratti di garanzia finanziaria*, French: *contrats de garantie financiéré*, German: *Finanzsicherheiten*). In order to improve the legal certainty of financial collateral arrangements, Member States should ensure that certain provisions of insolvency law do not apply to such arrangements, in particular, those that would inhibit the effective realization of financial collateral or cast doubt on the validity of current techniques such as bilateral close-out netting, the provision of additional collateral in the form of top-up collateral and substitution of collateral.

*Financial collateral arrangement* means a title transfer financial collateral arrangement or a security financial collateral arrangement whether or not these are covered by a master agreement or general terms and conditions.

*Title transfer financial collateral arrangement* means an arrangement, including repurchase agreements, under which a collateral provider transfers full ownership of financial collateral to a collateral taker for the purpose of securing or otherwise covering the performance of relevant financial obligations.

---

[117] O.J., L 168, 06/27/2002, to be implemented before December 27th 2003.

*Security financial collateral arrangement* means an arrangement under which a collateral provider provides financial collateral by way of security in favor of, or to, a collateral taker, and where the full ownership of the financial collateral remains with the collateral provider when the security right is established.

The Directive applies when the collateral taker and the collateral provider come within one of the following categories: a public authority, a central bank, the European Central Bank, the Bank for International Settlements, a multilateral development bank, a financial institution subject to prudential supervision, an investment firm (as defined in Dir. 93/22, repealed), an insurance undertaking (as defined in Dir. 92/49), an undertaking for collective investment in transferable securities (UCITS), and a management company (as defined in Dir. 85/611 as amended), a central counterparty, settlement agent or clearing house, (as defined respectively in Dir. 98/26), including a person other than a natural person, and including unincorporated firms and partnerships.

In order to be protected, financial collateral agreements must be in writing or in another legally equivalent form.

Dir. 2002/47 introduces the right of use by the collateral taker of the rights under the guarantee. Rapid, non-bureaucratic execution processes, are provided under the Directive, to safeguard financial stability and limit knock-on effects in the case of non-fulfillment by one of the parties. The Directive also leaves the option open to the Member States to maintain or introduce into the national legal systems an *a posteriori* checking system, through courts, to determine whether the evaluation of the financial collateral has been carried out under reasonable commercial conditions.

To ensure reinforced protection for the consumer, Dir. 2002/65 concerning the distance marketing of consumer financial services and amending Dir. 90/619/EEC, 97/7/EC, and 98/27/EC,[118] was adopted within a few years of being proposed.

As may be seen from the preamble to the Directive, its aim is to provide a high level of protection to consumers that will encourage consumer confidence, facilitate the development of innovative methods of selling with the introduction of new technologies, encourage cross-border sales of financial services, and encourage competition and facilitate market integration.

With a view to ensuring reinforced protection for the consumer, the Directive establishes a fundamental rule which has an impact on the for-

---

[118] O.J., L 271, 10/09/2002, p. 16. Member States must implement it by October 9th 2004.

mation of the contract, indeed precisely to do with the acceptance of the contractual offer: the absence of a reply (to the use of automated calling systems without human intervention) should not amount to consent:

> **25th Whereas, Dir. 2002/65**: "Consumers should be protected against unsolicited services. Consumers should be exempt from any obligation in the case of unsolicited services, the absence of a reply not being construed as signifying consent on their part."

The scope of the Directive's application is established under arts. 1 and 2: the provisions are related to all contracts for the provision of banking, insurance, investment or payment services made between suppliers and consumers (acting outside their trade, business or profession) that are concluded under an organized distance sales process exclusively by means of distance communication (i.e., telephone, internet, or post).

The Directive is intended to offer "optimum protection" of the consumer by means of two instruments: *information* and the right to *withdraw*.

The Directive seeks to ensure that all consumers are provided with sufficient information to make informed decisions. The consumer must be supplied with specific information before the contract is entered into, including a description of the main characteristics of the service, the total price including any applicable taxes, the arrangements made in relation to payment, delivery, and performance of the contract, the length of time the offer will remain open and valid, any factors that may cause the contract price to vary between the time the information is given and the time the contract is concluded, sufficient information to allow the customer to verify the price at the time the contract is concluded, and information on how to cancel the contract and any out-of-court redress procedures.

Art. 6 also gives consumers the right of withdrawal from the contract within a period of time without indicating the reasons and without penalty (14 to 30 days depending on the type of service) from the date of the conclusion of the contract or from receipt by the customer of the necessary information. This right of withdrawal will not apply to certain contracts, such as foreign exchange contracts, receipt, transmission and execution of order of transferable securities, financial futures and options or exchange and interest rate instruments, non-life insurance for less than two months, mortgages and real estate credit when monies have already been transferred to the seller of the property under the consumer's instruction, or where the consumer has validly executed and recorded a notarial act relating the real estate credit.

Another Directive which aimed at harmonizing the safeguards offered to investors was Dir. 97/9 of March 3rd 1997 on investor-compensation schemes.[119] It was developed with the aim of harmonizing the safeguards offered to investors should the enterprise become *insolvent.* It harmonized the protection mechanisms in the case of the insolvency of the enterprise in which investors have placed their own funds, analogous to the guarantee provisions for savers' deposits. The Directive was intended to make investor and saver protection homogenous and in this way to safeguard the economic stability of the European financial system as a whole.

## 12. Harmonization of National Laws on Financial Services

With the implementation of the *Investment Services Directive* (ISD) no. 93/22, the Member States harmonized their own national legislation in an extremely sensitive sector—the capital markets. The national implementing acts eliminated barriers which had up until then been preventing access to foreign intermediaries in the national territory, ensuring that these could operate in regulated national markets. However, in the light of the amendments introduced in the European framework by Dir. 2004/39, the optimism of academic commentators and financial operators, who saw the maturing of financial legislation as the highest expression and point of arrival of a long and labored reorganization process of the regulatory discipline, has to be reconsidered. Likewise, some of the cardinal provisions making up the *common core* of the still feeble investors' protection measures will have to be looked at anew.

While awaiting the transposition of new Dir. 2004/39, let us look at some examples of harmonization with regard to the ISD.

The Italian legislative decree which implemented the ISD was no. 415 of July 23rd 1996.[120]

The decree reconstructed the national regime for the financial markets and the exercise of investment services, previously regulated by act

---

[119] O.J., L 84, 05/26/1997. The Directive was implemented in Italy by *Decreto ministeriale del 06/30/1998, approvazione dello statuto e del regolamento operativo del Fondo nazionale di garanzia per la tutela dei crediti vantati dai clienti nei confronti delle società di intermediazione mobiliare e degli altri soggetti autorizzati all'esercizio di attività di intermediazione mobiliare, Gazz. Uff , Serie gen.*, 07/10/1998, n. 159, p. 22; in France by *Loi n° 99-532 du 25 juin 1999 relative à l'épargne et à la sécurité financière*; in Belgium by *Loi du 12/17/1998 créant un fonds de protection des dépôts et des instruments financiers et réorganisant les systèmes de protection des dépôts et des instruments financiers, Moniteur belge*, 12/31/1998, p. 42104. No reference is available for Germany, Ireland, Sweden, and the UK.

[120] *D. lgs.* no. 415, of July 23rd 1996, which came into force on September 1st 1996.

no. 1/91 of January 2nd 1991, which established the *società di intermediazione mobiliare* (*SIM*), namely those companies, distinct from banks and financial intermediaries listed under art. 107 of the consolidated banking legislation (Italian: *Testo unico bancario*), authorized to offer investment services, with head offices and general management in Italy.

Later, as a result of the numerous acts, administrative regulations, and circulars issued to transpose Community legislation, the entire *SIM* regime was gathered together in the consolidated financial legislation (Italian: *Testo unico delle disposizioni in materia di intermediazione finanziaria— TUF*), approved by legislative decree of February 24th 1998,[121] which came into force on July 1st 1998.

Supervision of the financial markets is carried out on the one hand by the Bank of Italy, which is responsible for the containment of risk and the stability of capital, and on the other by the Companies and Exchange Regulatory Committee (*Commissione nazionale per le società e la borsa, CONSOB*), which supervises the transparency and correct conduct of financial intermediaries. The Bank of Italy and CONSOB act in a coordinated way in order to reduce the burdens on the financial intermediaries to a minimum, and they exchange information concerning the provisions applied and irregularities which have come to light in the course of the supervisory activity.

The French pattern, after the implementation of the ISD by act no. 96-597 *de modernisation des activités financiers*, is arranged as follows: both the banks and investment companies are bound by the prudential regulation adopted by the Committee for Banking and Financial Regulation (*Comitè de la réglementation bancaire et financière)* and are regulated by the Bank Commission (*Commission bancaire)*.[122] Supervision is exercised under the aegis of the Financial Markets Council (*Conseil des marchés financiers)*, while observance of the prudential regulation is under the control of the Exchange Regulatory Commission (*Commission des opérations de borse)*.

Under the German pattern, supervision is exercised by the Exchange Supervisory Authority, a department of the *Länder* (*Börsenaufsichtsbehörde*).[123] The most important duties of the Exchange Supervisory Authority are the supervision of the price formation processes, the investigation

---

[121] *Gazz. Uff.*, n. 71, 03/26/1998, *Suppl. Ord.* no. 52/L. Amended by *D.lgs.* 09/25/01 no. 351, which became act no. 410 of 09/23/01 (*Gazz.Uff.*, n. 274, 11/24/01). Amended by *D.lgs.* no. 247, 08/01/2003 (*Gazz. Uff.* n. 233, 10/07/2003).

[122] See Banking Act, *loi* 84-46 of January 24th 1984 as amended by the 1996 Act.

[123] See *BörsenG*, as modified in 1994.

of violations of the exchange rules and regulations, the development of fraud prevention, and the supervision of lawful conduct by the exchange bodies. The Authority is also in charge of the supervision of trading participants admitted to exchange trading. Furthermore the Authority participates in the field of legislation and exchange policy.

The most important foundations for the tasks of the Exchange Supervisory Authority are contained in the Exchange Act of 2000 (*Börsengesetz)*[124] and the regulatory frameworks for the exchanges, such as the Exchange Rules and the Sanction Committee Regulations (*Sanktionsausschussverordnung*).

In the UK, the classic point of reference is the 1986 Financial Services Act,[125] which established a functional type of supervisory model: investment companies must belong to one of the country's Self-Regulatory Organizations (SROs), which regulate not only market activities but also prudential matters. The Bank of England acts as a banking supervisor and requires four-monthly reports from each SRO on the observance of the prudential rules by the companies. Investment firms that are not directly supervised by the Bank of England come under the prudential requirements as imposed by each SRO, according to the core rules set by the Securities and Investment Board (SIB), and for those not affiliated to any SRO, to the rules set by thc SIB itself. The SIB formally changed its name to the Financial Services Authority (FSA) in October 1997.

The first stage of the reform of financial services regulation was completed in June 1998, when responsibility for banking supervision was transferred to the FSA from the Bank of England.

The Financial Services and Markets Act, which received Royal Assent in June 2000 and was implemented on December 1st 2001,[126] transferred to the FSA the responsibilities of several other organizations: Building Societies Commission; Friendly Societies Commission; existing Self-Regulating Organizations; Personal Investment Authority; Register of Friendly Societies; Securities and Futures Authority; the Securities and Investment Board (SIB); the Insurance Directorate of the Treasury; the Supervision and Surveillance Branch of the Bank of England.

In addition, the legislation gives FSA some new responsibilities: in particular, regulating certain aspects of mortgage lending and setting up, and monitoring compliance with, a Code of Market Conduct. The FSA is an independent non-governmental body, a company limited by guarantee and financed by the financial services industry. The FSA operates as

---

[124] As amended in 2002, in *BGBl* 06/21/2002, p. 2010.

[125] 1986 c. 60, which came into effect as of April 1988.

[126] 2000 Chapter c.8 (June 14th 2000). It replaced the Financial Services Act 1986.

the UK's sole, statutory, financial services regulator. Its regulatory objectives are market confidence, public awareness, the protection of consumers, and the reduction of financial crime. To achieve these objectives, the FSA must have regard to such generally accepted principles of good corporate governance, as it is reasonable to regard their applicability.

## 13. Harmonization of CEECs Legal Systems

Financial markets are considered to be the visible symbol of the vitality of an advanced capitalist economy. Their establishment in Eastern Europe marks the passage from the planned economy, namely the centralized system based on non-market practices which lasted for more than forty years, to the western capitalist model. This is why their starting-up and functioning are, from the political viewpoint too, of fundamental importance for the East European countries emerging from their experience of communism.

To this can be added the fact that the great privatizations carried out during the 1990's in all the CEECs have required the establishment of Stock Exchanges as one of the fundamental mechanisms to the increase capital liquidity of privatized companies, providing means of company valuation and enhancing corporate governance.

In short, all credit activity was completely centralized under the planned economy, managed by each country's Central Bank. The latter was merely an instrument of planning and administrative control, to ensure, through the local branch network, that enterprises maintained a balance between investment, wages, and the cost of labor. To sum up, therefore, the socialist system turned on a "mono-bank," directly controlled by the State, whose main aim was to finance the planned economy.

The system of payment was notable for a peculiar institution, of so-called *inter-company credit*. By means of this mechanism, the undertakings (not the banks) on the one hand granted credit to their client-enterprises, and on the other became debtors of their supplier-enterprises.

Because of this, a large part of the activity of the enterprise consisted in the indebtedness of other enterprises which, following a spiraling process, were in their turn connected to other companies in the same way. The settlement of each individual debit/credit relationship was therefore related to those of previous dealings, and it was not in any way possible to verify which firms had a positive balance sheet.

In other words, banking practices in the former communist countries were largely characterized by inefficiencies that took the form of large bad debts, preferential allocation of credit and distortionary pricing of loans.

As a consequence, the original mono-bank was broken down, resulting in a number of different state-owned banks, with a number of them privatized, which specialized on different products and operations. Moreover, a large number of private foreign banks were granted operating licenses. Allowing the entry of the foreign banks was to produce positive externalities to the sector as a whole due to foreign banks' know-how and expertise, which domestic banks were lacking.

However, early in the 1990's, when the proper post-communist transitional phase had begun, the banking and financial sectors were still typified by aspects of *path dependence*, which bound these sectors' practices to the experience under the communist planned economy.

> The expression "path dependency" refers to the theory that states that historical, ideological, and behavioral circumstances follow the path by which institutions are formed and thereby condition their present state. "*Although formal rules may change overnight as the result of political or judicial decisions, informal constraints embodied in customs, traditions, and codes of conduct are much more impervious to deliberate policies" (D. North). Cf.* also chapter I, §11.2.

One could cite as an example the phenomenon of the *cross-ownership* between financial institutions and privatized companies. When the State enterprises were privatized and the two-tier banking system was introduced, the credit institutions often found themselves the owners of large numbers of shares in the privatized companies, operating a conversion of the company's debts into direct investments. However, the large enterprises were themselves shareholders in the banks, and so, in their role as shareholders these enterprises were able to insist on more favorable conditions for loans with respect to other clients, although this was in conflict with the true interests of the efficiency of banking management.

Given the rarity of a significant foreign banking presence, discouraged by an unfamiliar economic environment and the lack of domestic capital injection, the reform of the banking/financial sector was obliged to make only intermittent progress. The abuses and risks which threatened the growth of the financial markets could be summarized as follows:

- Fraud and insider trading.
- Monopolistic conduct.
- High-risk and uncalculated investment strategies.
- Lack of corporate governance.

---

[127] See in particular the Commission White Paper (1995): *cf.* chapter III, in the first volume of this *Guide, A Commom Law for Europe*.

For all these reasons, according to the Community institutions[127] it was first of all advisable to create an efficient banking system, which provided for the conversion of private savings into loans to the companies at market rates, alongside an efficient payment system and the establishment of collective investment or mutual funds.

Let us proceed to a rapid review of the features which characterize the reforms in this sector in some of the CEECs.

So far as the banking system is concerned, despite a reference model, namely the Community one (essentially based on the directives analyzed in the preceding paragraphs), the legislative choices of the countries in question are notable for a certain degree of heterogeneity.

In fact, the international experts who have offered (and continue to offer) advice and consultation to these countries have proposed the following:

- The state controlled French banking model.
- The American system of small and competitive banks, whose functions of commercial banking and investment banking are divided between entities.
- The German model of universal banks, according to which banks are closely related to industrial groups.

However, from among the characteristics common to the reform of these legal systems, in general we can recognize the introduction of a *two-tier banking system*, in which the Central bank of each country represents the first tier and the other financial institutions belong to the second tier.

The Central banks obtained considerable independence during the 1990's, on the model of the German *Bundesbank*. The objective was to respond to a two-fold need: to reduce the hyperinflation generated by the liberalization of prices and to some extent guarantee the credibility of company reform *vis-à-vis* the international financial community.

In four countries—the Czech Republic, Hungary, Estonia and Poland—the principle of the independence of the Central Bank, including its functions and its institutional structure, have been specifically laid down in the Constitution: respectively articles 98 Czech Constitution, 32 Hungarian Constitution, 111 Estonian Constitution, and 227 Polish Constitution.

In Bulgaria and the Slovakia, the Central Bank is only mentioned in the Constitution (art. 84 Bulgarian Constitution, art. 56 Constitution of Slovakia), but there are no rules which concern its functions or institutional set-up, whereas in the Romanian Constitution it is not mentioned at all. Safeguarding the independence of the Central banks by securing it in the Constitution is important in the case of a conflict with other organs of State, both in relation to the possibility of the latter influencing monetary policy, and to compromising the financial independence of the Bank itself.

### *13.1. Banking and Financial Services*

The adoption of the Community *acquis* in the banking, financial, and insurance sectors was later added to these initial objectives, with a view to accession to the EU.

In Poland, the first non state-owned bank, the *Bank Rozwoju Eksportu SA*, was founded in 1986, and the Program for strengthening the currency in 1987 introduced the two-tier banking system.

In 1989, the National Bank of Poland Act[128] established the National Bank of Poland as the central bank and has overseen the creation of nine independent regional banks, which subsequently were privatized and joined by a number of new private banks in the 1990's.

In the meantime, new legislation was introduced to allow private individuals, both Poles and foreigners, to form banks as limited stock companies.

Between 1989 and 1991, a total of seventy licenses were issued to private banks, including seven banks funded by foreign capital, two cooperative banks, and three branches of foreign banks. In October 1991, privatization of the Export Development Bank began, and the nine state commercial banks (which until that time still operated as they had under the old NBP) were transformed into limited stock companies. The State Treasury owned the banks for an intermediate period while they prepared for privatization.

Following its accession to the European Union, Poland is implementing reforms to deregulate, increase transparency, and promote competition, but these reforms remain as work in progress. The banking sector has been almost completely privatized, with 75% of the assets owned by foreign institutions. The controlling body is the General Inspectorate of Banking Supervision, whose statute was laid down on August 29th 1997, when the Act on the National Bank of Poland was passed.[129] It constitutes the executive agency of the Commission for Banking Supervision; as such, it is responsible for supervising the operations of the banks to ensure the safety of the deposits held by them and the stability of the banking system as a whole, while at the same time guaranteeing the banks sufficient freedom and flexibility in taking business decisions,

[128] Published in Polish Journal of Laws (*Dziennik Ustaw or Dz. U.*) of 1989, no. 4.
[129] Published in *Dz. U.* of 1997 no. 140, item 938.

along with a level playing field regarding the basic financial parameters of their participation in financial markets.

The new Banking Act was passed on August 29th 1997.[130] The Act specifies the principles applicable in conducting the business of banking, establishing and organizing banks, including branches and representative offices of foreign banks, and branches of credit institutions, and also the principles applicable to the performance of banking supervision, rehabilitation proceedings, and bank liquidations and bankruptcies. By art. 2 of the Banking Act, a bank shall constitute a legal person, established pursuant to the provisions of statute, operating on the basis of authorization to conduct banking operations that expose to risk funds which have been entrusted to the bank and which are in any way repayable.

In early 1991, important legislation, such as the Act on Public Trading, was also introduced to regulate securities transactions and establish a Stock Exchange in Warsaw (which was established for the first time in the 18th century).

At the same time, a Securities Commission was formed for fair competition and consumer protection. Restructuring the financial market was not only necessary for increasing the overall efficiency of the economy and accelerating privatization, but also was a precondition for the rapid influx of Western capital, critical to economic development. During the 1990s' the Stock Exchange Court was set up, acting more as a disciplinary body than as an arbitration panel, imposing fines on those companies which do not comply with the rules of the Stock exchange.

Recently, given the lack of effectiveness of the judgments of the Court against malpractices, the Polish legislature is modifying the functions and objectives of this Court, following the German model. The non-observance of the duty to disclose, or in other words, the diffusion of false information is to be made public (the Court acts through reprimands).

In 1997, the Act on Public Trading in Securities[131] regulated public trading in securities, including principles for the creation, organization, and supervision of entities conducting public trading in securities activities.

In 1993, the Act on the National Investment Funds and their Privatization[132] has set out principles for the establishment, operation, and privatization of national investment funds.

---

[130] Published in *Dz. U.* of 2002 no. 72, item 665. As amended by Art. 1, sub (1), of the Act Amending the Banking Act and other Legislation of August 23rd 2001 (as published in *Dz. U.* no. 111/2001, item 1195, which took effect on January 7th 2002).

[131] Published in *Dz. U.* of 1997, No. 118, item 754 dated October 3rd 1997.

[132] Published in *Dz. U.* of 1993, No. 44, item 202, dated May 31st 1993 (as later amended: No. 84 of 1994, item 385; No. 30 of 1997, item 164; No. 47, item 298).

In Hungary, the 1989 legislation (later amended in 1997) and the 1991 Banking Act (later amended in 1996) introduced the two-tier banking system which, in the European Commission's view, is based on Community requirements.[133]

A crucial point is the ownership structure of banks: the Banking Act has reduced state ownership in all the banks (with the exception of the National Savings Bank) to a level of less than 25%; according to the Banking Act, no entity (natural person or legal entity) may acquire more than 15% of the subscribed capital or the voting rights of a bank with the exception of the Hungarian State, other credit institutions, insurance companies, investment companies, and the National Deposit Insurance Fund.

With regard to the Community *acquis*, harmonization seems therefore to be complete so far as the first Directive on the activity of credit institutions, the own-funds Directive and the money-laundering Directive are concerned, and on large loans. Supervision of the whole sector is under the control of the State Financial and Capital Market Supervisory Board.

As regards stock exchanges and markets, a Commodities and Stock Exchange first opened in Budapest in 1864, and continued in its operation until 1948. In fact before World War II, Budapest was one of the major financial centers of the CEECs.

In 1990, with the Securities and Stock Exchange Act (Act VI), the Budapest Stock Exchange was reopened and became subject to a new regulatory framework: it is a self-regulating, non-profit organization, following the "open outcry" trading system. The executive body of the stock exchange, the Council of the Stock Exchange, manages the business, formulates the rules, and creates and controls the structures of the market under the supervision of the Supervisory Board of Securities. The Board is a State-administration body authorized to supervise public issues and brokerage of securities, and stock exchange transactions; it operates under the supervision of the Minister of Finance, who defines its structure and rules of procedure.

New rules on financial services capital markets and securities were enacted at the end of 1996 (Acts, CXI, CXII, CXIV of 1996): dematerialized securities have been admitted, the position of commercial banks has been changed, and rules on insider trading have been amended. The notion of financial institutions has been redefined: only companies limited by shares satisfying special requirements can function as a bank and only banks are entitled to take deposits (in addition some co-operatives). The Law on Investment Funds was enacted in 1991 (Act LXIII) and a

[133] See Commission Opinion COM(97) 2001 final.

new regulation enacted in 1993 enabled the first non-state pension funds to be established.

The Czech Republic passed the Banking Act in 1992,[134] when Czechoslovakia was still a federal State; the Securities Act[135] was enacted the same year, which regulated the new 'contracts on securities' and guaranteed the protection of the financial market.

The Czech National Bank Act[136] was enacted in 1993 (its counterpart in the Slovak Republic is the Act on the National Bank of Slovakia),[137] which determined the functions and management structure of the Central Bank. Conditions for access for foreign banks were considered "generally compatible with the first and second Directives on banking services."[138] The lack of conformity with Community legislation concerns another aspect, in relation to the deposit guarantee system, the adequacy of capital and consolidated supervision.

With regards to share trading, the Stock Exchange Act was enacted in 1992:[139] this established that the "stock exchange must be organized as a joint stock company, governed by the provisions of the Commercial Code,[140] apart from the exceptions stipulated in this Act" (Part one, Section 1, [3]).

The Investment Companies and Investment Funds Act was also passed in the same year.[141] The investment company may operate as a joint stock company or a limited liability company; an investment fund must have the legal form of a joint stock company (Part one, Section 2, [2 & 3]).

The Act further provides that an investment company accumulates capital through the sale of "participation certificates," from which it creates unit trusts (which are not legal entities). The unit trust assets are the joint property of holders of participation certificates, which do not carry voting rights. (Part one, Section 5 [1 & 2] and Section 11). The provisions of the Civil Code on co-ownership shall not apply to unit trust assets.

Because of its mixed provisions, transplanted from both civil and common law systems (as the provisions on unit trusts, an institution which is widespread throughout the Anglo–American world demonstrate), the

---

134 No. 21/1992 *Coll.*

135 No. 591/1992 *Coll.*

136 No. 6/1993 *Coll.*, subsequently amended.

137 No. 566/1992 *Coll.*, subsequently amended.

138 See Commission Opinion COM (97) 2009 final.

139 No. 124/1992 *Coll.*, as amended.

140 Sections 154 to 220 of the Commercial Code (no. 513/1991 *Coll.*)

141 No. 248/1992 *Coll.*, as amended.

Act has not been very warmly welcomed, so much so that legislative intervention was called for.

The legal framework and financial infrastructures are more fragile in other countries in the region. In Bulgaria, for example, a two-tier banking system was introduced in 1989, but a legal framework for this system was only established in 1992. Banking supervision has developed slowly, although new rules on capital adequacy and liquidity were introduced in 1993; however, these remained poorly enforced. A new Act was enacted in 1998, which reorganized the activity and functions of the Central Bank, called the Act on Reorganization of the State Savings Bank:[142] the State Savings Bank is reorganized into a commercial bank, acting under the rules of the Law on Banks. The State, represented by the Council of Ministers, is the sole shareholder of the Bank.

Also in 1998, the Act on Bank Deposit Guarantee[143] was enacted. This Act is applicable to all banks which have been given permission to accept deposits under the provisions of the laws. It is also applicable to branches of foreign banks in Bulgaria, provided that in the country of residence of the bank, either no bank deposit guarantee system exists, or the existing system guarantees a smaller rate of deposits than the rates guaranteed by this Act, or the existing systems does not cover the branches of the bank abroad.

As far as stock markets and exchanges are concerned, in 1994 there were two main functioning stock exchanges: the First Bulgarian Stock Exchange and the Sofia Stock Exchange. The Securities, Stock Exchanges and Investment Companies Act was adopted in July 1995 to consolidate the stock exchanges. It is intended to take into consideration the major EU securities legislation. Specifically, the introductory report of the Minister of Justice to the Cabinet refers to a number of directives to show how this framework is directly relevant to Bulgaria, even if it does not mean the EU legislation was, in fact, implemented. Among its provisions, the Act defines securities, including traded securities, dematerialized securities, investment contracts, and public offerings; provides provisions dealing with corporate control, including transfers, proxy issues, and tender offers; establishes stock exchange licensing mechanism and responsibilities; regulates investment intermediaries, including banks; establishes the Commission on Securities and Stock Exchange, which is responsible for both market regulation and development.

---

[142] State Gazette no. 48 of April 28th 1998.

[143] State Gazette no. 49 of April 29th 1998.

Moreover, the Act provides certain self-enforcing remedies to investors due to violations of certain securities laws, in addition to traditional criminal penalties and administrative enforcement efforts. The latest amendment to the legal framework is the Act for alteration and amendment of the Securities, Stock-Exchange Markets and Investment Companies Act,[144] which introduced, defined, and regulated the status of a "public company" and of the shares emitted by such a company (section IV, in Chapter 7 of the Act).

In the sector of non-bank financial intermediaries, new pension fund institutions have been formed, but according the EBRD[145] they remain weak. An act regulating investment funds was adopted in June 1995, and Privatization Investment Funds have begun operating under the Mass Privatization Scheme launched in 1996.

The Baltic States—Estonia, Latvia, and Lithuania—have all suffered serious bank collapses, due not only to 'bad loans' problems resulting from the traditional mono-bank practices (in particular, the funding of current expenditure and losses in state-owned enterprises in the form of bank loans, which were extremely unlikely ever to be repaid), but also to rapid creation of new banks, followed by subsequent restructuring.

However, recent legal reforms have brought the legislation in these countries into line with the Community provisions in the areas of banking, insurance, and finance.

Let us take, as an example, the case of Estonia.

The Credit Institutions Act was passed on February 9th 1999.[146] This Act provides the legal bases for the foundation, activities, and dissolution of credit institutions and the principles and legal bases for the supervision of credit institutions. It applies to all credit institutions founded or operating in Estonia and to parent companies, subsidiaries, branches, and representative offices thereof which are located in Estonia. This Act also applies to subsidiaries, branches, and representative offices of Estonian credit institutions in foreign states, unless otherwise prescribed by the legislation of the host country, and to subsidiaries, branches, and representative offices of foreign credit institutions in Estonia, unless oth-

---

144 State Gazette no. 42 of April 14th 1998.

145 On the EBRD see chapter III, in the first volume of this *Guide, A Commom Law for Europe*.

146 See the State Gazette (*Riigi Teataja* or *RT*) I 1999, 23, 349; consolidated text in *RT* I 2002, 17, 96; it entered into force July 1st 1999, amended by the following Acts: 06/19/2002 entered into force 09/01/2002 – *RT* I 2002, 63, 387; 06/05/2002 entered into force 07/01/2002 – *RT* I 2002, 53, 336; 02/20/2002 entered into force 07/01/2002 – *RT* I 2002, 23, 131; 01/29/2002 entered into force 03/04/2002 – *RT* I 2002, 21, 117.

erwise provided by international agreements entered into by Estonia. The Act defines the credit institution: a credit institution is a company the principal and permanent activity of which is to receive cash deposits and other repayable funds from the public and to grant loans for its own account and provide other financing. Credit institutions may operate as public limited companies or associations and the provisions of law regarding public limited companies or savings and loan associations, apply thereto unless otherwise provided by this Act. The Bank of Estonia is not deemed to be a credit institution.

The license to pursue the activity is granted (or revoked) by the 'Committee for Activity Licenses of Professional Securities Market Participants, Management Companies and Pension Management Companies,' under the control of the Ministry of Finance. The working procedures of this Committee have been amended more than once (in 1999 and 2000). These Working Procedures determine the activity license of professional securities market participants, management companies, and pension management companies,[147] and also provide, among other things, the procedure and forms for submission of information to the Committee and for submission of all the documents upon application for such activity licenses (i.e. copies of the memorandum of association and valid articles of association of the company; extract from the registry card of the commercial register; information on members of the supervisory board and management board, the management, and other responsible persons connected with the area of activity; information on the securities specialist, a copy of his or her certificate of qualification and an extract of the contract of employment).

The financial services sector is regulated by the following acts: the Investment Funds Act,[148] the Funded Pensions Act,[149] the Securities Market Act,[150] the Motor Third Party Liability Insurance Act,[151] the Estonian Central Register of Securities Act.[152]

As in all other countries,[153] the elements of imbalance in the bank–

[147] Pursuant to subsection 19 (4) of the Investment Funds Act (*RT* I 1997, 34, 535; 1998, 61, 979), subsections 5 (2) and 6 (6) of the Pension Funds Act (*RT* I 1998, 61, 979), subsection 18 (2) of the Securities Market Act (*RT* I 1993, 35, 543; 1996, 26, 528; 1997, 34, 535; 1998, 61, 979).

[148] *RT* I 1997, 34, 535; 1998, 61, 979; 2000, 10, 55; 57, 373; 2001, 48, 268; 79, 480; 89, 532; 93, 565; 2002, 23, 131.

[149] *RT* I 2001, 79, 480; 2002, 23, 131.

[150] *RT* I 2001, 89, 532; 2002, 23, 131.

[151] *RT* I 2001, 43, 238.

[152] *RT* I 2000, 57, 373; 2001, 48, 268; 79, 480; 89, 532; 93, 565; 2002, 23, 131.

[153] We have seen the case of Italy at § 7 of this chapter.

client relationship are in particular clearly demonstrated by the use of general contract terms unilaterally prepared by the credit institution and specifically approved in writing by the client. It follows that Estonian legislature also transposed what was expressly provided in Directive no. 93/13. Thus, the new Estonian national contract law allows certain exceptions precisely for the financial services sector: indeed, in June 2002 the Law of Obligations Act[154] was passed.

This Act, which has introduced a new definition of *obligation*[155] into the Estonian legal system, has transposed the Community *acquis* on consumer contracts (chapter I above), most evidently in the area of invalidity of unfair standard terms.

Clause 43 of the Act deals with credit institutions and supplier of financial services:

> **Estonian Law of Obligations Act** (**§ 43**): "(1) The terms specified in clause 42 (3) 14) of this Act is not deemed to be unfair for the other party if a credit institution or other supplier of financial services reserves the right under the standard terms to alter, with good reason and without advance notice, the rate of interest or other charge for financial services to be paid by the other party or to the other party, on the condition that the credit institution or other supplier of financial services is required to immediately inform the other party or other parties of such alteration and that the other parties have the right to terminate the contract immediately. (2) The terms specified in clause 42 (3) 14) of this Act is not deemed to cause unfair harm to the other party if a credit institution or other supplier of financial services reserves the right under the standard terms to unilaterally alter the terms of a long-term contract without a good reason specified in the contract if alteration of the terms is not unfair with regard to the other party and if the credit institution or other supplier of financial services undertakes to give advance notice to the other party of any alteration of the terms and to grant the other party the right to terminate the contract immediately."

---

[154] It entered into force 07/01/2002 – *RT* I 2002, 53, 336. See also above chapter I, § 11.2.

[155] *Cf.* § 2 of the Estonian Act: Definition of obligation: (1) An obligation is a legal relationship which gives rise to the obligation of one person (obligated person or obligor) to perform an act or omission (perform an obligation) for the benefit of another person (entitled person or obligee), and to the right of the obligee to demand that the obligor perform the obligation. (2) The nature of an obligation may oblige the parties to the obligation to take the other party's rights and interests into account in a certain manner. An obligation may also be confined thereto.

> "(§ **42(3)14**). Invalidity of standard terms: (3) In a contract where the other party is a consumer, a standard term is considered to be unfair if, in particular, the term:
>
> – 14) prescribes the right of the person supplying the term to alter the terms or conditions of the contract unilaterally for a reason or in a manner not provided by law or specified in the contract (…)."

Clause 58 of the Act also concerns rules relating to financial services:

> (§ **58**) "In the case of withdrawal from a contract for the provision of financial services, particularly investment, banking, insurance and securities transactions and services, the consumer may be required to compensate for the price of the financial services actually provided by the supplier if the price was predetermined by the supplier before entry into the contract. If the price was not predetermined by the supplier before entry into the contract, the consumer may be required to pay such part of the price of the financial services which were the object of the contract which corresponds to the period of time between entry into the contract and withdrawal from the contract."

In Slovenia, too, the legislative framework has undergone a second wave of reform, to bring the national legislation closer to the parameters required by Brussels. The Bank of Slovenia Act 1991 has been substituted by the Bank of Slovenia Act 2002, which has introduced the new *status* of the Central Bank of Slovenia.[156]

The Banking Act[157] was passed in 1999: it regulates the conditions for the establishing, operation, supervision and winding-up of banks and savings banks. According to the Act, a bank is a joint-stock company with a head office in the Republic of Slovenia, that has obtained an authorization from the Bank of Slovenia to provide banking services. The provisions of the Act on Commercial Companies that apply to joint-stock companies shall apply to banks, unless stipulated otherwise by the present law (art. 14).

Art. 3 defines which of those among financial services are to be treated as banking services:

- –Reception of deposits from legal and natural persons and granting credits from these resources for its own account.
- – Services that any other law stipulates may be provided only by banks.

---

[156] Respectively in Official Gazette the Republic of Slovenia, no. 1/91-I and in Official Gazette no. 58/02.

[157] Official Gazette of the Republic of Slovenia, no. 7/99 on February 5th 1999.

The deposits specified in the first point shall consist of a payment of money or other repayable resources, on the basis of which the depositor acquires the right to repayment by specific deadlines of the resources paid in.

According to this Act, other financial services are the following: factoring; financial leasing; issuing of guarantees and other commitments; lending, including consumer credits, mortgage credits, and financing of commercial transactions; trading in foreign means of payment, including foreign exchange transactions; trading in financial derivatives; collection, analysis and provision of information on the credit-worthiness of legal persons; mediation in sales of insurance policies, in accordance with the law governing the insurance sector; issuing and administering means of payment (e.g., debit and credit cards, travelers' checks, bankers' drafts); safe custody services; mediation in the conclusion of loan and credit transactions; services in connection with securities, in accordance with the law governing the securities market; administering pension or investment funds in accordance with the law governing pension and investment funds; performance of payment transactions. A bank may provide for these other financial services if it obtains an authorization from the Bank of Slovenia and if it fulfils the conditions stipulated by the law governing the particular services.

The adoption of the Community *acquis* for the purposes of accession has led to the adoption of the Regulation on Capital Adequacy of Banks and Savings Banks, which came into force on June 30th 2002, and of the Act on the Prevention of Money Laundering, entered into force October 25th 2001.[158]

## 13.2. Insurance Services

In Poland, the insurance system was reorganized in July 1990 with the Act on transacting the business of insurance in Poland.[159] The monopoly of the State Insurance Company (which had been responsible for all domestic insurance) was abolished, and also the Insurance and Reinsurance Company, which had been responsible for all foreign transactions, was abolished.

---

[158] Changes and Amendments in Official Gazette of the Republic of Slovenia no. 59/2002, published on July 5th 2002, entered into force July 25th 2002.

[159] Published in *Dz. U.* of 1991 No. 59, item 344, of 1993 No. 5, item 27; No. 44, item 201; of 1994 No. 4, item 17; No. 121, item 591; of 1995 No. 96, item 478; No. 118, item 574; of 1997 No. 43, item 272; No. 88, item 554; No. 107, item 685; No. 121, item 770.

Domestic and foreign-owned private limited stock and mutual insurance companies were then allowed to begin operating. At the same time, procedures were introduced to maintain adequate financial reserves and legal protection for people and assets insured. This Act lays down general provisions and principles of undertaking and carrying on the business of insurance against loss or damage and insurance of persons. Direct and indirect (re-insurance) insurance business may be carried on only upon a permit granted by the Minister of Finance.

Hungarian domestic insurance companies were among the first to be privatized, and foreign companies have successfully established themselves in Hungarian insurance sector since the early 1990's. An important step was taken with Act XCVI of 1995, which formulated the new regulation of insurance and new rules on the Board of Insurance Supervision. The 1996 Banking Act provides that banks may also perform insurance agency activities in accordance with the provisions of Act XCVI of 1995 on Insurance Companies and Insurance Activities (the Insurance Act).

In the Czech Republic, the insurance sector was regulated for the first time under free market conditions by the Insurance Act of 1991.[160] An insurance company may be established as a state enterprise, a joint stock company, a co-operative or a co-operative enterprise. Licenses for the pursuit of insurance business and supervision of the sector are delegated to the Ministry of Finance of the Czech Republic.

The Bulgarian private insurance sector is developing partly with support from the EBRD. In 1999, the Act on amendment of the Law on Insurance[161] was enacted, together with the Regulation on Insurance Brokers and Insurance Agents.[162]

In Estonia, the new Insurance Activities Act was passed on June 6th 2000.[163] This Act regulates insurance activities and supervision thereof. For the purposes of this Act, the following are insurance activities:

---

160 No. 185/1991 *Coll.*, as amended.

161 *S.G.* 88/99.

162 *S.G.* 111/99.

163 *RT* I 2000, 53, 343. It entered into force August 1st 2000 (later amended by the following Acts: 06/19/2002 entered into force 09/01/2002—*RT* I 2002, 63, 387; 03/27/2002 entered into force 06/01/2002—*RT* I 2002, 35, 215; 12/04/2002 entered into force 02/01/2002—*RT* I 2001, 93, 565; 10/24/2001 entered into force 11/09/2001—*RT* I 2001, 87, 529; 06/13/2001 entered into force 01/01/2002—*RT* I 2001, 59, 359; 05/09/2001 entered into force 01/01/2002—*RT* I 2001, 48, 268; 04/10/2001 entered into force 06/01/2001—*RT* I 2001, 43, 238).

This Act stands alongside the Insurance Act (*RT* 1992, 48, 601), later amended by other laws: (*RT* I 1995, 26–28, 355; 1996, 23, 455; 40, 773; 1998, 61, 979; 1999, 10, 155; 27, 389; 2000, 53, 343; 2001, 43, 238; 48, 268; 79, 480).

–Activities aimed at the conclusion or maintenance in force of insurance contracts or reinsurance contracts.
–Consultations relating to insurance contracts, except legal counseling by natural persons.
–Intermediation of the conclusion of insurance contracts.
–Maintenance, preservation, investment or lease of its property by an insurer or the purposes of insurance activities.
–Acts arising from insurance contracts, including acquisition, possession and transfer of property damaged in insured events.

An activity license is issued by a decision of the management board of the Financial Supervision Authority.[164] This Supervision Authority is an agency with autonomous competence and a separate budget, which operates at the Bank of Estonia and the directing bodies of which act and submit reports pursuant to the procedure provided for in this Act.

The Minister of Finance and the President of the Bank of Estonia are members of the supervisory board by virtue of office. One-half of the appointed members of the supervisory board shall be appointed and removed by the Government of the Republic on the proposal of the Minister of Finance and one-half by the Board of the Bank of Estonia on the proposal of the President of the Bank of Estonia.

---

[164] The Financial Supervision Authority Act passed May 9th 2001 (*RT1* I 2001, 48, 267), and entered into force June 1st 2001 (as amended in 2002).

# Bibliography Chapter III

## *Selected Commentary/Books/Articles:*

**§ *In English:***

PANOURGIAS L., *Banking Regulation and World Trade Law: GATS, EU and Prudential Institution-building,* Oxford, Hart Publishing, 2004; AVGERINOS Y.V., *Regulating and Supervising Investment Services in the European Union,* Basingstoke Hampshire, Palgrave, 2003; DUTZLER B., *The European System of Central Banks: An Autonomous Actor? The Quest for an Institutional Balance in EMU,* Vienna, Springer, 2003; SEATZU F., *Insurance in Private International Law, A European Perspective,* Oxford, Hart Publishing, 2003; ANDENAS M. & W.-H. ROTH (eds.), *Services and Free Movement in EU Law,* Oxford, University Press, 2002; USHER J., *The Law of Money and Financial Services in the EC,* Oxford Univ. Press., 2nd ed., 2000; CRANSTON R. (eds.), *European Banking Law, The Banker–Customer relationship,* 2nd ed., London, 1999; ID., *The Single Market and the Law of Banking,* 2nd ed., 1995; FERRARINI G., *European Securities Markets—The Investment Services Directive and Beyond,* London, 1998; ID. (ed.), *Prudential regulation of Banks and Securities Firms, European and International Aspects,* London, 1995; REIFNER, U., *Harmonisation of cost elements of the annual percentage rate of charge, APR,* Hamburg 1998; R. M. MERKIN, A. RODGER, *European Community Insurance Law,* Longman, 1997; LEA, M.J., WELTER, R., DÜBEL, A., *Study on the mortgage credit in the European Economic Area. Structure of the sector and application of the rules in the directives 87/102 and 90/88.* Final Report 1996; SECKELMANN R., *Methods of calculation, in the European Economic Area, of the annual percentage rate of charge,* Final Report 31 October 1995; J. ROTOWSKI (ed.), *Banking Reform in Central Europe and the Former Soviet Union,* Budapest, 1995; Czech Financial Services Legislation in 1995, *Banking, Foreign Exchange, Investment and Insurance,* ed. Trade Links, Prague, 1995; EDWARDS, K. FISHER, *Banks, Finance and Investment in Germany,* Cambridge Univ. Press, 1994; EECKHOUT P., *The European Internal Market and International trade,* Oxford Univ. Press, 1994; J. NORTON ET AL. (eds.), *International Banking Regulation and Supervision: Change and Transformation in the 1990s,* Graham & Trotman, Martinus Nijhoff Publishers, 1994; E. KARAILIEV, I. PETKOVA, *Removing the Financial System in Central and Eastern Europe,* in D. E. FAIR AND R. J. RAYMOND (eds.), *The New Europe: Evolving Economic and Financial Systems in East and West,* Dordrecht/Boston/London, 1993; R. M. BUXBAUM, K. J. *HOPT, Legal Harmonization and the Business Enterprise,* Berlin–New York, 1988.

**§ *In German:***

RÜHL G., *Obliegenheiten im Versicherungsvertragsrecht: auf dem Weg zum europäischen Binnenmarkt für Versicherungen,* Tübingen, 2004; SCHWINTOWSKY H.P, SCHÄFER F.A., *Bankrecht,* 2 Aufl., 2004; EKKENGA J., HADDING W., HAMMEN H.., *Bankrecht und Kapitalmarktrecht in der Entwicklung, Festschrift für Siegfried Kümpel zum 70. Geburtstag,* 2003; KRIEGNER J., *Die Fernabsatz-Richtlinie für Finanzdienstleistungen an Verbraucher,* Linz, 2003; VAN DE SANDE C., *Die Unternehmensgruppe im Banken- und Versicherungsaufsichtsrecht: eine Untersuchung zu den bank- und versicherungsaufsichtsrechtlichen Rahmenbedingungen der Gruppenbildung und Gruppenleitung im Finanzdienstleistungssektor,* Baden–Baden, 2003; BASEDOW J., *Verbraucherschutz durch und im Internet bei Abschluss von privaten Versicherungsverträgen: Altersvorsorgeverträge;* Baden–Baden, 2003; FENYVES A., KOBAN K., SCHAUER M., *Die Versicherungsvermittlungs-*

*Richtlinie: Umsetzung in das österreichische Recht*, Wien, 2003; CLAUSSEN, *Bank- und Börsenrecht*, 2nd ed., München 2002; SCHIMIKOWSKI, *Versicherungsvertragsrecht*, München 2001; KÜMPEL, *Bank- und Kapitalmarktrecht*, 2nd ed., 2000; HONSELL, HEINRICH, *Berliner Kommentar zum Versicherungsvertragsgesetz*, Berlin, 1999; SCHIMANSKYBUNTE, LWOWSKI, *Bankrechtshandbuch*, München, 1997.

***§ In Italian:***

MALATESTA A. L., *Unione monetaria, Banca centrale europea e allargamento dell'Unione europea,* Castellanza, Libero Istituto Universitario Carlo Cattaneo, 2004; SARTORI F., *Le regole di condotta degli intermediari fimanziani,* Milano, 2004; ANNUZIATA F., La disciplina del mercato mobiliare, *Torino, 2003;* MALATESTA A., *Gli aspetti istituzionali della banca centrale della Comunità europea,* Milano, 2003; ALPA G., CAPRIGLIONE F, *Diritto bancario comunitario,* Torino, 2002; AFFERNI V., *I servizi assicurativi,* in TIZZANO (ed.), *Il diritto privato dell'Unione europea,* in BESSONE, *Trattato di Diritto Privato,* vol. I, Torino, 2000, 421; PARTESOTTI-RICOLFI (ed.), *La nuova disciplina dell'impresa di assicurazione sulla vita in attuazione della terza direttiva,* Padova, 2000; PIVA A., *Assicurazioni,* in CHITI-GRECO (eds.), *Trattato di diritto amministrativo europeo, Parte speciale, vol.* I, Milano, 1997, 299; CORVESE C., *L'attuazione delle terze direttive CEE in materia di assicurazioni vita e danni,* Padova, 1997; ALPA G., *La "trasparenza" del contratto nei settori bancario, finanziario e assicurativo, Scritti in onore di PREDIERI A.,* Milano, 1996, 1; BUSNELLI F.D., *Fondamento costituzionale e linee di tendenza di uno "Statuto dei diritti del risparmiatore", in Scritti in onore di A. PREDIERI A.,* Milano, 207; CANDIAN A. D., *Il contratto di tutela giudiziaria, in I contratti del commercio, dell'industria e del mercato finanziario,* GALGANO F. (ed.) *Trattato,* vol. III, Torino 1995, 2645; GODANO G., *Le banche,* in TIZZANO (ed.), *Il diritto privato dell'Unione europea,* in BESSONE, *Trattato di Diritto Privato,* vol. I, Torino, 2000, 315; CRISOSTOMO M., *Le banche e le imprese di investimento,* in LIPARI (ed.) *Diritto Privato Europeo,* Padova 1997, 290; PUTTI P.M., *I fondi comuni di investimento,* in LIPARI (ed.), *Diritto Privato Europeo,* Padova, 1997, vol. I, 362; MACARIO F., *Il credito al consumo,* in LIPARI (ed.), *Diritto Privato Europeo,* Padova 1997, 827; CAPRIGLIONE F. (ed.), *Disciplina delle banche e degli intermediari finanziari,* Padova, 1995; GORGONI M., *Il credito al consumo,* Milano, 1994; PARDOLESI R., SQUILLACE N. (eds.), *Disciplina del credito al consumo,* Milano, 1993.

***§ In French:***

BRUCHER J., THIELTGEN N., *Le consommateur et sa banque: l'évolution depuis 1993 de la protection juridique du consommateur dans le domaine bancaire et financier, Droit bancaire et financier au Luxembourg,* Vol. 2, 2004; DOMONT-NAERT F., LACOSTE A.-C., *Etude sur le problème de l'usure dans certains états membres de l'espace économique européen,* Louvain-la-Neuve 1997; DOMONT-NAERT F., DEJEMEPPE P., *Etude sur le rôle et les activités des intermédiaires de crédit aux consommateurs,* Louvain-la-Neuve 1996; GAVALDA C., G. PARLEANI, *Droit des affaires de l'Union européenne,* Paris, 1995; SOUSI-ROUBI B., *Droit bancaire européen,* Précis Dalloz, 1995; GOLDMAN B., A. LYON–CAEN, L. VOGEL, *Droit Commercial européen,* Paris, 1994.

***Selected articles:***

DRAKOS KONSTANTINOS, *The Efficiency of the Banking Sector in Central and Eastern Europe,* 38 Russian and East European Finance and Trade 31, 2002; PISTOR K., *The standardization of law and its effect on Developing Economies,* 50 Am. J. Comp. L. 97, 2002; GRIFFIN P. B., *The Delaware Effect: Keeping in the Tiger in Its Cage. The Euro-*

*pean Experience of Mutual Recognition in Financial Services*, 7 Colum. J. Eur. L. 337, 2001; AVOGOULEAS E., *The Harmonization of Rules of Conduct in EU Financial Markets: Economic Analysis, Subsidiarity and Investor Protection*, 6 European Law Journal 72, 2000; WOUTERS J., *Conflict of Laws and The Single Market for Financial Services* (Part I) & (Part II), 4 Maastricht Journal of European and Comparative Law 161, 1997;

CERINI D., *Note in tema di esercizio dell'attività assicurativa in regime di libertà di prestazione di servizi e in regime di stabilimento*, Dir. econ. assicuraz. 155, 1999; MATUSCHE-BECKMANN, *Lo sviluppo del diritto privato europeo delle assicurazioni*, 1 Economia e dir. del terziario 285, 1998; RINELLA Z., *Servizi finanziari e tutela degli investitori nella Comunità Europea*, Società 357, 1998; BALZANO A., *Il contratto di assicurazione alla luce dei decreti legislativi nn. 174 e 175 del 17 marzo 1995*, Contratto impresa 777, 1997; FRIGESSI DI RATTALMA M., *La legge applicabile al contratto di assicurazione nell'attuazione delle direttive comunitarie*, Riv. dir. int. priv. 19, 1996; TUCCI G., *Norme bancarie uniformi e condizioni generali di contratto*, Contratti 152, 1996; GAGGERO P., *Diritto comunitario e disposizioni interne in materia di credito al consumo*, Contratto e impr./Europa 622, 1996; ALPA G., *Decreto Eurosim: la tutela dei consumatori*, Società 1062, 1996; COLAVOLPE A., *Decreto Eurosim: le modifiche al t.u. bancario*, Società 1086, 1996; LENER R., *Decreto Eurosim: il sistema di vigilanza*, Società 102, 1996; ZAMBELLI S., *Decreto Eurosim: la disciplina dei mercati*, Società, 1057, 1996; ZITIELLO L., *Decreto Eurosim: la disciplina degli intermediari e delle attività*, Società 1009, 1996; COSTI, *Libertà di tariffe e concorrenze, in Diritto ed economia dell'assic. 96, 1995; BIN M., Condizioni generali di contratto e rapporti assicurativi*, in CESÀRO E. (cur.), *Clausole abusive e direttiva comunitaria*, Padova, 1994, 140; CHIARLO M., *La tutela del consumatore di servizi assicurativi*, Assicurazioni 21, 1994; ALPA G., *L'attuazione della direttiva sul credito al consumo*, Contratto e impr. 6, 1994;

REIFNER U., *Empfehlungen zum Vorschlag einer EU-Richtlinie zum Konsumentenkredit*, 19 VuR Heft 1, 11, 2004; ZOBEL P., *Der Weg zu einem einheitlichen europäischen Versicherungsvertragsrecht: vom 5. und 6. Arbeitstreffen der Gruppe "Restatement of European Insurance Contract Law"*, 24 IPRax Heft 2, 169, 2004; SENN M., *Elektronischer Geschäftsverkehr und Finanzdienstleistungen*, European law reporter 37, 2004; GLAESNER A., *Finanzdienstleistungen in der Ära von Euro und elektronischem Handel funktioniert die Herkunftslandkontrolle?*, *EuR*, Beiheft 1,145, 2004; BRINKER I., SCHÄDLE A., *Kartellrechtliche Marktabgrenzung in der Versicherungswirtschaft*, 55 *VersR* Heft 16, 673, 2004; HEISS H., *Die Richtlinie über den Fernabsatz von Finanzdienstleistungen an Verbraucher aus Sicht des IPR und des IZVR*, 23, IPRax Heft 2, 100, 2003; WOLF M., *Die Beteiligung von Versicherungsunternehmen an Gesellschaften anderer Wirtschaftszweige: eine Untersuchung zur Reichweite des Verbots "versicherungsfremder Geschäfte" auf der Basis der neueren EuGH-Rechtsprechung am Beispiel von Beteiligungen an Finanzdienstleistungsgesellschaften*, 57 *WM* Heft 22, 1058, 2003;

MEHL A., *Les systèmes bancaires dans les PECO*, 1009 Le Courrier des pays de l'Est 48, 2000.

# CHAPTER IV

# Company Law

**KEY WORDS:** Company law – Sources – Policies – Harmonization – Limits – Transposition – Member States – CEECs – Requirements for disclosure, validity of obligations, and nullity of limited liability companies – Formation of public limited liability companies, maintenance and alteration of their capital – National mergers and divisions – Annual accounts – Consolidated accounts – Statutory audits of accounting documents – Branch offices – Single-member private limited-liability companies – Directives not yet approved – Supranational models – European Economic Interest Grouping – European Company – European Cooperative Society – Draft Regulations – European Mutual Society – European Association

## 1. Reasons for Harmonization of Company Law

The Communications, Green Papers, Recommendations and other Community declarations which all form part of the *soft law* of the Community, usually affirm that the internal market is achieved by means of protecting the *four freedoms* (movement of persons, services, goods, and capital) and, in particular, through *freedom of establishment.*

Since the end of 1995, see: Communication of November 14th 1995 on worker information and consultation, COM (95) 547; Communication on accounting harmonization: a new strategy vis-à-vis international harmonization, COM (95) 508; Communication of September 10th 1997 on participating of EEIGs in public contracts and programs financed by public founds, O.J., 1997, C 285/17; Interpretative Communication of January 7th 1998 on certain articles of the Fourth and the Seventh Directives, O.J., 1998, C 16/5; Communication of April 29th 1998 on the statutory audit in the European Union: the way forward, O.J., 1998 C 143/12; Communication from the European Commission: Towards an Internal Market without tax obstacles. A strategy for providing companies with a consolidated corporate tax base for their EU-wide activities, COM (2001) 582; A Modern Regulatory Framework for Company Law in Europe: A Consultative Document of the High Level Group of Company Law Experts at http://europa.eu.int/comm/internal_market/en/company/company/modern/consult/1_en.htm

All this is without a doubt essential, in order for the Member States to pursue the principle task, namely the functioning of the internal market, through the European Community legal framework. However, this is not enough.

To have an effective single market, it is also necessary that there be a sufficient degree of homogeneity between the national legal rules and practices governing entrepreneurial economic activity, including the tax regime, employment, and social security. Establishing a single market also implies adopting a set of legal rules common to all participating countries.

> **Art. 2 (ex Art. 2) TEC:** "The Community shall have as its task, by establishing a common market and an economic and monetary union and by implementing common policies or activities referred to in Articles 3 and 4, to promote throughout the Community a harmonious, balanced and sustainable development of economic activities, a high level of employment and of social protection, equality between men and women, sustainable and non inflationary growth, a high degree of competitiveness and convergence of economic performance, a high level of protection and improvement of the quality of the environment, the raising of the standard of living and quality of life, and economic and social cohesion and solidarity among Member States."

> **Art. 3 (ex Art. 3) TEC:** "(1) For the purposes set out in Article 2, the activities of the Community shall include, as provided in this Treaty and in accordance with the timetable set out therein: (a) the prohibition, as between Member States, of customs duties and quantitative restrictions on the import and export of goods, and of all other measures having equivalent effect; (b) a common commercial policy; (c) an internal market characterised by the abolition, as between Member States, of obstacles to the free movement of goods, persons, services and capital; (d) measures concerning the entry and movement of persons as provided for in Title IV; (e) a common policy in the sphere of agriculture and fisheries; (f) a common policy in the sphere of transport; (g) a system ensuring that competition in the internal market is not distorted; (h) the approximation of the laws of Member States to the extent required for the functioning of the common market; (i) the promotion of coordination between employment policies of the Member States with a view to enhancing their effectiveness by developing a coordinated strategy for employment; (j) a policy in the social sphere comprising a European Social Fund; (k) the strengthening of economic and social cohesion; (l) a policy in the sphere of the environment; (m) the strengthening of the competitiveness of Com-

> munity industry; (n) the promotion of research and technological development; (o) encouragement for the establishment and development of trans-European networks; (p) a contribution to the attainment of a high level of health protection; (q) a contribution to education and training of quality and to the flowering of the cultures of the Member States; (r) a policy in the sphere of development cooperation; (s) the association of the overseas countries and territories in order to increase trade and promote jointly economic and social development; (t) a contribution to the strengthening of consumer protection; (u) measures in the spheres of energy, civil protection and tourism. (2) In all the activities referred to in this Article, the Community shall aim to eliminate inequalities, and to promote equality, between men and women."

On the institutional level, the Commission has to take into account some constraints in the EC Treaty itself. As far as the competence of the EC to undertake harmonizing activities is concerned, we must mention, above all, art. 5 (ex art. 3 B), introduced by Maastricht Treaty.[1]

This provision makes it clear that the Community does not enjoy full competence, but may only act within the system of attributed competencies and objectives (principle of conferral).[2]

In addition, the subsidiarity principle means that in areas which do not fall within the exclusive competence of the EC, such as company law, the Community may legislate only if and in so far as the objectives of the proposed action cannot be sufficiently achieved by the Member States and therefore, by reason of the scale or effects of the proposed action, be better achieved by the Community. Finally, under the principle of proportionality, the Community action may not go beyond what is necessary to achieve the objectives of the Treaty.

In contrast, in the US, the States regulate many spheres of corporate, commercial, financial, and professional activity, with only limited intervention by the federal government. Except for banking and securities sector, there has been little attempt to "federalize" these fields or to harmonize the diverse state systems.

Bearing in mind the limits imposed by the founding Treaty (as amended), it is thought that the elimination of frontiers, customs, import tariffs, and quotas are not effective so long as important differences remain between the various systems in relation to corporate governance, competition and tax treatment which all affect economic activity. The European market will be neither "common" nor "single" until business and end-users can

---

[1] See chapter IV, of the first volume of this *Guide, A Common Law for Europe*.

[2] See previous footnote.

count on common legal principles and rules.[3] If this is not the case, a segmented market over the whole European territory will result, depending on the different kinds of treatment reserved for economic activity by the national legal systems.

Obviously, the greater the number of participating States in the internal market and the greater the diversity of their various legal systems, the harder it is to achieve the aim of standardization of legal rules in such vast sectors.

Therefore, besides eliminating customs barriers and the technical obstacles in the way of the movement of goods, persons, services and capital, the issues which the Community legislature must confront to achieve the single market are essentially linked to the development (or the selection, where they already exist) of standard legal models, which are above all efficient and which, at the same time, are accepted by all the Member States.

And it is precisely that necessity, of obtaining the consent of all the Member States before a standard model is adopted, which forms the greater obstacles to the harmonization and uniformization of the national legal rules and solutions.

As we have seen in preceding chapters, there is a constant danger that the Commission and the EC Council will meet resistance from some Member States, because the adoption of new rules is seen as some kind of cultural dominance, or at any rate as interference, by the EC or other Member States in its own sphere of national sovereignty.

In an attempt to overcome the differences, the Community legislature may be induced to adopt compromise models, which very often means less efficient ones.

Bearing these considerations in mind, the instruments which are normally used to achieve the single market, that is, to reach a sufficient parity of treatment among all the economic entities involved in the European common market, are essentially two:

– The harmonization of the rules of *private international law*.

– The harmonization of the rules of *substantive private law*.

### *1.1. Harmonization of the Rules of Private International Law*

The first system, which affects the *rules of private international law* in the Member States, tends to produce standard legal rules to determine the applicable law when certain factual circumstances have foreign aspects.

[3] See chapters I, II & VI on the various possibilities of harmonization/uniformization, in the first volume of this *Guide, A Common Law for Europe*.

Under this system, the Community determines the criteria for the choice of applicable law, but does not standardize the substantive law.

All this has some merit, in that the consent of Member States can be more easily obtained. In fact, while the new uniform rules do not affect substantive law, only the criteria of connection with, and choice of the *lex causae*, the States are less likely to put up resistance to uniformization.

Another advantage consists in the fact that this system allows any economic operator within the Union to know in advance which law will be applicable to the particular case.

For example, leaving aside whatever the reference criteria may be which, in fact, settle the conflict of laws in the field of contract,[4] in any case the parties involved in cross-border transactions are able to tell—right from the start of contractual relations—which law will apply to the contract.

However, such a system of uniformization also presents certain difficulties. Indeed, while it is true that the end-users of the conflict of law rules (that is, the rules of private international law), such as two commercial operators, are in a position to know at any time what law will apply in case of a dispute, it is also true that they must, sooner or later, come to terms with the differences in the rules of substantive law. The conflict between the various solutions therefore remains, since the rules of substantive law applicable to disputes are still the national ones. The solutions available to the same problem could be different, according to which national legal system is designated under the conflict of law rules.

Uniform rules of private international law are to be found in the Community Conventions, promoted under article 293 TEC. The Conventions are agreements entered into by and among the Member States in their separate sovereign capacities.

> **Art. 293 (ex art. 220) TEC** "Member States shall, so far as is necessary, enter into negotiations with each other with a view to securing for the benefit of their nationals: the protection of persons and the enjoyment and protection of rights under the same conditions as those accorded by each State to its own nationals; the abolition of double taxation within the Community; the mutual recognition of companies or firms within the meaning of the second paragraph of Article 48, the retention of legal personality in the

---

[4] Rules of private international law could establish that, in the field of contracts, the *lex causae* is *a)* the law of the place where the contract was concerned; *b)* the place where the contract is to be performed; *c)* the place where the seller (or selling company) resides/ has its head office.

> event of transfer of their seat from one country to another, and the possibility of mergers between companies or firms governed by the laws of different countries; the simplification of formalities governing the reciprocal recognition and enforcement of judgments of courts or tribunals and of arbitration awards."

Among these, we should recall the *Rome Convention* on the Law Applicable to Contractual Obligations, opened for signature on June 19th 1980,[5] the *Brussels Convention* of February 29th 1968 on the Mutual Recognition of Companies and Bodies Corporate,[6] and the *Brussels Convention* on Jurisdiction and the Recognition and Enforcement of Judgments in Civil and Commercial Matters concluded on September 27th 1968.[7]

> The rules of the Brussels Convention were extended to the States belonging to the European Free Trade Association by the Lugano Convention, signed on September 16th 1988. The Brussels Convention was extended successively to all the new Member States of the European Union and, most recently, by the Accession Convention of November 29th 1996 to Austria, Finland, and Sweden (O.J., 01/15/1997, C15). Art. 63 of the Convention provides that any State seeking membership in the EU is required to accept the Convention as a requirement of membership.

However, uniformizing the rules of private international law by means of Conventions has proved inadequate to the task of creating a single market.

A reason can initially be found in the fact that the Brussels Convention on Mutual Recognition of Companies and Bodies Corporate, i.e. the only Convention containing fundamental rules for the freedom of establishment of undertakings, has never come into force because it has not been ratified by all the States. The choice of law rules in this field are at present dictated by *ad hoc* provisions which each State has set down at the national level (generally contained in a specific national provision

---

[5] See above chapter I and VI of the first volume of this *Guide, A Common Law for Europe*.

[6] *EC Bull., Suppl.*, no. 2/1969, p. 7. The Convention has not yet come into force because of failure to ratify on the part of the Netherlands; its coming into force seems to have been postponed *sine die*.

[7] A consolidated version of the Convention was published in 1998: *cf.* O.J., C 27, 01/26/1998.

such as the Act on Private International Law, or directly in the Civil or Commercial Codes).

In general terms, the two doctrines to which the Member States generally refer are the *real seat theory* (the connecting factor is where the actual seat of administration is placed or, directly, the place of business) and the *incorporation theory* (the connecting factor is where the corporation is formed or incorporated). The latter prevails, for example, in the UK, Ireland, Denmark, Sweden and, to a certain extent, the Netherlands, although some important changes are in prospect as a result of the rulings of the Court of Justice in the *Centros* and *Uberseering* cases.[8]

The second reason lies in the fact that, regarding the uniformization of the law, the Convention (as an instrument agreed between the parties) lacks the capacity to bind the various legal systems of the Member States which the Community acts (adopted by the Community institutions according to the procedure established under the Treaty)[9] possess.

Indeed, it was in order to instill greater confidence in cross-border transactions (since the entrepreneur is more likely to buy and sell, work and invest abroad if s/he knows that in case of a dispute, s/he can rely on the application of rulings in her/his favor by the national courts in other Member States as well), that EC Council Regulation no. 44/2001 of December 22nd 2000 was issued, on jurisdiction and the recognition and enforcement of judgments in civil and commercial matters.[10]

This is a binding and directly applicable Community act, which has superseded, with effect from March 1st 2002, the Brussels Convention of September 27th 1968, ensuring a gradual transfer from one regime to another through various transitional provisions (arts. 66 and following). Denmark is the only exception to which the Brussels Convention still applies. Annexes I and II of Regulation 44/2001 have been amended by EC Commission Regulation no. 1496/2002 of August 21st 2002.[11]

## *1.2. Harmonization of the Rules of Substantive Private Law*

The second strategy employed by the Community institutions to achieve the single market consists in the harmonization of *private substantive law*, which means inducing the Member States to adopt common legal rules and persuading the national courts to interpret them in conformity with the principles developed by the Court of Justice.

---

[8] See below § 2.
[9] See Articles 251 and 252 TEC.
[10] O.J., L 12, 01/16/2001.
[11] O.J., L 225, 08/22/2002.

This is the method which the Community used in tandem with the first conventions at the end of the 60's, and which it has continued to use with increasing conviction, having seen the modest results of Community conventions in general and those concerning company law more particularly.

Starting with the assumption that the establishment of the single, internal market is essential, the EC Commission has taken the view that the main objective of harmonization of company law is the achievement of conditions of parity, in all the European countries, concerning both the position of third-party creditors and the shareholders themselves. A different guarantee scheme in favor of these groups would lead to disparity of treatment between stakeholders whose headquarters are in different countries, conflicting with the objective of a single internal market.

To achieve the single market without limitations on the flow of capital, investors, savers, and third parties to contracts are encouraged to invest and do business not only with undertakings which offer better terms on the merely economic level, but also with those who can offer greater transparency in their business dealings, thanks to the legal system governing them.

All the directives which we shall be considering, although they concern highly specific fields (on memorandum and articles of association, agency, mergers and divisions, accounts, etc.) have this objective as a common denominator.

## 2. Limits of Harmonization of Company Law

Harmonization of company law affects the new Community system of private law, characterized by a range of solutions and fundamental rules both for business activity itself and for the shareholders, workers, and third-party suppliers, or investors and consumers in general.

EC company law has been able to achieve an otherwise unimaginable degree of harmonization, through the use of directives and other Community provisions. What is more, the Community legislature has not only harmonized the rules of the various European legal systems, but has created new institutions of supra-national proportions, such as the well-known European Economic Interest Grouping (EEIG).[12]

Some of these institutions, such as the European Mutual Society and the European Association, are still at the development stage.[13]

---

[12] See § 19.

[13] See § 22.

The European Company (EC) and the European Cooperative Society (ECS),[14] on the other hand, have been recently regulated by the adoption of rules on their setting-up and functioning, and rules on worker participation in the creation and development of the company themselves.

However, it should be emphasized that, despite the efforts made to harmonize company law, the community strategy has seen a slowing-down compared to the enthusiastic start made in the 1960's. Owing to the absence of a precise and updated general program of intervention[15] and above all, because of the many obstacles put in its way by the Member States, the harmonization process is *fragmentary*, limited as to *sectors* and *poorly coordinated.*

The fact that Community intervention has concentrated upon public stock corporations (to use the 'neutral' American term, for the types of companies identified under the respective European legal systems, i.e. for example, the *societé anonyme* in France, the *Aktiengesellschaft* in Germany, the *public company* in UK, or the *Società per azioni* in Italy), leaving aside other categories of association, is a sign of the difficulties encountered by the European legislature in finding common solutions, owing to the diversity of the national legal systems.

The most obvious difficulties which the Community legislature has met (and still meets) concerning the harmonization criteria upon which to base directives, have, as a constant factor, the need to mediate between the various positions, which are to a greater or lesser degree rigid, taken up by the Member States in the finding of compromise solutions.

We should, first of all, recall the fact that the declared aim of the Community legislature is so-called *minimum harmonization.* It was soon combined with the principle of *mutual recognition* and the principle of *home country control.* This Community approach to harmonization is today the cornerstone of the single market.

The concept of mutual recognition was developed by the European Commission in the *White Paper on Completing the Internal Market,*[16] on the basis of the *Cassis de Dijon* judgment,[17] delivered in connection with the application of the former Article 30 (now Art. 28) TEC. It means

---

[14] See § 20 & 21.

[15] The program came into being in the 60's with the adoption by the Council of the General Programme for the abolition of restrictions on freedom of establishment and the General Programme for the abolition of restrictions on freedom to provide services. O.J., English Ed., 1974, IX, 3.

[16] COM (85) 310 final.

[17] Case C-120/78 of February 20th 1979, ECR 1979, p. 649.

that Member States cannot take a strictly national point of view when drawing up technical and commercial rules, and cannot prevent products or services that meet standards different from their national ones from being sold or provided on their territory, if the product or service concerned satisfactorily fulfils the legitimate objective specified in those regal rules. In this way, free movement of goods and the freedom to provide services may be achieved without requiring all regulations and standards in every area to be harmonized at Community level.

In other words, the Member States should adopt common rules and standards which, together, can permit sufficiently similar operating rules between the various Countries, and not a single legal model to cater for every aspect of company law. It is considered sufficient for harmonization to affect the main technical rules, so that all the undertakings and companies are subject to (more or less) similar regimes within the European market. The idea being that non-homogeneous territorial areas, regulated by different micro-legal regimes, should not be created within the internal market.

Another weak point in the Community intervention strategy is the system of *options*, which authorizes States to choose between two or more models proposed by the directive itself, on condition that the same result is achieved. It is clear that underestimating the differences between the proposed models may lead to even greater differentiation to the one which was to be eliminated. In other words, the more exposed the directive is to alternative solutions, the greater the risk of a lack of harmonization.

> In the US legal system, the same issue raised by harmonization (the extent to which a harmonizing directive prevents a Member State from supplementary regulation, whether stricter or simply different, in the field covered by the directive) has frequently arisen in application of the Interstate Commerce Clause and is characterized as one of the possible pre-emption of state rules by a federal law.
>
> The modern view of the Supreme Court is that federal and state regulation can readily coexist and pre-emption occurs only when there is "evidence of congressional intent to pre-empt the specific field covered by the state law."[18]

As far as company law is concerned, the policy of minimum harmonization is only sufficient to ensure the common purpose of minimal protec-

[18] *Wardair Canada, Inc. v. Florida Dept. of Revenue, 477 U.S. 1,6, 106 S.Ct. 2369, 2372, 91 L.Ed.2d 1 (1986).*

tion of shareholders and others who are drawn into the company's external sphere of action, such as suppliers and investors.

In addition, the policy of minimum harmonization in the field of company law causes paradoxical effects. In fact, Member States are allowed to adopt or maintain stricter measures[19] and the States often avail themselves of this possibility. The result is that business in the "stricter" State is penalized and competition is distorted, in that if measures are too severe, investment gravitates towards more "lenient" States, which have more relaxed regimes.

An effective antidote for the collateral effects of "minimum harmonization" can be found in the competition mechanism between national legal models,[20] which triggers the direct confrontation between legal rules and solutions adopted by Member States, or between legal rules from economically stronger countries.

It appears that the natural remedy of *competition* between legal systems or national micro-regimes was approved by the Court of Justice in the case of *Centros v. Erhvervs-og Selskabsstyrelsen*.[21]

Centros, a UK company without paid-up capital, with its registered office at a friend's home, with no intention to do business in the UK, applied to the Danish Companies Board to register a Centros branch in Denmark, in order to conduct a wine trading business. The Board rejected the application, deeming the creation of a branch to be an evasion of Danish company capital requirements. The Danish Court asked the Court of Justice whether the Centros' right of establishment was violated by the rejection.

> **Centros ruling**: see §§ 19, 20, 21, 26, 27, 28 and 39 of the Court decision:
>
> "(...) **19.** As to the question whether, as Mr. and Mrs. Bryde claim, the refusal to register in Denmark a branch of their company formed in accordance with the law of another Member State in which its has its registered office constitutes an obstacle to freedom of establishment, it must be borne in mind that that freedom, conferred by Article 52 of the Treaty on Community nationals, includes the right for them to take up and pursue activities as self-employed persons and to set up and manage undertakings under the same conditions as are laid down by the law of the Member

[19] Almost all the directives on the subject contain provisions of this sort, including those on consumer protection (for example the "door to door" sales directive, art. 8: see above chapter I).

[20] See above, chapters II and VI, of the first volume of this *Guide, A Common Law for Europe*.

[21] ECJ Judgment Case C-212/97 (1999), ECR I-1459.

State of establishment for its own nationals. Furthermore, under Article 58 of the Treaty companies or firms formed in accordance with the law of a Member State and having their registered office, central administration or principal place of business within the Community are to be treated in the same way as natural persons who are nationals of Member States. **20.** The immediate consequence of this is that those companies are entitled to carry on their business in another Member State through an agency, branch or subsidiary. The location of their registered office, central administration or principal place of business serves as the connecting factor with the legal system of a particular State in the same way as does nationality in the case of a natural person (see, to that effect, Segers, paragraph 13, Case 270/83 Commission v France [1986] ECR 273, paragraph 18, Case C-330/91 Commerzbank [1993] ECR I-4017, paragraph 13, and Case C-264/96 ICI [1998] I-4695, paragraph 20). **21**. Where it is the practice of a Member State, in certain circumstances, to refuse to register a branch of a company having its registered office in another Member State, the result is that companies formed in accordance with the law of that other Member State are prevented from exercising the freedom of establishment conferred on them by Articles 52 and 58 of the Treaty. (…) **26**. In the present case, the provisions of national law, application of which the parties concerned have sought to avoid, are rules governing the formation of companies and not rules concerning the carrying on of certain trades, professions or businesses. The provisions of the Treaty on freedom of establishment are intended specifically to enable companies formed in accordance with the law of a Member State and having their registered office, central administration or principal place of business within the Community to pursue activities in other Member States through an agency, branch or subsidiary. **27**. That being so, the fact that a national of a Member State who wishes to set up a company chooses to form it in the Member State whose rules of company law seem to him the least restrictive and to set up branches in other Member States cannot, in itself, constitute an abuse of the right of establishment. The right to form a company in accordance with the law of a Member State and to set up branches in other Member States is inherent in the exercise, in a single market, of the freedom of establishment guaranteed by the Treaty. **28**. In this connection, the fact that company law is not completely harmonised in the Community is of little consequence. Moreover, it is always open to the Council, on the basis of the powers conferred upon it by Article 54 (3)(g) of the EC Treaty, to achieve complete harmonisation. (…) **39**. The answer to the question referred must therefore be that it is contrary to Articles 52 and 58

> of the Treaty for a Member State to refuse to register a branch of a company formed in accordance with the law of another Member State in which it has its registered office but in which it conducts no business where the branch is intended to enable the company in question to carry on its entire business in the State in which that branch is to be created, while avoiding the need to form a company there, thus evading application of the rules governing the formation of companies which, in that State, are more restrictive as regards the paying up of a minimum share capital. That interpretation does not, however, prevent the authorities of the Member State concerned from adopting any appropriate measure for preventing or penalising fraud, either in relation to the company itself, if need be in cooperation with the Member State in which it was formed, or in relation to its members, where it has been established that they are in fact attempting, by means of the formation of a company, to evade their obligations towards private or public creditors established in the territory of the Member State concerned.

The European Court of Justice has created some turmoil in the EU with its *Centros* ruling. Does this ruling mean that there is no room anymore in Europe for the real seat theory (*Sitztheorie*)?[22] Does the ruling mean that companies can now transfer their seat by establishing their registered office in one Member State and doing their real business in another Member State? Does this ruling mean that we will have real competition among company laws in the EU? Is this the beginning of a European Delaware? How can we protect ourselves against a race to the bottom? These are some of the questions that are being raised after the Court's ruling.

> The *Centros* case has led to a number of new cases before the ECJ: 1) **C-410/99, *Challenger Trading,*** concerning a Dutch Act on formally foreign corporations. According to the Act, foreign companies with their main seat in the Netherlands must apply Dutch company law. Challenger Trading ltd. has been dissolved and the case has been withdrawn from the ECJ. 2) **C-86/00, *Wohnbau*** (Amtsgericht Heidelberg), concerning a Spanish company

[22] The country in which the main seat of the company's management is located. The theory was valid in all the Member States, except for the UK, the Netherlands, Denmark, and Sweden. These countries had adopted the incorporation theory: the country in which the company is registered, as a condition under company law for gaining legal personality. However, we should remember that the ECJ does not distinguish between the theory of incorporation and the real seat theory.

which acquired the entire capital of a German GmbH., and wished to change the nationality of the German company to become a Spanish company (it is allowed under Spanish law). Under German law a company formed under German law must be wound up, if its main seat is transferred out of Germany. 3) **C-115/00, *Hoves,*** concerning a German business incorporated as a Luxembourg SARL. The company operates a number of trucks driving in Germany. There are no facilities for the trucks in Luxembourg. All drivers are German. German authorities are seeking payment of German motor vehicles tax. 4) **C-208/00,** (Bundesgerichtshof): the fate of the *Sitztheorie* in Germany. 5) **C-447/00 *Holto ltd.*** (Landesgericht Salzburg): the fate of the *Sitztheorie* in Austria.

The end of the real seat theory,[23] at least to the extent it applies to the recognition of the legal capacity of companies incorporated in other EU States, has been signaled in a recent ruling.

Member States are now required to fully recognize the legal capacity a company enjoys under the laws of the State of incorporation. In the judgment, delivered on November 5th 2002, *Uberseering BV v. Nordic Construction Company Baumanagememtn GmbH (NCC)*,[24] the European Court of Justice ruled that a Member State can not deny legal capacity to a company formed in one Member State, which moves its central place of administration to another one, because it is incompatible with the freedom of establishment guaranteed by arts. 43 & 48 TEC. Following this ruling, a company incorporated in a EU State is entitled to rely on the principle of freedom of establishment to contest any refusal by a host State to recognize it as a legal person with the capacity to enter into contracts and to be a party to legal proceedings.

Those questions were raised in proceedings between Überseering BV, a company incorporated under Netherlands law, and Nordic Construction Company Baumanagement GmbH (NCC), a company established in the Federal Republic of Germany, concerning damages for defective work carried out in Germany by NCC on behalf of Überseering.

The *Oberlandesgericht* (High Regional Court) of Düsseldorf held that Überseering's action was inadmissible, because, as a company incorpo-

---

[23] Examples of cases where the real seat theory may still be applied by a Member State: 1. In respect of companies from non EU-States; 2. In respect of a company which is not yet formed in a Member State (see LG München, July 22nd, [ZIP 1999.1680]; 3. Under tax law (see the Danish Act no. 461, of May 31st 2000 [L. 212], which introduces a new tax law minimum capital requirement to enterprises doing business in Denmark: it affects, however, any business enterprise whose main seat is located in Denmark).

[24] ECJ Judgment, November 5th 2002, C-208/00 (2002), ECR I-9919.

rated under Netherlands law, Überseering did not have legal capacity in Germany and, consequently, could not bring legal proceedings there. In fact, the *Zivilprozessordnung* (German Code of Civil Procedure) provides that an action brought by a party which does not have the capacity to bring legal proceedings must be dismissed as inadmissible.

Under Paragraph 50(1) of the *Zivilprozessordnung* any person, including a company having legal capacity, has the capacity to be a party to legal proceedings: legal capacity is defined as the capacity to enjoy rights and to be the subject of obligations.

According to the settled case-law of the *Bundesgerichtshof*, which is approved by most German legal commentators, a company's legal capacity is determined by reference to the law applicable in the place where its actual center of administration is established (*Sitztheorie* or real seat principle). That rule also applies where a company has been validly incorporated in another State and has subsequently transferred its actual center of administration to Germany.

> **Überseering ruling**: "(**80**) Überseering, which is validly incorporated in the Netherlands and has its registered office there, is entitled under Articles 43 EC and 48 EC to exercise its freedom of establishment in Germany as a company incorporated under Netherlands law. It is of little significance in that regard that, after the company was formed, all its shares were acquired by German nationals residing in Germany, since that has not caused Überseering to cease to be a legal person under Netherlands law. (**81**) Indeed, its very existence is inseparable from its status as a company incorporated under Netherlands law since, as the Court has observed, a company exists only by virtue of the national legislation which determines its incorporation and functioning (see, to that effect, Daily Mail and General Trust, paragraph 19). The requirement of reincorporation of the same company in Germany is therefore tantamount to outright negation of freedom of establishment. (**82**) In those circumstances, the refusal by a host Member State ('B') to recognise the legal capacity of a company formed in accordance with the law of another Member State ('A') in which it has its registered office on the ground, in particular, that the company moved its actual centre of administration to Member State B following the acquisition of all its shares by nationals of that State residing there, with the result that the company cannot, in Member State B, bring legal proceedings to defend rights under a contract unless it is reincorporated under the law of Member State B, constitutes a restriction on freedom of establishment which is, in principle, incompatible with Articles 43 EC and 48 EC."

Questions arise as to what the implications may be regarding the recognition of the EC companies and of companies from CEECs in the context of the last enlargement. How does the notion of an EC company, implicit in the *Centros* and *Uberseering* judgments, affect CEECs' obligation to recognize such companies and to grant them national treatment regarding the right of establishment?

Since the criteria were literally the same under EC Law and under the Europe Agreements (and under the Treaty of Accession as well), there is room for applying the ECJ doctrine to the CEECs and for harmonizing their legal rules.

At present, Central and Eastern European States differ in their conflict of laws and rules for the determination of the proper law of companies.

The Czech Republic (§22 Comm. Code of 1991), Bulgaria (art. 282 Comm. Code of 1999), Slovakia (§21 (2) and 2 (3) Comm. Code of 1999) follow the incorporation doctrine.

Poland (art. 9 of the Act on Private International Law) and Romania (art. 40 (2) of the Act on Private International Law) follow the real seat doctrine.

Slovenia and Croatia (art. 17 and § 17 of their respective Act on Private International Law) follow an intermediate position: the incorporation doctrine is valid, however if another State applies its own laws to a company having its real seat within this State, then Slovenian and Croatian laws give way to the seat doctrine. Hungary follows the incorporation doctrine; however if the real seat is located in Hungary, then domestic company law is applied to the company according to the state doctrine (§ 18 of the Act on Private International Law and § 1 of Act on Business Association of 1997).

## 3. The Sources of Company Law

The Treaty provisions concerning company law cover only the bare essentials. Article 48 (*ex* art. 58) is of fundamental importance.

> **Art. 48 (ex art. 58) TEC "(1)** Companies or firms formed in accordance with the law of a Member State and having their registered office, central administration or principal place of business within the Community shall, for the purposes of this Chapter, be treated in the same way as natural persons who are nationals of Member States. **(2)** "Companies or firms" means companies or firms constituted under civil or commercial law, including cooperative societies, and other legal persons governed by public or private law, save for those which are non-profit-making."

The provision extends the same legal treatment to companies in general as that given to natural persons, as regards the right of establishment, and, in particular, the same rights as are recognized by articles 43 (*ex* art. 52) and 44 (*ex* art. 54) TEC. It ensures the gradual elimination of restraints on freedom of establishment of the citizens of one State in the territory of another Member State

Accordingly, the *right of establishment* includes three aspects, namely:
– To set up agencies, branches and subsidiaries.
– To conduct activities as a self-employed person.
– To set up and manage undertakings (companies or firms).

> **Art. 43 (ex art. 52) TEC** "**(1)** Within the framework of the provisions set out below, restrictions on the freedom of establishment of nationals of a Member State in the territory of another Member State shall be prohibited. Such prohibition shall also apply to restrictions on the setting-up of agencies, branches or subsidiaries by nationals of any Member State established in the territory of any Member State. **(2)** Freedom of establishment shall include the right to take up and pursue activities as self-employed persons and to set up and manage undertakings, in particular companies or firms within the meaning of the second paragraph of Article 48, under the conditions laid down for its own nationals by the law of the country where such establishment is effected, subject to the provisions of the Chapter relating to capital."

The Council and the Commission shall carry out their duties according to the following provision:

> **Art. 44 (ex art. 54) TEC** "**(1)** In order to attain freedom of establishment as regards a particular activity, the Council, acting in accordance with the procedure referred to in Article 251 and after consulting the Economic and Social Committee, shall act by means of directives. **(2)** The Council and the Commission shall carry out the duties devolving upon them under the preceding provisions, in particular:
>
> (a) by according, as a general rule, priority treatment to activities where freedom of establishment makes a particularly valuable contribution to the development of production and trade;
>
> (b) by ensuring close cooperation between the competent authorities in the Member States in order to ascertain the particular situation within the Community of the various activities concerned;
>
> (c) by abolishing those administrative procedures and practices, whether resulting from national legislation or from agreements

previously concluded between Member States, the maintenance of which would form an obstacle to freedom of establishment;

(d) by ensuring that workers of one Member State employed in the territory of another Member State may remain in that territory for the purpose of taking up activities therein as self-employed persons, where they satisfy the conditions which they would be required to satisfy if they were entering that State at the time when they intended to take up such activities;

(e) by enabling a national of one Member State to acquire and use land and buildings situated in the territory of another Member State, insofar as this does not conflict with the principles laid down in Article 33(2);

(f) by effecting the progressive abolition of restrictions on freedom of establishment in every branch of activity under consideration, both as regards the conditions for setting up agencies, branches or subsidiaries in the territory of a Member State and as regards the subsidiaries in the territory of a Member State and as regards the conditions governing the entry of personnel belonging to the main establishment into managerial or supervisory posts in such agencies, branches or subsidiaries;

(g) by coordinating to the necessary extent the safeguards which, for the protection of the interests of members and other, are required by Member States of companies or firms within the meaning of the second paragraph of Article 48 with a view to making such safeguards equivalent throughout the Community;

(h) by satisfying themselves that the conditions of establishment are not distorted by aids granted by Member States."

Finally, we should recall among the Treaty provisions, article 293 (*ex* art. 220) TEC, which forms the legislative basis for the Conventions in the field of company law.[25] The provision requires, among other things, that Member States adopt effective measures to ensure the reciprocal recognition of companies, the maintenance of legal personality should the head-office be transferred from one country to another, and the possibility of mergers between companies subject to differing national legislation.

Besides these articles, the Treaty does not contain any other measure concerning companies. In effect, the largest source of new Community company law is to be found in the harmonization directives and the regulations.

---

[25] For the text of and commentary on the article, see § 1, this chapter.

## 4. Community Strategies of Intervention

Two differing intervention strategies, therefore, are followed by the Community institutions in this field.

The first method used by the Community legislature is that of *uniformizing the rules*, which has given rise to a single set of legal rules for all the Members of the Union. At first, uniformization was pursued, as we saw earlier, by means of Conventions. However, this instrument was applicable only at trans-national level, namely, when the parties belong to two or more different States. It was therefore decided that Regulations should be used for uniformization.

This first strategy (uniformization) has an apparent notable advantage, in that the State is not required to adhere to a common model by revising all the national legal rules, as rules which are not affected by regulations or the Convention remain unchanged; this should more easily enable the consent of all the Member States to the adoption of the new legislation.

However, leaving aside the EEIG Regulation,[26] all other supranational legislative projects have met strong resistance, such as, for example, the drafts for the European Mutual Society and the European Association, (accompanied by a similar number of draft directives on employee participation in the management of such institutions).[27]

The use of regulations has bounced back recently, in a phase in which the Community legislators appear to want to pursue objectives of *maximum harmonization*, such as, for example, in the case of the European Company (*Societas Europaea)* and the European Cooperative Society,[28] or else that concerning Regulation no. 44/2001 which has superseded the Brussels Convention.[29]

The second strategy, *harmonization*, has been followed by the Community since the 1960's, by means of the large-scale use of directives. Originally there were to have been twelve directives,[30] but others have been added since, without particular ordinal numbers to identify them (unless you count the one corresponding to the date of publication in the *Official Journal*, obviously), either because they are complementary to

[26] See below, § 19.

[27] See below, § 22.

[28] See below, § 20 & 21.

[29] See above, § 1.

[30] They were identified by progressive numeration, (first, second, third, and so on) because the intervention program on the subject provided for a company law standardization plan subdivided in successive levels.

some of the projected twelve directives, or because they merely amend them.

We are going to analyze the following list of Directives, some of which have already been approved by the Council, and some of which await approval:

- First Directive, n. 68/151 concerning the disclosure of company information, the power of representation of the organs, and the nullity of companies with limited liability.
- Second Directive, n. 77/91 concerning the formation of public limited liability companies and the maintenance and alteration of their capital.
- Third Directive, n. 78/855, concerning mergers between public limited liability companies from the same Member State.
- Fourth Directive, n. 78/660, concerning the presentation and content of annual accounts and annual reports, the valuation methods used therein, and their publication in respect of all companies with limited liability.
- Proposal of Fifth Directive on the structure of public limited companies and the powers and obligations of their organs (awaiting approval).
- Sixth Directive, n. 82/ 891, concerning divisions of public limited liability companies from the same Member State.
- Seventh Directive, n. 83/349, concerning the coordination of national laws on consolidated (i.e. group) accounts.
- Eighth Directive, n. 84/253, defining the qualifications of persons responsible for carrying out the statutory audits of the accounting documents required by the fourth and seventh Directives.
- Draft Ninth Directive on the liability of a parent company for the debts of a subsidiary under its control (awaiting approval).
- Draft Tenth Directive on cross-border mergers of public limited companies (awaiting approval).
- Eleventh Directive, n. 89/666, concerning disclosure requirements in respect of branches opened in a Member State by certain types of companies governed by the law of another State.
- Twelfth Directive, n. 89/667, creating a legal instrument allowing the limitation of liability of the Single-member company throughout the Community.
- Thirteenth Directive n. 2004/25, on company law concerning takeover bids.
- Draft proposal of Fourteenth Directive on cross-border transfer of seat (awaiting approval).

Through the study of the harmonization Directives of company law, we will try to highlight the Community nature of the new domestic legal rules, to compare the degree of correspondence of the implementing legislation with the Community acts, and to verify whether the stated aims of harmonization have been achieved or not, as well as observing the various phenomena which occur as a result of the new approximation activity taking place within the national systems of both (old and new) Member States and the candidates for membership.

## 5. New Strategies of Intervention in Company Law

Before going on to analyze the harmonization directives mentioned above, it should be emphasized that the process of harmonizing company law has until now been carried out in a fragmentary and disjointed way, not in the context of a general framework of action, despite the fact that in the 1970's a coherent nucleus of action had been planned.

Today this approach seems destined to cease. Indeed, since the end of the 90's, the Community institutions have proceeded with the modernization of the legal framework using an *integrated type of approach*, which looks at the *capital markets*, fixing objectives in the short, medium, and long term. The reasons justifying the modernization of the Community legal framework of company law derive from the following:

- From the growing tendency of European enterprises to operate at cross-border level in the internal market and the consequent necessity to provide Community instruments to facilitate, for example, the freedom of establishment and cross-border restructuring.
- From the progress being made on the integration of European capital markets, which require a secure and transparent context, able to protect the position of investors and equivalent laws regulating companies.
- From the rapid development of new information and communication technology which is influencing the way information about companies is kept and disclosed, including the types of management (for instance, through the cross-border exercise of voting rights).
- From the enlargement of the Union to include ten new Member States, which increases the importance of an approach which can ensure a high level of certainty in the law in inter-Community dealings.
- From the negative repercussions arising from financial scandals including important European companies (the Italian *Parmalat* group, for example) which urgently need instruments to strengthen shareholders' rights and protect third parties.

The following initiatives feature among those forming part of this new *integrative type of approach*:

*a)* The *Financial Services Action Plan* (FSAP), 1999, which confirmed the general objectives which should guide policy in the field of financial services in the EU and which defined a framework for achieving an integrated capital market by the end of 2005.[31]

*b)* The *Communication* entitled *EU Financial Reporting Strategy: the way forward,* 2000, which proposes to ensure high quality information in the financial sphere through the adoption of a set of accounting principles and the establishment of a system which will ensure its effective application.[32]

*c)* The *Green Paper Promoting a European framework for Corporate Social Responsibility,* 2001, promoting a European framework for corporate social responsibility (CSR): according to the Commission, being socially responsible means not only fulfilling the applicable legal obligations, but also going beyond compliance and investing more into human capital, the environment, and relations with stakeholders. The experience with investment in environmentally responsible technologies and business practices suggests that in going beyond legal compliance companies can increase competitiveness and it can have a direct impact on productivity.[33]

*d)* The *Communication concerning corporate social responsibility: A business contribution to sustainable development*, 2002, which concerns the social and environmental aspects of enterprises and which aims at the adoption of responsible practices in the social and environmental fields.[34]

*e)* The *Action plan modernizing company law and enhancing corporate governance in the European Union*, 2003, which intervenes in the sectors of corporate governance, in the safeguarding and alteration of company capital, company groups, and company restructuring (mergers and divisions).[35]

*f)* The *Communication on reinforcing the statutory audit in the European Union*, 2003: these initiatives consist in modernizing the Eighth Company Law Directive; strengthening the regulatory framework in the EU; reinforcing at Community level public oversight of the audit profes-

---

[31] COM (1999) 232 final, 05/11/1999, not published in O.J.

[32] COM (2000) 359 final, 06/13/2000. Among the acts adopted there is Regulation 1606/2002 of July 19th 2002 on *International Accounting Standards*. See below §.

[33] COM (2001) 366 final. Not published in O.J.

[34] COM (2002) 347 final, 07/02/2002.

[35] COM (2003) 284 final, 05/21/2003.

sion; imposing the use of International Standards on Auditing (ISAs) for statutory audits in the European Union as of 2005; improving the systems of disciplinary sanctions; establishing the transparency of audit firms and networks of such firms; as regards corporate governance, reinforcing audit committees and internal control; strengthening auditor independence and introducing a code of ethics; facilitating the establishment of audit firms and examining auditor liability.[36]

## 6. Harmonization within Member States

Directives make up the largest part of company law harmonization and they have brought about much innovation in this field in most of the European States, in many cases causing a real *revolution in national company law*. The Member States have had to pass a number of statutes and implementing provisions to approximate their national laws to those of the Community. This has come about through the passing of special acts, and by means of the amendment, addition or repeal of numerous provisions of the civil and commercial Codes (depending on the State in question). In this way company law has been revolutionized and the resulting transplants among differing legal systems are very evident.

As we have seen, in France, Germany, and Spain, for example, company law is set out in the Commercial Codes (and sometimes in special acts).

Naturally, given that the Commercial Codes mainly date from the second half of the nineteenth century (the French *Code de commerce* 1807, the German *HGB* 1897, the Spanish *Codigo de comercio* 1886), many of the provisions in these codes have been repealed by special laws, which have brought the contents up to date to support altered trading needs.

In Italy, on the other hand, they are in the Fifth Book of the Civil Code, called "*Del Lavoro*" (on Labor Law) although the provisions relating to financial services, common investment funds and stock exchanges are to be found in special acts which complement the Civil Code.

However, in all cases the way the Codes work is based on a system of cross-references from one provision to another. Thus, reform of some of the Code's provisions has automatically involved the amendment of others, both literally as well as from the point of view of interpretation, causing problems related to the lack of internal coordination.

Under British law, notwithstanding the lack of Codes, the subject is governed by a coherent and organic body of legislation; the main statutes

---

[36] COM (2003) 286 final, 05/21/2003.

to consider, so far as the adoption of directives is concerned, are the Company Acts passed from the 1970's onwards.

As we shall see in the following pages, the implementation of a directive in domestic law requires the national legislature to opt not so much for a passive or a-critical transference of the Community legal text, as for an approximation which will integrate harmoniously into the pre-existing national legal system.

We shall also be observing the fact that the adoption of a statute or decree implementing a Community directive in the domestic law of each Member State, does not automatically mean that the domestic law conforms to what thc directive has laid down.

But before embarking on an analysis of the directives and their adoption, it may be useful to set out some preliminary considerations.

As this book is being written, many plans for the reform of company law are under way in the Member States. The general factor which these various projects have in common is uncertainty about the rate of the regulatory intervention by each State.

The trend seems to be in favor of deregulation, and in this way new, more flexible kinds of company have been constituted: in France, the *société par actions simplifiée (S.A.S.),*[37] in Germany, the *kleine AG– Gesetz,*[38] in the UK, the *limited liability partnership (LLP).*[39]

In Italy, too, the reforms taking place are aimed at simplifying the regulation of private limited liability companies and public companies limited by shares (*società a responsabilità limitata* and *società per azioni*).[40]

In general, the reforms increase flexibility and place central importance on the shareholders and on the relations between minority and majority shareholders; they simplify the procedure for the formation and dissolution and winding-up of companies, respecting the principles of certainty, and the safeguarding of third parties.

The European States are setting out the reform of national company law from the point of view of corporate governance, in the knowledge that the discipline is deeply rooted in national traditions and practices,

---

[37] *Loi n. 94-1 du 3 janvier 1994 instituant la société par actions simplifiée*, as modified by *Loi n. 99-586 du 12 juillet 1999.*

[38] *Gesetz von 08/02/1994 für kleine Aktiengesellschaften und zur Deregulierung des Aktienrechts* (*BGBl*, 1994, I, 1961).

[39] *Limited Liability Partnerships Act 2000*, which received Royal Assent on July 20th 2000 (c.12).

[40] *D. lgs.* 01/17/2003, no. 6, *Riforma organica della disciplina delle società di capitali e società cooperative, in attuazione della legge 3 ottobre 2001, n. 366*, which entered into force on January 1st 2004.

and these are strictly tied to the economic organization of the State and to the local structure of industrial relations and collective labor relations.

Often, however, the reforms being made do not always take into account the European context and the internationalization of the markets. To avoid national systems following different directions and also other events of the caliber of the American *Enron* and *Worldcom* cases, the EC has presented a plan of company law reform developed by a commission of seven experts, led by the Dutchman Jaap Winter, called *The High Level Group of Company Law Experts' Observations and Recommendations*,[41] which should then be recast as Community directives. The European path of reform gives greater weight to the rights of shareholders, who have the task of verifying all the delicate phases of the life of a company, with the possibility of appealing to tribunals, a watch-dog role which they share with independent agents. This path is a different one to that followed in the US, which has chosen the hard solution of sanctions as a deterrent to opaque management conduct.

## 7. Harmonization in the CEECs

The same problem of internal coordination is posed for the East European legal systems, but it assumes much greater proportions due to the stratification of rules, practices, and legal models which developed during the last century. In fact, it is worth recalling that stratification of domestic law is typical of the East European legal systems. The various strata may be recognized because they typify diverse legal and economic policies.

A rapid review of these, which we adopt here for ease of explanation, shows four phases:

- A *pre-communist* phase.
- A *communist* phase.
- A *post-communist* transitional phase.
- The present phase of *harmonization of internal law with Community law*, in order to accede to the European Union.

In the pre-communist era, there already were sources of law in existence which, often in some detail, regulated commercial law, often in conformity with the law of the Austro-Hungarian Empire, German, or

[41] The Commission's report is dated November 4th 2002 and is available on the website http://www.europa.eu.int/comm/internal_market/en/company/company/modern/consult/report_en.pdf.

French law. The remnants of a solid legislative substructure was the point of departure for the process of the emancipation of enterprises from State monopoly. The renewal process began before the reforms of the 1980's in Poland, Hungary, Romania, Bulgaria, and Yugoslavia.

Since the beginning, Yugoslavia followed an independent path when constructing its socialist economy.

Poland and Hungary had already departed from the classic model of State entrepreneurship and planned economy during the 1970's, revising and adjusting the regulation of companies: the Hungarian governmental Decree of 1967 on State enterprises; the Hungarian Act no. 6 of 1977 on State-owned enterprises and no. 33 of 1984 on the enterprise Councils; the 1981 Polish Act on self-management of State-owned enterprises, the 1982 Act on cooperatives, the Act on Economic activity of 1988, and so on.

A model arose which tended to take up the German system of codetermination and, partly, the Yugoslav system of self-management.

In Czechoslovakia, which was faithful to the policy of the centrally-planned economy, reforms began with the fall of the Communist regime in 1989: the act which amended the Economic Code, no. 103/1990, introduced some novelties in the area of company law, recognizing the main types of partnerships and joint stock companies. Moreover, the acts on share companies, no. 104/1990, on private enterprise, no. 105/1990, on foreign investments, no. 112/1990 (amending no. 173/1988), on foreign economic relations, no. 113/1990, which abolished the State monopoly on foreign trade and established the basis for an arbitration court for the international trade sector at the Czech Chamber of Trade and Industry, had radically reformed communist economic law.

During the 1990's, the emphasis placed by commentators at home and by foreign advisors on the need to rewrite the sources of commercial law, brought about a renewal of Commercial Codes and the adoption of special new acts, above all to satisfy the parameters imposed by the EU with the objective of harmonization and integration into the internal market.[42]

The legal systems of the CEECs, which are facing the challenge issued by harmonization and standardization of Community law, are different from one another, apart from a nucleus of common problems inherited from the previous organization of the economy (the centralized planning system, the monopolistic structure of business, the absence of financial markets, the negligible impact of domestic capital in the dismantling of State ownership).

---

[42] See chapter III, in the first volume of this *Guide, A Commom Law for Europe*.

The variety of legal solutions adopted during the transition phase has been determined by the differing economic policies launched by the governments and the impact produced by economic reform in the area under the adjustment policies imposed by international organizations.

In the second place, the diversity arose from the history of the reform strategies followed by the CEECs during the twentieth century, above all in the field of rights of ownership, a central plank of Marxist–Leninist ideology. Indeed, as is well known, the long process of liberation from the centralized planning system, which began in Poland and Hungary, reaching as far as the Soviet Union during the last phase of *perestroika*, significantly affected the activity of the privatization agencies during the 1990's.

In the third place, the variety is the result of the institutional framework of these systems. The evolution of the debate over institutions in the CEECs has recently demonstrated that there is a tendency, in the post-communist era, to move in the direction of an "imperfect presidency" (of French, rather than American inspiration), which concentrates ample power in the hands of the Head of State and the Prime Minister. The picture has become even more complex as a result of the amendments introduced into the Constitutional Charters of many East European countries between 1991 and 1994. It should be added that the conflict between the legislature and the executive is conditioned by the electoral rules. Faced with the goal of ensuring the governability of countries in transition through a new democratic mandate, the electoral law draftsmen mainly adopted mixed systems, combining proportional representation and simple majority. This has influenced the dynamics of interaction between parliament and the executive. Besides, the resolution of possible disputes between the highest institutions of State has been entrusted to the new Constitutional Courts, established in all these countries after 1989 and which, besides influencing the process of creating a market economy, have generated a system of checks and balances.

The diversity is also the result of the national characteristics that each East European government has given to the privatization of the State enterprises during the 90's, and which has been retained, with obvious repercussions on the rules of commercial law. The initial choice of intervening in the economic transformation by public auction rather than free distribution of coupons, or share participation of employees rather than the entry of foreign investors, has caused growing structural differences in the ownership structure of the new companies.

Lastly, the variety is determined by the types of legal models circulating in the CEECs, and the adoption of new ones from the Community.

The adoption of the Community *acquis* in the field of company law is taking place at the moment in all the CEECs[43] and is being integrated into an extremely complex context.

In the Czech Republic and Slovakia, the new Commercial Code (*obchodnì zakonìk*)[44] has been in force since January 1992. This has absorbed many areas of the law relating to obligations which traditionally formed part of the Civil Code,[45] and is divided into four sections: I. the first contains general provisions, rules relating to the definition of undertakings, entrepreneurial activity, the Register of companies, competition; II. the second concerns commercial companies (as they are known in the East European tradition), associations and cooperatives; III. the third identifies a range of common provisions in the most common types of contract in international trade and sets out the regulation of obligations; IV. the fourth collects together the transitional and final provisions.

The new Commercial Code has rescued concepts and rules which traditionally belonged to the countries' pre-communist legal culture: for example, the company management model is based on the Czech Commercial Code of 1863, and the Slovakian one of 1875, modeled in their turn on the Austrian Commercial Code.

Moreover, the Code recognizes the importance of standard models: the 1980 Vienna Convention on the international sale of goods has been adopted as far as the rules governing the delivery of goods and sellers' duties are concerned, in § 412 of the Commercial Code itself; this means that, in so far as the Code deals with them, the Convention provisions will regulate contracts of sale between domestic parties as well.

In 1992, the Commercial Code repealed its communist predecessors, the Economic Code, and the International Commercial Code, which came into force in Czechoslovakia in 1964. The new Commercial Code, moreover, has repealed the transitional provisions of the years just after 1989, contained in the 1990 Act on Commercial Companies and the 1988 Act on Companies with Foreign Participation.

To cope with the commitments undertaken with the EU, the Czech and Slovak Commercial Code has been repeatedly amended. A very

---

[43] We refer the reader to the Regular Reports which the Commission publishes every year to indicate the stage that adoption of the *acquis* has reached. *Cf.* chapter III, cit. at the previous footnote.

[44] Act no. 513/1991 Coll., approved by the Czechoslovak parliament when the Countries were still one entity.

[45] The Civil Code presently in force was adopted in 1964 during the communist period, on an Austrian model. The Civil Code has been amended several times in the light of the changeover from a planned to a market economy.

extensive amendment was adopted in 1996; in particular, the provisions regulating joint-stock companies were substantially changed.

The practical experience of the application confirmed the opinion of the experts: the newly adopted provisions complicated the day to day business of all entrepreneurs. Therefore, the substantive and large amendment was adopted in 2000.[46] Unfortunately, it was adopted in a hurry, and its impact has been rather problematic. As a consequence, another amendment, the so-called "technical amendment" correcting mistakes, was adopted in 2001.[47] In its commentary to this new Act, the Czech Parliament indicated that the main aim of the changes was to eliminate some technical errors in the Commercial Code, solve interpretation issues, and reflect changes in the Czech legal environment. Additionally, this Act also amended the Civil Code, the Act on Civil Proceedings, the Notarial Act, the Trade Licenses Act, and the Securities Act.

The fact that amendments to the Commercial Code continually follow one another affects the general principle of certainty in the law and may therefore have negative repercussions on economic trade.

For example, the Czech Commercial Code allows for the following methods when restructuring companies:

– Fusion (merger, consolidation).
– Absorption.
– Separation.
– Change of legal form.
– Disposition.

The amendment to the Czech Commercial Code that took effect on January 1st 2001, brought about a number of significant changes in the legal rules governing the transformation of companies. These changes included the introduction of new transformation methods for Czech companies, as well as the implementation of several new requirements regarding transformation procedures.

Another amendment of the Commercial Code that came into effect on January 1st 2002, however, restricted this means of restructuring: the amendment stipulates that at the general meeting of the company to be taken over, the main shareholder cannot vote on the take-over. Further,

---

[46] The amendment came into force as of January 1st 2001. Act No. 370/2000 *Coll.* See on-line documents of the Central European Advisory Group: http://www.ceag.cz/index.php?lang=en&main=archiv.php, and the site in German *FiFo Ost at* http://www.fifoost.org/slowakei/recht/sfln/2001/node102.php

[47] Act No. 501/2001 Coll., which came into force on January 1st of 2002. The above-mentioned amendment incorporated the following EU Directives: the First, Second, Third, Sixth, Eleventh, Twelfth Council Directives on company law.

the main shareholder in a joint stock company must have more than a 95% share in the company being absorbed.

In this field, the Slovak Ministry of Justice is actively using assistance provided by Austria within the scope of a twinning project. The achievement of harmonization of laws has been facilitated by a working group composed of representatives of the Ministry of Justice, Prosecution General Office and an Austrian expert provided under the twinning project. At its regular meetings, the working group analyzed the above-mentioned Directives and incorporated them into Slovak Commercial Code or into the Civil Code.

So far as Hungarian company law is concerned (*Társasági jog*), the country has recovered some parts of the 1875 Commercial Code, whose rules were based on German law. The Company Law Act VI of 1988 (as amended in 1991 and 1999) provides both for partnerships and capital companies, as in the most usual western tradition: public companies limited by shares, private limited liability companies (modeled on the German *GmbH)*, commercial partnerships, and limited partnerships. With respect to the pre-communist period, the law does not mention sleeping (or silent) partnerships (*csendes társaság*), given that it can be formed and operate as a limited partnership.

The principle of *numerus clausus (limited number)* of the legal types of companies operates. No other types can be chosen than ones enumerated by the Act and the types cannot be mixed. The Act has admitted the single member limited liability company and the single member company limited by shares. The Act of 1988 follows the two-tier system (board of directors and supervisory board) of German law in respect of the organization of companies limited by shares. In the Hungarian system, however, the supervisory board is different from the German one. The formation of the supervisory board is compulsory with limited liability company as well as with partnerships. The Act of 1988 follows the German model of co-determination, as well. The representatives of employees are members of the supervisory board if the number of employees of the company or the partnership is above 200. The influence of the German model is clear in the regulation of groups of companies. The rules concern only companies limited by shares and distinguishes three groups according to the proportion of shares or voting rights (more than 25%, more than 50%, more than 75%) acquired by a company limited by shares in another company.

It should be noted that in the Hungarian legal system, commercial law is not separated from civil law, although it is contained in an *ad hoc* Act, namely the Company Law Act VI of 1988. The connection between the Civil Code and the Act of 1988 has been expressed both in the Civil

Code (enumerating the legal types of companies and referring to detailed rules) and in the Act (referring to subsidiary application of the rules of the Civil Code).

The same principle of unity (of commercial and civil law) is to be found in Poland. The country has renewed its sources through the Code of Commercial Companies of 2000 (*Kodeks spòtek handlowych*), which came into force on January 1st 2001.[48] It repealed the Commercial Code of 1934, which followed a German model.

The preparatory work on the new Code dates from the time of the 1999 Act on Business Activity, which came into force on January 1st 2000, devoted, in particular, to defining the tasks of national and local bodies in economic activity, and to regulating the activity of foreign operators on Polish territory and the activity of new economic operators (the small and medium enterprises).

The Commercial Companies Code is composed of Title I on General Provisions, common to various types of company, Title II concerning Partnerships, (registered partnerships, professional partnerships, limited partnerships, limited joint-stock partnerships), Title III which regulates Companies (limited liability company and joint-stock company), Title IV on Mergers, Divisions, and Transformations of companies and partnerships, Title V on Penal Provisions (imprisonment and fines), and finally Title VI on Amendments to Provisions in Force and Final Provisions.

The new Code has affected the whole structure of Polish company law, given that the principle of unity of civil law is still in force, and it was therefore necessary to synchronize the new provisions with the previous special legislation and with the Polish private law system: the 1934 Bankruptcy Act, the 1964 Civil Code,[49] the 1997 Banking Act, and the 1997 Act on Public Trading in Securities[50] have all been amended, amongst others.

The Commercial Companies Code regulates matters included in at least six Directives: the First, Second, Third, Sixth, Eleventh, and Twelfth (68/151/EEC; 77/91/EEC; 78/855/EEC; 82/891/EEC; 89/666/EEC; 89/667/EEC, see in the following §§). The Directives concerning

---

[48] Act of 10/15/2000, Journal of Laws, 2000 /94/ 1037.

[49] The Civil Code dates from the communist era; it is eclectic, alternating French-style rules with ones of a German type, within a structure of Pandectist inspiration (the Code has a General Part). It was also influenced by the Swiss codification and has been amended many times to sustain the changeover to a market economy.

[50] See arts. 596 & *ff.* of Title VI of the Code of Commercial Companies "Amendments to Provisions in Force" and "Final Provisions."

financial reports and auditors were implemented in special acts.[51] The Polish Committee for European Integration confirmed the compatibility of Polish Commercial Companies Code with the directives concerning European company law.

Bulgaria has replaced its 1897 Commercial Code, obviously pre-communist in origin, with the 1991 Act on commerce.[52]

In Romania, the setting up and operation of companies are currently regulated by Act no. 31/1990 on companies (amended by Act no. 99/1999 on measures for accelerating the reform), and by Act no. 26/1990 on the trade register. These general provisions are to be combined with the provisions of Act no. 241/1998 for the approval of the Emergency Ordinance of the Government no. 92/1997 on direct investments in Romania; of Act no. 64/1995 on the procedure of judicial reorganization and bankruptcy, amended by Act no. 99/1999 on measures for accelerating the reform; of Banking Act no. 58/1998, amended by the Emergency Ordinance of the Government no. 186/1999; of Act no. 32/2000 on insurance companies and insurance supervision; and of Act no. 105/1992 on private international law relations.

These Romanian rules are, to a large extent, harmonized with European Directives in order to ensure the harmonization of Romanian legislation with the *acquis communautaire*: on the setting up of companies and the disclosure requirements these must comply with, on safeguards required for members and third parties when the registered capital is altered or the statutes are amended by means of merger or division of a company, on supplementary safeguards which have to be provided to third parties by single-member private limited-liability companies, and on disclosure requirements applicable to the branches of a company.

Slovenia has passed the Act on Commercial Companies, which came into force on July 10th 1993.[53] The types of companies follow those familiar in the Member States. The silent partnership has also been regulated (*Tiha druzba)*: this concerns a tacit agreement between two parties—the entrepreneur and the silent partner. The latter supplies the capital (on loan or by investment) and shares the profits in her/his own name, but s/he does not figure in the company/partnership name, otherwise the rules on limited liability are invalidated.

---

[51] See for example, the Accounting Act dated September 29th 1994 (Journal of Laws, no. 121, Item 591 and successive amendments); the Act on Expert Auditors and the Board of Expert Auditors dated October 13th 1994 (Journal of Laws no. 121, item 592 and successive amendments).

[52] Amended by Act 25/1992 and later, by Act 83/1996.

[53] Official Gazette 30/93, *Slovenian Business Report*.

Company operation has been regulated using the German model: a watchdog committee (the supervisory board) is mandatory for companies with an initial capital of more than 300 million Slovenian Tolar, with more than 500 employees and more than 100 registered shareholders, and for companies quoted on the stock exchange in Ljubliana. Act no. 6/99 has amended the rules for the setting up of companies: it has abolished the requirement of Slovenian citizenship for the sole director and for the majority of the members of the board of directors; it has established the requirement to provide communications within the company in the Slovenian language (saving the rules on the Hungarian and Italian minorities).

Estonia, once outside the USSR, re-codified both its private law (Civil Code 1994) and commercial law (Commercial Code 1995). Naturally these codes, too, have undergone constant amendments and modifications. In general it could be said that the reform of company law is coming to an end. The last transitional period ended in September 1999.

Since September 1st 1999, the Commercial Code has conformed to the EU requirements concerning the minimum amount of share capital or stock capital of companies.

A private limited company (the share capital of which was less than 40,000 EEK) or a public limited company (the share capital of which was less than 400,000 EEK) was deemed to have undergone compulsory dissolution, in the case where the company had not submitted an application to the registrar of the commercial register to increase the share capital to the amount specified by September 1st 1999, or the company had not submitted an application concerning the transformation of the company to the registrar of the commercial register by September 1st 1999 at the latest.

During 1999, the required draft of amendments to the Commercial Code to harmonize the Twelfth Council Company Law Directive 89/667/EEC on single-member private limited-liability companies was elaborated. The *Riigikogu* adopted those amendments on March 22nd 2000 and they came into force on April 17th 2000.

On November 2nd 1999 the Estonian Government decided to join the European Business Register which will allow the cross-usage of registered data via internet. The simultaneity of the entry and the accessibility of information entered into the commercial register will be assured when the information entered in registers is electronically accessible.

The Act implementing the European Economic Interest Grouping (EEIG) Regulation was prepared during 1999 as well, and adopted by the *Riigikogu* on May 31st 1999.

Lithuania regulates both commercial and civil law matters in a single

Code, the Civil one. Parliament passed the Civil Code in 2000, and it came into force on July 1st 2001. The Lithuanian Commission for drafting a new code started work in 1992, to replace the previous communist-inspired one, which had been modeled on the 1961 Soviet Basis of Civil Legislation.

The importance of the new Civil Code can be characterized by its priority over other sources of law. If there are any contradictions between the Code and other statute or decrees, the provisions of the Code are applied, unless the Code itself gives priority to provisions of other acts (Art. 1.3 (3) of the CC).

Among the novelties, the Civil Code has changed the concept of a legal person, expanding the list of enterprises considered to be legal persons. Under Art. 2.50 (4) CC, legal persons are considered to be persons of both limited and unlimited civil liability. It should be noted that individual (personal) enterprises and partnerships are already considered to be legal persons of unlimited civil liability, whether or not the incorporation documents of the enterprise stipulate otherwise. "Unlimited civil liability" means that a legal person is liable not only to the extent of its own assets, but also to the extent of its owners' or members' assets.

The new Civil Code simplifies requirements for the contents of articles of association of a legal person. According to the Art. 2.47 (3) CC, there is no further need to indicate the competence of shareholders' meeting, the order calling the meeting, the competence of other organs of the legal person, nor the procedure of their appointment and revocation in the articles of association of the legal person, if these factors do not differ from the ones established by law and if they are indicated in the articles of association. It is no longer mandatory to indicate the types of business activities undertaken.

Moreover, Lithuanian commercial companies matters are regulated by the Company Act of 1994 (as amended in 2000)[54] on the establishment, reorganization, and liquidation of public and private companies, their management and activities, as well as the rights and obligations of their shareholders.

Latvia has restored the pre-war Civil Code of 1937, which was familiar with institutions such as '*legal transaction*' (in German: '*Rechtsgeschäft*'). A Baltic Code of Private Law of 1864, with German legislation and jurisprudence partly as a model, served as the basic civil legislation in the Baltic region, including present Latvia. The Code was given con-

---

[54] Company Act, July 5th 1994, no. I-528 (as amended by July 13th 2000 no. VIII-1835).

tinued validity in Latvia after independence in 1920. In 1937 it was replaced by Latvian Civil Code.

The pre-war code has been in force since September 1st 1992 and has been amended several times. The new Commercial Code came into force on January 1st 2002.

## 8. The Requirements for Disclosure, Validity of Obligations, and Nullity of Limited Liability Companies

On March 9th 1968, the Council adopted First Directive no. 68/151/EEC on coordination of safeguards which, for the protection of the interests of members and others, are required by Member States of companies within the meaning of the second paragraph of art. 58 (now art. 48) TEC, with a view to making such safeguards equivalent throughout the Community.[55]

Directive 68/151 expressly refers to art. 54 (3) (g), (now art. 44) TEC.[56] The provision sets out, among the tasks of the Council and the Commission, the necessary coordination of the system of guarantees which each Member State must require of the company in order to provide better protection for third parties and the members themselves, so as to put them in equal positions.

To this end, a general comparison with US law seems opportune, given that the reference to art. 54 (3) (g), (now art. 44) TEC is constant in the later directives as well.

Whereas in Europe the main objective of company law seems to be the safeguarding of creditors, whose protection is to be found directly in the source of law, in the US, the main aim of company law is to provide the greatest degree of flexibility and autonomy to shareholders. Creditors who want to protect themselves from the opportunistic conduct of shareholders (in the case that shareholders reduce the fund which credi-

---

[55] O.J., L 65, 03/14/1968. Among the first States to implement the Directive: Germany, *Gesetz zur Koordinierung des Gesellschaftsrechts* vom 08/15/69, *Bundesgesetzblatt* Teile I vom 08/18/69, Seite 1146; France, *Ordonnance* no. 69-1176 du 12/20/1969 *modifiant la Loi* no. 66-537 du 07/24/1966; *Décret* no. 69-1177 du 12/24/1969, *modifiant le Décret* no. 67-236 du 03/23/1967 *sur les sociétés commerciales* et le *Décret* no. 67-237 du 03/23/1967 *relatif au registre du commerce*, in JO, 12/28/1969, p. 12680; Italy, *Decreto del Presidente della Repubblica* del 12/29/1969 n. 1127, *modificazioni alle norme del codice civile sulle società per azioni, in accomandita per azioni e a responsabilità limitata, in attuazione della direttiva 9 marzo 1968, n. 151 del Consiglio dei Ministri delle Comunità europee*, in *Gazz. Uff., Serie generale*, 02/10/1970, n. 35, p. 782. In the UK, *The European Communities* Act *1972*.

[56] We refer the reader to § 3, this chapter, for the text of art. 44 TEC.

tors are relying on, deciding on the payment of dividends in their own favor, acquisition of their own shares, excessive bonuses and salaries, or taking on further debts) must do so by means of contracts.

> To put it simply, the US company law system makes a distinction between partnerships and companies. A partnership has no legal personality and does not always undertake commercial activity.
>
> The term 'company' was replaced at the beginning of the nineteenth century by the word 'corporation,' in the body of laws created following the war of independence, which was intended to provide a single discipline covering legal persons (corporations, as the case in point).
>
> Thus in the US it is preferable to use the expression 'general business corporation.' The source is the *US Model Business Corporation Act* (passed for the first time in 1950, later remodeled) which represents the federal legislative model adopted in most of the States. Corporations are divided into private and public, the first meaning a company which offers shares for public investment and is usually listed on stock exchanges.

When the Directive was adopted, some commentators, however, raised a doubt: the reference to art. 54 (3) (g) TEC may not have been sufficient for harmonization, in that the proposal to reach the harmonization of company law on a European scale should be sustained by more detailed 'guideline criteria.'

Such guideline criteria would have inspired the task of the various working groups in the most opportune way, and would have provided for the study and the first outlines of a framework which would thereafter become binding directives for all the Member States. In other words, the prospect of protecting shareholders and third-party interests would have seemed, in the view of the distinguished legal scholars of the time, too restrictive to achieve the Community principle of freedom of establishment.

This doubt did not only touch the academic world, but the European Parliament as well, which interrogated the Commission on the point, and replied that the objective of art. 54 (3) (g) was of primary importance, even though it was not the only source of harmonization criteria.

When the Directive was adopted, the legislation in the Member States had rules and principles which were substantially different. As regards the procedure for incorporating companies, to which the problem of invalidity is closely connected, the situation (in extreme synthesis) was as follows: in Italy and Germany, a system of control by judicial authorities had been adopted, while in the Netherlands the principle of administrative control of legality was in force. In Belgium and Luxembourg the control process was carried out by a notary who drew up the articles of association in an official document. In France, the law was confined to the requirement of a notarial act attesting that capital had been subscribed and $^1/_4$ of the sum deposited in money. In the UK and Ireland, sufficient and incontrovertible proof of valid constitution was provided by an official document, the memorandum of association.

Consequently, nullity in some countries depended on the absence of a written document necessary for registering the company in the Register of Companies, or else by the absence of the official document with the administrative provision for recognition (a formal condition typical of the German system, followed by the Italian one, the French one after 1966, and the Dutch one).

In other countries, on the other hand, a company could be constituted orally and was effective both in regards to members and third parties, at least until the latter took the point of formal invalidity against the company (a substantial aspect which was given importance by the Belgian and Luxembourg systems).

Given that the legislative panorama was very varied, the First Directive proposed coordination among the legislatures of the Member States, but only in the context of capital companies (both public stock corporations and private limited liability companies, to use American terminology).

> **Art. 1 Dir. 68/151.** "The co-ordination measures prescribed by this Directive shall apply to the laws, regulations and administrative provisions of the Member States relating to the following types of company: *In Germany:* die *Aktiengesellschaft*, die Kommanditgesellschaft auf Aktien, die Gesellschaft mit beschränkter Haftung; *In Belgium:* de naamloze vennootschap, de commanditaire vennootschap op aandelen, de personenvennootschap met beperkte aansprakelijkheid; la société anonyme, la société en commandite par actions, la société de personnes à responsabilité limitée; *In France:* la société anonyme, la société en commandite par actions, la société à responsabilité limitée; *In Italy:* società per azioni, società in accomandita per azioni, società a responsabilità limitata; *In Luxembourg:* la société anonyme, la société en commandite par actions, la société à responsabilité limitée; *In the Netherlands:* de naamloze vennootschap, de commanditaire vennootschap op aandelen; *In the United Kingdom:* Companies incorporated with limited liability; *In Ireland:* Companies incorporated with limited liability; *In Denmark:* Aktieselskab; KommanditAktieselskab; *In Greece:* ανώνυμη εταιρία, εταιρία περιωρισμένης ενθύνης, ετερόρρυθμη κατά μετοχές εταιρία; *In Spain:* la sociedad anónima, la sociedad comanditaria por acciones,

> la sociedad de responsabilidad limitada; *In Portugal:* a sociedade anónima de responsabilidade limitada, a sociedade em comandita por acções, a sociedade por quotas de responsabilidade limitada; *In Austria*: die Aktiengesellschaft, die Gesellschaft mit beschränkter Haftung; *In Finland*: osakeyhtiö/aktiebolag; *In Sweden*: aktiebolag."

The goal pursued was to offer both to third-party creditors and members too, protection of their interests through adopting measures or provisions which are equivalent over the whole territory of the Community.

In the Preamble to Dir. 68/151, the main problem with which the Directive was trying to deal was explained: namely, the protection of third parties, either regarding the possible non-validity of obligations assumed by the company's representatives, or with reference to the effects of a possible judicial ruling of nullity against the company and to the consequences that all this might have regarding the certainty of legal relations and commercial trade.

> **Whereas Dir. 68/151:** "(4) Whereas the basic documents of the company should be disclosed in order that third parties may be able to ascertain their contents and other information concerning the company, especially particulars of the persons who are authorised to bind the company;
>
> (5) Whereas the protection of third parties must be ensured by provisions which restrict to the greatest possible extent the grounds on which obligations entered into in the name of the company are not valid;
>
> (6) Whereas it is necessary, in order to ensure certainty in the law as regards relations between the company and third parties, and also between members, to limit the cases in which nullity can arise and the retroactive effect of a declaration of nullity, and to fix a short time limit within which third parties may enter objection to any such declaration (…)"
>
> The Court of Justice, too, has placed emphasis on the protection of third parties; see the case of *Daihatsu Handler v. Daihatsu Deutschland*, Case C-97/96 (1997), ECR 1-6843.

In drafting Dir. 68/151, the Community legislature was greatly influenced by the German model. In its concern to identify standard criteria in relation to the nullity of company acts with regard to third parties and to guarantee the latter effective and equal protection in all the Member States, the Directive therefore established as follows:

– A general, standard system of *compulsory disclosure* through:

1. publishing (an extract of) the documents in the national official journal.

2. filing a central register (arts. 2, 3 and 4 Dir. 68/151), open to the public. The central register keeps on record a file for each company, comprising in particular the instruments of constitution (articles of incorporation and by-laws), a list of the managers and members of the board of directors, a description of the capital, the annual balance sheet and profit and loss statement. In the US, on the contrary, State law usually requires only the articles of incorporation to be filed with a State office.

In June 2002, the European Commission proposed simplifying and modernizing the provision of company information. The draft proposal to modify the First Company Law Directive makes company information more easily and rapidly available to the public while at the same time simplifying the disclosure formalities required from companies. The proposed modifications would allow full advantage to be taken of modern technology. Companies would be able to file their documents and particulars either by paper means or by electronic means. Interested parties would be able to obtain copies by either means. Companies will continue to file their documents and particulars in the language(s) of their Member State, but would be able voluntarily to file the same information in other EU languages, in order to improve cross-border access. The new proposal explicitly allows the national gazette to be published in electronic form. The new proposal means that letters and order forms must be posted on the company website.[57]

– Fundamental rules concerning the *validity of obligations* entered into by a company, in order to protect third parties (arts. 7, 8 and 9 Dir. 68/151).

**Art. 7 Dir. 68/151**: "If, before a company being formed has acquired legal personality, action has been carried out in its name and the company does not assume the obligations arising from such action, the persons who acted shall, without limit, be jointly and severally liable therefore, unless otherwise agreed."

**Art. 8, Dir. 68/151:** "Completion of the formalities of disclosure of the particulars concerning the persons who, as an organ of

---

[57] Brussels, June 3rd 2002, in IP/02/798, COM(02) 248 final.

the company, are authorised to represent it shall constitute a bar to any irregularity in their appointment being relied upon as against third parties unless the company proves that such third parties had knowledge thereof."

**Art. 9, Dir. 68/151** "**(1)** Acts done by the organs of the company shall be binding upon it even if those acts are not within the objects of the company, unless such acts exceed the powers that the law confers or allows to be conferred on those organs. However, Member States may provide that the company shall not be bound where such acts are outside the objects of the company, if it provcs that the third party knew that the act was outside those objects or could not in view of the circumstances have been unaware of it; disclosure of the statutes shall not of itself be sufficient proof thereof. **(2)** The limits on the powers of the organs of the company, arising under the statutes or from a decision of the competent organs, may never be relied on as against third parties, even if they have been disclosed. **(3)** If the national law provides that authority to represent a company may, in derogation from the legal rules governing the subject, be conferred by the statutes on a single person or on several persons acting jointly, that law may provide that such a provision in the statutes may be relied on as against third parties on condition that it relates to the general power of representation; the question whether such a provision in the statutes can be relied on as against third parties shall be governed by Article 3."

– The definitive list of the cases in which a company may be declared *null and void*. The reasons are heterogeneous and concern both the act and the procedure of constitution (arts. 11 and 12 Dir. 68/151).

**Art. 11, Dir. 68/151:** "The laws of the Member States may not provide for the nullity of companies otherwise than in accordance with the following provisions: 1. Nullity must be ordered by decision of a court of law; 2. Nullity may be ordered only on the following grounds: (a) that no instrument of constitution was executed or that the rules of preventive control or the requisite legal formalities were not complied with; (b) that the objects of the company are unlawful or contrary to public policy; (c) that the instrument of constitution or the statutes do not state the name of the company, the amount of the individual subscriptions of capital, the total amount of the capital subscribed or the objects of the company; (d) failure to comply with the provisions of the national law concerning the minimum amount of capital to be paid up; (e) the incapacity of all the founder members; (f) that, contrary to the national law governing the company, the number of founder members is less than two. Apart from the foregoing grounds of nullity, a company shall not be subject to any cause of non-existence, nullity absolute, nullity relative or declaration of nullity."

**Art. 12, Dir. 68/151** "**(1)** The question whether a decision of nullity pronounced by a court of law may be relied on as against third parties shall be governed by Article 3. Where the national law entitles a third party to challenge the decision, he may do so only within six months of public notice of the decision of the court being given. **(2)** Nullity shall entail the winding up of the company, as may dissolution. **(3)** Nullity shall not of itself affect the validity of any commitments entered into by or with the company, without prejudice to the consequences of the company's being wound up. **(4)** The laws of each Member State may make provision for the consequences of nullity as between members of the company. **(5)** Holders of shares in the capital shall remain obliged to pay up the capital agreed to be subscribed by them but which has not been paid up, to the extent that commitments entered into with creditors so require."

The scope of the rules on nullity in arts. 11 &12 of the First Directive has been interpreted restrictively by the ECJ: see Case C 136/87, *Ubbink Isolatie BV v. Dak- en Wandtechniek BV, (*1988*)* ECR I-4665*;* Case C 106/89, *Marleasing SA v. La Comercial Internacional de Alimentacion SA*, (1990) ECR I-4135.

The Directive is very strict, in the sense that it has left only small and unimportant waiver options to the Member States, ensuring a high level of harmonization among the European legal systems.

### *8.1. Examples of National Transposition*

The provisions contained in the First Directive have shaken up the national legal systems, forcing the amendment of provisions in the Commercial or Civil Codes or in the special statutes in this field.

In Italy, for example, the Directive was implemented by presidential decree no. 1127 of December 29$^{th}$ 1969 and, according to Italian academics, represented a "small reform" of the Civil Code.

This involved the introduction into the Italian Civil Code of a very wide range of matters for compulsory disclosure through publication in a Company Register called the *B.U.S.A.R.L.* (*Bollettino ufficiale delle società per azioni e a responsabilità limitata*). Compulsory disclosure was made less onerous by the provisions of the Act on administrative simplification, no. 340 of November 24th 2000,[58] whose contents where later confirmed by the reform of company law brought into force with the legislative decree no. 2003/6.[59]

Regarding the cases in which a company may be declared *null and void*, novel provisions introduced by Dir. 68/151 have been even more important. The Italian legislator, in adopting the Community provision, has been compelled, first of all, to redraft art. 2332 of the Civil Code on the nullity of limited liability companies.[60]

The transposition of the Community Directive brought legal solutions into the Italian system which are diametrically opposed to those previously in force.

Before the Community action, nullity of the instrument of constitution and registration in the Company Register would also overturn all the other actions taken by the directors. Today, if the appointment of a director is invalidated, but it has (in any case) been made public in compliance with the duty of disclosure introduced by the Directive, the declaration of nullity is of no effect against third parties who have relied on the presumed validity of the appointment of the director (art. 2383 (5) *C.C.*).

The novel provisions are also evident in the case where a director exceeds the authority vested in her/him by the company memorandum or articles of association (art. 2384 (2) *C.C.*). Before the Directive, the Civil Code placed the burden on the third parties to search the Companies Register to verify whether the articles or memorandum of association limited the directors' executive powers in any way. The protection this burden afforded to third-parties was inadequate and certainly did not encourage cross-border trade between businesses. Therefore, art. 2384 *C.C.* was amended by the insertion of a general rule in favor of third-parties who have not intentionally acted to the detriment of the company.

---

[58] *Disposizioni per la delegificazione di norme e per la semplificazione di procedimenti amministrativi – Legge di semplificazione 1999*," *Gazz. Uff.*, no. 275, 11/24/2000. See arts. 30 & *ff.*

Act no. 340/2000 repealed sub-clause 3 of paragraph (1) of art. 2332; repealed art. 2383 (5) and amended its paragraph (6) (7); repealed art. 2385 (3), art. 2400, art. 2436, art. 2449, & art. 2450 *bis* of the Civil Code. Prior to the Directive, compulsory disclosure was only provided for by art. 2456 C.C.

[59] *D. lgs.* 01/17/2003, no. 6, *Riforma organica della disciplina delle società di capitali e società cooperative, in attuazione della legge 3 ottobre 2001, n. 366*, which enters into force on January 1st 2004, cited above, footnote 40.

[60] Following the reform of company law mentioned before, the new wording of art. 2332 *C.C.* drastically reduces the circumstances for nullity of a company. The former clauses 1, 6, 7 & 8 of art. 2332 have been repealed; no. 4 has been amended, to the effect that only the illegality of the company purpose involves nullity of the company.

Other novel provisions concern the apportionment of risk in an action which exceeds the authority vested by law or the company articles: to encourage contract-making, trade and the market the new article 2384-*bis C.C.* has laid down that the limit of executive power (*acting ultra vires)* can never be used against third parties acting in good faith, except in the case where the company can prove that the third party has acted with the intention of causing detriment to the company itself.

Among the CEEC's, let us look at the provisions of the Lithuanian legal system for compulsory disclosure. The subject is of no small importance, as it touches upon the system of public access to documents, which is of extreme interest for private individuals and raises the problem of its practical functioning.

In Lithuania, as in Italy, the rules on disclosure are contained in the Civil Code, which entered into force on July 1st 2001.[61]

Moreover, the new Company Act[62] has enacted the rules on disclosure, taking into account the requirements of the Europe Agreement, the Accession Partnership, and the provisions of the Council Directives (the First Directive 68/151/EEC as well).

Art. 79 (1) of the Company Act provides that all public and private companies shall amend their articles of association according to the provisions of the Act, and shall register them following the procedure established by the Act on the Register of Enterprises[63] within 24 months starting from the date of entry into force of the Company Act itself (i.e. by July 1st 2003).

The new rules on disclosure obliges the Government to simplify the existing registers of legal entities and to merge them into one Centralized Register of Enterprises. The 'State Land Cadastre and Register Enterprise' is the Chief Administrator of the Register. Other administrators of the Register shall also be executive bodies of local authorities.

At present, company registration procedure in Lithuania is the responsibility of 60 municipalities, each of which maintains a local register; the Ministry of Economy registers enterprises with foreign capital; the Bank of Lithuania administers the register of commercial banks. A number of other registers of legal entities are being administered by various Government institutions.[64]

---

[61] *Cf.* above § 7, this chapter.

[62] *Cf.* above § 7, this chapter.

[63] Act on the Register of Enterprises, July 31st 1990, no. I-440, (as amended by May 30th 2002, no. IX-918).

[64] The Register of educational institutions is administered by the Ministry of Education and Science, the Register of health institutions is administered by the Ministry of Health Care, the Register of cultural institutions is administered by the Ministry of Culture, etc.

According to the Civil Code, the Central Register of Enterprises is the principal register of the State and the documents disclosed by companies should be entered into the Central Register (companies disclose memorandum, articles of association and every amendment of these documents, the balance sheet, profit and loss account for each financial year and other documents). The whole list of these documents, data of the Central Register and the complete procedure of the disclosure should be regulated by other legal acts.[65] Data about registered companies should be published in the Official Journal, pursuant to the Government Resolution on Approving the Statutes of the Register of Enterprises.

These changes in the legal system shall also help to simplify the administrative procedures for the registration of enterprises. Memoranda and articles of association of legal entities and confirmation of amendments of data and documents must be monitored and approved by notaries (instead of state and municipal civil servants) at the time of their formation. Third parties may receive copies of these documents and other information about the companies in all parts of Lithuania.

Data and documents of companies disclosed in the Register, especially data regarding the change in the legal or financial status of a company (restructuring, bankruptcy, but especially liquidity, which is not currently being disclosed) greatly improve the business environment. Moreover, the new rules on disclosure provide the possibility for the third parties to become acquainted with the accounting documents, particulars of the persons who are authorized to bind the company, and other information concerning companies.

---

[65] The new legal acts and the amendments of the existing legal acts covering all regulations on functioning and registration of different legal forms of legal entities need to be adopted.

# 9. The Formation of Public Limited Liability Companies and the Maintenance and Alteration of their Capital

On December 13th 1976 the Council adopted the Second Council Directive no. 77/91/EEC on coordination of the safeguards which, for the protection of the interests of members and others, are required by Member States of companies within the meaning of the second paragraph of art. 58 (now art. 48) TEC, in respect of the formation of public limited liability companies and the maintenance and alteration of their capital, with a view to making such safeguards equivalent.[66]

Unlike the First Directive, the Second Directive 77/91 was laid down exclusively to govern *one type of company*:

> **Art. 1, Dir. 77/91:** "The coordination measures prescribed by this Directive shall apply to the provisions laid down by law, regulation or administrative action in Member States relating to the following types of company: *in Belgium:* la société anonyme / de naamloze vennootschap; *in Denmark:* aktieselskabet; *in France:* la société anonyme; *in Germany:* die Aktiengesellschaft; *in Ireland:* the public company limited by shares, the public company limited by guarantee and having a share capital; *in Italy:* la società per azioni; *in Luxembourg:* la société anonyme; *in the Netherlands:* de naamloze vennootschap; *in the United Kingdom:* the public company limited by shares, the public company limited by guarantee and having a share capital; *in Grece* η ανώνυμη εταιρία; *in Spain:* la sociedad anónima; *in Portugal:* a sociedade anonima de responsabilidade limitada; *in Austria* die Aktiengesellschaft; *in Finland:*osakeyhtiö / aktiebolag; *in Sverige:* aktiebolag.

On the contrary, in the US, not long after the Directive in question was adopted, art. 6.21 of the *US Model Business Corporation Act* was amended to abolish the concept of 'capital,' serving no purpose and potentially misleading to creditors of the public stock corporation.

---

[66] O.J., L 26, 01/30/1977. Among the first to implement it were Germany, with the *Gesetz zur Durchführung der Zweiten Richtlinie des Rates der Europäischen Gemeinschaften zur Koordinierung des Gesellschaftsrechts* vom 12/13/1978, *Bundesgesetzblatt* Teil I vom 12/19/1978, Seite 1959; the UK with *The Companies Act* 1980 and with *The Companies Act 1985* (as amended by the *Companies Act 1989*); France, with *Loi Num. 81-1162* du 12/30/1981, *JO* 12/31/1981, p. 359; Italy, rather late, with *d.p.r. 02/10/1986, n. 30 modifica della disciplina delle società in attuazione della direttiva CEE n. 77/91 del 12/31/1976* (*infra* this chapter).

The reasons behind the limitation to just one type of company may be read in the first part of the Preamble, but the exclusion of other types of capital company has been criticized by academics.

> **Whereas, Dir. 77/91: "(1)** Whereas the coordination provided for in Article 54 (3) (g) and in the General Programme for the abolition of restrictions on freedom of establishment, which was begun by Directive 68/151/EEC (3), is especially important in relation to public limited liability companies, because their activities predominate in the economy of the Member States and frequently extend beyond their national boundaries; (...)"

As the First one was, so the Second Directive is founded upon art. 54 (3) (g) (now art. 44) TEC, following the course of the Community strategy directed towards freedom of establishment.

The aim of the Directive was to coordinate the legislation of the Member States in the area of *company share capital*, acquisition of its own shares, and other operations regarding its own shares.

Before the adoption of the Directive and its necessary transposition by the Member States, there was a profound difference between the common and civil law systems.

Countries in the Roman Law tradition, given the fundamental importance of share capital, recognized as a concept which is fundamental for company activity and its financial equilibrium, had a range of provisions for the safeguarding of this capital which were quite well developed (and of which traces may be found in the old Commercial Codes).

On the other hand, the Common Law tradition, confined itself to distinguishing between authorized (or nominal) capital and issued capital. As a rule, the company did not immediately issue a number of shares which corresponded to the whole of the authorized capital, but reserved the option of issuing shares at any time as to the remaining part of the unissued capital, without having to account for it to the shareholders. Contributions were allowed in kind and in the performance of services, with no particular check by reference to their value. The share capital could be increased by resolution at an ordinary shareholders' meeting and no option rights existed over newly-issued shares. The only existing provision to protect capital was represented by the prohibition on the distribution of dividends, if not within the profit margins, but this rule was very elastic in its application.

Dir. 77/91 aimed at standardizing the national laws so as to protect the rights and interests of members and third parties, as was set out in the Preamble:

**Whereas, Dir. 77/91:** "(**2**) Whereas in order to ensure minimum equivalent protection for both shareholders and creditors of public limited liability companies, the coordination of national provisions relating to their formation and to the maintenance, increase or reduction of their capital is particularly important; (**4**) Whereas Community provisions should be adopted for maintaining the capital, which constitutes the creditors' security, in particular by prohibiting any reduction thereof by distribution to shareholders where the latter are not entitled to it and by imposing limits on the company's right to acquire its own shares; (**5**) Whereas it is necessary, having regard to the objectives of Article 54 (3) (g), that the Member States' laws relating to the increase or reduction of capital ensure that the principles of equal treatment of shareholders in the same position and of protection of creditors whose claims exist prior to the decision on reduction are observed and harmonised (...)"

Dir. 77/91 contains detailed provisions which refer to important aspects of share company activity and which concern, in particular:

- The *minimum amount of share capital*, which must not be less than 25000 Euros (art. 6).
- *Increase in subscribed capital*:

**Art. 26, Dir. 77/91**. "Shares issued for a consideration, in the course of an increase in subscribed capital, must be paid up to at least 25% of their nominal value or, in the absence of a nominal value, of their accountable par."

**Art. 27, Dir. 77/91** "(1). Where shares are issued for a consideration other than in cash in the course of an increase in the subscribed capital the consideration must be transferred in full within a period of five years from the decision to increase the subscribed capital."

**Art. 29, Dir. 77/91** "(1). Whenever the capital is increased by consideration in cash, the shares must be offered on a pre-emptive basis to shareholders in proportion to the capital represented by their shares."

**Art. 29, Dir. 77/91** "(4). The right of pre-emption may not be restricted or withdrawn by the statutes or instrument of incorporation. This may, however, be done by decision of the general meeting, through a written report indicating the reasons for restriction or withdrawal of the right of pre-emption, and justifying the proposed issue price."

The rule contained in art. 29 refers to a right of pre-emption, i.e. that a shareholder has the option to subscribe to new shares whenever they are issued in cash, unless the shareholders meeting restricts or withdraws the right when it authorizes the new share issue. Art. 29 does not refer to any right of pre-emption when shares are issued for consideration other than cash (i.e. in kind). According to Court of Justice, however, the article leaves Member States at liberty to provide (or not) for a right of pre-emption in the latter case. See the Case *Siemens v. Nold*, C-42/95, (1996), ECR 1-6017.

On the contrary, since the early days of the twentieth century, the US corporate law view has been that pre-emption should not be required when shares are issued to acquire assets or to carry out a merger, to avoid a time-consuming and expensive process (see US Modern Business Corporation Act, art. 6.30).

– *Reduction in capital*:

**Art. 30, Dir. 77/91** "Any reduction in the subscribed capital, except under a court order, must be approved by a 2/3 majority of the shareholders' votes, in person or by proxy; such decision shall be published in the manner laid down by the laws of each Member State in accordance with Article 3 of Directive 68/151/EEC."

**Art 32, Dir. 77/91 "(1)** In the event of a reduction in the subscribed capital, at least the creditors whose claims antedate the publication of the decision to make the reduction shall be entitled at least to have the right to obtain security for claims which have not fallen due by the date of that publication."

– *Distribution of profits*:

**Art. 15, Dir. 77/91** "*(a)* Except for cases of reductions of subscribed capital, no distribution to shareholders may be made when on the closing date of the last financial year the net assets as set out in the company's annual accounts are, or following such a distribution would become, lower than the amount of the subscribed capital plus those reserves which may not be; *(b)* Where the uncalled part of the subscribed capital is not included in the assets shown in the balance sheet, this amount shall be deducted from the amount of subscribed capital referred to in paragraph (a); *(c)* The amount of a distribution to shareholders may not exceed the amount of the profits at the end of the last financial year plus any profits brought forward and sums drawn from reserves available for this purpose, less any losses brought forward and sums placed to reserve in accordance with the law or the statutes; *(d)* The expression 'distribution' used in subparagraphs (a) and (c) includes in particular the payment of dividends and of interest relating to shares."

– The *acquisition by a company of its own shares*. Where the laws of a Member State permit a company to acquire its own shares, either itself or through a person acting in her/his own name, but on the company's behalf, they shall make such acquisitions subject to (at least) the following conditions:

**Art. 19, Dir. 77/91** "**(1)** (a) authorization shall be given by the general meeting, which shall determine the terms and conditions of such acquisitions, and in particular the maximum number of shares to be acquired, the duration of the period for which the authorization is given and which may not exceed 18 months, and, in the case of acquisition for value, the maximum and minimum consideration. Members of the administrative or management body shall be required to satisfy themselves that at the time when each authorized acquisition is effected the conditions referred to in subparagraphs (b), (c) and (d) are respected; (b) the nominal value or, in the absence thereof, the accountable par of the acquired shares, including shares previously acquired by the company and held by it, and shares acquired by a person acting in his own name but on the company's behalf, may not exceed 10% of the subscribed capital; (c) the acquisitions may not have the effect of reducing the net assets below the amount mentioned in Article 15 (1) (a); (d) only fully paid-up shares may be included in the transaction. **(2)** The laws of a Member State may provide for derogations from the first sentence of paragraph 1 (a) where the acquisition of a company's own shares is necessary to prevent serious and imminent harm to the company."

**Art. 22, Dir. 77/91** "**(1)** Where the laws of a Member State permit a company to acquire its own shares, either itself or through a person acting in his own name but on the company's behalf, they shall make the holding of these shares at all times subject to at least the following conditions: (a) among the rights attaching to the shares, the right to vote attaching to the company's own shares shall in any event be suspended; (b) if the shares are included among the assets shown in the balance sheet, a reserve of the same amount, unavailable for distribution, shall be included among the liabilities. **(2)** Where the laws of a Member State permit a company to acquire its own shares, either itself or through a person acting in his own name but on the company's behalf, they shall require the annual report to state at least: (a) the reasons for acquisitions made

> during the financial year; (b) the number and nominal value or, in the absence of a nominal value, the accountable par of the shares acquired and disposed of during the financial year and the proportion of the subscribed capital which they represent; (c) in the case of acquisition or disposal for a value, the consideration for the shares; (d) the number and nominal value or, in the absence of a nominal value, the accountable par of all the shares acquired and held by the company and the proportion of the subscribed capital which they represent."

The uniformization of the national laws in this case did not come about solely on the basis of the text of the Directive, but also on the basis of a comparison between the legal rules and practices of the Member States, in order to avoid placing the national undertakings of one State in a position of disadvantage with respect to those of another State.

Take, for example, the issue of the distribution of dividend payments, that is, the possibility of making interim dividend payments (i.e. more frequently than just once a year).

The objective of providing maximum guarantees for third parties requires an express prohibition on the payment of interim dividends. But since some States were against an absolute ban, the Directive had to be limited to the following assertion:

> **Art. 15, Dir. 77/91:** "(2) When the laws of a Member State allow the payment of interim dividends, the following conditions at least shall apply: (a) interim accounts shall be drawn up showing that the funds available for distribution are sufficient; (b) the amount to be distributed may not exceed the total profits made since the end of the last financial year for which the annual accounts have been drawn up, plus any profits brought forward and sums drawn from reserves available for this purpose, less losses brought forward and sums to be placed to reserve pursuant to the requirements of the law or the statutes."

This meant that the Member States could even have prohibited the distribution of any interim dividends. However, if the national legislature had accepted an absolute ban, this would have constituted a disincentive to investment in shares of companies whose registered office was within the national territory, in favor of investing in countries where interim payments were permitted.

If, on the one hand, the Directive has in theory left the option open to the States to decide on the rule to be applied, in practice the States have approximated their law to the most widely accepted model which is more favorable to the undertakings. So, in general terms, we can say that even when the directive offers various options to the States, the national legislature cannot confine itself to making a choice without first examining the conduct and choices of the other States.

However, there is the surprising fact that the capital protection rules of the Second Directive have led to virtually no preliminary references to the ECJ, leaving aside the Greek continuing cases[67] and two specific German cases.[68]

The Second Directive 77/91 has been partly amended by Council Directive 92/101/EEC of November 23rd 1992 on the formation of public limited-liability companies and the maintenance and alteration of their capital.[69]

Dir. 92/101 has added art. 24-*bis* to the previous Directive, with the aim of extending the prohibition on a company buying its own shares to include operations carried out by one company through another company, where the first has a majority of voting rights or is in a position to exercise a *dominant influence*.

> **Art. 24 *bis*, Dir. 92/101**: "1. (a) The subscription, acquisition or holding of shares in a public limited-liability company by another company within the meaning of Article 1 of Directive 68/151/EEC in which the public limited-liability company directly or indirectly holds a majority of the voting rights or on which it can

---

[67] Joined cases C-19 and 20/90, *Karella and Karellas*, 1991, ECR I-2691; Case C-381/90, *Syndesmos Melon*, 1992, ECR I-2111; Joined Cases C-134 and 135/91, *Kerafina*, 1992, ECR I-5699; Case C-441/93, *Pafitis*, 1996, ECR I-1347; Case C-367/96 *Kefalas*, 1998, ECR I-2843; Case C-373/97, *Dionysios Diamantis v Elliniko Dimosio (Greek State) and Organismos Ikonomikis Anasygkrotisis Epicheiriseon* AE (OAE), 2000, ECR I-1705.

[68] Case C-83/91, *Meilicke*, 1992, ECR I-4871 ; case C-42/95, *Siemens*, 1996, ECR I-6017.

[69] O.J., L 347, November 28th 1992. On the harmonisation of some national legal systems to the Directive, reference is made to the following sources of law: in France, *Loi* no. 66-537 du 07/24/1966 *sur les sociétés commerciales*, *JO*, 07/26/1966, p. 6402; *Décret* no. 67-236 du 03/23/1967 *sur les sociétés commerciales*, *JO*, 03/24/1967, p. 2843. In the UK, *The Companies Act 1985*; *The Companies (Northern Ireland) Order* 1986, *Statutory Instruments no. 1032 of 1986*; *The Companies Act 1989*; *The Companies (No. 2) (Northern Ireland) Order 1990*, *Statutory Instruments no. 1504 of 1990*. In Italy, *Decreto legislativo* del 05/02/1994, n. 315, *attuazione della direttiva 92/101/CEE che modifica la direttiva 77/91/CEE per quanto riguarda la costituzione della società per azioni, nonché la salvaguardia e le modificazioni del capitale sociale delle stessa*, *Gazz. Uff.*, *Serie gen*, 05/26/1994, no. 121, p. 4. In Spain, *Ley* no. 2/95 de 03/23/1995 de *Sociedades de Responsabilidad Limitada*, *BOE* no. 71, 03/24/1995, p. 9181 (Marginal 7240).

directly or indirectly exercise a dominant influence shall be regarded as having been effected by the public limited-liability company itself (…). 2. However, where the public limited-liability company holds a majority of the voting rights indirectly or can exercise a dominant influence indirectly, Member States need not apply paragraph 1 if they provide for the suspension of the voting rights attached to the shares in the public limited-liability company held by the other company. 3. In the absence of coordination of national legislation on groups of companies, Member States may: (a) define the cases in which a public limited-liability company shall be regarded as being able to exercise a dominant influence on another company; if a Member State exercises this option, its national law must in any event provide that a dominant influence can be exercised if a public limited-liability company: has the right to appoint or dismiss a majority of the members of the administrative organ, of the management organ or of the supervisory organ, and is at the same time a shareholder or member of the other company or is a shareholder or member of the other company and has sole control of a majority of the voting rights of its shareholders or members under an agreement concluded with other shareholders or members of that company. Member States shall not be obliged to make provision for any cases other than those referred to in the first and second indents; (b) define the cases in which a public limited-liability company shall be regarded as indirectly holding voting rights or as able indirectly to exercise a dominant influence; (c) specify the circumstances in which a public limited-liability company shall be regarded as holding voting rights."

## *9.1. Examples of National Transposition*

Let us consider what has happened in some Member States after the implementation of the Second Directive on the subject of the acquisition of its own shares by the company. The reform of the national legal systems was wholly inspired by the desire to protect company capital as a means of guaranteeing the interests of the members and creditors in the face of the so-called watering-down of capital.

In France, the Directive was adopted by act no. 81-1162 of December 30th 1981. Well before this act entered into force, there was a regime already in existence concerning the conduct of the *société anonyme* in relation to its own shares. Legal scholars spoke (and still speak) of *rachat*, an expression used to render a share-issue equivalent to a sale.

In general, such acquisition was held to be legitimate, so long as it did not concern the share capital (or the unavailable reserves), and on condition that equality among shareholders was maintained. This principle had been sanctioned by precedents of the French Supreme Court, which took a somewhat relaxed attitude to the question. Moreover, the Court's approach was not accepted by the French legislature in act no. 66-537 of July 24th 1966. Article 217 of the act forbade the acquisition of its own shares by the company, either directly or by those acting in their own name, but on behalf of the company. Certain exceptions to the rule were, however, permitted: the prohibition did not apply where the acquisition of its own shares was as a result of the reduction of share capital not achieved through losses, or where the shareholders agreed, and acquisition by employees. Other exceptions were allowed for listed companies.

The present regime is governed by articles L225-206 to L225-217 of the Commercial Code (*Code de Commerce)*: the prohibition rule has so many and so varied exceptions that, in fact, a general principle of authorization[70] has replaced a general principle of prohibition, at least in terms of compatibility with the Second Directive.

In Germany the model of the *Aktiengesellschaft* (*AG*) is governed by the Act known as the *Aktiengesetz (AktG)* of September 6th 1965 (and later amendments).[71] Of particular interest for these purposes are the amendments introduced by the Act of December 13th 1985, which approximated German law to the Second Directive. As a result of this Act, the acquisition of its own shares by a company is only permitted when this is indispensable for avoiding damage to the company, or if the shares are destined for the employees, when there is an increase in subscribed capital, following a testamentary disposition, or else, in certain cases with the consent of the shareholders. There is a historical reason for the particularly strict rules provided by the German legislation. The practice, which prevailed between the wars, of exploiting share issues on multiple votes and the acquisition of their own shares by companies had noticeably distorted the relationship between risk, capital, and government in German society. Therefore, to remedy this, the legislature proposed an *ad hoc* statute for the *Aktiengesellschaft*, causing the abolition of the regime under the 1887 Commercial Code, where it had been enacted.

The regime has been further amended on several occasions, most recently with the Act on the improvement of controls and transparency of company management, (*Gesetz zur Kontrolle und Transparenz im*

---

[70] The regime has been amended by act no. 2001-420 of May 15th 2001, inserted into arts. from L225-177 to L225-187 of the Commercial Code.

[71] See also § 17.2. and above, § 6.

*Unternehemensbereich* or *KonTraG*) passed on April 27th 1998,[72] with the aim of strengthening the German financial market. The Act has had particular effect on the type of company known as the *Aktiengesellschaft (AG),* and has introduced more flexibility into the regime concerning the acquisition of its own shares by a company, supporting a tendency that is under way throughout Europe.

In Italy, the Directive was adopted by presidential decree no. 30/86 of February 10th 1986, notably delayed with respect to the deadline of November 1978[73] which had been set down. In this way, the multifarious difficulties which can occur in implementing a directive such as the one under consideration, are revealed as being very broad in scope and possessing not inconsiderable innovative force. From a formal point of view, the Italian legislature, instead of enacting a specific new act, favored intervening directly in the structure of the Civil Code, as had been done when the First Community Directive was implemented, amending, substituting and adding about thirty articles to the Civil Code.

Quantitative limits on the acquisition of their own shares by companies were introduced by the new text of art. 2357 (3) *C.C.* (1/10 of the share capital within the limits of the available income and reserves) by previous consent of the ordinary general meeting, which has to determine precisely the way in which the acquisition is to be made, in order to reduce the directors' margin of discretion. Other new articles (2357-2357-*ter* and 2357-*quarter C.C.)* have introduced, respectively, certain exceptions to the limitations on the acquisition by a company of its own shares: the prohibition on directors from disposing of the shares which have been acquired without the consent of the general meeting, the prohibition on a company from buying its own shares, a prohibition never before expressly laid down in Italian law but which has always been considered implicit by academics.

In the UK, the implementation of the Second Directive came about with the Companies Acts of 1980 and 1985. It should be pointed out straightaway that it was only after the implementation of the Community Directive that the British system attributed a degree of importance to the concept of capital. The expression 'authorized capital' is still used,

---

[72] This act has also introduced other amendments mainly aimed at reforming the functioning of the *Vorstand* (management body/board of directors), of the *Aufsichtsrat* (supervisory body), of *Hauptversammlung* (general meeting) and of *Abschlußprüfer* (external auditors). *Cf.* § 17.2.

[73] Only as a consequence of a ruling against Italy by the ECJ for failure to implement within the prescribed time-limit of December 16th 1978: Case C-136/81, *Commission of the European Communities v. Italian Republic*, (1982) ECR-1 3547.

and it may still happen that the capital is not fully issued at the time of the company's constitution, but in such case the issued capital must be equivalent to the authorized capital, unless there is a corresponding reduction of issued capital. Moreover, the concept of 'minimum capital' was introduced for the first time, by which a public limited company may not be constituted in the UK without a minimum capital of £50,000 sterling. To set up such a company, the capital must be wholly subscribed, even if here the subscription refers to capital actually issued and not to authorized capital.

The general prohibition on a company buying its own shares was also introduced into the UK system: the law lays down severe penalties in the case of violation of the prohibition. However, exceptions are allowed with the same tolerance admitted by the Directive. The provision contained in art. 76 of the Insolvency Act 1986 is noteworthy: this sets out that if the company goes into liquidation in the year following the acquisition of its own shares, and its trading is insufficient to pay its debts and cover the costs of the insolvency proceedings, every member whose shares have been purchased is personally liable to the extent that s/he has benefited from the operation.

Therefore, also on the subject of the safeguarding of capital (in the event of reduction or increase) and operations relating to a company's own shares, the major differences between the continental European legal systems and the Common law one have been overcome by means of the Directive we are considering.

## 10. National Mergers and Divisions

The Community intervention aimed at regulating the two fundamental aspects of companies, the constitution and the safeguarding of capital, finished with the First and Second Directives. The European legislature's attention, therefore, turned to more specific areas.

The particular development of the manufacturing and commercial sector which took place in Europe in the second half of the last century, following the lead of events in the United States, had induced entrepreneurs to carry out economic operations in association with one another. Such operations were aimed at increasing the productive capacity of the national enterprises, uniting economic resources and 'know-how' in order (among other aims) to confront competition from the huge Japanese and American conglomerates. In this way, arising out of a very concrete necessity, the ever-more frequent practice of mergers and divisions among the large and medium enterprises was begun.

Hence arose the necessity for regulating such phenomena, by means of institutions which could ensure greater transparency for operations in themselves delicate, in that they concealed practices very often side-stepping shareholders' and creditors' rights.

On October 9th 1978, the Council adopted the Third Council Directive 78/855/EEC based on Article 54 (3) (g) of the Treaty, concerning mergers of public limited liability companies.[74]

This was followed on December 17th 1982 by the Sixth Council Directive 82/891/EEC based on Article 54 (3) (g) of the Treaty, concerning the division of public limited liability companies.[75]

We will treat them both at once since, while they do not concern precisely identical cases, they nevertheless present the same problems:

– Protection of the previous positions and the weighting of the votes of members, who necessarily change.
– Protection of groups of creditors which have opposing interests.

Let us compare the Preambles of the two Directives:

> **Whereas, Third Dir. 78/855**: "(**4**) Whereas in the context of such coordination it is particularly important that the shareholders of merging companies be kept adequately informed in as objective a manner as possible and that their rights be suitably protected; (**5**) Whereas the protection of employees' rights in the event of transfers of undertakings, businesses or parts of businesses is at present regulated by Directive 77/187/EEC; (**6**) Whereas credi-

---

74 O.J., L 295, 10/20/1978. Among the first countries to adopt the Directive was Germany, by the *Gesetz zur Durchführung der Dritten Richtlinie des Rates der Europäischen Gemeinschaften zur Koordinierung des Gesellschaftsrechts* (*Verschmelzungsrichtilinie-Gesetz*) vom 10/25/1982, *Bundesgesetzblatt* Teil I, 10/30/1982, Seite 1425; France, by the *Loi* no. 88-17 du 01/05/1988 *relative aux fusions et scissions de sociétés commerciales* et modifiant la *Loi* no. 66-537 du 07/24/1966 *sur les sociétés commerciales*, *JO*, 01/06/1988, p. 227. Italy, only by the *decreto legislativo* 01/16/1991, n. 22, which implemented both Directives on mergers and divisions.

75 O.J., L 378, 12/31/1982. Among the first countries to adopt the Directive was Portugal, by *Decreto-Lei* n. 262/86 de 09/02/86, *Aprova o Código das Sociedades Comerciais*, *Diário da República I*, Série no. 201, 09/02/86, p. 2293; France, by *Loi* no. 88-17 du 05/01/1988 *relative aux fusions et aux scissions de sociétés commerciales et modifiant la Loi no. 66-537 du 07/24/1966 sur les sociétés commerciales*, *JO*, 01/06/1988, p. 227; the UK, by *The Companies (Mergers and Divisions) Regulations* 1987, *Statutory Instruments no. 1991 of 1987*; Spain, by *Ley* no. 19/89 de 07/25/1989, *de reforma parcial y adaptación de la legislación mercantil a las Directivas de la Comunidad Económica Europea (CEE), en materia de Sociedades*, *BOE*, no. 178, 07/27/1989, p. 24085 (Marginal 17832); Germany, by the *Gesetz über die Spaltung der von der Treuhandanstalt verwalteten Unternehmen (SpTrVG)* vom 04/05/1991, *Bundesgesetzblatt* Teil I, 04/11/1991, Seite 854.

tors, including debenture holders, and persons having other claims on the merging companies must be protected so that the merger does not adversely affect their interests; **(7)** Whereas the disclosure requirements of Directive 68/151/EEC must be extended to include mergers so that third parties are kept adequately informed; **(8)** Whereas the safeguards afforded to members and third parties in connection with mergers must be extended to cover certain legal practices which in important respects are similar to merger, so that the obligation to provide such protection cannot be evaded (…)."

**Whereas, Sixth Dir. 82/891:** "**(5)** Whereas the protection of the interests of members and third parties requires that the laws of the Member States relating to divisions of public limited liability companies be coordinated where the Member States permit such operations; **(6)** Whereas, in the context of such coordination, it is particularly important that the shareholders of the companies involved in a division be kept adequately informed in as objective a manner as possible and that their rights be suitably protected; **(7)** Whereas the protection of employees' rights in the event of transfers of undertakings, businesses or parts of businesses is at present regulated by Directive 77/187/EEC; **(8)** Whereas creditors, including debenture holders, and persons having other claims on the companies involved in a division, must be protected so that the division does not adversely affect their interests; **(9)** Whereas the disclosure requirements of Directive 68/151/EEC must be extended to include divisions so that third parties are kept adequately informed; **(10)** Whereas the safeguards afforded to members and third parties in connection with divisions must be extended to cover certain legal practices which in important respects are similar to division, so that the obligation to provide such protection cannot be evaded (…)."

In both hypotheses, there is a transfer of capital from one economic entity to another, with all that follows regarding the position of the shareholders (both before and after the operation), as well as the rights of third-party creditors of the companies participating in the operation.

In a merger, the transfer of capital takes place through the incorporation of one or more companies in another (the one which takes over having the benefit of the entire capital of the one taken over), or else through the constitution of a new company (whose capital will be formed from the aggregate sum of capital of the companies which will cease to exist). In a division, the transfer of capital takes place through distribution of part of the capital to pre-existing companies, or through the formation of an *ad hoc,* newly constituted company.

The Third Directive considers two types of merger: one which takes place through the incorporation of one or more companies in another (Chapter II, Dir. 78/855), and one which occurs through the constitution of a new company (Chapter III, Dir. 78/855).

> **Definitions of mergers (Third Directive n. 78/855): art. 3** "**(1)** For the purposes of this Directive, "merger by acquisition" shall mean the operation whereby one or more companies are wound up without going into liquidation and transfer to another all their assets and liabilities in exchange for the issue to the shareholders of the company or companies being acquired of shares in the acquiring company and a cash payment, if any, not exceeding 10% of the nominal value of the shares so issued or, where they have no nominal value, of their accounting par value."
>
> **Art. 4** "**(1)** For the purposes of this Directive, "merger by the formation of a new company" shall mean the operation whereby several companies are wound up without going into liquidation and transfer to a company that they set up all their assets and liabilities in exchange for the issue to their shareholders of shares in the new company and a cash payment, if any, not exceeding 10% of the nominal value of the shares so issued or, where they have no nominal value, of their accounting par value."

In either case, the Directive expressly provides that the merger process involves the winding-up of the incorporated company (art. 19 [1]). In any case, the winding-up does not involve the liquidation of capital.

In its turn, the Sixth Directive provides two forms of division: division by acquisition (Chapter I), and division by the formation of new companies (Chapter II).

> **Definition of division (Sixth Directive n. 82/891): art. 2** "For the purposes of this Directive, 'division by acquisition' shall mean the operation whereby, after being wound up without going into liquidation, a company transfers to more than one company all its assets and liabilities in exchange for the allocation to the shareholders of the company being divided of shares in the companies receiving contributions as a result of the division (hereinafter referred to as 'recipient companies') and possibly a cash payment not exceeding 10% of the nominal value of the shares allocated or, where they have no nominal value, of their accounting par value."
>
> **Art. 21** "For the purposes of this Directive, 'division by the formation of new companies' means the operation whereby, after being wound up without going into liquidation, a company trans-

fers to more than one newly-formed company all its assets and liabilities in exchange for the allocation to the shareholders of the company being divided of shares in the recipient companies, and possibly a cash payment not exceeding 10% of the nominal value of the shares allocated or, where they have no nominal value, of their accounting par value."

The two Directives are principally characterized by the merger (or division) scheme, which must be elaborated by the directors of the participating companies, made public and available to the shareholders at least one month before the date fixed for the shareholders' meeting which must decide on the advisability or otherwise of the scheme, and submitted to the shareholders' meeting for approval (arts. 5 and 6 Dir. 78/855; arts. 3 and 4 Dir. 82/891). The scheme must be accompanied by a directors' written report, which sets the merger project out in detail, justifying it from a legal and economic point of view, with particular reference to the share exchange ratio (art. 9 Dir. 78/855; art. 7 Dir. 82/891).

Of particular importance too is the rule which states that the merger/division scheme must be submitted for evaluation by "one or more independent experts," designated by the participating companies "or appointed by a judicial or administrative authority," with the task of examining the merger/division scheme and producing a written report for the attention of the shareholders (art. 10 Dir. 78/855; art. 8 Dir. 82/891).

The search for legal certainty both in the relationship between the companies participating in the merger or division, and between the companies and third parties and, finally, between the shareholders themselves, requires particular care in the issue of nullity: the nullity rules for mergers and divisions are reserved for particularly serious cases, and a special type of confirmation is provided for all the other cases.

In fact, as occurred in the case of the Second Directive, the two Directives we are considering here also list a range of strictly defined circumstances (art. 22 Dir. 78/855; art. 19 Dir. 82/891), setting a relatively short time-limit as the limitation period for bringing forward the nullification proceedings.

**Art. 22 Dir. 78/855** "**(1).** The laws of the Member States may lay down nullity rules for mergers in accordance with the following conditions only: (a) nullity must be ordered in a court judgment; (b) mergers which have taken effect pursuant to Article 17 may be declared void only if there has been no judicial or administrative preventive supervision of their legality, or if they have not been drawn up and certified in due legal form, or if it is shown that the decision of the general meeting is void or voidable under national law; (c) nullification proceedings may not be initiated more than six months after the date on which the merger becomes effective as against the person alleging nullity or if the situation has been rectified; (d) where it is possible to remedy a defect liable to render a merger void, the competent court shall grant the companies involved a period of time within which to rectify the situation; (e) a judgment declaring a merger void shall be published in the manner prescribed by the laws of each Member State in accordance with Article 3 of Directive 68/151/EEC; (f) where the laws of a Member State permit a third party to challenge such a judgment, he may do so only within six months of publication of the judgment in the manner prescribed by Directive 68/151/EEC; (g) a judgment declaring a merger void shall not of itself affect the validity of obligations owed by or in relation to the acquiring company which arose before the judgment was published and after the date referred to in Article 17; (h) companies which have been parties to a merger shall be jointly and severally liable in respect of the obligations of the acquiring company referred to in (g). ( **2**) By way of derogation from paragraph 1 (a), the laws of a Member State may also provide for the nullity of a merger to be ordered by an administrative authority if an appeal against such a decision lies to a court. Subparagraphs (b), (d), (e), (f), (g) and (h) shall apply by analogy to the administrative authority. Such nullification proceedings may not be initiated more than six months after the date referred to in Article 17. (**3**) The foregoing shall not affect the laws of the Member States on the nullity of a merger pronounced following any supervision other than judicial or administrative preventive supervision of legality."

**Art. 19 Dir. 82/891:** "(**1**) The laws of Member States may lay down nullity rules for divisions in accordance with the following conditions only: (a) nullity must be ordered in a court judgment; (b) divisions which have taken effect pursuant to Article 15 may be declared void only if there has been no judicial or administrative preventive supervision of their legality, or if they have not been drawn up and certified in due legal form, or if it is shown that the decision of the general meeting is void or voidable under national law; (c) nullification proceedings may not be initiated more than six months after the date on which the division becomes effective as against the person alleging nullity or if the situation has been rectified; (d) where it is possible to remedy a defect liable to render a division void, the competent court shall grant the companies involved a period of time within which to rectify the situation; (e) a judgment declaring a division void shall be published in the manner prescribed by the laws of each Member State in accordance with Article 3 of Directive 68/151/EEC; (f) where the laws of a Member State permit a third party to challenge such a judgment, he may do so only within six months of publication of the judgment in the manner prescribed by Directive 68/151/EEC; (g) a judgment declaring a division void shall not of itself affect the validity of obligations owed by or in relation to the recipient companies which arose before the judgment was published and after the date referred to in Article 15; (h) each of the recipient companies shall be liable for its obligations arising after the date on which the division took effect and before the date on which the decision pronouncing the nullity of the division was published. The company being divided shall also be liable for such obligations; Member States may provide that this liability be limited to the share of net assets transferred to the recipient company on whose account such obligations arose. **(2)** By way of derogation from paragraph 1 (a), the laws of a Member State may also provide for the nullity of a division to be ordered by an administrative authority if an appeal against such a decision lies to a court. Subparagraphs (b), (d), (e), (f), (g), and (h) shall apply by analogy to the administrative authority. Such nullification proceedings may not be initiated more than six months after the date referred to in Article 15. **(3)** The foregoing shall not affect the laws of the Member States on the nullity of a division pronounced following any supervision of legality."

## *10.1. Examples of National Transposition*

As far as the implementation of the Third and Sixth Directives are concerned, it can generally be said that the two Directives have marked a very important point for all the European legal systems, given that the rules previously in force were completely inappropriate with regard to the phenomena of mergers and fusions which were taking place in the internal market.

Before the Directives were implemented, mergers were regulated by a few provisions in the old Commercial Codes, and division was ignored, because, usually, recourse was had to liquidating the company which was to be wound up, with notable problems of coordination between aims pursuant to the rules on liquidation and those on division.

It is, however, difficult to estimate the impact on the domestic legislation of the Member States. According to some commentators, the national legislatures have 'over-legislated' (the so-called *spill over* or *reflex effect*), but according to others, they governed 'by default,' saving only the objective of achieving the result established by the Directives.

However, in this way, 'standard exceptions' rather than 'standard rules' have been achieved in relation to legal rules which have, in many cases, remained diverse. In other words, the activity of harmonizing domestic law to Community Directives has harmonized the most visible differences between national systems, to create a partially common background for mergers and divisions within Europe.

Let us take a few examples in this case, to demonstrate the mechanisms of 'excessive' or 'default' approximation.

The national implementing acts trace the provisions of the two Directives fairly faithfully; in some cases, however, they differ quite markedly:

– *'By excessive approximation'*

In Italy, for example, the Third and Sixth Directives were implemented by a single act: the legislative decree of January 16th 1991, no. 22, which amended the Civil Code once again and definitively, introducing twenty-four new articles.[76] The Italian implementing legislation has extended the application of the two Community Directives to all types of company, whether joint-stock companies or partnerships, including cooperatives, while the Directives limit the field of application to public companies limited by shares, and public companies limited by guarantee having a share capital only. The restrictive attitude of the Community legislature did not seem coherent with the fact that the Directives were inspired by art. 54 (now art. 44) (3) (g), referring to art. 58 (now art. 48) (2) TEC, which makes reference to the interests of members and third parties, not only of share companies but all types, including partnerships. The Community legislators' choice may perhaps be justified on the grounds of pragmatism, given the need to simplify an area which was of itself already complicated, such as the one concerning mergers. Besides, the most frequent cases of merger and division occur precisely among the large share companies.

The Dutch legislation goes further than the Third Directive: mergers are possible for all legal persons mentioned in Book 2 of the Civil Code, except for associations without full legal personality.

Other examples of 'excessive' implementation of Community legis-

---

[76] New articles on mergers, from 2501 to 2501-sexies *C.C.*; new articles on divisions, from 2504-septies to 2504-decies *C.C.* Note that the articles on disclosure of national mergers and divisions have been modified or repealed by Act no. 340/2000 (cited above note). Following the amendments brought about by the reform of company law by *D.lgs.* no. 6 of January 17th 2003, mentioned above, the numbering of the articles has changed and these provisions are to be found (and in some cases have been redrafted) in a new Section of the Civil Code "On transformation, merger, and division."

lation can be encountered among the CEECs, such as Poland. Here, the new Code of Commercial companies, which came into force in January 2001, regulates, under arts. 491 and *ff.*, mergers, divisions, and transformations of companies and partnerships.[77] Companies may merge with other companies or partnerships; however, a partnership may not be the acquiring company or the new company. Also partnerships may merge with other partnerships, but only by forming a company. On the other side, a company may be divided into two or more companies. A joint-stock company or a limited liability company may not be divided if their share capital has not been fully paid up, but a partnership shall not be divided. Moreover, four types of division are set out in art. 59: division by acquisition; division by formation of new companies; division by acquisition and formation of a new company; division by separation.

– *'By default approximation'*

There is no mention in the Italian legislation of a definite list of cases of nullity of mergers or divisions (art. 22 of the Third Dir.; art. 19 of the Sixth Dir., cited above). However, such provisions should be applicable to the Italian legal system as well, by virtue of the general principle which in fact concerns directives that are sufficiently precise and unconditional, but also as a result of art. 22 Third Dir. and art. 19 Sixth Dir. themselves, which provide that "The laws of the Member States may lay down nullity rules for mergers (and for divisions) in accordance with the following conditions only (…)." The Italian implementing provision did not take into account, either, of arts. 24, 25, 26 Third Dir. (acquisition of one company by another which holds 90% or more of its shares). Such detailed provisions, declared by the Directive non-binding upon Member States, have not been implemented by the Italian legislature which, by art. 2504-*quinquies* C.C. (now renumbered art. 2505 cc, following the 2003 reform of company law) has provided for the case of the incorporation of a company whose capital is wholly owned by the acquiring company.

---

[77] Poland has introduced new types of companies with regard to the previous pre-socialist tradition. According to art. 4, § 1 of the Polish Code of Commercial Companies, partnership shall mean a registered partnership, a professional partnership, a limited partnership, or a limited joint–stock partnership; company shall mean a limited liability company or a joint–stock company.

## 11. The Rules on Annual Accounts of Certain Types of Companies

Another key moment in the activity of any company is represented by the production of the annual accounts, where the Community legislature has intervened by issuing a special directive, with the aim of harmonizing the national laws governing both the form and the content.

Given that the annual accounts represent, in the great majority of cases, the main (if not actually the unique) means of judging a company's state of health, it is obviously necessary to establish a common language for all Member States, which can allow any interested party to read the balance sheet, whether the company be Norwegian, Portuguese, French, English, or else Polish, Hungarian, Estonian, Romanian, Slovenian etc., without having to have recourse to interpretative criteria which are always different, and which may falsify the correct view of the state of the capital and the productive potential of a company active in the European market.

The harmonized rules in the area of annual accounts were introduced by the Fourth Council Directive 78/660/EEC of July 25$^{th}$ 1978 based on art. 54 (3) (g) TEC on the annual accounts of certain types of companies.[78] They are obligatory for public companies limited by shares or by guarantee, and for private companies limited by shares or by guarantee only.

The Preamble of the Directive on annual accounts confirms the primary objective, consisting of the protection of members' and third-party interests.

---

[78] O.J., L 222, August 14$^{th}$ 1978. Among the first countries to implement the Directive: Denmark, *Lov* nr. 284 af 06/10/1981, *Ministerialtidende* j nr. 101-2-80, and *Lov* nr. 285 af 06/10/1981 Ministerialtidende j nr.101-2-80; Germany, *Gesetz zur Durchführung der Vierten, Siebenten und Achten Richtlinie des Rates der Europäischen Gemeinschaften zur Koordinierung des Gesellschaftsrechts (Bilanzrichtlinien-Gesetz-BiRiG)* vom 12/19/1985, *Bundesgesetzblatt* Teil I, 12/24/1985, Seite 2355; France, *Tables des commerçants et de certaines sociétés avec la IVe directive adoptée par le Conseil des Communautés européennes le 07/25/1978, JO*, 05/03/1983, p. 1335, *Arrêté ministériel du 04/27/1982 portant approbation du plan comptable général révisé, Num. complémentaire du JO*, 05/07/1982, p. 4355, *Décret no. 83-1020 du 11/29/1983 pris en application de la loi no. 83-353 du 04/30/1983 et relatif aux obligations comptables des commerçant et de certaines sociétés, JO*, 12/01/1983, p. 3461; the UK, *The Companies Act 1985*; Italy, *Decreto-legge del 04/09/1991 n. 127, di attuazione delle direttive n. 78/660/CEE e n. 83/349/CEE in materia societaria, relative ai conti annuali e consolidati, ai sensi dell'art 1, comma 1, della legge 26 marzo 1990, Supplemento ordinario, Gazz. Uff., Serie gen.*, 04/17/1991 n. 90, following a ruling against it for non-compliance: Case C-17/85, *Commission of the European Communities v. Italian Republic*, (1986) ECR I-1199.

Indirectly, the Directive also pursues an objective which is to the advantage of the company itself. Indeed, owing to the possibility of comparison and analysis of the company's activity carried on throughout the year, businessmen and investors may decide to place their faith in it again.

**Whereas, Dir. 78/660:** "**(1)** Whereas the coordination of national provisions concerning the presentation and content of annual accounts and annual reports, the valuation methods used therein and their publication in respect of certain companies with limited liability is of special importance for the protection of members and third parties; **(2)** Whereas simultaneous coordination is necessary in these fields for these forms of company because, on the one hand, these companies' activities frequently extend beyond the frontiers of their national territories and, on the other, they offer no safeguards to third parties beyond the amounts of their net assets; **(3)** Whereas, moreover, the necessity for and the urgency of such coordination have been recognized and confirmed by Article 2 (1) (f) of Directive 68/151/EEC; **(4)** Whereas it is necessary, moreover, to establish in the Community minimum equivalent legal requirements as regards the extent of the financial information that should be made available to the public by companies that are in competition with one another; **(5)** Whereas annual accounts must give a true and fair view of a company's assets and liabilities, financial position and profit or loss; **(6)** Whereas to this end a mandatory layout must be prescribed for the balance sheet and the profit and loss account and whereas the minimum content of the notes on the accounts and the annual report must be laid down; **(7)** Whereas, however, derogations may be granted for certain companies of minor economic or social importance (…)."

The Directive has excluded banks, insurance companies and financial institutions from its area of application, which are subject to specific rules.

Regarding the annual and consolidated accounts of banks and other financial institutions, the Council adopted Directive 86/635/EEC of December 8th 1986 on the annual accounts and consolidated accounts of banks and other financial institutions (O.J., L 372, 12/ 31/1986).

Regarding insurance companies, there is Council Directive 91/674/EEC of December 19th 1991 on the annual accounts and consolidated accounts of insurance undertakings (O.J., L 374, 12/ 31/1991).

> Neither directive contains an exhaustive regime on the annual accounts, but they both confine themselves to laying down some specific rules, given the special position such institutions have in the market. For the rest, the Directives in question refer to the rules contained in the fourth and seventh Directives.

The Fourth Directive establishes the following general criteria:

- The annual accounts, shall comprise the *balance sheet*, the *profit and loss account* and the *notes on the accounts*. These documents shall constitute a composite whole.
- The annual accounts shall give a *true and fair view* of the company's assets, liabilities, financial position and profit or loss.
- The annual accounts, shall be drawn up *clearly and in accordance with the provisions of this Directive*. The layout of the balance sheet and of the profit and loss account, particularly as regards the form adopted for their presentation, may not be changed from one financial year to the next. In the balance sheet and in the profit and loss account the items prescribed in arts. 9, 10, and 23 to 26 of the Directive must be shown separately, in the order indicated. The layout, nomenclature and terminology of items in the balance sheet and profit and loss account that are preceded by Arabic numerals must be adapted where the special nature of an undertaking so requires; such combination makes for greater clarity, provided that the items so combined are dealt with separately in the notes on the accounts. Any set-off between asset and liability items, or between income and expenditure items, shall be prohibited.
- The annual accounts of all companies to which this Directive applies must be published *in accordance with Directive 68/151/EEC* (i.e. the First Directive; see *supra* § 8).

On the basis of these principles, the Fourth Directive sets out the technical rules on drawing up the balance sheet, based on the accuracy and transparency of the accounts, which the company must offer for inspection by means of further documents with regard to the annual accounts.

> **Art. 46 Dir. 78/660**: "Contents of the annual report. **(1)** The annual report must include at least a fair review of the development of the company's business and of its position. **(2)** The report shall also give an indication of: (a) any important events that have occurred since the end of the financial year; (b) the company's likely future development; (c) activities in the field of research and development; (d) the information concerning acquisitions of own shares prescribed by Article 22 (2) of Directive 77/91/EEC."

The Fourth company-law Directive on annual accounts was later modified by some directives: Council Directive 84/569/EEC of November 27th 1984 revising the amounts expressed in ECU in Directive 78/660/EEC;[79] Council Directive 90/604/EEC of November 8th 1990 amending Directive 78/660/EEC on annual accounts and Directive 83/349/EEC on consolidated accounts as concerns the exemptions for small and medium-sized companies and the publication of accounts in ECUs;[80] Council Directive 90/605/EEC of November 8th 1990 amending Directive 78/660/EEC on annual accounts and Directive 83/349/EEC on consolidated accounts as regards the scope of those Directives;[81] last amendment by Council Directive 99/60/EC of June 17th 1999.[82]

More recently, it has been amended by Dir. 2003/38/EC of May 13th 2003[83] and by Dir. 2003/51/EC of June 18th 2003,[84] with the aim of bringing Community provisions into line with international accounting legislation provided for by the International Accounting Standards Board (IASB)[85] and to ensure coherence in accounting harmonization in the EU.

Among the most important amendments introduced by Dir. 2003/51 the following should be noted: it clarifies the treatment of off-balance-sheet financing (debts and loans) and extends beyond the financial aspects the risk analysis made in companies' management reports. Member States should be able to modify the presentation of the *profit and loss account* and of the *balance sheet* in accordance with international developments of IASB; furthermore, the Member States should be able to permit or require the application of revaluations and of *fair value* in accordance with international developments; moreover, the information contained in the annual report and the consolidated annual report should not be restricted to the financial aspects of the company's business. It is expected that, where appropriate, this should lead to an analysis of environmental and social aspects necessary for an understanding of the company's development, performance or position, annual report, and the consolidated annual report. However, taking into account the evolving nature of this area of financial reporting, and having regard to the poten-

---

[79] O.J., L 314, 12/04/1984.

[80] O.J., L 317, 11/16/1990.

[81] O.J., L 317, 11/16/1990.

[82] O.J., L 162, 06/26/1999.

[83] Amending Directive 78/660/EEC on the annual accounts of certain types of companies regarding amounts expressed in Euro, in O.J., L 120, 05/15/2003.

[84] Amending Directives 78/660, 83/349, 86/635 and 91/674 on the annual and consolidated accounts of certain types of companies, banks, and other financial institutions and insurance undertakings, in O.J., L 178, 07/17/2003.

[85] See next §.

tial burden placed on undertakings below certain sizes, Member States may choose to waive the obligation to provide non-financial information in the case of the annual report of such undertakings.

The Directive 2003/51 also spells out the compulsory content of an *audit report*. It aims to harmonize the accounting rules applying to companies and other bodies not subject to EC Regulation no. 1606/2002 on the application of international accounting standards to listed companies[86] (around 5 million such companies). It thus removes any discrepancy between the accounting directives and the Regulation on the application of international accounting standards (IAS),[87] since it makes it possible to apply the IAS accounting options to companies that retain the accounting directives as their basic legislation.

In the *US legal system*, the rules are partially different. US State laws generally contain no direct requirements on the nature of financial statements, although case law on the fiduciary duty of management to shareholders requires that financial reports be reliable and not misleading. Federal securities regulations set precise requirements for the financial statements, auditors' reports, and management operating reports of companies that issue shares to the public.

## *11.1. The Convergence of Accounting Standards at the International Level*

The convergence of national accounting standards has certainly been pursued at *international* rather than European levels:

- A source of *standardization* is to be found in the GAAP standards (Generally Accepted Accounting Principles), i.e. the American standards as established by the Financial Accounting Standard Board (FASB). Up until today, if a European company wishes to be listed on an American stock exchange, the SEC requires that it carry out its financial reporting in accordance with the GAAP.

  GAAP is a combination of authoritative standards set by standard-setting bodies as well as accepted ways of doing accounting. A comprehensive source of US GAAP information is available in internet at http://www.investopedia.com/offsite.asp?URL=http://cpaclass.com/gaap/gaap-us-01a.htm.

---

[86] See next §.

[87] See next §.

– Another source of *standardization* is to be found in the IAS (International Accounting Standards) as elaborated by the IASC, the professional body in the field of accountancy since 1973.

IAS (the International Accounting Standards) were developed by the International accounting standards committee (IASC, see www.iasc.org.), which proposed developing a single collection of accounting principles valid worldwide. On the 1st of April 2001, the IASC was renamed the International Accounting Standards Board (IASB); the International Accounting Standards (IAS) were renamed International Financial Reporting Standards (IFRS).

– An *alternative* is the compromise between the two types of standards, as elaborated in the IOSCO (International Organization of Securities Commissions) or the WTO (World Trade Organization).

See the websites respectively at http://www.iosco.org/about/ and http://www.wto.org/.

The idea that the European Community should retain a separate body of law, without taking into account international accounting principles, could not be entertained; this would have put at risk the sourcing of capital in foreign markets.

On July 19th 2002, EC Regulation no. 1606/2002 of the European Parliament and of the Council on the application of international accounting standards was adopted.[88] The provision requires listed companies and all companies, when preparing the prospectus for public subscription for the purposes of stock market listing, to apply the IAS when drafting the consolidated accounts, as from January 1st 2005. This requirement is backed by the option left to each Member State to allow (or prohibit) listed companies to draw up the annual accounts too, in conformity with the IAS. The choice made by the Community legislature supports the internationalization of the financial markets: the aim is to create a single market for financial services, which is efficient and transparent, where the investor is able to compare financial information easily.

Subsequently, Commission Regulation no. 1725/2003 of September 29th 2003 adopted certain international accounting standards in accordance with Regulation no. 1606/2002.[89]

In any case, EC law should further review its *acquis* in the field of

---

[88] O.J., L 243, 09/11/2002, p. 1.

[89] O.J., L 261, 10/13/2003, p. 1.

accounting to fit the increasing number of international standards, in order to prevent possible conflicts.

As we have already seen, on June 18th 2003, the Directive 2003/ 51 on the annual and consolidated accounts of certain types of companies, banks, and other financial institutions including insurance undertakings was approved,[90] with the aim of eliminating the discrepancies between the directives cited and the IAS, to bring the accounting directives up to date and to encourage approximation to international standards.

Among the amendments introduced by the Directive, the authorization given to Member States to permit (or order) the inclusion in the annual or consolidated accounts of certain supplementary documents, such as, for example, the cash-flow statement; the authorization given to Member States to allow the presentation of the capital assets according to the IAS scheme, as an alternative to that proposed by the Community Directive.

Still in the context of the strategy for reinforcing the statutory audit in the European Union, in 2004 the European Commission proposed a new Directive on the statutory audit of annual accounts and consolidated accounts and amending Council Directives 78/660/EEC and 83/349/ EEC,[91] with the object of ensuring the confidence of investors and interested parties in the accuracy of accounts checked by auditors and of strengthening safeguards against financial scandals such as those which have recently overtaken the *Parmalat* group.

The draft Directive is aimed at clarifying the duties of auditors and establishing some ethical principles to ensure objectivity and arm's length dealing, particularly where the auditing companies also provide other services to their clients. The draft proposes the use of international accounting standards (IAS) for all auditing of accounts in the EU and lays the foundation for effective collaboration between the regulatory authorities in Member States and those of third countries, such as the US *Public Company Accounting Oversight Board* (PCAOB). This is crucial because capital markets today are globally interconnected.

## *11.2. Examples of National Transposition*

The Community model represents a compromise between two different ways of setting out a balance sheet in Europe: the *Common-Law model*, more generic and de-regulated, and the *Civil-Law model*, stricter and involving binding, detailed, statutory acts. As with all compromises, the system proposed at Community level has not gathered great consensus,

---

[90] See above, the previous §. On banks and other financial institutions and insurance undertakings *cf.* chapter III.

[91] COM (2004) 177 final, 03/16/2004.

either in academic circles or among the entrepreneurial community, and its implementation has not always been very satisfactory, because of the large number of derogations and exceptions which have had to be inserted into Dir. 78/660 on the insistence of the States.

Take, for example, the standard for *corporate financial reporting*. The Directive provides for the prevalence of the *true and fair view standard* (in French: *image fidèle*; in German: *ein den tatsächlichen Verhoverältnissen entsprechendes Bild*; in Italian: *veritiero e corretto*) detailed rules in exceptional circumstances (art. 2 [5]).

In such a case, any departure "must be disclosed in the notes on the accounts together with the explanation of the reasons for it and a statement of its effect on the assets, liabilities financial position and profit or loss." The compromise reached among the Member States resulted in granting them the discretion to define the cases which would qualify as "exceptional" and to lay down the relevant specific rules.

Even where the Community rules have been quite faithfully implemented, as for example in France and Italy,[92] reservations and criticism have not been lacking, which may end up influencing accounting practice, to the point of jeopardizing the goal of harmonization which the Community has endeavored to pursue.[93]

It should be noted that, when drafting their own Accounting Acts, many of the post-communist countries which in 2004 became Members of the EU have drawn inspiration from the IAS, the Community model on offer in the Directive, and to the US GAAP model: this is so, for example, in the cases of Estonia, the Czech Republic, Hungary,[94] Poland,[95]

---

[92] For example, the Italian Civil Code has been completely renewed in articles 2423 to 2432, with the addition of articles 2423-*bis*, 2423-*ter*, 2424-*bis*, 2425-*bis*, 2435, 2435-*bis*, 2488, 2491, 2403 (1). On this legislative basis, the 2003 reform of company law has intervened with some important amendments, the most significant of which concerned arts. 2423-*bis*, 2426 & 2427 *C.C.* In the first article, the Community guidelines have been implemented, which are aimed at favoring the representation in the balance sheet of all the economic events *according to the economic reality underlying the formal aspects*. The amendments of the other articles essentially concern the possibility of using the (internationally valid) criterion of *fair value (Italian: valore equo)* in evaluating the financial elements of the capital of the company.

[93] A study by the *Fédération des Experts Comptable Européens, Conceptual Accounting Frameworks in Europe* (Brussels, 1997) has given a picture of the diversity, as for example, the divergent application of the principle of *true and fair view*.

[94] *Cf.* the Act on Accountancy no. XVIII/1991 and the Act on Accounting 2000: see respectively *Hungarian Rules of Law in Force*, no. II/15, 1991 and no. XII/3–4, XII/5–6, 2001.

[95] *Cf.* the Audit Act 1991, the Accountancy Act 1994 as revised in 2000 and 2001: see respectively *Dz. U.*, 1991, no. 10, item 35; and *Dz. U.*, 2000, no. 60, item 703; no. 94, item 1037; no. 113, item 1186.

Slovakia, and Romania (the latter two still candidate countries). Here we should note the case of Slovenia which, when reforming its domestic law on accounting principles,[96] has drawn largely upon the IAS, and the Fourth and Seventh Community Directives (see below, next §).

In 1993, the Slovenian legislature issued the Companies Act,[97] which by Chapter 7 governs the annual accounts (*letno poročilo*), drawn from Austrian and German models, as well as the Community directives. Almost at the same time, in the spring of 1993, the Slovenian Council of accountants approved the principles and published them in the specialist accountants' magazine, the *Review of Accounting and Business Finance* (IKS).[98] In addition to the law and accounting standards, Slovenian book-keepers, accountants, experts in company finance, and auditors must observe the following:

- The Code of accounting principles (*kodeks računovodskih načel),* approved on March 22nd 1995 by the Council of experts of the Slovenian Auditors' Institute[99] obligatory for members of the associations forming part of the Association of book-keepers, accountants, and company finance experts.[100]
- The professional accountants' code of ethics *(kodeks poklicne etike računovodje),* a set of rules of conduct which the members must respect in the exercise of their professional duties.
- The code of principles of financial management *(kodeks poslovno-finančnih načel),* approved by the Council of experts of the Slovenian Auditors' Institute on December 11th 1997, which also concerns mergers and divisions, and their failure and liquidation.
- The code of professional ethics of the experts in company finance *(kodeks poklicne etike poslovnega finančnika)* approved by the Council of experts of the Slovenian Auditors' Institute on April 17th 1998.

---

[96] In the communist era, there was a Yugoslav federal act on accounting practice already in existence, which was then ratified by amendment XCVI of the Constitution of the Republic of Slovenia, becoming the Slovenian Act on accounting procedure.

[97] Published in the Official Gazette of the Republic of Slovenia 30/93 of 06/10/94.

[98] This is a unofficial translation of the title of this journal. See no. 5/93 of the magazine.

[99] This is the Slovenia institute deputed to achieve and approve new accounting standards. Founded by the Association of book-keepers, accountants, and company finance experts in 1994, by express provision of the Slovenian Auditing Act of 1993.

[100] This is a national professional association on a voluntary basis, founded in 1957, which today unites 33 associations in all of Slovenia. It is often consulted by the Slovenian Government, for the preparation of legal texts concerning its professional activity.

So far, it seems that the application of the rules and standards for financial reporting are being achieved in practice, and not only in the rhetoric of the provisions of the law.

## 12. The Consolidated Accounts

We have already seen, in relation to company mergers, how fundamentally important it is for European companies to be able to join together, with a view to strengthening their own position both within the internal market and outside it, in order to compete against other Community entrepreneurs, as well as those coming from the Far East or America.

This need involves the increasingly frequent recourse to merger schemes or regroupings, normally called *holdings* or simply *groups*, often of extremely large dimensions, whose economic activity is carried on beyond national boundaries and involves the interests of a huge number of both large and small investors and/or savers.

For this reason, the objective pursued by the Community legislators has been to oblige the groups of companies to present a truthful picture of the situation regarding capital, not just of the single enterprises which make up the group, but also the group in its entirety.

The annual accounts present the accounting position of a particular business. But if the business forms part of a group, its real economic situation may no longer correspond to its valuation in the annual accounts, in that it is strongly affected by the way the rest of the group to which it belongs is going.

In other words, examining just the annual accounts of a single company, the investor or any other third-party creditor may obtain information from it which does not correspond to the truth. For example, an enterprise may give the impression of enjoying a flourishing economic state of health, but not so the group to which it belongs; or, on the contrary, an enterprise which presents a negative balance-sheet may, however, when analysed in the context of the group of which it forms part, offer certain safeguards precisely because its contractual and economic relations of credit/debit with the other businesses in the group lead to the conclusion that the business is certainly not losing money.

Hence the need to create a balance-sheet which is additional to the individual ones of the companies forming a group, and which gives a precise picture of the whole.

The main problem encountered by the Community legislatuie was that not all the States possessed specific legislation on groups (for instance, France and Italy).

In the Italian system, the phenomenon of groups and consolidated accounts had never been regulated, but were recognized in practice, to the extent that a 1974 Act permitted the independent Italian authority, *CONSOB* (*Commissione nazionale per le società e la borsa)*, when they considered it necessary, to require certain groups of companies to draw up consolidated accounts (of which, however, no definition was supplied).

In France, the term *groupes* began being used by legal scholars to reflect the economic reality from the beginning of the 80's. During that period, many corporations, mostly privately owned, engaged in cross-participation with each other. The *groupe* had not been codified under the Act no. 66-537 of July 24th 1966, partly because, unlike a corporation, it was not regarded as a legal entity.

Under the French Act of 1966, there is control only to the extent that the controlling corporation owns stock representing at least 50% of the voting rights of other corporations in the network (L. 355-1). However, in certain cases, control could result from either a contract between shareholders and the controlling corporation or the *de facto* voting power the controlling corporation enjoys (although it holds less than 50% of stock of the other corporations).

In 1985, the *Cour de Cassation* provided some guidance as to the definition of a group.[101] In practice, a *groupe* denotes a network of corporations that are financially linked through participation (and not mere placement) with each other and subject to the control of one of them.

In those systems which provide for group/consolidated accounts (Germany, and Portugal, which has followed the German example) the legal rules were different. In Germany, the *Konzernrecht* has been the object of systematic study. The Stock Corporation Act of 1965 was the first to codify a law of groups for stock corporations.

This was the origin of the need to put the various rules of each Member State in order, and to encourage the States which had not as yet done it, to adopt legal rules aimed at protecting members of various group companies and third parties, providing them with a homogenous collection of financial information on the group.

The Community system was inspired by the German model, which was among the first countries in Europe to regulate the phenomenon.

The Community rules on the subject of consolidated accounts were

---

[101] In its famous decision, the *Cour de Cassation* defined a *groupe* as being a social and economic unit. See *Soc*. 27 mars 1985, *Bull. Civ. V*, n. 221 at 158.

introduced by the Seventh Council Directive 83/349/EEC of June 13th 1983 based on the art. 54 (3) (g) TEC on consolidated accounts.[102]

The Seventh Directive requires parent undertakings of "bodies of undertaking to produce consolidated accounts concerning such bodies as a whole, so that financial information concerning such bodies of undertakings may be conveyed to members and third parties."

It should be noted that the Directive does not define undertaking (the expression goes wider than company, and probably includes any business, whether incorporated or not). But this is subject to art. 4, which provides, in effect, that groups of undertakings are caught only if either the parent undertaking or at least one subsidiary undertaking is a limited company. Furthermore, art. 4 allows Member States to limit the requirement to produce consolidated accounts to those parent undertakings which are limited companies.

The Community act is important, besides having established the principles and criteria for the drawing-up of consolidated accounts, above all for having identified the so-called *consolidation area*. Substantially, this identifies the entities obliged to produce consolidated accounts and, as a result, has influenced the national legislatures in forming the concept of control of one undertaking over one or more others:

> **Art. 1, Dir. 83/349** "**(1)** A member state shall require any undertaking governed by its national law to draw up consolidated accounts and a consolidated annual report if that undertaking (a parent undertaking): (a) has a majority of the shareholders' or members' voting rights in another undertaking (a subsidiary undertaking); or

---

[102] O.J., L 193, 07/18/1983. Among the first to approximate their own domestic law to the Directive: Germany, *Gesetz zur Durchführung der Vierten, Siebenten und Achten Richtlinie des Rates der Europäischen Gemeinschaften zur Koordinierung des Gesellschaftsrechts (Bilanzrichtlinien-Gesetz-BiRiG)* vom 12/19/1985, *Bundesgesetzblatt* Teil I, 12/24/1985, Seite 2355; *Gesetz zur Änderung des D-Markbilanzgesetzes und anderer handelsrechtlichen Bestimmungen* vom 07/25/1994, *Bundesgesetzblatt* Teil I, 07/29/1994, Seite 1682; France, *Loi* no. 85-11 du 01/03/1985 *relative aux comptes consolidés de certaines sociétés commerciales et entreprises publiques*, *JO*, 01/04/1985, p. 101; *Décret* no. 86-221 du 02/17/1986 *pris pour l'application de la Loi* no. 85-11 du 01/03/1985 *relative aux comptes consolidés de certaines sociétés commerciales et entreprises publiques et portant dispositions diverses relatives à l'établissement des comptes annuels*, *JO*, 02/19/1986, p. 2729; *Arrêté ministériel* du 02/01/1991 *portant homologation de règlements du Comité de la réglementation bancaire*, *JO*, 02/22/1991, p. 1660; the UK, *The Companies Act 1989*; Italy, *Decreto legislativo of 12/30/1992 no. 526, implementing directive 90/604/CEE on annual accounts and 83/349/CEE on consolidated accounts so far as waiver for small and medium enterprises are concerned, including publication of accounts in ECU, Gazz. Uff., Serie gen., Supplemento ordinario n. 5.*

(b) has the right to appoint or remove a majority of the members of the administrative, management or supervisory body of another undertaking (a subsidiary undertaking) and is at the same time a shareholder in or member of that undertaking; or (c) has the right to exercise a dominant influence over an undertaking (a subsidiary undertaking) of which it is a shareholder or member, pursuant to a contract entered into with that undertaking or to a provision in its memorandum or articles of association, where the law governing that subsidiary undertaking permits its being subject to such contracts or provisions. A member state need not prescribe that a parent undertaking must be a shareholder in or member of its subsidiary undertaking. Those member states the laws of which do not provide for such contracts or clauses shall not be required to apply this provision; or (d) is a shareholder in or member of an undertaking, and: (aa) a majority of the members of the administrative, management or supervisory bodies of that undertaking (a subsidiary undertaking) who have held office during the financial year, during the preceding financial year and up to the time when the consolidated accounts are drawn up, have been appointed solely as a result of the exercise of its voting rights; or (bb) controls alone, pursuant to an agreement with other shareholders in or members of that undertaking (a subsidiary undertaking), a majority of shareholders' or members' voting rights in that undertaking. The member states may introduce more detailed provisions concerning the form and contents of such agreements. The member states shall prescribe at least the arrangements referred to in (bb) above. They may make the application of (aa) above dependent upon the holding's representing 20% or more of the shareholders' or members' voting rights. However, (aa) above shall not apply where another undertaking has the rights referred to in subparagraphs (a), (b) or (c) above with regard to that subsidiary undertaking. **(2)** Apart from the cases mentioned in paragraph 1 above and pending subsequent coordination, the member states may require any undertaking governed by their national law to draw up consolidated accounts and a consolidated annual report if that undertaking (a parent undertaking) holds a participating interest as defined in article 17 of directive 78/660/EEC in another undertaking (a subsidiary undertaking), and: (a) it actually exercises a dominant influence over it; or (b) it and the subsidiary undertaking are managed on a unified basis by the parent undertaking."

**Art. 17, Fourth Directive** states that "a participating interest means (…) rights in the capital of other undertakings (….) which by creating a durable link with those undertakings, are intended to contribute to the company's activities. The holding of part of

> the capital of another company shall be presumed to constitute a participating interest where it exceeds a percentage fixed by the Member States which may not exceed 20%."
>
> It should be noted that under **Arts. 4 to 11, Dir. 83/349**, Member States may grant exemption (and sometimes must) from the obligation to produce consolidated accounts, in a number of cases.

The significance of the definition of *consolidation area* derives from the fact that the identification of the entity under obligation is not (and could not be) made on the basis of the type of company (share company, private limited liability company, etc.), but on the basis of the particular relationship which binds that individual company to the group, and which goes beyond a simple numerical relationship among shareholders.

Indeed, such valuation criteria mainly take into account the effective and concrete power of control which an undertaking enjoys.

The Seventh Community Directive is very innovative because it sketches out the Community model of the '*controlled undertaking*,' refocusing the interpreter's attention from a quantitative to a qualitative criterion.

In referring to the control of one undertaking over another, what counts is not so much a question of a majority of shares, rather the '*de facto*' power which is indicated by many other circumstances.

Whenever a company, for whatever reason, possessing a sufficient number of votes to exercise *in fact* a dominating influence, is in a position to bring influence to bear over the decisions of another company, there exists, without doubt, a situation of control, and hence the parent company will be obliged to produce consolidated accounts.

## *12.1. Examples of National Transposition*

In adopting the Seventh Directive, the Member States have introduced new definitions of control into the national systems. Let us look at some examples.

In Italy, the Seventh Directive was adopted by legislative decree no. 127 of April 9th 1991, which also adopted the Fourth Directive on the annual account.[103] The difference lies in the fact that the rules on consolidated accounts were not inserted into the Civil Code because, as there was no existing provision in the Code, it was preferable to avoid problems of coordination which might have arisen from the introduction of a

---

[103] See above, § 11.

new element of commercial law into the Code. Therefore, while the provisions on the annual accounts are collocated within the Civil Code, the ones on consolidated accounts are in a special act, the legislative decree no. 127/91. Article 26 of the decree defines the concept of control, affirming that, apart from the cases under art. 2359 CC on "controlled corporations," (Italian: *societá controllate)* they are to be considered "controlled" in any case under two circumstances:[104]

- A contract or statutory condition between the controlling company (parent company) and the company forming part of the group (subsidiary), by which a dominating influence is exercised.
- An agreement between the parent company and the members of the other company in the group, whereby it exercises sole control of the majority of voting rights.

In France, after the passing of the Act 85-11 of January 3rd 1985 on consolidated accounts (French: *comptes consolidés*), which adopted the Seventh Directive, the Act of July 12th 1985 was passed, which has been incorporated in art. L. 358 of the Act of 1966. The latter Act has limited the scope of cross-participation between publicly-held stock corporations: a corporation (X) cannot hold another corporation's stock (Y) if the latter (Y) already owns more than 10% of the former corporation's stock (X).

Moreover, under French law, when a corporation holds a controlling (or substantial) amount of shares of its own stock, either directly or through one or several wholly-owned corporations, it is deemed to be controlling itself. In order to remedy the potential inability of shareholders to control the board, art. L. 359-1 of the Act of 1966, deprives the shares of a corporation's stock, which are owned by the same corporation, of any voting power. Infringement of this rule makes managers and executives liable for damages falling within art. 1382 of the Civil Code, as well as a fine laid down under L. 482 Act of 1966.

In the UK, Seventh Directive was adopted by the Companies Act 1989, passed on November 16th 1989. The Act has inserted a new section 227 in Part VII of the Companies Act 1985, prefaced *Duty to prepare group accounts.*[105] The Companies Act 1989 also introduced a new

---

[104] Following the 2003 reform of company law, the national legislature has intervened in the field of groups of companies, introducing new rules (from arts. 2497 to 2497–*sexies*) into Book V of the Civil Code. However, the new provisions do not introduce any definition of 'company group' or of 'control,' so both art. 2359 *CC* and the definition contained in *D.lgs* no. 127/91 remain unchanged.

[105] See art. 5, The Companies Act 1989, 1989 c. 40.

Section 258, still in Part VII of the Companies Act 1985, entitled *Parent and subsidiary undertakings*.[106]

Among the provisions laid down in Section 258,[107] which faithfully transposes the Directive, is the following.

The expressions "parent undertaking" and "subsidiary undertaking" shall be construed as follows: an undertaking is a "parent undertaking" in relation to another undertaking, a "subsidiary undertaking," if: (a) it holds a majority of the voting rights in the undertaking, or (b) it is a member of the undertaking and has the right to appoint or remove a majority of its board of directors, or (c) it has the right to exercise a dominant influence over the undertaking (i) by virtue of provisions contained in the undertaking's memorandum or articles, or (ii) by virtue of a control contract, or (d) it is a member of the undertaking and controls alone, pursuant to an agreement with other shareholders or members, a majority of the voting rights in the undertaking. A "parent company" means a parent undertaking which is a company.

For the purposes of Subsection (2), an undertaking shall be treated as a member of another undertaking, (a) if any of its subsidiary undertakings is a member of that undertaking, or (b) if any shares in that other undertaking are held by a person acting on behalf of the undertaking or any of its subsidiary undertakings.

An undertaking is also a parent undertaking in relation to another undertaking, a subsidiary undertaking, if it has a participating interest in the undertaking and (a) it actually exercises a dominant influence over it, or (b) it and the subsidiary undertaking are managed on a unified basis.

A parent undertaking shall be treated as the parent undertaking of undertakings in relation to which any of its subsidiary undertakings are, or are to be treated as, parent undertakings; and references to its subsidiary undertakings shall be construed accordingly.

The meaning of "undertaking" is specified in Section 259: (a) a body corporate or partnership, or (b) an unincorporated association carrying on a trade or business, with or without a view to profit.

The meaning of other related expressions are contained in Section 260: "Participating interest" means an interest held by an undertaking in the shares of another undertaking which it holds on a long-term basis for the purpose of securing a contribution to its activities by the exercise of control or influence arising from or related to that interest.

---

[106] See art. 21, The Companies Act 1989, 1989 c. 40.

[107] Schedule 10A contains provisions explaining expressions used in this Section and otherwise supplementing this Section.

A holding of 20% or more of the shares of an undertaking shall be presumed to be a "participating interest" unless the contrary is shown. "Interest in shares" includes: (a) an interest which is convertible into an interest in shares, and (b) an option to acquire shares or any such interest; and an interest or option falls within paragraph (a) or (b) notwithstanding that the shares to which it relates are, until the conversion or the exercise of the option, unissued. An interest held on behalf of an undertaking shall be treated as held by it.

By the end of the 90's, the CEECs had harmonized their national laws, approximating them to the Seventh Directive which we are considering. In Romania, for example, the Directive has been transposed into the Romanian legislation by the Methodological Norms for Consolidated Accounts, approved by the Order n. 772/2000 issued by the Minister of Finance; in Estonia the requirements of the Directive have been incorporated into Estonian legislation through the Accounting Act and the Business Code Amendment Act in 2000; in Bulgaria, accounting and financial reporting is regulated by the new Accountancy Act, enforced in the beginning of 2002. This Act also transposed the International Accounting Standards (IAS), adopted by the International Accounting Standards Board (IASB), as a primary basis of accounting and preparation of the financial statements for all Bulgarian companies. The introduced accounting principles are, in general, in accordance with the Fourth Directive. The change is to be effective from 2003 for financial institutions and companies listed on the Bulgarian Stock Exchange and from 2005 for all other enterprises.

## 13. The Directive on Persons Responsible for Carrying out the Statutory Audits of Accounting Documents

Once standard rules on the subject of producing annual accounts and consolidated accounts had been made, which also required that the relevant accounts should, by any type of company, be submitted for auditing by people authorized to do this, it became necessary to regulate the conditions for the exercise of the auditing activity in a standardized way as well.

This is the significance of the Eighth Council Directive 84/253/EEC of April 10th 1984 based on art. 54 (3) (g) TEC on the approval of persons responsible for carrying out the statutory audits of accounting documents.[108]

---

[108] O.J., L 126, 05/12/1984. Among the first countries to transpose the directive: Belgium, *Loi* du 02/21/1985 *relative à la réforme du révisorat d'entreprises*; *Arrêté royal* du 05/15/1985 *portant exécution des dispositions transitoires insérées par la loi du 02/21/*

**Whereas, Dir. 84/253: (3)** Whereas the qualifications of persons entitled to carry out the statutory audits of accounting documents should be harmonised; whereas it should be ensured that such persons are independent and of good repute; **(4)** Whereas the high level of theoretical knowledge required for the statutory auditing of accounting documents and the ability to apply that knowledge in practice must be ensured by means of an examination of professional competence; **(5)** Whereas the Member States should be given the power to approve persons who, while not fulfilling all the conditions imposed concerning theoretical training, nevertheless have engaged in professional activities for a long time, affording them sufficient experience in the fields of finance, law and accountancy and have passed the examination of professional competence (…)

This Directive has raised the quality of accounting standards and auditors in all the Member States. In June 2000, the Commission indicated that it intended to propose amendments to the accounting Directives in order to adopt international accounting standards.[109] In November 2000, the Commission recommended that all company auditors be subject to regular quality reviews, either peer reviews or periodic monitoring, to ensure more reliable audits, especially of quoted companies and financial institutions.[110] In May 2002, the Commission recommended a set of fundamental principles for protecting Statutory Auditors' independence (objectivity, integrity, and independence).[111]

**Recommendation of November 15th 2000:**
**Whereas:** "**(6)** The current national quality assurance systems differ in several aspects such as the scope of the quality review, being mandatory or voluntary, the cycle of coverage and the existence of public reporting. Such differences make it difficult to

---

*1985 dans la loi du 07/22/1953 créant l'Institut des Réviseurs d'Entreprises*; *Arrêté royal* du 04/15/1985 *portant désignation des membres du Conseil supérieur du Révisorat d'Entreprises*; Germany, *Gesetz zur Durchführung der Vierten, Siebenten und Achten Richtlinie des Rates der Europäischen Gemeinschaften zur Koordinierung des Gesellschaftsrechts (Bilanzrichtlinien-Gesetz-BiRiG)* vom 12/19/1985, *Bundesgesetzblatt* Teil I vom 12/24/1985, Seite 2355; Italy, *decreto legislativo* 01/27/1992 n. 88/1992; the UK, *The Companies Act 1989*.

[109] See §§ 11 & 11.1.

[110] Recommendation of November 15th 2000 on quality assurance for the statutory audit in the European Union: minimum requirements, (2001/256/EC), O.J., L 91, 03/31/2001.

[111] O.J., L 191, 07/19/2002, p. 22.

assess whether national quality assurance systems meet relevant minimum requirements. **(7)** At this moment there is no internationally accepted standard defining minimum requirements for quality assurance which could be used as a benchmark for national quality assurance systems. **(8)** The scope of this initiative on quality assurance is the EU statutory audit profession as a whole and it aims at setting a benchmark for Member State quality assurance systems throughout the European Union. (…)"

**Art. 4:** "Scope of the quality review. **(1)** Quality assurance relates to statutory audits of financial statements carried out by statutory auditors in public practice. The scope of the quality review should include an assessment of the internal quality control system of an audit firm with sufficient compliance testing of procedures and audit files to verify its adequate functioning. All Member States have already required audit firms to implement an internal quality control in line with the International Standard on Auditing 220 "Quality Control for Audit work". In addition to the black-lettered paragraphs of ISA 220 it could be necessary to establish at Member State level more specific requirements on the internal quality control of statutory auditors underpinning the quality reviews. These additional requirements could be based on the quality control procedures as mentioned in point 6 of ISA 220, dealing with the objectives of internal quality control systems of audit firms. **(2)** The scope of quality review should include the following subjects for testing individual audit files: the quality of the evidence from the audit working papers as a basis for assessing the quality of the audit work; compliance with auditing standards; compliance with ethical principles and rules, including independence rules; audit reports: 1. appropriate format and type of opinion; 2. compliance of financial statements with the financial reporting framework as referred to in the audit report; 3. failure to mention non-compliance of financial statements with other legal requirements as referred to in the audit report. A statutory audit carried out in compliance with legal requirements, established auditing standards and respecting ethical rules is crucial to users of audited financial information because it ensures a certain level of credibility of audited financial statements. Specific requirements are laid down concerning the audit report because of its importance as the public product of a statutory audit. Compliance with a financial reporting framework is included to underline the instrumental role of the statutory audit for the enforcement of accounting standards."

**Recommendation of May 16th 2002:**

**Whereas:** "(**1**) The independence of statutory auditors is fundamental to the public confidence in the reliability of statutory auditors' reports. It adds credibility to published financial information and value to investors, creditors, employees and other stakeholders in EU companies. This is particularly the case in companies which are public interest entities (e.g., listed companies, credit institutions, insurance companies, UCITS and investment firms). (**2**) Independence is also the profession's main means of demonstrating to the public and regulators that statutory auditors and audit firms are performing their task at a level that meets established ethical principles, in particular those of integrity and objectivity. (**5**) Member States' national rules on statutory auditors' independence currently differ in several respects such as: the scope of persons to whom independence rules should apply, both within an audit firm and outside the firm; the kind of financial, business or other relationships that a statutory auditor, an audit firm or an individual within the firm may have with an audit client; the type of non-audit services that can and cannot be provided to an audit client; and the safeguards which need to be put in place. This situation makes it difficult to provide investors and other stakeholders in EU companies with a uniformly high level of assurance that statutory auditors perform their audit work independently throughout the EU. (**6**) At present there is no internationally accepted ethics standard for statutory auditors' independence that could be used as a benchmark for national independence rules throughout the EU."

**Art. 1:** "(**1**) Objectivity and professional integrity should be the overriding principles underlying a statutory auditor's audit opinion on financial statements. The main way in which the Statutory Auditor can demonstrate to the public that a Statutory Audit is performed in accordance with these principles is by acting, and being seen to act, independently. (**2**) Objectivity (as a state of mind) cannot be subjected to external verification, and integrity cannot be evaluated in advance. (**3**) Principles and rules on statutory auditors' independence should allow a reasonable and informed third party to evaluate the procedures and actions taken by a Statutory Auditor to avoid or resolve facts and circumstances that pose threats or risks to his objectivity."

## *13.1. Examples of National Transposition*

In transposing the Eighth Directive, all the CEECs have regulated principally the *status* and *activity of auditors*, and Chambers of auditors have been established.

In the Czech Republic, for example, Act no. 524/1992, later amended by Act no. 63/1996, has reformed the subject. An auditor is defined as a person (a natural person or a company), enrolled in the register of Auditors held in the Chamber of Auditors. Before the reform, the professional body was represented by the group of employed accountants working for the Ministry of Finance.

In order to be registered in the list, it is necessary to be in possession of the requirements set out in art. 4 of Act no. 524/92 (and later amendments). The auditor's task is substantially to verify and form a judgment about the reliability of the accounts; this judgment is subject to scrutiny as to its accuracy.

The *independence* of the auditing activity is one of the fundamental principles expressed by the law. The Chamber of Auditors ensures the independence of the whole professional body against the power of the State: it is governed by a proper Assembly, which deliberates the decisions which the Council, the executive body, has the task of putting into effect, under the control of the Supervisory Board; finally, the fourth branch of the Chamber of Auditors, the disciplinary Commission, is competent to adopt any disciplinary measures for failure to observe the provisions of Act no. 524/1992.

The most significant requirements and principles defined in the Estonian Auditing Act are as follows. The Institute of Authorized Auditors is the body to govern the development of the profession. It is an independent body of auditors that counsel and monitor auditors' activities in Estonia. The program for the authorization examination is prepared by this Institute and approved by the Minister of Finance. The Minister of Finance has the right and obligation to supervise the activities of the Institute.

An *auditor* can be either a physical person or an audit firm; a person applying for authorization must have a university degree and three years of work experience under the supervision of an authorized auditor. A person authorized as an auditor in another state must pass an examination on Estonian legislation (the examination can be passed in English language). An *audit firm* can be either a partnership or a limited liability company. At least three fourths of the votes in an audit firm must belong to authorized auditors or another audit firm, and the majority of the Board of Directors of an audit firm must be authorized auditors. An auditor/an audit firm is liable for damage wrongfully caused to a client or a third person as a result of his/her professional activities; an auditor must insure his/her professional risks at least in the minimum amount and insurance conditions defined by the Board of the Institute; in order to maintain the authorization, an auditor must report once in three years to the Board of the Institute.

The Authorization Committee for Auditors, which was established by Government Order no. 1194 on November 2th 1999, consists of four representatives of the Institute of Authorized Auditors, 2 from the Ministry of Finance and 1 from the Bank of Estonia, the State Audit Office and the Tax Board. In 1999, the training of auditors, buying and translating international auditing, and accounting standards and literature was carried on. It is essential to raise the professional qualification of auditors. The Authorization Committee is financed from the State budget.

## 14. Disclosure of Branch Offices

An undertaking which wants to carry on part of its own business activity in a stable way, or, at least over some period of time, in another country as well, usually makes use of subsidiary or branch offices, or else an agency.

In the Community context, these three types of offices have been defined by the Court of Justice:

> Judgment of the ECJ of November 22th 1978, C-33/78, **Somafer SA v. Saar-Ferngas AG**; see § 12 of the judgment: **12.** "(…) the concept of branch, agency or other establishment implies a place of business which has the appearance of permanency, such as the extension of a parent body, has a management and is materially equipped to negotiate business with third parties so that the latter, although knowing that there will if necessary be a legal link with the parent body, the head office of which is abroad, do not have to deal directly with such parent body, but may transact business at the place of business constituting the extension."

However, whereas the *branch office*, having no legal personality, is not considered as a separate entity with respect to the parent undertaking, but only as its operational arm, on the other hand the *subsidiary* is understood as an entity possessing legal personality and independent assets. It concerns, substantially, an undertaking distinct from the parent company which merely has a controlling interest in it.

This means that, if a company operates in another country through *subsidiaries*, then the entire body of company law (as constituted following the harmonization process carried out in relation to the Community directives), will be applicable to these, in that they have independent legal personalities, i.e. in that they are, to all effects, national companies.

On the other hand, if the company operates through *branch offices,* these latter, in that they are entities which are not distinct from the parent company, could escape the harmonization process, and, in particular, could shirk precisely those fundamental rules which were introduced by the First Directive on the subject of disclosure of company information, to protect members and third parties.

This, then, is the significance of the Eleventh Council Directive 89/666/EEC of December 21st 1989[112] concerning disclosure requirements in respect of branches opened in a Member State by certain types of company governed by the law of another State.

The Directive closes the circle on the problem of disclosure by companies which operate in other States as well:

- If the company operates through an independent entity with legal personality, or a subsidiary, this will be subject to the rules under the First Directive.
- If it operates through other establishments, mere 'extensions,' such as branch offices, these will be subject to the rules under the Eleventh Directive.

The aim of the Eleventh Directive is the same as that underlying all the other directives to do with company law, namely the protection of members and, in this case, contracting third parties with whom the branch office comes into contact. Protection is ensured through making known, in the State in which the branch office operates, the relevant information

---

[112] O.J., L 395, 12/30/1989. Among the first States to implement the Directive: Spain, *Real Decreto* no. 1597/89 de 12/29/1989, *por el que se aprueba el Reglamento del Registro Mercantil, BOE* no. 313, 12/30/1989, p. 40407 (Marginal 30592); Germany, *Gesetz zur Durchführung der Elften gesellschaftsrechtlichen Vorschriften* vom 07/22/1993, *Bundesgesetzblatt* Teil I, no. 39, 07/29/1993, Seite 1282; France, *Décret* no. 92-521 du 06/16/1992 *relatif à la mise en harmonie du décret Numéro 84-406 du 05/30/1984 relatif au registre du commerce et des sociétés avec la onzième directive du Conseil des Communautés européennes* du 12/21/1989, *JO*, 06/17/1992, p. 7894; Italy, *Decreto-legge del 12/29/1992 n. 516, attuazione della direttiva 89/666/CEE relativa alla pubblicità delle succursali create in uno Stato membro da taluni tipi di Società soggette al diritto di un altro Stato, Supplemento ordinario n. 138 alla Gazz. Uff., Serie gen.,* 12/31/1992, n. 306; the UK, *The Companies Act 1985 (Disclosure of Branches and Bank Accounts), Regulations 1992, Statutory Instruments no. 3178 of 1992*; Northern Ireland, *Regulations 1993, Statutory Rules of Northern Ireland no. 199 of 1993, The Branch Disclosures Regulations 1993, Statutory Instruments no. 395 of 1993.*

concerning the parent company, whose registered office is in another country.

Consider, for example, the importance of information concerning the identity of the directors, their powers, statutory limits, and so on. The implementation of the Dir. 89/666, among other things, avoids unjust discrimination against businesses which operate abroad through subsidiaries and those which operate through branch offices. Hence, the Directive lays down that acts and information concerning branch offices operating within the EC are subject to disclosure in the Member State in which the branch office is situated.

The requirement of publicity concerns information such as the address of the branch office, the kind of business activity undertaken, the register in which the branch office is kept, the name and nature of the parent company, including the appointment, termination of office, and particulars of the people who have authority to represent the company in dealings with third parties, the dissolution of the company, and its accounting documents.

> **Art. 2, Dir. 89/666**: "The compulsory disclosure provided for in Article 1 shall cover the following documents and particulars only: (a) the address of the branch; (b) the activities of the branch; (c) the register in which the company file mentioned in Article 3 of Council Directive 68/151/EEC is kept, together with the registration number in that register; (d) the name and legal form of the company and the name of the branch if that is different from the name of the company; (e) the appointment, termination of office and particulars of the persons who are authorised to represent the company in dealings with third parties and in legal proceedings; as a company organ constituted pursuant to law or as members of any such organ, in accordance with the disclosure by the company as provided for in Article 2 (1) (d) of Directive 68/151/EEC; as permanent representatives of the company for the activities of the branch, with an indication of the extent of their powers; (f) the winding-up of the company, the appointment of liquidators, particulars concerning them and their powers and the termination of the liquidation in accordance with disclosure by the company as provided for in Article 2 (1) (h), (j) and (k) of Directive 68/151/EEC; insolvency proceedings, arrangements, compositions, or any analogous proceedings to which the company is subject; (g) the accounting documents in accordance with Article 3; (h) the closure of the branch."

In the second place, Member States have the option, if they consider it advisable, to require disclosure of the representatives' signatures as well, and the act of association and company statutes. Besides, in case of divergence between disclosure requirements in the State where the branch office operates and those in the State where the registered office is, the former always takes precedence concerning transactions carried out with the branch.

> **Art. 1, Dir. 89/666:** "**(1)** Documents and particulars relating to a branch opened in a Member State by a company which is governed by the law of another Member State and to which Directive 68/151/EEC applies shall be disclosed pursuant to the law of the Member State of the branch, in accordance with Article 3 of that Directive. **(2)** Where disclosure requirements in respect of the branch differ from those in respect of the company, the branch's disclosure requirements shall take precedence with regard to transactions carried out with the branch."

Finally, Member States are permitted to require that the act of constitution, statute, and accounts must be published in an authorized translation.

> **Art. 4, Dir. 89/666:** "The Member State in which the branch has been opened may stipulate that the documents referred to in Article 2 (2) (b) and Article 3 must be published in another official language of the Community and that the translation of such documents must be certified."

## *14.1. Examples of National Transposition*

Member States have harmonized domestic law to Dir. 89/666 with very different results from the point of view of rules introduced.

In Italy, for example, the Eleventh Directive was implemented by means of the legislative decree no. 516 of December $29^{th}$ 1992, which amended arts. 2428 (adding paragraph 4), 2506, 2626 e 2627 of the Civil Code, and adding art. 101-*ter* e 101-*quarter* to the implementing provisions of the Civil Code.

The implementation of the Directive could have been an opportunity to resolve some doubts on interpretation raised by art. 2506 CC, in particular whether or not it was necessary to have a judgment recognizing the foreign company operating in Italy through branch offices ("secondary offices" in the terminology of the Italian Civil Code), given that courts considered such a check as indispensable. But the Italian legislature, in harmonizing the content of art. 2506 CC to the provisions of the Eleventh Directive, was silent on this point, and left the problem of interpretation practically as it was.

A direction more in line with the practice in favor in other European legal systems was taken in the Act no. 340 of November 24th 2000, and lastly in the legislative decree no. 6 of January 17th 2003.[113] The reforms in company law make the process of constituting both a share company and a joint-stock company less cumbersome, with the aim of improving competitiveness of national companies.

As far as concerning this area, the reforms have replaced the former procedure of recognition of joint-stock companies by the courts (art. 2330 *CC*), slow and variable in length owing to the different practices among the Italian courts, for a new system of verifying the legality in advance, carried out by a notary who monitors both the formal regularity and the substantial legitimacy of the act of constitution. The reforms have also repealed a part of the first clause of art. 2506 *CC* (now art. 2508 *CC)*, which provided that the foreign company had to deposit the authenticated signatures of its permanent representatives in the territory of the Italian State, in the Italian register of business enterprises in the place where the branch office/secondary office was established. Furthermore, the new art. 2507 *CC* introduced by the reform of company law of 2003 provides that the interpretation and application of the civil code regime for companies set up abroad should be carried out on the basis of principles of the European Community legal system.

In the UK, implementation of the Eleventh Directive was achieved by means of Statutory Instrument no. 3178 of 1992, which came into force on January 1st 1993.

The principal purpose of these Regulations was to implement art. 11 of the Eleventh Company Law Dir. 89/666.

> **Art. 11 Dir. 89/666, Eleventh Directive**. "The following subparagraph is added to Article 46 (2) of Directive 78/660/EEC: «(e) the existence of branches of the company»."

> **Art. 46 Dir. 78/660, Fourth Directive**. "Contents of the annual report. 1. The annual report must include at least a fair review of the development of the company's business and of its position. 2. The report shall also give an indication of: (a) any important events that have occurred since the end of the financial year; (b) the company's likely future development; (c) activities in the field of research and development; (d) the information concerning acqui-

[113] Respectively *"Disposizioni per la delegificazione di norme e per la semplificazione di procedimenti amministrativi," Gazz. Uff.* no. 275, 11/24/2000, and *"Riforma organica della disciplina delle società di capitali e società cooperative, in attuazione della legge 3 ottobre 2001, n. 366,"* cited above.

sitions of own shares prescribed by Article 22 (2) of Directive 77/91/EEC."

In accordance with that provision, Regulation 3 has amended Schedule 7 to the Companies Act 1985,[114] which dealt with the content of the directors' report which accompanies a company's annual accounts, by inserting into paragraph 6 an additional requirement, *sub-paragraph (d)*, that the directors' report of a company (unless it is an unlimited company) contain an indication of the existence of any branches of the company outside the United Kingdom.

## 15. Single-Member Private Limited Liability Companies

The single-member private limited liability company was regulated to meet the needs of individual small and medium enterprises, to enable entrepreneurial activity to be undertaken without risking the entire sum of private capital.[115]

In systems where this institution was unknown, recourse was had, in order to obtain the same result, to dummy partners, holders of a minimum number of shares, men of straw or fiduciaries, by virtue of whom a limited company could be set up, so obtaining the advantage of limited capital liability. This brought about an unreal situation, concealing the true position, which never came to light unless the company's activities were closely examined, with fruitless added costs, dangers of disagreement and difficulty in running the business, which all had repercussions for third parties and creditors.

The Community, therefore, considered it more consistent to satisfy a widespread and real need, by regulating the phenomenon, on the basis that regulation and control was more effective than a general prohibition.

In the context of the Community policy which aimed at encouraging small and medium enterprises, the Community legislature issued the Twelfth Council Company Law Directive 89/667/EEC of December 21st 1989 on single-member private limited-liability companies.[116]

---

[114] Later amendments made to the Companies Act 1989.

[115] See *The small and medium-sized enterprises (SME) action programme*, approved by the Council Resolution of November 3rd 1986 (O.J., C 287, 11/14/1986).

[116] O.J., L 395, 12/30/1989. In Portugal, the issue was already regulated by the *Decreto-Lei* n. 248/86 de 08/25/1986, *Cria o establecimiento individual de responsabilidade limitada, Diário da Republica I* Série n. 194 de 08/25/1986, p. 2148; in Belgium as well, by the *Loi* du 07/14/1987 *relative à la société d'une personne à responsabilité limitée*; in France by *Loi* no. 85-697 du 07/11/1985 *relative à l'entreprise unipersonnelle à responsabilité limitée et à l'exploitation agricole à responsabilité limitée*, *JO*, 07/12/1985,

From a formal point of view, Dir. 89/667 is certainly essential and lacking in padding (there are only nine articles), but from the point of view of its contents, it was the harbinger of revolutionary effects for all those systems which did not already have similar company models.

The Preamble offers a very clear explanation of the reasons and criteria which were behind the Directive:

> **Whereas, Dir. 89/667:** "**(3)** Whereas the small and medium-sized enterprises (SME) action programme was approved by the Council in its Resolution of 3 November 1986; **(4)** Whereas reforms in the legislation of certain Member States in the last few years, permitting single-member private limited-liability companies, have created divergences between the laws of the Member States; **(5)** Whereas it is important to provide a legal instrument allowing the limitation of liability of the individual entrepreneur throughout the Community, without prejudice to the laws of the Member States which, in exceptional circumstances, require that entrepreneur to be liable for the obligations of his undertaking; **(6)** Whereas a private limited-liability company may be a single-member company from the time of its formation, or may become one because its shares have come to be held by a single shareholder; whereas, pending the coordination of national provisions on the laws relating to groups, Member States may lay down certain special provisions and penalties for cases where a natural person is the sole member of several companies or where a single-member company or any other legal person is the sole member of a company; whereas the sole aim of this provision is to take account of the differences which currently exist in certain national laws; whereas, for that purpose, Member States may in specific cases lay down restrictions on the use of single-member companies or remove the limits on the liabilities of sole members; whereas Member States are free to lay down rules to cover the risks that single-member companies may present as a consequence of having single members, particularly to ensure that the subscribed capital is paid; **(7)** Whereas the fact that all the shares have come to be held

p. 7082 and *Décret* no. 88-909 du 07/30/1988, *JO*, 08/04/1988, p. 9869. In Italy, the new type of company was introduced following implementation of the Directive: *Decreto legislativo* del 03/03/1993 n. 88, *di attuazione della direttiva 89/667/CEE in materia di diritto delle società relativa alla società a responsabilità limitata con un unico socio, Supplemento ordinario n. 34 alla Gazz. Uff., Serie gen,* 04/03/1993, n. 78, p. 5; so it was too in the common law systems, *Statutory Rules of Northern Ireland no. 405 of 1992: The Companies (Single Member Private Limited Companies) Regulations (Northern Ireland) 1992*; in the UK, *Statutory Instruments no. 1699 of 1992: The Companies (Single Member Private Limited Companies) Regulations 1992.*

> by a single shareholder and the identity of the single member must be disclosed by an entry in a register accessible to the public (…)."

To achieve this objective, the Community legislature had two models available for reference.

The first consisted in allowing the constitution of a single-member company with capital separate from the individual's and intended for the needs of the business activity; only this separate capital could be liable to possible seizure by creditors, in the case of insolvency. This was the model used in Portugal.

The second consisted in allowing the possibility of constituting a company which, from the outset, lacked the usual plurality of members. This model was already known and used in many countries of the Community: Denmark had passed its own act on the subject in 1973, Germany in 1980, France in 1985, Holland in 1986, and Belgium in 1987.

The Community legislators opted for the second solution. In this way it approved and, at the same time, also harmonized the choice made by some countries which had already regulated this institution.

The choice of the company model is justified on several counts.

First and foremost, all the Community legal systems already had a sufficiently harmonized set of rules in the area of company law because of the directives already issued in previous years and developed with a view to protecting third parties. Thus, it was possible to make use of this body of law which had been sufficiently tried and tested as to ensure that third parties had a range of information similar to that available for joint-stock companies, avoiding the need to lay down totally new rules, as would have been necessary had the option been chosen of the single entrepreneur with separate capital.

In the second place, the choice of the company model is justified for practical reasons too, such as, for example, its flexibility, in that the single partner/entrepreneur can have recourse at any time to the collaboration of other investors or entrepreneurs using the existing company structure. In the same way, should there is a shortfall in the number of members, the remaining member is not obliged to replace the members or dissolve the company.

The concern that this innovative instrument could be used to create inextricable links between companies, to the detriment of creditors and third parties, has profoundly affected the course of the Directive, which has been amended several times.

The original draft provided for certain severe restrictions. First of all, there was a prohibition on a single-person company, whose single member was a joint-stock company, from being in its turn the single member of another company. Besides, unlimited liability was laid down for company obligations arising from the period when the single member was a legal person; finally, size limits were set and there was a requirement of a minimum capital sum. In the final version, however, pending a Community regime on the subject of group companies, the option was preferred of a law which gave Member States the option of setting down some specific provisions on the point, without, however, giving precise indications.

This is the significance of art. 2 (2) Dir. 89/667, which states that "Member States may, pending coordination of national laws relating to groups, lay down special provisions or sanctions for cases where: (a) a natural person is the sole member of several companies; (b) a single-member company or any other legal person is the sole member of a company."

Dir. 89/667 first of all defines its field of application:

> **Art. 1, Dir. 89/667:** "The coordination measures prescribed by this Directive shall apply to the laws, regulations and administrative provisions of the Member States relating to the following types of company: in Germany*: Gesellschaft mit beschraenkter Haftung;* in Belgium*: Société privée à responsabilité limitée/de besloten vennootschap met beperkte aansprakelijkheid;* in Denmark*: Anpartsselskaber; in Spain: Sociedad de responsabilidad limitada;* in France*: Société à responsabilité limitée; in Greece: Etaireia periorismenis efthynis;* in Ireland*: Private company limited by shares or by guarantee;* in Italy*: Società a responsabilità limitata;* in Luxembourg*: Société à responsabilité limitée;* in the Netherlands*: Besloten vennootschap met beperkte aan- sprakelijkheid;* in Portugal*: Sociedade por quotas;* in the United Kingdom*: Private company limited by shares or by guarantee."*

Then, art. 2 (1) establishes that a company may have a sole member when it is formed and also when all its shares come to be held by a single person (single-member company). The Community regime follows, establishing that where a company becomes a single-member company because all its shares come to be held by a single person, that fact, together with the identity of the sole member, must either be recorded in the file or entered in the register within the meaning of art. 3 (1) and (2) Dir. 68/151, or be entered in a register kept by the company and accessible to the public (art. 3).

As far as relations between the single member and the company are concerned, the legislation, clearly motivated by protection of third parties, governs the powers of the single member with the same rigor as that used in multi-member companies: the sole member shall exercise the powers of the general meeting of the company and the decisions taken by the sole member shall be recorded in minutes or drawn up in writing (art. 4).

Similar strictness is required for contracts which the single member draws up with the company s/he represents: contracts between the sole member and her/his company as represented by her/him shall be recorded in minutes or drawn up in writing. The Member States need not apply this rule to current operations concluded under normal conditions (art. 5).

The Community regime ends with these few provisions, but at the same time opens up other possibilities for the Member States.

Hence the Directive allows Member States to provide for single-member companies within its own system of company law, as defined by art. 2 (1), in the case of public limited companies as well (art. 6). Germany, for example, was a country which availed itself of this possibility. The new rule, introduced as a result of implementation of the Directive, has been an important new feature for German company law in that, up till then, the *Aktiengesellschaften* could only be constituted with a minimum of five persons.

Moreover, Dir. 89/667 allows the States to lay down various kinds of companies apart from the limited company, but similar in effect, such as the single-person company with separate capital, designated for just the company business, on condition, however, that the guarantees and safeguards, set down by the Community legislators for the single-member private limited-liability company for third parties, are respected:

> **Art. 7, Dir. 89/667**: "A Member State need not allow the formation of single-member companies where its legislation provides that an individual entrepreneur may set up an undertaking the liability of which is limited to a sum devoted to a stated activity, on condition that safeguards are laid down for such undertakings which are equivalent to those imposed by this Directive or by any other Community provisions applicable to the companies referred to in Article 1."

The exception inserted by art. 7 was put into the Directive to meet the needs of the Portuguese who had opted, in 1986, for the single-member company with capital separate from the individual entrepreneur's, understood as a natural person.

### *15.1. Examples of National Transposition*

Let us look at the effects of harmonization in Member States which, before the Directive, had no such provision for this kind of company.

So far as the Italian system was concerned, not only were such forms of company not allowed, but also any prototypes involving a lack (even temporarily) of multiple members, were regarded with suspicion.[117] As far as the Italian system was concerned, any company should necessarily be constituted with a multiple membership. The absolutely exceptional and provisional case of continuing the business activity with anything less than multiple membership, involved unlimited liability for company obligations on the part of the single member.

This diffidence at the prospect of single-member companies reappeared in the implementation decree which, while allowing the new institution, laid down a series of rules all aimed at safeguarding the position of third parties and at suppressing any situation whatsoever which could also be a prelude to a possible abuse which not even the Directive itself had foreseen. The legislative decree no. 88 of March 3rd 1993, in implementing the Twelfth Directive, introduced important amendments to the articles of the Civil Code laid down on the subject of joint stock company (Italian: *Società a responsabilità limitata, S.r.l.*).[118] In the first place the implementation decree, operating on the original structure of company law, unhinged the basic concept of a company by amending art. 2247 *CC* which now is entitled 'Company Contract' (Italian: *contratto di società*) and no longer 'Definition of Company' (Italian: *nozione di società*), precisely in order to highlight the fact that a company may originate in a contract but also by unilateral act (art. 2475 (3) *CC*, now, after the reform of 2003, art. 2463 (1) *CC*). Also the *S.r.l.* may originate by the act of a single person, and not just become one, but above all may maintain the single member's benefit of limited responsibility. However, in 1993 the Italian legislature did not consider it advisable to make use of the option allowed to Member States to permit the existence of the single-person share company, revealing its small liking for the introduction of the single-person company and the entrepreneur with limited liability. The possibility of setting up a share company with one single-member was introduced later, in 2003 (see below).

It is important to underline the importance given by the new legisla-

---

[117] Indeed, before the Directive was implemented, the only references to a situation involving a single member were to be found in art. 2497 (2) *CC* (now art. 2484 CC) , and art. 2272, no. 4, *CC*.

[118] In particular, arts. 2475 (2), 2476, and 2497, and added arts. 2475-*bis* and 2490-*bis*.

tion to the problem of information available to third parties of acts concerning the single-person company, as well as the amendments which refer to the presence or otherwise of multiple membership.[119] In particular, the Italian legislature has strictly regulated the disclosure aspect, providing that the failure to observe this provision represents one of the causes for the extinction of the benefit of limited liability.

In fact, art. 2497 (2) *CC* (now, following the 2003 reform, the provision is to be found partly under art. 2462 *CC* and partly under art. 2484 *CC*), making use of the option allowed by the 5th "whereas" clause in the Preamble of the Twelfth Directive, sets out three cases of unlimited liability of the single member:

> Note that the option (or exception) is set out not in one of the Directive's articles, but in one of the 'whereas clauses,' a fact which confirms the importance of the Directives' Preamble, which takes on fundamental importance not only from the point of view of interpretation, but also from the point of view of the contents, whether of directives or regulations.

- When the single member is a legal person, or, if a natural person, is at the same time the single member of another joint-stock company.
- When the money has not been paid in full relative to the act of constitution or increase in capital, or within three months of its ceasing to be a multiple membership company.
- Until the identity of the single member has been disclosed in the business register.

Another form of disclosure is envisaged by the additional clause 4 of art. 2250 *CC*, whereby every act and article of correspondence of the company must indicate that it concerns a company with a single member.

Whereas art. 4 Dir. 89/667 concerns the form of the decisions taken by the single member, requiring the taking of minutes or the drawing-up of a written document of the resolutions adopted by the sole member exercising the powers of the general meeting of the company, nothing is said, in this regard, by the Italian implementing provision.

The reason can be found in the fact that the Civil Code already expressly provides for a written form of the meeting (art. 2375 *CC* & art. 2486 (2)

---

[119] The rules are contained in art. 2475-bis *CC* (now art. 2470 CC), which imposes disclosure in the business register (by the directors or the single member) regarding the identity of the single member, requiring the deposit (in order to be registered) of a declaration indicating name, surname, date and place of birth, citizenship, and domicile.

CC [now art. 2479 bis CC]). However, it should be recalled that the requirement to reduce into writing the resolutions taken by a single member exercising the powers of the general meeting, assume significance above all when the will of the member and that of the company must be kept distinct, or when the management of the company is not in the hands of the single member but in those of a third party.

The reform of company law in 2003, taking up the chance offered by the Community Directive (and as yet not exploited by the legislature), has introduced another novelty into the Italian legal system. We are referring here to the possibility of setting up a share company with one single member, something which is feasible under the new sub-clause of art. 2328 of the Civil Code.[120]

This, then, is a brief account of the characteristics of the regime of single-person limited liability and share companies in Italy. If the primary objective is to encourage the development of small and medium enterprises, the very evident concern for the protection of third parties emerges, through devices for safeguarding the company capital, for forcing the identity of the single member to be revealed, and for putting up obstacles to complex participation in other companies, devices which have gone well beyond the minimum requirements of the Directive.

The UK implemented the Eleventh Directive by Statutory Instrument 1992 no. 1699, *The Companies (Single Member Private Limited Companies) Regulations 1992*, which amended various legal provisions contained in the Companies Act 1985 and Insolvency Act 1986.

A single-member company is a private company, limited by shares or by guarantee, which is incorporated with one member, or whose membership is reduced to one person.

Under British law, the single-member company has the following characteristics:

- A single member cannot run the company.
- The company must still have at least one director and a secretary who cannot also be the sole director.
- Unless the company's articles of association specify anything to the contrary, a single member (present in person or by proxy) constitutes a quorum.
- If such a meeting is held, it must be recorded in the minutes.
- If a single member takes a decision, except by written resolution, then the decision must be given to the company in writing.

---

[120] This regime is to be found in art. 2331(2) *CC*, in art. 2342( 2) and (4) *CC* and in art. 2362 *CC*.

– If the company enters into an unwritten contract with the sole member who is also a director of the company (and the contract is not in the ordinary course of the company's business), the company must ensure that the terms of the contract are set out in a memorandum or are recorded in the minutes of the next directors' meeting.

A faithful harmonization of the Directive's provisions has taken place in the CEECs, where, from the Baltic States to the other Central–Eastern Countries of Europe, all have issued special statutes or amended their own Codes in the field of company law to accommodate the single-member company or single-member partnership. The single-member company was introduced to deal with the needs of privatization, in particular to legitimize the activity of the tax authorities, which often acted as a single member–founder of new private-owned commercial entities.

## 16. Takeover bids

The first Proposal of Thirteenth Directive on company law concerning takeover bids (or tender offers) dates from 1989[121] and was very ambitious. It was intended to establish the procedure for initial takeover bids, their revision and competing bids, and to prescribe in great detail the information that both the bidder and the company subject to the bid (the *target company*) must provide to shareholders. The draft governed the powers of Member State supervisory authorities, laying down certain principles and criteria which had to be observed, notably the equal treatment of shareholders and the obligation of the target board to act "in the interests of all the shareholders." The draft also barred the target management from employing several common defensive tactics without the consent of the shareholders, such as the issuing of new securities, the acquisition of the target's own shares, and the acquisition or sale of significant assets. The draft contained a compulsory buy-out provision to protect minority shareholders: any person who acquires 1/3 of a company's voting rights had to make a bid to buy the securities of all other shareholders.

Only the French and English systems already had significant experience on the subject of hostile takeovers and already had legislation governing takeover bids. In the UK, for example, takeover bids are still regulated by a City Code with which all public companies voluntarily comply, since the British experts in the field believe that to take legal action to resolve any conflicts in takeover bids is completely ineffective, above

[121] O.J., C 64, 03/14/1989.

all from the point of view of the time involved for a judge to find out all the facts surrounding the event and then decide on the merits.

In other countries such as Germany, Italy, and the Netherlands, on the other hand, takeover bids had (and still have) only a very insignificant role, leaving room for different legal instruments which, in fact, make hostile takeovers arduous tasks. Without doubt, an explanation of this difference lies in the eclectic makeup of the capital markets in the different European countries. In Germany, reference has to be made to the part played by the universal banks, employee codetermination laws, and the role of other creditor-protection provisions of German company law.

In 1997, a substantially revised and shorter version of the draft was formulated.[122] Under art. 5, target companies must give all security holders "equivalent treatment" and "act in all the interests of the company including employment." Under art. 8 (a), the target company may not take "any action which may result in the frustration of the offer" without approval of the shareholders meeting given during the term of the bid. Under art. 3, a compulsory purchase of outstanding shareholders after a bidder takes control is still required, but not if there are "equivalent means" to protect them. Under art. 4 (at the UK's insistence), the supervisory authority may be a private body, and judicial review is not required if the injured party enjoys appropriate and adequate remedies.

The draft seemed to be near to being approved in 2000, but during the co-decision process, Parliament tabled an amendment to the draft, which set out specific rights for target companies to create anti-takeover defenses in advance of any bid (called the 'poison pill' defense) which was not accepted by the Council. Finally, a proposal of the Conciliation Committee was rejected in July 2001, putting an end to the complex Community legislative procedure for adoption of the Directive.

The Proposal was presented again in 2002 and on April 21st 2004 it was approved as Directive 2004/25/EC of the European Parliament and of the Council on takeover bids (Thirteenth Directive).[123]

The Directive, which Member States must transpose by May 20th 2006, applies to companies subject to the law of a Member State, whose shares are listed in one or more States of the European Union. The new regime concerns both mandatory bids, which the State imposes to protect minority shareholders when a change in control of their company occurs, as well as voluntary bids, namely those made to acquire a controlling share in the company.

---

[122] O.J., C 378, 12/13/1997.

[123] O.J., L 142, 04/30/2004, p. 12.

The Directive excludes the following in particular from its own sphere of application.

- Takeover bids for securities issued by companies, the object of which is the collective investment of capital provided by the public, which operate on the principle of risk-spreading and the units of which are, at the holders' request, repurchased or redeemed, directly or indirectly, out of the assets of those companies.
- Takeover bids for securities issued by the Member States' central banks.

Member States are invited to designate authorities who will be charged with the duty to supervise the development of bids and to ensure that the regime established in conformity with the directive is respected. The authorities thus designated shall be either public authorities, associations, or private bodies recognized by national law or by public authorities expressly empowered for that purpose by national law. Member States shall inform the Commission of those designations.

## 17. Directives not yet Approved

The draft Directives which we will be considering, presented by the Commission but have yet to be approved by the Council because of various obstacles placed in their way by some Member States, are as follows:

- Proposal of Fifth Directive on the structure of public limited companies and the powers and obligations of their organs.
- Proposal of Ninth Directive on liability of a parent company for the debts of a subsidiary under its control.
- Proposal of Tenth Directive on cross-border mergers of public limited companies.
- Proposal of Fourteenth Directive on cross-border transfer of seat.

### *17.1. Draft Fifth Directive*

The Fifth Directive sets itself the goal of harmonizing the laws of the Member States with regard to shareholders rights and management structure for public limited liability companies.

It has now been in preparation for 30 years, but the chances of adoption seem rather slim. A first draft was presented to the Council on October 9th 1972.[124]

---

[124] O.J., C 131, 12/13/1972.

This initial version of the draft would have required stock corporations to adopt the German *AG* model of split management, with a supervisory board and a management board, and employee participation on each. As a result of frequent and heavy criticism made by almost all the States, besides that of the Economic and Social Committee, a second draft was presented in 1983,[125] followed by two further amendments, one in December 1990 and the other in November 1991.[126]

There were substantially two crucial points where the margins of agreement between Member States seemed to be very small indeed:

- The first concerned the management structure.
- The second concerned the problem of employee participation in management.

Under the original 1972 formulation, the draft provided that the management of a share company must be entrusted to separate bodies, according to the typical scheme of the German legal system, which is characterized by the so-called *two-tier system*, the management or executive board (*Vorstand)*, with the task of managing the company, and the supervisory board, (*Aufsichtrat)*, to which the task of controlling the work of the management body should be given.

Based on the German model, the draft Directive provided that the supervisory body nominate the members of the management body, which, in its turn, would be nominated by two thirds of the members' meeting and a third of the company's employees. This system of nomination would have applied to share companies with at least 500 employees.

The model proposed was too close to the German one involving *labor codetermination* (*Mitbestimmung*), and took no account of other possibilities: the French and Belgian codetermination, through separate organs representing the personnel of the enterprise *(Comité d'enterprise)* and the Swedish codetermination model, based upon contractual arrangements between labor and management.

In addition to this, it was too far from the experience of other countries, where a *one-tier* system was in operation, such as Italy, where there was no such body as a supervisory board, (rather, a specific kind of audit committee, the *collegio sindacale*), or France, (at least in part, given that art. L 118-150 of the 1966 Act allows, in a *societé anonyme* the alternative of *a directoire et conseil de sorveillance*).

In France, until a new Act was passed in 2001, it was mandatory, with-

---

[125] O.J., C 240, 09/09/1983.

[126] O.J., C 7, 01/11/1991, C 321 and O.J., 12/20/1991, respectively.

in the one-tier board structure, to be chief executive officer and chairman of the board at the same time, thus empowering one person with all management tasks. This *président-directeur-général* selected the board members and submitted her/his choice to the shareholders. Recently, corporate governance Codes encouraged the introduction of subcommittees and the election of independent directors. These directors must be independent of the controlling stakeholders which can be the majority shareholder or the management. A large number of companies created subcommittees and nominated independent board members.

In the Netherlands, the members of the board of directors of corporations satisfying certain requirements (over 60% of the listed companies) were appointed by the independent supervisory board, the latter selecting their own members. This is called the co-optation system. The shareholders only have a non-binding recommendation right.

In the UK, the board structure could be compared with the US organizational structure of corporations, where the board is elected by shareholders and composed of insider and outsider directors. The latter provide oversight while the former manage the day-to-day business. Directors are selected by nomination committees. These committees consist of a majority of outsider directors. The fiduciary duty law system offers a response for directors' acts of negligence or undue self-interest. Internal audit investigations is the task of another committee—the audit committee. In the majority of corporations, the same person undertakes both the roles of chief executive officer and chairman of the board. As an advantage of this duality, understanding and knowledge of the company's operating environment is mentioned. However, in a large majority of UK listed corporations, the practice of duality of *chairman* and *chief executive officer* (CEO) is regarded as undesirable, as it concentrates too much power and it is difficult to exercise control over this inside director.

Thus many models were in circulation in Europe and due to the difficulty in combining all these rules, principles, and practices, the draft Directive based on the German model was rejected by the majority of the Member States.

The later draft of 1983, in the desire to reach a compromise, gave the Member States the opportunity to choose between the two systems—two-tier or one-tier. But the amended draft was not able to overcome the real obstacles which were put in place by systems such as the French and Italian ones, which took into account the lack of inclination to accept the restructuring of company management, which could have endangered the unity of the board of directors and, above all, the hostility towards direct or indirect schemes of participation by the employees in the running of the company.

However, actually confronting the problem of worker participation, a theme beloved of German labor law and industrial relations, it did not intend to do without what is still seen as the 'pride and joy' of its own legal system, the draft Directive allowed Member States to choose between four different participation models for the *two-tier system*, and three models, should the *one-tier system* be chosen.

In this way the draft Directive offered the most reluctant States a broad range of solutions, and partially maintained the chance to conserve their own diversity, deeply rooted in political–institutional history and the law of each individual State. Moreover, it supported the political, entrepre-neu-rial and trade–unionist lobbying, which has always been pressed upon national legislators in this sector.

In spite of the amendments, the draft Directive did not achieve the necessary consensus. The further draft amendments of 1990 and 1991, although they left the essential points set out above substantially unchanged, showed some acceleration imposed by the Community on the harmonization program and the Commission's strong desire to bring another ambitious project to completion, namely the one concerning the European Company. This, based on the draft scheme of the Fifth Directive, concerning both the management structure and worker participation, was regulated by two Community instruments in 2001. We will be dealing with both the Regulation and the Directive on the *Societas Europaea* later.[127] For present purposes, we would like to note the fact of the 'historic compromise' concerning the *Societas Europaea,* in the area of participation by and representation of the workforce, determined the decision of the Commission to withdraw the draft Fifth Directive.[128]

> There is a curious coincidence to note, perhaps not completely random, in the evolving situation at Community level and an important ruling from the Italian Supreme Court. In a 1993 judgment,[129] the Italian Supreme Court for the first time expressly affirmed an important principle, namely that in a share company, the auditors' supervisory responsibility is not confined to performing tasks of mere accounting and formal control, but also extends to the area of management, with consequent liability of the auditors for failure to supervise.
>
> This specific clarification by the Supreme Court leads to a re-evaluation of the role of the audit committee in the of management

---

[127] See below § 20.

[128] Communication of December 11th 2001 (COM/2001/763(2) final) on the withdrawal of Commission proposals which are no longer topical.

[129] *Cass. civ., Sez. I,* May 7th 1993, no. 5263, in *Società*, 1994, no. 7, p. 897.

of a company, confined until now to the merely formal task of control, with few possibilities, or none at all, of intervening in the resolutions adopted by the board of directors. The judgment was the prelude to the restructuring of the share company, whose shape is emerging ever more clearly at Community level and with which national actors have had to come to terms, following the reform of company Law in 2003. So far as the CEECs are concerned, it should be noted that in reforming their national Commercial Codes (or special acts), they have all adopted the German model of corporate governance.

## *17.2. Draft Ninth Directive*

In most countries, groups of companies have not given rise to a specific codified "law of groups." As we know, this is different in Germany. The Stock Corporation Act of 1965 was the first to codify a law of groups for stock corporations. More recently, similar rules have been developed by German courts for limited liability companies (*Gesellschaft mit beschrankter Haftung, GmbH*) and even commercial partnerships.

This is not to say that there is no law of groups in other countries. Upon closer examination there is even extensive group law, though it is found in specific fields (such as bank and insurance supervision, labor law, and, of course, tax law) rather than in general company law. In addition, there is a considerable body of case law as to limited liability companies. But the approach is different. There is no coherent body of specific provisions; instead, the controlling shareholder has specific duties toward the minority shareholders, whether in the independent company or in a group.

Most recently, principles and proposals for a European group company law were elaborated by the *Forum Europaeum Konzernrecht* in a cooperative effort by many European academics, legislators, and practitioners.[130] Their starting point is that the existence of company groups has long been an economic reality everywhere. To cope with this, framework rules by both European and national legislators are necessary. While full harmonization of the law of company groups within the EU is neither feasible nor advisable, a certain degree of uniformity in the European single market is indispensable. Rules proposed by the *Forum Europaeum* include disclosure; legal recognition of group management under certain

---

[130] *Forum Europaeum Konzernrecht,* Corporate Group Law for Europe, Stockholm 2000; also in: *European Business Organization Law Review* (EBOR) I (2000) 165–264.

safeguard conditions; special investigation in the independent company as well as in the group; mandatory bid; buy-out and withdrawal rights; and, ultimately, liability for wrongful trading.

The phenomenon, as we have shown in relation to the Directive on consolidated (or group) accounts, is spreading ever more widely and involves the interests of members and creditors in ever-increasing numbers.

In the face of this widespread need, the Commission has, since the 1960's, been developing a draft of a Ninth Directive on the structure of groups of companies, aimed at coordinating the few and diverse rules in existence in this area and to establish the same conditions throughout the Member States. The draft, clearly based on a German model, has never been officially published in the Community Gazette.[131]

The objective pursued by the Ninth Directive is the protection of shareholders, above all of controlled companies or subsidiaries, and creditors. Substantially, the Directive should regulate the opposing interests of minority shareholders and the controlling shareholders in a balanced way, starting logically in any case with transparency in the relationship between group companies and controlling shareholders, and placing the burden of liability upon the parent company for damage suffered by the subsidiary company consequent upon blameworthy conduct of the parent company's directors.

First of all, the draft scheme separates groups of companies into two sub-divisions: one made up of groups formed on a contractual basis and the other of *de facto* groups.

In the first case, one or more companies are placed under the control of another by means of a written *contract of affiliation*, or a declaration by the controlling company affirming it owns 90% of the shares of the controlled company.

In the second case, the controlling company limits itself to *owning the majority of shares* in one or more companies, or, at least, the option in fact to exercise directive powers in the affairs of another company, according to the concept of control already set out in the Seventh Directive on consolidated accounts.[132]

The legal regimes which govern the two cases envisaged are different.

The contract of affiliation, which gives rise to a relationship of control by one party and legitimizes in all effects the power to direct on the part of the parent company vis-à-vis the group (including the power to

---

[131] The French version, from the mid 1980s, with explanations, is available in: CDVA (ed.), *Modes de rapprochement structurel des enterprise. Tendences actuelles en droit des affaires* (Brussels, 1986), p. 223–263.

[132] See above, § 12.

manage company capital), obliges the parent company to be additionally liable for obligations assumed by the controlled companies. Moreover, in the terms of the affiliation contract, the minority shareholders of the affiliated company must be allowed to opt for the purchase of shares on a basis which reflects their true value, or for an annual indemnity.

The *de facto* relationship of control by one party, on the other hand, obliges the parent company to be liable for the acts of the subsidiary which are against the parent company's interests, given that the management activity of the head company should be carried out with the interests of the whole group in mind. Every company which is head of a group is further obliged to produce annual and consolidated accounts, the directors' report and the auditors' report, as provided by the Fourth and Seventh Directives.

The draft of the Ninth Directive has not yet begun its usual journey towards approval by the Council, but the numbering of the other directives has not been updated, a sign of the will of the Community institutions not to abandon standardized regulation of this essential element in the economic and productive activity of the internal market. On this point, the Commission, in the recent *Communication on the strategy for modernising company law and enhancing corporate governance in the European Union—A plan to move forward,*[133] recognized that the consultation relating to the proposal for the Ninth Directive had demonstrated that there was very little support: the document states that an approach of this kind was quite unknown in the greater part of the Member States and that businesses considered it too complex and rigid. For this reason the Commission decided not to make the proposal official.

It should be noted in this connection that, although a directive with which domestic law must be harmonized is not in existence, the CEECs have for some time begun to prepare the legislation with regard to this phenomenon, setting up academic contacts with some German study centers which are well-known for their profound knowledge of the subject: this, for example, is the case with Hungary (Act on joint-stock companies, 1997), Slovenia (Companies Act, 1993), Croatia (Companies Act, 1995), and Poland (Code of Commercial Companies, 2000). The *Max-Plank-Institut* in Hamburg[134] is very active in this field, where German academics and those from the various CEECs have met (and still meet) to discuss possibilities for transplanting the German model into the post-communist legal systems.

---

[133] See above COM (2003) 284 final, 05/21/2003.

[134] See the website at http://www.mpipriv-hh.mpg.de/.

As we noted above, the German legislation on groups is set out in the Act of September 6th 1965 on share companies (*Aktiengesetz* o *AktG*).[135] The *AktG* is very analytical and lays down four types of company relationships:[136] *de facto* groups, company contracts,[137] company incorporations,[138] and reciprocal participation companies.[139] The Act also covers in detail the guarantees which the company must provide to company creditors and shareholders and the liabilities of the various bodies. This legislation has been partially amended by the Act of April 27th 1998 on improvement of control and transparency in company management, with the aim of strengthening the German financial markets (*Gesetz zur Kontrolle und Transparenz im Unternehemensbereich* o *KonTraG*), which has introduced novel developments both in the area of *de facto* groups and company cross-participation.

### *17.3. Draft Tenth Directive*

Concentrations among companies and the formation of group companies represent some of the most effective means of dealing with competitors, either within the common internal market or in the form of outside competition from North America and the Far East.

Since the earliest days, the Commission has grasped the importance of concentration schemes among the big commercial forces, especially if they belong to different States, and has endeavored to encourage integration by the research and development of a standard legal model for company mergers with registered offices in different States, ensuring the simplification of operations and ease of use.

In earlier times, the Community sought to achieve this by means of Conventions, as laid down by art. 220 (now 293) TEC, as was done in the area of recognition of foreign companies and legal persons, or recognition of foreign judgments in the civil and commercial fields.[140]

A first draft for a Convention was developed in 1967; the scheme was not confined to enabling Member States to make trans-national mergers, but also put forward a standard model for mergers between foreign States, which would have become the unique legal model of reference for the Member States. However, the lukewarm reception by many Member

---

[135] See above § 9.1.

[136] The concept of a related company is supplied by § 15 of the *AktG*.

[137] § 291–292 *AktG*.

[138] § 319 ff. *AktG*.

[139] § 328 *AktG*.

[140] See above, § 1.

States did not make for easy trans-national mergers, either because of the legal problems (such as the rules on worker participation) or, above all, for the strictly tax-related aspects which presented themselves. The desire by Member States not to yield prerogatives of control over such important economic operations made the Commission give up the scheme; perhaps it was too far ahead of its time.

A second scheme amending the Convention on international mergers of share companies, presented in 1973,[141] had no better luck than its predecessor.

The perplexity of the States resulted in the Commission abandoning the idea of standard regulation. It was decided to proceed in a simpler way, through harmonization of national law, on the basis of the well-known art. 54 (3) (g) (now art. 44) TEC, according to the same methods used in other directives in the field of company law.

Thus in 1985, a draft Directive was presented on cross-border mergers between public limited liability companies, which was designated as the Tenth Directive. The choice at once appeared favorable, given the relative success of the other directives which had harmonized a good number of company institutions, and, in particular, the national mergers themselves, to which the draft in question amply referred.[142]

In effect, the draft Tenth Directive, presented to the Council on January 14th 1985,[143] uses the same scheme devised for the Third Directive on national mergers, and makes particular provision for the production of a merger scheme for international mergers to be submitted to the general meeting, the approval by the competent bodies of each company, the directors' and experts' reports, and so on, including safeguarding of the creditors' interests of the companies involved in the merger.

It should be noted that, with respect to national mergers, those between companies from different States have a particular characteristic: one part of the operation is to be carried out individually, by each participating country, according to the domestic law of the Member State to which each of them is subject; another part is carried out in common by all the companies, and therefore must be governed by a single rule.

For this reason it is usually said that the draft Tenth Directive comes within the ambit of private international law, given that it principally concerns the laying down of linking criteria to identify which law is applicable to the various aspects and problems which may arise in inter-

---

141 *Bull. E.C., Supp.* 13/73.

142 See art. 2 of the draft.

143 O.J., C 23, 01/25/1985.

national mergers. For instance, the draft establishes that the merger project must take the form of a public act, even when only one of the legal systems to which the companies are subject has such a requirement; the choice of date from which the merger takes effect is determined by reference to the law of the country to which the newly-merged company belongs; nullity proceedings for a trans-national merger can only take place if the legal system to which the new company is subject provides for the nullification of the merger for failure to check its legitimacy or in the absence of a public act. Besides provisions of private international law, the draft Directive also contains standard rules, some of which amend or except provisions regarding national mergers in the Third Directive, and which involve greater strictness regarding the particulars to be included in the scheme, or the non-effectiveness of the whole operation until all necessary steps have been taken and all necessary formalities required for members' and third-party protection have been carried out.

In spite of encouraging early signs, the draft Directive has not been adopted.

It was thought that the tax treatment aspect of the trans-national merger represented one of the main obstacles to the approval of the new legislation. But even after the approval of Directive no. 90/434 of July 23rd 1990[144] concerning the taxation scheme applicable to mergers, divisions, transfers of assets, and exchanges of shares concerning companies of different Member States, the draft stayed where it was. It was revised and amended as the result of the adoption of the regulation on the European Company,[145] with which it had to be coordinated, given the aspects that the two cases have in common. In 2003, the Commission presented a new proposal for the Tenth Directive on cross-border mergers of companies with share capital,[146] developed on analogous principles to the preceding ones, apart from certain novel features. The new proposal, in fact, extends the field of application to include all companies with share capital, public limited companies, and incorporated private companies, which in Member States are characterized by the possession of a legal personality and separate assets. The draft Directive is mainly concerned with enterprises which are not involved in setting up a European Company, in particular the small and medium-sized enterprises (SMEs) which want to merge, in order to operate in two Member States.

The purpose of the proposed of Directive is to facilitate cross-border

---

[144] O.J., L 225, 08/20/1990.

[145] See below § 20.

[146] O.J., C 96, 04/21/2004.

mergers of commercial companies without the national laws governing them forming an obstacle. In particular, it will tend to benefit mergers of SMEs which, since they do not want to operate in all Member States, have no interest in adopting a European Company Statute (which is more appropriate for large companies, which have greater capitalization and operate throughout the Community). Once the new entity resulting from the merger has been set up, it will be subject to the national law of only one Member State—that in which it is established. The purpose of the basic principle is to bring the cross-border merger procedure more into line with domestic merger procedures.

Moreover, the proposal provides that the rules on employee participation must be governed by the national law applicable to the company created by the merger. Where at least one of the merging companies is governed by rules on employee participation and the company created by the merger establishes its head office in a Member State where such rules do not apply, the new entity must hold negotiations on an employee participation system. In such cases, the negotiation procedure laid down for the European Company will apply.

## *17.4. Draft Fourteenth Directive*

In 1997, the Commission drafted a proposal for the Fourteenth Directive on cross-border transfer of seat (the center of activities and/or registered office of the companies). The proposal has been circulating since 1997, but this has yet to be officially discussed by the Community institutions. The proposal of Directive states a specific procedure for the transfer of the seat of a company. The company would have to register in the new Member State and change its charter in accordance with the company law of this Member State. Moreover the company would have to give a guarantee to its creditors before transferring the seat.

This proposal is still at the center of a broad debate among the legal scholars. On the one hand, in fact, in the absence of specific legislation, the cross-border transfer of company seat is subject to a complex set of legal provisions. This is due to the fact that the national laws of the Member States do not possess suitable instruments; for this reason, when a transfer is feasible by virtue of the simultaneous application of national laws, there are frequent conflicts with these laws caused by the different rules applied by Member States.

On the other hand, case-law developed by the Court of Justice since the 1980's has established that Member States have the right to establishment and to carry on their own economic activities in a Member State, where the registered office is not located, apart from cases of abuse which are ascertained on a case-by-case basis. Since the original ruling in *Segers,* the principle has been developed and refined in the *Daily Mail*, *Centros*, *Uberseering* cases, and recently in *Inspire Art*, and *Huges.*[147]

## 18. New Supra-National Models

When the Community legislators wish to intervene in a particular case or legal institution, intending to bring closer together diverse national practices, they have two options: to *harmonize the existing regime* in the individual systems, or *create new supranational legal instruments and institutions* valid throughout the Community, characterized by the same rules in every country.

The first instrument is used to harmonize certain rules in States where their diversity could harm the unification of the common market. This is the purpose of directives, such as we have considered above in relation to company law; these tend to establish minimum, substantially standard rules and criteria, in order to ensure equality of treatment of members, as well as contracting third parties, as an essential requirement for an effective single market.

The second instrument is used, on the other hand, with the aim of encouraging integration among European enterprises by means of reciprocal collaboration and the exchange of projects, ideas, and knowledge. This is the purpose of new institutions such as the *European Economic Interest Grouping*, the *European Company*, the *European Cooperative,* and the *European Mutual Societies*, regulated in principle by Community provisions and in a subsidiary way by domestic laws which are applicable by analogy.

> The European Company, the Association, the Cooperative, and the Mutual Societies will always keep their own national characteristics that correspond to the place where the head office and central administration is, and will be subject to the provisions of their own domestic law, in addition to Community rules, in so far as expressly provided by the regulation or applicable in a subsidiary way, where rules are lacking.

The main characteristic which is common to all these institutions is that they may only be used exclusively in the context of a relationship between

---

[147] Respectively ECJ, July 10th 1968, C-79/85, ECJ, September 27th 1988, C-81/87, ECJ, March 9th 1999, C-212/97, ECJ, November 5th 2000, C-208/00, ECJ, September 30th 2003, C- 167/01, ECJ, March 11th 2004, C-09/02 . *Cf.* above § 1 in this chapter.

enterprises belonging to different States. They are new forms of association which are justifiable only if at least two participating enterprises do not belong to the same State. This is the sense in which the word 'Community' is to be understood when applied to such institutions. They, therefore, have nothing to do with other (apparently similar) situations, where a standard model is superimposed on a national one.

Another special feature is that they are governed not by directives, but by regulations. Indeed, the Community legislature's intention is not to harmonize the various rules prevailing in Member States, but to give rise to new institutions, with original features, to different institutions as opposed to the national ones—which will still be valid, only more or less harmonized amongst each other, thanks to the company law directives—applied to domestic relationships in the sense of being between enterprises from the same State. The new Community institutions, however, far from substituting for the national ones, will work alongside them and can be used only when a relationship of collaboration arises between undertakings or subjects of differing nationalities.

These therefore concern, as was illustrated in the first chapter of the first volume of this *Guide, A Common Law for Europe,* an activity which tends towards uniformization of the rules between Member States instead of harmonizing them. The source of law of the new supranational institution, being set out in a Community regulation, is exactly the same in every Member State. The only differences may concern aspects connected with administrative and bureaucratic requirements, tax liability and in general, the necessary adjustments for inserting the institution into the domestic mechanism of each legal system.

## 19. The European Economic Interest Grouping

The EEIG was developed with a view to offering enterprises, and other economic entities of the Member States, an innovative instrument aimed at creating, by means of a special scheme, an institutional framework for projects of international cooperation within a Community context. This instrument for companies was introduced and regulated at Community level by Council Regulation (EEC) no. 2137/85 of July 25th 1985 on the European Economic Interest Grouping (EEIG),[148] and came into force in all the States on July 1st 1989.[149]

---

[148] O.J., L 199, 07/31/1985.

[149] The new instrument for trans-national collaboration is enjoying quite considerable favor. About 800 or so EEIGs were registered in 2001, constituted throughout the EU.

The EEIG is not the child of the Community legislature's imagination. The reference model is the French *Groupement d'intérêt économique* (*Gie*) introduced in 1967 for similar reasons to those which motivated the Community, representing the encouragement of collaboration between companies, and creating services and common structures to improve and increase productivity in the enterprises.

As usual, the recitals in the Preamble of the Community acts are of great assistance to a better understanding of the real significance of the institution:

> **Reg. 2137/85:** "(**1**) Whereas a harmonious development of economic activities and a continuous and balanced expansion throughout the Community depend on the establishment and smooth functioning of a common market offering conditions analogous to those of a national market; (**2**) whereas to bring about this single market and to increase its unity a legal framework which facilitates the adaptation of their activities to the economic conditions of the Community should be created for natural persons, companies, firms and other legal bodies in particular; (**3**) whereas to that end it is necessary that those natural persons, companies, firms and other legal bodies should be able to cooperate effectively across frontiers (…)."

*– The aim of the institution*

The aim of the Grouping is to facilitate or develop the economic activity of its members, to improve or increase the profit from its activity. For this reason, the EEIG does not list among its aims that of making profits on its own account. Its activity must be related to the economic activity of its members and must not be more than ancillary to these.

> **Art. 3, Reg. 2137/85** "(**1**). The purpose of a grouping shall be to facilitate or develop the economic activities of its members and to improve or increase the results of those activities; its purpose is not to make profits for itself. Its activity shall be related to the economic activities of its members and must not be more than ancillary to those activities. (**2**) Consequently, a grouping may not: (a) exercise, directly or indirectly, a power of management or supervision over its members' own activities or over the activities of another undertaking, in particular in the fields of personnel, finance and investment; (b) directly or indirectly, on any basis whatsoever, hold shares of any kind in a member undertaking; the holding of shares in another undertaking shall be possible only in so far as it is necessary for the achievement of the grouping's objects and if it is done on its members' behalf; (c) employ more

> than 500 persons; (d) be used by a company to make a loan to a director of a company, or any person connected with him, when the making of such loans is restricted or controlled under the Member States' laws governing companies. Nor must a grouping be used for the transfer of any property between a company and a director, or any person connected with him, except to the extent allowed by the Member States' laws governing companies. For the purposes of this provision the making of a loan includes entering into any transaction or arrangement of similar effect, and property includes moveable and immoveable property; (e) be a member of another European Economic Interest Grouping."

An EEIG is therefore not an instrument for the exercise of economic activity, but one which has an ancillary function to the participants, directed at improving and coordinating the activity of the members themselves. The 5th "whereas" clause of the Preamble reads thus:

> "(**5**) Whereas a grouping differs from a firm or company principally in its purpose, which is only to facilitate or develop the economic activities of its members to enable them to improve their own results; whereas, by reason of that ancillary nature, a grouping's activities must be related to the economic activities of its members but not replace them so that, to that extent, for example, a grouping may not itself, with regard to third parties, practise a profession, the concept of economic activities being interpreted in the widest sense (…)."

For this reason, the Grouping may not:

- Exercise, directly or indirectly, a power of management or supervision over its members' own activities or over the activities of another undertaking, in particular in the fields of personnel, finance, and investment.
- Directly or indirectly, on any basis whatsoever, hold shares of any kind in a member undertaking; the holding of shares in another undertaking shall be possible only in so far as it is necessary for the achievement of the grouping's objects and if it is done on its members' behalf.
- Employ more than 500 persons; the rule exists because if the EEIG had more than 500 employees, the German rule regarding worker participation in management (*Mitsbestimmung*) (art. 3, no. 2, *c*) would have been triggered.
- Be used by a company to make a loan to a director of a company, or any person connected with him, when the making of such loans is restricted or controlled under the Member States' laws governing

companies. Nor must a grouping be used for the transfer of any property between a company and a director, or any person connected with him, except to the extent allowed by the Member States' laws governing companies.

– Be a member of another European Economic Interest Grouping; art. 32 of the Regulation has, among the reasons for the dissolution of the grouping, the infringement of the limits cited in art. 3 in contemplation. In such a case, the national judicial authorities, or an authority recognized as competent for these purposes, must declare the EEIG dissolved, on the application of interested parties.

– *The law applicable to the institution*

The Regulation contains the nucleus of the new institution's regime. Although Reg. 2137/85 allows ample negotiating freedom to the parties as far as regulating their reciprocal relationship is concerned, the majority of the rules cannot be derogated by national laws; the Court of Justice has jurisdiction over their interpretation.

Besides the Community source of law, the national laws of the State where the head office is established by the EEIG contract, apply, in so far as not expressly regulated:

> **Art. 2, Reg. 2137/85:** "**(1)** Subject to the provisions of this Regulation, the law applicable, on the one hand, to the contract for the formation of a grouping, except as regards matters relating to the status or capacity of natural persons and to the capacity of legal persons and, on the other hand, to the internal organization of a grouping shall be the internal law of the State in which the official address is situated, as laid down in the contract for the formation of the grouping. **(2)** Where a State comprises several territorial units, each of which has its own rules of law applicable to the matters referred to in paragraph 1, each territorial unit shall be considered as a State for the purposes of identifying the law applicable under this Article."

Compare, too, some points in the judgment of the ECJ (Fifth Chamber) of December 18th 1997, *European Information Technology Observatory, Europäische Wirtschaftliche Interessenvereinigung*.[150]

> ***Cf.*** **§§ 20-22 of the ruling**: "(...) **20** It is clear from Article 2(1) that, subject to the provisions of the Regulation, the law

150 Case C-402/96, (1997) ECR I-7515. Reference for a preliminary ruling: *Oberlandesgericht* Frankfurt am Main, Germany.

applicable is the internal law of the State in which the official address is situated, as laid down in the contract for the formation of the grouping. **21** As the Advocate General has indicated (…), all that Article 5(a) requires is that the business name of an EEIG should contain either the words "European Economic Interest Grouping" or the initials "EEIG". The purpose of that provision is to enable the grouping to be identified and distinguished in its relations with third parties by means of the reference to the type of association established by the Regulation. It does not, however, impose any other requirement as to the content of the grouping's business name. In particular, the phrase "unless those words or initials already form part of the name" is simply intended, where appropriate, to avoid any pointless repetition. **22** The Regulation thus provides that the business name of an EEIG must include the words "European Economic Interest Grouping" or the initials "EEIG", but is silent as to the content of the name. It follows that requirements in that connection may, in accordance with Article 2(1) of the Regulation, be imposed by the provisions of internal law applicable in the Member State in which the grouping has its official address. (…)."

*– Competing sources of law regulating the EEIG*

It should be added that in many cases the national legislators have issued laws to be integrated with Regulation 2137/85, applicable to all the EEIGs constituted within or having their registered office in national territory.

The two sources, the Community regulation and the national integration provisions,[151] to which are added the provisions of the 'contract for the formation' of the EEIG, complete the sources of law regulating EEIGs. As to the rest, national provisions which relate to any other entity carrying out similar functions and activity, apply: social security and employment law, taxation provisions and competition rules and so on, come to mind.

We are dealing here with a Regulation which is not complete in all its aspects, in that it leaves it open to the States to choose to integrate certain elements of the institution, as they see fit.

For example, according to Reg. 2137/85, the EEIG has legal personality:

**Art. 1 (2), Reg. 2137/85.** "A grouping so formed shall, from the date of its registration as provided for in Article 6, have the

[151] See, for example in Italy, the legislative decree of July 23rd 1991, no. 240 which contains rules for the application of Regulation no. 85/2137/CEE relating to the establishment of an EEIG published in the Italian Official Gazette, (*Gazz. Uff.*) of August 5th 1991, no. 182.

> capacity, in its own name, to have rights and obligations of all kinds, to make contracts or accomplish other legal acts, and to sue and be sued."

As regards the further aspect of legal personality, the option is left to the States as to whether this is conferred or not (art. 1 [3]).[152] Art. 1 (3) of the Regulation states: "The Member States shall determine whether or not groupings registered at their Registries, pursuant to Article 6, have legal personality."

However, the fact remains that the wholesale referral to national law by the Regulation could not auger well for the standardization of the EEIG regime, nor to create the best conditions for effective equality of treatment for business and businessmen; it is highly likely, in fact, that most of the EEIGs will form, or establish their headquarters, in those countries where the laws on taxation, contributions and employment are the most favorable.

> Such considerations lead us to ask, more generally, where exactly the borderline between a regulation and a directive is. If, in principle, the former is obligatory in all its aspects and is directly applicable within the Member States, as laid down by art. 249 TEC, in fact a regulation may not always be applicable unless there is a domestic law which makes it compatible with the complex of national laws in force. Besides, it is often the regulation itself which establishes a minimum of obligatory rules from which Member States may not derogate, and then leaves to the States the option of laying down stricter rules.
>
> Against this, the directives bind not only the Member States as to the result to be achieved, but, as we have seen in the first volume of this *Guide, A Common Law for Europe*, their rules prevail over any incompatible domestic ones.
>
> The line of demarcation between the two Community acts therefore becomes extremely indistinct, with the potential consequence of leading the interpreter to confuse the two legislative acts and to attribute a different weight to them, based on a formal rather than substantive reading.

For example, concerning the taxation aspect, the Community legislature confined itself to sanctioning the fact that the profits of the EEIG's activity are to be apportioned to individual members (art. 21 Reg. 2137/85):

---

[152] Italy, by the decree of 1991 cited above, preferred to exclude legal personality, whereas in France this possibility is expressly allowed.

**Art. 21 Reg. 2137/85** "**(1)** The profits resulting from a grouping's activities shall be deemed to be the profits of the members and shall be apportioned among them in the proportions laid down in the contract for the formation of the grouping or, in the absence of any such provision, in equal shares. **(2)** The members of a grouping shall contribute to the payment of the amount by which expenditure exceeds income in the proportions laid down in the contract for the formation of the grouping or, in the absence of any such provision, in equal shares."

Procedure, obligations and tax liability are left to the laws of individual Member States. The space left to the national legislatures concerning insolvency and cessation of payments by the EEIG is even greater, given that art. 36 leaves the Regulation of the consequences to them.

**Art. 36 Reg. 2137/85** "Groupings shall be subject to national laws governing insolvency and cessation of payments. The commencement of proceedings against a grouping on grounds of its insolvency or cessation of payments shall not by itself cause the commencement of such proceedings against its members."

*– Who can participate in an EEIG*

Regarding who may participate, the Regulation leaves the possibility open to a huge range of legal persons, exercising commercial, industrial, or professional activity in the private or public field. The only requirement of the Community Regulation is that at least two of the participants should belong to different States.

**Art. 4, Reg. 2137/85** "**(1)** Only the following may be members of a grouping: (a) companies or firms within the meaning of the second paragraph of Article 58 of the Treaty and other legal bodies governed by public or private law, which have been formed in accordance with the law of a Member State and which have their registered or statutory office and central administration in the Community; where, under the law of a Member State, a company, firm or other legal body is not obliged to have a registered or statutory office, it shall be sufficient for such a company, firm or other legal body to have its central administration in the Community; (b) natural persons who carry on any industrial, commercial, craft or agricultural activity or who provide professional or other services in the Community. **(2)** A grouping must comprise at least: (a) two companies, firms or other legal bodies, within the meaning of paragraph 1, which have their central administrations in different Member States, or (b) two natural persons, within the

> meaning of paragraph 1, who carry on their principal activities in different Member States, or (c) a company, firm or other legal body within the meaning of paragraph 1 and a natural person, of which the first has its central administration in one Member State and the second carries on his principal activity in another Member State. **(3)** A Member State may provide that groupings registered at its registries in accordance with Article 6 may have no more than 20 members. For this purpose, that Member State may provide that, in accordance with its laws, each member of a legal body formed under its laws, other than a registered company, shall be treated as a separate member of a grouping. **(4)** Any Member State may, on grounds of that State's public interest, prohibit or restrict participation in groupings by certain classes of natural persons, companies, firms, or other legal bodies."

EEIGs certainly represent a response to the needs of international cooperation, between subjects who may be private or public, it does not matter so long as they are exercising some kind of economic activity. The question raised by some commentators is whether participation by public, non-economic institutions in an EEIG may be considered legitimate.

For example, a French municipality in Savoy set up an EEIG together with an Italian ski-lift company to encourage the development of a cross-border ski-area; some French and British universities pooled their technical expertise in a new center for innovation situated at *Caen* (in *Normandy, France*); the European Community itself participates in an EEIG for research and development called EMARC, in the field of research into advanced materials.

This all supports anything but a restricted interpretation of the concept of economic subjects which the Community itself has given, as further anticipated in the 5th whereas clause of the Preamble to the Regulation, which affirms "the concept of economic activities being interpreted in the widest sense."

*– How an EEIG can be established*

The procedure for establishing an EEIG goes through the following stages:

– Drawing-up of the contract by the founder–members.

– Registration of the contract as provided for in art. 6:

> **Art. 6, Reg. 2137/85** "A grouping shall be registered in the State in which it has its official address, at the registry designated pursuant to Article 39 (1)."

> **Art. 39, Reg. 2137/85** "**(1)** The Member States shall designate the registry or registries responsible for effecting the registration referred to in Articles 6 and 10 and shall lay down the rules governing registration. They shall prescribe the conditions under which the documents referred to in Articles 7 and 10 shall be filed. They shall ensure that the documents and particulars referred to in Article 8 are published in the appropriate official gazette of the Member State in which the grouping has its official address, and may prescribe the manner of publication of the documents and particulars referred to in Article 8 (c). **(2)** The Member States shall also ensure that anyone may, at the appropriate registry pursuant to Article 6 or, where appropriate, Article 10, inspect the documents referred to in Article 7 and obtain, even by post, full or partial copies thereof. The Member States may provide for the payment of fees in connection with the operations referred to in the preceding subparagraphs; those fees may not, however, exceed the administrative cost thereof."

A grouping so formed shall, from the date of its registration as provided for in art. 6, have the capacity, in its own name, to have rights and obligations of all kinds, to make contracts or accomplish other legal acts, and to sue and be sued (art. 1 (2), Reg. 2137/85). If activities have been pursued on behalf of a grouping before its registration in accordance with art. 6 and if the grouping does not, after its registration, assume the obligations arising out of such activities, the natural persons, companies, firms or other legal bodies which carried on those activities shall bear unlimited joint and several liability for them (art. 9 (2), Reg. 2137/85).

Notice that a grouping has been formed, or that the liquidation of a grouping has been concluded, stating the number, date, and place of registration, and the date, place, and title of publication, shall be given in the Official Journal of the EU after it has been published in the Gazette referred to in art. 39 (1) (art. 11, Reg. 2137/85).

*– The internal organization governing the EEIG*

Regarding the organs, art. 16 (1) Reg. 2137/85, with the aim of simplifying as far as possible the internal organizational structure, requires only two obligatory organs: the members acting collectively and the manager(s). Nothing prevents the 'contract for the formation' of the EEIG providing for other organs.

At the members' meeting, each member has one vote. However, the contract may allocate more than one vote to some members, on condition that no one member has a majority of votes (art. 17 (1), Reg. 2137/85). Decisions are on a majority, except for some cases expressly provided by art. 17 Reg. 2137/85 (altering the grouping's objects, altering the conditions for taking decisions, extending the duration of the grouping, altering the contribution payment, etc.) where unanimity is required instead.

> **Art. 16 , Reg. 2137/85** "**(1).** The organs of a grouping shall be the members acting collectively and the manager or managers. A contract for the formation of a grouping may provide for other organs; if it does it shall determine their powers. 2. The members of a grouping, acting as a body, may take any decision for the purpose of achieving the objects of the grouping."

> **Art. 17, Reg. 2137/85** "**(1)** Each member shall have one vote. The contract for the formation of a grouping may, however, give more than one vote to certain members, provided that no one member holds a majority of the votes. **(2)** A unanimous decision by the members shall be required to: (a) alter the objects of a grouping; (b) alter the number of votes allotted to each member; (c) alter the conditions for the taking of decisions; (d) extend the duration of a grouping beyond any period fixed in the contract for the formation of the grouping; (e) alter the contribution by every member or by some members to the grouping's financing; (f) alter any other obligation of a member, unless otherwise provided by the contract for the formation of the grouping; (g) make any alteration to the contract for the formation of the grouping not covered by this paragraph, unless otherwise provided by that contract. **(3)** Except where this Regulation provides that decisions must be taken unanimously, the contract for the formation of a grouping may prescribe the conditions for a quorum and for a majority, in accordance with which the decisions, or some of them, shall be taken. Unless otherwise provided for by the contract, decisions shall be taken unanimously. **(4)** On the initiative of a manager or at the request of a member, the manager or managers must arrange for the members to be consulted so that the latter can take a decision."

The manager represents the Grouping regarding third parties, and binds it even when s/he acts outside the Grouping's objects; unless the Grouping can show that the third party cannot have been unaware that the act went beyond the objects:

> **Art. 20, Reg. 2137/85** "Only the manager or, where there are two or more, each of the managers shall represent a grouping in respect of dealings with third parties. Each of the managers shall bind the grouping as regards third parties when he acts on behalf of the grouping, even where his acts do not fall within the objects

> of the grouping, unless the grouping proves that the third party knew or could not, under the circumstances, have been unaware that the act fell outside the objects of the grouping; publication of the particulars referred to in Article 5 (c) shall not of itself be proof thereof."

Finally, the Community Regulation introduced another important new feature, concerning the option of making legal persons managers, on condition that one or more natural persons are designated as their representative(s).

> **Art. 19, n. 2, Reg. 2137/85** "A Member State may, in the case of groupings registered at their registries pursuant to Article 6, provide that legal persons may be managers on condition that such legal persons designate one or more natural persons, whose particulars shall be the subject of the filing provisions of Article 7 (d) to represent them. If a Member State exercises this option, it must provide that the representative or representatives shall be liable as if they were themselves managers of the groupings concerned."

*– Members Liability and EEIG insolvency*

An EEIG need not necessarily be equipped with guarantee capital for third parties. To set against this advantage, however, the Regulation prescribes unlimited joint and several liability of members for all obligations assumed in the name and on behalf of the Grouping. To this end, art. 24 provides for a *beneficium excussionis* in favor of the Grouping's members.

> **Art. 24, Reg. 2137/85** (...) "the members of a grouping shall have unlimited joint and several liability for its debts and other liabilities of whatever nature. National law shall determine the consequences of such liability. Creditors may not proceed against a member for payment in respect of debts and other liabilities, in accordance with the conditions laid down in paragraph 1, before the liquidation of a grouping is concluded, unless they have first requested the grouping to pay and payment has not been made within an appropriate period."

Members' liability also extends to obligations arising from acts outside the purposes of the Grouping or in any case, acts which are *ultra vires* the directors.

The new members are liable for obligations arising before they joined, unless otherwise agreed, which operates as a defense against third parties if it has been properly recorded and disclosed. After leaving the Grouping, or after its liquidation, the members continue to be liable for a maximum period of five years from the publication of the liquidation (arts. 34 and 37, Reg. 2137/85).

> **Art. 34, Reg. 2137/85** "Without prejudice to Article 37 (1), any member who ceases to belong to a grouping shall remain answerable, in accordance with the conditions laid down in Article 24, for the debts and other liabilities arising out of the grouping's activities before he ceased to be a member."
>
> **Art. 37, Reg. 2137/85** "**(1)** A period of limitation of five years after the publication, pursuant to Article 8, of notice of a member's ceasing to belong to a grouping shall be substituted for any longer period which may be laid down by the relevant national law for actions against that member in connection with debts and other liabilities arising out of the grouping's activities before he ceased to be a member. **(2)** A period of limitation of five years after the publication, pursuant to Article 8, of notice of the conclusion of the liquidation of a grouping shall be substituted for any longer period which may be laid down by the relevant national law for actions against a member of the grouping in connection with debt."

An EEIG may become insolvent if it carries on commercial activity:

> **Art. 36, Reg. 2137/85** "Groupings shall be subject to national laws governing insolvency and cessation of payments. The commencement of proceedings against a grouping on grounds of its insolvency or cessation of payments shall not by itself cause the commencement of such proceedings against its members."

*– The EEIG in commercial practice*

An EEIG may be used in a vast range of situations: from data banks for entrepreneurs in certain sectors (with the aim of gathering and distributing information about official advertisements for posts, offers for tenders, community facilities and aid, etc.) to service centers common to several enterprises or professionals, to research and documentation centers for entrepreneurs in the public and private sector, which are the center for coordination between regional bodies, and/or private individuals about to undertake a project or scheme of common interest, to coordination centers for law firms which undertake legal, fiscal or tax consultation at international level, to study centers of common interest, individuals, either legal or natural persons, in any sector at all, and so on. The nature of an EEIG is essentially that of a mutual, non-profit-making body, since it does not have profit making among the purposes of the activity it carries out. However, it is necessary to determine whether it is true that an EEIG must not aim at making a profit; there is no legislative rule which states that an EEIG may not also make a profit from its activity.

Indeed, art. 21 of the Regulation expressly mentions profit, and provides that the profits resulting from a Grouping's activities shall be deemed to be the profits of the members and shall be apportioned among them in the proportions laid down in the contract for the formation of the grouping or, in the absence of any such provision, in equal shares. It further provides that the members of a Grouping shall contribute to the payment of the amount by which expenditure exceeds income in the proportions laid down in the contract for the formation of the Grouping or, in the absence of any such provision, in equal shares.

One might consider an EEIG which manages a data bank that can be used by all its members; there is nothing to prevent the EEIG charging the members for use of the service, nor to the service being offered to third parties for a fee. The important thing is that the activity carried out continues to be directed mainly, if not exclusively, towards rendering a useful service for the Grouping's members, so that they can improve their activity.

The success of the new institution goes well beyond the confines of the European Community; many ex-communist countries, during the phase of approximation of commercial law to the rules of the EC and with a view to accession to the Union, adopted the EEIG legislation (see, for example, Estonia and Hungary). In other countries in the region, some problems have come to light.

In Slovakia, for instance, Regulation no. 2137/85/EEC is close to the notion of a Grouping of persons governed by Chapter XVI of the Slovak Civil Code. What makes the implementation of this Regulation more difficult is the fact that, traditionally, such Grouping has the nature of property without legal personality. On the other hand, Regulation 2137/85 in its art. 1 (2), refers to the legal capacity of a Grouping from the date of its registration, although paragraph 3 of the same article gives the Member States freedom to make decisions as to the legal personality of such Groupings or not. Taking into account the above mentioned articles (as well as art. 4 [1]) referring to registered offices within the European Union, and not outside the Union, for instance in an associated country), the transposition of the Regulation into Slovak civil law will be addressed during the process of re-codification (for instance, as a specific type of Grouping). Another option to be considered is the implementation of this Regulation into Slovak commercial law, if the re-codification committee decides to do so.

## 20. The European Company

The instituting Regulation of the European Company was adopted on October 8th 2001, no. 2157/2001.[153] On the same day, Council Directive 2001/86/EC of October 8th 2001 was also adopted, supplementing the Statute for a European Company with regard to the involvement of employees.[154]

The European Company (known by its Latin name of *Societas Europaea* or SE) has become a reality, some 30 years after it was first proposed. The SE gives companies operating in more than one Member State the option of being established as a single company under Community law, and so able to operate throughout the EU with one set of rules and a unified management and reporting system rather than all the different national laws of each Member State where they have subsidiaries. For companies active across the internal market, the European Company therefore offers the prospect of reduced administrative costs and a legal structure adapted to the internal market as a whole.

This concerns the second institution, after the EEIG, to be governed from within by Community rules, standard throughout the Member States. The advantages are remarkable for Community multinationals, in terms of costs and simplification of bureaucracy, starting with the chance for the new company structure to rely on one set of internal rules. Set against this, the approval of the regulation of the SE has not brought benefits in regards to taxation, contributions, and the satisfaction of bureaucratic procedures, which continue to be governed by the specific rules in force in each State.

The French government advanced the idea of a trans-national share company in the early 1960's, promoted in a report sent to the European Commission, about an initiative aimed at creating a unique company structure to facilitate collaboration between companies belonging to different States, and designed to overcome the diffidence of businessmen, forced to maneuver among the various models and rules of the respective legal systems.

In 1970, the Commission presented a first draft regulation to the Council, which was later partly amended in 1975, in view of opinions expressed by the Social and Economic Committee. In 1989,[155] after stalling for more than a decade, the Commission presented the Council with a sec-

---

[153] O.J., L 294, 11/10/2001. It came into force on October 8th 2004 (art. 70 Reg.).

[154] O.J., L 294, 11/10/2001. Member states should adopt the laws, regulations, and administrative provisions necessary to comply with this Directive no later than October 8th 2004 (art. 14 Dir.).

[155] COM (89)268 final; O.J., C 236/1989, p. 41.

ond draft, which contained some important aspects: the new project was no longer based on art. 235 (now art. 308) TEC, but on the new text of art. 100a (now art. 95) TEC, introduced by art. 18 of the Single European Act of February 17th 1986.[156] In substance, the unanimity rule for Council decisions concerning the achievement of the single market gave way to the qualified majority rule. In addition, the European Parliament took on a new role of co-legislator, together with the Council.

> **Art. 95 TEC:** "(...) The Council shall, acting in accordance with the procedure referred to in Article 251 and after consulting the Economic and Social Committee, adopt the measures for the approximation of the provisions laid down by law, regulation or administrative action in Member States which have as their object the establishment and functioning of the internal market (…)."

In 1991, the Council also presented a draft directive,[157] to complement the statute of the European Company, relating to the role of the employees.

The Preamble of Reg. 2157/2001 sets out the objectives which the Community legislation hopes to pursue:

> **Whereas, Reg. 2157/2001:** "**(1)** The completion of the internal market and the improvement it brings about in the economic and social situation throughout the Community mean not only that barriers to trade must be removed, but also that the structures of production must be adapted to the Community dimension. For that purpose it is essential that companies the business of which is not limited to satisfying purely local needs should be able to plan and carry out the reorganisation of their business on a Community scale; **(3)** Restructuring and cooperation operations involving companies from different Member States give rise to legal and psychological difficulties and tax problems. The approximation of Member States' company law by means of Directives based on Article 44 of the Treaty can overcome some of those difficulties. Such approximation does not, however, release companies governed by different legal systems from the obligation to choose a form of company governed by a particular national law; **(4)** The legal framework within which business must be carried on in the Community is still based largely on national laws and therefore no longer corresponds to the economic framework within which it must develop if the objectives set out in Article 18 of the Treaty

---

[156] And later partially modified by art. G22 of the Maastricht Treaty and the Treaty of Amsterdam.

[157] COM (91)174 final; O.J., C 138, 05/29/1991.

> are to be achieved. That situation forms a considerable obstacle to the creation of groups of companies from different Member States; **(9)** Since the Commission's submission in 1970 of a proposal for a Regulation on the Statute for a European public limited-liability company, amended in 1975, work on the approximation of national company law has made substantial progress, so that on those points where the functioning of an SE does not need uniform Community rules reference may be made to the law governing public limited-liability companies in the Member State where it has its registered office; **(10)** Without prejudice to any economic needs that may arise in the future, if the essential objective of legal rules governing SEs is to be attained, it must be possible at least to create such a company as a means both of enabling companies from different Member States to merge or to create a holding company and of enabling companies and other legal persons carrying on economic activities and governed by the laws of different Member States to form joint subsidiaries."

The Preamble of the Regulation also expressly refers to Directive 86/2001, requiring coordination of the two sources:

> **Whereas, Reg. 2157/2001:** "**(19)** The rules on the involvement of employees in the European company are laid down in Directive 2001/86/EC, and those provisions thus form an in-dissociable complement to this Regulation and must be applied concomitantly; **(21)** Directive 2001/86/EC is designed to ensure that employees have a right of involvement in issues and decisions affecting the life of their SE. Other social and labour legislation questions, in particular the right of employees to information and consultation as regulated in the Member States, are governed by the national provisions applicable, under the same conditions, to public limited-liability companies; **(22)** The entry into force of this Regulation must be deferred so that each Member State may incorporate into its national law the provisions of Directive 2001/86/EC and set up in advance the necessary machinery for the formation and operation of SEs with registered offices within its territory, so that the Regulation and the Directive may be applied concomitantly."

Under the European Company Statute,[158] a European Company can be set up by the creation of a holding company or a joint subsidiary, by the

[158] For the purposes of this Regulation, the statutes of the SE shall mean both the instrument of incorporation and, where they are the subject of a separate document, the statutes of the SE (art. 6 Reg.).

merger of companies located in at least two Member States, or by the conversion of an existing company set up under national law.

In particular, the SE may not be constituted by natural persons, but only legal ones, and in conformity with the following methods (arts. 1–3 and Title II, arts. 15–37, Reg. 2157/2001):

- Merger between several public limited-liability companies, which have their registered offices and head offices within Community territory, so long as at least two of them have their head offices in two different States.
- Constitution of a holding company between several share companies (or else private limited-liability companies), on condition that at least two of them have their head offices in different States, or else that each of at least two of them has, for at least two years, had a subsidiary company governed by the law of another Member State or a branch situated in another Member State.
- Constitution by the companies of a subsidiary SE in common, under art. 58 (2) (now art. 48) TEC,[159] on condition that they have their registered offices and head offices in different States, and each of at least two of them has, for at least two years, had a subsidiary company governed by the law of another Member State or a branch situated in another Member State.
- Transformation of a share company (a public limited-liability company) into an SE if, for at least two years, it has had a subsidiary company governed by the law of another Member State, on condition that it has its registered office and head office within the Community.
- Merger or creation of a new holding or a subsidiary SE in common by one European Company with another European Company, or with another national share company.

Non-European undertakings can, therefore, also constitute an SE, so long as they have had a subsidiary or associated company in a State of the Union for at least two years, and that the SE itself is registered in a Member State.

In any case, the companies and entities which participate in the formation of a SE should have been constituted in their turn under rules of law of one of the Member States, and should have the company headquarters within the Community.

The registered office of the SE, which necessarily corresponds to the

---

[159] See § 3 of this chapter.

place where the head office is, must be situated in one of the Community States (art. 7 Reg. 2157/2001).

The transfer from one State to another within the Community is allowed, without the necessity for the liquidation of the existing company and reconstitution of a new one (art. 8 Reg. 2157/2001).

The minimum subscribed capital for an SE has been fixed at 120,000 Euro (art. 4 Reg. 2157/2001); the laws of a Member State requiring a greater subscribed capital for companies carrying on certain types of activity (for example credit institutions) shall apply to SEs with registered offices in that Member State (art. 4 (3), Reg. 2157/2001). The capital of an SE, its maintenance and changes thereto, together with its shares, bonds and other similar securities, shall be governed by the provisions which would apply to a public limited-liability company with a registered office in the Member State in which the SE is registered (art. 5 Reg. 2157/2001).

There follow many other rules concerning the structure and administration of the SE. The administration rules reflect what has already been laid down in the draft Fifth Directive on company law:[160] articles 38 & *ff.* provide that the SE be constituted by:

- A general meeting of shareholders.
- Either a supervisory organ and a management organ (two-tier system), or an administrative organ (one-tier system) depending on the form adopted in the statutes.

Article 9 Reg. 2157/2001 has an important provision, which states that the SE shall be governed in principle by the Regulation, and secondly by the will of the contracting parties, and only in a subsidiary way by the provisions of law applicable to public limited liability companies in the State where the SE has its registered office.

> **Art. 9, Reg. 2157/2001:** "**(1)** An SE shall be governed: (a) by this Regulation, (b) where expressly authorised by this Regulation, by the provisions of its statutes or (c) in the case of matters not regulated by this Regulation or, where matters are partly regulated by it, of those aspects not covered by it, by: (i) the provisions of laws adopted by Member States in implementation of Community measures relating specifically to SEs; (ii) the provisions of Member States' laws which would apply to a public limited-liability company formed in accordance with the law of the Member State in which the SE has its registered office; (iii) the provisions

160 See above § 17.1.

> of its statutes, in the same way as for a public limited-liability company formed in accordance with the law of the Member State in which the SE has its registered office. **(2)** The provisions of laws adopted by Member States specifically for the SE must be in accordance with Directives applicable to public limited-liability companies referred to in Annex I. **(3)** If the nature of the business carried out by an SE is regulated by specific provisions of national laws, those laws shall apply in full to the SE."

The regime for disclosure of the SE's acts is left to the national laws, as is the protection of creditors and shareholders, the acquisition of its own shares, insolvency, cessation of payments, winding-up, liquidation, and other important aspects in the life of an SE.

The numerous other rules (the Regulation has a total of 70 articles, including transitory and final provisions) which concern the SE's organization and activity do not add anything of special importance with respect to what is already set out in the national laws.

It is most important, however, to address the other subject-area strictly connected to the SE's statute, which concerns the position and participation of the workforce in the management of the company. Given the difficulties of the Member States in reaching a consensus concerning the European Company, and the experience of the Fifth Directive on the structure of national public limited liability companies (which has never come into force),[161] it has been thought preferable since 1989 to leave all reference to rules on worker-participation out of the draft Regulation on the SE, in order to put them in a directive which specifically concerns this issue.

Hence in 2001, Council Directive 2001/86/EC of October 8th 2001 was adopted, supplementing the Statute for a European company with regard to the involvement of employees. As was noted above, the Directive, together with the regulation on the SE, constitutes a single body of law.

Since the old 1991 draft, the choice of one participation model from among those proposed in the draft itself was an essential requirement in order to constitute a European Company.

The participation models to which Dir. 2001/86 refer are essentially the two provided by the draft Fifth Directive: there is also a general reference to other models established by the collective agreements, with the sole condition that the minimum safeguard requirements in the first two proposed models are observed. The two proposed models in the Directive respectively provide:

---

[161] See above, § 17.1.

- That employees have the right to nominate from one third to a half of the supervisory body (the two tier system) or the management structure (the one-tier system).
- That there should be a specific employee representation body, with a right to be kept informed periodically on the progress of the undertaking's activity and to receive information and written reports directly from the managers.

Under the Directive on worker involvement, the creation of a European Company would require negotiations on the involvement of employees with a body representing all employees of the companies concerned. If it proved impossible to negotiate a mutually satisfactory arrangement then a set of standard principles, laid down in an annex to the Directive, would apply. Essentially these principles oblige SE managers to provide regular reports on the basis of which there must be regular consultation of and information to a body representing the companies' employees. These reports must detail the companies' current and future business plans, production and sales levels, implications of these for the workforce, management changes, mergers, divestments, potential closures, and layoffs.

At this point it is clearer than ever that the model for the SE has moved even further away from the original concept of creating a standard model for all the Member States, and has assumed the more modest, but more realistic, appearance of a new, harmonized model of a commercial company.

In effect, either because of the referral to the national law of the company's registered office, or to the company law harmonization directives, or the choice itself of operating through directives rather than regulations in the area of employee participation, or, finally, the possibility of choosing the model of employee participation, these are all indications of a low level of standardization of the rules, certainly less than the first drafts of the regulation led us to expect.

As we have had cause to note more than once, there are political and economic reasons behind the legal problems, which very often prevent over-ambitious projects from being achieved. The lower the uniformization threshold and the greater the possibilities left to the States for creating exceptions to the Community regime, the easier it is to reach the necessary agreement to adopt a Community provision. For this reason, too, Community regulations rarely intervene to regulate the legal systems, compared to directives, and, where they are used, they leave much more room for national peculiarities than a superficial reading of the provisions would lead one to believe.

## 21. The European Cooperative Society

This concerns the third institution after the EEIG and the European Company to be governed through Community rules. The special characteristics of the *non-profit* organizations could not permit the use of the other supra-national institutions just described above.

The intrinsic characteristics of a public limited liability company could not be adapted to the principle governing the *non-profit movement* (which has a purely mutual scope, the pre-eminence of people over capital, solidarity, indivisibility of reserves, and the designation of assets to socially beneficial ends, in the case of liquidation).

Moreover, the unlimited liability of members of an EEIG as well as the auxiliary nature of its activity with respect to that of its members, were sufficient reasons to suppose that operators in the mutual sector would have had little use for it.

Concerning *cooperative aims* and considering that its activity, though entrepreneurial in nature, presupposed a *minimum of capital*, the cooperative was, by necessity, achieved in the form of a company, and, as such, was governed by national laws which fixed certain limitations and conditions on its constitution and activity (a ceiling on the number of shares for each participant; maximum limit on profit on subscribed capital, equal to the fixed interest rate; each member to belong to the social category in whose favor the society promotes itself as operating, the principle of *one man, one vote;* registration and non-transferability at will of shares).

However, with time, these conditions and limitations represented an ever-greater obstacle to the development of the individual cooperatives, which were unable to keep pace in a market dominated by capital enterprise.

The incurable difference between the two activities, *entrepreneurial* on the one hand, and *mutualistic* on the other, was behind the legislative revision process throughout Europe, becoming ever more pressing with the progress being made not only in the technical and organizational means of production, but also in the economy and affluence in general.

The members themselves of those cooperatives, who found that they had great economic potential, aspired to a greater supply of capital in the cooperative society. Thus, by developing its productive capacity, the cooperative would be able to assure its members, in addition to specific advantages or services (so-called *pure mutuality*), a somewhat higher return, even though this aspiration was ancillary to the cooperative's aim of saving costs or of a greater economic reward from the activity (the so-called *cooperative patronage dividend*).

The problem of finding the financial means necessary to compete, independently, with capitalist enterprise on equal terms, without the subsidies available to public undertakings, was faced everywhere and resolved in the Member States with greater or lesser determination in favor of the capital factor, sacrificing the mutual aspect.

The European Community itself, in light of the guidance given by academic lawyers in the individual Member States, brought the study of a model cooperative to a conclusion at the beginning of the 1990's; common to all—supranational—it took form in the draft Regulation of December 1991,[162] together with the draft proposals for the Mutual Society and the European Association.

> Almost at the same time, and drawing inspiration from the same modern Community principles, France issued Act no. 643 of July 13th 1992, concerning the *modernization* of the cooperative enterprises, after comparing closely all the various solutions adopted or in the course of adoption in States of the European Community such as Portugal, Spain, Belgium, and Italy. The first organic regime for a modern cooperative was formulated by Portugal, with the passing of the *Codigo cooperativo* of 1980. In Italy, the act no. 59 on cooperative societies was passed on January 31st 1992, following a process of innovation and modernization of the cooperative societies begun in 1983 with the so-called *legge Visentini-bis* (act no. 72/83).

It was adopted twelve years later with Council Regulation (EC) no. 1435/2003 of July 22nd 2003.

As happened in the case of the European Company, Directive no. 2003/72/EC of July 22nd 2003 supplementing the Statute for a European Cooperative Society (ECS) with regard to the involvement of employees was placed alongside the Regulation.[163]

The main feature, both in the national European laws and the Community Regulation, consists in the greater regard for the 'capitalistic' element as opposed to the purely 'mutual' one. The result has been achieved by adopting certain expedients and innovative solutions with respect to tradition.

Take, for instance, the limit on shares which each member may hold. The Community Regulation does not impose any 'maximum limit' on the ownership of shares, and establishes that any such limit imposed by

---

[162] O.J., C 99, 04/21/1992; see below § 22.

[163] The provisions are the same: for a general framework of reference see above § 20.

national laws must be indicated in the statute of the cooperative (arts. 1 (2), 4, 5, Reg. 1435/2003). Again, both in national laws and the Regulation, there is the option of increasing the cooperative's finance through the input of venture-capital, either by the cooperative members themselves or by third parties who are not involved in the services offered by the cooperative, who are known as '*supporting members*,' with no voting rights, but possessing special advantages as regards the allocation of profits and the payment of share dividends (art. 64, Reg. 1435/2003).

The usual, typical rule of '*one man–one vote*' still remains in principle, but may be subject to certain exceptions, both in favor of members for whom the statutes may provide a number of votes determined by their participation in the cooperative activity other than by way of capital contribution (but this attribution shall not exceed five votes per member or 30% of total voting rights, whichever is the lower), or to non-users or supporting members, who are not involved in using the cooperative's services (art. 59 (2) & (3) Reg. 1435/2003).

A particularly significant rule which increases 'capitalist interest' of the participants who see the revaluation of both the contribution and the dividends in proportion to the revalued capital, is contained in art. 67 of the Regulation of the European Cooperative Society: this permits the increase of capital by allocating the available surplus to ECS capital.

The Preamble of the Regulation sets out the aims of the European Cooperative Society:

> **Whereas, Reg. 1435/2003:** "(7) Cooperatives are primarily groups of persons or legal entities with particular operating principles that are different from those of other economic agents. These include the principles of democratic structure and control and the distribution of the net profit for the financial year on an equitable basis. **(8)** These particular principles include notably the principle of the primacy of the individual which is reflected in the specific rules on membership, resignation and expulsion, where the "one man, one vote" rule is laid down and the right to vote is vested in the individual, with the implication that members cannot exercise any rights over the assets of the cooperative. **(9)** Cooperatives have a share capital and their members may be either individuals or enterprises. These members may consist wholly or partly of customers, employees or suppliers. Where a cooperative is constituted of members who are themselves cooperative enterprises, it is known as a "secondary" or "second-degree" cooperative. In some circumstances cooperatives may also have among their members a specified proportion of investor members who do not use their services, or of third parties who benefit by their activities

> or carry out work on their behalf. **(10)** A European cooperative society (hereinafter referred to as "SCE") should have as its principal object the satisfaction of its members' needs and/or the development of their economic and/or social activities, in compliance with the following principles: its activities should be conducted for the mutual benefit of the members so that each member benefits from the activities of the SCE in accordance with his/her participation; members of the SCE should also be customers, employees or suppliers or should be otherwise involved in the activities of the SCE; control should be vested equally in members, although weighted voting may be allowed, in order to reflect each member's contribution to the SCE; there should be limited interest on loan and share capital; profits should be distributed according to business done with the SCE or retained to meet the needs of members; there should be no artificial restrictions on membership; net assets and reserves should be distributed on winding-up according to the principle of disinterested distribution, that is to say to another cooperative body pursuing similar aims or general interest purposes."

The European Cooperative Society shall be set up in conformity with the following methods (arts. 1 & 2 and Chapter II, art. 17 *ff.*, Reg. 1435/2003):

- By five or more natural persons resident in at least two Member States.
- By five or more natural persons and companies and firms within the meaning of art. 48 (2) TEC and other legal bodies governed by public or private law, formed under the law of a Member State, resident in, or governed by the law of, at least two different Member States.
- By companies and firms within the meaning of art. 48 (2) TEC and other legal bodies governed by public or private law formed under the law of a Member State which are governed by the law of at least two different Member States.
- By a merger between cooperatives formed under the law of a Member State with registered offices and head offices within the Community, provided that at least two of them are governed by the law of different Member States.
- By conversion of a cooperative formed under the law of a Member State, which has its registered office and head office within the Community if, for at least two years, it has had an establishment or subsidiary governed by the law of another Member State.

The subscribed capital shall not be less than EUR 30,000 (art. 3, Reg. 1435/2003).

The administration rules reflect those contained in the Community Regulation concerning the European Company: the ECS shall be constituted with a general meeting of shareholders, and either a supervisory organ and a management organ (two-tier system), or an administrative organ (one-tier system) depending on the form adopted in the statutes (art. 36, Reg. 1435/2003).

According to art. 8, the law applicable is, in principle, the Regulation, secondly the will of the contracting parties expressed in the statutes, and only in a subsidiary way the provisions of law applicable to the cooperative in the State where the ECS has its registered office.

The statutes may provide for the payment of a dividend to members in proportion to their business with the ECS, or the services they have performed for it (art. 66). The balance of the surplus after deduction of the allocation to the legal reserve (art. 65), of any sums paid out in dividends and of any losses carried over, with the addition of any surpluses carried over and of any sums drawn from the reserves, shall constitute the profits available for distribution of so called 'allocation of available surplus' (art. 67). The general meeting which considers the accounts for the financial year may allocate the surplus in the order and proportions laid down in the statutes, and in particular: carry them forward; appropriate them to any legal or statutory reserve fund; provide a return on paid-up capital and quasi-equity, payment being made in cash or shares. The statutes may also prohibit any distribution.

It is true that the *non-profit* sector is in net expansion, but it is also undergoing profound and rapid evolution. This involves a greater degree of caution in accepting solutions and new Community rules, which could prove to be inappropriate. This makes it subject to continual evaluation by academic lawyers and by case law throughout the Member States.

## 22. Draft Regulations for the European Mutual Society and the European Association

On December 18th 1991, the Commission of the Community adopted three draft regulations concerning respectively the Statute for European Cooperative Society (ECS),[164] the Statute for the European Mutual Society (EMS), and the Statute for European Association (EA).[165]

The enormous success being enjoyed over almost the whole of Europe in the cooperative company sector[166] and the great, almost exponential, increase in the so-called *non-profit* organizations over the last twenty years, has induced Parliament, the Economic and Social Committee, as well as the European Commission, to take these type of institutions into consideration too.

The objective should be to permit the exercise of these activities no longer just at national, but at cross-border levels as well, by making a single, Community model available, the same for all Member States.

The aim is not only to encourage greater integration among Members of the Union, but also to create incentives for the use of these mutual formats through bigger, stronger bodies and organizations which are able to compete more efficiently in the market against profit-making organizations which undertake similar activity.

The absence of approval, as things currently stand, of the draft Regulations concerning the European Mutual Society and European Association should be attributed to at least two reasons.

It should be kept in mind that the mutual sector, though highly developed throughout all the Member States, is not as yet sufficiently homogeneous nor has it been harmonized by any Community directives.

Whereas a plan of more than thirteen directives has been developed in the context of commercial companies, whose almost complete implementation has given rise to a now closely harmonized series of national laws, at least in their essential elements, the sector we are now considering has, on the other hand, never been even partially harmonized.

No directive has ever endeavored to lay down or establish a certain

---

164 See § 21.

165 O.J., C 99, 04/21/1992. Later, on the basis of observations made by Parliament and the Economic and Social Committee (O.J., C 223, 08/31/1992 and C 42, 02/15/1993), they were amended by the Commission on July 6th 1993, and presented again to the Council.

166 If one thinks, for instance that almost 60% of agricultural production in Europe is produced or sold through cooperatives; or the fact that cooperative banks and mutual societies receive 1/5 of European savings.

number of fundamental ground-rules, which are essential to bring together legal models which are sometimes very different. Thus, when the Regulations on Mutual Societies and Associations refer to the national laws on the subject, where no provision is made by the draft Regulations themselves, national differences re-emerge all-powerful.

The strengthening of the 'capitalistic' element of the mutual society which is to be found in the Community drafts (which draw on the German model) is not reflected in the legislation of some of the Member States, which has tended to develop along more 'mutualistic' lines. Such differences of approach lead one to believe that the process of harmonization to Community law will be long and arduous for the Member States.

Beyond these considerations, there remains the fact that the European Community has set itself the task of creating certain new institutions, so that operators in the mutual sector may have instruments at their disposal which allow them to carry out and develop, at Community level too, the same activity which is pursued in all the Member States, and which also, to a large degree, helps to fill the gaps and remedy the deficiencies in the area of social security, which are noticeable in many national systems.

It also allows the mutual sector to exploit the advantages offered by the single market and creates the conditions under which the operators in these sectors can compete at the same level as other economic and manufacturing organizations: this is a necessary step to avoid the situation where disparity of treatment can marginalize these non-profit making activities in favor of purely capitalistic ones.

The models proposed by the Commission, the European Mutual Society, and the European Association, are constituted partly by some rules in common and partly by special ones, adapted to the particular entity concerned.

In this way, the draft proposals provide that the respective entities of a European nature may be constituted by at least two legal persons/ organizations (mutual societies for the European Mutual Society, associations and foundations for the European Association), which have their head offices in two or more Member States, or through transforming themselves, on condition that they have a branch in another Member State. The European Association may, on the other hand, be constituted directly by natural persons (at least 21).

These institutions have legal personality, which is acquired upon registration in the State where the registered office is.

They are regulated by the provisions in the respective Community draft Regulations, by the rules of their Statute and, in a secondary way, by the laws of the State where the registered office is, which govern corresponding national institutions of this kind.

They may transfer their registered office, upon previous approval of the transfer scheme by the general meeting, from one State to another, without having to go into liquidation.

With regard to the management structure, there is in regard to the Mutual Society the option of choosing either the two-tier system (a management body and a supervisory one), or the one-tier system (a single administrative body).

In the European Mutual Society, unless otherwise provided by the Statute, the managers may not receive any form of remuneration or any share of the profits, apart from reimbursement of expenses incurred in the performance of their duties. There is no provision for supporting members, and the members may be required to pay "relevant supplementary contributions" in addition to the fixed ones. The principle of 'one man–one vote' is approved.

The European Association may be constituted, besides the minimum of 21 natural persons, by two or more legal non profit-making bodies, which have common professional or sectoral interests, on condition that they have their registered offices or head offices in at least two Member States. Before registration, and hence before acquiring legal personality, those acting on behalf of the Association have complete and unlimited liability for obligations assumed, unless ratified by the Association itself which may intervene only after registration. The proceeds of the economic activity are exclusively designated for the achievement of its purposes, with no division of the profits among the associates (art. 1 (2) draft Reg. 1991).

As was done in the case of the draft for the European Company and the Cooperative Society, draft Directives have also been placed alongside the draft Regulations in question, with the purpose of regulating employee participation in the management of the organization. The rules on employee participation are applicable in default, in the absence of relevant national regimes.

# Bibliography Chapter IV

## *Selected Commentary/Books/Articles:*

**§ *In English:***

WILLES J.H & WILLES J.H, *International Business Law,* McGraw Hill/Irwin, 2004; LOMBARDO S., *Regulatory Competition in Company Law in the European Community,* Bern, Peter Lang, 2002; HOPT K., E. WYMEERSCH, *Company Law and Financial Markets,* Oxford Univ. Press., 2003; EDWARDS V., *EC Company Law,* Oxford Univ. Press, 1999; MATHIJSEN P.S.R.F., *A Guide to European Union Law, London 1999; HARMATY A. (ed.), Introduction to Hungarian Law,* (Chapter 8, Business Law) Kluwer, The Hague, 1998; *Law Series: Developments in European company law,* Kluwer law Int., (1997–); FOLSOM R. H. & M. P. CLOES, *European Union Business Law: A Guide to Law and Practice,* 1995; BAUMS T., BUXBAUM R. M., HOPT K. J., (eds)., *Institutional Investors and Corporate Governance,* Berlin, New York, 1993; BUXBAUM R. M., HERTIG G., HIRSCH A., HOPT K. J., (eds.) *European Business Law—Legal and Economic Analyses on Integration and Harmonization,* Berlin, New York (de Gruyter) 1991; SCHMITTOFF C. M. (ed.), *Harmonization of European Company Law,* 1973.

**§ *In German:***

GRUNDMANN S., *Europäisches Gesellschaftsrecht: eine systematische Darstellung unter Einbeziehung des europäischen Kapitalmarktrechts*, Heidelberg, 2004; HÜFFER U., *Kommentar zum Aktiengesetz*, München, 2004; LUTTER M., *Umwandlungsgesetz*, Köln, 2004; LUTTER M., HOMMELHOFF P., *Kommentar zum GmbH-Gesetz*, Köln, 2004; LIND M., *Die Europäische Aktiengesellschaft: eine Analyse der Rechtsanwendungsvorschriften*, Wien, 2004; ALTMEPPEN R., *GmbHG*, 4th ed., München, 2003; KOLLER I., ROTH W.-H., MORCK W., *Handelsgesetzbuch. Kommentar*, München, 2003; HIRTE H., *Kapitalgesellschaftsrecht*, Köln, 2003; HABERSACK M., *Europäisches Gesellschaftsrecht*, München, 2003; ROTH G., ALTMEPPEN H., *Kurzkommentar zum GmbH-Gesetz*, München, 2003; WINTER S., *Management- und Aufsichtsratsvergütung unter besonderer Berücksichtigung von Stock Options – Lösung eines Problems oder zu lösendes Problem?* Arbeitstitel, in: HOMMELHOFF P., HOPT K. J., VON WERDER A. (eds.), *Handbuch Corporate Governance*, Köln und Stuttgart, 2002; SCHMIDT, *Gesellschaftsrecht*, 4th ed., Köln 2002; HOMMELHOFF P., HELMS D., *Neue Wege in die Europäische Privatgesellschaft,* Köln, 2001; BAUMBACH-HOPT, *Handelsgesetzbuch*, 30th ed., München, 2000; EISENHARDT, *Gesellschaftsrecht*, 9th ed., München 2000; CANARIS, *Handelsrecht*, 23rd ed., München, 2000; SCHNEIDER U.H., HOMMELHOFF P., SCHMIDT K., TIMM W., GRUNEWALD B., DYRGALA T. (eds.), *Festschrift für Marcus Lutter zum 70.Geburtstag*, Köln 2000; *Münchener Kommentar zum Aktiengesetz*, 2nd ed., München 2000–2003 (Kommentar – 5 vol.); SCHMID, *Handelsrecht*, 5th ed., Köln 1999; EISELSBERG M. (ed.) *Gesellschaftsrecht in Europa,* Wien, 1997; SCHMIDT (ed.), *Münchener Kommentar zum Handelsgesetzbuch* (from 1996–).

**§ *In French:***

RACLET A. (préface de H. Gaudemet-Tallon), *Droit communautaire des affaires et prérogatives de puissance publique nationale,* Dalloz, Paris, 2002; GAVALDA C., PARLEANI G., *Droit des affaires de l'Union européenné,* Litec, 3ème ed. 1999; MAGNIER V. (préface de P. Didier), *Rapprochement des droits dans l'Union Européenne et viabilité d'un droit commun des sociétés,* LGDJ Paris, 9 ed., 1999; CORRUBLE P, *Droit européen des affaires,* Dunod, 1998; POILLOT-PERUZZETTO S., M. LUBY, *Le droit communautaire appliqué à l'entreprise,* Dalloz, Paris, 1998; GOLDMAN B., LYON-CAEN A., VOGEL L., *Droit commercial européen,* Précis Dalloz 1994.

**§ *In Italian:***

BENAZZO PATRIARCA, PRESTI (eds.), *Il nuovo diritto societario fra società aperte e società private,* Milano, 2003; GENCO (ed.), *La riforma delle società cooperative, collana Diritto delle societȧ e dei mercati finanziari,* Milano, Ipsoa, 2003; AMBROSINI (ed.) *La riforma delle società. Profili della nuova disciplina,* Torino, 2003; ASSOCIAZIONE PREITE (OLIVERI, PRESTI, VELLA eds.), *Il nuovo diritto delle società,* Bologna, 2003; BERTUZZI, MANFEROCE, PLATANIA, *Società per azioni. Costituzione, patti parasociali, conferimenti (artt. 2325-2345 c.c.),* in: *La riforma del diritto societario* LO CASCIO (ed.), vol. 3, Milano, 2003; BIANCHI (G.), *Amministrazione e controllo delle nuove societá di capitali – Metodi alternativi di gestione dopo la riforma del diritto societario,* Milano, Ipsoa, 2003; BUONOCORE (ed.), *La riforma del diritto societario. Commento ai d.lgs. n. 5-6 del 17 gennaio 2003,* Torino 2003; GALGANO, *Manuale di diritto commerciale. Le società,* Bologna, 2003; SANDULLI, SANTORO (eds.) *La riforma delle societá. Commentario del. D. Lgs. 17 gennaio 2003, n. 6,* Torino, 2003; CASSOTTANA, NUZZO, *Lezioni di diritto commerciale comunitario,* Torino, 2002; BENAZZO, GREZZI, PATRIARCA, *Verso un nuovo diritto societario: contributi per un dibattito,* Bologna, 2002; LAMANDINI M., *Struttura finanziaria e governo nelle società di capitali: le prospettive di riforma,* Bologna, 2001; CORAPI-DE DONNO, *Le società,* in TIZZANO (ed.), *Il diritto privato dell'Unione Europea,* in BESSONE, *Trattato di diritto privato,* 2000, vol. II, 1027; COTTINO G., *Diritto commerciale,* vol. I, (2000), vol. II (1999), Padova; CALÌ S., *Questioni in tema di scissione,* Milano, 2000; RONDINONE N., *I gruppi di imprese fra diritto comune e diritto speciale,* Milano, 1999; ROSAPEPE R., *La società a responsabilità limitata unipersonale,* Milano, 1996; SANTA MARIA A., *Diritto commerciale comunitario,* Milano, 1995; SACERDOTI G. & FRIGO M., (eds.), *La Convenzione di Roma sul diritto applicabile ai contratti internazionali,* Milano, 1994; BALLARINO T. (ed.), *La Convenzione di Roma sulla legge applicabile alle obbligazioni contrattuali,* Milano, 1994; ID., *Le direttive comunitarie sull'armonizzazione del diritto delle società,* in DRAETTA (ed.), *Verso un diritto europeo delle società,* Milano, 1991, 31; POCAR F., *La Convenzione di Bruxelles sulla giurisdizione e l'esecuzione delle sentenze,* Milano, 1989; MARLETTA M., *La cogestione delle imprese nella CEE – La partecipazione dei lavoratori nelle proposte di società europea e di V direttiva sulle società per azioni,* Napoli 1983; AA. VV., *La partecipazione dei lavoratori alla gestione delle imprese,* Rimini, 1982.

***Selected articles:***

DRAGNEVA R. & E. MILLAN, *Transposing the "true and fair view" concept in the legislation of Hungary and Poland in the context of the EU Enlargement,* 28 Rev. of Central and Eastern European Law 183, 2003; MACHEK J., *Merger law reduces interest in corporate absorptions,* Pricewaterhouse Coopers Publication, Prague Business Journal (No. 11), 18 March, 2002, available at http://www.pwcglobal.com/cz/eng/ins-sol/exec-pers/Squeezeout_JM.html; FISCHER J., *Code untangles corporate restructuring options, PricewaterhouseCoopers Publication,* Prague Business Journal (No. 15), 15 April, 2002, available at http://www.pwcglobal.com/cz/eng/ins-sol/exec-pers/Restructuring _JF.html; BAELZ K., BALDWIN T., *the European Court of Justice Decision in Ueberseering of 5 November 2002 and its Impact on German and European Company Law,* 3 German Law Journal 2002, available at http://germanlawjournal.com/article.php?id=214; DRAGNEVA R.O., JERSILD T.N., *Perspectives on company law reform in Central and Eastern Europe: an Introduction,* Rev. of Central and Eastern Europe, 1, 2001; KLINE C. L., *Pro-*

*tecting Minority Shareholders in close corporations: modelling Czech Investor protections on German and United States Law*, available at http://www.bc.edu/bc_org/avp/law/lwsch/journals/bciclr/23_2/03_TXT.htm, 2000; SCHWEISFURTH T., ALLEWELDT R., *New Constitutional Structures in Central and Eastern Europe*, Review of Central and East European Law 289, 1999;· LEVY D.A., *Developments in European Company Law*, available at E-Journal on May 17, 1997, at http://www.ili.org/pubeuro.html#28; EBKE W. F., *Company law and the EU: Centralized versus Decentralized Lawmaking*, 31 The International Lawyer 961, 1997; ZAPHIRIOU G. A., *Unification and Harmonization of Law Relating to Global and Regional Trading*, 14 N. Ill. U.L. Rev. 407, 1994; BLACKBURN T. L., *The Societas Europaea: The Evolving European Corporation Statute*, 61 Fordham L. Rev. 695, 1993; EBKE W. F., GOCKEL M., *European Corporate Law*, 24 Int'l Law 239, 1990; GROSSFELD B., W. F. EBKE, *Controlling the Modern Corporation: A Comparative View of Corporate Power in the United States and Europe*, 26 Am. J. Comp. L. 397, 1978;

PERNAZZA F, *Libertà di stabilimento delle società in Europa e tutela dei creditori*, Societá 373, 2004; CONTALDI G., *Il diritto comunitario delle società tra evoluzioni giurisprudenziali e legge di riforma della materia*, Il Diritto dell'Unione Europea 711 2003; GHERA E., *Azionariato dei lavoratori e democrazia economica. Relazione al convegno "Sviluppi e occupazione tra europeismo e localismi"* Napoli, 3-4 maggio 2002, Rivista italiana di diritto del lavoro, pt. 1, pp. 413, 2003; Portale G.B. *"Armonizzazione" e "concorrenza" tra ordinamenti nel diritto societario europeo*, Il Corriere giuridico 95, 2003; ROSSI, STABILINI, *Virtù del mercato e scetticismo delle regole: appunti a margine della riforma del diritto societario. Relazione al Convegno "Diritto societario: dai progetti alla riforma," Courmayeur 27-28 settembre 2002*, Rivista delle società 1, 2003; WYMEERSCH E., *Il trasferimento della sede della società nel diritto societario europeo*, Rivista delle società 723, 2003; BIANCA M. *La società europea: considerazioni introduttive, Contratto e* impresa/Europa 453, 2002; POGGI A.M., *L'impresa sociale tra Stato e mercato e necessità di una identificazione all'interno del terzo settore*, Non Profit 223, 2002; FORTUNATO S., *Una recente sentenza della Corte di Giustizia in tema di libertà di stabilimento delle società*, Dir. Unione Eur. 83, 2000; VALENTE-ROLLE. *Liberttà di stabilimento e controllate estere nell'interpretazione della Corte di Giustizia*. Società 497, 2000; GIULIANI THOMPSON L., *Il conflitto nell'applicazione del diritto di stabilimento primario e secondario delle società europee*, Contratto e impr./Europa 229, 2000; FORTUNATO S., *La mobilità transfrontaliera delle società nel diritto comunitario: il caso 'Centros'*, osservazioni a Corte giust., 9 marzo 1999, causa C-212/97, Foro it., IV, 317, 2000; PORTALE G.B., *La scissione nel diritto societario italiano: casi e questioni*, Riv. soc. 480, 2000; ROSSI A., *Spunti sulla nuova disciplina della revisione contabile*, Società 1034, 1999; CATERINO D., *Collaboratori del sindaco e organizzazione del controllo contabile nelle società di capitali*, Giur. comm. I, 183, 1999; ANNUNZIATA F., *La tredicesima direttiva CE sull'OPA: nuova proposta*, Riv. soc. 664, 1998; DEZZANI F., PISONI P., & PUDDU L., *Le fusioni: aspetti civilistici dopo l'attuazione della terza direttiva CEE*, Impresa 414, 1996; VISMARA F., *Prime applicazioni giurisprudenziali delle norme attuative dell'undicesima direttiva comunitaria in tema di società*, Riv. dir. internaz. priv. e proc. 87, 1995; POCAR F., *Sull'attività del Geie costituito tra liberi professionisti*, Riv. dir. civ. II, 387, 1996; CATALDO C., *Il gruppo europeo di interesse economico (Geie)*, Impresa, 505, 1995; ALBY E., *Geie (gruppo europeo di interesse economico)*, Digesto comm., Appendice, vol. X, Torino, 1994, 495; CICOGNANI A., *Il codice civile e l'attuazione della quarta direttiva Cee*, Giur. it. IV, 263, 1994; BALZARINI P., *Bilancio consolidato*, in Digesto comm., Appendice, vol. XI, Torino, 1995, 577; FORTUNATO S., *La funzione del bilancio consolidato nella tutela degli interessi correlati al gruppo*, Riv. dir.

comm. I, 51, 1993; *La riforma dei bilanci annuali e consolidati delle società*, contributors: COLOMBO G.E., JAEGER P.G., SACCHI R., DEZZANI F., TANTINI G., CAGNASSO O., FALSITTA G., SBISÀ G., VIGANÒ A., TESSITORE A., BIANCHI L.A., LIBONATI B., Padova, 1993; OPPO G., *Diritto delle società e attuazione della 2ª direttiva CEE – Il decreto di attuazione in Italia. Rilievi sistematici*, Riv. dir. civ. I, 565, 1986; CORAPI D., *L'influenza della produzione giuridica delle Comunità Europee e del Consiglio d'Europa sul diritto italiano: il diritto delle società*, Riv. soc. 849, 1981; SANTA MARIA A., *L'attuazione negli ordinamenti interni delle direttive comunitarie in materia di società*, Giur. comm. I, 927, 1980.

EIDENMÜLLER H., *Mobilität und Restrukturierung von Unternehmen im Binnenmarkt: Entwicklungsperspektiven des europäischen Gesellschaftsrechts im Schnittfeld von Gemeinschaftsgesetzgeber und EuGH*, 59 JZ 24, 2004; SPINDLER G., BERNER O., *Inspire Art: der europäische Wettbewerb um das Gesellschaftsrecht ist endgültig eröffnet: Anmerkung zu EuGH, Urteil vom 30.9.2003, Rs. C-167/01*, 49 RIW Heft 12, 949, 2003; SPINDLER G., *Deutsches Gesellschaftsrecht in der Zange zwischen Inspire art und Golden shares? Anmerkung zu EuGH, Urteile vom 13.5.2003, Rs. C-463/00, Kommission/Spanien und Rs. C-98/01, Kommission/Vereinigtes Königreich Großbritannien und Nordirland*, 49 RIW Heft 11, 850, 2003; VEIL R., *Das Konzernrecht der Europäischen Aktiengesellschaft*, 57 WM Heft 45, 2169, 2003; EBERT S., *Das anwendbare Konzernrecht der Europäischen Aktiengesellschaft*, 58 BB Heft 36, 1854, 2003; MAUL S., TEICHMANN C., WENZ M., *Der Richtlinienvorschlag zur grenzüberschreitenden Verschmelzung von Kapitalgesellschaften*, 58 BB Heft 50, 2633, 2003.

# CHAPTER V

# Industrial and Commercial Property Rights

KEY WORDS: Industrial and commercial property rights – European patent – Community patent – European trademark – Industrial designs – Utility models – Copyright/Author's rights – Designations of origin – Biotechnological inventions – Genetically modified organisms – Harmonization – CEECs

## 1. Industrial and Commercial Property Rights in the Single Market

First of all, attention should be drawn to the question of *terminology*, given that, outside the context of the Community, "intellectual property rights" is favored as the generic expression.

In art. 30 (*ex* art. 36) TEC, the expression "industrial and commercial property" is used to denote one of the reasons justifying some limitation on the free movement of goods, but does not define what it means.

> **Art. 30 TEC:** "The provisions of Articles 28 and 29 shall not preclude prohibitions or restrictions on imports, exports or goods in transit justified on grounds of public morality, public policy or public security; the protection of health and life of humans, animals or plants; the protection of national treasures possessing artistic, historic or archaeological value; or the protection of industrial and commercial property. Such prohibitions or restrictions shall not, however, constitute a means of arbitrary discrimination or a disguised restriction on trade between Member States."

More precise reference to the first part of the expression (*industrial property*) can be found in the *Paris Convention* for the protection of industrial property, signed on March 20th 1883.[1] Industrial property is defined in art. 1 (2): "The protection of industrial property has as its object patents, utility models, industrial designs, trademarks, service marks, trade names,

---

[1] As revised at Brussels on December 14th 1900, at Washington on June 2nd 1911, at The Hague on November 6th 1925, at London on June 2nd 1934, at Lisbon on October 31st 1958, and at Stockholm on July 14th 1967, and as amended on September 28th 1979. See below, § 3 in this chapter.

indications of source or appellations of origin, and the repression of unfair competition."

The meaning of the second adjective (*commercial*) is attributed (not by all legal academics, however) to the need to suppress unfair competition, as provided both under the Paris Convention and the GATT, signed in 1947.[2] Hence, article XX (d) of the GATT states: "Subject to the requirement that such measures are not applied in a manner which would constitute a means of arbitrary or unjustifiable discrimination between countries where the same conditions prevail, or a disguised restriction on international trade, nothing in this Agreement shall be construed to prevent the adoption or enforcement by any contracting party of measures: necessary to secure compliance with laws or regulations which are not inconsistent with the provisions of this Agreement, including those relating to customs enforcement, the enforcement of monopolies operated under paragraph 4 of Article II and Article XVII, the protection of patents, trademarks and copyrights, and the prevention of deceptive practices (...)."

Therefore, in speaking of *industrial and commercial property rights,* we refer to rights such as patents, trademarks, copyrights and related issues (neighboring rights, service marks, industrial design rights), and other forms of protection concerning software, biotechnological inventions, geographical indications of origin, plant variety rights, and trade secrets. They concern rights which permit exclusive economic exploitation by their proprietor in the context of the exercise of manufacturing activity or the supply of goods and services.

As mentioned, article 30 (*ex* art. 36) TEC represents the legislative foothold which gives entry to the protection of all these rights under the Treaty. According to the provision, the restriction on the movement of goods is not considered illegal where it is justified by the "*protection of industrial and commercial property*," on condition that the prohibitions and restrictions "*shall not, however, constitute a means of arbitrary discrimination or a disguised restriction on trade between Member States*."

The provision should be read and interpreted as an exception to the general rule imposed under art. 28 (*ex* art. 30) TEC: this concerns the fundamental principle under which "*quantitative restrictions on imports and all measures having equivalent effect shall be prohibited between Member States*."

Protection of industrial and commercial property rights has developed, as we shall see, by means of the ECJ's interpretation of this Treaty provision, with this objective in mind.

---

[2] As amended through 1966. See below, § 3 in this chapter.

The subject may be approached from two different aspects.

The first, which can be defined as the *'static profile,'* concerns the substantive rights (patents, trademarks, etc.,) which a given legal system (national, supranational, international) accords to the proprietor.

The second, which can be called the *'dynamic profile,'* on the other hand, concerns the context in which these rights provide effective protection in relation to other rights protected by the legal system: in particular, the important aspect, at Community level, is to determine the point to which a proprietor of such rights (patents, trademarks, etc) can limit or suppress the free movement of goods, free competition and, finally, the development and integration of the single market.

The protection of industrial and commercial rights concerns two different aspects, since the first tends to involve the *particular interests* of individual proprietors, (concerning the relationship between the owner of the right and the concessionaire or licensee; between the owner and third-party counterfeiters, and so on) and gives them the possibility of making a profit through the economic exploitation of the exclusive use of the distinctive logo (in the case of a trademark), invention (in the case of a patent), or a work of a literary or artistic kind (in the case of copyrights). The other aspect, conversely, tends to involve *collective interests* too, those of other undertakings, competition between manufacturers, the market and consumers.

It is not always the owner of the right who undertakes directly the production or commercialization of the intangible product of her/his activity (invention, new technology, song, etc) to which the right refers. Often the owner, rather than exploiting the product directly, cedes the opportunity of use and commercial exploitation to others, with the objective of reaching a greater number of users in the market, and increasing profits.

To this end, s/he subjects the concessionaire to a range of binding conditions to avoid conflicts with other economic operators and exploit to the full the profit-making possibilities which derive from the monopoly of the product of which s/he is the owner.

Industrial and commercial property rights are therefore rights which allow their owner to impose conditions and limitations on the exploitation and use of the goods or products. These rights can of themselves cause a restriction on the free movement of goods.

Historically, in effect, it is really the various national laws for the protection of intellectual property were in conflict with Community rules that govern the free movement of goods.

It could happen that certain commercial practices or entrepreneurial activity (by the owners of these rights), if put in place within the State of origin, were considered lawful and were protected by the legal system, whereas, if imposed in the context of interstate trading, were prohibited as being harmful to the free movement of goods or free competition. Among the most frequently used clauses in licensing contracts, which could bring about an infringement of Community rules, we draw attention to those concerning the following: territorial limits on manufacture or marketing; the prohibition on parallel importation; limitations on technical applications and selection of clients; the prohibition on the grant of sub-licenses; limitations on quantities produced and pricing; limitations on manufacturing locations; the prohibition on challenging the patent.

A different situation exists in the US, where federal legislation defining the nature and scope of patents, trademarks, and copyrights is in place, such that State legislation cannot restrict the exploitation of these rights on the national marketplace.

In the European Community, it was the State which provided protection and governed by means of national laws, and the monopolistic power which they recognized as extending was over the national territory and not beyond it: this was the so-called '*territorial principle.*' In other words, this means that the owner exhausted (in the sense of uses up) the right when s/he placed the product on the market and, as a result, lost all chance of controlling the possible resale and later circulation of the product. This principle applied within each individual national territory.

The owner had the chance to enjoy the exclusive rights conferred by law, through the monopoly price which s/he had been able to impose, on the first sale. For expediency, this chance was conceded only once for each product unit.

It did not matter that the first market launch occured in another State because, the national regime and the monopolistic nature of the right being what it was, the owner could oppose the parallel importation of the product, that is, third parties who, profiting from price differences, try to obtain the product in the State where the product was offered at a lower price and sell it where it was offered at a higher price, in competition with the owner of the inherent rights in the product.

To resolve the conflict between national legislation on industrial and commercial property rights and the common market, the Community institutions, beginning with the ECJ,[3] have developed and refined a principle which guarantees the owner of the right one single opportunity to obtain the monopoly profit within the whole of the Community territory, extending the exhaustion of the intellectual property to the context of the whole of the EC (the so-called '*exhaustion of rights doctrine*').

---

[3] See above, chapter II, on the role of the ECJ, in the first volume of this *Guide, A Common Law for Europe*.

In concrete terms, this principle has produced the effect of preventing the owner of the right from dividing the common market along national boundaries. According to the ECJ, the owner exhausts her/his right over the whole of Community territory, once s/he has put the product into circulation in one Member State (it does not matter which one) and has as a result obtained some form of economic recompense; however, it is essential that the first time the goods are put into circulation in Community territory, it should have been done by the owner her/himself, or with her/his consent.

## 2. The Doctrine of Exhaustion of Rights

In summary, the basic problem concerning the exercise of such rights in the context of the EC consists precisely in reconciling opposing needs and balancing opposing interests: on the one hand, the owner's need to make the best economic use of his own right; on the other, the need to avoid situations which, by dividing the market or hindering commercial exploitation in certain areas, may compromise (or even just impede) the free movement of goods or free competition, so creating circumstances prohibited by articles 81 and 82 (*ex* arts. 85 and 86) TEC in the areas of restrictive agreements and the abuse of a dominant position.[4]

In the search for balance between the different viewpoints, the part played by the ECJ, through the mechanism of preliminary references under art. 234 TEC, has been crucial. The ECJ and the Commission have had recourse to various criteria: at times they relied on the *'rule of reason,'* typical of the American system, and have held admissible, as reasonable, a limitation on circulation of the product which seems to be proportionate to the economic advantage which the owner hopes to gain. At other times, the position adopted by the Community bodies seems to rest upon the application of *prohibitions* imposed under arts. 81 and 82 TEC, even if the conditions for the application of these rules have often been shown to be lacking in cases of parallel importation.

The *exhaustion of rights doctrine,* whose content has just been explained, underlies the rather rigid attitude of the European Community. Let us now look at how the principle has been developed by the ECJ, interpreting the Treaty provisions on the free movement of goods.

The process of erosion of the area of national jurisdiction and the specific contents of national laws began with the *Consten–Grundig*[5] case,

[4] See chapter I.

[5] Joint Cases C-56-58/64, (1966) ECR I-458.

and continued with the judgments in *Parke Davis*[6] and *Sirena*.[7] The practice of importing trademarked goods from another country of the Community, when they are then sold in the country of import at a higher price, was "regulated" under the doctrine of exhaustion of rights by the ECJ. As a result of these two judgments, *Consten–Grundig* and *Sirena*, which dealt with trademarks, the ECJ did not allow trademark law to be used to prevent the practice of parallel imports, provided that the trademarked goods were initially sold with the consent of the proprietor or licensee. This result was reached indirectly, aimed in the first place at protecting a regime of free competition.

The impact of Community law reached its zenith with the comprehensive development of the exhaustion of rights doctrine (although the term "exhaustion" is not used in the judges' reasoning), formulated in the *Deutsche Grammophon GmbH v. Metro*[8] case, in relation to patent rights.

The *Hanseatisches Oberlandesgericht* of Hamburg referred to the ECJ, under art. 177 of the EEC Treaty, certain questions on the interpretation of the second paragraph of art. 5, art. 85 (1) and art. 86 of the EEC Treaty (now arts. 10, 81 & 82 TEC).

The ECJ, however, decided the case on the basis of art. 30 (now art. 28) and 36 (now art. 30) TEC, placing particular emphasis on the first clause of art. 30, which provides an exception in general terms:

> The ECJ held that when ***Deutsche Grammophon***, owner of a German music copyright, sold records through its French subsidiary Polydor S.A. in Alsace, it could not take advantage of art. 30 EC Treaty to bar the re-import and resale of the records in Germany. **See §§ 7, 12, 13 of the ruling**:
>
> "(**7**) If, however, the exercise of the right does not exhibit those elements of contract or concerted practice referred to in article 85 (1) it is necessary, in order to answer the question referred, further to consider whether the exercise of the right in question is compatible with other provisions of the treaty, in particular those relating to the free movement of goods. (**12**) If a right related to copyright is relied upon to prevent the marketing in a member state of products distributed by the holder of the right or with his consent on the territory of another member state on the sole ground that such distribution did not take place on the national territory, such a prohibition, which would legitimise the isolation of national

[6] Case C-24/67 (1968) ECR I-76.
[7] Case C-40/70 (1971), ECR I-69.
[8] Case C-78/70 (1971), ECR I-487.

> markets, would be repugnant to the essential purpose of the treaty, which is to unite national markets into a single market. That purpose could not be attained if, under the various legal systems of the member states, nationals of those states were able to partition the market and bring about arbitrary discrimination or disguised restrictions on trade between member states. (**13**) Consequently, it would be in conflict with the provisions prescribing the free movement of products within the common market for a manufacturer of sound recordings to exercise the exclusive right to distribute the protected articles, conferred upon him by the legislation of a member state, in such a way as to prohibit the sale in that state of products placed on the market by him or with his consent in another member state solely because such distribution did not occur within the territory of the first Member State."

Later, in the cases of *Centrafarm v. Sterling Drug, Centrafarm v. Winthorp,* and *Warner Brothers Inc. and Metronome Video,*[9] the ECJ extended the doctrine to all other industrial and commercial property rights, using the *criterion of 'specific object.'*

The 'specific object' is represented by the rights which cannot be sacrificed to achieve the aim of the free movement of goods, at the risk of not recognizing the existence of the trademark, patent, copyright, etc.

In this way, the ECJ has created a complex body of case law, which is at times contradictory. Its intervention was legitimized on the basis of interpreting the aims to be achieved by the Treaty: to avoid industrial and commercial property rights being exercised in a way that conflicted with the goal of a common market. With these judgments, the Court also defined the basis for the limitation of its intervention, affirming that establishing the content aspect of the protection remained the prerogative of the Member States. In fact, the Court did not reduce the contents of the national laws to nothing, but rather clarified that industrial and commercial property rights *are not a subject reserved* for national legal systems:

> Patent law: ***Centrafarm BV et Adriaan de Peijper v Sterling Drug Inc.;* cf. §§ 9, 15, 19, 20 of the ruling**:
>
> "(**9**) In relation to patents, the specific subject matter of the industrial property is the guarantee that the patentee, to reward the creative effort of the inventor, has the exclusive right to use an invention with a view to manufacturing industrial products and

[9] Respectively: Case C-15/74 (1974), ECR I-1147; Case C-16/74 (1974), ECR I-1183; Case C-158/86 (1988), ECR I-2605.

putting them into circulation for the first time, either directly or by the grant of licences to third parties, as well as the right to oppose infringements. (**15**) The question referred should therefore be answered to the effect that the exercise, by a patentee, of the right which he enjoys under the legislation of a member state to prohibit the sale, in that state, of a product protected by the patent which has been marketed in another member state by the patentee or with his consent is incompatible with the rules of the EEC treaty concerning the free movement of goods within the common market. (**19**) It follows (...) that the factor which above all else characterizes a restriction of trade between member states is the territorial protection granted to a patentee in one member state against importation of the product which has been marketed in another member state by the patentee himself or with his consent. (**20**) Therefore the result of the grant of a sales licence in a member state is that the patentee can no longer prevent the sale of the protected product throughout the common market."

Trade mark law: ***Centrafarm BV et Adriaan de Peijper v Winthrop BV.;* cf. §§ 8, 9, 10, 12 of the ruling**:

"(**8**) In relation to trade marks, the specific subject-matter of the industrial property is the guarantee that the owner of the trade mark has the exclusive right to use that trade mark, for the purpose of putting products protected by the trade mark into circulation for the first time, and is therefore intended to protect him against competitors wishing to take advantage of the status and reputation of the trade mark by selling products illegally bearing that trade mark. (**9**) An obstacle to the free movement of goods may arise out of the existence, within a national legislation concerning industrial and commercial property, of provisions laying down that a trade mark owner's right is not exhausted when the product protected by the trade mark is marketed in another member state, with the result that the trade mark owner can prevent importation of the product into his own member state when it has been marketed in another member state. (**10**) Such an obstacle is not justified when the product has been put onto the market in a legal manner in the member state from which it has been imported, by the trade mark owner himself or with his consent, so that there can be no question of abuse or infringement of the trade mark. (**12**) The question referred should therefore be answered to the effect that the exercise, by the owner of a trade mark, of the right which he enjoys under the legislation of a member state to prohibit the sale, in that state, of a product which has been marketed under the trade mark in another member state by the trade mark owner or with his consent is incompatible with the rules of the EEC Treaty concerning the free movement of goods within the common market."

The facts and the parties in these two judgments are substantially the same.

*Sterling Drug Inc.* was a New York company, the owner of patents on the preparation method for a pharmaceutical product in various European countries, among which were Holland and the UK. The product was sold under the brand name Negram, which was owned by the *Sterling Winthrop Group Limited*, (an affiliate of Sterling Drug Inc.) in the UK and *Winthorp BV* (an affiliate of the Sterling Winthrop Group Limited) in Holland. Furthermore, the British affiliated company had a license for the production and manufacture of the product in the UK, while the Dutch subsidiary only had a license to sell the product in Holland and imported it from the UK. The product was sold at a lower price in the UK with respect to Holland, owing to a price-control policy imposed by the British government.

*Centrafarm*, exploiting this loophole, imported the product, which had been bought in the UK and in Germany, where it was put on the market by a subsidiary of the New York parent company. Sterling Drug and Winthrop brought an action against Centrafarm in the Rotterdam court for violation of patent rights in the first place and of the trademark in the second. The court referred the case to the Court of Justice.

The ECJ applied the *doctrine of exhaustion*: the right in the industrial property is exhausted the first time the goods are put into circulation by the owner of the right, or with her/his consent, within the Community, and not in the more limited sense of a national territory.

> Copyright law: ***Warner Brothers Inc. and Metronome Video ApS v Erik Viuff Christiansen; cf.*** §§ **11, 12, 13, 14, 15, 16 of the ruling**:
>
> "(**11**) Consideration should therefore be given to whether such legislation may be considered justified on grounds of the protection of industrial and commercial property within the meaning of Article 36—a term which was held by the Court, in its judgment of 6 October 1982 in Case 262/81 Coditel v Ciné-Vog (1982), ECR 3381, to include literary and artistic property. (**12**) In that connection it should first be noted that the Danish legislation applies without distinction to video-cassettes produced in situ and video-cassettes imported from another Member State. The determining factor for the purposes of its application is the type of transaction in video-cassettes which is in question, not the origin of those video-cassettes. Such legislation does not therefore, in itself, operate any arbitrary discrimination in trade between Member States. (**13**) It should further be pointed out that literary and artistic works may be the subject of commercial exploitation, whether by way of pub-

> lic performance or of the reproduction and marketing of the recordings made of them, and this is true in particular of cinematographic works. The two essential rights of the author, namely the exclusive right of performance and the exclusive right of reproduction, are not called in question by the rules of the Treaty. (**14**) Lastly, consideration must be given to the emergence, demonstrated by the Commission, of a specific market for the hiring-out of such recordings, as distinct from their sale. The existence of that market was made possible by various factors such as the improvement of manufacturing methods for video-cassettes which increased their strength and life in use, the growing awareness amongst viewers that they watch only occasionally the video-cassettes which they have bought and, lastly, their relatively high purchase price. The market for the hiring-out of video-cassettes reaches a wider public than the market for their sale and, at present, offers great potential as a source of revenue for makers of films. (**15**) However, it is apparent that, by authorizing the collection of royalties only on sales to private individuals and to persons hiring out video-cassettes, it is impossible to guarantee to makers of films a remuneration which reflects the number of occasions on which the video-cassettes are actually hired out and which secures for them a satisfactory share of the rental market. That explains why, as the Commission points out in its observations, certain national LAWS HAVE RECENTLY PROVIDED SPECIFIC PROTECTION OF THE RIGHT TO HIRE out video-cassettes. (**16**) Laws of that kind are therefore clearly justified on grounds of the protection of industrial and commercial property pursuant to Article 36 of the Treaty."

The facts of the case concern *Warner Brothers Inc.*, the holder of copyright on a film produced by it. This company had conceded the video production rights for the whole Danish national territory to the *Metronome* company. The legislation in the two countries differed regarding protection of lending rights: in the UK the copyright holder, once the first sale has been made, could not prohibit hiring; in Denmark, on the other hand, the holder's authorization was required for the purposes of hire in any case. On the basis of this law, Warner and Metronome sued the *Christiansen* company, which had bought video cassettes in the UK, imported them into Denmark and intended to hire them out there, without authorization. The Danish Tribunal asked the ECJ whether the Treaty provisions on the free movement of goods allowed the Danish national legislation to prevail, when the goods had been put into circulation in another Member State (namely the UK), which did not have this particular regime.

The ECJ in its judgment started from the assumption that the author of a work may have an interest in the new forms of exploiting it provided under national law. The issue turned on the importance of the copyright holder's remuneration. Hence the Danish law, which protected the lending rights regarding videocassettes, seemed justified for reasons of the protection of commercial and industrial property.

> In later years, the ECJ maintained the same position on copyright and related rights (rental and lending right) *cf*:
>
> – Case C-200/96, *Metronome Musik GmbH v Music Point Hokamp GmbH*, (1998), ECR I-1953.
> – Case C-61/97, *Foreningen af danske Videogramdistributører, acting for Egmont Film A/S, Buena Vista Home Entertainment A/S, Scanbox Danmark A/S, Metronome Video A/S, Polygram Records A/S, Nordisk Film Video A/S, Irish Video A/S and Warner Home Video Inc. v Laserdisken*, (1998), ECR I-5171.

In these judgments, by means of the specific objective criterion, the ECJ formulated a definition for every right (trademark, patent, copyright), with a view to guaranteeing the owner the first market launch of the product and protection against counterfeiting. These are not exhaustive definitions: the Court itself has admitted the possibility (by the use of the expression "amongst other things" in the ruling) that the specific objective may be wider.

In later judgments, the ECJ paused to consider whether the prohibition on parallel importation in the individual case creates a hidden restriction or arbitrary discrimination in trade between Member States, basing its own analysis on the second clause of art. 30 TEC. This permits an evaluation as to whether the national provisions violate the Treaty or not. At the same time, the definition of 'specific object' has lost importance and appears as *obiter*, mere repetition of the previous rulings. In the area of patents, an example of this new reasoning is to be found in the case of *Allen & Hansburys v. Generics*.[10]

The Court gave a preliminary ruling on a reference from the House of Lords, in a case concerning *licenses of right*. The 1977 Patent Act had extended the validity period of British patents from 16 to 20 years, in order to bring Britain into line with European legislation. For patents granted since July 1st 1967, the British Parliament introduced licensing rights to counterbalance the increased number of years of protection.

---

[10] Case C-434/85, (1988), ECR I-1245.

Under this system, the patent-holder had to grant a license to whomever requested one, either on terms to be agreed between the parties or, in default, on terms established by the relevant authority, the Comptroller General of Patents.

This regime of licenses of right was applied to a patent belonging to a company, *Allen & Hansburys Ltd.* The company was a subsidiary of *Glaxo* and was owner of a patent in the UK of a pharmaceutical product for asthma. Throughout the Member States, owners of the patent on the product were all companies which were part of the Glaxo group, apart from Italy, where, at that time, the patenting of medicines and their respective manufacturing processes was not permitted by law. In this case, the product was being made by a company which was in no way connected to the Glaxo group.

*Generics Ltd.*, a UK subsidiary of a Panamanian company, was cited in the case before the ECJ. Generics Ltd. had requested a license of right from Allen & Hansburys, expressing the intention to import the product from Italy. Consequently, Allen & Hansburys obtained an injunction against them, on the grounds of the threatened passing-off of the product.

In the British judges' view, the provisions of the Patent Act 1977 allowed Allen & Hansburys to oppose the importation by Generics Ltd.

However, the Court of Justice held that this Act created arbitrary discrimination in trade between the Member States, since it did not permit an analogous prohibitory injunction to be taken out with regard to a national manufacturer.

> ***Allen & Hansburys v. Generics* ruling:** "**(1)** Articles 30 and 36 of the Treaty preclude the courts of a member state from issuing an injunction prohibiting the importation from another member state of a product which infringes a patent endorsed "licences of right" against an importer who has undertaken to take a licence on the terms prescribed by law where no such injunction may be issued in the same circumstances against an infringer who manufactures the product in the national territory. Those provisions prohibit the competent administrative authorities from imposing on a licensee terms impeding the importation from other member states of a product covered by a patent endorsed "licences of right" where those authorities may not refuse to grant a licence to an undertaking which would manufacture the product in the national territory and market it there. The fact is wholly immaterial that the product in question is a pharmaceutical product and comes from a member state where it is not patentable. **(2)** It is only where they apply without distinction to both domestic and imported products that

> national rules impeding imports do not fall under the prohibition laid down by article 30 of the treaty if they are necessary in order to satisfy imperative requirements relating in particular to consumer protection or fair trading. A prohibition on importation cannot be justified on grounds of such requirements where the national legislation on which it is based is not applicable without distinction to domestic and imported products."

The ECJ had the opportunity of clarifying the extent of the principle of exhaustion of rights with respect to countries outside the Community, too, during the 1970's; this involved three distinct cases, with similar facts but adjudicated upon by the Court in three separate rulings on the same day, June 15th 1976, *EMI Records Limited v. CBS United Kingdom Limited, EMI Records Limited v. CBS Grammophon,* and *EMI Records Limited v. CBS Schallplatten GmbH.*[11]

A company which owned a trade-mark took action to protect its right to import goods from the US which were the same as those produced by the company and which carried the same trade-mark. The plaintiff was the British company *EMI Records Limited*; the defendants were three subsidiaries of a US company, *American CBS Inc.*, which had head-offices in three different Member States (the UK, Denmark, and Germany).

The ECJ held that the Treaty provisions, under which the doctrine of exhaustion had been invoked, did not apply to trade between countries outside the Community and Member States.

It further held that the Treaty did not impede a holder of an industrial property right in one or more of the Member States from exercising her/his exclusive right to prevent the importation of goods from third countries, thereby limiting the effect of the doctrine of exhaustion of rights only to the case where the first sale has been made within the Community.

There was still a need to clarify what the consequences would be of putting a product into circulation which was protected by an intellectual property right by a non-Member country, but with which the Community had signed a free-trade Agreement within the meaning of art. 133 TEC. The main case in which the Court had adjudicated upon this question was that of *Polydor*,[12] concerning the importation into the UK of records and cassettes containing recorded music from Portugal, (which, in 1972, at

---

[11] Respectively Case C-51/75, (1976) ECR I-811; Case C-86/75 (1976) ECR I-871; Case C-96/75, (1976) ECR I-913.

[12] Case C-270/80, *Polydor v. Harlequin & Simons*, (1982), ECR I-329.

the time of these facts, was not yet a Community member, but had signed a free-trade Agreement with the EEC).

The ECJ held that the exhaustion doctrine developed under arts. 28–30 TEC is limited only to goods which are put into circulation in one of the Member States. It is irrelevant whether they have entered Community territory and are now freely available and whether they come from a country with which a free trade agreement has been signed. There is no exhaustion of the right when the goods are traded in any non-Member State and the signing of an agreement between the non-Member State and the Community is of no relevance at all.

During the 1980's, the ECJ defined the limits on its own intervention, or, in other words, the sphere of jurisdiction within which Community law operates with regard to the national laws of Member States, affirming in several judgments[13] that fixing the conditions for extending national protection remains the prerogative of the Member States.

Similar rulings recur in later judgments concerning industrial designs and utility models, where Community judges assert that they cannot evaluate individual aspects of the content of domestic laws, which, conversely, remains the prerogative of the States.

> See the judgment *Consorzio italiano della componentistica di ricambio per autoveicoli and Maxicar v. Régie nationale des usines Renault*, C-53/87 (1988), ECR I-6039.

In summary, the principle of the exhaustion of rights may be expressed in these terms: the holder of a patent or, as we have seen, any other type of intellectual property rights may not, once a product has been put on to the market or s/he has given consent for its marketing, hinder or place limitations upon its circulation, either in the original market or in that of the other Member States.[14]

The practical application of the principle of exhaustion of rights means that anyone, having obtained a license or a product covered by a right such as a patent, copyright, or trade mark may market or distribute the product in any other country in the Community, including one where the intellectual property right-holder has given exclusive rights to another person. This principle also applies to the parties of a licensing agreement

---

[13] *Keurkoop v. Nancy Gifts* [Case C-144/81 (1981), ECR I-2853] and *Thetford v. Fiamma* [Case C-35/87, (1988), ECR I-3585].

[14] See above, for references to the ECJ case-law.

in the sense that any clause prohibiting marketing in other countries is treated as void in law, within the meaning of art. 81 of the Treaty.

The potential for expansion of this principle has been such that, once developed (as we have noted, in connection with patents), not only was it extended to all other industrial and commercial property rights, but it was also adopted in all the national legal systems and also applied to cases arising exclusively within the particular market of one Member State.

Beyond the exhaustion of rights principle and the criteria which may be developed and used by the Court of Justice or the Commission, the problem of the admissibility of limitations on the exploitation and circulation of patents, trademarks, inventions, etc. (also called Intellectual Property or IP rights), cannot be resolved without taking into account other important sources of legislation, which are:

- Exemption rules, issued by the Commission under art. 81 (3) TEC, which fix the criteria for taking advantage of waivers to the prohibition on the placing of restrictions.[15]
- International and Community Conventions in this field.
- Directives and regulations issued by the Council to govern certain procedural and substantive aspects of the individual variants (patents, trademarks, author's rights, etc.).

The different types of sources reflect the differing objectives of Community intervention:

- With the exemption regulations, the Community was concerned with the problem of the circulation of the IP right and the admissibility of restrictions placed upon its circulation according to EC competition rules.
- With the Conventions (and later directives and regulations), it endeavored to standardize the contents of the law, namely the rules for the protection which the owner of the IP right receives, or the means and procedure for acquiring the right itself.

## 3. The European Patent and the Community Patent

A patent is a right granted to the inventor of a technological product or process that is new or novel, useful or capable of industrial application, and involves an inventive step. The patent entitles the inventor to exclude others from making, using, selling or importing the invention for a peri-

[15] See below, chapter VI.

od of time (generally twenty years from the date the patent application is filed).

Historically, national governments were free to define the aims and contents of this intellectual property right, and, indeed, large parts of Europe and North America equipped themselves with specific laws on the subject during the course of the nineteenth century. With the development and spread of industrialization and technology, the need for international cooperation also grew. The first fundamental means for harmonizing the procedural patent rules of the various States dates from 1883: the Paris Convention for the Protection of Industrial Property.[16]

It provides minimal rules of protection. Art. 2 contains the rule of national treatment: foreign investors shall be treated in the same way as their domestic counterparts and their inventions shall be granted the same level of protection.

The impact of the Paris Convention has been enlarged even further by TRIPs Agreement.[17]

Art. 2 of that Agreement obliges all contracting States to comply with the main substantive provisions of the Paris Convention, even if they are not members of it. Articles 27 to 34 of the Agreement contain, for the first time, substantive minimum rules in relation to patents (covering points such as patentable subject matter, the rights that are conferred by a patent, exceptions, and the right to use the patent without the consent of the rightholder).

Other international measures which should be mentioned in connection with patents are the Patent Co-operation Treaty (Washington 1970, PCT), which provides for the filing of a single application to improve the protection for patent rights; the Strasburg Convention on the International Classification of patents (Strasburg 1971, IPC), which provides an uniform system of classification; the Patent Law Treaty (Geneva, 2000, opened for signature on June 2nd 2000, but still not into force), which streamlines national patent procedures.

Cooperation at the supranational level was strengthened by the European initiatives, which sought further harmonization of procedural and substantive rules regarding patents.

---

[16]The Convention was amended at various times during the course of the twentieth century: see § 1.

[17] On the TRIPs Agreement, see the website at http://www.wto.org/english/tratop_e/trips_e/t_agm0_e.htm.

There are *three supranational Conventions* concerning patents:

– The *Strasbourg Convention*, on the standardization of certain legislative principles concerning patents for inventions; it was signed on November 27th 1963 by all the Members of the European Economic Community and other European States.[18] Although it is not a Community Convention in that it was promoted by the Council of Europe, nevertheless it cannot be ignored by the Community. Indeed, not only does it involve many of the Community States, but it is the only one of the three Conventions on the subject to lay down standard substantive rules concerning certain essential requirements for the 'patentability' of inventions (the possibility for any inventions to be susceptible to industrial application): *novelty*, *originality,* and *industrial potential.* Besides, the Strasbourg Convention introduced some principles which then reappeared both in the later Munich and Luxembourg Conventions, and in national laws. Substantially, the Convention has carried out harmonization activity regarding laws not only in the signatory states, but also in other Member States of the Community, which has proved essential for the later Community provisions.

– The *Munich (Bavaria) Convention*, dated October 5th 1973, better known as the *European Patent Convention*, was signed by all the Member States of the European Community and other European States.[19] This, which is not a Community Convention promoted on the basis of article 220 (now 293) TEC, came into force on October 7th 1977. The Convention on the European patent established a Central Patent Office (in Munich, with a separate office at the Hague), which has jurisdiction over all patent applications, in fact known as 'European,' which permits the holder to enforce her/his own right in every State, according to each system's own rules. The Convention on the European Patent has, therefore, not introduced a new patent right which is different from those of the signatory states, nor has it standardized national laws. The Convention's scope is to standardize only the procedure for the granting of national patents; whoever is granted an application becomes the holder

---

[18] On the Strasbourg Convention see the website at http://conventions.coe.int/Treaty/en/Treaties/Word/047.doc.

[19] On the Convention see the website at http://www.european-patent-office.org/legal/epc/e/ma1.html. The signatories States are: Austria, Belgium, Denmark, Finland, France, Germany, Great Britain, Greece, Ireland, Italy, Liechtenstein, Luxembourg, Monaco, The Netherlands, Portugal, Spain, Sweden, and Switzerland. Among the candidate States the following are currently members of the European Patent Organization: Cyprus, Turkey, Bulgaria, Czech Republic, Slovak Republic, Slovenia, Estonia, Hungary, Romania. A revised version of the European Patent Convention was agreed on November 29th 2000 and is awaiting ratification.

not of a single patent right, but of as many rights as there are states in respect of which s/he has requested registration. The holder, therefore, receives a collection of various national patents. The advantage of the European Patent, which is also very well known for its practical effects for anyone who deals regularly with the Community countries, lies, however, in the fact that all relevant rights may be activated in a single operation, in every other European State which has signed the Convention, so reducing time and expenditure in the procedure of registering a patent.

– The *Luxembourg Convention*, dated December 15th 1975,[20] which established the *Community Patent Convention*, has never come into force due to the lack of a sufficient number of signatories. This is the only one of the three which is a Community Convention, promoted under art. 220 (now art. 293) TEC. The Convention's aim was to establish a standard patent in the true sense for the whole Community, with a single content for all the States. The failure of the Convention to come into force has been attributed to two main reasons: on the one hand, the cost of the Community patent, made heavier by having to be translated into all the languages of the Community; on the other, the fact that a judgment given by one national judge, nullifying the patent, could have a Community-wide effect, with all the attendant consequences for certainty in the law and from the point of view of national sovereignty.

In June 1997, given the stalled position of the Luxembourg Convention, practically static since 1975, the Commission tried a new tack to activate the standardization program. To this end it published a *Green Paper on the Community Patent and Patent system in Europe*,[21] to identify, with the help of observations made by interested parties, the essential aspects of the intervention and to assemble suggestions for overcoming the impasse. The idea of intervening by means of a Council Regulation was launched in this document, completely abandoning the Luxembourg Convention, which was by then in any case outdated in some of its contents. According to the comments collected, the Regulation, compared to the Convention, would have the great advantage of being immediately effective and applicable within Member states, without the complex ratification procedure conversely required by the Convention. Moreover, the unanimous consent of the State representatives would not be necessary for its approval.

---

20 Community Patent Convention (CPC) 76/76 CEE, in O.J., L 17, 01/26/1976, as modified in O.J. L 401/10, 12/30/1989.

21 COM(97) 314, June 1997.

In effect, the Commission presented a draft Community Patent Regulation on July 5th 2000,[22] whose fundamental feature lies in its strict connection with the Munich Convention, which the European Community signed. Indeed, the draft Regulation has reproduced the essential content (patentability requirements, conditions, nullity and other remedies, and so on).

> It should also be noted that the Treaty of Nice, precisely in anticipation of the imminent adoption of the draft Regulation on the Community Patent, inserted art. 225a into the EC Treaty, authorizing the Council to create a specialized judicial panel in this field, and a new art. 229a on the basis of which the Council may adopt provisions to confer jurisdiction, to the extent that it shall determine, on the Court of Justice in disputes relating to the application of acts adopted on the basis of the Treaty which create Community industrial property rights.

In addition, thanks to a modification of the Munich Convention, the European Patent Office will have competence to accept applications regarding the Community Patent, too. To limit registration costs, and therefore, to make the new patent more attractive, the draft Regulation provides that the patent be granted in one language only, from a choice of English, French or German. It will have a lifetime of twenty years.

Finally, a specific Community Tribunal will be established, specializing in the adjudication of patent cases, concerning the interpretation of the Regulation and other Community provisions in the patent field, whose rulings will be subject to review by the Court of Justice, thus eliminating the risk of divergent interpretation of the national courts.

When the Regulation is approved, the Community Patent will become a new patent, distinct from and also in part differing from those of the Member States, with a different content. Whoever obtains a Community Patent will be certain that s/he will receive equal protection, as there is only one substantive law to refer to, in whichever State s/he should choose to bring an action to defend his own right.

The new patent will not, therefore, replace the ones in the individual States, but will stand alongside them, representing a valid alternative when dealing at a trans-national level. It will be utilized only by those wanting to enlarge the protection of their own right to include other Community countries.

---

[22] COM (2000) 412 final.

This is not the first time that a similar solution has been encountered in private Community law. We have already seen the Community supranational institutions (the European Company, the European Cooperative Society, and the draft proposal on the European Mutual Society and Association),[23] and, in the next section, we shall be looking at the Regulation on the Community trade mark.

These are institutions which stand alongside the respective national ones, without replacing them. These models seem to be based on the idea that European Community law does not require the replacement of national laws with a single Community law, in order to establish a single European market.

This *uniformization technique* represents a possible alternative to the progressive harmonization of domestic laws, with the undoubted advantage in the fact that it allows many of the obstacles, which certain States may place in the way of the adoption of a harmonization directive, to be avoided. Within the Member State the laws remain unchanged, with all their specificity and distinguishing features, but still on condition that they do not prejudice trade and the common market. Cases involving a Community aspect, however, will be subject to supra-national law, which is equal for all undertakings which carry on activity at an international level.

## 4. The Community Trade mark

A trade mark[24] is a sign used on a product or in connection with the marketing of a product, including goods and services. It confers on the proprietor the exclusive right to prevent all third parties not having the consent of the owner from using, in the course of trade, any sign which is identical with the trade mark or any sign whose similarity to the trade mark is such that there exits a likelihood of confusion on the part of the public between the sign and the trade mark. For the consumers, a trade mark is a symbol needed to distinguish between competing products and services in a market economy; for the investment companies a trade mark is needed for the goodwill achieved through it, referring to a particular quality of products for which the trade mark is used and stands for.

The minimum international rules for trade marks were set out, for the first time, in the Paris Convention as we saw in the case of patent rights.

---

[23] See above chapter IV.

[24] In the US "trademark" is generally spelled as a single word; within the Community legal system, "trade mark" in generally spelled as two words.

Moreover, the TRIPs Agreement has added other rules (articles 15 to 21), to that Convention.

From the point of view of simplifying the procedure for registration in order to exploit the trade mark in several states, the Madrid Agreement Concerning the International Registration of Marks (Madrid, 1892) should be born in mind, to which a Protocol was added (Madrid, 1989), without the presence of which some States, such as the UK, would not have participated in the Convention. Another attempt at harmonization was made with the Trade Mark Law Treaty (Geneva, 1994). A standard system of classification, based on classes of goods and services and lists of goods and services that fall within each of the classes, is provided by the Nice Agreement Concerning the International Classification of Goods and Services for the Purposes of Registration of Marks (Nice, 1861, revised in Geneva, 1977) and by the Vienna Agreement Establishing the International Classification of the Figurative Elements of Marks (Vienna, 1985).

There have been recent important changes in the area of trade mark protection, which, deriving from the new Community measures, has radically altered the previous national legislative landscape in the Member States.

The collection of Community sources of law in relation to trade marks is very straightforward and, perhaps for this very reason, full of impact. These consist of two acts:

- First Council Directive 89/104/EEC of December 21st 1988 to approximate the laws of the Member States relating to trade marks.[25]
- Council Regulation (EC) no. 40/94 of December 20th 1993 on the Community trade mark.[26] To this, the Commission Regulation (EC) no. 2868/95 of December 13th 1995 can be added, implementing Council Regulation (EC) no. 40/94 on the Community trade mark.[27]

Before these Community legislative provisions came into effect, the functioning of trademarks and the relationship between Community rules relating to it and national laws had been developed by the Court of Justice. The ECJ had first of all extended to trademarks the exhaustion of rights doctrine, which had been developed in relation to patents.[28] Later it returned to the question of the exhaustion of rights doctrine, develop-

---

[25] O.J., L 40/1, 02/11/1989.
[26] O.J., L 11/1, 01/14/1994.
[27] O.J., L 303/1, 12/15/1995.
[28] See above, § 1, the case of *Centrafarm v. Winthorp,* C-16/74 (1974), ECR I-1183.

ing it further in two cases, *Hoffman-La Roche v. Centrafarm* and *Centrafarm v. American Home Products Corp.*:[29]

> In the first case, ***Hoffman-La Roche*** the ECJ confronted the problem of the reapplication of the trade mark. Parallel importations were legitimate under certain conditions (where the holder is informed in advance of the marketing of the repackaged product and the declaration by name on the new packaging of whoever has repackaged the product). The Court ruled:
>
> "**1.** (**a**) the proprietor of a trade mark right which is protected in two member states at the same time is justified pursuant to the first sentence of article 36 of the EEC treaty in preventing a product to which the trade mark has lawfully been applied in one of those states from being marketed in the other member state after it has been repacked in new packaging to which the trade mark has been affixed by a third party. (**b**) However, such prevention of marketing constitutes a disguised restriction on trade between member states within the meaning of the second sentence of article 36 where: it is established that the use of the trade mark right by the proprietor, having regard to the marketing system which he has adopted, will contribute to the artificial partitioning of the markets between member states; it is shown that the repackaging cannot adversely affect the original condition of the product; the proprietor of the mark receives prior notice of the marketing of the repackaged product; and it is stated on the new packaging by whom the product has been repackaged. **2.** To the extent to which the exercise of a trade mark right is lawful in accordance with the provisions of article 36 of the Treaty, such exercise is not contrary to article 86 of the treaty on the sole ground that it is act of an undertaking occupying a dominant position on the market if the trade mark right has not been used as an instrument for the abuse of such a position."
>
> In the second case, ***Centrafarm v. American Home Products Corp.***, the ECJ was concerned with a case of the substitution of a trade mark. Subsequently, the Court had another occasion to rule on cases of repackaging, without altering the reasoning set out in the case of *Hoffman La Roche*: C-427/93, C-429/93, C-436/93; C-71/94, C-72/94, C-73/94, C-232/94.

However, before these rulings, the functioning of the trade mark had been

[29] Respectively Case C-102/77, (1978), ECR I-1139 and Case C-3/78, (1978), ECR I-1823.

made less effective by the theory of '*common origin*,' set out in the *Hag* case.[30]

In this case, the ECJ had allowed two identical trade marks to coexist, where the holders were entirely unconnected with one another in the new market. The Court justified this by reference to the fact that originally, before the Second World War, there had been a single proprietor of the trade mark, and it was only later that the ownership of the trade mark had been sub-divided. The judgment had been criticized both by legal scholars, who emphasized above all the risk of confusion which would be met by consumers, and the national courts, which sought to avoid applying the doctrine set out in the case.

In the judgment in *Hag* (*no. 2*),[31] the ECJ rejected the theory of common origin, relying on the essential function played by a trade mark, which allows the specific subject-matter of the trade mark to be clearly identified:

> ***Cf.* §§ 13–14 of the *Hag (no. 2)* ruling:** "**(13)** Trade mark rights are, it should be noted, an essential element in the system of uny-distorted competition which the Treaty seeks to establish and maintain. Under such a system, an undertaking must be in a position to keep its customers by virtue of the quality of its products and services, something which is possible only if there are distinctive marks which enable customers to identify those products and services. For the trade mark to be able to fulfil this role, it must offer a guarantee that all goods bearing it have been produced under the control of a single undertaking which is accountable for their quality. **(14)** Consequently, as the Court has ruled on numerous occasions, the specific subject-matter of trade marks is in particular to guarantee to the proprietor of the trade mark that he has the right to use that trade mark for the purpose of putting a product into circulation for the first time and therefore to protect him against competitors wishing to take advantage of the status and reputation of the trade mark by selling products illegally bearing that mark. In order to determine the exact scope of this right exclusively conferred on the owner of the trade mark, regard must be had to the essential function of the trade mark, which is to guarantee the identity of the origin of the marked product to the consumer or ultimate user by enabling him without any possibility of confusion to distinguish that product from products which have another origin (see, in particular, the judgments in Case 102/

---

[30] Case C-192/73, *Van Zuylen Feres v. Hag AG*, (1974), ECR I-731.

[31] Case C-10/89, *SA CNL SUCAL NV v. Hag Gf Ag.*, (1990), ECR I-3711.

> 77 *Hoffmann-La Roche v Centrafarm* [1978] ECR 1139, paragraph 7, and in Case 3/78 *Centrafarm v American Home Products Corporation* [1978] ECR 1823, paragraphs 11 and 12).

Any doubt was finally resolved by the ruling in the *Ideal Standard* case,[32] which definitively rejected the doctrine of common origin. According to the ECJ "there is no unlawful restriction on trade between Member States within the meaning of Articles 30 and 36 where a subsidiary operating in Member State A of a manufacturer established in Member State B is to be enjoined from using as a trade mark the name 'Ideal Standard' because of the risk of confusion with a device having the same origin, even if the manufacturer is lawfully using that name in his country of origin under a trade mark protected there, he acquired that trade mark by assignment and the trade mark originally belonged to a company affiliated to the undertaking which, in Member State A, opposes the importation of goods bearing the trade mark 'Ideal Standard.'"

### *4.1. Directive 89/104*

Besides the evolution of the institution brought about by case-law, the rules developed by the Community legislature should be evaluated. The latter has proceeded, as we have seen, in two parallel directions: firstly, towards the harmonization of national legislation (Directive 89/104); secondly, towards a uniform regime (Regulation 40/94).

The methodology employed is the same as we have encountered several times in this exploration of European Community private law, and rests upon the assumption that standardization is only possible when there is a sufficient degree of homogeneity among the respective legal regimes. Before issuing the Regulation on the Community trade mark, it was in fact considered essential to harmonize the various national trade mark rules.

The situation which had been brought about in the patents sector by the Strasbourg Convention, namely the harmonization of the national regimes of the majority of European States as well as some who were not Community members, was conversely achieved in the context of trade marks by means of a Community Directive.

Directive 89/104, strongly influenced by Benelux law, has been imple-

---

32 Case C-9/93, *IHT Internazionale Heiztechnik GmbH v. Ideal Standard GmbH*, (1994), ECR I-2789.

mented in all the Member States, which, in transposing it into the national systems, have amended their previous laws on the subject.[33]

The Directive is not concerned with procedural issues, but defines the function and scope of a trade mark, governs the content of the rights conferred by the trade mark, introduces the principle that misleading use of the trade mark may bring about the loss of the right, regulates licenses, collective trade marks, as well as the loss of the right through non-use. Finally it also harmonizes the time-limits for expiry through non-use of the trade mark, increased to five years (in place of the three provided, for example, under Italian law).

> **Art. 1, Dir. 89/104** "Scope. This Directive shall apply to every trade mark in respect of goods or services which is the subject of registration or of an application in a Member State for registration as an individual trade mark, a collective mark or a guarantee or certification mark, or which is the subject of a registration or an application for registration in the Benelux Trade Mark Office or of an international registration having effect in a Member State."

> **Art. 2, Dir. 89/104** "Signs of which a trade mark may consist. A trade mark may consist of any sign capable of being represented graphically, particularly words, including personal names, designs, letters, numerals, the shape of goods or of their packaging, provided that such signs are capable of distinguishing the goods or services of one undertaking from those of other undertakings."

> **Art.4 (4), Dir. 89/104** "Any Member State may furthermore provide that a trade mark shall not be registered or, if registered, shall be liable to be declared invalid where, and to the extent that:
> *a)* The trade mark is identical with, or similar to, an earlier national trade mark within the meaning of paragraph 2 and is to be, or has been, registered for goods or services which are not similar

---

[33] See, for example, the implementation of the Directive in France: *Loi no. 91-7 du 01/04/1991 relative aux marques de fabrique, de commerce ou de service, JO,* 01/06/1991, p. 316; in Germany: *Gesetz zur Reform des Markenrechts und zur Umsetzung der ersten Richtlinie 89/104 EWG des Rates* vom 12/21/1988 *zur Angleichung der Rechtsvorschriften der Mitgliedstaaten über die Marken (Markenrechtsreformgesetz)* vom 10/25/1994, *Bundesgesetzblatt* Teil I, Nr. 74, 10/28/1994, Seite 3082; *Verordnung zur Ausführung des Markengesetzes (Markenverordnung – MarkenV)* vom 11/30/1994, *Bundesgesetzblatt* Teil I, Nr. 85, 12/06/1994 Seite 3555; in Italy: *d.lgs. 12/04/1992, no. 480, which amended the Regio decreto of June 21st 1942 no. 929, Gazz. Uff.*, no. 295, 12/16/1992.

to those for which the earlier trade mark is registered, where the earlier trade mark has a reputation in the Member State concerned and where the use of the later trade mark without due cause would take unfair advantage of, or be detrimental to, the distinctive character or the repute of the earlier trade mark; ***b)*** rights to a non-registered trade mark or to another sign used in the course of trade were acquired prior to the date of application for registration of the subsequent trade mark, or the date of the priority claimed for the application for registration of the subsequent trade mark and that non-registered trade mark or other sign confers on its proprietor the right to prohibit the use of a subsequent trade mark; ***c)*** the use of the trade mark may be prohibited by virtue of an earlier right other than the rights referred to in paragraphs 2 and 4 (b) and in particular: a right to a name; a right of personal portrayal; a copyright; an industrial property right; ***d)*** the trade mark is identical with, or similar to, an earlier collective trade mark conferring a right which expired within a period of a maximum of three years preceding application; ***e)*** the trade mark is identical with, or similar to, an earlier guarantee or certification mark conferring a right which expired within a period preceding application, the length of which is fixed by the Member State; ***f)*** the trade mark is identical with, or similar to, an earlier trade mark which was registered for identical or similar goods or services and conferred on them a right which has expired for failure to renew within a period of a maximum of two years preceding application, unless the proprietor of the earlier trade mark gave his agreement for the registration of the later mark or did not use his trade mark; ***g)*** the trade mark is liable to be confused with a mark which was in use abroad on the filing date of the application and which is still in use there, provided that at the date of the application the applicant was acting in bad faith."

**Art. 5 (1) & (2), Dir. 89/104** "Rights conferred by a trade mark. **(1)** The registered trade mark shall confer on the proprietor exclusive rights therein. The proprietor shall be entitled to prevent all third parties not having his consent from using in the course of trade: a) any sign which is identical with the trade mark in relation to goods or services which are identical with those for which the trade mark is registered; *b)* any sign where, because of its identity with, or similarity to, the trade mark and the identity or similarity of the goods or services covered by the trade mark and the sign, there exists a likelihood of confusion on the part of the public, which includes the likelihood of association between the sign and the trade mark. **(2)** Any Member State may also provide that the proprietor shall be entitled to prevent all third parties not having his consent from using in the course of trade any sign which is identical with, or similar to, the trade mark in relation to goods or services which are not similar to those for which the trade mark is registered, where the latter has a reputation in the Member State and where use of that sign without due cause takes unfair advantage of, or is detrimental to, the distinctive character or the repute of the trade mark."

The Court has set wide standards for the rather elusive concept of "*confusion*" through its interpretation of arts. 4 and 5: see *Sabel v. Puma*, Case C-251/95 (1997), ECR I-6191; *Lloyd Schufabrik Meyer v. Klijsen Handel*, Case C-342/97 (1999), ECR I-3819.

**Art. 7, Dir. 89/104** "Exhaustion of the rights conferred by a trade mark. **(1)** The trade mark shall not entitle the proprietor to prohibit its use in relation to goods which have been put on the market in the Community under that trade mark by the proprietor or with his consent. **(2)** Paragraph 1 shall not apply where there exist legitimate reasons for the proprietor to oppose further commercialisation of the goods, especially where the condition of the goods is changed or impaired after they have been put on the market."

See before the ECJ ruling in *Bristol-Myers Squibb v Paranova A/S* (C-427/93); *C. H. Boehringer Sohn, Boehringer Ingelheim KG and Boehringer Ingelheim A/S v Paranova A/S* (C-429/93); *Bayer Aktiengesellschaft and Bayer Danmark A/S v Paranova A/S* (C-436/93), joined cases C-427/93, C-429/93 and C-436/93, ECR I-3457.

Under art. 7 Dir. 89/104 *cf.* also §§ **47, 60, 66, and operative part 1–3** of the ruling *Zino Davidoff SA v A & G Imports Ltd. and Levi Strauss & Co. and Others v Tesco Stores Ltd. and Others*, joined cases C-414/99 to C-416/99, (2001) ECR I-8691:

"(**47**) The answer to the first question referred in each of Cases C-414/99 to C-416/99 must therefore be that, on a proper construction of Article 7(1) of the Directive, the consent of a trade mark proprietor to the marketing within the EEA of products bearing that mark which have previously been placed on the market outside the EEA by that proprietor or with his consent may be implied, where it is to be inferred from facts and circumstances prior to, simultaneous with or subsequent to the placing of the goods on the market outside the EEA which, in the view of the national court, unequivocally demonstrate that the proprietor has renounced his right to oppose placing of the goods on the market within the EEA. Whether implied consent may be inferred from the mere silence of a trade mark proprietor. **(60)** The answer to be given to the second question and to Question 3(a)(i), (vi) and (vii) in Cases C-415/99 and C-416/99, and to the second question in Case C-414/99, must therefore be that implied consent cannot be inferred: from the fact that the proprietor of the trade mark has not communicated to all subsequent purchasers of the goods placed on the market outside the EEA his opposition to marketing within the EEA; from the fact that the goods carry no warning of a prohibition on their being placed on the market within the EEA; from the fact that the trade mark proprietor has transferred the ownership of the products bearing the trade mark without imposing any contractual reservations and that, according to the law governing the contract, the property right transferred includes, in the absence of such reservations, an unlimited right of resale or, at the very least, a right to market the goods subsequently within the EEA. **(66)** The answer to be given to Question 3(a)(ii) to (v), raised in Cases C-415/99 and C-416/99, must therefore be that with regard to exhaustion of the trade mark proprietor's exclusive rights, it is not relevant: that the importer of goods bearing the trade mark is not aware that the proprietor objects to their being placed on the market in the EEA or sold there by traders other than authorised retailers, or that the authorised retailers and wholesalers have not imposed on their own purchasers contractual reservations setting out such opposition, even though they have been informed of it by the trade mark proprietor."

The Court, in answer to the questions referred to it by the High Court of Justice of England and Wales, Chancery Division (Patent Court), by orders of 24 June 1999 and 22 July 1999, hereby rules: "**1.** On a proper construction of Article 7(1) of First Council Directive 89/104/EEC of 21 December 1988 to approximate the laws of the Member States relating to trade marks, as amended by the Agreement on the European Economic Area of 2 May 1992, the consent of a trade mark proprietor to the marketing within the European Economic Area of products bearing that mark which have previously been placed on the market outside the European Economic Area by that proprietor or with his consent may be implied, where it follows from facts and circumstances prior to, simultaneous with or subsequent to the placing of the goods on the market outside the European Economic Area which, in the view of the national court, unequivocally demonstrate that the proprietor has renounced his right to oppose placing of the goods on the market within the European Economic Area. **2.** Implied consent cannot be inferred: from the fact that the proprietor of the trade mark has not communicated to all subsequent purchasers of the goods placed on the market outside the European Economic Area his opposition to marketing within the European Economic Area; from the fact that the goods carry no warning of a prohibition of their being placed on the market within the European Economic Area; from the fact that the trade mark proprietor has transferred the ownership of the products bearing the trade mark without imposing any contractual reservations and that, according to the law governing the contract, the property right transferred includes, in the absence of such reservations, an unlimited right of resale or, at the very least, a right to market the goods subsequently within the European Economic Area. **3**. With regard to exhaustion of the trade mark proprietor's exclusive right, it is not relevant: that the importer of goods bearing the trade mark is not aware that the proprietor objects to their being placed on the market in the European Economic Area or sold there by traders other than authorised retailers, or that the authorised retailers and wholesalers have not imposed on their own purchasers contractual reservations setting out such opposition, even though they have been informed of it by the trade mark proprietor."

### *4.2. Some Examples of National Transposition*

There are many new features introduced into the legal systems which have adopted the Directive.

For example, in Italy the subject of intellectual property was governed by a few articles of the Civil Code, (arts. 2569–2573), in addition to the 1942 Royal Decree (*Regio decreto),* and 1939 and 1940 Royal Decrees on patents for industrial inventions.[34]

In transposing the Directive,[35] the so-called *marchio di rinomanza* was introduced, to stand alongside the normal one. From the point of view of terminology, Dir. 89/104 uses the expression "*a trade mark which has a reputation in the Community*," while the Italian legislature decided to opt for the "*marchio di rinomanza.*" It is a more highly protected trade mark, in that it is safeguarded in a way that goes beyond the marketing of the product (and enters into the Italian system of classification of goods for taxation purposes); it is possible to protect it against the use of a similar trade mark for products which have nothing to do with the products which it identifies.

---

[34] As amended by the D.P.R. no. 338 of June 22nd 1979 (*Gazz. Uff.*, 08/07/1979, n. 215) after the ratification of the Strasburg Convention by act n. 260 of May 26th 1978 (*Gazz. Uff.*, 06/07/1978 n. 156).

[35] D.lgs. December 4th 1992, n. 480, in *Gazz. Uff.* n. 295, 12/16/1992, *cit* above.

On the significance of this and its implications of the concept of *reputation*, see the ECJ case *General Motors Corporation v Yplon SA*.[36]

> ***Cf.* §§ 12, 20, 24, 28, 31 of the *General Motors Corporation v Yplon SA* ruling:** "**12.** By its question the national court is essentially asking the Court of Justice to explain the meaning of the expression 'has a reputation' which is used, in Article 5(2) of the Directive, to specify the first of the two conditions which a registered trade mark must satisfy in order to enjoy protection extending to non-similar goods or services and to say whether that condition must be satisfied throughout the Benelux countries or whether it is sufficient for it to be satisfied in part of that territory. **20**. The Court observes that the first condition for the wider protection provided for in Article 5(2) of the Directive is expressed by the words 'er renommeret' in the Danish version of that provision; 'bekannt ist' in the German version; '÷áßñåé öÞiçò' in the Greek version; 'goce de renombre' in the Spanish version; 'jouit d'une renommée' in the French version; 'gode di notorietà' in the Italian version; 'bekend is' in the Dutch version; 'goze de prestigio' in the Portuguese version; 'laajalti tunnettu' in the Finnish version; 'är känt' in the Swedish version; and by the words 'has a reputation' in the English version. **24.** The public amongst which the earlier trade mark must have acquired a reputation is that concerned by that trade mark, that is to say, depending on the product or service marketed, either the public at large or a more specialised public, for example traders in a specific sector. **28.** Territorially, the condition is fulfilled when, in the terms of Article 5(2) of the Directive, the trade mark has a reputation 'in the Member State'. In the absence of any definition of the Community provision in this respect, a trade mark cannot be required to have a reputation 'throughout' the territory of the Member State. It is sufficient for it to exist in a substantial part of it. **31**. The answer to be given to the question referred must therefore be that Article 5(2) of the Directive is to be interpreted as meaning that, in order to enjoy protection extending to non-similar products or services, a registered trade mark must be known by a significant part of the public concerned by the products or services which it covers. In the Benelux territory, it is sufficient for the registered trade mark to be known by a significant part of the public concerned in a substantial part of that territory, which part may consist of a part of one of the countries composing that territory."

---

[36] C-375/97, September 14th 2000, *General Motors Corporation v Yplon SA*, (2000), ECR I-5421.

Another important new feature introduced by the Directive through the Italian implementing provision concerns the expiry of the right. Until 1992, the trade mark could only be given up in circumstances of transfer of the undertaking (see also the former article 2573 (1) *CC*, before amendment), and served to identify a certain number of products. However, it may now be transferred independently of the transfer of ownership of the firm or even in respect of only a part of the products for which it has been registered. The concession contracts for the trade mark (in a broad sense, to include licensing agreements, too) are today free both of the firm and the product.

The introduction of the principle of exhaustion of the trade mark right, provided under a special article (art. 1-*bis*) added to the Italian 1942 Royal Decree, was very innovative.

> On the exhaustion of trade mark see: Case C-173/98, July 1st 1999, *Sebago Inc. and Ancienne Maison Dubois & Fils SA v G-B Unic SA*, (1999), ECR I-4103; Case C-379/97, October 12th 1999, *Pharmacia & Upjohn SA v Paranova A/S.*, (1999), ECR I-6927; C-355/96, July 16th 1998, *Silhouette International Schmied GmbH & co. C. Hartlauner Handelgesellschaft GmbH*, (1998) ECR I-4799.

### *4.3. Regulation 40/94*

If Directive 89/104 did not give rise to the creation of a new trade mark, different from that of the Member States, but was confined to harmonizing the diverse national legislation, the aims and objectives of Regulation 40/94, which introduced the Community trade mark, are very different, equipping it with standard rules for all Member States.

Thus, as in the case of the Community patent, the Community trade mark places itself alongside the domestic laws of the States, confirming the legislators' option in favor of what we can call a *two-track system.*

Regulation 40/94, in fact, introduces a standard regime for all undertakings operating at inter-state level within the Community, giving rise to a new type of trade mark, distinct from those in force in the Member States. It contains substantive rules (content, length, amendment, nullity, etc) as well as procedural ones (method of registration, appeals, judicial action).

The Community trade mark is acquired through registration at the Alicante Office in Spain, where the Office for Harmonization in the Internal Market (Trade marks and Designs) is situated (OHIM).[37] This Com-

---

[37] See the web page at http://oami.eu.int/.

munity Office has legal personality, which is distinct from the other Community institutions. The Trade mark Office has a Board of Appeal, with a further appeal possible to the Court Justice (art. 63 Reg. 40/94). The Court of Justice has jurisdiction to alter or annul the contested decisions.

> *Cf.* for example, the case C-383/99, September 20th 2001, *Procter & Gamble v. OHMI* (2001) ECR I-6251.

The three fundamental features of the Community trade mark are substantially as follows: *unitary character, autonomy,* and *accessibility*.

*Unity* means that, by means of a single application, presented to one competent authority, it is possible to obtain effective registration throughout Community territory and it has equal effect throughout the Community. According to art. 1 (2) Reg. 40/94, the trade mark in question can be transferred, surrendered, or be the subject of a decision revoking the rights of the proprietor or declaring it invalid, and its use may be prohibited by one unique action in respect of the whole territory. However, it may be licensed either exclusively or non-exclusively for part of the Community (art. 22).

*Autonomy* means the fact that the Community trade mark system is governed by a single regime, under art. 1 (1) and art. 14 (1) Reg. 40/94.

*Accessibility* concerns the entitlement to the trade mark in question: only the persons mentioned in art. 5 may, upon request, become holders of a right to a Community trade mark.

The Community trade mark shall be registered for a period of ten years from the date of filing of the application, renewable for other ten-year periods (art. 46).

Even if the regime is not substantially very different from the now harmonized regime in Member States, there is no shortage of reasons for emphasizing the advantages and opportunities which the new Community trade mark offers for entrepreneurs.

It concerns not only procedural simplification, which means that nowadays it is possible to obtain registration of a single trade mark, valid throughout the States, by following one single procedure, whereas previously it was necessary to present as many applications as there were States in which one wanted the trade mark registered.

The Community trade mark has brought about a remarkable improvement in the level of certainty of the right as well as tangible advantages for the holder.

Indeed, from the point of view of certainty and predictability, the advantage of knowing that in any State of the Community, the regime which the judge has to apply is the same for every country is not of secondary importance.

From the point of view of advantage for the proprietor or the holder of the trade mark, the benefits deriving from the supranational character itself of the new model ought not to be overlooked. Let us take as an example, the case of non-use of the trade mark for a certain period of time.

Before the Regulation, the holder of the trade mark right had to take care that the time-limit of five years was not overrun in each European country, on pain of expiry of the right. Following Reg. 40/94, conversely, it is only necessary for the holder to exercise his/her right in any one of the Community States in order not to lose the right in any of the other States.

There is a new procedural rule, equally useful and economically advantageous, which makes it possible to bring all actions (or consolidate those already possibly started) for passing-off of the trade mark, even where this has occurred in several different States.

Several thousand applications for the registration of a Community trade mark are presented every year to the OHIM at Alicante. It should be noted that many of the numerous applications which are made come from American companies who have understood the advantage to be gained from protecting their trade mark in all the States of the Community by a single registration and with much lower costs compared to a series of national registrations.

## 5. Industrial Designs and Utility Models

An attractively designed product may command a significantly higher price in the market than an ordinary product. For this reason producers may invest heavily in creating an outward appearance of their products which they believe will appeal to consumers. Design has also a relationship with function. On the one hand, design possibilities are limited by function; on the other hand, design can facilitate function (see for example, extravagance *versus* aerodynamics in certain designs of motor vehicles).

In this case too, as with other intellectual property rights, protection has been guaranteed above all at the international level. An industrial design can be deposited internationally and will attract protection in all Member States of the Hague Agreement Concerning the Deposit of Industrial Designs (The Hague, 1925; updated by the Geneva Act, 1999). An international classification was established in the Locarno Agreement

Establishing an International Classification for Industrial Designs (Locarno, in force since 1970).

In the field of industrial design, the Community, following the same criteria adopted in the area of patents, moved in two directions at the same time.

On one side, the Community moved towards harmonizing the laws of Member States in order to create a minimum common legal basis, which would allow for substantially uniform rules within the common market so far as the essential requirements for the protection of such rights are concerned. Hence, with the objective of harmonization of the national provisions, Directive 98/71/EC of the European Parliament and of the Council of October 13th 1998 on the legal protection of designs was approved,[38] implemented in the national legal systems in the course of 2001.[39]

The Directive proposes a definition of *design* which is acceptable in all the States of the European Union; thus, by the term design, the following is meant: the appearance of the whole or a part of a product resulting from the features of, in particular, the lines, contours, colors, shape, texture and/or materials of the product itself and/or its ornamentation (art. 1 [b]).

> **Art. 5, Dir. 98/71:** "Individual character. **(1)** A design shall be considered to have individual character if the overall impression it produces on the informed user differs from the overall impression produced on such a user by any design which has been made available to the public before the date of filing of the application for registration or, if priority is claimed, the date of priority. **(2)** In

---

[38] O.J., L 289/28, 10/28/1998.

[39] In Germany: *Gesetz zur Bereinigung von Kostenregelungen auf dem Gebiet des geistigen Eigentums, Bundesgestzblatt* nr 69, Teil I, Jahrgang 2001, 12/19/2001, Seite 3656; in France: *Ordonnance no. 2001/670 du 25 juillet 2001, JO*, 07/28/2001, p. 12132; the UK: *The Registered Designs Regulations 2001, S.I.* no 3949 of 2001, 12/08/2001; *The Patents Regulations 2000 (articles 1 – 11), S.I.* no. 2037 of 2000, coming into force 07/28/2000; *The Patents and Plant Variety Rights (Compulsory Licensing) Regulations 2002 (article 12), S.I.* no. 247 of 2002, coming into force 03/01/2002; *The Patents (Amendment) Rules 2001 (articles 13 et 14), S.I.* no. 1412 of 2001, coming into force 07/06/2001; in Italy *Decreto legislativo* 02/02/2001 no. 95, *Supplemento ordinario alla Gazz. Uff., Serie gen.*, no. 79, 04/04/2001, p. 23; *Decreto legislativo* 04/12/2001, no. 164 (*disposizioni integrative al decreto legislativo 02/02/2001, no. 95*) *Gazz. Uff., Serie gen*, no. 106 of 05/09/2001. p. 4; *Decreto legislativo* 02/02/2002. no. 26, *Disposizioni integrative al decreto legislativo 02/02/2001 no. 95*, recante *attuazione della direttiva 98/71/ CE sulla protezione giuridica dei disegni e dei modelli, Gazz. Uff. Serie gen.*, no. 58, 03/09/2002, p. 3.

assessing individual character, the degree of freedom of the designer in developing the design shall be taken into consideration."

**Art. 10, Dir. 98/71:** "Term of protection. Upon registration, a design which meets the requirements of Article 3 (2) shall be protected by a design right for one or more periods of five years from the date of filing of the application. The right holder may have the term of protection renewed for one or more periods of five years each, up to a total term of 25 years from the date of filing."

**Art. 12, Dir. 98/71:** "Rights conferred by the design right. **(1)** The registration of a design shall confer on its holder the exclusive right to use it and to prevent any third party not having his consent from using it. The aforementioned use shall cover, in particular, the making, offering, putting on the market, importing, exporting or using of a product in which the design is incorporated or to which it is applied, or stocking such a product for those purposes. **(2)** Where, under the law of a Member State, acts referred to in paragraph 1 could not be prevented before the date on which the provisions necessary to comply with this Directive entered into force, the rights conferred by the design right may not be invoked to prevent continuation of such acts by any person who had begun such acts prior to that date.

**Art.15, Dir. 98/71:** "Exhaustion of rights. The rights conferred by a design right upon registration shall not extend to acts relating to a product in which a design included within the scope of protection of the design right is incorporated or to which it is applied, when the product has been put on the market in the Community by the holder of the design right or with his consent."

The chief dispute during the drafting of the Directive concerned the treatment of *automotive spare parts*. The Directive in the 19th "whereas" clause (or recital) indicates that States will retain their present rules governing spare parts, which in many States permit car manufacturers to retain their design rights monopoly over spare parts:

**Whereas, Dir. 98/71:** "**(19)** Whereas the rapid adoption of this Directive has become a matter of urgency for a number of industrial sectors; whereas full-scale approximation of the laws of the Member States on the use of protected designs for the purpose of permitting the repair of a complex product so as to restore its original appearance, where the product incorporating the design or to which the design is applied constitutes a component part of a complex product upon whose appearance the protected design is dependent, cannot be introduced at the present stage; whereas the lack of full-scale approximation of the laws of the Member States on the use of protected designs for such repair of a complex product should not constitute an obstacle to the approximation of those other national provisions of design law which most directly affect the functioning of the internal market; whereas for this reason Member States should in the meantime maintain in force any provisions in conformity with the Treaty relating to the use of the design of a component part used for the purpose of the repair of a complex product so as to restore its original appearance, or, if they introduce any new provisions relating to such use, the purpose of these provisions should be only to liberalise the market in such parts; whereas those Member States which, on the date of entry into force of this Directive, do not provide for protection for designs of component parts are not required to introduce registration of designs for such parts; whereas three years after the implementation date the Commission should submit an analysis of the consequences of the provisions of this Directive for Community industry, for consumers, for competition and for the functioning of the internal market; whereas, in respect of component parts of complex products, the analysis should, in particular, consider harmonisation on the basis of possible options, including a remuneration system and a limited term of exclusivity; whereas, at the latest one year after the submission of its analysis, the Commission should, after consultation with the parties most affected, propose to the European Parliament and the Council any changes to this Directive needed to complete the internal market in respect of component parts of complex products, and any other changes which it considers necessary (…)."

*Cf.* the ECJ rulings: *KeurKoop v. Nancy Kean Gifts* (Case C-144/81, 1982, ECR I-2853); *Consorzio Italiano v. Regie Nazionale Des Usines Reanult* (Case C-53/87, 1988, ECR I-6039).

The monopoly granted by a national industrial or commercial property law to the owner of the right is a classic example of a potential dominant position in a competitive marketplace.

If, on the one hand, the path of harmonization is being ventured, on the other the Community is encouraging a different initiative, which consists in the institution of a new legal instrument of an industrial design patent, a single one for the whole of the Community.

The achievement of this objective is demonstrated by Council Regulation (EC) No 6/2002 of December 12th 2001 on Community designs,[40] as can be deduced from the draughtsmen's intentions, set out in the 9th recital of the Preamble: "The substantive provisions of this Regulation on design law should be aligned with the respective provisions in Directive 98/71/EC."

Among the objectives of the *Community design* is both the desire to avoid compartmentalization of the internal market (4th recital of the Preamble), and to ensure a more accessible and adequate protection system for the needs of the internal market, an indispensable condition to achieve a corresponding safeguard in the main export markets of the Community (7 & 8th recitals of the Preamble):

> **Whereas, Reg. 6/2002** "**(4)** The effect of design protection being limited to the territory of the individual Member States whether or not their laws are approximated, leads to a possible division of the internal market with respect to products incorporating a design which is the subject of national rights held by different individuals, and hence constitutes an obstacle to the free movement of goods; (...); **(7)** Enhanced protection for industrial design not only promotes the contribution of individual designers to the sum of Community excellence in the field, but also encourages innovation and development of new products and investment in their production. **(8)** Consequently a more accessible design-protection system adapted to the needs of the internal market is essential for Community industries."

Reg. 6/2002 provides for two forms of protection, the first short-term, granted in respect of non-registered industrial designs, the second for a longer term in respect of registered industrial designs.

In the same way as is already happening with the Community trade mark, Reg. 6/2002 offers undoubted advantages for anyone intending to exploit the right beyond their own borders, such as, for example, obtaining effective protection throughout the European Community through a single registration at a specific office, instead of registering as many times as there are States in which protection of the right is to be enforced.

The registration of the industrial design is permitted without previous examination by any authority (that is, without ascertaining whether it is the object of prior rights within the European Community). However, it is possible to request nullity of the industrial design at the OHIM.[41]

---

40 O.J., L 3/1, 01/05/2002.

41 The OHIM performs the tasks of registering Community Trade marks and Community Designs. *Cf.* also previous §.

The Community Regulation on industrial designs stands alongside the analogous national regime and will not replace it until the level of harmonization of the latter has reached a satisfactory standard.

As far as utility models are concerned, the Commission published a Green Paper, *The Protection of Utility Models in the Single Market,* dated July 19th 1995.[42] As an outcome of that session, the Commission reached a Proposal for a European Parliament and Council Directive approximating the legal arrangements for the protection of inventions by utility model.[43] Among the reasons for it delay in the harmonization process is the fact that it encounters concrete limits: the institution of the *utility model* is not provided for at all throughout the legal systems of the Member States, and its differences *vis à vis* the *patent* are much debated, as we have seen.

According to art. 1 of the Community draft, *utility model* means the registered right which confers exclusive protection for technical inventions.

Under art. 3 of the Proposal, there is a definition of an invention which is capable of being protected: "Utility models shall be granted for any inventions which are susceptible to industrial application, which are new and which involve an inventive step. The following in particular shall not be regarded as inventions: (a) discoveries, scientific theories and mathematical methods; (b) aesthetic creations; (c) schemes, rules and methods for performing mental acts, playing games or doing business; (d) presentations of information."

The requirement of *novelty* is stated in art. 5 of the Proposal: "An invention shall be considered to be new if it does not form part of the state of the art." Paragraph 2 of art. 5 provides that "the state of the art shall be held to comprise everything made available to the public by means of a written or oral description, by use, or in any other way, before the date of filing of the utility model application." Additionally, it continues, "the content of utility model applications as filed, of which the dates of filing are prior to the date referred to in paragraph 2 and which were published on or after that date, shall be considered as comprised in the state of the art."

---

[42] COM(95)370 final.

[43] O.J., C 36/13, 02/03/1998. In the course of 2000, an amended draft was presented, in O.J., C 248, 08/29/2000.

## 6. Copyright and Author's Right

Amongst intellectual property rights, copyright presented characteristic features which were peculiarly tied to its historical development, when two schools of thought ran counter to one another in Europe: the English one, emphasizing the entrepreneurial/exploitation aspect of the copyright, and the French, who, by the use of the term *author's right* (in French *droit d'auteur)* and not *copyright*, highlighted the respect felt for the artistic act of creation brought about by the author of the work, which expresses the personality of the author her/himself.

However, we shall see that today there is no longer anything to be gained from drawing a clear distinction between purely industrial property rights and purely artistic rights. If by the first expression we mean the kind of activity which, while nonetheless creative, is achieved in the context of economic activity, and by the second we mean the cases which are expressions of creative activity of a literary or artistic kind, it is not easy to categorize the sort of activity connected with the development of programs for computer programmers, or those to do with the setting-up of data banks or even more, that of the production and sale of broadcast programs and products.

Historically, copyright was connected with the protection of written literary works: from the second half of the fifteenth century onwards, when it was possible to reproduce many copies of a manuscript, stationers began to acquire authors' works and to arrange for the printing and distribution of the resulting works. These entrepreneurs assumed the commercial risk involved in exploiting the author's work, and obtained protection through the exclusive right to publish the work. Such copyright steadily began to be extended to include other types of work as well: engravings, lithographs, sculpture, dramatic, and musical works. Moreover, a right of use was sought by authors such as playwrights and composers. However, in these last instances, the copyright as understood to mean the right to produce copies of a work and to prevent others from doing so, did not operate as a safeguard, given that the exploitation of these works relied on the representations of the work and not from the sale of copies.

At an international level, the most important agreement in this field is the *Berne Convention for the Protection of Literary and Artistic Works* (Berne, 1886, whose contents were radically amended during the 1960s); the Convention's effect was reinforced by the TRIPs Agreement, which requires its contracting states to comply with most of the provisions of the Berne Convention. Supplementary safeguards are offered in the specific sectors of rights of performers, recorder, and broadcasting organizations: see the Convention on the Protection of Performers, Producers of Phonograms, and Broadcasting Organizations (signed in Rome in 1961), and the WIPO Performance and Phonograms Treaty (signed in Geneva in 1996 but not yet in force).

All these Conventions are administered by the World Intellectual Property Organization (WIPO), a specialized Agency of the United Nations, with headquarters in Geneva.

Furthermore, it should be noted that as part of the Uruguay Round of the world trade negotiations, the GATT (now World Trade Organization, WTO) contracting states reached an agreement on the TRIPs initiative. The TRIPs Agreement entered into force on January 1st 1995. On January 1st 1996 the rules of the TRIPS Agreement became obligatory for developed country Members. At the same time, provision with respect to national and most favored nation treatment become obligatory for all WTO Members.

The WTO is the principal arena for the negotiation of primary international intellectual property standards. Disputes arising under TRIPs are now subject to resolution by the WTO Dispute Settlement Body, in accordance with the terms of the Dispute Settlement Understanding. Trade sanctions may be collectively authorized to assure compliance by WTO Members with TRIPs obligations.

In general terms, in order to understand the concept, we can say *copyright* not only safeguards the artist's creation from unauthorized copying or reproduction, but also guarantees some additional personal rights of the author (the right of attribution and the right to prevent a mutilation or other abuse of the work that would disparage the reputation of the author).

These *moral rights* are considered inalienable, and they are not subject to sale or transfer in connection with the author's economic rights in a work. They have always been one of the essential requisites of the French *droit d'auteur*; in Britain they were incorporated for the first time in The Copyright, Designs, and Patents Act 1988 (Part I, Chapter 4).

Unlike the patent, a copyright does not establish a monopoly in relation to the content of the created work: the ideas remain in the public domain and may be freely used in different forms of expression. A copyright protects the particular expression of a literary work, in a piece of music, in a sculpture, etc. The idea in itself is not protected by copyright.

The regime for copyright is therefore considered as an integral part of the more general theme of intellectual property.[44]

---

[44] Some legal scholars doubt whether the institution can be made part of intellectual property, preferring instead the concept of competition rules, or entrepreneurial activity in general (such as in the case of the institutions of patent and trade mark).

In recent times, because of new technologies and new systems of exploiting creative works, it has undergone such radical transformation as to cause doubt as to the existence of a clear distinction from the field of intellectual property. The fact is that the European Community has made a remarkable contribution to the extension of its own range of action in the competition and intellectual property fields, applying many of the principles and rules, typical of patents and trade marks, to copyrights as well.

The lack of any reference whatsoever to the protection of copyrights in the Treaty provisions has allowed a good number of European legal scholars and Member States' legislatures to assert that the Community had no legitimate basis upon which to intervene in this sector. They drew strength from the fact that art. 222 (now art. 295) TEC declares the intention of leaving the system of property ownership in the Member States unprejudiced:

> **Art. 295 (ex art. 222) TEC**: "This Treaty shall in no way prejudice the rules in Member States governing the system of property ownership."

The reliance upon a purely literal reading of this provision concealed the real intention: to prevent the Community increasing a jurisdiction which many felt was already too great. With this position being taken by State representatives, the Commission and the Council of the Community were unable to intervene in the field of copyright for very long, and the sporadic initiatives of draft directives could make no further headway.

Once again, it fell to the Court of Justice to break the logjam, the true protagonist in the first important Community moves on copyright from the beginning of the 1970's.

In those years there was a conviction that the Community competition provisions, namely arts. 85 and 86 (now arts. 81 and 82 TEC),[45] could be applied to copyrights as well, and, consequently, to the activity of a group of authors and editors:[46]

> ***Deutsche Grammophon Gesellschaft mbh v. Metro Grossmärkte GmbH.* ruling:** "(**§ 3**) the exercise of an industrial property right falls under the prohibition set out in article 85 (1) of the Treaty each time it manifests itself as the subject, the means or

---

[45] *Cf.* below, chapter VI.

[46] See C-78/70, *Deutsche Grammophon Gesellschaft mbh v. Metro Grossmärkte GmbH.*, cited above in § 2 of this chapter.

> the result of an agreement which, by preventing imports from other member states of products lawfully distributed there, has as its effect the partitioning of the market."

On the other hand, in the *Coditel* case,[47] the Court reasoned by using the principle of the free movement of goods, inferred from arts. 28 and 30 (ex 30 and 36) TEC.

In this case, *Cine Vog Films SA*, a Belgian film-distribution company, asserted that its author's rights had been violated by three Belgian television distribution companies, known as *Coditel*, and a French film-production company, *Les Films la Boetié*.

> In its ruling, the Court of Justice traced the fundamental distinction between the various forms of exploitation of copyrights.
>
> ***Coditel v. Cine Vog Films* ruling: "(§ 12)** a cinematographic film belongs to the category of literary and artistic works made available to the public by performances which may be infinitely repeated. In this respect the problems involved in the observance of copyright in relation to the requirements of the treaty are not the same as those which arise in connection with literary and artistic works the placing of which at the disposal of the public is inseparable from the circulation of the material form of the works, as in the case of books or records."

> Although the text of the provision being considered by the ECJ was art. 49 (*ex* art. 59) TEC, the Court's reasoning literally reproduces the text of art. 30 (*ex* art. 36) TEC: the assignee may enjoy his exclusive right in so far as such a right does not constitute a means of arbitrary discrimination or a disguised restriction on trade:
>
> "(§ **15**) whilst article 59 of the Treaty prohibits restrictions upon freedom to provide services, it does not thereby encompass limits upon the exercise of certain economic activities which have their origin in the application of national legislation for the protection of intellectual property, save where such application constitutes a means of arbitrary discrimination or a disguised restriction on trade between member states. Such would be the case if that application enabled parties to an assignment of copyright to create artificial barriers to trade between member states. (§ **16**) The effect of this is that, whilst copyright entails the right to demand fees for any showing or performance, the rules of the Treaty cannot in principle constitute an obstacle to the geographical limits

---

[47] Case C-62/79, *Coditel v. Cine Vog Films*, (1980), ECR I-881.

which the parties to a contract of assignment have agreed upon in order to protect the author and his assigns in this regard. The mere fact that those geographical limits may coincide with national frontiers does not point to a different solution in a situation where television is organised in the member states largely on the basis of legal broadcasting monopolies, which indicates that a limitation other than the geographical field of application of an assignment is often impracticable. (§ **17**) The exclusive assignee of the performing right in a film for the whole of a member state may therefore rely upon his right against cable television diffusion companies which have transmitted that film on their diffusion network having received it from a television broadcasting station established in another member state, without thereby infringing community law."

Applying the rules and principles of the free movement of goods and services to the production and marketing of works protected by national copyrights, the ECJ maintained that, while it is true that former art. 36 (now art. 30) TEC allowed the States to create an exception to the rules on the free movement of goods in order to safeguard industrial and commercial property rights, it is equally true that this option is not without limits. In particular, limitations which could constitute arbitrary discrimination or a disguised restriction on trade between Member States (art. 30, ex art. 36 TEC) would not be permitted.[48]

Indeed, the Court **in *Musik Vertrieb Membran GmbH*** v. ***G.E.M.A*** has held that "the proprietor of an industrial or commercial property right protected by the law of a member state cannot rely on that law to prevent the importation of a product which has been lawfully marketed in another member state by the proprietor himself or with his consent. The same applies as respects copyright, commercial exploitation of which raises the same issues as that of any other industrial or commercial property right. Accordingly neither the copyright owner or his licensee, nor a copyright management society acting in the owner's or licensee's name, may rely on the exclusive exploitation right conferred by copyright to prevent or restrict the importation of sound recordings which have been lawfully marketed in another Member State by the owner himself or with his consent."

---

[48] ECJ January 20th 1981,C-55/80, *Musik Vertrieb Membran GmbH* v. *G.E.M.A.*, (1981), ECR I-147.

In this judgment, the ECJ applied the doctrine of exhaustion of copyright, even though confined to cases where the work circulates by electronic means. Some commentators have, however, emphasized that the same work may be exploited in a number of different ways. Hence a series of successive judgments concerning the distribution of videocassettes of a film or of some other performance, have clarified the issue: according to the Court, the cassette can be offered for sale (so immediately extinguishing the author's right), or it may be rented out over and over again. Video-rental is aimed at a different market and, by its nature, can be achieved through an unlimited number of repeat hiring, each of which involves a right and a recompense. For these reasons it is comparable to the method of exploiting the work by performances: the right to recompense is not exhausted the first time it is hired out, since it is subsumed into the existing copyright in the film.

See Case C-158/86 *Warner Brothers Inc. and Metronome Video ApS v. Erik Viuff Christiansen*, (1988) ECR I-2605; C-200/96 *Metronome Musik GmbH v. Music Point Hokamp GmbH*, (1998) ECR I-1953; C-61/97, *Foreningen af danske Videogramdistributører, acting for Egmont Film A/S, Buena Vista Home Entertainment A/S, Scanbox Danmark A/S, Metronome Video A/S, Polygram Records A/S, Nordisk Film Video A/S, Irish Video A/S and Warner Home Video Inc. v Laserdisken*, (1998) ECR I-5171.

***Cf.* ruling C-61/97**: "§§ **(1)** It is not contrary to Articles 30 and 36 of the EC Treaty for the holder of an exclusive rental right to prohibit copies of a film from being offered for rental in a Member State even where the offering of those copies for rental has been authorised in the territory of another Member State. The principle of exhaustion of distribution rights where copyright works are offered for sale by the rightholder or with his consent is expressed in the settled case-law of the Court according to which the exclusive right guaranteed by the legislation of a Member State on industrial and commercial property is exhausted when a product has been lawfully distributed on the market in another Member State by the actual proprietor of the right or with his consent. However, literary and artistic works may be the subject of commercial exploitation, whether by way of public performance or of the reproduction and marketing of the recordings made of them. By authorising the collection of royalties only on sales to private individuals and to persons hiring out video cassettes, it is impossible to guarantee to makers of films a remuneration which reflects the number of occasions on which the video cassettes are actually hired out and which secures for them a satisfactory share of the

> rental market. The release into circulation of a picture and sound recording cannot therefore, by definition, render lawful other acts of exploitation of the protected work, such as rental, which are of a different nature from sale or any other lawful act of distribution. Just like the right to present a work by means of public performance, rental right remains one of the prerogatives of the author and producer notwithstanding sale of the physical recording. The same reasoning must be followed as regards the effects produced by the offer for rental. The specific right to authorise or prohibit rental would be rendered meaningless if it were held to be exhausted as soon as the object was first offered for rental. **(2)** It is not contrary to Directive 92/100 on rental right and lending right and on certain rights related to copyright in the field of intellectual property for the holder of an exclusive rental right to prohibit copies of a film from being offered for rental in a Member State even where the offering of those copies for rental has been authorised in the territory of another Member State."

It was only with great difficulty that the European Commission was able to proceed with a minimal program of directives to harmonize this extremely complex sector. The difficult situation in which the Commission found itself was also caused by the fact that from a technical and commercial point of view, this sector is continually evolving and is made more complex by the arrival of new means of transmission and communication and completely innovative technical ideas, at such speed that the normal time required by the Commission to develop legislation cannot manage to keep pace.

For these reasons, those few initiatives which endeavored to harmonize some aspects of this sector, were welcomed enthusiastically, and up to now they represent the only legal frame of reference.

## *6.1. Copyright and Neighboring Rights in the Community Directives*

The initial impetus came from a study made by the Commission, the *Green Paper on Copyright and the Challenge of Technology,*[49] which was followed by the *White Paper on Copyright and Neighboring Rights*, also by the Commission.[50]

[49] COM (1988) 172 final.
[50] COM (1990) 584 final.

Later, the following provisions were issued:

– Council Directive 91/250/EEC of May 14th 1991 on the legal protection of computer programs.[51] The legislation supported that branch of academic and judicial opinion which, in the choice of possible options for the protection of software (whether it should be in the context of the regime for industrial design patents or the context of copyright), preferred the second alternative. The national legislating bodies, which adopted the Directive, were obviously conditioned by this choice. Art. 1 of the Directive requires all States to give copyright protection to a computer program that is "original in the sense that it is the author's own intellectual creation." However the principles which underlie a 'program,' as well as the 'interface' between the software and hardware, are not protected. Art. 4 indicates the scope of protection: the reproduction of the program, its translation, adaptation, alteration, its sale, rental, or other form of contractually authorized use. However art. 5 permits persons who have a right of use to make back up copies as well as to study or test the program and to determine its underlying ideas and principles. Art. 8 sets the term as the life of the author plus 50 years. The controversial proposal for a Directive of the European Parliament and of the Council on the patentability of computer-implemented inventions, which would imply a radical reform of the system, should also be noted.[52] The current legal situation regarding patent protection in the field of computer-implemented inventions is ambiguous, and lacks legal certainty. In fact, computer programs as such are excluded from patentability by Member States' patent laws and the European Patent Convention (EPC). The proposal covers inventions which involve the use of a computer and the use of a computer network or any other programmable device, i.e. inventions created by running a computer program or a similar device. The inven-

---

[51] O.J., L 122, 05/17/1991. The Directive has been implemented in all Member States; in particular, in the UK with the *The Copyright (Computer Programs) Regulations 1992, S.I.* no. 3233 of 1992; in Italy with *d.lgs.* 12/29/1992, no. 518, which amended the Act of 04/22/1941 *protezione del diritto d'autore edi altri diritti connessi*, no. 633, *Supplemento ordinario* no. 138, *Gazz. Uff., Serie gen.*, 12/31/1992 no. 306; in Germany with the *Zweites Gesetz zur Änderung des Urheberrechtsgesetzes vom 06/09/1993, Bundesgesetzblatt* Teil I, 06/23/1993, Seite 910; in Spain with *Ley* no. 16/93 of 12/23/1993, *de incorporación al Derecho español de la Directiva 91/250/CEE, de 14 de mayo de 1991, sobre la protección jurídica de programas de ordenador, BOE* no. 307, 12/24/1994, p. 36816 (Marginal 30621); in France with *Loi* no. 94-361 of 05/10/1994 *portant mise en oeuvre de la directive (CEE) num. 91-250 du Conseil des Communautés européennes en date du 05/14/1991 concernant la protection juridique des programmes d'ordinateur et modifiant le code de la propriété intelectuelle, JO*, 05/11/1994, p. 6863.

[52] COM (2002) 92 final, O.J., C151 E, 06/25/2002.

tion may be a product (for example, a programmed computer) or a procedure. The proposal has had extraordinary resonance, provoking a debate which has involved the mass media as well. The delicacy of the issues surrounding the patents is even more in evidence in this case, because the numerous supporters of "open source software" have always criticized the political pressure aimed at limiting the freedom to use inventions for computers, especially through circulation on-line. On the other hand, it is championed by those who highlight the need to protect the rights of European software authors, particularly in the face of US competition.

– Council Directive 92/100/EEC of November 19th 1992 on rental right and lending right and on certain rights related to copyright in the field of intellectual property, which has been adopted in all the countries of the EU.[53] This created such rights in several States which had not previously recognized them. The Directive established a common system for recognition and protection of rights of authors, performing artists, and the producers of films or records when their works are the subject of commercial exploitation by rental or lending.

– Council Directive 93/83/EEC of September 27th 1993 on the coordination of certain rules concerning copyright and rights related to copyright applicable to satellite broadcasting and cable re-transmission, which has been implemented in all EU countries.[54]

---

[53] In O.J., L 346, 11/27/1992. In France, *Loi no 92-597 du 07/01/1992 relative au code de la propriété intellectuelle (Partie législative)*, *JO*, 07/01/1992, p. 8801; in Italy, *d.lgs.* 11/16/1994, no. 685, *Gazz. Uff., Serie gen.*, 12/16/1994, no. 293, p. 4; in Spain, *Ley no. 43/94 de 12/30/1994, de incorporación al Derecho español de la Directiva 92/100/CEE, de 19 de noviembre de 1992 sobre derechos de alquiler y otros derechos afines a los derechos de autor en el ámbito de la propiedad intelectual, BOE* no. 313, 12/31/1994, p. 39504 (Marginal 28969); in Germany, *Drittes Gesetz zur Änderung des Urheberrechtsgesetzes vom 23/06/1995, Bundesgesetzblatt* Teil I, 06/29/1995, Seite 842; in UK, *The Copyright and Related Rights Regulations 1996, S.I.* no. 2967 of 1996.

[54] In O.J., L 248, 10/06/1993. In the UK the Directive has been implemented using the same act which adopted Directive no. 92/100, namely *The Copyright and Related Rights Regulations 1996, S.I.* no. 2967 of 1996; in Italy by *d.lgs.* 10/23/1996, no. 581 *implementation of directive 93/83/CE for the coordination of certain laws in the field of copyrights and related rights applicable to broadcasting and cable rediffusion, Gazz. Uff., Serie gen.*, 11/18/1996 no. 270, p. 3, amending the Act on copyrights of 04/22/1941, no. 633; in France by *Loi no. 97-283 du 03/27/1997 portant transposition dans le code de la propriété intellectuelle des directives du Conseil des Communautés européennes Num. 93-83 du 09/27/1993 et 93-98 du 10/29/1993, JO*, 03/28/1997, p. 4831; in Germany by *Viertes Gesetz zur Änderung des Urheberrechtsgesetzes vom 05/08/1998, Bundesgesetzblatt* Teil I, 05/20/1998, Seite 902.

– Council Directive 93/98/EEC of October 29th 1993 harmonizing the term of protection of copyright and certain related rights, which has been implemented in all EU countries.[55] The Directive, following the German model, raised the duration to 70 years from the author's death for the protection of literary and artistic works, including films. In this second case, the protection runs from the death of the last surviving person among the director, the scenographer, the scriptwriter, and the composer of the music, whereas the actors' and artists' rights expire 50 years after the release of the film. The paradoxical result achieved by the Directive has been to create a longer period during which a division of the common market is possible, where different parties are holders of copyright in different Member States. In fact, under art. 10, the revival of rights which have already expired in some States is possible, if the term is still running for example, in Germany or another longer term State.

– Directive 96/9/EC of the European Parliament and of the Council of March 11th 1996 on the legal protection of databases.[56] The Member States

---

[55] In O.J., L 290, 11/24/1993. Among the first to transpose the Directive: Belgium: *Loi du 06/30/1994 relative au droit d'auteur et aux droits voisins - Wet van 06/30/1994 betreffende het auteursrecht en de naburige rechten, Moniteur belge* 07/27/1994, p. 19297; Denmark: *Lov nr. 395 af 06/14/1995 om ophavsrettigheder*; the UK: *The Duration of Copyright and Rights in Performances Regulations 1995, S.I.* no. 3297 of 1995; Ireland: *the European Communities (Term of Protection of Copyright) Regulations, 1995, S.I.* no. 158 of 1995; Spain: *Ley no. 27/95 de 10/11/1995, de incorporación al Derecho español de la Directiva 93/98/CEE del Consejo, de 29 de octubre de 1993, relativa a la armonización del plazo de protección del derecho de autor y de determinados derechos afines, BOE* no. 245, 10/13/1995, p. 30046 (Marginal 22380); Italy: *d.lgs.* 05/26/1997, no. 154 (which amended once again the Act of 04/22/1941, no. 633) implementation of Directive 93/98/CEE concerning the harmonisation of the duration of protection of copyrights and certain connected rights, *Gazz. Uff., Serie gen.*, 06/13/1997, no. 136, p. 9.

[56] In O.J., L 77, 03/27/1996. In Germany: *Gesetz zur Regelung der Rahmenbedingungen für Informations- und Kommunikationsdienste (Informations- und Kommunikationsdienste-Gesetz-LuKDG) vom 07/22/1997, Bundesgesetzblatt* Teil I, 07/28/1997, Seite 1870; Denmark: *Lov nr. 407 af 06/26/1998 om ændring af ophavsretsloven. Kulturmin., 5.kt.*, j.nr. 1998, 7001-7; Spain: *Ley no. 5/98 de 03/06/1998, de incorporación al Derecho español de la Directiva 96/9/CE, del Parlamento Europeo y del Consejo, de 03/11/1996 sobre la protección jurídica de las bases de datos, BOE no.* 57, 03/07/1998, p. 7935 (Marginal 5568); Austria: *Bundesgesetz, mit dem das Urheberrechtsgesetz geändert wird (Urheberrechtsgesetz-Novelle 1997 – UrhG-Nov 1997), Bundesgesetzblatt für die Republik Österreich*, Nr. 25/1998 ausgegeben 01/09/1998; Belgium: *Loi du 08/10/1998 transposant en droit judiciaire belge la directive européenne du 11 mars 1996 concernant la protection juridique des bases de données, MB*, 11/14/1998, p. 36913; *Loi du 08/31/1998 transposant en droit belge la directive européenne du 11 mars 1996 concernant la protection juridique des bases de données*; Italy: *d. lgs.* 05/06/1999, n. 169, *Gazz. Uff.* no. 138, 06/15/1999.

have encountered various difficulties in transposing the Directive within the prescribed time limits (January 1st 1998); however, certain important omissions have been rectified. For example, the Italian legislative decree implementing the Directive has involved a full range of important amendments to the Act of April 22nd 1941 no. 633 concerning copyright (Italian: *diritto d'autore*). It is sufficient to recall the provisions which establish in detail the rights of an *author* of a data bank (*i diritti dell'autore di una banca di dati)* (arts. 64 *quinquies* e 64 *sexies*), or those which govern, in extreme detail, the rights of the *creator* of a data bank (*diritti del creatore di una banca di dati)* (art. 102 *bis*), or those which govern the rights and obligations of those who use data-banks (art. 102 *ter*). In fact, many of the national systems, with the previous instruments available, were incapable of efficiently confronting and resolving the new legal problems arising from the use of data-bases, which were accessible through electronic and computerized means. This Directive has created a new species of exclusive economic right for the contents of a database, thus protecting the investment costs of its maker, if it cannot qualify for copyright protection (e.g. a telephone directory).

– Directive 2001/29/EC of the European Parliament and of the Council of May 22nd 2001 on the harmonization of certain aspects of copyright and related rights in the information society.[57] The Directive, which leaves unaltered the provisions contained in the previous directives on the subject, endeavors to widen the range of Community action and to harmonize national rules allowing the holder to authorize or prohibit the reproduction of her/his own work, as for instance, their publication and transmission to the public, including by cable or satellite, so far as radio and television broadcasting is concerned, as well as the distribution of the works themselves through sales, or by some other method.

– Directive 2001/84/EC of the European Parliament and of the Council of September 27th 2001 on the resale right for the benefit of the author of an original work of art.[58] Although the Berne Convention for the protection of literary and artistic works has in contemplation the rights of an author of a work of art on the later sales of the original, this

---

[57] In O.J., L 167, 06/22/2001. Up to now transposed in Greece by *Act* no. 3057/2002, *FEK A* no. 239, 10/10/2002 p. 4535; in Denmark by *Lov om aendring af ophavsretsloven, Lov* no. 1051, 12/17/2002 p. 7881; in Italy by *D. lgs.* 04/09/2003, n. 68, *Attuazione delle direttiva 2001/29/CE sull'armonizzazione di taluni aspetti del diritto d'autore e dei diritti connessi nella società dell'informazione, Gazz. Uff., Serie gen.*, no 87, 04/14/2003; in Austria by *Bundesgesetz, mit dem das Urheberrechtsgesetz geändert wird (Urheberrechtsgesetz-Novelle 2003 – UrhG-NOV 2003), BGBl für die Republik Österreich* Teil I, no. 32, 06/06/2003 p. 149.

[58] O.J., L 272, 10/13/2001.

is not an obligation and therefore some Member States have not implemented the relevant provisions. According to data supplied as a result of research conducted on behalf of the Commission on resale rights in the legislation of eleven Member States, in practice there are nine States which apply them, but by substantially different methods (works subject to this right, operations which involve a payment, taxes which apply, and so on). The Directive aims at establishing a harmonized legal framework in the field of resale right aimed at guaranteeing the working of the market in modern and contemporary works of art within the Union. The resale right permits the creator of an original work of art, and, after her/his death, her/his heirs, to obtain a percentage of the price of a work of art when it is sold again following the first transfer of the original work of art, except where the resale is between private parties. The resale right aims at giving artists some economic share in the success of their creations. The desired effect is to re-establish the balance between painters, sculptors and designers on the one hand, and composers or authors of literary works on the other, in that the latter are already protected in this way by the laws in force.

## 7. Designations of Origin

Many European States have adopted rules to protect the *provenance of certain products* (e.g. Champagne, Cognac, Rioja, Grana Padano, etc.). These are not trade marks or trade-names because they do not identify a specific product, nor do they even represent property rights as such. States traditionally protect designations of origin since they play a fundamental part in identifying products which possess certain characteristics or special qualities.

The first step in this direction was taken in the wine sector, with Council Regulation (EEC) no. 823/87 on quality wines produced in specific regions.[59] The sector was then standardized with two regulations, Council Regulation (EEC) No 2081/92 of July 14th 1992 on the protection of geographical indications and designations of origin for agricultural products and foodstuffs, and Council Regulation (EEC) No 2082/92 of July 14th 1992 on certificates of specific character for agricultural products and foodstuffs.[60]

---

[59] O.J., L 84/59, 03/27/1987.

[60] O.J., L 208, 07/24/1992. In Italy, the Regulation was made applicable by the *Community Act for 1999*, under which art. 14 provides an amendment to the previous legislation (art. 53 of the Act of April 24th 1998, no. 128) concerning controls and monitoring for designations of origin on agricultural and food products.

The Community legislation is not of secondary importance, in that it has a decisive impact in a sector which is particularly sensitive in the common market, namely the common agricultural policy; moreover, from the technical viewpoint, it forms part of the well-known problem, much debated in academic circles as well as in case-law, of the legitimacy of *regional quality marks*. In other words, those marks which make some reference to a region, a country, a territory or to a certain geographical area.

The European Community has for some time, through the Commission and the ECJ, held the belief that regional quality marks are incompatible with Treaty provisions, and in particular with arts. 28 and 30 (ex arts. 30 and 36) TEC.

As already noted in connection with these Treaty provisions, the Commission and the ECJ have always tended to circumscribe and restrict the cases and situations which might constitute a limitation on the principles of the free movement of goods and competition. All situations in which certain people make use of geographical indications as an extra attribute to give to their product, figure in this sort of case. Whenever an entrepreneur uses a territorial designation to give a further attribute to the product, s/he creates discrimination against businesses which belong to different territorial areas, discrimination which is not permitted by the EC Treaty.

These considerations have given rise to the particular caution of the Community institutions in conceding the possibility of using geographical indications which make reference to a precise territorial area (region, province, municipality, or other precise geographical district), even when they are the self-same public bodies in the territory which guarantee the quality and provenance of the product.

> See, for example, *Pistre et al.*, judgment of the ECJ (Fifth Chamber) of May 7th 1997, Criminal proceedings against Jacques Pistre (C-321/94), Michèle Barthes (C-322/94), Yves Milhau (C-323/94) and Didier Oberti (C-324/94). Reference for a preliminary ruling: *Cour de cassation,* France, concerning domestic legislation on the use of the description 'mountain' for agricultural products and foodstuffs: Joined cases C-321/94, C-322/94, C-323/94 and C-324/94, ECR 1997, I-2343.
>
> The ECJ in ***Pistre et al*** **held that:** "(**§ 54**) (…) Article 30 of the Treaty precludes application of domestic rules, such as those laid down by Article 34 of Law No 85-30 and Decree No 88-194, which restrict use of the description 'mountain' to products manufactured on national territory and prepared from domestic raw materials. (**§ 45**) (…) the application of the national measure may also have effects on the free movement of goods between Member States, in particular when the measure in question facilitates the

marketing of goods of domestic origin to the detriment of imported goods. In such circumstances, the application of the measure, even if restricted to domestic producers, in itself creates and maintains a difference of treatment between those two categories of goods, hindering, at least potentially, intra-Community trade."

See also the precedent constituted by the ***Eggers*** **case**, judgment of the Court of October 12th 1978, *Joh. Eggers Sohn & Co. v Freie Hansestadt Bremen*, reference for a preliminary ruling: *Verwaltungsgericht Bremen*, Germany, on designations for quality of spirits [Case C-13/78, (1978) ECR I-1935]:

"(§ **23**) As for the prohibition of measures having an effect equivalent to quantitative restrictions, article 30 of the treaty prohibits all such measures in trade between member states. For the purpose of this prohibition it is sufficient that the measures in question are likely to hinder, directly or indirectly, actually or potentially, imports between member states. According to the sixth recital of the preamble to Commission Directive no. 70/50/EEC of December 22th 1969 on the abolition of measures which have an effect equivalent to quantitative restrictions, measures 'which, at any marketing stage, grant to domestic products a preference, other than an aid, to which conditions may or may not be attached, and where such measures totally or partially preclude the disposal of imported products', must be considered to be included among such measures and are consequently prohibited. Having regard to these considerations article 2 (3) (s) of the directive rightly classifies measures which 'confine names which are not indicative of origin or source to domestic products only' as measures having an effect equivalent to quantitative restrictions and therefore prohibited. (**24**) In order to be effective the prohibition on the reserving of certain designations (other than those indicative of origin or source), and in particular designations of quality, for domestic products only must extend to measures which distinguish between domestic products according to whether or not the raw materials or the semi-finished products from which they are manufactured have been produced or semi-finished products, treated on national territory, special designations such as to give them an advantage in the opinion of the traders or consumers concerned. In fact in a market which, as far as possible, must present the features of a single market, entitlement to a designation of quality for a product can—except in the case of the rules applicable to registered designations of origin and indications of origin—only depend upon the intrinsic objective characteristics governing the quality of the product compared with a similar product of inferior quality, and not on the geographical locality where a particular production stage took place. (**25**) However desirable may be the introduction of a policy on quality by a member state, such a policy can only be developed within the community by means which are in accordance with the fundamental principles of the Treaty. Consequently, the member states are empowered to lay down quality standards for products marketed on their territory and may make the use of designations of quality subject to compliance with such standards, but only on the condition that such standards and designations—unlike the position in the case of registered designations of origin and indications of origin—are not linked to a requirement that the production process for the products in question be carried on within the country but are dependent solely on the existence of the intrinsic objective characteristics which give the products the quality required by law. A presumption of quality which is linked to a requirement that the whole or part of the production process should take place on national territory, thereby restricting or treating unfavourably a process some or all of the phases whereof are carried out in other member states is, always excepting the rules relating to registered designations of origin and indications of origin, incompatible with the common market. This is more particularly the case where the requirement that the whole or part of the production process should take place on national territory is, in substance, justified only by a rule which, by introducing the principle of 'undivided responsibility', is intended to facilitate quality controls whereas such controls may be carried out just as effectively by means which are less restrictive of trade between member states. **(26)** It follows from all the foregoing considerations that a national measure which makes the right to use a designation of quality for a domestic product subject to the condition that the semi-finished product from which it was manufactured was either produced or treated on national territory, and refuses to allow the use of that designation simply because the semi-finished product was imported from another member state, is a measure having an effect equivalent to a quantitative restriction."

The use of geographical names to distinguish agricultural/food products is only feasible in the context of Community Regulation 2081/92, on *designations of origin* and *typical geographical indications.*

In reply to a parliamentary question, a Commission member affirmed that Regulation 2081/92 is the "exclusive instrument for exploiting and promoting quality regional products identified by means of their geographical origin."[61]

---

[61] Written question no. 316/99 by McCARTIN to the Commission. Recipients of investments in the pig meat sector in Ireland. O.J., C 207, 07/21/1999, p. 177. Answer of the Commissioner Fischler.

The are two well-known cases, *Grana Padano* and *Prosciutto di Parma*,[62] essentially concerned with the question whether the Community Regulation referred to above can protect:

- The grating and packaging of Grana Padano cheese in the region of production.
- The slicing and packaging of Parma ham in the region of production.

The Court has prohibited third parties from slicing, grating or packaging the original product outside the geographical area of origin, so sustaining the notion of regional/national gastronomic traditions.

> ***Cf. the operative part of the ruling Prosciutto di Parma***: "On those grounds, the Court, in answer to the question referred to it by the House of Lords by order of 8 February 2001, hereby rules: **(1)** Council Regulation (EEC) No 2081/92 of 14 July 1992 on the protection of geographical indications and designations of origin for agricultural products and foodstuffs, as amended by the Act concerning the conditions of accession of the Republic of Austria, the Republic of Finland and the Kingdom of Sweden and the adjustments to the Treaties on which the European Union is founded, must be interpreted as not precluding the use of a protected designation of origin from being subject to the condition that operations such as the slicing and packaging of the product take place in the region of production, where such a condition is laid down in the specification. **(2)** Where the use of the protected designation of origin 'Prosciutto di Parma' for ham marketed in slices is made subject to the condition that slicing and packaging operations be carried out in the region of production, this constitutes a measure having equivalent effect to a quantitative restriction on exports within the meaning of Article 29 EC, but may be regarded as justified, and hence compatible with that provision. **(3)** However, the condition in question cannot be relied on against economic operators, as it was not brought to their attention by adequate publicity in Community legislation."

However, the rulings have not been warmly welcomed by consumers' associations because they do not ensure that consumers' interests are safeguarded. The prohibitions established by the Court substantially introduce a producers' monopoly on processes such as slicing Parma ham,

---

[62] C-469/00 *Ravil SARL v Bellon import SARL and Biraghi SpA*, (2003), ECR I-1, and C-108/01, *Consorzio del Prosciutto di Parma and Salumificio S. Rita SpA v Asda Stores Ltd and Hygrade Foods Ltd.*, (2003), ECR I-1.

or grating and packaging parmesan cheese, with the clear risk of price increases for consumers. It should be added that the Italian State's position in this sector, as we have noted, is in stark contrast with the Community.

Substantially, geographical (quality) indications are considered completely legitimate under Italian legislation as long as they are '*collective*' *(in Italian: marchi collettivi)*.[63] However, they are not considered as legitimate under Community law if the reference to a geographical area is a precondition for attributing an '*additional feature*' to the product, since this would be contrary to the competition rules.

Reg. 2081/92 on designations of origin represents the affirmation of this desire on the part of the Community to contain the use of designations of origin in the agricultural sector and to place the centralized control of restrictions on the circulation of products exclusively with the Community authorities, according to standard rules for all the States in the Community.

Despite the implementation of Regulations 2081/92 and 2082/92 on the protection of geographical indications and on designations of origin, by means of national legislation which has made them concretely applicable within the various legal systems of the Member States, the internal practice within the States does not seem to match up to the expectations of the Community.

Let us consider, for example, the case relating to olive oil: according to a 1998 Regulation,[64] the criterion for assigning the designation of origin was to be determined by the place where the oil was obtained and pressed. However, given that this criterion seemed contrary to the free movement of goods, in that it favored only those companies which had the good fortune to find themselves within that particular territory pertaining to that variety of olive oil, where the natural conditions (of sun, type of soil etc.) play a decisive part, the Community issued a new Regulation in 2001.[65] The new Regulation stated that the designation of origin shall correspond to the geographical area in which the olives concerned or the oil extracted from the olives were obtained. For the purposes of this Regulation, an extra virgin or a virgin olive oil shall be deemed to

---

[63] See art. 2 of *Regio Decreto* June 21st 1942, no. 929, as amended by *D.Lgs.* December 4th 1992, no. 480.

[64] Commission Regulation (EC) No 2815/98 of December 22th 1998 concerning marketing standards for olive oil, O.J., L 349, 12/24/1998, p. 56.

[65] Commission Regulation (EC) No 2152/2001 of October 31st 2001 amending Regulation (EC) No 2815/98 concerning marketing standards for olive oil, O.J., L 288, 11/01/2001, p. 36.

have been obtained in the geographical area where the mill in which the oil was extracted from the olives is located. In the case of olives harvested in a Member State or a third country different from the geographical area in which the oil from those olives was obtained, the designation of origin shall indicate both the area where the olives were harvested and the area where the oil was obtained, using the following wording: (Extra) virgin olive oil obtained in (name of the European Community or of the member State concerned) from olives harvested in (name of the European Community, the Member State or the country concerned).

Now in Italy, for example, the designation of origin corresponds to the criteria established by an administrative act, which each Region (the territorial and administrative areas into which the Italian State is divided) can pass: businesses operating outside that precise territory may also come within the criteria and enjoy the protection of the designation of origin.

## 8. Biotechnological Inventions and Genetically Modified Organisms

With respect to biotechnological inventions, the production and marketing of genetically modified organisms present problems which are distinct from the legal perspective, even though they may be linked conceptually to the patentability of biotechnological innovations.

Directive 98/44/EC of the European Parliament and of the Council of July 6th 1998 on the legal protection of biotechnological inventions[66] deals with the legal issues of patentabiliy.

However, it concerns not only the context of intellectual property rights over such organisms, but also the law of contracts, as well as numerous questions of constitutional and administrative law, ethics, and general policy, as it is explained in the 9th recital (out of 63) in the Preamble:

> **Whereas, Dir. 98/44:** "**(9)** Respect for ethical principles recognised in a Member State is particularly important. Member States may take into consideration ethical aspects when GMOs are deliberately released or placed on the market as or in products."

Under art. 3, inventions which are *new*, which involve an *inventive step* and which are susceptible of *industrial application* shall be patentable even if they concern a product consisting of or containing biological

---

[66] O.J., L 213, 07/30/1998.

material or a process by means of which biological material is produced, processed, or used.

*Biological material* which is isolated from its natural environment or produced by means of a technical process may be the subject of an invention even if it previously occurred in nature. Under art. 4, on the other hand, these are not patentable.

- Plant and animal varieties.
- Essentially biological processes for the production of plants or animals.

*Inventions* which concern plants or animals shall be patentable if the technical feasibility of the invention is not confined to a particular plant or animal variety.

The inventions which concern a microbiological or other technical process, or a product obtained by means of biological processes for the production of plants or animals, are patentable.

Under art. 5, the *human body*, at the various stages of its formation and development, and the simple discovery of one of its elements, including the sequence or partial sequence of a gene, cannot constitute patentable inventions. On the contrary, an element isolated from the human body or otherwise produced by means of a technical process, including the sequence or partial sequence of a gene, may constitute a patentable invention, even if the structure of that element is identical to that of a natural element.

Finally, Dir. 98/44 provides that inventions whose commercial exploitation is contrary to *public order or public morality* are not patentable: inventions shall be considered unpatentable where their commercial exploitation would be contrary to public order or morality; however, exploitation shall not be deemed to be so contrary merely because it is prohibited by law or regulation.

The following, in particular, shall be considered *unpatentable*:

- Processes for cloning human beings.
- Processes for modifying the germ line genetic identity of human beings.
- Uses of human embryos for industrial or commercial purposes.
- Processes for modifying the genetic identity of animals which are likely to cause them suffering without any substantial medical benefit to man or animal, and also animals resulting from such processes.

It should be noted that the Directive, which should have been implemented by July 30th 2000, is still a long way from its transposition. The potential industrial exploitation of genetic engineering is in fact the subject of various kinds of debate—scientific, ethical, and economic—also for reasons to do with the risk of the future dependence of European research structures on American and Japanese ones.

*Cf.* for instance, the ECJ Judgment of October 9th 2001, C-377/98, (2001) ECR I-7079, *Kingdom of the Netherlands v. European Parliament and Council of the European Union.* Application for annulment of Directive 98/44/EC of the European Parliament and of the Council of July 6th 1998 on the legal protection of biotechnological inventions, in the light of the opposition expressed there to genetic manipulation involving animals and plants, and to the issuing of patents for the products of biotechnological procedures liable to promote such manipulation.

The Court said: "**(6)** It is for the Court of Justice, in its review of the compatibility of acts of the institutions with the general principles of Community law, to ensure that the fundamental right to human dignity and integrity is observed. As regards living matter of human origin, Directive 98/44 on the legal protection of biotechnological inventions frames the law on patents in a manner sufficiently rigorous to ensure that the human body effectively remains unavailable and inalienable and that human dignity is thus safeguarded. First, Article 5(1) of the Directive provides that the human body at the various stages of its formation and development cannot constitute a patentable invention. Second, the elements of the human body are not patentable in themselves and their discovery cannot be the subject of protection. Only inventions which combine a natural element with a technical process enabling it to be isolated or produced for an industrial application can be the subject of an application for a patent. Thus, an element of the human body may be part of a product which is patentable but it may not, in its natural environment, be appropriated. That distinction applies to work on the sequence or partial sequence of human genes. The result of such work can give rise to the grant of a patent only if the application is accompanied by both a description of the original method of sequencing which led to the invention and an explanation of the industrial application to which the work is to lead, as required by Article 5(3) of the Directive. In the absence of an application in that form, there would be no invention, but rather the discovery of a DNA sequence, which would not be patentable as such. Thus, the protection envisaged by the Directive covers only the result of inventive, scientific or technical work, and extends to biological data existing in their natural state in human beings only where necessary for the achievement and exploitation of a particular industrial application. Moreover, reliance on the right to human integrity, which encompasses, in the context of medicine and biology, the free and informed consent of the donor and recipient is misplaced as against a directive which concerns only the grant of patents and whose scope does not therefore extend to activities before and after that grant, whether they involve research or the use of the patented products. (see paras. **70–75, 77–79**."

Given this range of extremely up to date issues, the Community legislature passed another Directive, which makes certain ethically (rather than merely legally) important distinctions.

Directive 2001/18/EC of the European Parliament and of the Council of March 12th 2001 on the deliberate release into the environment of genetically modified organisms,[67] and repealing Council Directive 90/220/EEC provides for a range of time-limits which will end on December 31st 2008, at the conclusion of its transposition in the Member States. Meanwhile, the States will have the opportunity to examine the range of views which divides public opinion domestically and representative views throughout the various EU States, before proceeding to the required modification and integration of their domestic rules.

Art. 24 Dir. 2001/18 provides for the need to put mechanisms in place which allow *individual citizens* to present their own comments since, according to the wording of the 10th recital of the Preamble, for a comprehensive and transparent legislative framework, it is necessary to ensure that the public is consulted by either the Commission or the Member States during the preparation of measures and that they are informed of the measures taken during the implementation of this Directive.

As in the case of the Directive on E-commerce,[68] the resistance of States to radical intervention in a field with social implications, which is still in a state of evolution, leads to the issuing of directives which are decidedly prudent, from the point of view of time-limits for implementation.

In part, this divergence also derives in this case from the fact that Community law should take account of the rules and solutions found in other countries outside the EU, such as the United States. Globalization and internationalization of markets force the twentyfive to take into account the diversity of legal solutions, in that the non-EU enterprises have to deal with these differences. And this constitutes an indispensable factor for the maintenance by European industry of a high level of competitiveness in international markets.

---

[67] O.J., L 106/1, 04/17/2001.

[68] See chapter I.

## 9. Industrial and Commercial Property Rights in the CEECs

We must finally pose the question as to how Community legislation thus far described (inspired in many cases by the international sources cited) may affect the legal systems of the CEECs.

Historically, the majority of these countries were able to boast a long tradition in the copyright protection sector, which followed the systems of safeguard in force in the legal systems of continental Europe, namely the approach taken in respect of *copyright* (*author's rights*, *droit d'auteur)* which has been already discussed.[69]

In the pre-communist era of the 1920's, the majority of these countries passed copyright acts, affording a high level of protection, which allowed Bulgaria, Hungary, Poland, Romania, Yugoslavia, and Czechoslovakia to participate in the Berne Convention for the protection of Literary and Artistic Works. Many of these countries developed legislation to protect copyright even further, through case law and through academic commentary upon those acts, which later influenced the drafting and interpretation of the statutes and regulations of the communist era.

The features of communist legislation for copyright protection in the 1950's, which reproduced a particular system of protection of a communist stamp, turned on the principle by which the copyright was largely restricted, for the *benefit of the general public*.

Citizens were to participate in their nations' cultural products without authorization and without payment. Four fundamental categories of so-called "free uses" were permitted:

- Free personal and professional use.
- Use for the purpose of information (i.e. news reports).
- Lending by public libraries or use of works in school books.
- Free non-commercial uses (i.e. performance of a work of music at a non commercial event).

The principle characteristics were as follows:

- Low standards of protection (in particular the terms of protection were significantly reduced).
- Limited range of activities for *collecting societies (*certain collective rights administration bodies*)*, according to the lack of technological innovation (such as personal computers or copying machines).
- Close association between collecting societies and the government,

[69] See above, § 6.

that led to *censorship* (for example, the All Union Agency for Copyright, VAAP, created in 1973, as the sole agent in the Soviet Union for all Soviet authors and entities, was the sole licensing authority for the use of domestic works in foreign countries).

- Intense regulation of the relationship between authors and the State; in particular, the State established tariffs which remunerated authors when state enterprises exploited their works, fixing minimum and maximum remuneration. The main purpose of the tariffs was to guarantee authors a certain social standard, that freedom of contract might have failed to afford.
- Only Czechoslovakia, and to a very limited extent, Hungary and Yugoslavia, provided for some neighboring rights protection.

After the abandonment of communism, with the passing from a planned economy to a market one, all the legal rules and solutions which had characteristics typical of that time, were as a consequence transformed. A large number of the changes in the copyright sector in these countries were attributable to the signing of multilateral or bilateral agreements, as a result of Western pressure. The two principal actors of this approximation process between post-communist law and the law of the (so-called) 'advanced capitalist economies' were, on the one hand, the US and on the other, the European Community.

Under pressure from the first of these, the bi-lateral agreement (so called "Business and Economic Relation Treaty") attained importance in the sector of the computer software industry, both because of the pre-eminent position of US software manufacturers in many international markets including Eastern European markets, and because of the enormous potential that CEECs' computer industry offers for US software producers.

Conversely, under pressure from the EC, three separate moments should be distinguished, given that the first generation bi-lateral agreements have made way for the signing of second and third-generation agreements, in view of the accession of the CEECs to the European Union.

The first generation agreements on trade, commercial, and economic cooperation (between 1988 and 1991) contained only limited provisions on intellectual property. The second generation of bilateral trade, commercial, and economic cooperation agreements (initiated in 1992) were more precise: the notion of "effective and adequate protection" was specified by the words "at a level similar to that which exists in the European Community," reflecting the long-term goals of rapprochement of laws of integration. The third generation of agreements were the Europe

Agreements:[70] these oblige the CEECS to adapt their copyright laws to the EC copyright law, namely the harmonization directives.

It should be remembered that many of these countries, even back in the pre-communist era, had ratified some Conventions, usually the Berne Convention and the Rome Convention such as, for example Poland, respectively in 1919 and 1928, and Hungary in 1922.

The recent membership of certain CEECs of the World Trade Organization (WTO) and the Agreement on Trade-Related Aspects of Intellectual Property Rights (TRIPs Agreement) has effectively raised the standard of protection to the prevailing international level.[71]

Following the ratification of international Conventions and the adoption of the Community model of protection, supplied with regulations and directives, many of these countries have adopted new laws on copyright (among those for imminent accession, Estonia, Latvia, Poland, Slovenia, Romania, and Bulgaria); others, amongst which are Hungary and Lithuania, have opted to amend previous statutes and/or Codes.

These laws are almost always extremely detailed.

In Poland, the Polish Copyright and Neighboring Rights Act of February 4th 1994[72] replaced the communist-model copyright law, which dated from 1952, which in its turn had repealed a statute which had been in force since 1926, based on a continental model.

This Act represents the effort at mediation between public and private requirements (recalled in the first few pages of this chapter), achieved by the Polish legislature. The final objective remains that of integration with European and international law, developed in large measure by the Western industrialized countries. The Act, among other things, protects computer programs, following, in particular, the US model.

In Lithuania, the Amendment and Supplement of the Civil Code of the Republic of Lithuania of May 17th 1994, altered chapters 4 and 5 of the Civil Code (arts. 5151 and following) concerning copyright general provisions and author's contract types.

In 2000, Latvia adopted the new Copyright Act.

In Slovenia, the Copyright and Related Rights Act of 1995[73] has its roots in the Slovenian pre-communist tradition, namely the pre-1918 era. In fact, the law was in the Austrian mould, since before becoming

---

[70] See chapter III, in the first volume of this *Guide, A Commom Law for Europe*.

[71] See Internet website of the WTO for the most recent list of WTO members: http://www.wto.org. All the CEECs are currently members of the WTO and WIPO: http://www.wipo.org/treaties/ip/index.html.

[72] *Dz. U.* 1994, no. 24, item 83.

[73] Official Gazette of Slovenia, no. 21/1995.

part of Yugoslavia, Slovenia was part of the Austro-Hungarian Empire, whose 1811 Code (the Austrian Civil Code) had been in force up until independence, after the First World War. Moreover, although Communism had defined the political climate after the Second World War, Tito immediately broke away from the orthodoxy of the Soviet system, and established a judicial system inspired by moderately 'liberal' principles, articulated by the issuing of the Constitutions of 1953, 1963, and 1974.[74]

The new Slovenian Act on copyright protection was preceded by the Industrial Property Act, of April 4th 1992, the first Slovenian statute to put the basis for protection of intellectual property rights in place. The 1995 Copyright Act stands out in the legislative panorama because it concentrates attention on the 'enforcement phase' of the right, allowing the author to seek punitive damages. Accordingly, an author may claim up to two hundred percent of either the agreed remuneration or the customary royalty or remuneration for such use, regardless of whether the right-holder suffered actual pecuniary damage from the infringement of his/her right. To this end, a special court, the District Court of Lubljana, has been established under Slovenian law, to have exclusive jurisdiction in all cases concerning intellectual property rights. The court's judges receive special training in copyright law before taking office.

Generally, however, this very issue of the low level of enforcement remains open in all the CEECs, with regard to trade in 'pirate' goods and illegally distributed software products. Amendments to existing laws have been passed in order to strengthen the protection of intellectual property rights.

Let us take as an example the system in the three Baltic States. In 2001 Estonia enhanced the protection of copyright by way of introducing the possibility of prohibiting legal persons from trading in certain goods, if they are found to have been trading in "pirate" goods. A precedent worth noting occurred on June 18th 2001, set by the Tallinn City Court. It decided to sentence a person to 10 months' imprisonment for trading in pirate copies without the authorization of the author of the work, the holder of copyright or the holder of related rights.

As far as the law on *patents* and *trade marks* is concerned, they are regulated by separate normative acts. These areas of the law had little significance in the communist era, given that the State owned both the

[74] Art. 169 of the Yugoslav Constitution 1974, which remained valid until 1990, enumerated the rights granted to investors, which included the investor's moral and material rights, to their achievement.

means of production and also the inventions used in the production process.

Practically all workers were employed by the State, which meant that there was very little demand for the protection of intellectual property, at least not until the end of the 1980's, when foreign investors began to operate in those markets.

Nowadays, these rights find protection either in amended statutes dating from the communist period, or in new ones such as the Polish Industrial Property Act of 2000,[75] and receive additional protection by way of registration administered by governmental agencies: the Patent Offices in Estonia and Latvia, the State Patent Bureau in Lithuania,[76] the National Patent Office in Poland and Hungary, and so on.

In short, the legislation in the CEECs in this sector is heading towards a higher order of protection, to the point where the level of supranational protection (motivated by the prospect of joining the EU) meets the level of international protection (motivated by the adoption of protection standards fixed by the aforementioned international Conventions, in which they all participate). These are the stimuli which keep the protection of intellectual property rights high in the CEECs, on a level which is comparable, at least on paper, to that of the other Member States.

[75] *Dz. U.* 2001/49, item 508. It entered into force on August 22nd 2001.

[76] See respectively internet websites: www.epa.ee and www.is.lt/vbp/eng/index.htm.

# Bibliography Chapter V

## *Selected commentary/books:*

*§ In English:*

EASTAWAY N. A., *Intellectual property law and taxation*, Thomson-Sweet & Maxwell, 2004; MARLIN-BENNETT R., *Knowledge Power: Intellectual Property, Information, and Privacy*, Reinner Publishers, 2004; SELL S. K., *Private power, public law: the globalization of intellectual property rights*, Cambridge University Press, 2003; WARREN JONES A., *Human and Animal Biotechnology in the UK and Europe*, Lawtext Publsh., 2001; PRIME T. & BOOTON D., European *Intellectual Property Law*, Ashgate, 2000; WADLOW C., *Enforcement of Intellectual Property in European and International Law: The New Private International Law of Intellectual Property in the United Kingdom and the European Community*, Sweet & Maxwell, 1998; ZIELINSKA-GLEBOCKA A., A. STEPNIAK (eds.), *EU Adjustment to Eastern Europe, Polish ad European Perspective*, Gdansk, 1998; TRITTON, *Intellectual property in Europe*, London, 1996; OECD, *Intellectual Property, Technology Transfer and Genetic Resources: An OECD Survey of Current Practices and Policies*,1996; DIETZ A., *Protection of intellectual property in Central and Eastern European countries : the legal situation in Bulgaria, CSFR, Hungary, Poland, and Romania*, Paris, Organisation for Economic Co-operation and Development, 1995; EPSTEIN M. A., LAURIE R. S., ELDER L. E., *International Intellectual Property: The European Community and Eastern Europe*, Aspen Law & Business, 1994.

*§ In German:*

LUO L., *Verwertungsrechte und Verwertungsschutz im Internet nach neuem Urheberrecht: Vergleich des internationalen, europäischen, deutschen und US-amerikanischen Rechts*, München, 2004; GAMM E.-I., *Die Problematik der Gestaltungshöhe im deutschen Urheberrecht: unter besonderer Berücksichtigung europarechtlicher Vorgaben und der Überschneidung mit dem deutschen Geschmacksmuster-, Wettbewerbs- und Kennzeichnungsrecht*, Baden–Baden, 2004; EBNER M., *Markenschutz im internationalen Privat- und Zivilprozessrecht*, Köln, 2004; INGERL R., ROHNKE C., *Markengesetz: Gesetz über den Schutz von Marken und sonstigen Kennzeichen*, München, 2003; CHEN H.-H., *Die Nutzung urheberrechtlich geschützter Werke auf Individualabruf nach den WIPO-Verträgen, der EU-Richtlinie sowie deutschem und taiwanesischem Recht*, München, 2003; STÖCKEL M., LÜKEN U., DEIGENDESCH T., *Handbuch Markenrecht*, Berlin, 2003; HUBMANN H., GÖTTING, H.-P., *Gewerblicher Rechtsschutz*, Beck, 2002; REHBINDER; *Urheberrecht*, 12th ed., München 2002; HOEREN; *Grundzüge des Internetrechts*, 2nd ed., München 2002; SCHRICKER, DIETZ; *Urheberrecht – Kommentar*, 2nd ed., München 1999; Wadle, Elmar; *Geistiges Eigentum*, 1996; FROMM, NORDEMANN; *Urheberrecht* (Kommentar), 9th ed., Stuttgart 1998; MÖHRING, NICOLINI; *Urheberrechtsgesetz, Kommentar*, 2nd ed., München 2000; MÜHLENDAHL-VON OHLGART, *Die Gemeinschaftsmarke*, München, 1998.

*§ In Italian:*

CHIMIENTI, L., *Lineamenti del nuovo diritto d'autore aggiornato con la direttiva 2001/29/CEE* e con il D. lgs. 68/2003, Milano, 2004; COMBA M. E., *I diritti civili: verso una nuova funzione della proprietà privata, Diritti e Costituzione nell'Unione europea*, Torino, 2003; FOGLIA R., *La proprietà intellettuale*, in TIZZANO (ed.), *Il diritto privato dell' Unione europea, Trattato di diritto privato diretto da BESSONE M.*, Torino, 2000, Tomo II, 1065; CHIMIENTI L., *Lineamenti del nuovo diritto d'autore - Direttive comunitarie e normativa interna,* Milano, 3rd ed., 1999; BORRUSO R., *La tutela giuridica del software - Diritto d'autore e brevettabilità* (commento al d.leg. n. 518/1992 e all'art. 7 d.p.r. n. 338/1979 sui programmi per elaboratori elettronici), Milano, 1998; SENA G., *Il nuovo diritto dei marchi,* Milano 1998; GUGLIELMETTI G., *L'invenzione di software – Brevetto e diritto d'autore,* 2 ed., Milano, 1997; MACARIO F., *La proprietà intellettuale e la circolazione delle informazioni,* in LIPARI (ed.), *Diritto privato europeo,* Padova 1997, vol. I, 398; SGARBANTI G., in COSTATO (ed.), *Trattato breve di diritto agrario italiano e comunitario,* Padova, 1997, 574; GHIDINI G., HASSAN S., *Diritto industriale e della concorrenza nella CEE,* Milano, 1991.

*§ **In French:***

BERTRAND A., *Droit à la vie privée et droit à l'image, Litec 2000; Code de la Propriété Intellectuelle,* Dalloz, 2000; LUCAS A., *Droit d'auteur et numérique, Litec,* 1998; COLOMBET C., *Propriété littéraire et artistique et droits voisins,* Dalloz, 8ème éd., 1997; GAUTIER P.Y., *Propriété littéraire et artistique,* PUF, 2ème éd., 1996; LUCAS A.& H.J., *Traité de la propriété littéraire et artistique, Litec,* 1994; EDELMAN B., *Droits d'auteur droits voisins,* Dalloz, 1993.

*§ **In Spanish:***

ROGEL C., *Anuario de propiedad intellectual 2003,* Reus, 2004; FERNÁNDEZ-NOVOA, C., *Tratado sobre derecho de marcas,* Marcial Pons, 2001.

***Selected articles:***

AERTS ROB J., *The industrial applicability and utility requirements for the patenting of genomic inventions: a comparison between European and US law,* 26 European intellectual property review 349, 2004; GUADAMUZ GONZÁLEZ A., *Viral contracts or unenforceable documents?: contractual validity of copyleft licences,* 26 European Intellectual Property Review. 331, 2004; HANSEN M., SHAH O., *The new EU technology transfer regime: out of the straightjacket into the safe harbour?,* 25 European Competition Law Review 465, 2004; GOLD R., *The European Biotech Directive: Past As Prologue,* 7 European Law Journal 328, 2001; LLEWELYN, M., *The Patentability of Biological Material: Continuing Contradiction and Confusion,* 22 European Intellectual Property Review 191, 2000; DRAHOS P., *Biotechnology, Patents, Markets and Morality,* 21 European Intellectual Property Review 441, 1999; SCOTT A., *The Dutch Challenge to the Bio-Patenting Directive,* 21 European Intellectual Property Review 212, 1999; STERCKX S., *Some Ethically Problematic Aspects of the Proposal for a Directive on the Legal Protection of Biotechnological Inventions,* 20 European Intellectual Property Review 123, 1998; WARREN A., *A Mouse in Sheep's Clothing: The Challenge to the Patent Morality Criterion posed by 'Dolly,'* 20 European Intellectual Property Review 445, 1998; FORD R., *The Morality of Biotech Patents: Differing Legal Obligations in Europe?,* 19 European Intellectual Property Review 315, 1997; HARMS D., *Drafting Claims Around Morality,* 18 European Intellectual Property Review 424, 1996; JONES N., *The New Draft Biotechnology Directive,* 18 European Intellectual Property Review 363, 1996; ROBERTS T., *Draft Directive on Legal Protection of Biotechnical Inventions,* 17 European Intellectual Property Review 116, 1995; NOTT R., *The Proposed EC Directive on Biotechnological Inventions,* 16 European Intellectual Property Review 191, 1994; On GMOs Biotechnology, Food Safety, see also the documents available at http://food-traceability.net/interno.php?sez=biblio&nr=1

Bécourt D., *Vers une révolution du droit d'auteur?*, 72 Droit et Patrimoine 46, 1999; Sirinelli P., *Le droit d'auteur en cyberespace*, Journées d'étude de l'ALAI, 1998, 108; *Passa J., La protection des droits patrimoniaux de l'auteur sur l'Internet en droit français*, RRJ 79, 1999; Sirinelli P., *Les autoroutes de l'information*, RIPIA 147, 1996;

Galli C., *I limiti di protezione dei marchi rinomati nella giurisprudenza della Corte di giustizia CE*, Rivista di diritto industriale II, 60, 2004; Fittante A., *La tutela giuridica dell' "industrial design": il recepimento della Direttiva 98/71/CE*, Dir. ind. 5, 2001; Calboli I., *"Marchio che gode di notorietà": una discutibile pronuncia della Corte di Giustizia delle Comunità Europee (nota a Corte di Giustizia delle Comunità europee*, 14 settembre 2000, *C-375/97)*, Riv. dir. ind. II, 261, 2000; Guidetti B., *L'esaurimento internazionale del marchio nella giurisprudenza italiana e comunitaria (Nota a Cass. Civ. Sez. I.* 18/11/1998 *n. 11603; Trib.* Milano *Sez. I. civ. 23/11/1998; Trib.* Busto Arsizio 3/7/1998), Riv. dir. Ind. II, 45, 2000; Pavoni R., *Brevettabilità genetica e protezione delle biodiversità: la giurisprudenza dell'Ufficio europeo dei brevetti*, Riv. dir. internaz. 429, 2000; Guidetti B., *La direttiva 98/44/Ce sulle invenzioni biotecnologiche*, Contratto e impr./Europa 482, 1999; Rambelli P., *La direttiva europea sulla protezione delle invenzioni biotecnologiche*, Contratto e impr./Europa 492, 1999; Mondini G., *La direttiva comunitaria sulla protezione giuridica di disegni e modelli*, Nuove leggi civ. 947, 1999; Floridia G., *La nuova direttiva sulla protezione giuridica dei disegni e dei modelli, Dir.* Ind. 284, 1998; Barbuto M., *Brevetto europeo e brevetto comunitario*, Impresa 25, 1998; Beghè Loreti-Marini, *La protezione giuridica delle invenzioni biotecnologiche*, Dir. Unione europea 773, 1998; Quaia P., *Il marchio d'impresa tra libera circolazione delle merci e tutela dei consumatori*, Dir. comun. scambi internaz. 655, 1997; Guglielmetti G., *La tutela delle banche dati con diritto sui generis nella direttiva 96/9/CE*, Contratto e impresa/Europa 177, 1997; Frignani A., *Proprietà intellettuale e regole di concorrenza nell'UE – Recenti sviluppi*, Riv. dir. ind. I, 151, 1996; Zambrano V., *Il marchio, il consumatore e l'Ecolabel*, Rass. dir. civ. 170, 1996; Floridia G., *La nuova legge marchi*, Corriere giur. 255, 1993; Todaro N., *La nuova disciplina italiana dei marchi*, Dir. comm. internaz. 457, 1993; Carlotti G., *La "novella" della legge sui marchi e il diritto d'autore*, Dir. autore 98, 1993; Ubertazzi L.C., *Diritto d'autore, Digesto comm., vol.* IV, Torino, 1989, 457; Benussi F., *Brevetto europeo*, Digesto comm., vol. II, Torino, 1987, 324.

Berger C., *Elektronische Pressespiegel und Informationsrichtlinie: zur Vereinbarkeit einer Anpassung des Paragr. 49 UrhG an die Pressespiegel-Entscheidung des BGH mit europäischem Urheberrecht*, 20 CR 360, 2004; Schuhmacher F., *Marktaufteilung und Urheberrecht im EG-Kartellrecht, 53 GRUR (Internationaler Teil)* Heft 6, 487, 2004; Frey D., Rudolph M., *EU-Richtlinie zur Durchsetzung der Rechte des geistigen Eigentums: Anmerkungen zur Harmonisierung des immaterialgüterrechtlichen Sanktionsrechts aus urheberrechtlicher Perspektive*, 48 ZUM Heft 7, 522, 2004; Schenk M., *Entwicklungen und Stand der absoluten Schutzhindernisse im europäischen Markenrecht*, European law reporter, 133 & 160, 2004; Grünzweig C., *Neueste Entwicklungen im EU- und internationalen Markenrecht*, 15 Ecolex Heft 5, 343, 2004; Streinz R., Herrmann C., *Vorabentscheidungsverfahren und Vorlagepflicht im europäischen Markenrecht*, 53 GRUR (Internationaler Teil), Heft 6, 459, 2004; Hotz A., *Die rechtsverletzende Markenbenutzung in der neueren Rechtsprechung von EuGH und BGH*, 105 GRUR Heft 12, 993, 2003; Mühlendahl A., *Markenschutz zu Beginn des 21. Jahrhunderts: Rückblick, Bestandsaufnahme, Ausblick*, 56 NJW Sonderheft, 74, 2003.

# CHAPTER VI

# Competition Law

**Key words**: Competition law – Historical development – Community intervention – Sources of Community law – Community competence – National competence – Undertakings – Agreements – Concerted practices – Exemptions – Negative clearances – Abuse of dominant position – State aid – Concentrations – Harmonization – Member States – CEECs

## 1. Origins and Reasons for Competition Law

From the beginning, the European Economic Community has placed importance on free competition as a *sine qua non* of common economic policy.

The meaning and importance which such principles as the free movement of goods, persons, capital, and services (the *four fundamental freedoms*) have in the development of common policies and Community legal systems, is well known, which have allowed the gradual dismantling of customs barriers and the overcoming, albeit with great difficulty, of obstacles standing in the way of achieving these freedoms. The synergy created between *these fundamental freedoms* and the convergence between *these* and *competition policy* are made possible through the interpretative activity of the Court of Justice. The Court sees them as distinct aims of the internal market, to be pursued by these means.

If the principles of fair competition, of freedom of economic initiative, and the independence of business actors are expressions of the market economy upon which Western Europe was founded and has developed, this, however, does not exclude their encountering limitations and adjustments made in order to preserve their existence.

Ensuring that competition in the common market is free and not distorted, is not at all in conflict with the imposition of a regulatory framework, which indeed represents the basis upon which competition may remain effective and efficient in the long term. The contrast between *freedom of economic initiative* and the restraints placed on *free competition* is more apparent than real.

Other important reasons also exist, such as political ones, for example, which tend to favor the regulation of competition. Just consider the large cartels, which may have, and, in certain cases, have had an important impact on the political life of a State, to the point of conditioning the choices of the legislature; or else consider the problem of the interests of consumers in the variety of choice and the quantity of goods on offer, and the consequent lowering of prices, which only a truly competitive market is able to provide. The negative influence which a lack of control of certain economic behavior could exert over this spirit of cooperation is obvious. States could favor their own undertakings which could then proceed, through agreed practices, to parcel out the market, creating barriers between one State and another, thus impeding the achievement of a true single market.

The inclusion of competition policy among the subjects coming under the competence of the EEC since its formation is not, therefore, a surprise element, all the more since the first and, even nowadays, the strongest unifying factor in the old continent is cooperation at the economic level.

The Community legislature was not the first to confront these difficulties.

The prize for originating the model for competition rules goes to the USA, which had already learned, back in the late nineteenth century, to develop a complex, sophisticated, and efficient system of rules in this regard.

1890 is generally considered to be the year in which antitrust law was born, the year which saw the Sherman Act passed in the US, even though the problem of cartels (in particular, the transport companies) had already led to the Interstate Commerce Act of 1887. Various important acts followed these, among which the Clayton Act and the Federal Trade Commission Act, both in 1914, should be remembered.[1]

The American legislation had illustrious forbears: the English common law, for example, had held unreasonable restraint of trade as unlawful for a long time. However, this concerned piecemeal regulation of limited application.

The reasons which induced such a young country to pass acts protecting competition so quickly are linked to the particular history of the US, indeed to the very fact of being a developing nation.

Large, organized cartels sprang up, generally in the East and North, which had won the Civil War and which had advanced industrial development for some time. To avoid the consequences of dangerous competition, given that the supply of goods and services exceeded demand, causing price decreases which were at times dramatic, some undertak-

---

[1] See website http://www.findlaw.com/01topics/01antitrust/gov_laws.html.

ings fixed prices by agreement, preventing small and medium-sized businesses from entering the market. Besides, it is not surprising that the issue of economic freedom should have become one of the main talking points in American society, considering that the ideal of liberty was the foundation underpinning the creation of the US, and today is still an integral part of the 'American Way of Life.' In other words, the issue of antitrust legislation was no longer just an economic one, but had become a political and ideological question.

The word *antitrust* itself dates from the early history of competition law, a term which defines a complex set of rules used to repress activity which is harmful to competition. In order to achieve dominance of the market by a chosen few, the large undertakings in fact made use of a common law institution, the trust or '*cartel,*' which came to be indissolubly linked to restrictive practices.

Most industrialized countries, including the Member States of the European Community itself, have, in the light of the American experience, begun to equip themselves with legislation in this sector, referring almost always to the model and solutions which have been developed by the United States' legal system.

The legislation in the various European countries, which has developed over the years, has, however, separate and different origins and development, with no special form of collaboration among the States themselves, or any common or standardized planning.

Within the European Community, this has caused competition law to develop on two parallel levels: that of the *Community*, governed by the Treaty and the Regulations, strongly unified and centralized, managed by the Commission and the Court of Justice, but applicable only to situations which have a dimension and impact at European Community level; and the *national* level, governed by domestic law, not harmonized, within the jurisdiction of the relative judicial authorities and applicable to situations which are of exclusively domestic relevance.

A general tendency towards a true integration of the internal market has only begun to be noticeable in the last few years.

The fact is that collaboration, exchange of information, and coordination among the various national bodies responsible for protecting competition are now indispensable, given the global dimension of many economic and fiscal issues. Consultative committees involving the Competition Directorate General of the European Commission[2] and the national bodies responsible for this field are provided for within the European

[2] See http://www.europa.eu.int/comm/dgs/competition/index_en.htm.

Community. The latter collaborate, in differing ways, with the Community authorities, and the form such collaboration takes is the object of increasing interest.

The phenomenon concerns not only the Member States, but involves the East European countries which, in the last ten years, have filled a gap left over from the previous ex-communist regime by introducing competition rules based on the Community model, which is followed more or less completely and faithfully, as we shall see in the following pages.

The phenomenon also involves, beyond the European panorama, the same relationship between the European Union and the United States, where, due above all to international cooperation agreements, the 'global' dimension of the competition policy is evident.

For example, in the 1990's Asian and American producer of Lysine, an amino acid used in animal foodstuffs for nutrition, fixed prices and sales quotas and carried on an extensive information exchange to support the price and quota fixing for sales worldwide, including Europe. The cartel members were prosecuted in the US, resulting in high fines and terms of imprisonment. In Europe, the Commission brought proceedings and fines against the US, Japanese, and Korean conspirators totaling nearly 110 million Euro.

## 2. Sources of Community Law for Regulating Competition

The fact to be highlighted is that, as regards EC private law, the competition sector is the only one to have been completely unified.

Indeed, other legislation of general importance has been added to the Treaty provisions (which represent the main body of competition law), such as rules on concentrations, patents or other areas which lie between industrial law and competition law, which make use of regulations as well as directives as instruments.

As distinct from the situation we have already seen in other sectors of EC private law, directives are practically non-existent in the framework of sources which govern competition; the Community legislature has favored the use of *regulations* as an instrument to ensure the unification of legal rules.[3]

Besides this, not only have uniform rules been imposed, but the power to interpret them in a binding way has been conferred upon a single jurisdiction, namely the Court of Justice. Every national judge has to apply

---

[3] See in chapter II, in the first volume of this *Guide, A Commom Law for Europe.*

Treaty provisions and the Regulations, following the *precedents of the Court of Justice* on the point, just as the Commission must.[4]

The Treaty of Rome (as amended) is not limited to declaring the principle of guaranteeing and protecting competition, but provides a set of provisions designed to impede or suppress any behavior which may have the effect of restricting or distorting competition.

These provisions are set out and regulated in various sources.

*– The area of competition law is almost entirely governed by the Treaty.* In general, art. 3 (g) TEC provides for "a system ensuring that competition in the internal market is not distorted."

In particular, there are three fundamental articles. Art. 81 (*ex* art. 85), concerning practices and agreements made between undertakings; art. 82 (*ex* art. 86) concerning behavior resulting from the abuse of dominant position of undertakings in the market; art. 87 (*ex* art. 92), which aims instead at outlawing certain kinds of aid and subsidies by Member States to their own undertakings.

There are other provisions in the Treaty of a procedural and transitional nature; these, however, are of secondary importance compared to the first three, which are principal provisions, in that they identify the three circumstances relevant to the scope of protecting competition: arts. 83, 84, and 85 (*ex* arts. 87, 88, and 89) TEC contain procedural provisions relating to arts. 81 and 82; arts. 88 and 89 (*ex* arts. 93 and 94) TEC concern procedural provisions in relation to State aids; art. 86 (*ex* art. 90) TEC concerns public undertakings.

*– Regulations from the Council and the Commission.*
Historically, the most important has been the Council Regulation no. 17 of February 6th 1962, called First Regulation Implementing Articles 85 and 86 of the EC Treaty,[5] which has represented the main source of procedure and application of the provisions relating to competition law until 2003. It ensured the uniform application throughout the common market of arts. 85 and 86 (now arts. 81 and 82) TEC and it empowered the Commission to address to undertakings or associations of undertakings decisions designed to bring any infringements of those articles to an end.

This Regulation has been repeatedly amended: one of the most impor-

---

[4] See below, §12 of this chapter, on the relationship between the Commission, on the one hand, and the national judges and administrative authorities, on the other.

[5] O.J., L 13, 02/21/1962.

tant amendments was introduced under Council Regulation no. 1216/1999 of June 10th 1999.[6] Following the Regulation, a failure to notify a vertical agreement that is not covered by a group exemption regulation (because the parties' market share exceed the ceiling provided for in the group exemption regulation) no longer prevents that agreement from being retroactively exempted (i.e. when it is notified after taking effect), if it fulfils the conditions of art. 81 (1) and (3) TEC.

However, this whole area has undergone further far-reaching reform, both procedurally and in substance, with the Council Regulation of the December 16th 2002, no. 1/2003,[7] which incorporates the proposals made by the Commission in the *White Paper on Modernization of the Rules Implementing Articles 81 and 82 of the EC Treaty,* of April 28th 1999.[8]

The general aims of Regulation no. 1/2003 is to increase the effectiveness of competition policy and to simplify procedures.

The reform involves a greater number of institutions with responsibility for competition policy in ensuring coherent application of the EU competition rules.

Therefore the Commission has abolished both its own monopoly over exemptions and the current notification system; it has involved the national authorities in monitoring competition *a posteriori* in the internal market and national judges in the application of Community competition rules. The jurisdictions of the Member States competition authorities are enlarged in order to enforce the prohibitions under arts. 81 (1) and 82 TEC, as well to as ensure that the conditions established by art. 81 (3) are fulfilled. The Member States must designate the relevant national authorities to apply the Regulation: they may choose administrative or/and judicial authorities but, once designated, the latter must apply European competition law (which shall always prevail over national law) independently.

Finally the Commission has strengthened its powers of investigations and increased its own powers in cases of infringement. The Commission is now entitled to impose any behavioral or structural remedies like disinvestments, scissions, etc., when there is no other measure proved as effi-

---

[6] O.J., L 148, 06/15/1999, no. 148.

[7] O.J., L 1, 01/04/2003. This Community act came into effect on May 1st 2004, replacing the Regulation 17/1962. Regulation no. 1/2003 was likewise amended by EC Council Regulation no. 411/2004, of February 26th 2004 (O.J., L 68, March 6th 2004), which put an end to an abnormal situation where the Commission lacked full enforcement powers in connection with air transport between the European Community and non-EU countries.

[8] O.J., L 132, 05/12/1999.

cient to be found; moreover, the Commission may impose higher procedure fees.

Among the Commission's regulations, those inherent in institutions and contracts such as franchising, distribution, and technology transfer agreements should be noted, which are regulated only in order to encourage waiver of the provisions of articles 81 and 82 TEC. In such cases the Commission issues regulations on the basis of a mandate conferred by the Council in conformity with art. 211 (*ex* art. 155) TEC, as it does not possess its own independent regulation-making power in the area of competition law.

– *The provisions and practice of the Commission.*

The Commission exercises its own competence first and foremost through the issuing of 'individual decisions,' that is, directed at individual undertakings to whom irregularities regarding competition are notified. They concern acts of an administrative nature which provide interpretation of Community law on the subject and from which the Commission's viewpoint is discernable. The individual decisions of the Commission are without binding force *erga omnes*, but are, in fact, highly persuasive for all those involved in business activities.

In addition to the decisions, the 'communications' of the Commission should be remembered. These concern declarations which express the Commission's opinion and the direction it is taking in relation to problems of a general, not individual, nature. For these reasons, they are published in the Official Gazette of the European Union, in a specific section;[9] they are, among other things, of limited binding application in the sense that, if the Commission wants to depart from an opinion set down in a previous communication, it must justify its own differing assertion.

The Report on competition policy, which the Commission publishes every year, and in which all its most important judgments are summarized, including the relevant ones of the Court of Justice, is also an important informative source.

– *The judgments of the Court of Justice and the Court of First Instance.*

As we have seen in the previous chapters, the Court of Justice had, and still has, a fundamental role in the development of the Community legal system.

In the more specific sector of competition, precedent created by the

---

[9] The communications are contained in the C Series of the Official Journal (O.J.), on a daily basis.

European Courts has a function which is of more fundamental importance than ever, both in interpreting Treaty law, and indicating to Member States and the Commission what the guidelines to follow are in identifying, and if necessary suppressing, anti-competitive behavior by business and the States themselves.

The combination of these four differing sources and their reciprocal concerted effect has contributed to forming the system and the model for protecting competition in the European Union.

It concerns a model which, having as a starting point a basic distinction, namely whether the acts which are harmful to competition have been done by private individuals or the States themselves, is based on the 'system of prohibition.'

Traditionally, models for protecting competition provide for two possible versions:

- The "control type," which starts with the presumption that all activity, even if harmful to competition, is considered lawful unless it is expressly forbidden.
- The "prohibitory type," by which any activity that restricts competition is always considered unlawful, leaving intact the possibility of exceptions.

The system chosen by the European Community derives from the formulation of art. 81 TEC relating to restrictive practices which, having affirmed that "the following shall be prohibited as incompatible with the common market (...)," specifies in paragraph 3 that "the provisions of paragraph 1 may, however, be declared inapplicable " in some instances.

The advantages of the prohibitory system are that it allows greater control on the part of the authorities who have to safeguard this sector, as well as a more thorough consideration of their activity on the part of the undertakings, in that any activity which theoretically involves cases considered as prohibited cannot be considered lawful, unless previously expressly authorized by the Commission. To this point, and in particular to the problem concerning exceptions (known as 'exemptions' in the language of the Community), we shall be returning later on.

## 3. The Competence of the Commission

If the Council has the task of tracing the evolutionary line of Community competition law, the main actor of Community competition law is the Commission.

As noted above, Regulation 1/2003[10] introduces some radical amendments of the rules regarding the Commission's powers and those of the national authorities in the application of arts. 81 and 82 (*ex* arts. 85 and 86) TEC.

One of the principle objectives of the Regulation is precisely that of limiting the Commission's area of intervention to include only the most serious cases, and at the same time widening that of the national courts, thereby decentralizing the application of competition rules.

In this new framework, the Commission has renounced its own exclusive competence to grant exemptions under art. 81 (3) TEC, and has eliminated the system of prior notification and authorization in favor of a tightening of controls *ex posteriori* (after the event occurs).

Moreover, the protection of private individuals' rights in this area has been strengthened by recognizing the right to compensation for damages incurred by anti-competitive activity, to be the province of the national civil courts. However, this last attempt is plainly inadequate, since no account is taken of tortious or other restitutionary claims which may arise.

The Commission still ascertains violations of arts. 81 and 82 (*ex* 85 and 86) TEC, and prevents or stops them, on the basis of powers conferred under art. 85 (ex art. 89) TEC, which contains the fundamental procedural rules, and under Council Regulation 1/2003, which, from May 1st 2004, replaced the previous rules contained in Council Regulation 17/62.

In carrying out this task, the Commission has the power, in the first *investigation* or *evidence-gathering phase*, to assemble the required information, check books and documents, have access to business premises or other places in case of reasonable suspicion, and request police intervention at the place where the inspection takes place.

As we shall see in the following pages, the evidence-gathering phase may conclude with negative clearance, individual or block exemption, a prohibition decision, or a decision to reject the violation complaint. In all these circumstances, the parties may appeal against the Commission's decisions by applying to the European Community Courts.

However, in the majority of cases, the Commission replies informally, simply filing the case by means of *comfort letter,* where it believes either that Community law does not apply in the particular case, or there is no relevant Community interest at stake, or else that the case is covered by an exemption. The comfort letter is like an informal individual exemption, based on the supposition that the party notified has accepted

---

[10] See § 2.

this alternative way of closing the evidence-gathering phase. Sometimes the Commission sends a *discomfort letter,* that is, a letter which notifies the party that the case will be filed, despite the existence, in fact, of reasons which put the particular agreement or practice under consideration in breach of Community law, so that the national authorities may deal with it.

After the evidence-gathering phase, and whatever infringement has been ascertained, the Commission sends *recommendations* to the business(es), aimed at stopping the effects of the agreement or concerted practice which is considered damaging to competition, or rather bring an end to unilateral activity which constitutes abuse of its own dominant position on the market.

If the undertaking(s) do not take heed of the recommendations contained in the warning letter, the Commission may send a *decision* addressed to them, which gives formal notice to cease the infringement.

If the undertaking(s) do not conform to the Commission's decision, each State where the undertaking has its headquarters must adopt all the measures necessary to remedy the situation (art. 85, [2]) TEC. Where the Member State fails to intervene, the Commission has no other alternative than to take action in the Court of Justice under the infringement procedure of art. 226 (*ex* art 169) TEC.

The sanctions which the Commission may impose at the conclusion of the evidence-gathering phase, are as follows:

- Nullify the whole agreement, or else just individual clauses, if it concerns an agreement which infringes competition law (art. 81 (2) TEC).
- Order the prohibited activity to cease through the imposition of any "behavioral or structural remedies." This has the double effect of preventing the company from proceeding with the anti-competitive activity and of returning to the *status quo ante* (art. 7 Reg. 1/2003).
- High fines: the maximum sum that the Commission can impose is now 1% of the total turnover of the relevant undertaking in the preceding business year (art. 23 (1) Reg. 1/2003), with the option of increasing the sum to up to 10% of the total turnover in the preceding business year by the relevant undertaking, having regard to the gravity and duration of the anti-competitive behavior (art. 23 (2) Reg. 1/2003).
- For every day's delay in complying with the Commission's instructions, periodic penalty payments may be imposed, varying from 50,000 Euro per day to 5% of the daily average turnover of the relevant undertaking in the preceding business year, calculated from the date fixed by the decision (art. 24 Reg. 1/2003).

The recent fine of 497 million Euro imposed on the American *Microsoft Corporation* for abuse of dominant position has caused much comment. The ruling against *Microsoft* has arrived after five years of investigations, at the end of which the Commission concluded that the company has exploited its virtual monopoly in PC operating systems in the markets for work group server operating systems and Media Player for PC systems.

Cf. COM(2004)900 final, Commission Decision of 03/24/2004 relating to a proceeding under Art. 82 TEC (Case COMP/C-3/37.792 Microsoft).

- *Microsoft Corporation*, a company based in Redmond, state of Washington, USA, manufactures, licenses and supports a wide variety of software and products for many computing devices. Microsoft Europe Middle East & Africa controls its activities in the European Economic Area from Paris *La Défense*. Microsoft is present in all countries within the EEA.
- *Sun Microsystems Inc.*, a company based in Palo Alto, California, USA, provides network computing infrastructure solutions that comprise computer systems (hardware and software),[11] network storage systems (hardware and software), support services, and professional and educational services.

On December 10th 1998, Sun made an application to the Commission pursuant to art. 3 of Regulation No. 17/62 for the initiation of proceedings against Microsoft. Sun alleged that Microsoft enjoyed a dominant position as a supplier of a certain type of software product called "operating systems for personal computers." Sun further contended that Microsoft infringed art. 82 of the Treaty by reserving to itself information that certain software products for network computing, called "work group server operating systems," need to interpolate fully with Microsoft PC operating systems. According to Sun, the withheld interoperability information is necessary to viably compete as a work group server operating system supplier.

---

[11] Computer systems are constituted of hardware and software. The word hardware refers to the set of physical components that can constitute computer systems (such as e.g. a display, a keyboard, a hard disk or a processor), while the word software refers to the instructions that direct the hardware operations, also designated as computer programs. A hard disk is a device containing one or more inflexible platters coated with material in which data can be recorded magnetically, together with their read/write heads, the head-positioning mechanism and the spindle motor in a sealed case that protects against outside contaminants. See Microsoft™ Computer Dictionary, on page 246.

In addition, *Microsoft* has been ordered to supply, within 90 days, a version of its Windows operating system, without the Windows Media Player, and to pass over to its competitors, within 120 days, the information necessary to make their players compatible with Windows.

## 4. Article 81 TEC: Agreements and Concerted Practices between Undertakings

Articles 81 and 82 are probably the most important ones in the Treaty of Rome (ex arts. 85 and 86), whether for the consequences they have had for business behavior or for the gradual acceptance of a standardized model for safeguarding competition.

This system governing competition in the Community has been proposed and debated by legal scholars, lawyers, and practitioners of European law, accustomed to a common jargon and syntax, who, together with the Court of Justice, have collaborated in the uniform development of antitrust legislation.

The first manifestation of anti-competitive conduct to be governed by the Treaty concerns *agreements and concerted practices between undertakings*.

The following are incompatible with the common market and are prohibited:

– All agreements between undertakings.
– Decisions by associations of undertakings.

A futher prohibition extendeds to concerted practices which may affect trade between Member States and which have as their object or effect the prevention, restriction or distortion of competition within the common market (art. 81(1) TEC).

All the cases listed in the provision, that is, agreements, decisions and concerted practices, have two features in common: that they involve the renouncing of competition within a competitive system, and that they are created by at least two entities, which may be without legal personality, so long as they are legally and economically distinct and equipped with their own independent executive power.

This means, for example, that a potential agreement between a company and its subsidiary within a group is not included among the cases contemplated under art. 81, but may possibly come within those in art. 82, abuse of dominant position (*infra* next §).

The entity under consideration in art. 81 TEC is defined as an *under-*

*taking* or *associations of undertakings*. Neither term, as has been pointed out, is defined in the Treaty, but both have been given a very broad meaning by the Court of Justice:[12] the concept of an undertaking includes every type and variety of entity involved in economic activity, whether or not for profit, whether a company, group, association, a natural person, a public law entity, or a pension fund.

The concept of an agreement between undertakings is generic and characterized solely by the effects which the agreements are capable of producing (to restrict or distort the competition within the European market).

The looseness of the definition under consideration is confirmed by the fact that, in the third case contemplated by art. 81 TEC, namely *concerted practices*, no reference whatever is made to the concept of undertaking.

> The concept of concerted practices was defined by the Court of Justice in the *Dyestuffs* case, Joined Cases 48/49, 51-57/69, (1972), ECR I-619, as a form of co-ordination between undertakings which, without having reached a stage where an agreement properly so called has been concluded, knowingly substitutes practical co-operation between them for the risks of competition.

The recourse to concerted practices serves to avoid the difficulty the Commission may have in producing proof of the existence of an *agreement* between the undertakings.

In this connection, the affirmation by the Court of First Instance is interesting:[13]

> *Cf.* the Court of First Instance ruling in ***Limburgse Vinyl Maatschappij NV, Montedison SpA, et al. v. Commission* § 22**: "Although Article 85 of the Treaty distinguishes between 'concerted practices', 'agreements between undertakings' and 'decisions by associations of undertakings', the object is to bring within the prohibitions laid down in that provision a form of coordination between undertakings which, without having reached the stage where an agreement properly so-called has been concluded, knowingly substitutes practical cooperation between them for the risks of competition. The criteria of coordination and cooperation,

---

[12] On the concept of undertaking in Community case law and academia, see above, chapter II, in the first volume of this *Guide, A Commom Law for Europe*.

[13] See the case T-305/94 and others, on April 20th 1999, *Limburgse Vinyl Maatschappij NV, Montedison SpA, et al. v. Commission*, (1999) ECR II-931.

> far from requiring the elaboration of an actual 'plan', must be understood in the light of the concept inherent in the Treaty provisions relating to competition, according to which each economic operator must determine independently the policy which he intends to adopt on the common market. Although that requirement of independence does not deprive economic operators of the right to adapt themselves intelligently to the existing and anticipated conduct of their competitors, it strictly precludes any direct or indirect contact between such operators with the object or effect either to influence the conduct on the market of an actual or potential competitor or to disclose to such a competitor the course of conduct which they themselves have decided to adopt or which they contemplate adopting on the market."

If there is no particular doubt over the concept of *decisions* by associations of undertakings, some query may arise, on the other hand, in relation to the term *agreements*.

> See the ECJ, June 18th 1998, C-35/96 ***Commission v. Italian Government*** (1998), ECR I-3851: *cf.* §§ **9–10** of the ruling: "(**9**) The decisions by which a professional body sets a uniform, compulsory tariff for all customs agents restrict competition within the meaning of Article 85 of the Treaty where the tariff directly sets the prices for customs agents' services, provides, for each separate type of operation, the maximum and minimum prices which can be charged to customers, lays down various scales on the basis of the value or the weight of the goods to be cleared through customs or of the specific type of goods, or type of professional service, and is mandatory, so that a customs agent may not depart from it on his own initiative. Those decisions are capable of affecting intra-Community trade where the tariff, by extending over the whole of the territory of a Member State, has, by its very nature, the effect of reinforcing the compartmentalisation of markets on a national basis, thereby holding up the economic interpenetration which the Treaty is designed to bring about. That effect is all the more appreciable because the various types of import or export operations within the Community, as well as transactions between Community traders, require customs formalities to be carried out and may, in consequence, make it necessary for an independent registered customs agent to be involved. (**10**) Although Article 85 of the Treaty is, in itself, concerned solely with the conduct of undertakings and not with measures adopted by Member States by law or regulation, the fact nevertheless remains that that article, in conjunction with Article 5, requires the Member States not to introduce or maintain in force measures, even of

> a legislative nature, which may render ineffective the competition rules applicable to undertakings. Such would be the case if a Member State were to require or favour the adoption of agreements, decisions or concerted practices contrary to Article 85 or to reinforce their effects, or to deprive its own rules of the character of legislation by delegating to private economic operators responsibility for taking decisions affecting the economic sphere. A Member State thus fails to fulfil its obligations under Articles 5 and 85 of the Treaty by adopting and maintaining in force a law which, in granting the relative decision-making power, requires a professional body to adopt a decision by an association of undertakings contrary to Article 85 of the EC Treaty, consisting of setting a compulsory tariff for all customs agents."

Here too the concept is normally given a broad meaning, including not only contracts made with the precise aim of controlling the parties' activity in the market place, but also any economic fetter which has been agreed between at least two undertakings. The form the agreement takes is irrelevant: its existence may be deduced even from correspondence. It concerns both horizontal agreements, that is, between firms at the same level of production, and vertical ones, that is, between manufacturing companies and those involved in product distribution.

Art. 81 (1) groups together, for merely illustrative purposes, some categories of agreement and/or anti-competitive activity, which may consist in the following:

- Directly or indirectly fix purchase or selling prices or any other trading conditions.
- Limit or control production, markets, technical development, or investment.
- Share markets or sources of supply.
- Apply dissimilar conditions to equivalent transactions with other trading parties, thereby placing them at a competitive disadvantage.
- Make the conclusion of contracts subject to acceptance by the other parties of supplementary obligations which, by their nature or according to commercial usage, have no connection with the subject of such contracts.

Such conduct, as is the case with any such conduct demonstrated by any other kind of agreement which has the effect of impeding, restricting or distorting the competition, is only prohibited if it has a significant impact on inter-Community trade, and has effect within the common market.

The agreement, therefore, is not forbidden unless there is an appreciable effect on the common market or if such effect is only felt at the national level. In such cases it will if anything be for the national authorities to intervene, by means of their own national law applicable to acts which are harmful to internal competition.

Some precise definitions in this regard were reached by the Court of Justice in the early 1970's.

In the first place, it was established that "agreements which are not capable of significantly affecting trade between Member States are not caught by art. 81 (ex art. 85);"[14] in the wake of the Court's rulings, the Commission has drawn up a list of quantitative criteria to determine the definition of 'appreciable': these criteria have been available since 1997 in the Commission's Notice of Agreements of minor importance, which do not appreciably restrict competition under Article 81 (1) TEC, better known as the *de minimis* Notice.[15]

> The European Commission has adopted a new Notice on agreements of minor importance,[16] which replaced the previous one of 1997. It aims to reduce the compliance burden for smaller undertakings in particular, as well as to free up the Commission's time allowing it to focus on more problematic agreements.

In the second place, the Court of Justice has held it to be unnecessary that the agreements in question should distort competition within the market of the Community. They may also be considered prohibited when they distort competition within a single Member State, so long as their effects are felt on trade between the States.[17]

This rule continues to be widely applied: we cite some examples of conduct by businesses which have been held by the Commission, in some of its decisions, to be harmful to competition in violation of art. 81 TEC (*ex* art.85).

> **1999/271/EC: Commission Decision** of December 9th 1998 relating to a proceeding pursant to Article 85 of the EC Treaty, in O.J., L 109, 04/27/1999, p. 24:
>
> "**Article 1.** 1. Minoan Lines, Anek Lines, Karageorgis Lines, Marlines SA and Strintzis Lines have infringed Article 85 (1) of the EC Treaty by agreeing prices to be applied to roll-on–roll-off

[14] Case 5/69, *Volk v. Vervaecke*, (1969) ECR 298.

[15] O.J., C-372/13, 1997.

[16] O.J., C-368 of 12/22/2001.

[17] Case C-8/72, *Vereniging van Cementhandelaren v. Commission*, (1972) ECR I-977 at § 29.

ferry services between Patras and Ancona. The duration of these infringements is as follows: (a) in the case of Minoan Lines and Strintzis Lines, from 18 July 1987 until July 1994; (b) in the case of Karageorgis Lines, from 18 July 1987 until 27 December 1992; (c) in the case of Marlines SA, from 18 July 1987 until 8 December 1989; (d) in the case of Anek Lines, from 6 July 1989 until July 1994. 2. Minoan Lines, Anek Lines, Karageorgis Lines, Adriatica di Navigazione SpA, Ventouris Group Enterprises SA and Strintzis Lines have infringed Article 85 (1) of the EC Treaty by agreeing on the levels of fares for trucks to be applied on the Patras to Bari and Brindisi routes. The duration of these infringements is as follows: (a) in the case of Minoan Lines, Ventouris Group Enterprises SA and Strintzis Lines, from 8 December 1989 until July 1994; (b) in the case of Karageorgis Lines, from 8 December 1989 until 27 December 1992; (c) in the case of Anek Lines, from 8 December 1989 until July 1994; (d) in the case of Adriatica di Navigazione SpA, from 30 October 1990 until July 1994.

**Article 2.** The following fines are hereby imposed on the following undertakings in respect of the infringement found in Article 1: Minoan Lines, a fine of ECU 3.26 million; Strintzis Lines, a fine of ECU 1.5 million; Anek Lines, a fine of ECU 1.11 million; Marlines SA, a fine of ECU 0.26 million; Karageorgis Lines, a fine of ECU 1 million; Ventouris Group Enterprises SA, a fine of ECU 1.01 million; Adriatica di Navigazione SpA, a fine of ECU 0.98 million.

**Article 3.** The fines shall be paid within three months of the date of notification of this Decision to the following account: Account No 310-0933000-43. European Commission Banque Bruxelles–Lambert Agence Européenne Rond-Point Schuman/ Schumanplein 5 B-1040 Brussels. After three months, interest shall automatically be payable at the rate charged by the European Central Bank on its ecu transactions on the first working day of the month in which this Decision was adopted, plus 3.5 percentage points, namely 7.5%.

**Article 4.** This Decision is addressed to: Minoan Lines 25th August 17 GR 71202 Heraklion, Crete; Strintzis Lines 26 Akti Possidonos GR 18531 Piraeus; Anek Lines Nikolaou Plastira & Apokoronou GR Hania, Crete; Marlines SA 38 Akti Possidonos GR 18531 Piraeus; Karageorgis Lines Karageorgis Buildings Akti Kondyli 26–28 GR 18503 Piraeus; Ventouris Group Enterprises SA 91 Leoforos Pireos & Kithiron 2 GR 18541 Piraeus; Adriatica di Navigazione SpA Zattere 1411 I 30123 Venice."

**1999/210/EC: Commission Decision** of October 14th 1998 relating to a proceeding pursuant to Article 85 TEC, Case IV/F-

3/33.708; British Sugar plc., Case IV/F-3/33.709; Tate & Lyle plc., Case IV/F-3/33.710; Napier Brown & Company Ltd., Case IV/F-3/33.711; James Budgett Sugars Ltd., in O.J., L 76 03/22/1999, p. 1:

"**Article 1.** British Sugar plc., Tate & Lyle plc., Napier Brown & Company Ltd. and James Budgett Sugars Ltd. have infringed Article 85 (1) by participating in an agreement and/or concerted practice the object of which was to restrict competition by the coordination of the parties' pricing policy on the market for industrial sugar in Great Britain. In the case of British Sugar plc. and Tate & Lyle plc. this participation lasted from 20 June 1986 until 2 July 1990. In the case of Napier Brown & Company Ltd. and James Budgett Sugars Ltd. the participation lasted from late 1986 until 2 July 1990.

**Article 2.** British Sugar plc. and Tate & Lyle plc. have infringed Article 85 (1) by participating from 20 June 1986 until 2 July 1990 in an agreement and/or concerted practice the object of which was to restrict competition by the coordination of the parties' pricing policy on the market for retail sugar in Great Britain.

**Article 3.** A fine of ECU 39.6 million is hereby imposed on British Sugar plc in respect of the infringement referred to in Articles 1 and 2. A fine of ECU 7 million is hereby imposed on Tate & Lyle plc. in respect of the infringement referred to in Articles 1 and 2. A fine of ECU 1.8 million is hereby imposed on Napier Brown & Company Ltd. in respect of the infringement referred to in Article 1. A fine of ECU 1.8 million is hereby imposed on James Budgett Sugars Ltd. in respect of the infringement referred to in Article 1.

**Article 4.** The fines imposed under Article 3 shall be payable in ECU within three months of the date of notification of this Decision to the following bank account of the European Commission: 310-0933000-43, Banque Bruxelles Lambert, Agence Européenne, Rond-Point Schuman 5, B-1040 Brussels. After the expiry of that period, interest shall automatically be payable at the rate charged by the European Central Bank for transactions in ECU on the first working day of the month in which this Decision was adopted, plus 3.5 percentage points, namely 7.50%.

**Article 5.** This Decision is addressed to: British Sugar plc., Oundle Road, Peterborough PE29QY, United Kingdom; Tate & Lyle plc., Sugar Quay, Lower Thames Street, London EC3R 6DQ, United Kingdom; Napier Brown & Company Ltd., International House, 1 St. Katharine's Way, London E1 9UN, United Kingdom; James Budgett Sugars Ltd., Beacon House, Rainsford Road, Chelmsford, Essex CM1 2PY, United Kingdom.

This Decision shall be enforceable pursuant to Article 192 of the Treaty."

**98/273/EC: Commission Decision** of January 28th 1998 relating to a proceeding under Article 85 TEC, Case IV/35.733—VW, in O.J., L 124, 05/25/1998, p. 60.

"**Article 1.** Volkswagen AG and its subsidiaries Audi AG and Autogerma SpA have infringed Article 85 (1) of the EC Treaty, by entering into agreements with the Italian dealers in their distribution network in order to prohibit or restrict sales to final consumers coming from another Member State, whether in person or represented by intermediaries acting on their behalf, and to other authorised dealers in the distribution network who are established in other Member States.

**Article 2** Volkswagen AG shall bring to an end the infringements established in Article 1 immediately upon notification of this Decision and shall not replace restrictions of that kind with restrictions having similar objectives. In particular, Volkswagen AG shall, within two months of notification of this Decision: (a) amend the contract with the authorised Italian dealers so that bonus payments are not granted according to whether sales are made within the contract territory or to another Member State; (b) inform the authorised Italian dealers by circular that the margins scheme introduced in the circulars of 20 October and 2 November 1994 has been abolished wherever the margins are smaller for a sale concluded within the contract territory; (c) inform the authorised Italian dealers by circular that all restrictions on cross-deliveries to network dealers in the other Member States have been abolished, pointing out that it is no longer necessary to obtain the prior consent of the importer and that no penalties in the form of restricted supply or termination of the dealer's contract need be feared if the dealer sells to final consumers from other Member States who act either for themselves or through an intermediary appointed by them; (d) inform all authorised dealers in the VW/Audi distribution network in the European Community, by circular, that all restrictions on cross-deliveries from Italy to the other Member States are abolished; (e) instruct its subsidiary, Audi AG, to send circulars setting out points (a) to (d) to its contract dealers in the European Community and shall instruct its subsidiary Autogerma SpA to send circulars setting out points (a) to (c) to its Italian contract dealers.

**Article 3**. In view of the gravity of the infringement of Article 85(1) of the EC Treaty a fine of ECU 102 million (one hundred and two million ecus) is imposed on Volkswagen AG.

**Article 4.** The fine determined in Article 3 shall be paid in ecus within months following the date of notification of this Decision into the following bank account of the Commission of the European Communities: 310-0933000-43 Banque Bruxelles Lambert

> Agence Européenne Rond Point Schuman 5 B-1040 Bruxelles. After the expiry of that period, interest shall become payable. The rate applicable shall be that which the European Monetary Institute applies for transaction in ecus. The interest shall be payable from the first working day of the month in which this Decision was adopted. A supplement of 3.5 (three and a half) percentage points shall be charged. In total, the interest rate shall be 7.75%.
>
> **Article 5.** With regard to the obligations mentioned in Article 2, a penalty payment of ECU 1 000 shall be imposed on Volkswagen AG for each day of delay in implementing this Decision. Such delay shall start from the expiry of the two-month period specified for their implementation.
>
> **Article 6.** This Decision is addressed to Volkswagen AG, D-38436 Wolfsburg.
>
> This Decision shall be enforceable pursuant to Article 192 of the EC Treaty."
>
> This decision has been partly amended, solely as regards the amount of the fine, by the judgment of the Court of First Instance, July 6th 2000, *Volkswagen AG* v. *Commission*, T-62/98, (2000) ECR II-2707.

Finally, it should be remembered that art. 81 (1) TEC leaves room not only for the suppression of existing, but also potential anti-competitive conduct. According to some decisions of the Commission, potential anti-competitive conduct exists when it is obvious that the entry of an undertaking into the market is a "natural and reasonably foreseeable extension of its business activities."[18]

## 5. The Exemptions

Every agreement or concerted practice between two or more undertakings which tends to distort the competition is to be considered, in principle, incompatible with the common market.

However, when it can be ascertained that certain conduct, of itself likely to distort competition, is able to provide certain advantages for the market or consumers themselves, it may be excluded from the prohibition.

This is the sense of paragraph 3 of art. 81 TEC, which provides that the Commission may allow an exception to the prohibition contained in

[18] Commission Decision of July 14th 1986, *Optical Fibres*, O.J., L 236/30, 1986; Commission Decision of December 17th 1986, *Mitchell Cotts*, O.J., L 41/31, 1987.

the first part, by means of creating an exemption, provided that the agreement, decision or concerted practice contributes " to improving the production or distribution of goods or to promoting technical or economic progress, while allowing consumers a fair share of the resulting benefit (...)."

Further provided, art. 81 (3) continues, that such agreements or practices do not "(a) impose on the undertakings concerned restrictions which are not indispensable to the attainment of these objectives; (b) afford such undertakings the possibility of eliminating competition in respect of a substantial part of the products in question."

Until the entry into force of the Reg. 1/2003, the previous system, founded on Reg. 17/62, provided that the Commission alone could grant exceptions to the prohibition contained in the first part of the provision, exceptions which are known as individual exemptions.

*Individual exemptions* were those permitted from time to time, at the request of interested parties, after the Commission had examined all the essential elements of the agreement. They could be permitted for a limited period or renewed at the request of the parties, provided that the preconditions exist. The decision, in favor or against, was published in the Official Gazette, obviously bearing in mind the parties' interests in not publishing items considered confidential.

The allowance of an exemption could be accompanied by certain conditions, instructions, and duties which could concern the terms of the contract itself or the conduct of the undertakings when carrying on their activity. For instance, the exemption granted to KLM, the Dutch airline company, regarding the acquisition of 40% of Transavia, was subject to KLM giving up a certain number of principle and secondary routes; to the concession of charter licenses on competitive terms; to not acquiring other shares in other companies involved in the running of airlines.

With effect from the application date of Reg. no. 1/2003 (May 1st 2004), the Commission will no longer issue individual exemption but, for reasons of Community public interest, may, on its own authority, take decisions objecting to *'inapplicability'* under art. 81, concerning certain agreements or concerted practices.[19] In those cases, where the Community public interest relating to the application of arts. 81 and 82 TEC so requires, the Commission, acting on its own initiative, may by decision find that art. 81 TEC *is not applicable* to an agreement, a decision by an association of undertakings or a concerted practice, either because the conditions of art. 81 (1) TEC are not fulfilled, or because

---

[19] See art. 10 of Reg. 1/2003.

the conditions of art. 81 (3) TEC are satisfied. The Commission may likewise make such a finding with reference to art. 82 TEC.

In addition, Reg. 1/2003 has eliminated the system of previous notification of agreement or draft agreement to the Commission, which was required so that the latter could carry out investigations into the compatibility or otherwise of the agreement, or the possibility of its exemption. Today, thanks to the provision in Reg. 1/2003 (art. 1), a transfer has taken place from a regime of necessary prior authorization to one of automatic legal exception (or exemption).

> **Art. 1, Reg. 1/2003:** "**1.** Agreements, decisions and concerted practices caught by Article 81 (1) of the Treaty which do not satisfy the conditions of Article 81 (3) of the Treaty shall be prohibited, no prior decision to that effect being required. **2.** Agreements, decisions and concerted practices caught by Article 81 (1) of the Treaty which satisfy the conditions of Article 81 (3) of the Treaty shall not be prohibited, no prior decision to that effect being required. **3.** The abuse of a dominant position referred to in Article 82 of the Treaty shall be prohibited, no prior decision to that effect being required."

Where the preconditions for not applying the prohibition on an agreement which violates competition rules are not present, the Commission and the national authorities can always take action under art. 81 (2) TEC. Such an approach is a complete reversal of the model previously in force, according to which "in any national or Community proceedings for the application of Articles 81 and 82 of the Treaty, the burden of proving an infringement of Article 81 (1) or of Article 82 of the Treaty shall rest on the party or the authority alleging the infringement. The undertaking or association of undertakings claiming the benefit of Article 81 (3) of the Treaty shall bear the burden of proving that the conditions of that paragraph are fulfilled."

Furthermore, in order to lighten the workload which up until now has been borne exclusively by the Commission, the new Regulation transfers a great number of the competencies to the national legal authorities, which "where the competition authorities of the Member States or national courts apply national competition law to agreements, decisions by associations of undertakings or concerted practices within the meaning of Article 81 (1) of the Treaty which may affect trade between Member States within the meaning of that provision, (they) shall also apply Article 81 of the Treaty to such agreements, decisions or concerted practices" (art. 3 (1) Reg. 1/2003).

Substantially, the new model abandons both the concept and practice of the exclusive competence of the Commission in the area of agreements and exemptions, in order to involve the national authorities as well in this activity of controlling the conduct of enterprises, be they the competition authorities of the Member States (art. 5, Reg. 1/2003), or the national courts (art. 6, Reg. 1/2003).

It is an indication that now, after almost fifty years of the Community bodies applying the competition rules, and the adoption of approximated laws in all the Member States, the States have gained sufficient experience and maturity to operate in perfect harmony with the Commission and the Court of Justice.

If the new Regulation has eliminated *individual exemptions,* it has left the *group exemptions* intact (art. 29, Reg. 1/2003).

*Group exemptions*, also known as *block exemptions*, are set out in special regulations issued by the Commission on a mandate from the Council, often added to later by further communications by the Commission itself.

Some of these exemption regulations have indeed been directly adopted by the *Council.*

> For example, Regulation (EEC) 2821/71 of the Council of December 20th 1971 on application of Article 85 (3) of the Treaty to categories of agreements, decisions and concerted practices, in O.J., L 285, 12/29/1971, p. 46*;* Regulation 19/65/EEC of March 2th of the Council on application of Article 85 (3) of the Treaty to certain categories of agreements and concerted practices, in O.J., L 36, 03/06/1965, p. 533.

The phenomenon of block exemptions was not provided for by the Treaty, but was developed later with the aim of resolving the problem caused by thousands of individual exemption requests arriving each year at the Commission, paralyzing its progress. Thus the Council gave the Commission the task of providing some regulations which identified typical cases, corresponding to the contractual and commercial practice of the operators, within which certain contractual terms or commercial practices, identifiable in the abstract as prohibited within the meaning of art. 81 TEC, could be held to be equally compatible with the common market.

Since the middle of the 1960's the *Commission* has adopted many block exemption regulations.

> Among which the following should be recalled:
>
> **Commission Regulation (EC) No 772/2004** of April 27th 2004 on the application of Article 81 (3) of the Treaty to cate-

gories of technology transfer agreements. Replaces Regulation no. 240/96, O.J., L 123, 04/27/2004, p. 11.

**Commission Regulation (EC) No 358/2003** of February 27th 2003 on the application of Article 81 (3) of the Treaty to certain categories of agreements, decisions and concerted practices in the insurance sector, O.J., L 53, 02/28/2003, p. 8.

**Commission Regulation (EC) No 1400/2002** of July 31th 2002 on the application of Article 81(3) of the Treaty to categories of vertical agreements and concerted practices in the motor vehicle sector, O.J., L 203, 08/01/2002, p. 30.

**Commission Regulation (EC) No 2659/2000** of November 29th 2000 on the application of Article 81 (3) of the Treaty to categories of research and development agreements, O.J., L 304, 12/05/2000, p. 7. It came into force on January 1st 2001. It replaced Regulation no. 418/85.

**Commission Regulation (EC) No 2658/2000** of November 29th 2000 on the application of Article 81(3) of the Treaty to categories of specialization agreements, O.J., L 304, 12/05/2000, p. 3. It came into force on January 1st 2001. It replaced Regulation no. 418/85.

**Commission Regulation (EC) No 240/96** of January 31th 1996 on the application of Article 85 (3) of the Treaty to certain categories of technology transfer agreements, in O.J., L 031, 02/09/1996, p. 2.

**Commission Regulation (EEC) No 4087/88** of November 30th 1988 on the application of Article 85 (3) of the Treaty to categories of franchise agreements, in O.J., L 359, 12/28/1988, p. 46.

**Commission Regulation (EEC) No 418/85** of December 19th 1984 on the application of Article 85 (3) of the Treaty to categories of research and development agreements, in O.J., L 53, 02/22/1985, p. 5

**Commission Regulation (EEC) No 417/85** of December 19th 1984 on the application of Article 85 (3) of the Treaty to categories of specialization agreements, in O.J., L 53, 02/22/1985, p. 1.

One of these is the group exemption Regulation of the Commission, no. 2790/1999, which concerns some categories of vertical agreement and concerted practices, soon followed by the Commission Notice entitled *Guidelines on Vertical Restraints*,[20] which provide analytical criteria that complements the current rules on approved vertical restraints. The guidelines provide a detailed analysis of the regulation, particularly as regards the granting and withdrawal of exemption.

---

[20] O.J., C 291, 10/13/2000, p. 1.

The most common vertical restraints are *single branding* (which results from an obligation or incentive which makes the buyer purchase practically all her/his requirements on a particular market from only one supplier); *exclusive distribution agreements* (in which the supplier agrees to sell her/his products only to one distributor for resale in a particular territory. At the same time, the distributor is usually limited in her/his active selling into other exclusively allocated territories); *exclusive customer allocation agreements* (in which the supplier agrees to sell her/his products only to one distributor for resale to a particular class of customer. At the same time, the distributor is usually limited in her/his active selling into other exclusively allocated classes of customer); *selective distribution agreements* (like exclusive distribution agreements, they restrict the number of authorized distributors, on the one hand, and the possibilities of resale on the other; the difference *vis-à-vis* exclusive distribution is that the restriction of the number of dealers does not depend on the number of territories, but on selection criteria linked, in the first place, to the nature of the product and the restriction on resale is not a restriction on active selling to a territory, but a restriction on any sales to non-authorized distributors, leaving only appointed dealers and final customers as possible buyers); *franchising* (franchise agreements contain licenses of intellectual property rights relating, in particular, to trade marks or signs and know-how for the use and distribution of goods or services); *exclusive supply* (there is only one buyer inside the Community to which the supplier may sell a particular final product); *tying* (it exists when the supplier makes the sale of one product conditional upon the purchase of another distinct product from the supplier or someone designated by the latter. The first product is referred to as the tying product and the second is referred to as the tied product); *recommended and maximum resale prices* (the practice consists in recommending a resale price to a reseller or requiring the reseller to respect a maximum resale price).

The *negative effects* on the market that may result from vertical restraints which EC competition law aims to prevent are as follows: foreclosure of other suppliers or other buyers by raising barriers to entry; reduction of inter-brand competition between the companies operating on a market; reduction of inter-brand competition between distributors; limitations on the freedom of consumers to purchase goods or services in a Member State.

However, vertical restraints often have *positive effects,* in particular by promoting non-price competition and improved quality of services. Consequently, the application of certain vertical restraints may be justifiable for a limited period where: one distributor may *free-ride* on the promotion efforts of another distributor; a manufacturer wants to enter a new geographic market, for instance by exporting to another country for the first time. This may involve certain first-time investments by the distributor to establish the brand in the market; certain retailers in some sectors have a reputation for stocking only *quality* products; client-specific investments have to be made by either the supplier or the buyer, such as in special equipment or training; know-how, once provided, cannot be taken back, and the provider of the know-how may not want it to be used for or by her/his competitors; in order to exploit economies of scale and thereby see a lower retail price for her/his product, the manufacturer may want to concentrate the resale of her/his product on a limited number of distributors; the usual providers of capital (banks, equity markets) provide capital sub-optimally when they have imperfect information on the quality of the borrower or there is an inadequate basis to secure the loan; a manufacturer increases sales by imposing a certain measure of uniformity and quality standardization on her/his distributors. This may enable her/him to create a brand image and thereby attract consumers. This can be found, for instance, in selective distribution and franchising.

Any undertaking engaged in activity which comes within the categories provided by the exemption rules no longer needs to request individual exemption, since this is implicit in the issue of the regulation.

The advantages of block exemptions are obvious. First and foremost they lighten the load of the Commission; besides this, they speed up a procedure which is considered highly complex and afflicted by an excess of control which demands futile attempts at conformity on the part of the undertakings, creating problems and difficulties which are mostly unjustifiable. Furthermore, the fact should not be overlooked that block exemptions noticeably reduce the risk of disparity of treatment among competing undertakings.

## 6. Negative Clearances

Negative clearances, provided by Council Regulation 17/1962 and by Council Regulation 1/2003, (but see the new expression *finding of inapplicability* used by the second Regulation), should not be confused with individual exemptions.

The difference between *negative clearance/finding of inapplicability* and *exemption* lies in the declaratory nature of the former and the substantive nature of the latter.

Negative clearance/finding of inapplicability serves only to ascertain that a particular kind of conduct is not, of itself, incompatible with the single market, whereas the exemption serves to render legitimate conduct which would otherwise be incompatible with the market.

In other words, the issuing of an exemption serves to legitimize an otherwise unlawful agreement or course of conduct. In such a case, what is desired to be sanctioned is not the anti-competitive conduct, so much as the fact that undertakings should be subject to control, having omitted to request exemption.

A negative clearance/finding of inapplicability serves only to ascertain whether a particular agreement is not of itself, incompatible with the single market.

> **Art. 10, Reg. 1/2003**: "Where the Community public interest relating to the application of Articles 81 and 82 of the Treaty so requires, the Commission, acting on its own initiative, may by decision find that Article 81 of the Treaty is not applicable to an agreement, a decision by an association of undertakings or a concerted practice, either because the conditions of Article 81 (1) of the Treaty are not fulfilled, or because the conditions of Article 81 (3) of the Treaty are satisfied. The Commission may likewise make such a finding with reference to Article 82 of the Treaty."

These findings of inapplicability are issued at the request of interested parties following a procedure by which the petitioners formulate a query for the Commission's consideration, as to whether a particular agreement or concerted practice, not yet in operation but which they intend to agree to or put into place, falls under those prohibited by Community law.

Of course, since the request for an opinion is voluntary, it is not necessary for the parties to wait for a response from the Commission before going ahead with the agreement in question. Previously, should negative clearance be refused, the parties had to submit to the required sanctions for not having sought individual exemption. Now, since there is no longer an obligation to request an individual exemption, the consequences of failing to obtain a negative clearance/finding of inapplicability have also been altered.

## 7. Article 82 TEC: The Abuse of Dominant Position

The second phenomenon of anti-competitive conduct governed by the Treaty is known as the *abuse of dominant position*.

Any abuse by one or more undertakings of a dominant position within the common market or in a substantial part of it shall be prohibited as incompatible with the common market insofar as it may affect trade between Member States (art. 82 (1), ex art. 86 (1) TEC).

The purpose of the signatory parties to the Treaty was not to suppress dominant positions in the market place *per se*. The achievement of a dominant position in the market place may, in fact, be the result of deserving entrepreneurial activity, and as such it is not punished. In many production sectors, only huge undertakings, which easily attain a dominant position in at least one part of the market, are in a position to withstand European and worldwide competition.

What the signatory parties wanted, and still want today, is to avoid some undertakings taking unfair advantage of their dominant position and harming others, when this prejudices the common market. The concept of dominant position in the market, not made explicit in art. 82 TEC, has been defined by the Court of Justice, keeping in constant touch with legal scholars and the European Commission.

The simplest and most precise definition, which has had the largest following, is the one laid down in the judgment in *Metro-Saba*, of October 25th 1977,[21] where the Court of Justice held that an undertaking may be considered to be in a dominant position when it is able to operate to a large extent without having to take account of the behavior of its competitors.

This implies that it is not necessary to have a large share of the market to be considered to be in a dominant position. In some cases, according to the structure of the market, companies have been held to be in a dominant position with a market share of less than 50%, bearing in mind the fact that the remainder was subdivided amongst a high number of small undertakings, none of whose individual shares exceeded 2–3%.

The concept of dominant position is therefore *relative*, requiring a case-by-case evaluation, based on the following structural criteria:[22] market share of the firm considered; market share of the firm's competitors; development of the market over the time; barriers to the entry of competitors on the market; financial power; absence of countervailing power on the purchasers' side.

Moreover, there cannot be an abstract dominant position: it exists only in relation to a specific market, the *relevant market*.

---

[21] Case 26/76, *Metro–Saba*, (1977) ECR I-1875, §§ 17–21. See also Case 27/76, *United Brands v. Commission*, (1978) ECR 207, at § 17.

[22] Deduced from Court of Justice rulings in well-known cases, the *Metro–Saba* case of 1977 (cit. *supra*), the *Hoffman–La Roche* case of 1979 (C-85/76, (1979) ECR 461), the *Akzo* case of 1991 (C-62/86, (1991) ECR I-3359), from Commission decisions in the fields of concentrations, and from regulatory legislation (art. 2 1. b) Reg. 4064/89).

This has been defined by case law of the Court of Justice and by the Commission Notice on the definition of the relevant market for the purpose of EC competition law,[23] whether in terms of products or services (*relevant product* market), or geographical extent (*relevant geographic market*), or time dimension (*relevant market in time*):

> "A relevant product market comprises all those products and/or services which are regarded as interchangeable or substitutable by the consumer, by reason of the products' characteristics, their prices and their intended use."[24]

> "The relevant geographic market comprises the area in which the undertakings concerned are involved in the supply and demand of products or services, in which the conditions of competition are sufficiently homogeneous and which can be distinguished from neighbouring areas because the conditions of competition are appreciably different in those areas."[25]

> "The different time horizon considered in each case might lead to the result that different geographic markets are defined for the same products depending on whether the Commission is examining a change in the structure of supply, such as a concentration or a cooperative joint venture, or issues relating to certain past behaviour."[26]

Regarding the concept of abuse, here too the Treaty avoids declarations and prefers rather to provide a non-exhaustive list of examples of cases which could include the phenomenon in question. Such abuse may, in particular, consist in:

- Directly or indirectly imposing unfair purchase or selling prices or other unfair trading conditions.
- Limiting production, markets, or technical development to the prejudice of consumers.
- Applying dissimilar conditions to equivalent transactions with other trading parties, thereby placing them at a competitive disadvantage.
- Making the conclusion of contracts subject to acceptance by the other parties of supplementary obligations which, by their nature or according to commercial usage, have no connection with the subject of such contracts (art. 82 [2]).

---

[23] O.J., C-372/5, 12/09/1997.

[24] Commission Notice cit. *supra*.

[25] Commission Notice cit. *supra*.

[26] Commission Notice cit. *supra*.

By way of example, we shall cite some of the examples of the conduct of undertakings in a dominant position, most frequently held to be abusive by the Commission, which have been prohibited (so called *exploitative conduct* and *anti-competitive conduct*):

- Binding exclusive supply agreements: these occur when the dominant undertaking expressly obliges the distributors to obtain their entire requirement from itself.
- Incentives for exclusive supply: these are not expressly imposed, as in the preceding case, but may be formulated in the such a way (for example, annual bonuses on acquisitions or promotional offers to supply on advantageous conditions) as to force the supplier not to seek out competitors.
- The loyalty discount clause: if the client–company goes to another undertaking, even if only for a small order, it loses the whole discount which it had earned from the supply-company. Besides ensuring the loyalty of the other party, the dominant undertaking may also impose a price-rise on the distributor, assuring itself a percentage of the profit margin which the other party might have expected.
- The alignment clause: the client–company may go to the competitor whenever it likes, but must give reasons for its choice, on pain of a fine or other sanctions.

In all these examples, the undertakings put in place acts which are included in the range of normal commercial activity. They are only prohibited if they are put in place by an undertaking in a dominant position, and where prejudice results to trade among Member States.

Finally, as far as the last requirement of prejudice to trade among Member States is concerned, the Commission and the Court hold that this occurs when, voluntarily or not (hence there is no requirement of intention), an undertaking creates a situation where, objectively, it is difficult for other companies to enter the market or to maintain their own position in that market.

In the Decision of *Tetra Pak* of July 26th 1988,[27] the Commission held that "Tetra abused its dominant position by the acquisition of exclusive license which had the effect of strengthening its already dominant position, further weakening existing competition and rendering even more difficult the entry of any new competition."

The Court of First instance, in the following *Tetra Pak* case, where Tetra Pak claimed that the Court should annul the Commission's deci-

---

[27] O.J., 1988, L 272, p. 27. Point 60 of the Decision.

sion of July 26th 1988 relating to a proceeding under arts. 85 and 86 of the EEC Treaty, held that "the mere fact that an undertaking in a dominant position acquires an exclusive patent license does not per se constitute abuse within the meaning of Article 86 of the Treaty. For the purpose of applying Article 86, the circumstances surrounding the acquisition, and in particular its effects on the structure of competition in the relevant market, must be taken into account. The acquisition by an undertaking in a dominant position of an exclusive patent license for a new industrial process constitutes an abuse of a dominant position where it has the effect of strengthening the undertakings already very considerable dominance of a market where very little competition is found and of preventing, or at least considerably delaying, the entry of a new competitor into that market, since it has the practical effect of precluding all competition in the relevant market."[28]

Previously, in the case of *Continental Can* of February 21st 1973[29] the Court of Justice had held that the fact of reinforcing a dominant position to the point of creating such a position of superiority that every chance of competition by other companies was hindered, constituted an abuse under (former) art. 86 TEC.

The abuse of *economic dependence* as such is not prohibited by the Treaty. However, the existence of a relationship of economic dependence between suppliers or customers of a company and the company itself may indicate that the undertaking is in a dominant position and so is subject to art. 82 TEC.

No exemptions to the abuse of dominant position can be countenanced, either on an individual or block basis; however, the undertakings may request a specific *negative clearance* (now *finding of inapplicability,* under art. 10 (2), Reg. 1/2003), regarding the lack of incompatibility of their conduct with art. 82 TEC.

## 8. Article 87 TEC: State Aid

The third case to be considered harmful to competition and provided for in the Treaty of Rome is that of State aid for undertakings: "Save as otherwise provided in this Treaty, any aid granted by a Member State or through State resources in any form whatsoever which distorts or threatens to distort competition by favoring certain undertakings or the pro-

---

[28] Case T-51/89, Judgment of the Court of First Instance of July 10th 1990, *Tetra Pak Rausing SA v Commission of the European Communities*, (1990), ECR II-309, § 1.

[29] Case C-6/72, *Europemballage and Continental Can v. Commission*, (1973), ECR 215.

duction of certain goods shall, insofar as it affects trade between Member States, be incompatible with the common market" (art. 87 (1), *ex* art. 92, TEC).

The aid in question may take many varied forms: free subsidies, low-interest loans, low or zero tax arrangements, deferment of tax or social security contributions, grants of land or buildings at below market price, export assistance, advertising campaigns which favor certain manufacturers, and so on.

More generally, aid which is incompatible with the common market is considered to consist in any State intervention which, under various guises, may relieve the burdens which normally fall on a company's balance sheet, involving at the same time, a reduction in payments to the Treasury. Substantially, it concerns easy terms offered by the State to its own national undertakings which distort competition in the common market, favoring national companies over foreign competition.

Some examples are supplied by rulings of the European courts, the Court of Justice and Court of First Instance:

> ECJ (Sixth Chamber), June 29th 1999, C-256/97, ***Déménagements-Manutention Transport SA (DMT),*** (1999) ECR I-3913: ***cf.* the operative part of the ruling**: "Payment facilities in respect of social security contributions granted in a discretionary manner to an undertaking by the body responsible for collecting such contributions constitute State aid for the purposes of Article 92 (1) of the EC Treaty (now, after amendment, Article 87 (1) EC) if, having regard to the size of the economic advantage so conferred, the undertaking would manifestly have been unable to obtain comparable facilities from a private creditor in the same situation vis-à-vis that undertaking as the collecting body."

> ECJ, June 17th 1999, C-295/97, ***Piaggio SpA v. Ifitalia & Ministero della Difesa,*** ECR I-3735: ***cf.* the operative part of the ruling**: "Application to an undertaking of a system of the kind introduced by Italian Law No 95/79 of April 3th 1979, and derogating from the rules of ordinary law relating to insolvency, is to be regarded as giving rise to the grant of State aid, within the meaning of Article 92 (1) of the Treaty, where it is established that the undertaking has been permitted to continue trading in circumstances in which it would not have been permitted to do so if the rules of ordinary law relating to insolvency had been applied, or has enjoyed one or more advantages, such as a State guarantee, a reduced rate of tax, exemption from the obligation to pay fines and other pecuniary penalties or de facto waiver of public debts wholly or in part, which could not have been claimed by another

insolvent undertaking under the application of the rules of ordinary law relating to insolvency (…).”

ECJ, May 19th 1999, C-6/97, ***Italian Government v. Commission,* ECR I-2981: *cf.* §§ 1–2 of the ruling:** “(§ **1**) The concept of aid within the meaning of Article 92 (1) of the Treaty (now, after amendment, Article 87 (1) EC) embraces not only positive benefits, such as subsidies, but also measures which, in various forms, mitigate the charges which are normally included in the budget of an undertaking and which, therefore, without being subsidies in the strict sense of the word, are similar in character and have the same effect. A measure whereby the public authorities grant to certain undertakings a tax exemption which, although not involving a transfer of State resources, places the persons to whom the exemption applies in a more favourable financial position than other taxpayers constitutes State aid within the meaning of Article 92 (1) of the Treaty. (§ **2**) A tax credit scheme for the benefit of road hauliers from a particular Member State has adverse effects on their competitors—namely road hauliers established in other Member States, whether operating on their own account or for hire or reward—in so far as, even if the legislation of the Member State concerned provides for the latter to receive compensatory payments, they cannot, in the absence of any provisions laying down detailed rules for granting those payments, usefully avail themselves of the right to claim them.”

Court of First Instance, April 30th 1998, T-214/95, ***Vlaams Gewest* v. *Commission,*** ECR II-717: “(§ **10**) The relatively small amount of State aid or the relatively small size of the undertaking which receives it does not as such exclude the possibility that intra-Community trade might be affected. Even aid of a relatively small amount is liable to affect trade between Member States where there is strong competition in the sector in which the recipient operates. When State financial aid or aid from State resources strengthens the position of an undertaking compared with other undertakings competing in intra-Community trade, the latter must be regarded as affected by that aid. That is particularly so where the aid benefits an airline which is geared to international trade, since it provides air transport between towns situated in different Member States and competes with airlines established in other Member States, and the aid is designed to facilitate the development and operation of European routes so that its potential to affect trade between Member States is increased.”

Court of First Instance, April 30th 1998, T-16/96, ***Cityflyer Express ltd.* v. *Commission,*** ECR II-757: “(§ **5**) In order to deter-

> mine whether financial assistance granted by a Member State to an undertaking has the character of State aid, the relevant criterion is whether the undertaking receiving the aid could have obtained the amounts in question on the capital market. In particular, the relevant question is whether a private investor would have entered into the transaction in question on the same terms and, if not, on which terms he could have entered into the transaction. In the case of a loan granted at a preferential rate, the Commission may rightly classify as aid incompatible with the common market the difference between the interest which would have been paid at the market rate and the interest actually paid, and not the sum lent. The private investor test also enables the Commission to determine the measures to be taken under Article 93 (2) of the Treaty in order to remove any distortions of competition which are found and to restore the situation prevailing prior to payment of the unlawful aid, having due regard to the principle of proportionality (...)."

It should be added that, in this particular context, the national courts do not always express themselves in conformity with Community case law. Not infrequently the Italian Supreme Court, for example, justifies financial concessions on the grounds of "collective needs," even though this harms free competition.

> See *Corte Cassazione*, ruling no. 5087 of 2000; in the case of *Fallimento Traghetti Mediterraneo S.p.a v. Tirrenia di Navigazione S.p.a e il Ministero dei Trasporti*. The latter were held guilty of having received and conceded state aid on the basis of which it was possible to offer low tariffs on the shipping routes between Sicily, Sardinia, and the Italian mainland. According to the Supreme Court, state aid, prohibited as being a technique which distorts competition, may be compatible with the market depending on the case, when indeed free competition has to be balanced in favor of satisfying certain collective needs. Thus the Italian Court of last resort in private law matters has held such aid to be completely legitimate, denying that the issue should be referred to the Court of Justice.

What is more, the phenomenon of state aid, which occurs frequently in every country, is extremely complex and beset with delicate issues which involve the relationships between the States and national companies. It therefore concerns a problem which would have to be resolved at the political level, before the legal one.

At any rate, there is not a complete prohibition under Community legislation on state aid to undertakings, but it is subject to a series of checks and limitations.

In fact, all new state aid or new systems for aid to companies must be previously notified by member States to the Commission, so that this body can evaluate its compatibility with the competition rules and in this way authorize it. Special conditions, representing a greater degree of tolerance with regard to the prohibitions laid down in art. 87 TEC, are allowed in the case of aid in the areas of agriculture (art. 36 TEC, *ex* art. 42), transport (art. 73 TEC, *ex* art. 77), national security (art. 296 TEC, *ex* art. 223), environmental protection, and education.

The fact remains that under art. 88 (*ex* art. 93) TEC, whenever a State intends to provide certain sorts of aid for its own undertakings (or modify that already in existence or authorized), it must notify the grant (or the grant proposal) to the Commission to obtain authorization. Where the Commission ascertains the existence of aid which is not compatible with the common market, it will invite the Member State not to adopt the aid provision, or to revoke it if it has already been adopted; in this case the Commission may also order the complete or partial recovery of the incompatible and unlawfully provided aid. If the State fails to comply, the Commission (and any other Member State) can apply to the Court of Justice to prosecute the State for non-compliance.

Aid is considered '*incompatible*' if it involves distortion to competition in the context of the single market; it is considered '*unlawful*' when it has not been the subject of prior communication to the Commission and obtained its approval; it is considered '*abusive*' when it is used in another way than that authorized or established by the Commission.

An appeal lies to the Court of Justice or the Court of First Instance against Commission decisions which declare the aid to be incompatible, unlawful or abusive, either by the State or the undertaking which has received the aid declared unlawful. Where the Commission has declared aid to be unlawful, the prohibition has direct effect, in the sense that interested parties may challenge the grant of state aid before any national judge. On the other hand, the other States, as well as the undertakings which are the competitors of those benefiting from the grant of aid, may appeal against a Commission decision declaring aid to be compatible.

Moreover, **art. 88 (1) TEC** provides that "The Commission (...) shall keep under constant review all systems of aid existing in those States, with the aim of proposing to the latter any appropriate measures required by the progressive development or by the functioning of the common market."

Existing aid means: *a)* that which has already been authorized by the Commission; *b)* that which was already in place before the coming into force of the EEC Treaty or before the State joined the EC; *c)* that in respect of which the prescribed ten-year period provided by art. 15 of the Council procedure Regulation no. 659/99[30] on the subject of state aid has expired.

Confirmation of the fact that the Community antitrust model is based on the prohibition principle is also to be found in the rules governing State aid, since the format of the law indicates the various exceptions to the general prohibition rule.

As art. 87 (1) TEC affirms, aid is prohibited only in so far as it impinges on *trade between Member States*. However, contrary to what one might suppose, for this to happen it is not necessary that the undertaking to which aid is given also operates outside the national market.

In fact, according to the Commission, aid may have an effect on trade between Member States even if the beneficiary undertaking operates exclusively within one State, and even if it does so exclusively in a local, regional, or provincial context. What counts is to establish whether that particular market, limited and circumscribed as to geographical extent, may be attractive to undertakings from other countries as well, who may find it economic or be interested in supplying their own services or selling their own products there. And it is not even necessary for there actually to be other firms coming from other states of the Community; it is enough that the possibility exists for other Community undertakings to come and operate in that particular territory, in order to make aid in favor of a national undertaking be treated as capable of impinging on trade between member States.

According to art. 87 TEC, State aid must be considered to be incompatible when it *distorts or threatens to distort* competition. It is not thereby necessary that the aid should actually have distorted competition, it is sufficient to show its harmful potential. The expression "distort competition" is open to many interpretations. However, according to a respected opinion, it is thought that it is in the very nature of State aid to distort competition: any economic support in favor of one undertaking and not in favor of all the other competitors, self-evidently distorts or risks distorting competition. Given that competitiveness is based on the criteria of the organizational capacity of the entrepreneur and the efficiency of the organization, any external measure which favors one company over another spoils the rules of the game.

[30] O.J., L 83/1 03/27/1999.

Finally, art. 87 (2) and (3) TEC distinguishes two situations.

Paragraph 2, art. 87, indicates three categories of aid which are always compatible with the common market, in the sense that there is no room for discretionary evaluation by the Community authorities:

- Aid having a social character, granted to individual consumers, provided that such aid is granted without discrimination related to the origin of the products concerned.
- Aid to make good the damage caused by natural disasters or exceptional occurrences.
- Aid granted to the economy of certain areas of the Federal Republic of Germany affected by the division of Germany, insofar as such aid is required in order to compensate for the economic disadvantages caused by that division.

The first hypothesis for example, permits the State to intervene by giving incentives for the consumption of certain types of goods; the second is obviously exceptional; finally, the third hypothesis is specifically addressed to post-war Germany, but today, following reunification, it could regain its strength.

Paragraph 3, art. 87, on the other hand, indicates five categories of aid which may be declared compatible by the Community authorities:

- Aid to promote the economic development of areas where the standard of living is abnormally low or where there is serious underemployment.
- Aid to promote the execution of an important project of common European interest or to remedy a serious disturbance in the economy of a Member State.
- Aid to facilitate the development of certain economic activities or of certain economic areas, where such aid does not adversely affect trading conditions to an extent contrary to the common interest.
- Aid to promote culture and heritage conservation where such aid does not affect trading conditions and competition in the Community to an extent that is contrary to the common interest.
- Such other categories of aid as may be specified by decision of the Council acting by a qualified majority on a proposal from the Commission.

The natural destination for Community sanctions, provided by art. 88 TEC, is the State which has behaved in an anti-competitive way. However, this apparently obvious solution conceals a problem of no little account, namely, what is to become of the aid already received by the undertakings. Reasons of justice make one conclude that it would always be necessary to force the State to recover the unjustifiably granted aid. However, the political and economic consequences deriving from the forced restitution of the subsidies which have been spent cannot be ignored. It is sufficient to recall the problems encountered in the payment of the fines on companies which went beyond the so-called 'milk quotas,' and all the argument which that provoked over recent years.

It is for this reason that the Commission has left a wide margin of discretion to the States.

The Council has, under Regulation no. 994/98 of May 7th 1998,[31] issued a series of rules regarding the application of arts. 87 and 88 TEC to certain categories of horizontal State aid; amongst these, provision is made for the Commission to remove the necessity of prior notification from some categories of aid.

On January 12th 2001 the Commission issued the first three regulations to be applied regarding the area of law just mentioned. These are Regulation no. 68/2001, concerning aid for training,[32] Regulation no. 69/2001, concerning aid of minor importance (*de minimis*),[33] and Regulation no. 70/2001, concerning aid for small and medium enterprises,[34] so defined on the basis of criteria set out in the Recommendation of April 3rd 1996, no. 96/280/CE. Regulation no. 2204/2002, of December 12th 2002 on the application of Articles 87 and 88 TEC to State aid for employment[35] followed on from these. The aim of the Regulation is to exempt from the notification requirement State aid for job creation and aid to promote the recruitment of disadvantaged and disabled workers. Other types of employment aid are not prohibited, but they must be notified to the Commission in advance. In accordance with Article 87 (1) TEC, aid exempted by the Regulation must have as its object and effect the promotion of employment, while leaving trade unaffected. Export aid is not covered by the Regulation.

[31] O.J., L 142, 05/14/1998, p. 1.

[32] O.J., L 10, 01/13/2001, p. 20.

[33] O.J., L 10, 01/13/2001, p. 30. In principle, apart from some activity and production under art. 1, aid which does not exceed 100,000 Euro per undertaking over three years, need not be notified.

[34] O.J., L 10, 01/13/2001, p. 33. The aid in question is that for investment in material and non-material assets, so long as they do not exceed the sum, respectively, of 15% (for small enterprises) and 7.5% (for medium enterprises), of the investment sum.

[35] O.J., L 337, 12/13/2002.

## 9. Community Regulations on Concentrations

The last big issue to do with competition governed by Community law concerns concentrations. This term means the merger of two or more undertakings, or the acquisition by one undertaking of control of one or more undertakings.

Such operations are not prohibited *per se*, indeed they are encouraged, since they allow the companies to reinforce their economic position and to increase their capacity to confront competition coming from huge industrial groups outside the Community, such as those in Japan or the United States.

These operations lead, in any case, to a decrease in the number of companies in the market, and become incompatible with the common market when they threaten its balance by distorting competition.

Mergers and acquisitions were not expressly governed at Community level until 1989, and no Treaty provisions, regulations, or directives existed on the subject. This did not prevent the Commission from applying the rules of arts. 85 and 86 (now arts. 81 and 82) TEC to mergers and acquisitions, declaring merger agreements void or seeking to identify a situation of abuse of dominant position in the merger operation.

The forced application of legislation which had not been specifically developed for mergers and acquisitions, implied a series of difficulties. First of these was a consequence of the concentration that such rules only allowed the Commission to intervene after the fact, when the agreement had already been made, or the abuse had manifested itself, and could not be used in a preventative way.

Council Regulation no. 4064/89 of December 21st 1989 on the control of concentrations between undertakings,[36] better known as the *Concentration Control Regulation* was inserted into this context, so avoiding the technical difficulties set out above, by providing for the necessity of a prior intervention by the controlling authorities, before the acquisition became effective.

> **Art. 3 (1), Reg. 4064/89.** "A concentration shall be deemed to arise where: (a) two or more previously independent undertakings merge, or (b) one or more persons already controlling at least one undertaking, or one or more undertakings acquire, whether by purchase of securities or assets, by contract or by any other means, direct or indirect control of the whole or parts of one or more other undertakings."

[36] O.J., L 395/1, 12/30/1989, (as corrected in O.J., L 257/14, 09/21/1990).

The aversion felt by some Member States in the face of this systematic meddling by Community authorities in the financial and economic life of national companies was one of the main reasons for the delay, thirty years after the approval of the Treaty of Rome, in filling the legislative gap in this area. The difficulties met in the approval phase of Regulation 4064/89 on concentrations were obvious in art. 9, which contained the so-called 'German clause,' a mechanism by which the authorities in the Member States had the opportunity, in certain cases, to involve themselves in merger operations which should really have fallen within the sphere of competence of the Community, and in art. 22, containing the 'Dutch clause,' which provided for the opposite possibility, by which the States could call upon the Commission to examine a merger proposal which had no Community dimension at all.

In particular, the thing that fixed the determined opposition to the adoption of this Regulation was the compulsory provision, for every undertaking taking part in mergers, to give prior notification to the Commission, both of their intention to proceed with a merger and the terms of the relevant agreement.

The Member States' veto of the compulsory notification of mergers was removed only when a compromise was reached by which the threshold of Community interest was defined, which in turn determines the Community dimension of the phenomenon. For operations which exceeded the minimum threshold, the competence and control of the Commission was envisaged, whereas for those which remained below the threshold, competence was conferred on the State authorities.

The *Community threshold of interest* consisted of two elements.

The first referred to the combined aggregate worldwide turnover of all interested undertakings, which had to exceed the sum of 5 billion ECU.

The second referred to the aggregate Community-wide turnover of at least two of the undertakings participating in the operation, which had to supersede 250 million ECU, unless each of the undertakings concerned achieved more than two-thirds of its aggregate Community-wide turnover within one and the same Member State.

These minimum thresholds should have been reviewed and lowered before the December of the fourth year of the Regulation coming into force (art. 1 (3), Reg. 4064/89), that is before 1993, with the aim of increasing the Community's competence and of placing a greater number of merger operations under its control. However, the failure to reach agreement by Member States prolonged the timetable for review.

It was only on June 30th 1997 that the Council adopted Regulation

1310/97,[37] which amended the preceding Reg. 4064/89. However, apart from lowering the threshold of Community interest, the Regulation has introduced new weighting elements which limit in concrete terms the Commission's competence.

The new Regulation has left unaltered the former thresholds provided under Reg. 4064/89, and has introduced a new provision which widens the ambit of the Commission's competence, as follows: "(…) a concentration that does not meet the thresholds laid down in paragraph 2 has a Community dimension where: (a) the combined aggregate worldwide turnover of all the undertakings concerned is more than ECU 2,500 million; (b) in each of at least three Member States, the combined aggregate turnover of all the undertakings concerned is more than ECU 100 million; (c) in each of at least three Member States included for the purpose of point (b), the aggregate turnover of each of at least two of the undertakings concerned is more than ECU 25 million; and (d) the aggregate Community-wide turnover of each of at least two of the undertakings concerned is more than ECU 100 million; unless each of the undertakings concerned achieves more than two-thirds of its aggregate Community-wide turnover within one and the same Member State (art. 1 (3) Reg. 1310/97)."

The fact remains that in all other cases, that is when the thresholds provided by the two Regulations are not reached and, therefore, the concentration does not have a Community dimension, the Member States' authorities will have jurisdiction, and will be able to apply their own competition rules.

This solution, in harmony with the subsidiarity principle,[38] has uncovered a series of concentrations which are of purely 'national' interest, attributable to the lack of law which typified the legal systems of some States in this field, amongst which, for example, is Italy.

Besides the minimum thresholds, which serve to identify the Community dimension of concentrations, other relevant aspects of the new Community discipline concern the definition of *control*.

Reg. 4064/89, in defining concentrations, indirectly supplied the concept of control which one undertaking exercises over another, a concept which has had much importance in the context of the analogous situation in the national legal systems:

---

[37] O.J., L 180, 07/19/1997, p. 1, *corrigendum* in O.J., L 40/17, 02/13/1998. The Regulation came into force on March 1st 1998, the date that the Commission adopted the new Implementing Regulation no. 447/98 (O.J., L 61/23, 1998) replacing the Commission Regulation no. 3384/94 of December 21st 1989.

[38] See chapter IV, in the first volume of this *Guide, A Commom Law for Europe.*

> **Art. 3 (3), Reg. 4064/89:** "(…) control shall be constituted by rights, contracts or any other means which, either separately or in combination and having regard to the considerations of fact or law involved, confer the possibility of exercising decisive influence on an undertaking, in particular by: (a) ownership or the right to use all or part of the assets of an undertaking; (b) rights or contracts which confer decisive influence on the composition, voting or decisions of the organs of an undertaking."

It was the Commission, with its Notice of 1998[39] on the concept of concentration under Regulation no. 4064/89, which definitively clarified what was meant by concentration and the acquisition of control.

A merger arises where undertakings cease to exist as separate legal entities (merger in the legal sense) or where a single economic unit is created (merger in the economic sense), e.g. by the creation of a common economic management. The different forms of control that may occur are sole control, joint control, control by a single shareholder on the basis of veto rights, and changes in the structure of control.

Thus there may be a concentration when two undertakings acquire joint control of another company: typically this occurs when a joint venture is established. However, only the so-called 'full function' joint venture qualifies as a concentration.

> **C.f. Art. 3(2), Reg. 4064/89**: "The creation of a joint venture performing on a lasting basis all the functions of an autonomous economic entity, shall constitute a concentration within the meaning of paragraph 1 (b)."

The other important aspect of the new Reg. 1310/1997 is the fact that the system is so structured as to suppress incompatible concentrations in advance, rather than later. Indeed, undertakings which intend to proceed with a merger are obliged to *notify* such an operation immediately to the Commission.

> **C.f. Art. 4(1), Reg. 4064/89**: "Concentrations with a Community dimension defined in this Regulation shall be notified to the Commission not more than one week after the conclusion of the agreement, or the announcement of the public bid, or the acquisition of a controlling interest. That week shall begin when the first of those events occurs."

---

[39] O.J., C 66/5, 1998.

In the meantime, the effectiveness of the operation remains in suspense until such time as the Commission finishes the examination procedure.

Fines and penalties for default are provided for in the following cases:

- Failure to notify the operation to the Commission.
- Where the validity of the operation has been suspended by the Commission and such suspension has been violated by the undertaking.
- Failure to observe the Commission's directions and requests.

Concentration operations, since they are judged to be incompatible with the market and competitiveness, cannot partake in the exemptions scheme.

The enlargement of the European Union to twenty-five States, the new 'European Company' and 'European Cooperative' entities, which should encourage trans-national collaboration between enterprises, the recent draft Directive on cross-border mergers, the completion of the internal market and of economic and monetary union, and the lowering of international barriers to trade and investment will continue to result in major corporate reorganizations, particularly in the form of concentrations.

The prospect itself of a huge increase in such operations by business enterprises led the Commission to fine-tune the system set out in Reg. 4064/89 (as amended), to make it more efficient and speed up the procedure. Hence Regulation no. 139/2004 on the control of concentrations between undertakings (the EC Merger Regulation)[40] was approved by the Council on January 20th 2004; this repealed and replaced the 1989 Regulation with effect from May 1st 2004 (the date of entry for the ten new European Union States).

The new Regulation, while maintaining the structure of the previous legislation, has introduced some changes into the Community system for controlling mergers. Amongst these, certainly the most important is the one concerning the concept of a *merger* which is incompatible with the common market.

Indeed, if the previous 1989 Regulation turned attention on those operations which created or reinforced a dominant position (art. 2 (3) Reg. 4064/89), the new 2004 Regulation instead highlights "concentrations which would significantly impede effective competition, in the common market or in a substantial part of it, in particular as a result of the creation or strengthening of a dominant position" (art. 2 (3) Reg. 139/2004).

Therefore, a criterion has been opted for which is similar to the *Slc* test (*substantial lessening of competition*). This is typical of the US legal system, by which ascertaining any eventual damage to the market is the

---

[40] O.J., L 24, 01/29/2004.

preferred approach; whereas ascertaining dominant position (the so-called *dominance test*), while it appears among the control parameters to be utilized by the Commission, becomes simply a specified feature of the first ascertainment criterion.[41]

The 2004 Regulation, taking up the same formulation of the previous Regulation, also indirectly provides the definition of the *'control'* exercised by one enterprise over others (art. 3 (3), Reg. 139/2004), a concept which has had great importance within the national legal systems, influencing the interpreter's activity.

> **Art. 3(3) Reg. 139/2004:** "Control is acquired by persons or undertakings which: (a) are holders of the rights or entitled to rights under the contracts concerned; or (b) while not being holders of such rights or entitled to rights under such contracts, have the power to exercise the rights deriving therefrom."

An important aspect of the Community legislation is the fact that the system is so structured as to prevent incompatible concentrations rather than to suppress them later. Indeed, enterprises which intend to merge must give *prior notification* of such an intention to the Commission. In the meantime, the operation remains ineffective and in suspension until the Commission has finished examining the case. Unless that Member State disagrees, the Commission, where it considers that such a "distinct market" within a Member State exists, and that competition in that market may be "significantly affected" by the concentration, may decide to refer the whole or part of the case to the competent authorities of that Member State with a view to the application of that State's national competition law. In the 2004 Regulation, the period of one week "following the conclusion of the agreement, the announcement of the public bid, or the acquisition of a controlling interest" has been eliminated, to meet the request by business enterprises for greater flexibility.

## 10. Competition Law in the Member States

A distinction must firstly be made between the European States which boast a long tradition of applying competition rules (Germany, France, United Kingdom), and those which, although legal rules in the field

---

[41] It should be noted that this is a further important example of the circulation into the European legal system of models from outside its territory, and, most probably, from the supranational into the national systems in the future.

exist, do not have suitable mechanisms for the enforcement of competition rules and finally, those States for whom antitrust legislation has only recently been introduced.

German law traditionally distinguishes between activity which constitutes unfair competition and activity which limits competition. The distinction is reflected by two legislative provisions which govern this area, the Act Against Unfair Competition (*Gesetz gegen den unlauteren Wettbewerb*) and the Act Against Restraints of Competition (*Gesetz gegen Wettbewerbsbeschränkungen*), also known as the Antitrust Act. The latter was passed in 1958, but has been amended several times: the Sixth Amendment Act came into force on January 1st 1999 to rationalize the legal stratifications occurring as a result of the five previous reform initiatives and, finally, further to approximate German law to Community competition law.

It is interesting to note that German antitrust law, as distinct from what is to be seen in the legal systems of other States and the EC Treaty, provides a definition of *undertaking* (in German: *Unternehmen*). All individuals, associations and companies involved in commercial activity relating to the sale of goods or the setting-up and supply of services are undertakings. The intention to make a profit is not a pre-requisite of the German law. In this way architects, lawyers, engineers, physicists, mathematicians, and other professionals, along with scientific, artistic, or sporting organizations (including soccer clubs) constitute undertakings when they undertake commercial activity. Even public entities, such as the local authorities or the State(s), are considered as undertakings when they carry on commercial activity.

German rules regarding *agreements and concerted practices* fundamentally coincide with those under art. 81 TEC.

On the other hand, the rules on the *abuse of dominant position* are more detailed with respect to the rules under art. 82 TEC. Indeed, under German law we find various situations where a dominant position is presumed by law: an undertaking is presumed to have a dominant position if it has a market share of at least one third. Three or fewer undertakings with a combined market share of one half or more of the market, and five or fewer undertakings with a combined market share of two thirds or more of the market, are also presumed to have a dominant position. The presumption is rebuttable; the burden, however, is on the undertaking to prove to the contrary.

Other differences with respect to Community law are evident too, in relation to *exemptions*: German law does not have a system of group exemptions comparable to that of the Community. Concerning, for example, vertical agreements, to which a good part of the Community block exemptions apply, there is no general prohibition under German law and so there is no need for exemptions. Concerning horizontal agreements, on the other hand, they must be notified to the German controlling authorities, in order to be eligible for individual exemptions and to avoid the general prohibition under German antitrust law.

The Sixth Amendment Act of 1999 introduced significant changes, above all in the context of the control of *concentrations*. It should be noted, first and foremost, that the German concept of concentration differs noticeably from the corresponding concept under art. 3 (1) of Reg. 4064/1989. The rules regarding the control of concentrations apply to concentrations between undertakings including acquisitions of assets or shares, the formation of joint ventures and certain other transactions as defined in Section 37 of the Act, provided the worldwide and domestic turnover of the undertakings concerned exceeds the thresholds as defined in Section 35.

There are three institutions charged with ensuring that the law is correctly applied, known as Cartel Authorities: the Federal Cartel Office (*Bundeskartellamt*), an independent federal authority responsible for the application of the law;[42] the Federal Minister of Economics (*Bundesminister für Wirtschaft*), responsible for German competition policy direction; and the State Cartel Offices (*Landeskartellbehörden*), with limited responsibility for minor issues. The Monopoly Commission, (*Monopolkommission*), is a consultative institution, not directly involved with the application of the law. However, it participates in the development of German competition law and its interpretation: in fact every two years it has to give an opinion (*Hauptgutachten*) on the progress of the merger and takeover markets and the application of concentration control provisions.

British competition law underwent profound changes with the *Competition Act 1998*,[43] which introduced a regime modeled on the Community system as set out in arts. 81 and 82 TEC. The new Act repealed the previous legislation governing British competition law which was based on the Restrictive Trade Practices Acts 1976 and 1977 (the *RTPA*) and derivative legislation, the Resale Prices Act 1976 (the *RPA*), the Compe-

---

[42] It is made up of 10 Divisions, organized in bodies composed of a chairman and two associate members, each made up of lawyers and economists who work on a collegiate basis in industry-differentiated sectors.

[43] The Competition Act 1998, in force from March 1st 2000. *Cf.* the proposal for further amendment published in July 2001, by the UK Government: "White Paper—Productivity and Enterprise: a world class competition regime," available in internet at http://www.dti.gov.uk/ccp/topics2/ukcompref.htm.

tition Act 1980, and some clauses of the Fair Trading Act 1973 (the *FTA*), which, at least in part, are still in force today.

The Competition Act 1998, besides faithfully reproducing the contents of articles 81 and 82 TEC in the *prohibitions chapters* (Chapters I and II ), expressly sets out the procedure for notification of agreements and the conduct of undertakings to the regulatory authorities for the grant of exemptions or negative clearances; moreover the Act confers new powers of investigation and for application of the provisions on those authorities; finally, it provides for a new Appeals institution so that the parties may appeal against the rulings of the regulatory authorities under the new prohibitions.

The Fair Trading Act 1973 concerns the regulation of *concentrations* (or mergers, as they are known in British legal terminology) and the investigation of monopolies.

As regards the *institutions* involved in the monitoring and application of British competition rules, essentially there are three. First and foremost, the Secretary of State for Trade and Industry. This is the government department responsible for competition policy, which has several fundamental functions: it is responsible for the block exemptions under the Chapter I prohibitions; may modify certain exclusions from the Chapter I and II prohibitions; must approve the guidance on levels of fines and procedural rules made by the Director General of Fair Trading; may make regulations for the exercise of the concurrent powers of the Director General of Fair Trading and sectoral regulations; is responsible for the appointment of members of the Competition Commission, its Chairman, President, and Appeal Tribunal Chairmen, and for the Director General of Fair Trading (who may be removed only in cases of incapacity or misdemeanor).

The Competition Act 1998 also established the Competition Commission, the second fundamental institution for the protection of competition. It is an independent body, in which the British government may not interfere, although it is financed by public funds. The Commission's main task is to function as an Appeal Tribunal against the rulings of the Director General of Fair Trading. The latter body, set up by the 1998 Act, is supported by the Office of Fair Trading, which is the office which organizes the seven sectors of competition policy under its own surveillance, namely:

- Policy coordination.
- Mergers.
- Cartel investigations.
- Media, sport and information industries.
- Service industries.

– Basic industries, energy and vehicles.
– Consumer goods industries.

The Directorate General of Fair Trading is the body with the principal powers of investigation and application of the prohibitions set out in the 1998 Act; it has the task of providing advice to the Secretary of State for Trade and Industry in relation to block exemptions. Besides this, it has a special function regarding competition, being a recognized source of soft law, which is spread by means of publishing its own non-binding opinions (better known as *Guidelines*) addressed to institutions as well as the courts, with the aim of interpreting the Competition Act 1998.

In France, the competition legislation helped reconstruct the country's economy after the Second World War and was set up by the Ordinance of June 30th 1945, which introduced a regime of price regulation, followed by the Decree of August 9th 1953, which concerned agreements restricting competition. Political and economic conditions having changed, the subject was newly regulated by the Ordinance of December 1st 1986, followed by the implementing Decree of December 29th 1986.[44] The new rules regulate both *antitrust* activity in the true sense (restrictive practices, abuse of dominant position, mergers, and acquisitions), as well as *other activity* which could distort or otherwise harm free competition (such as below-price sales, rules on invoicing, transparency of the conditions of sale).

The Ordinance does not contain any definition of *undertaking*. Legal scholars, interpreting the general trend of case law on the point in a very shorthand way, have identified it (and consequently have defined the contextual limits for the application of the law), in the following way: an undertaking is any entity which carries on commercial activity with sufficient decision-making and managerial independence, whether a natural or legal person, or a combination of human and financial resources, without a separate legal personality.

The 1986 Ordinance also provides for the formation of an *independ-*

---

[44] Ordinance no. 86-1243 of December 1st 1986 and Decree no. 86-1309 of December 29th 1986, amended several times during the 90's. The French competition legislation was amended by the Act on New Economic Regulations (NER), [*Décret no. 2002-689 du 30 avril 2002 fixant les conditions d'application du livre IV du code de commerce relatif à la liberté des prix et de la concurrence, OJ 03/05/2002, p. 8055*], which entered into force on May 18th 2002. It substantially modified French merger control and introduced important changes to the procedures and penalties in cases of anticompetitive agreements and abuses of dominant positions before the French *Conseil de la Concurrence* (the Competition Council).

*ent administrative authority,* the Competition Council (*Conseil de la Concurrence*). This is composed of 17 members, of whom 8 have been past members of the *Conseil d'Etat* (the Supreme Court for Administrative Tribunals) or of the *Cour de Cassation* (the Supreme Court in civil law matters) or of every other lower court; 4 members are well-known experts for their distinction in economic or competition matters; 5 are entrepreneurs from the world of business, whose careers have excelled in the production, distribution, or manufacturing sectors.

The Competition Council has the following wide powers:

- Consultative: the Council may be called to give its opinion on the matter at the request of the Minister for the economy, to be consulted by local government and consumer organizations as well.
- Of investigation and opinion: parties in disagreement may appear before the Council and, if the ruling goes against them, may appeal to the first chamber of the Court of Appeal in Paris. The latter's judgments may be appealed, only on a point of law, in the commercial chamber of the French Supreme Court (*Cour de Cassation*).

The civil and commercial courts have concurrent jurisdiction with the Council in deciding on the practices which fall within the scope of Title III of the Ordinance (agreements and the abuse of dominant position); moreover, they have exclusive jurisdiction in the areas governed by Title IV (commercial transparency); finally, the courts may set sums by way of compensation for the victims of anti-competitive conduct.

Among Member States which, while having legislation in this area of law, lack suitable methods for the enforcement of competition rules, one can take the example of Greece. In 1977 the Greek Parliament adopted Act no. 703 on the control of monopolies and oligopolies and the protection of free competition.[45] Previously there only existed a provision to prevent unfair competition, modeled on the French rule on *concurrence déloyale*. The reason which induced Greece to legislate all at once in the area of competition was essentially a political one: in order to join the EEC it was indispensable to adopt and assimilate the *acquis communautaire,* which also includes competition rules.

The 1977 Act is still in force today, although amended several times, most recently by Act no. 2837/2000.[46] The 2000 Act introduced many changes to the Greek competition rules system, taking into account above all the experience and practice of the Greek Competition Commission

[45] Published in the Government Gazette, Vol. A, no. 278, 09/26/1977, and came into force from 03/27/1978.

[46] Published in the Government Gazette, Vol. A, no. 178, 03/08/2000.

gained over the preceding five years (the Commission already existed, but was reconstituted in 1995[47] and given new powers, which follow those of the European Commission).

Let us turn finally to the third set of Member States, those in which competition law has only recently been introduced, at a distance of some forty years from the ratification of the Treaty of Rome and about a century after the Sherman Act.

By subscribing to the Single European Act, all the Member States had to engage in the removal of physical, fiscal, and technical barriers, which gave renewed impulse to the introduction of new rules for the protection of competition. Let us recall the case of Belgium, for example, where the Act on the protection of economic competition came into force on April 1st 1993.[48] This represents a novelty for the Belgian legal system, in that this act introduces, for the first time, a complete set of provisions on competition. The 1999[49] amendments remedied the inadequate functioning of the regulatory authorities, which were concerned almost exclusively with mergers, omitting the area of restrictive practices and agreements.

In the Netherlands, competition rules are mainly to be found in the *Mededingingswet*, the Competition Act of January 1st 1998,[50] which transposed *verbatim* the contents of arts. 81, 82, and 86 TEC and the rules relating to block exemptions. The enforcement of the rules is under the control of the Competition Authority (*Nederlandse mededingingsautoriteit or NMa*), which is equipped to and does act in the same way as the European Commission in competition cases. The *NMa* is organized in 4 departments:

- Investigation, control and exemptions.
- Concentration control.
- Decisions, administrative appeals, and appeals.
- Support services. The *NMa* publishes an Annual Report along the lines of the one produced by the European Commission, with the complete transcript of the relevant judicial decisions.

The Competition Authority, as distinct from the authorities in other

---

47 Act 2296/1995, published in the Government Gazette, Vol. A, no. 43, 02/24/1995.

48 Act of August 5th 1991, *Belgisch Staatblad/Moniteur belge* (Belgian State Gazette), October 11th 1991, amended by two Acts of April 26th 1999 (Belgian State Gazette,April 27th 1999).

49 A consolidated version of the Competition Act has been published: Royal Decree of June 14th 1999, Belgian State Gazette, September 1st 1999.

50 Published in the *Staatsblad* (Statute Book), 1997, n. 242.

Member States which are independent of government, operates under the auspices of the Ministry of Economic Affairs; however, there is news of reform under way, by which it seems that the *NMa* is to be transformed into an independent administrative agency. The *NMa*'s decisions can be appealed in the first instance, to the District Court of Rotterdam, and in the second, to the Court of Appeal for Trade and Industry.

Italy harmonized national law with Community provisions by the Antitrust Act no. 287/90. Before 1990, draft legislation in the competition field followed fast upon one another. The debate began as soon as the Constitution of the Italian Republic of 1942 came into force, in the context of a deeply divided ideological climate, which had formed around the interpretation of some provisions of the Constitution regarding economic relations. Italian lawyers were divided over the role to be assigned to art. 41 of the Constitution which protects freedom of economic initiative, which, according to some, was a mere declaration of principle and to others laid down real obligations to be implemented by the legislature. But despite various draft laws and debates, competition law occupied a secondary place in Italian legal system up to the 1990s.

The 1942 Civil Code had some rules of reference on competition: art. 2105 *CC* prohibits an employee from competing with her/his own employer; art. 2125 *CC* defines the terms of post-contract agreements preventing competition (restraint of trade) between employer and employee; art. 2301 *CC* prohibits competition by a member of a partnership against the partnership itself; art. 2390 *CC* lays down the same prohibition for directors of a share company; art. 2557 *CC* prohibits competition on the part of the vendor of an undertaking and the purchaser of that undertaking, for a period of five years.

Notwithstanding the sometimes frenetic alterations which occurred in related disciplines, such as company law or intellectual property, the competition area remained unchanged.

Hence only articles 2595-2601 in Book V of the Civil Code presented any interesting analogies to the Community regime we considered above.

For example, art. 2595 *CC* establishes that competition "must take place in a way which does not damage national economic interests," thus affirming a principle which recalls the fundamental one underlying the Community legislation in this area. Article 2596 *CC*, which is concerned with defining some limits to restrictive competition agreements, recalls the essence of art. 81 (*ex* art. 85) TEC. Art. 2597 *CC* affirms, in the same way, that "whoever operates an undertaking under terms of legal monopoly, is obliged to contract with whomsoever requests the services offered by the undertaking, applying equality of treatment," in fact taking into consideration one of the many possible situations involving abuse of dominant position.

However, this clearly represents an inadequate basis of legislation to regulate so complex a sector as competition. For their part, Italian courts have never, either because of the technical complexity or the delicacy of the economic and social aspects which are involved, played a decisive part in proposing new models for competition rules, confining itself to "ordinary administration" of the now obsolete provisions of the Civil Code. This happened notwithstanding the experience of the Community and other systems, which could have supplied valid assistance in the formation of new competition rules.

It was in this context that the Competition and Fair Trading Act, better known as the Antitrust Act, (Italian: *Norme per la tutela della concorrenza e del mercato*) no. 287 of October 10th 1990, was passed.

This represents another macroscopic example of the *communitarization* of the law. In fact, the Italian legislature faithfully adopts the Community competition model. The important instances, from a substantive and procedural point of view, are precisely those to be found in the Community legal system. The actors change, obviously, but the structure and functions remain the same.

First and foremost, the terminology and contents of the Italian Act are identical to the respective Community provisions, in particular arts. 81 and 82 (*ex* arts. 85 and 86) TEC, as well as the mergers Regulation, 4064/1989.

Secondly, the Italian Act introduces the principle, signaling a fundamental shift in the national legal system, whereby a domestic provision can and must be interpreted according to criteria and categories of altogether another system. Article 1 (4) of the Act, in fact, affirms that "the interpretation of the law in the present Title shall be undertaken on the basis of the principles of the European Community legal system in the field of competition law."

This means that the authority of competition and fair trading, also known as the *Antitrust Authority* (Italian: *Autorità garante della concorrenza e del mercato),* to whom the task of applying the new provisions has been assigned, cannot exclude reference to Community judgments in this field, either by the Court of First Instance and the interpretative judgments of the Court of Justice. Thus Community case law and the practice of the Commission have formally and by express legislative provision become indispensable elements in the interpretation and application of provisions of a national law.

The Antitrust Authority is an independent authority which acts outside the power or influence of executive bodies (or the Government) and is subject only to the law. It presents notable similarities, in its role concerning anti-competitive activity, to the European Commission. Its structure is governed by the 1990 Act; it is a collegiate body constituted by a president and four members who hold office for a period of seven years with no possibility of a second term of office, chosen from among persons of proven independence, to be selected from judges in the Council of State (Italian: *Consiglio di Stato*), State Auditor's Court (Italian: *Corte dei Conti*) or the Supreme Court, permanent University professors in economic or legal fields, and persons from economic sectors who have an excellent track record of proven professionalism.

The Antitrust Authority may also grant exemptions in the same way as the Commission, derogating from the general provisions of the discipline. Moreover, it has increased its power with respect to the Commission, namely the ability to order the suspension of the undertaking's activity for up to thirty days, a sanction which may only be imposed when the undertaking fails to obey the Authority's instructions or abide by its prohibitions.

As distinct from the Commission, the Antitrust Authority may not impose emergency or preventative measures (such as obliging the parties to resume supply, or restoring a price-list) with the aim of forcing the parties to stop the anti-competitive conduct. According to Italian law, action of this kind may only be taken by judicial authorities, in particular by Court of Appeal judges with national jurisdiction.

As regards the jurisdiction of the courts, the law confers general and exclusive competence for identifying and punishing anti-competitive conduct, but actions for nullity and damages should be taken to the relevant Court of Appeal for the area. Appeals against the Authority's rulings should, on the other hand, be taken to the *TAR del Lazio* (Regional Administrative Tribunal) (Art. 33 (1), & (2), Act 287/90).

## 11. Competition Law in the CEECs

As we have seen, Community competition law has this special characteristic, that it possesses an international or *extra-territorial dimension*. This applies even when the anti-competitive conduct is not exhibited by undertakings with registered offices in one or more Member States, if such conduct affects the working of the common market.

From another and different point of view, the extra-territorial dimension means that the Community's competition rules have effect well beyond the common market as defined by the boundaries of the Member

States. In this second sense, we would like to shed some light on a two-fold phenomenon.

From one side, on the fact that Community competition law was the legal model which inspired the Central and Eastern European countries after the communist dogma of centralized planning was abandoned, at the beginning of the 90's, to regulate this field, (even though, in some cases, for example Poland and Bulgaria, the legislators availed themselves of advice supplied by the Antitrust Division of the US Department of State and the American Bar Association).

> During the communist era, some of these countries had anti-monopoly acts, some of which also contained rules preventing unfair competition: in Poland, the Act of January 1987, in force from January 1st 1988; in Hungary, Act no. IV of October 1984, in Yugoslavia the Act of May 1974.
>
> Before the communist era, therefore before the Second World War, some statutes governing cartels were in force in some East European systems. For instance, in Poland, Act no. 31 of March 1933 placed cartels under the Ministry for Industry and Commerce, and established a cartel Court, which had jurisdiction to hear cases in which cartels may be "against the public interest," that is, could cause harmful effects on prices, above all any unjustified rises. In Czechoslovakia too, Act no. 141 of 1933 regulated cartels and private monopolies, providing for their registration in the Cartel register (eliminated only in 1993) and suppressing abuses against the national interest. In Hungary, Act V of 1923 governed the area of unfair competition and Act XX of 1931 regulated cartel agreements, which were permitted as long as were not of an "abusive nature."

From another angle, on the fact (evident above all in the 'second generation' of competition rules put in place at the end of the decade of transformation of the centrally-planned economy) that the reception of the Community rules has had—as a consequence—the direct applicability of these rules, by the Courts and the Competition Authorities in the CEECs, even though the latter have just (or, in some cases, not yet) become members of the European Union.

The *'first generation' of competition laws* have been in force since early 1990. The Act on counteracting monopolistic practices, and the Act on the anti-monopoly court in Poland (1990), Act LXXXVI on the prohibition of unfair market practices in Hungary (1990), Act no. 15 on the reorganization of State economic units as autonomous management units and commercial companies (Chapter V—Association and Free Competition) in Romania (1990), the Act on protection of competition in Bulgaria (1991), the Act on competition and restriction of monopoly activity in Latvia (1991), the Competition Protection Act in the Czech Republic and the Slovak Republic (1991), amended in the Czech Republic by Act no. 286 on Economic Competition (1993) and replaced in Slovakia by Act no. 188 on Protection of Economic Competition (1994), the Competition Act in Lithuania (1992), the Competition Act in Slovenia (1993).[51]

The economic transformation and consequent legal reforms which the CEECs had to undergo concerned the privatization of the communist State enterprises, the distortion of the price system due to the planned economy, the elimination of large monopolies and the liberalization of the economy, in order to ensure the development of fair competition.

Precisely because the issues to be addressed concerning the economic transformation of these countries were the same, the 'first generation laws' had a very *similar structure*.

They were detailed and left much space for:

- Counteracting restrictive business practices and anti-competitive agreements between undertakings.
- Circumscribing the abusive conduct of undertakings in a dominant position by setting minimum thresholds with differing percentages, creating a presumption of dominance.
- Controlling privatizations, mergers, amalgamations, acquisitions, and organizational restructuring.

They did not, however, regulate State aid.

The objectives of these acts, therefore, were those which are usually cited as constituent elements of competition: to eliminate barriers artificially put up against the entry of new economic operators in the market and to ensure freedom of action to undertakings offering products and services on the market, to benefit freedom of choice for consumers.

Freedom of enterprise and private ownership became fundamental principles.

There were some *differences*, both concerning the legal model represented by the Community competition rules and among the various legal systems of the ex-communist bloc.

---

[51] Poland: Journal of Laws (*Dziennik Ustaw*) no. 14/1990, item 89, of 03/13/90 and *Dziennik Ustaw* no. 27/1990, item 157; Hungary: Journal of Laws (*Magyar Közlöny*) no. 121/1990; Bulgaria: Journal of Laws (*DV*) 39/1991; Lithuania: Act no. I-2878 of September 15th 1992 (translation available in *East European Business Law*, September 1993, 93-IX, p. 12); Latvia: Republic of Latvia Supreme Council and Government Bulletin, 1991, no. 51 and 1993, no. 16/17; Czech Republic and Slovakia: Bull. of Czechoslovak Law, 1991, no. 1-2, Act no. 63/1991 Coll.; Slovakia: Act no. 188/1994 Coll.; Slovenia: Official Gazette of the Republic of Slovenia no. 18/93 (translation available in *East European Business Law*, August 1993, 93-VIII, p. 46).

The *differences* concerned the *sectors* regulated by the acts: in Hungary and Bulgaria, for example, competition law was much concerned with unfair competition; as indeed it was in Romania, where the legislature later resolved to issue a separate act in this field, no. 11 of January 1991, a provision adopted in Poland, as well, the following year; another difference concerns the entities which must apply these rules: the first *ad hoc* agencies for the protection of competition are recent creations, namely the Competition Offices, which operated (and still operate) through the Competition Council or Competition Commission.

In some cases the *differences* concerned *substantive competition law*: for example, in Romania, as distinct from what is envisaged at Community level, there was no clear distinction between the regime governing agreements between undertakings and the abuse of dominant position; take the cases of Poland, the Czech Republic and Slovakia as other examples, where the legislation did not clearly distinguish between horizontal and vertical agreements, whereas in Hungary there were some specific provisions (§§14–18), which prohibited horizontal agreements and which seemed to take into account the directions expressed by the European Commission in its Communications. Other examples of diversity are to be found in the Polish act at art. 2 (6)–(7), which, distancing itself from the model provided by art. 86 (now art. 82) TEC, introduced a further distinction between undertakings "in a monopolistic position" and those occupying "a dominant position;" the same distinction could also be seen in the Bulgarian act at art. 3, as well as in the Czech and Slovak provisions. Another example of novel law-making was represented in the Slovak act, which, as distinct from what was envisaged by Community law whereby in certain cases individual exceptions are allowed, had provided for the so-called "automatic exception": according to this, agreements restricting competition are not banned if they satisfy certain criteria (the same criteria for the ex-"individual exception" under EU law).

Finally, another sign of diversity was represented by the fact that the Community concept of block exemptions was generally absent from all these acts.

In other cases, the *differences* concerned the *context of the application* of competition law: thus, the Romanian provisions, for example, applied only to State undertakings reorganized into independent units and commercial companies, and made no reference whatever to its applicability to private enterprise.

The principal problems with these competition rules were twofold: *implementation* and *enforcement*.

A prime reason for dissatisfaction was the absence of secondary-level regulation, i.e. through acts of the Council of Ministers or Competition

Agencies which would clarify the interpretational difficulties inevitably arising from the application of the principles and general regulations contained in the competition laws. A second shortcoming was the lack of recognition of the independence of the competition authorities, which depended on the political entities in any case, and the absence of powers of sanction which would have rendered their control effective. In some cases, the shortcoming was in the failure to establish such control authorities at all. A third reason for criticism derived from the lack of coordination between the competition rules and the provisions of the civil and/or commercial codes.

These 'first generation laws' were amended at various times during the 90's, in the course of a continuous process of harmonizing domestic law with Community law. These provisions were modified and integrated to satisfy the commitments undertaken by signing the Europe Agreements and then with the signing of the Accession Partnerships and the candidature for accession of the East European countries.[52]

Given that, as we have seen, the special characteristics of the Community, since its founding in the 50's, have been competition policy and competition rules, it may be said that these rules represent the indispensable technical apparatus for the entry of these countries into the Union's internal market. In this connection, some provisions contained in the "Title V" section of each Europe Agreement "on payments, capital, competition, and other economic provisions, approximation of laws," faithfully reproduced (not without gaps in some cases, however,) articles 85, 86, 92 (now 81, 82 e 87) TEC.

The provisions contained in the respective Europe Agreements had, as a common denominator, the approximation of legislation to the EC Treaty provisions and only to these, not to the entire *acquis communautaire*; in fact, the third area of Community competition law introduced by Reg. 4046/89 on the control of concentrations was outside the scope of the Europe Agreements.

These competition rules were commonly defined as "the major precondition" or "an important condition for the parties' economic integration into the Community."[53]

In every case, by express provision of the Europe Agreements, competition rules did not apply to agricultural products and fisheries.

The provision concerning the regulation and protection of competi-

---

[52] See chapter III, in the first volume of this *Guide, A Commom Law for Europe*.

[53] Compare on the one hand Hungary (art. 67) and Poland (art. 68), and on the other the Czech Republic (art. 69), the Slovak Republic (art. 69), Romania (art. 69), Bulgaria (art. 69), Estonia (art. 68), Latvia (art. 69), and Lithuania (art. 69).

tion had the same structure in all the Agreements, and the articles were respectively the following: Hungary (art. 62), Poland (art. 63), Czech Republic (art. 64), Slovak Republic (art. 64), Romania (art. 64), Bulgaria (art. 64), Estonia (art. 63), Latvia (art. 64), Lithuania (art. 64).

Each article consisted of a first paragraph which set out the limits for the correct functioning of the Europe Agreement: restrictive agreements and practices between undertakings, abuses of a dominant position in the Community or in the other Party territories as a whole or in a substantial part thereof, public aid which distorts competition by favoring certain undertakings or the production of certain goods. The second paragraph recalled arts. 85, 86, 92 (now 81, 82 e 87) TEC as guidelines for establishing possible violations. The third paragraph was certainly the one which raised most questions, for at least two reasons:

- In that it established that each candidate State should have adopted implementing rules compatible with Community rules and provides that each Association Council should have adopted the measures necessary to protect competition within three years of the coming into force of each Europe Agreement. The calculation of the time available to adopt the legislation in question was specified more comprehensively in each Agreement: also taking into account the Interim Agreements signed by all the States in question (time expired in December 1994 for Hungary, Poland, the Czech Republic, and the Slovak Republic, in December 1995 for Romania and Bulgaria, and in December 1997 for the three Baltic Republics).
- In that each Europe Agreement had a partially different paragraph formulation of the part which established what the applicable law was, until such time as the implementing rules were adopted: *a) international law*; according to Polish, Estonian, Latvian, and Lithuanian Agreements, the provisions contained in the Agreement on interpretation and application of Arts. VI, XVI and XXIII of the GATT (it should be emphasized that the three Baltic Republics have never participated in the GATT). On the other hand, the same provision was not to be found in the Agreements of the Czech Republic and the Slovak Republic, Romania, and Hungary which were, respectively, founder members of the GATT, a member since 1971 and a member since 1973; *b) internal law*; other Agreements referred explicitly to domestic law. These were the cases of the Czech Republic and the Slovak Republic, which, until they adopted the implementing rules in 1996, applied the provisions of the Competition Protection Act of January 30$^{th}$ 1991, and replaced in Slovakia in 1994 by the Act on Protection of Economic Competition. It was extraordinary that it was only these Agreements which referred to

domestic law, especially as these two Republics were not the first or at least not the only ones to have introduced competition rules in the early 1990's.

Although the temporary recourse to domestic competition law served, from one point of view, to fill the gaps left in the articles of the Europe Agreements,[54] from another it has caused divergent interpretation of the very competition rules contained in the Agreements, also caused by the fact that it was not possible for the CEECs' courts to obtain a hearing at the Court of Justice for a preliminary ruling on interpretation. On the other hand, the systems for dispute settlement contained in the Agreements (Hungary art. 107, Poland art. 105, Czech Republic art. 107, Slovak Republic art. 107, Romania art. 109, Bulgaria art. 108, Estonia art. 112, Latvia art. 113, Lithuania art. 114) did not represent a valid alternative able to ensure the uniform interpretation of the competition provisions.

In respecting the provisions of the Europe Agreements concerning competition, Poland, the Czech Republic, and Hungary adopted—between 1995 and 1996—the competition implementing rules which applied to all cases of interstate trade, either towards Member States or among the associated States. The new rules tended to fill possible gaps as well, introducing, for example, a formula which apparently allows the Commission to deal with Reg. 4046/89 cases.

> **Decision No 1/96** of the Association Council, between the European Communities and their association Member States, of the one part, and the Republic of Poland, of the other part, of 16/7/1996 adopting the implementing rules necessary for the application of Article 63 (1)(i), (1)(ii) and (2) of the Europe Agreement between the European Communities and their Member States, of the one part, and the Republic of Poland, of the other part, and the rules implementing Article 8 (1)(i), (1)(ii) and (2) of Protocol No. 2 on ECSC products to that Agreement.
>
> **Decision No 2/96** of the Association Council of November 6th 1996, between the European Communities and their association Member States, of the one part, and Hungary, of the other part, adopting the rules necessary for the implementation of Article 62 (1) (i), (1) (ii) and (2) of the Europe Agreement and the rules implementing Article 8 (1) (i), (1) (ii) and (2) of Protocol No. 2 on ECSC products to that Europe Agreement.

---

[54] These articles did not contain a sanction for incompatibility with the proper functioning of the Agreements, for example. The national courts established that any such sanction was that of nullity.

**Decision No 1/96** between the European Communities and their Member States, of the one part, and the Czech Republic, of the other part, of January 30th 1996 adopting the implementing rules for the application of the competition provisions referred to in Article 64 (1) (i), (1) (ii) and (2) of the Europe Agreement establishing an association between the European Communities and their Member States, of the one part, and the Czech Republic, of the other part, and in Article 8 (1) (i), (1) (ii) and (2) of Protocol No. 2 on ECSC products to that Agreement.

The '*second generation*' process of approximation to Community law began with the Hungarian Act LVII of 1996 on the Prohibition of Unfair and Restrictive Market Practices, in force from January 1st 1997, which repealed the 1990 Act.[55] The Act aligned the domestic provisions with the content of art. 85 (now 81) TEC, including with respect to the possible approval of block exemptions, and the content of art. 86 (now 82) TEC, with a list of examples of abuse taken from letters *a)* to *d)* of the Community provision; moreover the Hungarian law adopted the definition of dominant position expressed by the Court of Justice in the *United Brands v. Commission*[56] case, and replaced the rules on mergers in the 1990 Act with provisions which more accurately reflect the EC Concentration Control Regulation; finally, it updated the competence and procedures of the Competition Office, following the model of some Member States (in particular Germany and Austria).

The 1996 Hungarian Act also took due account of "soft law," as well: indeed, it established that the President of the *Gazdasági Versenyhivatal* (*GVH*), the Hungarian competition authority, together with the President of the Competition Council, could issue notices describing the basic principles of the law enforcement practice of the GVH. These notices were non-legislative means which indicated for the undertakings the interpretation of the vague notions of the Competition Act (for example, making clear the guiding principles for the imposition of fines).

The notices, besides being based on former decisions, could also reflect law enforcement policy or the view of the Council on competition matters. Notices were not legally binding on undertakings, their function was to indicate the development of the practice concerning competition law issues.

---

[55] Declared by Act No. CXXXII of 1997 which is in force from 01/01/1998. Last amended in 2000, declared by Act No. CXXXVIII of 2000, which is in force from 02/01/2001. See at http://www.gvh.hu/index.php?id=118&l=e.

[56] Case 27/76 *United Brands v. Commission* (1978) ECR 207, at § 38, cited above.

Finally, the 1996 Act had (with some exceptions) extraterritorial effect, in the sense that it was applicable to all commercial practices carried on outside Hungarian territory but which could have direct consequences in relation to it.

Later, in order to keep up with the continual amendments of Community law, those implementing rules were repealed and substituted by new rules.[57]

The Hungarian Parliament, by Act X of 2002, declared Decision no. 1/2002 of the Association Council, replacing Decision no. 2/96 of the Association Council, on the implementation of the competition rules adopted under Article 62 (3) of the Europe Agreement establishing an association between the Republic of Hungary, of the one part, and the European Communities and their Member States, of the other part.[58] Later, the Government (authorized by point a. of § 4 (2) of Act X of 2002 on the declaration of Decision no. 1/2002) adopted Government Regulation no. 39/2002, where space was made for the official translation into Hungarian of the Community acts listed in the Appendix to the Decision.

This represents the first step to their complete adoption and is interesting from the point of view of form, because it comes about by way of the complete recognition of the Community sources involved:

> **Hungarian Government Regulation no. 39/2002:** "Appendix. Acts referred to in Article 2 (4) of the Annex: A. Vertical agreements: Commission Regulation (EC) No 2790/1999 of 22 December 1999 on the application of Article 81(3) of the Treaty to categories of vertical agreements and concerted practices (OJ L 336, 29.12.1999 p. 21). Commission Regulation (EC) No 1475/95 of 28 June 1995 on the application of Article 85(3) of the Treaty to certain categories of motor vehicle distribution and servicing agreements (OJ L 145, 29.6.1995, p. 25). B. Licensing agreements for the transfer of technology: Commission Regulation (EC) No 240/96 of 31 January 1996 on the application of Article 85(3) of the Treaty to certain categories of technology transfer agreements (OJ L 31, 9.2.1996, p. 2). C. Specialisation and research and development agreements: Commission Regulation (EC) No 2658/2000 of 29 November 2000 on the application of Article 81(3) of the

---

[57] Among the Baltic States, Decision no. 1/99 of the Association Council between European Communities and their Member States and Republic of Estonia on adopting the Implementing Rules for Competition Provisions Applicable to Undertakings ( *RT* II 1999, 15, 94) should be recalled.

[58] O.J., L 145, 06/04/2002, p. 16.

Treaty to categories of specialisation agreements (OJ L 304, 5.12. 2000, p. 3). Commission Regulation (EC) No 2659/2000 of 29 November 2000 on the application of Article 81(3) of the Treaty to categories of research and development agreements (OJ L 304, 5.12.2000, p. 7). D. Insurance sector: Council Regulation (EEC) No 1534/91 of 31 May 1991 on the application of Article 85(3) of the Treaty to certain categories of agreements, decisions and concerted practices in the insurance sector (OJ L 143, 7.6.1991, p. 1). Commission Regulation (EEC) No 3932/92 of 21 December 1992 on the application of Article 85(3) of the Treaty to certain categories of agreements, decisions and concerted practices in the insurance sector (OJ L 398, 31.12.1992, p. 7). E. Transport: Council Regulation (EEC) No 1017/68 of 19 July 1968 applying rules of competition to transport by rail, road and inland waterway (OJ L 175, 23.7.1968, p. 1) (in particular Article 4: exemption for groups of small and medium-sized undertakings). Council Regulation (EEC) No 4056/86 of 22 December 1986 laying down detailed rules for the application of Articles 85 and 86 of the Treaty to maritime transport (OJ L 378, 31.12.1986, p. 4) (in particular Articles 3 and 6: exemption for agreements between carriers concerning the operation of scheduled maritime transport services, and exemption for agreements between transport users and conferences concerning the use of scheduled maritime transport services). Commission Regulation (EC) No 823/2000 of 19 April 2000 on the application of Article 81(3) of the Treaty to certain categories of agreements, decisions and concerted practices between liner shipping companies (consortia) (OJ L 100, 20.4. 2000, p. 24). Commission Regulation (EEC) No 1617/93 of 25 June 1993 on the application of Article 85(3) of the Treaty to certain categories of agreements and concerted practices concerning joint planning and coordination of schedules, joint operations, consultations on passenger and cargo tariffs on scheduled air services and slot allocation at airports (OJ L 155, 26.6.1993, p. 18 (as amended by Regulation (EC) No 1523/96, OJ L 190, 31.7.1996, p. 11 and Regulation (EC) No 1083/1999, OJ L 131, 27.05.1999 p. 27). F. Notices of the Commission of the European Communities. Notice concerning its assessment of certain subcontracting agreements in relation to Article 85(1) of the EEC Treaty (OJ C 1, 3.1.1979, p. 2). Notice on the application of the EC competition rules to cross-border credit transfers (OJ C 251, 27.9.1995, p. 3). Commission Communication on clarification of Commission recommendations on the application of competition rules to new transport infrastructure projects (OJ C 298, 30.9.1997). Notice on the definition of the relevant market for the purposes of Community competition law (OJ C 372, 9.12.1997, p. 5). Commission notice: Guidelines on vertical restraints (OJ C 291, 13.10.2000, p.

1). Commission Notice: Guidelines on the applicability of Article 81 of the EC Treaty to horizontal cooperation agreements (OJ C 3, 06/01/2001, p. 2)."

A new Antitrust Act was also adopted in Romania in 1996: "The scope of this act is to protect, maintain, and stimulate competition and a normal, competitive environment, with a view towards promoting consumers' interests."[59] On coming into force, it repealed arts. 36–38 of Act 15/1990 concerning the reorganization of state companies as "*regies autonomes*" and commercial companies, art. 4, (a) of Act 11/1991 concerning the control of unfair competition, as well as other provisions contrary to the law.

In 1998, Bulgaria adopted the Act on Protection of Competition, replacing of the previous one of 1991.[60]

In Latvia, the 'second generation competition law' took legal effect on January 1st 1998.[61] The drafting technique used was unusual: the first article of the Act, even before setting out the purposes, provides the interpreter with a list of legal terms and the respective contents to which s/he must refer in applying these provisions.

**Latvian Competition Act 1998**, *cf.* the following definitions:

"(…) 1) *Natural monopoly*: the exceptional economic position of a market participant in the relevant market in which the possibilities for the development of competition are restricted due to objective conditions; 2) *Dominant position*: the exceptional economic position of a market participant, if its market share in the relevant market exceeds forty percent (40%) and if it has the possibility to significantly prevent, restrict or distort competition in the relevant market by acting in full or partial independence from competitors, customers or purchasers; 3) *Decisive influence*: such an influence in which a market participant must include by law another market participant in its annual accounts or in which a market participant (participants), directly or indirectly, has: the control of more than one-half of the parts, shares or voting rights of another market participant, or the right to dispose of part of the assets of another market participant, or the right to make decisions which are binding on another market participant, or the right to appoint the majority of the members of the managing bodies of another market participant (…)."

---

[59] See art. 1 of the Act, at http://www.oficiulconcurentei.ro/legea2_english.htm.

[60] See the act at http://www.cpc.bg/law.htm.

[61] The Act has been adopted by the *Saeima* on June 18th 1997 and published on July 8th, 1997: see at http://www.competition.lv/eng/matter/matter.htm.

The objectives are set out at art. 2 of the Act and follow the Community ones: "(...) to ensure the opportunity for each market participant to undertake economic activity under the conditions of free and fair competition and favorable conditions for the protection, maintenance and development of competition in the public's interest, by restricting market concentration, terminating activities which are prohibited by the normative acts regulating competition, and by taking action against the persons responsible, under the procedures prescribed by normative acts."

A Competition Council has been established, to achieve these objectives and apply the law correctly. Its legal status and competence is regulated by this and other normative acts. The Competition Council, as well as other state government institutions and local governments, has the obligation to promote the development of free and fair competition and to not allow unfair competition, when taking decisions within the realm of their competence. It does not, therefore, concern an independent agency, as happens, conversely, in other countries; in this case, the role of guarantor of competitiveness has been conferred directly upon the State.

With a view to harmonizing its own laws with those of the Community, Lithuania passed a new Antitrust Act in March 1999.[62] The purpose of the Act is to protect freedom of fair competition in the Republic of Lithuania.

> **Lithuanian Antitrust Act 1999, Art. 1 (1)**: "(... ) the actions of the public and local authorities and undertakings, which restrict or may restrict competition as well as actions of unfair competition, it shall establish the rights, duties and liabilities of the said institutions and undertakings and the legal basis for the control of competition restriction and unfair competition in the Republic of Lithuania (...)". Moreover, art. 1 provides that this act "(...) shall prohibit undertakings from performing actions which restrict or may restrict competition, regardless of the character of their activity, except in cases where this Law or laws governing individual areas of economic activity provide for exemptions and permit certain actions prohibited under this Law."

As to the context for the application of the Act, as in the other cases, it shall also be applicable to the activity of undertakings registered beyond the territory of the Republic of Lithuania if the said activity restricts competition in the domestic market.

---

[62] Act on Competition, March 23th 1999, no. VIII-1099 Vilnius, at http://www.konkuren.lt/english/antitrust/legal.htm.

The new Polish Act of December 2000, on the Protection of Competition and Consumers,[63] well represents the 'second generation legislation' for protecting competition and is a suitable example of the harmonization of domestic law through adoption of the *acquis communautaire*.

The Act of 2000 repealed the previous one of 1990. Besides protecting competition, the legislation dictates new consumer protection rules which are in conformity with Community law.[64] Article 2 defines some terms: undertaking, association of undertakings, agreements, product prices, relevant market, dominant position, competitors.

> **Polish Competition and Consumers Act of 2000**:
> Definitions of *Undertaking*: "a natural and legal person or organisational unit without legal status, organising or rendering services of public utility, which are not business activity within the meaning of provisions on business activity, a natural person exercising a profession on his own behalf and account and a natural person being in possession of stocks and shares ensuring at least twenty-five percent of votes in organs of *(sic)* at least one undertaking."
> *Relevant market*: "a market of products, which by reason of their intended use, price and characteristics, including quality, are regarded by the buyers as substitutes, and are offered in the area in which, by reason of their nature and characteristics, existence of market access barriers, consumer preferences, significant differences in prices and transport costs, the conditions of competition are sufficiently homogeneous."
> *Dominant position* is a position of the undertaking that "allows it to prevent the efficient competition on the relevant market thus enabling it to act in a significant degree independently from competitors, contracting parties and consumers."

These definitions are the result of rulings of the Polish Anti-Monopoly Court and the case law of the Court of Justice and, (as in the case of the term 'undertaking'), refer to those contained in the Act on Business Activity.[65]

Article 5 of the 2000 Act is equivalent of art. 81 TEC: when drafting it, the Polish legislature has eliminated references contained in the 1990 Act to "monopolistic practices," a very ill-defined concept. Article 6 introduces a new provision which follows the European *de minimis* rule

---

63 Journal of Laws, 2000/122, item 1318.

64 See above, chapter I.

65 Act on Business Activity, of November 19th 1999, Journal of Laws, 1999/101, item 1178, (as amended 2000/ 86, item 958).

for prohibited agreements of five percent market share for horizontal agreements and ten percent market share for vertical agreements.[66]

While it did not exist in the previous competition Act of 1990, its introduction had been considered extensively, mostly to ensure that the Competition Office (now Office for Competition and Consumer Protection) would not find itself overburdened with cases that, in fact, had no significant impact on the market. The 2000 Act contains no "rule of reason" or exemption from the prohibitions, which art. 81 (3) TEC does provide.

Article 8 of the 2000 Polish Act is the equivalent of art. 82 TEC. With respect to the 1990 Act, the new one prohibits the practice of imposing onerous contract conditions that yield unjustified profits to the undertaking, the imposition of unfair prices, including predatory prices, glaringly low prices, and significantly delayed payments. The catalogue is comprehensively more detailed than the equivalent catalogue of art. 82 TEC.

Article 8 goes beyond what is contemplated by art. 82 TEC in expressly providing a nullity clause which provides a sanction in all cases of abuse of dominant position.

> The Office for Competition and Consumer Protection has been conducting an investigation against the Polish Telecommunication (now a public listed company of which the principal shareholder is France Telecom) for abuse of a dominant position. For years, the former state company tried to prevent a new competitor from entering the market for long-distance phone calls. Polish Telecommunication has previously been found guilty of abuse of a dominant position: in 1993, for imposing excessive prices on consumers (being the then sole provider of services), in 1997 for imposing unfair contract conditions on one mobile operator and suddenly breaking the inter-operator's contract with the other one (as a result the users could not call to land-line phones from mobiles) and in 1998 for imposing excessive prices for long-distance phone calls on consumers (it was the sole provider of services).

As regards concentrations, the new 2000 Act not only raises the thresholds for notifications, but also introduces a range of exceptions, which

---

[66] In the meantime the Commission adopted a new notice on block exemptions with different *de minimis* depending on the type of agreement: Commission Notice on agreements of minor importance which do not appreciably restrict competition under Article 81 (1) of the Treaty establishing the European Community (*de minimis*), O.J., C 368, 12/22/2001, p. 13.

will prevent the competition authority from being overburdened by notifications of small concentrations.

> **Art. 12, Polish Competition and Consumers Act of 2000**: "Concentration is defined by the act as: merger of two or more independent undertakings; creation of one joint undertaking by other undertakings; take-over by acquisition or entering into possession of stocks, other securities, shares or in any other way obtaining direct or indirect control over one or several undertakings; take-over or acquisition of stock and shares resulting in achieving at least twenty-five percent of votes; assumption of functions in managing or controlling bodies in the competing undertakings by the same person.
>
> "Notification is not required where: A) the undertaking, over which control is taken or whose stocks and shares are acquired, is quite small (its turnover for the two years preceding notification cannot exceed ten million Euro); B) combined market share of the undertakings intending to merge does not exceed twenty percent; C) financial institution, which normally invests in stocks for its own account and the accounts of others, acquires stocks on temporary basis with a view to resell them within one year; D) undertaking acquires stocks and shares on a temporary basis to secure debts and does not exercise the rights arising from acquired stocks and shares; E) concentration arises because of bankruptcy, unless control is assumed by the competitor; F) concentration takes place within one capital group."

The new Act of 2000 fills some gaps in the 1990 legislation. In particular, it deals with the Office for Competition and Consumer Protection's organizational and procedural aspects of its activity and introduces individual or block exemptions and negative clearances for specific agreements. The rules on the powers of investigation of the President of the Office are inspired by Reg. 17/ 62[67] and the wording is often similar. The President is appointed and dismissed by the Prime Minister, who also supervises his activity. The appeals against its decisions are lodged with a special court, the Anti-Monopoly Court. Judgments of the Anti-Monopoly Court are final and can be only appealed to the Supreme Court under specific conditions, namely the interpretation of laws.

On June 30th 2000, Poland also adopted an act on state aid that harmonizes this area with the EC law (assessment under art. 87 TEC): the Act on the conditions of admissibility and supervision of State aid for

---

[67] See above § 2.

undertakings.[68] However, legislation on public undertakings and undertakings granted special or exclusive rights is still lacking.

In Estonia, the Competition Act was passed on June 5th 2001 and entered into force on October 1st 2001.[69] An important step was made towards approximation of legislation with that of the European Union: the new Competition Act fully corresponds to the EC competition rules. The preparation of this bill has been a very time-consuming task for the members of the working group, and one which required much effort. Simultaneously with the draft of the Competition Act, the officials of the Competition Board prepared a number of related drafts of secondary legislation, that had to come into force at the same time as the Competition Act.

According to § 1 (1) of the Act: "The scope of application of this Act is the safeguarding of competition in the interest of free enterprise upon the extraction of natural resources, manufacture of goods, provision of services and sale and purchase of products and services (hereinafter goods), and the preclusion and elimination of the prevention, limitation, or restriction (hereinafter restriction) of competition in other economic activities."

A peculiarity of the Estonian act is represented by Chapter 6, dedicated entirely to State aid, an area with which the competition rules of other countries generally do not occupy themselves.

> **Estonia Competition Act 2001; § 30 of Chapter 6 is as follows:** "**(1)** State aid is an advantage granted directly or indirectly in any form whatsoever by the state or a local government (hereinafter grantor of state aid) or from their resources which distorts or threatens to distort competition by favouring certain undertakings or the production or sale of certain goods. Such aid may be financial aid, postponement of the payment of tax arrears, debt write-offs and the grant of loans under more favourable terms than usually granted to other undertakings, and other forms of aid. **(2)** The following shall also be deemed to be grantors of state aid: 1. foundations which directly or indirectly use the resources of the state or a local government; 2. non-profit associations which directly or indirectly use the resources of the state or a local government; 3. legal persons in public law which directly or indirectly use the resources of the state or a local government; 4. companies in which the state, a local government or any other legal person in public law holds more than one-half of the share capital or

[68] Journal of Laws 2000/ 60, item 704.

[69] *RT* 1 I 2001, 56, 332. See at http://www.konkurentsiamet.ee/eng/index.html?id=763.

votes represented by shares; 5. companies belonging to the same group as a company specified in clause 4) of this subsection."

Moreover, the Estonian Competition Act introduces the concept of concentration. Pursuant to the new Competition Act, as a concentration shall be also considered an acquisition of control over a part of an undertaking or an acquisition of joint control over a third undertaking or a part thereof.

**Estonia Competition Act 2001, § 19** "Concentration. **(1)** Concentration is deemed to arise where: 1. previously independent undertakings merge within the meaning of the Commercial Code (RT I 1995, 26–28, 355; 1998, 91–93, 1500; 1999, 10, 155; 23, 355; 24, 360; 57, 596; 102, 907; 2000, 29, 172; 49, 303; 55, 365; 57, 373; 2001, 34, 185); 2. an undertaking acquires control of the whole or part of another undertaking; 3) undertakings jointly acquire control of the whole or part of a third undertaking; 4. a natural person already controlling at least one undertaking acquires control of the whole or part of another undertaking; 5. several natural persons already controlling at least one undertaking jointly acquire control of the whole or part of another undertaking. **(2)** The creation, by persons specified in clauses (1) 3. and 5. of this section, of a joint venture performing on a lasting and independent basis is also deemed to be acquisition of control within the meaning of clauses (1) 3. and 5. of this section. **(3)** If the creation of a joint venture specified in subsection (2) of this section has as its object or effect the co-ordination of the competitive behaviour of the founders amongst themselves or if the joint venture does not perform on a lasting and independent basis, the provisions of § 4 of this Act apply to the creation of the joint venture. **(4)** For the purposes of this Chapter, a part of an undertaking is the assets of the undertaking or an organisationally independent part of the undertaking, including an enterprise which constitutes a basis for business activities and to which market turnover can be clearly attributed. **(5)** Transactions specified in subsection (1) of this section are not deemed to be a concentration if the transactions are carried out as an internal restructuring of a group of undertakings."

Pursuant to subsection 21 (1) of the new Competition Act a concentration shall be subject to control if, during the previous financial year, the aggregate worldwide turnover of the parties to the concentration exceeded 500 million kroons and the aggregate worldwide turnover of each of at least two parties to the concentration exceeded 100 million kroons and if the business activities of at least one of the merging undertakings or of the whole or a part of the undertaking of which control is acquired are carried out in Estonia.

The new Competition Act stipulates that the Competition Board has the authority to prohibit a concentration, provided that it may create or strengthen a dominant position, as a result of which competition would be significantly restricted in the goods market.[70] The Competition Board developed cooperation with neighboring countries, as well as with EU Member States' competition agencies and with international organizations.

It is interesting to note that, to gain knowledge and experience in order to carry out the supervisory tasks in respect of the Competition Act, the officials of the Competition Board participated in seminars, conferences and training events in Austria, Hungary, Belgium, France, Germany, Sweden, Slovenia, Finland, Korea, Slovakia, Latvia, Netherlands, Ireland, Denmark, and Great Britain.

In the Czech Republic, Parliament has enacted the Act on the Protection of Competition no. 143 of April 4th, 2001, in force from July 1st 2001. The new provisions repeal some previous legislation of the 1990s.[71]

The objectives pursued by the Czech legislature are set out in art. 1: "(1) This Act regulates the protection of competition on the market of products and services (…) against its elimination, restriction, other distortion, or, on conditions laid down by this Act, against its threat (…) by: agreements between undertakings, abuse of dominant position of undertakings, or concentration of undertakings."

Following art. 2 (1): "Undertakings under this Act shall be deemed to mean natural or legal persons, associations thereof, associations of such associations and other groupings, including where such associations and groupings are not legal persons, provided the same take part in competition or may influence competition by their activities, although they are not entrepreneurs."

Czech law, as distinct from other legislation on the subject, is concerned to provide the interpreter with a definitive grid for distinguishing between horizontal and vertical agreements. Article 5 in fact provides that: "Agreements between undertakings operating at the same market

---

[70] The Estonian Competition board publishes an annual report with references to domestic case law. See at http://www.konkurentsiamet.ee/dokumendid/annualreport2001.pdf.

[71] Act No. 63/1991 *Coll.*, on the Protection of Competition; Act No 495/1992 *Coll.*, amending Act No. 63/1991 *Coll.*, on the Protection of Competition; it also modifies Act No. 286/1993 *Coll.*, amending Act No. 63/1991 *Coll.* on the Protection of Competition.

level are horizontal agreements. Agreements between undertakings operating at different market levels are vertical agreements. Mixed agreements between undertakings operating at the same horizontal level as well as at different vertical levels shall be deemed to constitute horizontal agreements; in case of any doubt, any such agreement shall be deemed to be a horizontal agreement."

## 12. The Relationship between Community and National Level in the Field of Competition

What has been highlighted in paragraphs 10 and 11 demonstrates not only the advanced state of *integration* between national and Community law, but also the way in which the circulation and transplant of legal rules and legal models are phenomena of first importance for understanding the present-day structure of competition law in the various legal systems.

The internal market of the Community and the obligations derived from it, both for Member States and the candidates who will become Members, could act as a more effective stimulus than an international convention for the creation of uniform rules within the European legal systems.

As we have seen above, with Reg. 1/2003, the competition authorities (administrative and judicial) of the Member States have been more closely concerned than before with the enforcement of Community competition rules in order to ensure that they are effectively applied. The competition authorities and courts of the Member States have the power to apply not only art. 81 (1) and art. 82 TEC, which have direct applicability by virtue of the case law of the Court of Justice, but also art. 81 (3) TEC.

In particular, national courts have an essential part to play in applying Community competition rules. When deciding disputes between private individuals they protect the individual rights under Community law, for example by awarding damages to the victims of infringements.

The role of the national courts complements that of the competition authorities of the Member States and that of the Commission, which has the power to impose any remedy, whether *behavioral* or *structural*, which is necessary to bring the infringement effectively to an end, having regard to the principle of proportionality.

In other words, the enforcement procedures of Community competition law have been decentralized, but it is unrealistic to expect that the newly established system will work uniformly.

The problems which may arise are the same as those which arose before, when there was a division of competence between the Community and Member States.

Indeed, the possibility cannot be excluded that a particular type of conduct on the part of one or more undertakings may provoke the simultaneous intervention of both the Community and the national authorities, bringing to light problems derived from a *potential clash of the Commission's and the national authority's adjudications.*

One might consider the undertaking which finds itself in a dominant position both in the European and the national market, and which abuses its position; furthermore, consider the situation where the Commission is of the view that the preconditions do not exist to start proceedings for abuse of dominant position, whereas the national authorities are of the opposite view and consequently prohibit the undertaking from continuing that particular type of conduct.

> The issue ought not to arise in relation to concentrations, since well-defined limits have been drawn between national and Community competence, based on objective criteria such as the annual turnover of the undertakings.[72]

The problem raised above regarding the debate between supporters of the 'single barrier theory' (also known as reciprocal exclusion theory) and those who support the 'double barrier theory' (or theory of competition) has now (theoretically, at least) been resolved.

According to the '*single barrier theory,*' Community law always prevails over the legal systems of Member States; as a result, the law of individual States cannot derogate either from the Commission's prohibitions or the exemptions it has permitted. The reasoning of those who seek to support the single barrier theory can be understood. They attribute particular importance to the EC's "guiding" role in competition law, and fear that this role will become too restricted if it becomes identified with just a power to prohibit an illicit commercial practice.

> For example, the Italian Act no. 287/90, which implicitly recognizes the supremacy of the Community legal system, openly welcomes the single barrier theory, establishing that its provisions are only applicable in cases which are not considered to come under the competence of the Commission. Article 1, in fact, affirms that "the provisions of this law (...) apply to agreements, abuses of dominant position and concentrations of undertakings which

[72] See above, § 9.

> do not fall within the ambit of the application (...) of articles 85 and 86 of the Treaty (...) of EC Regulations or Community acts with equivalent legal effect."
>
> This remissive behavior on the part of the Italian legislature, unique throughout the EC, where other States have still not given up consideration of the double barrier theory, is made even more explicit in the two subsequent clauses, where two important rules are laid down.
>
> The first provides that the Italian Antitrust authority whenever it considers that a particular case under examination is beyond its competence and falls within that of the Community, must stay all proceedings and send all the documentation in its possession to the Commission (art. 1 [2]).
>
> The second considers the circumstance where the Antitrust authority, having decided that Italian law applies, has started inquiry proceedings; however, an analogous procedure has later begun before the Commission. In such a case, the law requires the Italian Antitrust authority to suspend the inquiry and await the findings of the Commission (art. 1 (3) of the Italian Act).

The '*double barrier theory*' starts with the assumption that the national and Community systems, albeit complementary, are independent from one another; consequently, the fact that a particular course of conduct comes under the competence of the Community authorities does not of itself exclude the competing competence of the national authorities, which, since they have different aims and interests to serve, may disregard a possible contradictory precedent set by a Community body. In principle, therefore, the Commission has competence to determine whether a particular course of conduct is or is not in breach of the Community competition rules. Vice versa, if it concerns facts which are only of relevance to domestic law, the national administrative authorities will have competence. The national administrative authorities' competence to determine whether or not a particular act is compatible with the competition rules, should not be confused with a national judge's competence, who always has jurisdiction to adjudicate upon a dispute between two parties.

In this way, for example, if in a civil action the argument is as to whether an agreement between two undertakings is valid and which may be harmful to competition, there is nothing to stop the national judge from ruling, without waiting for a possible ruling from the Commission or the national administrative authorities.

For its part, the Court of Justice has developed a theory which may be considered a *compromise* between the two opposing theories. The Court holds that whenever there is a divergence between a State's ruling and the Commission's, the latter must prevail where a prohibition has been imposed. In other words, the national authority cannot authorize something which has been prohibited at Community level.

Conversely, if the Commission should authorize or exempt certain conduct, there is nothing to prevent the national authorities from prohibiting it within their own territory.

The solution proposed by the ECJ would not be in conflict with the requirements of Community law, since this is safeguarded, provided that the Commission's prohibitions, imposed to protect the common market, are not disregarded by Member States. The only real interest that the Community has, in fact, is in preventing anti-competitive conduct from being carried on at the single market level. If an individual State then wishes to impose stricter rules within its own system, there is nothing to stop it from doing so.

Regulation 1/2003, too, is a *compromise* between the two theories, the 'single barrier' and the 'double barrier.' According to the Preamble of the Regulation, the Commission and the competition authorities of the Member States should together form a *network* of public authorities applying the Community competition rules in close cooperation.

For that purpose, it is necessary to set up arrangements for *information* and *consultation*. To this end, further modalities within the network will be laid down and revised by the Commission, in close cooperation with the Member States. Notwithstanding any national provision to the contrary, the exchange of information and the use of such information in evidence should be allowed between the members of the network even where the information is confidential. This information may be used for the application of arts. 81 & 82 TEC as well as for the parallel application of national competition law, provided that the latter application relates to the same case and does not lead to a different outcome.

When the information exchanged is used by the receiving authority to impose sanctions on undertakings, there should be no other limit to the use of the information than the obligation to use it for the purpose for which it was collected, given the fact that the sanctions imposed on undertakings are of the same type in all systems.

The rights of defense enjoyed by undertakings in the various systems can be considered as sufficiently equivalent. However, as regards natural persons, they may be subject to substantially different types of sanctions across the various systems. Where that is the case, it is necessary to ensure that information can only be used if it has been collected in a way which respects the same level of protection of the rights of defense of natural persons as provided for under the national rules of the receiving authority.

If the competition rules are to be applied consistently and, at the same time, the network is to be managed in the best possible way, it is essential to retain the rule that the competition authorities of the Member States are automatically relieved of their competence if the Commission initiates its own proceedings. Where a competition authority of a Member State is already acting on a case and the Commission intends to initiate proceedings, it should endeavor to do so as soon as possible. Before initiating proceedings, the Commission should consult the national authority concerned.[73]

An open question remains, namely that of ensuring compliance with the principles of legal certainty and the uniform application of the Community competition rules in a system of 'parallel powers' (at Community and national level). To this end, conflicting decisions must be avoided. It is therefore necessary to clarify, in accordance with the case law of the Court of Justice, the effects of Commission decisions and proceedings on courts and competition authorities of the Member States. Commitment decisions adopted by the Commission do not affect the power of the courts and the competition authorities of the Member States to apply arts. 81 & 82 TEC.

The breadth of the debate which is developing around this issue and the diversity of academic and judicial opinion, lead us to believe that this is still an open question and that we can expect further developments in the future.

---

[73] *Cf.* 15–17 of the Preamble, Reg. 1/2003.

# Bibliography Chapter VI

## *Selected commentary/books*


*§ In English:*

GERARDIN D. (ed.), *Remedies in Network Industries: EC Competition Law vs. Sector Specific Regulation*, Intersentia, 2004; ID., *Modernisation and Enlargement: Two Major Challenges for EC Competition Law*, Intersentia, 2004; KUAN J. S. *Competition and Antitrust Law & Practice in Europe*, Worldtrade Executive, Inc., 2004; RITTER D. L., BRAUN W. D., *European Competition Law: A Pracrtitioner's Guide*, Kluwer Law International, 3rd ed., The Hague, 2004; VAN BAEL & BELLIS, *Competition Law of European Community*, 4th Edition, Kluwer Law International, 2004; BAVASSO A., *Communications in EU Antitrust Law. Market Power and Public Interest*, The Hague, Kluwer Law International, 2003; HARDING CH. & J. JOSHUA, *Regulating Cartels in Europe. A Study of Legal Control of Corporate Delinquency*, Oxford University Press, 2003; VAN DER WOUDE M., *EC Competition Law Handbook 2002/2003*, London, 2003; VEDDER H., *Competition Law and Environmental Protection; Towards Sustainability*, Groningen, Europa Law Publishing, 2003; WHISH, R., *Competition law*, 5th ed., London, Butterworths, 2003; WISHLADE F.G., *Regional State Aid and Competition Policy in the European Union, European*, The Hague, Kluwer Law International, 2003; BASEDOW J. (ed.), *Limits and Control of Competition with a View to International Harmonization*, The Hague, Kluwer Law International, 2002; BAQUERO CRUZ J., *Between Competition and Free Movement*, Hart Publishing, 2002; JONES C., BASEDOW J., BAUM H., HOPT K. J., KANDA H., KONO T., (eds.), *Economic Regulation and Competition—Regulation of Services in the EU, Germany and Japan*, The Hague/London/New York, 2002; VEDDER H., *Competition Law, Environmental Policy and Producer Liability, Experience in the Netherlands from a European perspective*, Groningen, 2002; VOGELAAR O.W., STUYCK J., REEKEN B.L.P. (eds.), *Competition Law in the EU, its Member States and Switzerland*, Vol. 2–I (2000) and Vol. 2-II (2002), Kluwer Law Int./WEJ Tjeenk Willink; DRAHOS M., *Convergence of Competition Laws and policies in the European Community*, Kluwer Law Int., 2001; EHLERMANN C.D., ATANASIU I. (eds.), *European Competition Law Annual 2000: The Modernisation of EC Antitrust Policy*, Oxford–Portland Oregon, 2001; RIVAS M., HORSPOOL J. (eds.), *Modernisation and Decentralisation of EC Competition Law*, Kluwer law Int., European Business law and Practices Series, vol 16, 2000; O'KEEFE & BAVASSO, *Four freedoms, one market and national competence. In search of a dividing line, in Liber amicorum in Honour of Lord Slynn of Hadley*, The Hague, 2000, 548; OLIVER, *Goods and Services: two freedoms compared, in Melanges en hommage à Michel Waelbroek*, Brussels, 1999; RITTER L., BRAUN W. D., RAWLINSON F., *European Competition Law: A Practitioner's Guide*, Kluwer Law Intl, 1999; VERLOOP P., DUTILH N., *Merger Control in the EU: A Survey of European Competition Laws*, Kluwer Law Intl, 1999; GOYDER D. G., *EC Competition Law*, Oxford University Press, 1999; OTTERVANGER T. R., STEENBERGEN J., VAN DER VOORDE S., *Competition Law of the European Community, t*he Netherlands and Belgium, Kluwer Law Intl, 1998; FRAZER T., WATERSON M., *Competition Law and Policy*, Harvester Wheatsheaf, 1994; FEJO J., *Monopoly Law and Market—Studies of EC Competition Law with US American Antitrust Law as a frame of reference and supported by basic market economics*, Kluver, 1990; GARDNER N., *A Guide to United Kingdom and European Community Competition Policy*, Macmillan, 1990.

***§ In French:***

MAIL-FOUILLEUL S., *Les sanctions de la violation du droit communautaire de la concurrence*, LGDJ, 2002; WAELBROECK M., FRIGNANI A., *Commentaire Mégret – Concurrence*, 2ème ed., 1997; STUYCK, *Libre circulation et concurrence: les deux piliers du Marché commun, in Mélanges en hommage à M. WAELBROECK*, Brussels, 1999, 1478.

***§ In German:***

MESTMÄCKER E.-J., SCHWEITZER H., *Europäisches Wettbewerbrecht*, München, 2004; HEINEKE T., *Entlastungsgründe in der europäischen und US-amerikanischen Fusionskontrolle*, Baden–Baden 2004; LIEBSCHER C., FLOHR E., PETSCHE A., *Handbuch der EU-Gruppenfreistellungsverordnungen*, München, 2003; POHLMEIER J., *Behinderungsmissbrauch im Plattformmarkt*, Tübingen 2003; LÜCKENBACH A., *Nebenabreden nach europäischen Fusionskontrollrecht*, München, 2003; ULSHÖFER M., *Kontrollerwerb in der Fusionskontrolle. Eine Untersuchung im europäischen, deutschen und US-amerikanischen Fusionskontrollrecht*, Baden–Baden, 2003; BAHR C., *Verbundgruppenfranchising*, Baden–Baden, 2002; BOESCHE K. V., *Die zivilrechtsdogmatische Struktur des Anspruchs auf Zugang zu Energieversorgungsnetzen. Eine Untersuchung der Zugangsregelung der §§ 6, 6a EnWG und 19, 20 GWB*, Baden–Baden, 2002; HEMPEL R., *Privater Rechtsschutz im Kartellrecht – Eine rechtsvergleichende Analyse*, Baden–Baden 2002; HUBMANN, GÖTTING, *Gewerblicher Rechtsschutz*, 7th ed., München 2002; KÖHLER, PIEPER, *UWG–Kommentar*; 3rd ed., München, 2002; CASPAR U., *Wettbewerbliche Gesamtwürdigung von Vereinbarungen im Rahmen von Art. 81 Abs. 1 EGV*, Köln, 2001; HEFERMEHL, *Wettbewerbsrecht*, 22nd ed., München 2001; HOHMANN H., *Die Essential Facility-Doctrine im Recht der Wettbewerbsbeschränkungen*, Baden–Baden, 2001; JACOBS, LINDACHER, TEPLITZKY, *UWG–Großkommentar;* IMMENGA, MESTMÄCKER, *GWB, Kommentar zum Kartellgesetz*, 3rd ed., München 2001; EKEY, *Heidelberger Kommentar zum Wettbewerbsrecht*, Heidelberg 2000; KNIEPS G., BRUNEKREEFT G. (EDS.), *Zwischen Regulierung und Wettbewerb Netzsektoren in Deutschland*, Heidelberg, 2000; GRABBE H., *Nebenabreden in der europäischen Fusionskontrolle*, Baden–Baden, 2000; FEZER, *Markenrecht* (Kommentar), 2nd ed., München 1999; PASTOR, AHRENS, *Der Wettbewerbsprozess*, 4th ed, Köln, 1999; LIEBMANN H., *Vertriebsverträge in der EU*, Wien, 1998.

***§ In Italian:***

TOSATO G.L., BELLODI L., *Il nuovo diritto europeo della concorenza*, Milano, 2004; PORCHIA O., *Il procedimento di controllo degli aiuti pubblici alle imprese tra ordinamento comunitario ed ordinamento interno*, Torino, 2002; PINOTTI C., *Gli aiuti di Stato alle imprese nel diritto comunitario della concorrenza*, Padova, 2000; ROBERTI G.M., *La disciplina delle concentrazioni tra imprese*, in TIZZANO (ed.), *Il diritto privato dell'Unione Europea*, in BESSONE (ed.), *Trattato di diritto privato.*, Torino, Tomo II, 2000, 1211; MUNARI F, *Le regole di concorrenza nel sistema del Trattato*, in TIZZANO (ed.), *Il diritto privato dell'Unione Europea*, in BESSONE (ed.), *Trattato di diritto privato*, Tomo II, Torino, 2000, 1149; ROBERTI G.M., *Le procedure applicative delle regole di concorrenza*, in TIZZANO (ed.), *Il diritto privato dell'Unione Europea*, in BESSONE (ed.), *Trattato di diritto privato*, Torino, 2000, Tomo II, 1223; GHIDINI G., HASSAN S., *Diritto industriale e della concorrenza nella CEE*, Milano 1991.

***Selected articles:***

KEKELEKIS M., *The "statement of objections" as an inherent part of the right to be heard in EC merger proceedings: issues of concern*, 25 European Competition Law Review, 518, 2004; MCCURDY, GREGORY V.S., *The impact of modernisation of the EU competition law system on the courts and private enforcement of the competition laws: a comparative perspective*, 25 European Competition Law Review 509, 2004; PETIT, N., *The Commission's contribution to the emergence of 3G mobile communications: an analysis of some decisions in the field of competition law,* 25 European Competition Law Review, 429, 2004; DEKEYSER K., LAURILA M., *The new era of European antitrust enforcement: the main principles and mechanisms of the new regime for the enforcement of articles 81 and 82 of the EC Treaty,* Competition law yearbook 2003, 11, 2004; DOLMANS J.F.M., GRAF T., *Analysis of tying under Article 82 EC: the European Commission's Microsoft decision in perspective,* 27 World competition 27, 2004; AHLBORN C., EVANS D.S., PADILLA A.J., *The antitrust economics of tying: a farewell top er se illegality, The Antitrust Bulletin,* Vol. XLIX, 287, 2004; COPPI L., WALKER M., *Substantial convergence or parallel paths?: similarities and differences in the economic analysis of horizontal mergers in U.S. and EU competition law,* The Antitrust Bulletin, Vol. XLIX, 101, 2004; BAVASSO, A. F., *Essential facilities in EC law: the rise of an "epithet" and the consolidation of a doctrine, in the communication sector,* 21 Yearbook of European law 63, 2001– 2002; GRUNDMANN S., *Information, Party autonomy and economic agents in European Contract law,* 39 CMLRev. 269, 2002; KOMNINOS A P., *New Prospective for Private enforcement of EC competition law: Courage v. Crehan and the Community right to damage,* 39 CMLRev. 447, 2002; BAUDENBACHER C., HIGGINS I., *Decentralization of EC competition law enforcement and arbitration,* 8 Columbia Journal of European Law 1, 2002; MONTI G., *Anticompetitive agreements: the innocent party's right to damages,* 27 EL Rev.282, 2002; MCCARTHY N., *Proposed New UK Merger Regime, Revue de droit des affaire internationales/IBLJ* 603, 2002; VAGLIASINDI M., *Competition Policy across Transition Economies, Revue d'Economie Financière* 215, 2001; MORTELMANS K., *Towards convergence in the application of the rules on free movement and on competition?* 38 CMLR 613, 2001; EHLERMANN, *The modernization of EC Antitrust Law: A legal and cultural revolution,* 37 CML Rev. 537, 2000; SCHMID, *Diagonal competence conflicts between European competition law and national regulation—a conflict of laws reconstruction of the dispute on book price fixing,* ERPL 155, 2000;

LE ROUX S., *La réforme des règles d'application des articles 81 et 82 du Traité CE: le nouveau règlement de procedure/ Reform of the rules implementing Articles 81 & 82 of the EC Treaty: the new procedure regulation,* RDAI /IBLJ 543, 2003; LÜBBIG T., HAEHNEL A., *Les droit des parties et des tiers dans la procedure de controle des concentrations: les systemes continentauw communautaire et allemande/The rights of parties and third parties in mergers control proceedings: the European and German litigation systems,* RDAI/IBLJ 569, 2002; JALABERT-DOURY N., *Le nouveau contrôle francais des concentrations: entre convergence et maintien d'une exception francaise/The new French merger regime: between convergence and subsisting Frenc exception,* RDAI/IBLJ 583, 2002; MCCARTHY N., *Proposed new UK merger regime: le projet d'un nouveau regime des concentrations au Royaume-Uni,* RDAI/IBLJ 603, 2002; *Le livre blanc de la Commission sur la modernisation des règles de concurrence, Actes de la Journée d'études organisée le 26 mai 2000 à l' occasion du 35 anniversaire des Cahiers de droit européen,* 37 Cahiers de droit européen 133, 2001;

KÖHLER H., *Kartellverbot und Schadensersatz,* GRUR 99, 2004; BECHTOLD R., *Zulassungsansprüche zu selektiven Vertriebssystemen unter besonderer Berücksichtigung der Kfz-Vertriebssysteme,* NJW 3729, 2003; KOENIG C., KÜHLING J., RASBACH W., *Das energierechtliche Unbundling-Regime,* RdE 221, 2003; HOSSENFELDER S., LUTZ M., *Die neue Durchführungsverordnung zu den Artt. 81 und 82 EG-Vertrag,* WuW 118, 2003;

KOENIGS F., Die VO Nr.1/2003: *Wende im EG-Kartellrecht*, DB 1237, 2003; WEITBRECHT, A., *Das neue EG-Kartellverfahrensrecht*, EuZW 69, 2003; LETTL T., *Der Schadensersatzanspruch gemäß 823 Abs. 2 BGB in Verbindung mit Art. 81 Abs. 1 EG*, 167 ZHR 473, 2003; EMMERICH V., *Fusionskontrolle 2002/2003*, AG 649, 2003; BERGER C., *Urheberrechtliche Erschöpfungslehre und digitale Informationstechnologie*, GRUR 198, 2002; KÜHNE G., *Gemeinschaftsrechtlicher Ordnungsrahmen der Energiewirtschaft zwischen Wettbewerb und Gemeinwohl*, RdE 257, 2002; BAUDENBACHER K., *Erschöpfung der Immaterialgüterrechte in der EFTA und die Rechtslage in der EU*, GRUR (Internationaler Teil) 583, 2000; GASTER G., *Die Erschöpfungsproblematik aus der Sicht des Gemeinschaftsrechts*, GRUR (Internationaler Teil) 571, 2000; MARKERT K., *Langfristige Bezugsbindungen für Strom und Gas nach deutschem und europäischem Kartellrecht*, EuZW 427, 2000; ROTH, *Diskriminierende Regelungen des Warenverkehrs und Rechtfertigung durch die „zwingenden Erfordernisse" des Allgemeininteresses*, WRP 979, 2000; SACK R., *Der Erschöpfungsgrundsatz im deutschen Immaterialgüterrecht*, GRUR 610, 2000; JARASS, *Elemente einer Dogmatik der Grundfreiheiten*, 30 EuR, 1995, 202 & 35 EuR, 2000, 705; BEHRENS, *Die Konvergenz der wirtschaftlichen Freiheiten im...* 27 EuR, 1992, 145.

ALFARO ÁGUILA-REAL J., *Autorizar lo que no está prohibido: una crítica a la regulación de los acuerdos verticals, in Gaceta jurídica de la Unión Europea y de la competencia.* No. 229 (2004),p. 51–67; ALONSO SOTO R., *The modernisation of EU competition law enforcement in the European Union: FIDE 2004 (Spain) national reports*. 2004, p. 541–553; MARTÍNEZ LAGE, SANTIAGO, *El nuevo reglamento comunitario sobre el control de concentraciones, in Gaceta jurídica de la Unión Europea y de la competencia.* No. 229 (2004),p. 3–13;

CASSINIS P., SABA P., *La riforma comunitaria sul controllo delle concentrazioni, Le nuove leggi civili commentate*, Anno XXVII, 405, 2004; CASSINIS P., *La sentenza della Corte nel caso del "consorzio industrie fiammiferi"(CIF): prevalenza del diritto comunitario e tutela della concorrenza in contesti regolamentati, Il foro amministrativo*, Vol. III, 291, 2004; CHIEFFI I., *Competenze dell'Autorità per le garanzie nelle comunicazioni e della Commissione nel nuovo quadro normativo comunitario e italiano per le comunicazioni elettroniche, Rivista italiana di diritto pubblico comunitario*, Anno XIV, 267, 2004; DE FALCO V., *Il rinvio del controllo sulle concentrazioni all'autorità antitrust nazionale: alcune riflessioni sul caso spagnolo del mercato delle telecomunicazioni*, Diritto pubblico comparato ed europeo, I, 358, 2004; D'ALBERTI M., *Libera concorrenza e diritto amministrativo*, Rivista trimestrale di diritto pubblico 347, 2004; FAELLA, G., *Incompatibilità tra normativa interna e disciplina antitrust comunitaria:gli incerti equilibrismi della Corte di giustizia nel caso "Cif"*, Il foro it., IV, 325, 2004; NIVARRA L., *Il "Libro bianco sulla modernizzazione delle norme per l'applicazione degli articoli 85 e 86 del Trattato": quale futuro per il diritto europeo della concorrenza?*, Europa e dir. priv. 1001, 2000; CAPELLI F., *La riforma della disciplina comunitaria della concorrenza e i nuovi compiti affidati ai giudici nazionali (con particolare riferimento alla situazione italiana)*, Dir. comun. scambi internaz, 395, 2000; DI VIA L., *Considerazioni sulle "mobili frontiere" del diritto della concorrenza*, Contratto e impresa/Europa 1, 2000; GHEZZI F., *Il libro bianco della Commissione sulla Modernizzazione del diritto della concorrenza comunitario*, Concorrenza e mercato III, 175, 2000; LONGU T., *Il divieto dell'abuso di dipendenza economica nei rapporti tra le imprese*, Riv. dir. civ. II, 345, 2000; PINTO V., *L'abuso di dipendenza economica "fuori dal contratto" tra diritto civile e diritto antitrust*, Riv. dir. civ. II, 389, 2000; RIZZA C., *La posizione dominante collettiva nella giurisprudenza comunitaria*, Concorrenza e Mercato 509, 200; TODINO M., *Le riforme del Regolamento CEE 4064/89, sul controllo delle concentrazioni fra imprese. Una prima verifica,* Dir. comm. internaz. 515, 2000; ALBANESE A., *Abuso di dipendenza economica: nullità del contratto e riequilibrio del rapporto,* Europa e diritto privato 1179, 1999; SPOLIDORO M.S., *Riflessioni critiche sul rapporto fra abuso di posizione dominante e abuso dell'altrui dipendenza economica,* Riv. dir. ind I, 191, 1999; AUTERI P., *I rapporti tra la normativa antitrust nazionale e quella comunitaria dopo la legge comunitaria 1994,* Contratto e impresa / Europa 535, 1996.

***In the CEECs:***

*Forum: Eastward Enlargement of the Euro Zone,* 39 Review of European Economic Policy 236, 2004; *Forum: The EU on the Threshold of Enlargement: How Well Prepared are the Participants?* 39 Review of European Economic Policy 60, 2004; MAKS J. A. H., WITTE C., *Romanian Competition Policy: Taking over the European Model?* 39 Review of European Economic Policy 314, 2004; FORNALCZYK, A., *The Enforcement of Competition Policy in the Candidate Countries,* 37 Review of European Economic Policy 52, 2002, 52; OPRESCU G., *The modernisation of EC Competition Law: the case of an Associated Country (Romania),* in European Competition Law Annual 2000: *The modernisation of EDC Antitrust Policy,* C.D. EHLERMANN, I. ATANASIU (eds.) Oxford, Portland Oregon, 2001, 387; HOEKMAN, B. & SIMEON D., *Competition Law in Post-Central-Planning Bulgaria,* The Antitrust Bulletin 227, 2000; DUTZ, M. A. & M. VAGLIASINDI, *Competition Policy Implementation In Transition Economies: An Empirical Assessment,* 44 European Economic Review 762, 2000; KEPINSKI M., HARDING C., *Polish Legislation on Competition and its Harmonisation with the EU competition law,* Droit Polonais Contemporain/Polish Contemporay Law 121, 1999; PLANAVOVA–LATANOWICZ J., HARDING C., *The Control of Concentrations in the Czech Republic and Poland,* 20 ECLR 265, 1999; ZINSMEISTER U., VASILE D., *Romania's New Competition Law,* ECLR 164, 1998; ENE ILJA M., ED. H. PISUKE (transl.) *Estonia Competition Act,* 94 I East European Business Law 20, 1994; JUHASZ J., *Slovakia Competition Rules Modernised,* 94-X East European Business Law 6, 1994.

***CEECs competition legislation in English:***

*Bulgaria: "Law on the Protection of Competition,"* www.cpc.bg/englaw.htm.

*Czech Republic: "Act on the Protection of Economic Competition,"* www.compet.cz/Zakony/zakonHseng.htm.

*Estonia: "Competition Act,"* www.konkurentsiamet.ee/gb/eng-law.rtf.

*Hungary: "Act on Prohibition of Unfair and Restrictive Market Practices,"* www.gvh.hu/angol/ineto6aa.htm.

*Lithuania: "Law on Competition,"* www.konksuren.lt/english/antitrust/legal.htm.

*Romania: "Competition Law,"* www.oficiulconcurentei.ro/legea2_english.htm.

*Slovakia: "Act on Protection of Economic Competition,"* www.antimon.gov.sk/default_a.htm.

*Slovenia: "Prevention of the Restriction of Competition Act,"* www.sigov.si/uvk/ang/2legal/1basis.htm

*Poland*: *competition policy regulations*, http://www.uokik.gov.pl/

*Latvia: State aid policy,* http://www.fm.gov.lv/page.php?id=113

# List of Abbreviations

| | |
|---|---|
| AG | Advocate General |
| AP (s) | Accession Partnership (s) |
| C- | Case |
| CEECs | Central and Eastern European Countries |
| CFI | Court of First Instance |
| CMEA | Council for Mutual Economic Assistance |
| COREPER | Committee of Permanent Representatives of the Member States |
| EA | European Agreement |
| EBRD | European Bank for Reconstruction and Development |
| ECJ | European Court of Justice |
| ECR | European Court Reports |
| ECS | European Cooperative Society |
| ECSC | European Coal and Steel Community |
| EC | European Community |
| EEA | European Economic Area |
| EEC | European Economic Community |
| EEIG | European Economic Interest Grouping |
| EFTA | European Free Trade Association |
| EIB | European Investment Bank |
| EMS | European Mutual Society |
| EP | European Parliament |
| EURATOM | European Atomic Energy Community |
| EU | European Union |
| FDI | Foreign Direct Investments |
| FTA | Free Trade Agreements |
| GATT | General Agreement on Tariffs and Trade |
| GIE | Groupement d'Intéréte économique |
| IBRD | International Bank for Reconstruction and Development (World Bank, WB) |
| IGC | Intergovernmental Conference |
| ILO | International Labor Organization |
| IMF | International Monetary Fund |
| ISPA | Instrument for Structural Policies for Pre-Accession |
| MDBs | Multilateral Development Banks |
| NPAA(s) | National Programme(s) for the Adoption of the Acquis |
| OECD | Organization for Economic Cooperation and Development |
| OEEC | Organization for European Economic Cooperation |
| OJ | Official Journal of the European Union |
| SAA | Stabilization and Association Agreements |

| | |
|---|---|
| SAPARD | Special Accession Programme for Agriculture and Rural Development |
| SE | Societas Europaea (European Company) |
| SEA | Single European Act |
| SIGMA | Support for Improvement in Governance and Management |
| TAIEX | Technical Assistance Information Exchange Office |
| TEC | European Community Treaty |
| TEU | European Union Treaty |
| UNCITRAL | United Nations Commission on International Trade Law |
| UNIDROIT | International Institute for the Unification of Private Law |
| WIPO | World Intellectual Property Organisation |
| WTO | World Trade Organization |

***Miscellaneous***

| | |
|---|---|
| *ABA* | American Bar Association |
| *ABGB* | Allgemeines Burgerliches Gesetzbuch fur Osterreich (Austrian General Civil Code) |
| *AC* | Appeal Cases (English Law Reports) |
| *AG* | Aktiengesellschaft |
| *AGB Gesetz* | German Act on General Terms and Conditions in Business |
| *art.* | article |
| *BGB* | Bürgerliches Gesetzbuch (German Civil Code) |
| *BGH* | Bundesgerichtshof (Supreme Court, Ordinary Jurisdiction) |
| *BGHZ* | Reports of civil cases of the German Federal Supreme Court |
| *CEELI* | Central and East European Law Initiative |
| *Cass.* | Corte di Cassazione |
| *Cass. S.U.* | Cassazione, Sezioni Unite |
| *Cf.* | compare, see |
| *Civ.* | Camera civile della Corte di Cassazione |
| *Com.* | Camera commerciale della Corte di Cassazione |
| *Cod. civ.* | Codice civile |
| *CONSOB* | Commissione nazionale per le società e la borsa |
| *C. consom.* | Code de la consommation |
| *Corte cost.* | Corte costituzionale |
| *d.lgs.* | decreto legislativo |
| *d.l.* | decreto legge |
| *Dir.* | Directive |
| *DM* | Decreto Ministeriale |
| *DPR* | Decreto del Presidente della Repubblica |
| *ff.* | followings |
| *Gazz. Uff., Suppl. Ord., Serie gen.* | Gazzetta Ufficiale, Supplemento Ordinario, Serie generale (Italian Official Journal) |
| *GTZ* | German organisation for technical cooperation |
| *HGB* | German Commercial Code |
| *Ibid.* | Ibidem |
| *ID.* | Idem |
| *L.* | Legge |
| *MICECO* | French inter-ministerial mission for Central and Eastern Europe |
| *NBW* | Nieuw Burgerlijk Wetboek (Dutch Civil Code) |

| | |
|---|---|
| *Para(s).* | Paragraph(s) |
| *S.A.* | Société Anonyme |
| *S.A.R.L* | Société a responsabilité limitée |
| *R.D.* | Regio Decreto |
| *Reg.* | Regulation |
| *TAR* | Tribunale amministrativo regionale |
| *Trib.* | Tribunale |
| *Sez.* | Sezione |
| *ZPO* | German Code of Civil Procedure |

***Law Reviews***

| | |
|---|---|
| *All ER* | *All England Reports* |
| *Am J.Comp.L.* | *American Journal of Comparative Law* |
| *AJIL* | *American Journal of International Law* |
| *Bull.* | *Bulletin des arrêts de la Cour de Cassation* |
| *Cal. L. R.* | *California Law Review* |
| *CMLR* | *Common Market Law Review* |
| *Colum.L. R.* | *Columbia Law Review* |
| *Cornell L. R.* | *Cornell Law Review* |
| *EC Bull.* | *European Community Bulletin* |
| *EJIL* | *European Journal of International law* |
| *EL Rev.* | *European Law Review* |
| *ERPL* | *European Review of Private Law* |
| *European Competition L. Rev.* | *European Competition Law Review* |
| *Harv. L. R.* | *Harvard Law Review* |
| *Hastings LJ* | *Hastings Law Journal* |
| *ICLQ* | *International and Comparative Law Quarterly* |
| *JBL* | *Journal of Business Law* |
| *J Leg. Stud.* | *Journal of Legal Studies* |
| *J Pub Law* | *Journal of Public Law* |
| *LQR* | *Law Quarterly Review* |
| *LS* | *Legal Studies* |
| *Mich.L.R.* | *Michigan Law Review* |
| *MLR* | *Modern Law Review* |
| *NYULR* | *New York University Law Review* |
| *OJLS* | *Oxford Journal of Legal Studies* |
| *Stan.L.R.* | *Stanford Law Review* |
| *Texas L Rev* | *Texas Law Review* |
| *Tulane L Rev* | *Tulane Law Review* |
| *YaleLJ* | *Yale Law Journal* |
| *WLR* | *Weekly Law Reports* |

| | |
|---|---|
| *AG* | *Die Aktiengesellschaft* |
| *AöR* | *Archiv des öffentliches Rechts* |
| *BB* | *Betriebs-Berater* |
| *BKR* | *Zeitschrift für Bank- und Kapitalmarktrecht* |
| *CR* | *Computer und Recht* |

| | |
|---|---|
| *DB* | *Der Betrieb* |
| *DVBl.* | *Deutsches Verwaltungsblatt* |
| *EuR* | *Europarecht* |
| *EuZW* | *Europäische Zeitschrift für Wirtschaftsrecht* |
| *EWS* | *Europäisches Wirtschafts- & Steuerrecht* |
| *GRUR* | *Gewerblicher Rechtsschutz und Urheberrecht* |
| *IPRax* | *Praxis des internationalen Privat- und Verfahrensrechts* |
| *JA* | *Juristische Arbeitsblätter* |
| *Jura* | *Juristische Ausbildung* |
| *JZ* | *Juristenzeitung* |
| *NJW* | *Neue juristische Wochenschrift* |
| *RdE* | *Recht der Energiewirtschaft* |
| *RIW* | *Recht der internationalen Wirtschaft* |
| *RRa* | *Reise Recht aktuell* |
| *VersR* | *Versicherungsrecht* |
| *VuR* | *Verbraucher und Recht* |
| *WM* | *Wertpapiermitteilungen* |
| *WRP* | *Wettbewerb in Recht und Praxis* |
| *WuW* | *Wirtschaft und Wettbewerb* |
| *ZEuP* | *Zeitschrift für Europäisches Privatrecht* |
| *ZEuS* | *Zeitschrift für Europarechtliche Studien* |
| *ZHR* | *Zeitschrift für das gesamte Handelsrecht* |
| *ZLR* | *Zeitschrift für das gesamte Lebensmittelrecht* |
| *ZÖR* | *Zeitschrift für öffentliches Recht* |
| *ZRP* | *Zeitschrift für Rechtspolitik* |
| *ZUM* | *Zeitschrift für Urheber- und Medienrecht* |

| | |
|---|---|
| *AJDA* | *Actualités juridiques du droit adiministratif* |
| *Cah. dr. eur.* | *Cahier de droit européen* |
| *Contrats, conc., consomm.* | *Contrats, concurrence, consommation* |
| *D.* | *Dalloz* |
| *D. Aff.* | *Dalloz Affaires* |
| *Defrénois* | *Répertoire du notariat Defrénois* |
| *Dr. et patrim.* | *Droit et patrimoine* |
| *Gaz. Pal.* | *La Gazette du Palais* |
| *I. R.* | *Informations rapides* |
| *J. C. P.* | *Juris-classeur périodique* |
| *JCP* | *Semaine Juridique* |
| *JCP(E)* | *JCP édition Entreprise* |
| *P. A.* | *Les Petites Affiches* |
| *Rec.* | *Recueil Lebon* |
| *Rev. crit. dr. internat. privé* | *Revue critique de droit international privé* |
| *Rev. eur. dr. consomm.* | *(REDC) Revue européenne de droit de la consommation* |
| *Rev. du dr. de l'U. E.* | *Revue du droit de l'Union européenne* |
| *Rev. int. dr. comp.* | *Revue internationale de droit comparé* |
| *Rev. trim. dr. civ.* | *Revue trimestrielle de droit civil* |
| *Rev. trim. dr. com.* | *Revue trimestrielle de droit commercial* |
| *Rev. trim. dr. eur.* | *Revue trimestrielle de droit européen* |

| | |
|---|---|
| *Rev jur. dr. aff.* | *Revue de jurisprudence de droit des affaires* |
| *Rev. rech. jur.* | *Droit prospectif, revue de la recherche juridique* |
| *RIDC* | *Revue internationale de droit comparé* |

| | |
|---|---|
| *Arch. Civ.* | *Archivio civile* |
| *Contratti I* | *Contratti* |
| *Contr. e Impr.* | *Contratto e Impresa* |
| *Contr. e Impr./Europa* | *Contratto e Impresa/Europa* |
| *Corriere Giur.* | *Corriere Giuridico* |
| *Danno e resp.* | *Danno e responsabilità* |
| *Dir. comun. e scambi internaz.* | *Diritto comunitario e degli scambi internazionali* |
| *Foro amm.* | *Foro amministrativo* |
| *Foro It.* | *Foro Italiano* |
| *Giornale dir.amm.* | *Giornale di diritto amministrativo* |
| *Giur.amm.sic.* | *Giurisprudenza amministrativa siciliana (ora Giustizia amministrativa siciliana)* |
| *Giur. di merito* | *Giurisprudenza di merito* |
| *Giur. It.* | *Giurisprudenza italiana* |
| *Giust. civ.* | *Giustizia civile* |
| *Giust. Cost.* | *Giustizia Costituzionale* |
| *Guida al dir.* | *Giuda al diritto* |
| *Resp. civ. prev.* | *Responsabilità civile e previdenza* |
| *Riv. crit. dir. priv.* | *Rivista critica di diritto privato* |
| *Riv. dir. civ.* | *Rivista di diritto civile* |
| *Riv. dir. comm.* | *Rivista di diritto commerciale* |
| *Riv.it.dir.pubbl.com.* | *Rivista italiana di diritto pubblico comunitario* |
| *RTDP civ.* | *Rivista trimestriale di diritto e procedura civile* |

# Index